STATE & LOCAL
POLITICS

STATE & LOCAL
POLITICS

Charles R. Adrian
University of California, Riverside

Michael R. Fine
University of Wisconsin–Eau Claire

Lyceum Books/Nelson-Hall Publishers
Chicago

Project Editor: Anita Samen
Cover Painting: *Baraboo Revisited,* by Rosemary Zwick.

Library of Congress Cataloging-in-Publication Data

Adrian, Charles R.
    State and local politics / Charles R. Adrian, Michael R. Fine.
      p.   cm.
    Includes bibliographical references and index.
    ISBN 0-8304-1285-9
    1. State governments–United States. 2. Local government–United
States. I. Fine, Michael R. II. Title.
JK2408.A33 1991
320.8'0973–dc20   91-10113
                                                CIP

Manufactured in the United States of America

10 9 8 7 6 5 4 3 2 1

 ™ The paper used in this book meets the
minimum requirements of American
National Standard for Information
Sciences—Permanence of Paper for
Printed Library Materials, ANSI
Z39.48-1984.

Contents

3 Rules for Rule Making   69

4 Federalism and Intergovernmental Relations   93

5   The Electorate and Interest Groups   123

6   Parties, Elections, and Direct Democracy   145

7   Forms of Government   171

8   Government in Metropolitan Areas   211

9   Executive Officers   245

10   Administration and the Bureaucracy   283

11 Legislative Organization, Functions, and Membership   309

12 The Legislative Process and Representation   337

Preface

The subject of this book is politics, the political process that leads to the actions and policies of government. Our foundation is the American federal system, which we examine and on which we build in detail the important contributions made by state and local governments.

The topics presented are those that a mainstream political scientist would expect to cover in a course on state and local politics. Yet our emphasis is not that which is generally found in textbooks on the subject. We present a considerable amount of primary historical background, which is also used in the analysis. We emphasize the ideology that holds us together as a nation and ties the political candidate and officeholder to the voter and resident. Political thought is used in other ways as well, especially in relation to federalism. We examine the peculiarities of structure and the ways in which forms of government affect political power.

We believe that our inclusion of considerable detail about the history of apportionment and the process of redistricting to be used in both states and localities following the 1990 census is especially useful. We also give recognition to the emerging trend toward social-class analysis as a basis for understanding much of politics, providing another method for clarifying the process. And in many ways throughout the book we have integrated public-policy matters—the end products—into the political process itself. Our goal, overall, has been to include as many aspects of the total mechanism of politics as possible within the available space.

By way of acknowledgments, we offer thanks to Dean Lee Grugel and Patrick George, department chair at UWEC, for their assistance in finding the resources for preparation of the manuscript, and to Lois Morrison for organizing the typing. Though the medium may seem pedestrian for such a purpose, thanks also to Audrey Nelson Adrian for nearly half a century of love and support and to Helen K. Adrian, who, in her ninety-eighth year as this is written, continues to take a keen interest in her son's work and in American politics. Thanks to Kerry Kinney Fine for putting up with Mike through this project and for her willingness to give excellent, honest editorial comments. In memorial, thanks to Gilda Richter Fine (1923–1990) for inspiring those around her to observe, write, and improve.

Copyright, 1987, The Courier-Journal. Reprinted with permission, Hugh S. Haynie

1

The Nation We Live In

The automobile; the telephone; the suburb; the owner-occupied, heavily mortgaged, single-family home; the expectation of a right to a high standard of living; public education from kindergarten to the doctorate; a superb medical profession, jealous of its profits and of the sphere of activity it has staked out for itself; a feeling of inferiority despite enormous wealth and power; urbanism; social conflict; professional entertainment; mass culture; heroes made to order on Madison Avenue; ambivalence toward governmental services and administration, civil rights, and subcultures other than one's own; confidence in an ability to meet crisis situations, even to the point of overconfidence; resentment toward an involuntary world leadership role and the insecurities it produces; neuroticism over neuroses, faddism; social climbing; a scramble for prestige and security, and an opportunity to achieve both; public servants of greater ability than is their credit—this is all a part of America.

Culture: **The pattern of arrangements, material or behavioral, that have been adopted by a society as traditional ways of solving the problems of its members. In a "mass" culture this pattern is determined more by the collective values of the common person than by an aristocratic elite.**

All this and much more—the demagogue; the traffic accident; inadequate protection for those who fail in the socioeconomic struggle; the homeless; the condominium and the multifamily apartment, which collectively shelter some in luxury, others in utter poverty; the jail cells, which hold nearly a million people each year; assault rifles and comic books; huge metropolitan areas, decaying in places; demonstrations and riots; racial tensions; poverty in the midst of plenty; bright neon signs; impatient traffic; puritanical soul-searching and self-doubt; a political system designed to give us the kind of government and governors we deserve. This is all a part of America.

Every aspect of American culture, every social need, every problem affects government and is in turn affected by government—national, state, and local. Because this is so, and because state and local government agencies deserve special

1

attention in their important social activities, this book was written. Although many approaches could be taken to the study of political institutions, the emphasis here is on a study of the *political process* as a method by which individual wants, which become social wants, are met by government. When they are accepted or rejected, sociopolitical policies emerge as imperfect compromises among the conflicting claims, interests, and wants of citizens and organized political, economic, or social groups.

Encyclopedic detail concerning each of the thousands of local units of government in America is not to be found here. Such detail is available in the nearest library, amply cited with footnotes. Neither is there an effort here to outline a set of ethical norms for the reader's guidance, because an objective collection of relevant data is necessary before understanding politics is possible. A word of warning, however: Values are essential ingredients in understanding politics and in the decision-making process. Therefore, the authors attempt to provide sufficient choices so the reader can understand the value options involved in state and local governments. When we choose what to study, we use values; when we provide choices about governmental structure, we use values; when we demonstrate, vote, or join a group to influence governmental policy or otherwise take political action, we rely on our moral sense of what is right or wrong, good or bad, in deciding what to do. At such times, personal values are of critical importance. No reader should assume, as so many voters do, that ''one choice is as good as another,'' or that ''no matter what I do, things will turn out the same way.'' The analysis in this book does not imply or justify such simple conclusions.

Government, which sets the boundaries of action for other social groups and for government itself, is the final means of enforcing controls. The decision makers in government, therefore, select which groups and ideas will be favored and which will not. They do this even while generally permitting groups to decide their relative places in society; for at any point in the process government decision makers may intercede and make rules that help or handicap a particular individual, group, or idea. They have done so, for example, in holding that relations among races will no longer be determined without involving formal governmental regulations in the process. Similarly, governmental policy has imposed a rule against plural marriages (polygamy) of the type once practiced within the Mormon church.

In a democracy, government exercises controls or gives rewards that are favored by the effective social forces—subject, however, to certain procedures and to certain rights of minorities. As in other forms of government, the actions of government in a democracy remold social forces; however, as society is modified, it also modifies government. Society and the life-styles of persons within it are in turn sharply affected by changes in technology. Thus, the development and marketing of the automobile for the common person permitted great changes in life-styles (rapid growth of suburbia, development of cities outward along major streets instead of in concentric circles of increasingly older homes, the ''weekend at the lake,'' independence for young couples). It also vastly changed or gave rise to governmental activities (the traffic officer and traffic court, giant highway programs, new types of state taxes, environmental controls, enlargement of state park systems, more emergency rooms at municipal hospitals).

Society: **A group of people who share a (roughly) common culture.**

Life-Style: **A concept that refers to the kind of life lived by people in differ-ent situations. It includes the ways of living that accompany life cycles, sta-tuses, career stages, changes through time resulting from technological de-velopments, tastes, and other stages of individual or group development.**

In recent years developments in computerization and telecommunication have had a similar effect on life-styles (too much home entertainment and too much information to process). The impact on state and local governments again has been great. For example, state legislatures that can write new thirty-page statutes at noon and pass them at 1 P.M. may let many mistakes pass through the pages. Questions regarding the balance between censorship and the right to view pornography may shift from the courts to local cable boards. Public libraries may spend more on computer disks than on books. Police officers may exercise discretion to stay out of whole new areas of computer crime, which may cost far more than street-level property crime. And the same officers now—for the first time in American history—know about and are able to arrest felons or traffic offenders who committed crimes far away from the jurisdiction of arrest.

Changing technology also makes possible changes in life-style, for example from single-family to apartment-house living. But the present trend toward more apartments and condominiums further complicates governmental policies and plan-ning because it causes problems, for example, with streets and highways (apartments increase parking-space and street-use demands in the area), fire departments (high-rise buildings require complex, expensive equipment and professional firefighters), child care (high density creates overcrowding), and police (adequate protection be-comes difficult within a private building complex).

Changes in technology may also alter the number and types of persons involved in the decision process. Chemical herbicides and insecticides, auto exhausts, mounds of garbage too large or hazardous for landfills, industrial effluent affecting the ecology of water, and many similar signs of technological changes and their results, combined with increasing population concentration in metropolitan areas, became matters of con-cern to many citizens, young and old, who had previously ignored or were unaware of such problems. Their interest began to influence the decisions and behavior of many professional personnel who previously had carried out most of their work well below the visibility level of most citizens. State foresters and water-quality engineers, county public health officers, air pollution control technicians, and municipal environmental sanitarians were among those who found themselves monitored by concerned, politi-cized amateurs. In turn, they became more highly politicized in their governmental roles. Thus, technology and its interrelated partner, life-style, help determine govern-ment's agenda. So do the politically powerful, the particular actors with their varying abilities and goals, and the structure of governmental institutions itself.

Agenda: **Items of business to be disposed of, in this case, by government. The agenda may be "overt" (e.g., the senate calendar or the governor's budget message) or "hidden" (e.g., the confidential goals of a party fac-tion, of a reform organization or of a revolutionary group).**

Structure and Process in Politics

The process of public policy making is modified by the structure of government, just as the path of a turbulent river is modified by natural and artificial barriers. But the process influences the character of a culture, and the interests of powerful groups shape the policies a government will follow, The institutional arrangements themselves modify the outcome of the policy-making process.

The structure of American government includes an independently elected governor. This fact allows the chief executive to behave differently from the way he or she would if chosen by the legislature (as is the practice in many cities where the council chooses the city manager). The seniority system in the legislative body, which often determines who will head a committee, produces a different pattern of legislative leadership and a different set of leaders with different values and policy goals from what would be the case if these leaders where chosen by a political party committee, for example. The seniority system most commonly produces conservatives from ''safe'' or noncompetitive districts who face little competition while staying in office and who, therefore, have little incentive to be concerned about the most recent political demands or policy issues.

The point is, then, that the structure of government is only one influence on policy and hence only one thing to be studied in an examination of the workings of American government. Structure, on the other hand, is not to be dismissed lightly, for it, too, affects the pattern of decision making.

American Panorama

The states and their subdivisions are individual communities with distinctive characteristics. The nation, a collection of geographic areas and subcultures, is a land of infinite variety. It is in many ways an enigmatic nation, seemingly with a uniform mass culture but also with great regional and local diversity. The individual speaks of an American way of life, but the sociologist sees a collection of cultural groupings based on geographic location and ethnic associations, each with its own values and behavior patterns. America is at once a nation of uninspired place names and romantic and beautiful ones—Sixteenth Street and Perdido Pass; of two political parties and dozens of parties masquerading under well-known labels or using no labels at all.

Sociologists often argue that formal political boundaries are artificial, but political activity within those boundaries produce cultural patterns. Thus, most Americans simultaneously reflect the values of many subcultures, some legal entities (city, state), some traditional (region, metropolis, or neighborhood). When the high school basketball game is at stake, a resident of Van Nuys is a fierce competitor to a resident of neighboring Sherman Oaks. But a week later, the loser of that rivalry boisterously supports the winner at the state tournament 400 miles away. When asked by a New Yorker where he or she lives, a resident of Roseville, Minnesota, replies ''the Twin Cities'' although living neither in St. Paul nor Minneapolis; and that ''New Yorker'' might actually live in Yonkers, New York, or even Stamford, Connecticut. A presidential candidate visiting Oklahoma becomes a ''fellow Southwesterner,'' not a Texan, while an opponent visiting Vermont is a ''fellow New Englander,'' no longer from Massachusetts. Each of these labels is shorthand for a subculture of values that need not be explained in full because they are meaningful, albeit frequently in mis-leading ways. Even though such values can be deliberately contrived, they create significant differences in the images between adjoining cities and states, not to men-tion among regions.

Too often the differences among states and among regions are not noted. That is, we speak of the "American way" as if all Americans have much in common. The dangers of oversimplifying are many. Yet, in the twentieth century the convergence of regional cultures has reduced some of the differences described below.[1] The high school movement and the professional training of teachers following World War I provided somewhat of a common basis to education for the first time. By 1927, na-tional radio networks were in operation; and from the mid-1950s television was fur-ther homogenizing American culture. The New Deal under Franklin Roosevelt moved far in the centralizing direction and reformers wanted federal legislation that in time would produce national uniformity in policy and social values. Frequently the states, ever concerned with receiving more funding from the national government, conform to national legislative trends. Welfare, public health, public administration, civil rights, education, and transportation, to name only a few areas of governmental policy, continue to move toward uniformity. Even Ronald Reagan, who claimed re-luctance to use national policy in this way, could be found leading the fight for a uni-form national drinking age, something that could not be accomplished directly through national legislation but could be done by requiring that states pass such legis-lation in return for national dollars. Differences among the states and regions will always exist and always affect public policy in the states, but convergence of cultures is the tendency in the twentieth century.

The States as Cultural Entities

Every state has a different political, social, and economic tradition. Behavior patterns and practices of the past can be dominant as they affect decisions of the present. In some states, political elites pride themselves on leadership in policy innovation; oth-ers traditionally look with satisfaction toward the past and therefore view proposed changes with skepticism as to their potential contribution to "progress." Although economic development and wealth seem to be the two most important factors in deter-mining the extent and pattern of state social policies, local traditions of experimenta-tion are also factors.[2] Indeed, willingness to be innovative seems to vary by particular function of government (for example, education or welfare) within a single state.[3]

It is useful to think of each state as representing in varying degrees one or more of three model political cultures that have been dominant in the United States. Each model first moved westward, in early America, then into suburbia. One cul-ture, based on *individualism,* sees democratic government as a marketplace. Gov-ernments exist for strictly practical reasons, to perform functions demanded by sig-nificant segments of the public. Private decision making and reduced government involvement dominate, and it is not government's task to bring about the good life, only to aid in the struggle to attain it, which takes place primarily in the private sector. Another model centers on the *moralistic* concept of a commonwealth of persons seeking the good life through democracy. According to this thinking, politics is one of the higher human activities designed to achieve such a society; and public policies ought to be in the "public interest," but individualism is secondary to the "good of all." The third concept is *traditionalistic* and reflects an older attitude that accepts a hierarchical order of things, with the expectation that the elite should lead through a sense of noblesse oblige. Government has a positive task to perform but is restricted by its obligation to maintain the existing social order.[4] It is from these differing concepts of the task of state (and local) government that much political conflict arises.

Although sociologists have tended to ignore the states as units, seeing them as arbitrary structures, they are not entirely correct. Time and differing laws, ethnic settlements, racial and rural–urban balances, and economic combinations have all contributed toward the creation of vast differences among adjoining states, not to mention among states of different regions of the nation. Thus Washington State, strongly influenced by the gold rush, Scandinavian settlement, and populism, is liberal and Democratic; and Oregon, first settled by New Englanders, is conservative and traditionally Republican.

Anomalous arrangements are found within states, too, Northern Idaho is within the area dominated by Spokane, Washington, and the politics of the state centers on a north-south split. West central Wisconsin faces toward the Twin Cities of Minneapolis–St. Paul, while Michigan's Upper Peninsula has long felt isolated from the rest of the state and has tended to identify with Wisconsin. Oregon is divided by the Cascades, with one economy in the humid western and another in the dry eastern potion of the state. California has two cultures, north and south; and numerous attempts, from the first days of statehood to the present, have been made to divide the state at the Tehachapi Mountains.[5]

Immense dissimilarities exist among the states, of course (see table 1–1). These include differences in area, population, urbanization, per capita income, and period of settlement. Alaska is almost five hundred times the size of Rhode Island. California has more than fifty-eight times the population of Wyoming. Some 90 percent of California's people are considered urbanites (1986), whereas over 65 percent of Vermont's live in rural areas. The first permanent settlement in Virginia was in 1607; in Oklahoma, 1889. Social and economic differences in the culture of the states lead to differences in their political culture. Differences in political culture lead to differences in public policy. But the differences in populations alone will never explain public policy. Attitudes and values toward the role of government must be known. Yet once established, population differences can help shape policies. Can Florida's very low per capita spending on education in 1987 ($574) be partially explained by the small percentage of its population that is of school age? But in Mississippi, where we find one of the highest percentages of school-age children, we also find one of the lowest per capita expenditures for education ($496). When we compare the *effort* made by the two states in terms of per capital annual income, we find they make a greater effort than at first seems the case. Demographic differences among the states cannot be ignored, but they can be confusing and should not be overstated. Perhaps cultural differences explain more than does population of the variation in state public policy.

TABLE 1-1 Selected Characteristics of States and the Nation

	Vermont	New York	Indiana	Minnesota	Florida	Mississippi	Oklahoma	Arizona	California	HIGH	LOW	United States
Population (1,000) (1990 est.)	562	17,773	5,550	4,324	12,818	2,699	3,285	3,752	29,126	29,126 (CA)	502 (WY)	249,891
Area (sq. mi.)	9,614	49,108	36,185	84,402	58,664	47,689	69,956	114,000	158,706	591,004 (AK)	1,212 (RI)	3,618,770
Population (per sq. mi.) (1986)	58.3	375.1	153.2	53.0	215.6	55.6	48.1	29.2	172.6	1,020.3 (NJ)	0.9 (AK)	68.1
Percent Metro (1986)	23.1%	90.5%	68.0%	65.8%	90.9%	30.0%	58.5%	75.4%	95.7%	100.0% (NJ)	19.4% (ID)	76.6%
Percent Urban (1980)	33.8%	84.6%	64.2%	66.9%	84.3%	47.3%	67.3%	83.8%	91.3%	91.3% (CA)	33.8% (VT)	73.7%
Percent White (1990 est.)	98.7%	80.7%	90.6%	95.7%	84.4%	63.6%	84.9%	89.8%	82.1%	98.7% (VT,ME)	63.6% (MS)	84.1%
Percent Black (1990 est.)	0.4%	17.7%	8.4%	1.6%	14.2%	35.6%	6.8%	2.7%	8.2%	35.6% (MS)	0.2% (MT)	12.4%
Birth Rate per 1,000 (1986)	13.9	14.9	14.5	15.4	14.3	15.8	14.5	18.4	17.1	23.2 (AK)	12.7 (CT)	15.5
Death Rate per 1,000 (1986)	8.9	9.7	9.3	8.3	10.7	9.0	8.7	8.0	7.3	10.7 (FL)	4.1 (AK)	8.7
Percent of Pop. over 65	11.9%	12.8%	11.9%	12.5%	17.7%	12.0%	12.4%	12.3%	10.6%	17.7% (FL)	3.4% (AK)	12.1%
Percent of Pop. under 18	25.3%	24.6%	26.8%	26.3%	22.5%	30.5%	27.2%	27.4%	26.3%	37.2% (UT)	22.5% (FL)	26.2%
Per Capita Income (1986)	$13,348	$17,111	$13,136	$14,994	$14,646	$9,716	$12,283	$13,474	$16,904	$19,600 (CT)	$9,716 (MS)	$14,641
Education Spending per Capita (1987)	$ 721	$ 859	$ 606	$ 717	$ 574	$ 496	$ 535	$ 480	$ 641	$ 1,809 (AK)	$ 480 (AZ)	$ 666
Education Spending per Pupil (1987)	$ 4,459	$ 6,299	$ 3,379	$ 3,954	$ 4,056	$ 2,534	$ 2,701	$ 2,784	$ 3,751	$ 8,842 (AK)	$ 2,534 (MS)	$ 3,970

Source: U.S. Bureau of the Census, Statistical Abstract of the United States: 1988.

Regions and Sectionalism

For all the talk about American uniformity and conformity, the diet, dialect, language, degree of urbanization, ethnic patterns, and political traditions of the various regions of the country differ considerably. Perhaps the similarities among regions are greater than their differences, but the differences *are* important to understand cultural trends and political variations.[6]

An initial problem exists in reaching some consensus on aggregating the states into regions. The Census Bureau groups states into four regions and nine subregions for purposes of statistical analysis. Even though these groupings are not arbitrary, they do not follow many of the historical settlement patterns, cultural patterns, or intraregional conflicts that different authors use in aggregating the states. For example, reference to "sunbelt" or "Midwest" means different things to different authors. Thus care should be taken in comparing studies that variously aggregate the states.

Despite such inconsistencies, Daniel Elazar's writing on regions and sections has been widely used. He summarizes his arguments by highlighting the conceptual distinction between sectionalism and regionalism:

> Sectionalism is not the same as regionalism. The latter is essentially a phenomenon—often transient—that brings adjacent state, substate, or interstate areas together because of immediate and specific common interests. The portions of the nine states from Georgia to Pennsylvania that are located within the Appalachian Mountains represent one kind of region. The Mississippi Valley is another. Ties between the political entities in such regions are expediential only, a product of their common interest in overcoming very specific problems.
>
> Sectionalism involves arrangements of much greater permanence which, as essentially political phenomena, link whole states and persist despite the emergence of immediate conflicts or divergences among its component states from time to time. For example, New England is a section bound by the tightest of social and historical ties. . . . Their cooperative efforts have been sufficiently institutionalized to create what is essentially a six-state "community" like the European Community, a veritable confederation within the larger American Union. It is through such acts of political will that sectionalism best manifests itself.[7]

The regional distinction that attracted the greatest attention in the past decade is between the sunbelt of the South and West and the frostbelt of the North and East.[8] The housing shortage, brought on by a falloff in new home construction between the stock market crash of 1929 and the end of World War II, led to a postwar suburban building boom. Whereas government could stimulate housing growth through a variety of programs (most important the VA and FHA mortgage guarantees), the choice of where to build was often determined by the location of the cheapest vacant land. At first, most of this was found in the West; later, in the South. The perception that the West had come "closer" to the East was nourished by increased availability and greater speed of air travel (commercial jets were introduced in 1959) and by increased use of and declining charges for the telephone. These advances reduced the difficulties in keeping in touch with distant family and friends.[9] The perception that regions were discouragingly different also was challenged by the increasingly nation-alized mass media, particularly the creation and expansion of television networks. Cheaper power, labor, and raw materials advanced the South as an attraction for the new industries of the postwar economy. Air conditioning made it possible to control the climate in the South and the West, much as heating did in the colder climates. The myth of the better life in the South and West was born, a myth that reinforced the other advantages of the sunbelt. The middle- and working-class population move-ment was—and continues to be—dramatically toward the South and West. And indus-tries (particularly the service, high-tech, and non-"smokestack" types) continue their move to the sunbelt.[10]

> *Political Myth:* **A political belief that may or may not be supported by facts, but that leads people to act. This is a result of the *perceived* reality of the belief rather than some objective statement or measure of reality.**

In American politics, myths have always been influential in explaining popula-tion movement. The belief in "cities paved with gold" launched the movement of immigrants to the United States at the end of the nineteenth century. The myth of a small-town life-style was one factor that drove Americans to the suburbs following World War II. People will not move simply because of the attractiveness of the myth, but without the belief in enhanced quality of life, population movements rarely would be pronounced or long sustained.

Another myth about America brought to the nation, beginning around 1970, large numbers of immigrants from Latin America and many of the nations abutting the Pacific Ocean. As always with immigrant groups, large numbers settled where they arrived, having no money to move onwards. As a result, Florida, Texas, and especially California have replaced New York as the principal states of entry and settlement for immigrants.

The realities of life in the sunbelt helped create a myth held by many that that area had a higher quality of life than did the frostbelt. Climate, newness and layout of physical plant, temporarily lower taxes, and popular life-styles reinforce these be-liefs. Despite the decline of some economic advantages of the sunbelt, the myth of a better life-style should center growth in the sunbelt cities well into the twenty-first century.

Nevertheless, a number of mitigating factors suggest that the present trends will not continue unabated. As the sunbelt population becomes more urban and suburban—more like the frostbelt—many problems that sunbelt movers came to the South and West to escape will be created. Crime in South Florida, gang wars and traffic jams in Los Angeles, water shortage in Tucson, and unemployment in Hous-ton are but a few already realized examples. As consumers move to states with lower levels of services, they will soon demand the service levels they left behind. Such demands inevitably lead to higher taxes and even though sunbelt residents enjoyed lower taxes during the period of transition, taxes in the sunbelt are moving toward the national mean. (California's taxes are already among the nation's highest.) Once the tax-climate bubble bursts, one underlying motivation for businesses to move will be reduced. But the climate and geography will remain. By then, the sunbelt's proximity to labor forces, raw materials, and markets probably will sustain the trend to those regions for some time.

Politically, sunbelt states are taking in more federal dollars than they are sending out in taxes, whereas frostbelt states are sending out more dollars than they are taking in. Furthermore, the Constitution requires Congressional seats to follow the movement of people. Because western members are generally more conservative than the Easterners they are replacing, the former will become more important in shaping the Congress of the early twenty-first century. But the significance of the increases in the South are reduced somewhat by changes in party relationships. Southern Congressional power formerly came from the likelihood that southern Democrats would have the safest seats and therefore garner the greatest seniority. Today, the southern states have become more competitive between Democrats and Republicans, thus reducing the force of seniority, which at the same time has become less important in Congress.

The sunbelt is demonstrating little cultural distinction as it grows; it is a region, not a section, as defined earlier. As will be discussed later in this chapter, the cultural differences among states and localities are being reduced by a variety of factors. Ironically, the differences may eventually become more important to the demographer than to the sociologist or political scientist, as Theodore Roosevelt anticipated decades ago. The longer-lasting vitality of the sunbelt ultimately may depend more on the weight of the Pacific Rim and Latin American countries in world affairs than on the attractiveness of the region to mobile citizens.

Local Cultural Variations

For years, students of local affairs have attempted to define the particular cultural characteristics that distinguish localities. At one end is a school of thought that views a group as an integrated body, a *Gemeinschaft* (German for "community"), seeing individuals only in terms of their function in a larger organic whole.[11] Authors with this view tend to lament the seeming lack of identity in the modern metropolis, city, or neighborhood. Nevertheless, they attempt to define these localities in terms of those characteristics that make them distinct from other forms, special in their capacity to encapsulate a certain life-style. On the other extreme, students view the group as an artificial entity, an aggregation of no particular character, contrived for vote-keeping or policy-making purposes, or as a convenient research repository where variables for study are readily accessible. Neither extreme can accurately describe American localities. The metropolis, the city, the suburb, or the neighborhood each generates myths and realities that attract people.[12] Nevertheless, within each type of area some people see great distinction and character in the places they call home or choose to visit, whereas others find only a dull monotony of interchangeable places.

John C. Bollens and Henry J. Schmandt argue that metropolises should be thought of as communities, "in the sense that they constitute settlements of people living within a specified geographical space and interacting with each other in terms of daily needs."[13] Metropolises can be distinguished by the *decentralization* of their people, facilitated by the expanded technologies of power, water, communication, and transportation since World War II; the *fragmentation* of the government, which gives advantages to some and disadvantages to others in some parts of the metropolises; and the *specialization* of their sections, which produces the *interdependence* of parts of the metropolis despite the lack of a metropolitan-area government. Norton Long describes this metropolis as an "unwalled city," beset by the needs of communities with no corresponding governments and the problems of governments with no corresponding communities.[14]

Although metropolises certainly are distinguishable, few identify a life-style that can be studied as unique to that community. *Cities* on the other hand, produce a unique life-style. Louis Wirth provided the classic description of urbanism as a way of life distinguished by the size, density, and homogeneity of its population.[15] Unfortunately, since Wirth's statement in 1939, little has been agreed upon in characterizing the life-style that follows. Some see it as cold and depersonalized, with individuals moving about like so many programmed atoms. Others see particular communities blessed with fraternal neighbors working in harmony to produce the abundance of a well-ordered machine. Neither view is correct. American cities collectively are most distinguishable by the *variety* of life styles we find in them. But like kinds tend to cluster to create some semblance of community feeling. Sometimes this clustering corresponds to the borders of a city, as in the traditional suburb that served as a bedroom community for its inhabitants, who worked in the central city. At other times the city is a collection of neighborhoods segregated on the basis of social class, religion, race, or family structure. The traditional model can be seen in Boston and Philadelphia, for example.

Perhaps the oldest cultural community is the neighborhood, which is difficult to define but is usually meaningful to its inhabitants.[16] Its boundaries often date back to when the neighborhood was a separate city or when ethnic groups were segregated into separate areas. Neighborhoods remain meaningful for a variety of reasons, but particularly if new groups move in or challenge these perceived borders. With the exception of those cities with city council wards conforming to neighborhoods, most do not have formal governmental powers but do have the capacity for deliberative decision making. Radical groups in poor neighborhoods have espoused neighborhood organization as a means of achieving greater power, whereas middle-class groups frequently form neighborhood groups to enforce neighborhood norms and to lobby government to maintain their special life-styles. Whatever its definition, the neighborhood remains important to many of its residents in terms of familiarity, security, and orientation to daily affairs.

Suburbanism highlights the process by which people seek out their counterparts in an effort to recapture a sense of community. Robert Wood defined suburbanism as a life-style characterized by people seeking conformity and fraternity while ever engaged in conspicuous consumption.[17] People moved to suburbs to pursue the myth of the small town while also enjoying the benefits of metropolitan diversity, jobs, and abundant amenities. Government greatly encouraged such movement through middle-class housing subsidies, mortgage guarantees, and exclusionary zoning practices. More so than in a core city, which many visit, suburbanites could benefit from services without sharing with those in the core. Banks financed suburban home membership, making payments manageable for the family of moderate means—particularly if financing was coupled with national government guarantees.

Suburbs have continued to expand in population and diversity and, as they have grown older, have taken on some problems typical of all well-used cities (the proto-typical Levittown, started in a Long Island potato field, was 40 years old in 1990). In addition, suburbs have continued to contain the bulk of the American middle classes, working classes, industry, commerce, social institutions, and indeed (in most large metropolises) virtually everything else deemed urban (except for our oldest historic monuments, some public offices and structures, the majority of the poor, and many of the institutions that service the poor).[18]

Population Patterns and Politics

All state governments and 80,000-odd local units of U. S. government are social ser-vice agencies. Their size, shape, and reason for being are a result of historical acci-dent and tradition. Often they are a heritage from more simple and primitive times. But their tasks, functions, and problems are posed by the populations they contain. Population, of course, does not merely mean numbers of people; it encompasses den-sity, ethnic and racial patterns, rate of growth, population by age groups, rural or urban dwellers, and stability and mobility. Before inquiring into services performed at the state and local levels of government or into the politics surrounding those ser-vices, we must consider the general pattern of demographic trends.

> *Urban Population:* **All persons living in cities or villages with a population of 2,500 or more, or otherwise living in** *urbanized areas* **(those comprised of cities, villages, and adjacent densely settled surrounding areas with a com-bined minimum population of 50,000). That segment of the population not classified as urban constitutes the** *rural population.* **(The Census Bureau adds a number of complicated criteria to define these areas and changes them from census to census. For this reason, unlike other categories, no intercensus estimates of these populations are made.)**

> *Metropolitan Statistical Areas (MSAs):* **Geographical areas consisting of a large population, together with adjacent counties that have a high degree of economic and social integration with that nucleus. The MSA must have a city of at least 50,000 people or a Census Bureau–defined urbanized area of 50,000 and an areawide population of at least 100,000 (75,000 in New England). The nucleus of the area is the county (or counties) containing a** *central city.* **The central city is the largest city, but additional cities may be designated central if they are of large size and are employment hubs, meet-ing the criteria set by the Census Bureau. An MSA also includes outlying counties that have close economic and social relationships with the central counties. The outlying counties must have a specified level of commuting to the central counties and must also meet certain standards regarding met-ropolitan character, such as population density, urban population, and population growth. In New England, MSAs comprise cities and towns rather than counties. The area outside the central city is generally de-scribed as suburban.**

MSAs were known as Metropolitan Districts in 1910, became Standard Metropolitan Areas (SMAs) in 1949, and were dubbed Standard Metropolitan Statistical Areas (SMSAs) from 1959 through 1983. Criteria for definition change with each census or periodically whenever estimates are made.

Consolidated Metropolitan Statistical Areas (CMSAs): In some parts of the nation, metropolitan development has progressed to the point where adjoining MSAs are socially and economically interrelated. These extended population areas, designated as consolidated metropolitan statistical areas, were described as early as 1961 by Jan Gottmann, who coined the term *megalopolis.* The distinct MSAs or former SMSAs in a CMSA are designated as *primary metropolitan statistical areas* (PMSAs).

Urbanization, the Metropolis, and the United States

Fewer than 4 million persons lived in the United States at the time of the first census in 1790. This figure thereafter doubled approximately every twenty-five years for the next century. Rural America had a high birthrate, and immigrants arrived from abroad with little restriction. An all-time high of 1,285,349 foreigners reached our shores in 1907. This figure dropped sharply following a post–World War I quota system for immigration. For a while the rate of population increase declined sharply, especially during the Great Depression of the 1930s. Although decade increases would never approach the 20 to 40 percent of the nineteenth century, a 10 to 15 percent rise in population has occurred since World War II. The Census Bureau showed over 226 million residents in 1980, estimated 242 million for 1987, and projects 260 million by 1995.

The history of America has been almost continuously one of urbanization. In every decade since the Constitution went into effect, the urban percentage has increased. The population of American cities, which doubled between the beginning of the Civil War and 1900, doubled again over the next twenty-five years. By 1920, more than one-half (51.2 percent) of Americans were living in urbanized areas; in 1980, nearly three-fourths were.

It was not cities but metropolitan areas that were undergoing the most rapid change in the second half of the twentieth century (see table 1–2). One American in five lives in the CMSAs of New York, Los Angeles, Chicago, Philadelphia, and San Francisco; over 40 percent live in MSAs of 1 million or more; and over 76 percent live within the 332 metropolitan areas defined in 1987. Yet, these areas cover less than 20 percent of the land area of the continental United States.

Suburban growth continues to be noteworthy. Before 1920, core cities grew faster than did their suburbs. Both increased their populations at about the same rate in the 1920s, but since the census of 1930 suburban growth has been faster. Between 1970 and 1980, core-city populations remained almost constant (0.1 percent growth), with northeastern and north central core-city declines being offset by southern and western growth. The suburban growth, however, continued spectacularly in all regions. By 1986, over 46 percent of all Americans lived in suburbs, which con-

TABLE 1–2   Metropolitan Population

	1950 Census	1960 Census	1970 Census	1980 Census	1986 Estimate
Population					
United States	151.3	179.3	203.2	226.5	238.5
Inside MSAs	84.9	112.9	139.4	169.4	184.8
Central City	49.7	58.0	63.8	67.9	73.7
Outside Central City	35.2	54.9	75.6	101.5	111.1
Outside MSAs	66.5	66.4	63.8	57.1	53.7
Percent of U.S.					
United States	100.0%	100.0%	100.0%	100.0%	100.0%
Inside MSAs	56.1%	63.0%	68.6%	74.8%	77.5%
Central City	32.8%	32.3%	31.4%	30.0%	30.9%
Outside Central City	23.2%	30.6%	37.2%	44.8%	46.6%
Outside MSAs	43.9%	37.0%	31.4%	25.2%	22.5%

Source: U.S. Bureau of the Census.

tinue to have higher than average percentages of whites, Anglos, and wealthier Americans (see table 1–3). The conventional wisdom that describes suburbs as wholly white, middle class, or homogeneous is incorrect today. Some suburbs tend to follow the old stereotypes, but these towns may now be found in great variety. Specialized suburbs primarily of working class, black, Hispanic, or other ethnic groups are quite commonplace.[19]

Metropolitan growth patterns are often statistically misleading. A few people moving from a city of 1 million to a town of two hundred demonstrates a minuscule percentage change in the city but a significant percentage change in the town. Be-

TABLE 1–3   Metropolitan Characteristics

	Central City		Suburb		Outside MSA	
	1980**	1986***	1980	1986	1980	1986
Percent of Race Living in:						
White	24.9%	26.7%	48.4%	49.9%	26.7%	23.4%
Black	57.8%	57.0%	23.3%	24.6%	18.9%	18.4%
Hispanic*	50.3%	54.2%	37.3%	38.3%	12.4%	7.6%
Percent of Area:						
White	69.2%	73.2%	89.7%	90.9%	88.0%	88.2%
Black	22.5%	22.3%	6.1%	6.4%	8.8%	9.9%
Other	8.3%	4.5%	4.2%	2.7%	3.2%	1.9%
Hispanic*	10.8%	n.a.	5.4%	n.a.	3.2%	n.a.
Below Poverty Line	16.7%	18.0%	7.5%	8.4%	14.5%	18.1%

Source: U.S. Bureau of the Census.
*Hispanics may be of any race.
**Poverty figures are for 1982.
***Hispanic figures are for 1987 families.
N.a.: not available.

cause the people remain the same few, care must be taken not to overstate the importance of the patterns that emerge.

One population group that has gotten attention in the past decade is the "gentrified," a high-income segment who have stayed in or moved into neighborhoods of the core city with the effect of reversing—or at least halting—the deterioration of the central city. Given the relatively small number of people involved, the attention given is probably overstated. Nevertheless, the movement is important insofar as it demonstrates a change in postwar trends and may prove to be more apparent after the analysis following the 1990 census can properly measure it. Gentrification demonstrates a small trend countering the movement of the middle class to the suburbs. For some, the core city has always offered the myth of excitement in diversity and abundance. For idealistic others, people of all classes, races, or life-styles ought to live together in the core city. But since the inception of suburbanization, the core cities have been poorer than their suburbs, and the movement of those who could afford it has been outward.[20] Difficulty in measuring gentrification has led to its examination primarily through case studies.[21] These suggest that many of the new core-city middle class are childless (see the section later in this chapter on new family structures) and that some of the new neighborhoods are made possible by changes in urban design that allow the middle class a perception of protection from the poor who live close by. Furthermore, governments are favoring a variety of schemes to encourage gentrification because it will either increase the tax base within the city (see chapter 14) or increase its middle-class population (or both), changing the life-style of the city.[22] Gentrification is likely to be an underlying factor in the conflicts among social classes (see chapter 2). Furthermore, it represents a sense of neighborhood within the middle-class core city.[23]

A small number of people also have moved out of the *metropolitan* area in recent years, although this exodus is greatly offset by the growth within the area. Many explanations can be given for this movement,[24] but it is in part a result of a spillover of metropolitan people, not yet counted in a growing metropolitan area. Others who contribute to this perception are retirees who move to the growing number of small specialized retirement towns, and middle-class Americans who enjoy the amenities of a middle-class life-style in the small town because of new technologies that earlier had been available only in the metropolitan area.

The Effects of Physical Mobility

Ours is a nation of seminomadic people. Opportunity for advancement, the necessity for going to the job that will not come to the individual, the practice of businesses and industries that operate over the entire nation or even larger areas of sending men and women from assignment in one city to assignment in another while they move up the organizational ladder, all contribute to this mobility. And some families have to contend with two wage earners following this pattern of mobility, which compounds decision-making dilemmas. Some people move more often than the average, of course, and some Americans still are born, live, and die in the same house; but nearly one-half of all Americans now move every five years. Chapter 8 will examine the fragmentation of government, which exists when people move within the metropolitan area.

High amounts of physical and social mobility have characterized American society from colonial times. Physical mobility has offered new opportunities for people who fear they have reached a stalemate in their present location. It permits workers to go wherever they may be needed and gives variety to otherwise jaded life interest.

But high physical mobility can also create serious social problems. Within the core city, for example, the breakdown of primary controls in the residential hotel and deteriorated apartment-house areas of the zone of transition leads to higher crime rates, increased insecurity feelings, and other personal and social problems. Because low-skilled migrants to core cities usually are marginal workers—last hired and first fired—their presence in large numbers exacerbates the public welfare problem. These problems have been compounded by the increasing number of homeless Americans who, in this area particularly, may have been made homeless by changes in governmental programs regarding the mentally ill.

> *Primary Groups:* **Population segments characterized by behavior controlled through shared values and goals of persons in small groups who deal with one another on a personal basis, rather than on the basis of functions they perform in society.**

> *Secondary Groups:* **Population segments, usually larger and more dispersed in space, that share fewer values than primary groups. The individual is seen not as a whole person but as someone performing a particular role. Secondary group controls emphasize formal rules and procedures.**

> *Zone of Transition:* **The area outside the central business district (CBD), where retreating residents have left an area now consisting of deteriorating apartments, hotels, and business places. The decline of the CBD and the rise of shopping centers have modified this traditional urban area, which often was an early target of urban renewal.**

From the point of view of those concerned with participation in democratic government, high mobility is important in that large numbers of migrants fail to identify with their adopted communities. Their civic pride is likely to be almost nonexistent, with no loyalty to the city as such. A migrant living in a suburb may not even know whether that location is actually an independent unit of government, so that political appeals to community responsibility will fall on deaf ears. Government will be left in the hands of others—others who may be grossly unrepresentative of the interests of the newer arrivals.

The Changing American Family

As recently as 1970, the conventional image of the American family was still valid. By the age of 25, all but 14 percent of women had married, 85 percent of children lived with two parents, and less than one-third of the mothers with preschool children worked outside the home. By the 1980s these and other factors relating to the stereotypical American family had greatly changed. These changes have presented new policy questions for governments (how to pay for more child care, what to do with underused or unused school buildings, where the poor will go when or if the ''yuppies'' want the central city). These issues will be among the most important in the final decade of the twentieth century.

The changing role of American women began when they moved into the labor force. In every decade since 1940 a larger percentage of women have worked outside the home (see table 1–4). At first, this movement was largely reserved for childless women or those with grown children, but in the past decade this has not been the case. By 1982, for the first time, roughly one-half of all mothers with preschool children and nearly two-thirds of those with school-age children were in the labor force. These figures then rose steadily throughout the decade, affecting many related demographic trends.[25]

The decade of the 1980s saw the restructuring of the American family. The two-parent household became the exception; about one-fifth of all adult Americans were single, nearly one-half of all families had no children, and little more than one-third of all households had children (35.8 percent in 1986, down from 45 percent in 1970). In the 1980 census, 20 percent of families with children under age 18 had only one parent in the home; a number estimated to have risen to 23 percent by 1986 (twice that of 1970). A major reason for this trend is the deterioration of urban family values (often religious). Divorce rates climbed from 3.5 per 1,000 population in 1970, to over 5.0 in the 1980s, and births to unmarried women grew from roughly one in five in 1960 to one in three in the mid-1980s.

Changes in family structure explain in part the widened gap between rich and poor families. In the 1980s families with both parents in the work force had over two and one-half times the average family income of a family headed by a single woman. Even in the two-parent family, when one spouse was not in the labor force, family income was reduced by about one-third. Thus the family with income above the median is almost always there today because both spouses work. Conversely, poverty is increasing. In 1969, the poorest (the bottom one-fifth of the population) received 5.6 percent of the national income; in 1987 the figure was only 4.6 percent—and poverty had become most predominant in families headed by women (see table 1–5). This means that a larger percentage of children are growing up in poverty than ever before, despite rising national wealth—one-fifth of all children, including one-half of black children, as the decade of the 1990s began.

As will be seen in later chapters, the political process at the state and local levels often devises public policies based on the social class structures of their communities.

TABLE 1–4   Percent of Women in the Labor Force

1940	27%
1950	31%
1960	35%
1970	43%
1980	51%
1987	55%

Source: U.S. Bureau of the Census.

TABLE 1–5   Median Family Income

	1960	1965	1970	1975	1980	1985
Family type:						
Married couple	$5,873	$7,330	$10,516	$14,867	$23,141	$31,100
wife employed	$6,900	$8,633	$12,276	$17,237	$26,879	$36,431
wife not employed	$5,520	$6,706	$9,304	$12,752	$18,972	$24,556
Female parent only	$2,968	$3,535	$5,093	$6,844	$10,408	$13,660
Female parent only income as						
percent of married couple income	51%	48%	48%	46%	45%	44%
wife employed	43%	41%	41%	40%	39%	37%
wife not employed	54%	53%	55%	53%	55%	56%

Source: Computed from Census Bureau, Statistical Abstract of the United States: 1988, p. 430.

Suburbs and neighborhoods within the larger cities are heavily segregated on the basis of race and social class. America's poor consists mostly of families with children headed by single women, abandoned by the man who fathered the children. Conservatives have long argued that welfare policies for the poor may make poverty even worse by rewarding the breakup of the family. But national conservative leadership since about 1980 has brought little change in basic approaches to poverty relief. This suggests that innovation may not be forthcoming or may await the demands of those in the middle class who share the need for child care and government assistance. In the meantime, state and local governments will have to contend with the new realities in regard to work and family structure with piecemeal solutions (e.g., extended school hours, public-employee contracts that provide maternity leave, publicly supported day-care services). The ideologies that support such programs will be the topic of the next chapter.

The Changing Demographics of American Blacks

The black population in the United States is demographically distinct from the white population on the basis of social class, family structure, and political power (see table 1–6). In diverse ways, Hispanics also differ from Anglos. Unfortunately, Hispanic demographics are badly documented because the Census Bureau has had difficulty defining Hispanics and because immigration problems unique to Hispanics have created skepticism and suspicion within the population with regard to demographers. It is likely that, as Hispanics emerge as a greater political force in the next decade, the measuring difficulties will diminish so that more informed discussion of Hispanic demographics will become possible. What follows, therefore, is principally a discussion of black patterns.

    Perhaps the most dramatic population shift in American history has been made by blacks, many of whom are descendants of persons brought to the New World as slaves. Their ancestors labored on plantations in the South; nearly all of them were rural dwellers. After the Civil War, most blacks remained in the Deep South, becoming sharecroppers on land subdivided when the great plantations were broken up. Their numbers increased with each census, but a lower economic standard lead to a higher death rate. This, combined with an almost all-white immigration, caused the black percentage of the population (nearly 20 percent in 1790) to drop from 14 percent in 1860 to about 10 percent in 1930. But higher birth rates among blacks since 1950 has led to an increasing black percentage of the total population. In 1989, the Bureau of the Census estimated the black population to be 12.3 percent, with projections estimated to exceed 13 percent by the year 2000.

Even before slavery was abolished, some movement of blacks out of the South took place. However, as late as 1900, only 10 percent of the black population lived in the North. This began to change with the demand for unskilled labor in the urban factory, which first came during World War I. When a shortage of factory hands caused an imbalance in supply and demand of labor, it was the younger, more adventuresome blacks who first made the long trek to Chicago, Detroit, or New York. The word they sent back was that one could make far more money in less time and under better conditions in a factory than in the almost hopeless atmosphere of the tenant farm. As early as 1914, Henry Ford created a sensation when he offered a $5-a-day wage. He also established a quota for black employees.

After World War I, only the Great Depression served temporarily to stop the urbanization of blacks. Every other important economic and political consideration—the closing of the gates to immigration (1924), World War II (1941–1945), and the prosperous years after 1945—encouraged movement to the cities. In the decade following 1940, 3 million blacks made the rural-to-urban change. By 1950, 28 percent of the black population lived in the North; nearly 60 percent of the total was urban, for southern blacks also moved into southern cities. By 1970, the percentage of blacks located in urban areas had surpassed that of urban whites and by 1980, 85 percent of the black population (compared with only 71 percent of the white) was urban. In the 1970s and 1980s the migration of blacks out of the South slowed, but the percentage of blacks in core cities continued to reach new highs. Almost one-third of the core city population is black, and blacks comprise the majority in four core cities of the twenty largest MSAs (Atlanta, Detroit, Newark, and Washington); in another three core cities (Baltimore, Chicago, and Cleveland) 40 percent of the population is black. Hispanic movement has also been to the core city in recent years. In three of the 100 largest-populated U.S. cities (El Paso, Miami, and San Antonio) Hispanics exceed 50 percent. A dramatic consequence of this has been the emergence of minority mayors in many American core cities.

The diversity of black experience in America makes it dangerous to overgeneralize. Large numbers of blacks are considerably different from the statistical

TABLE 1–6   American Black Population Trends

Year	Black Population	Percent of Total Population Black	Urban Black Population	Percent Urban	Percent Outside South
1910	9,800,000	10.7%	2,700,000	28%	9%
1980	26,495,000	11.7%	22,500,000	74%	47%
1989	30,597,000	12.3%	n.a.	n.a.	47%

Source: Compiled from U.S. Bureau of the Census.
N.a.: not available.

averages. But blacks continue to be at a disadvantage in comparison with urban whites by almost any standard of measurement. Lower levels of education, fewer marketable skills, lower average income, smaller dwelling places, poorer sanitary facilities, poorer health and less medical care, fewer avenues for social or economic advancement, and poorer schools, all contribute to this imbalance. The late arrival of blacks to American cities partially explains the disadvantages.[26] The latest ethnic or racial group to come to a city has always held the position of lowest status. Blacks, arriving in cities without job skills and in large numbers, often were reduced to competing with one another.

But this alone does not explain black disadvantage. Higher incidence of the breakup of black families and lower education levels continue to reinforce the likelihood of a gap between black and white income levels. And the breakup of the black family is even more severe than the general breakup of families discussed above. Although this pattern dates back to slavery, it is on the rise again. In 1986, 54 percent (29 percent in 1970) of black children were raised in single-parent households headed by mothers only; and 60 percent of black children (37 percent in 1970) were born outside of marriage. Even though black income levels remain below those of whites in any family structure, the larger number of black single-parent families headed by a woman exaggerates the income disparities between white and black households.

To the degree that higher education levels pave the way for higher incomes, disparities in education levels between whites and blacks suggest that income differences will continue to exist. For example, the percentage of blacks who had not completed high school was reduced from 68.6 percent in 1970 to 35.3 percent in 1988, but the corresponding drop among whites was from 45.5 percent to 22.1. Thus, on the one hand black education levels are rising more quickly than white, but on the other they remain significantly below white levels. These differences will continue to institutionalize disadvantages to undereducated blacks.

Although disparities between blacks and whites continue, a gap is growing among blacks, too (see in table 1-7). The percentages of upper-income ($50,000 above) and upper-middle-income ($35,000–$49,999) blacks have increased despite black income remaining constantly at around 60 percent of white income. Furthermore, while the proportion of the poorest whites has gone down during this time, that of poorest blacks has gone up. Thus, not only are blacks becoming both poorer *and* wealthier at the same time, compared with whites; but the gap between poor and upper-middle-class blacks also is widening. Actually, the gaps between poor and upper-middle class have increased for whites, blacks, and Hispanics. Each has seen an increase in the upper-middle incomes and upper incomes, fluctuating a bit for economic hard times. But unlike whites, the minority groups have seen this happen while the proportion of their poor increases. Although the Hispanic numbers can be explained by the influx of poorer immigrants, the black disparities suggest an ever-increasing gap between blacks who have moved up socially and economically and blacks who remain poor. The variety of life-style differences that accompany this gap suggests that one must use considerable caution when treating blacks as a single interest group in today's political process.

In a federal system that values democratic equality of condition, conflict will always survive when serious income gaps exist. The valid normative questions are whether the gaps between black and white are being closed at a satisfactory rate, and whether the widening gaps among blacks will shift the focus of conflict away from the racial dimension that often has dominated American life since the Civil War. Regardless of the focus, state and local governments will have to respond to the demands created by new relationships among and within the races.

Population: In Summary

America entered the 1990s as an industrial nation with two-thirds of its population living in urban areas and chiefly in metropolitan communities. Large core cities have

TABLE 1–7   Income of the Population*

	Less than $5000	$5000– $19,999	$20,000– $35,999	$35,000– $49,999	$50,000 and above	Median Income
All Households						
1970	8.2%	34.2%	33.3%	12.8%	11.5%	$24,662
1975	6.8%	34.7%	31.3%	14.8%	12.3%	$24,039
1980	8.3%	34.2%	28.4%	16.4%	12.7%	$23,565
1982	8.5%	35.7%	27.8%	15.4%	12.7%	$22,913
1984	7.6%	35.0%	26.9%	15.8%	14.6%	$23,661
1986	7.4%	33.1%	26.2%	16.5%	16.8%	$24,897
White						
1970	7.3%	32.8%	34.2%	13.4%	12.2%	$25,687
1975	6.0%	33.4%	32.0%	15.5%	13.2%	$25,139
1980	7.1%	32.8%	29.1%	17.3%	13.7%	$24,862
1982	7.2%	34.3%	28.6%	16.1%	13.7%	$23,988
1984	6.3%	33.8%	27.7%	16.7%	15.6%	$24,962
1986	6.0%	31.9%	26.7%	17.3%	17.9%	$26,175
Black						
1970	15.5%	47.8%	25.7%	6.9%	4.0%	$15,635
1975	14.5%	47.2%	25.7%	8.3%	4.3%	$15,092
1980	17.7%	45.9%	22.4%	9.3%	4.7%	$14,323
1982	19.1%	45.9%	22.2%	9.0%	3.7%	$13,595
1984	17.5%	46.3%	21.2%	9.0%	5.8%	$14,220
1986	18.6%	42.1%	22.2%	10.2%	6.9%	$15,080
Hispanic**						
1970	n.a.	n.a.	n.a.	n.a.	n.a.	n.a.
1975	9.4%	45.5%	30.4%	9.8%	4.9%	$18,060
1980	11.0%	42.6%	26.9%	12.0%	6.5%	$18,164
1982	11.3%	46.0%	25.7%	10.8%	6.1%	$17,241
1984	11.8%	42.4%	26.8%	11.8%	7.1%	$17,937
1986	11.1%	42.4%	25.6%	11.8%	9.2%	$18,352

Source: U.S. Bureau of the Census.
*Income in constant 1986 dollars.
**Hispanic persons may be of any race.
N.a.: not available.

slowed their growth; nearly all the population increase after 1950 has been centered in the suburban areas.

In the 1980s small-town population continued to hold its own and even to grow; but farm population, which had reached an all-time high of 32.4 million in 1915 and had been declining almost without interruption since, continued to drop, falling to 5.2 million in 1986.

In the metropolitan areas, the flight to the suburb by the bulk of the middle class and many working-class families still was being counterbalanced by the continuing arrival of immigrants, migrants from rural and small-town areas, and some gentrification. Blacks are still moving into the core cities of all regions, and the increasing number of Hispanic and Asian immigrants is leading to renewed ghettoization of some neighborhoods. Asians accounted for almost half of the immigrants to the United States between 1980 and 1985, although political changes in Asia and in immigration law slowed that immigration in the latter part of the decade.

The aging of America, which began around 1970, continued through the 1980s. The percent of the population under age 5 remained uniform in the 1980s (around 7.5 percent), but the proportion of the population over age 65 rose slowly but steadily (to about 12.5 percent). The number of persons age 18 to 21 peaked in 1981 and will continue to decline through the early 1990s. But after the birthrate reached bottom in the mid-1970s, it increased slightly in the early 1980s and is projected to hold that increase well into the 1990s. Despite all of the changes, the total U.S. population will continue to increase at near the present birth-death rates.

Political Consequences

A great many aspects of state and local government are affected by the changing population pattern in America. To name a few:

1. Urbanization has produced successful demands for increased urban and suburban representation in legislatures; rural and, more recently, core cities have lost a rearguard action against this.[27]
2. The suburban trend has resulted in political conflict and service problems in metropolitan areas, which contain dozens, sometimes hundreds, of governmental units.[28]
3. The movement of blacks into cities has been accompanied by a growing awareness of their potential political power, particularly when blacks vote as a block against a split white electorate. Among other results, this has led to the election of a number of black mayors in cities without a black majority.[29]
4. People of many subcultures and living arrangements have found themselves living in close physical proximity in urban areas. This is contributing to increased social conflict, which becomes political conflict.[30]
5. The insecurities created because the urbanite is dependent for work upon someone else—the employer—have produced demands for governmental programs of many kinds.[31]
6. The agricultural transformation is causing economic distress to many farmers. Farmers, agricultural workers, and rural-to-urban migrants, are looking to

government at all levels for several types of assistance.[32] This is especially true of the less successful farmers and those who seek to preserve the increasingly less efficient family-size farm.

7. Gentrification and creative tax breaks for the middle class are leading to some middle-class return to the core cities and a slight slowing of the movement to the suburbs. These changes demonstrate renewed middle-class attraction to the core city and some recovery of lost tax base.[33]

8. Americans are becoming more and more alike by virtue of their attention to common or homogenized communication and entertainment media, homogenized education, the mix of people created by movement among all geographic regions, major SMSAs and large cities, and the federal government's attempts to equalize through grants-in-aid. As a result, all state and local governments face similar demands on scarce resources.[34]

9. Americans are, however, becoming more distinguished by class as measured by education, occupation, and life-style. The wealthy are becoming wealthier and the poor are becoming poorer; middle-income groups are not improving their positions as rapidly as they once did. Average income growth which slowed sharply in 1973, has not rallied to its old rate. The level of education (and hence kinds of skills) achieved has become more important than ever in determining personal income. The earnings of women relative to those of men have improved since 1979, but this has been more than offset for many women by their greater responsibilities as single parents. The causes of these trends— which span the Carter, Reagan, and Bush administrations and have transcended all levels of government—are not well understood. They are probably related to worldwide economic developments.[35]

These phenomena, which, among others, will be explored in later chapters, indicate an expanded task for state and local governments.

Notes

1. For a discussion of the continuing divergence and convergence in relation to urbanism, see Charles R. Adrian, *A History of American City Government: The Emergence of the Metropolis, 1920–1945* (Lanham, MD: University Press of America, 1987), chapter 1.

2. See a variety of accounts of the cultural differences among states and regions in Jerry Hagstrom, *Beyond Reagan: The New Landscape of American Politics* (New York: W. W. Norton, 1988); and Neal Pierce and Jerry Hagstrom, *The Book of America: Inside Fifty States Today* (New York: W. W. Norton, 1984); also Jack L. Walker, "The Diffusion of Innovation among the American States," *American Political Science Review* 63 (Sept. 1969): 867–79.

3. Virginia Gray, "Expenditures and Innovation as Dimensions of 'Progressivism': A Note on the American States," *American Journal of Political Science* 18 (Nov. 1974): 693–99.

4. Daniel J. Elazar, *American Federalism; A View from the States,* 3d ed. (New York: Thomas Y. Crowell, 1984).

5. Attempts to measure statistically the differences can be seen in Susan Welch and

John G. Detus, "State Political Culture and the Attitudes of State Senators Toward Social, Economic, Welfare and Corruption Issues," *Publius* 10 (Spring 1980): 3, 59–67; Charles A. Johnson, "Political Culture in American States: Elazar's Formulation Examined," *American Journal of Political Science* 20 (Aug. 1976): 3, 491–509; and Norman Luttbeg, "Classifying the American States: An Empirical Attempt to Identify Internal Variations," *Midwest Journal of Political Science* 15 (Nov. 1971): 703–22. See also Samuel C. Patterson, "The Political Cultures of the American States," *Journal of Politics* 30 (Feb. 1968): 187–209; and Raymond E. Wolfinger and Fred I. Greenstein, "Comparing Political Regions: The Case of California," *American Political Science Review* 63 (Mar. 1959): 74–85.

6. See Hagstrom, *Beyond Reagan*; and Ira Sharkansky, *Regionalism in American Politics* (Indianapolis: Bobbs-Merrill, 1970); Wolfinger and Greenstein, "Comparing Political Regions"; Ira Sharkansky, "Regionalism, Economic Status and the Public Policies of American States," *Southwestern Social Science Quarterly* 49 (June 1968): 9–26, together with comments by Charles R. Adrian, Clarence E. Ayers, A. L. Bertrand, and J. B. Frantz.

7. Elazar, *American Federalism,* 137–38. Also see David B. Walker, "New England and the Federal System," *Publius* 2 (Fall 1972): 4, 9–50.

8. See Kirkpatrick Sale, *The Power Shift: The Rise of the Southern Rim and Its Challenge to the Eastern Establishment* (New York: Random House, 1975); a series appearing in the *New York Times*, Feb. 8–12, 1976; and another in the *Minneapolis Star and Tribune*, Apr. 9–15, 1984; also for background, Carl Abbott, *The New Urban America: Growth and Politics in Sunbelt Cities* (Chapel Hill: University of North Carolina Press, 1982); and R. M. Miller and G. E. Pozzetta, eds., *Shades of the Sunbelt* (Westport, CT: Greenwood Press, 1988).

9. Gerald R. Nash, *The American West Transformed: The Impact of the Second World* (Bloomington: Indiana University Press, 1985).

10. Elazar, *American Federalism*, p. 97; and Larry Sawyers and William K. Tabb, eds., *Sunbelt/Snowbelt: Urban Development and Regional Restructuring* (New York: Oxford University Press, 1984).

11. The distinction was popularized by Ferdinand Toennis in *Gemeinshaft Und Gesellshaft* [first published in 1887]. It can be found in Toennis's text translated by Charles P. Loomis, *Fundamental Concepts in Sociology* (New York: American Books, 1940).

12. The relationship among local governments is the subject of chapter 8.

13. John C. Bollens and Henry J. Schmandt, *The Metropolis: Its People, Politics, and Economic Life,* 4th ed. (New York: Harper & Row, 1982), 11.

14. Norton Long, *The Unwalled City* (New York: Basic Books, 1972).

15. Louis Wirth, "Urbanism as a Way of Life," *American Journal of Sociology* 44 (July 1938):1, 1–24. For the life-style centering on the specialization of labor, which emerged with the coming of cities, Dora Jane Hamblin and others, *The First Cities* (New York: Time-Life Books, 1973).

16. Milton Kotler, *Neighborhood Governments,* (New York: Bobbs-Merrill, 1969).

17. Robert C. Wood, *Suburbia: Its People and Their Politics* (Boston: Houghton Mifflin, 1959).

18. We will return to the values of suburbia in chapter 2.

19. Public choice theory best explains suburban specialization. See Robert L. Bish, *The Public Economy of Metropolitan Areas,* (Chicago: Markham Publishing Co., 1964); and Robert L. Bish and Vincent Ostrom, *Understanding Urban Government* (Washington, D.C.: Domestic Affairs Studies, 1973).

20. See Edward Banfield, *The Unheavenly City Revisited* (Boston: Little, Brown, 1974), particularly chapter 2, "The Logic of Metropolitan Growth"; and, for a different

perspective, Anthony Downs, *Opening Up the Suburbs* (New Haven, CT.: Yale University Press, 1973).

21. A recommended collection is by S. Laska and D. Spain, eds., *Back to the City* (New York: Pergamon, 1980).

22. See chapter 14.

23. These kinds of conflicts are developed in J. Anthony Lukas, *Common Ground: A Turbulent Decade in the Lives of Three American Families* (New York: Alfred A. Knopf, 1985). This study centers around the failed Boston school-busing experiment and controversy of the 1970s.

24. See Claude Fischer, *The Urban Experience,* 2d ed. (San Diego: Harcourt Brace Jovanovich, 1984).

25. *U. S. Children and Their Families: Current Conditions and Recent Trends,* 1983, 1987, and 1989 (Washington, D.C.: U. S. Congress, House of Representatives Select Committee on Children, Youth, and Families).

26. George G. Grier, *Region in Transition* (Philadelphia: Penjerdel, 1964), 41. An excellent discussion of the black poor as part of a larger pattern is offered in Banfield, *Unheavenly City*; also see Charles R. Adrian and Charles Press, *American Politics Reappraised* (New York: McGraw-Hill, 1974), chapters 1 and 2. The inability of the unskilled to advance economically in an age of technology is portrayed in Sar A. Levitan and Isaac Shapiro, *Working but Poor—America's Contradiction* (Baltimore, MD: Johns Hopkins University Press, 1987).

27. See chapter 11 in particular.

28. See chapter 8 in particular.

29. See chapters 5 and 9 in particular.

30. See chapter 2 in particular.

31. See chapter 14 in particular.

32. Ibid.

33. Ibid.

34. Ibid.

35. Census Bureau data are summarized and examined in Jonathan Rauch, ''Downsizing the Dream,'' *National Journal* (Aug. 12, 1989), 2038–43.

Historical Pictures Service, Chicago

2

Ideology at the Grass Roots

Ideas affect politics. So do emotions. Effective politicians know how to mix the two in the proper proportion. They seek ideas that will make the most effective appeal in a given situation. They know too that the typical citizen often responds more readily to an emotional appeal than to a closely reasoned argument. Because of this, the politician becomes interested in ideas as weapons, as devices for manipulating people. Stated in terms that reflect existing social values, ideas are repeated with variations and elaborations and tied to established clichés that produce a desired response. Through skillful reiteration, ideas are boiled down until they become slogans or proverbs that produce a conditioned response in the individual exposed to them. But politicians, in seeking to influence people, are restrained by the existing value structure and thus cannot move effectively except within that structure.

Understanding ideas, attitudes, ideas as goals, and cultural values is important not just to the politician seeking to sway the minds of citizens, however. Some knowledge of these concepts is vital to anyone who wishes to understand the political process. Therefore, the material in this chapter includes key analytical tools that allow citizens to examine meaningfully—as participants *and* observers—political events that affect them.

The Nature of Political Ideology

Philosophers attempt to explain social phenomena—including, of course, political phenomena—in terms of ultimate causes, and they seek to develop logical relationships among the various phenomena they observe. In pursuing an understanding of life's meaning, philosophers frequently write about the function of government and its politics; yet the effect that these writings may have on the general public or on the structure and functioning of government has not been clearly determined. Certainly some philosophers influence the actions of future generations, as Thomas Jefferson did in setting the scene for a frontier democracy and as John Dewey did in influencing the public schools. Others, however, probably reflect the values of their own day or of a past or future day, expressing them in more formal and systematic terms than would the politician or the journalist. Whatever their ultimate effect on government, the writings of those whose views were so painstakingly set out by Sabine and Parrington are not read by the typical citizen.[1] His or her views on politics stem from far more visceral impressions than those created by the systematic and rational (though not always unemotional) writings of philosophers, even though the "temptation to assign a controlling influence to the place of ideas in the operation of democracy is very great."[2] For the ordinary person in any society, far more important than philosophy is the network of less systematic values that social scientists call ideology.

Symbolism, which underlies philosophy and ideology, is any term or concept intentionally used to represent something else. Symbols have meaning both because they appeal to the emotions and because they are outward shorthand expressions of the loosely clustered ideological values that hold society together and enable the political system to function. Symbols are important in the development of public policy, for whenever they are used ineffectively to justify policy, widespread dissatisfaction results.[3]

Ideologies: The Web of Government

Politics has its "rituals, sacred objects, saints, dogmas, devotions, feasts, fanaticisms, mummeries and its Bible of sacred writing."[4] That is, it has an elaborate system of symbols, not as pervasive or enduring as those of religion, perhaps, but certainly similar. As suggested in the previous chapter, these symbols influence people to act, even people who scarcely understand the myths on which the symbols are based.

An *ideology* is a system of beliefs that provide a distinctive way of evaluating some aspect of political life and a preference for the future condition or direction of that aspect. An ideology may be beyond the scope of a single idea. For example, an individual may demonstrate one ideology on a particular aspect of political life (for instance, the localistic belief in neighborhood schools) while simultaneously demonstrating a more encompassing ideology (for instance, the democratic belief in racially integrated schools). Ideologies simplify the understanding process; they allow individuals to act without making all of the difficult and time-consuming decisions about the likely ramifications of a particular political act. Information management—a problem of such concern to scientists that separate university departments are formed for the purpose of training specialists to organize the subject matter, is a lesser problem to the ideologist who, instead of preparing exhaustive indexes, operates with a short list of truths that are accepted on faith.

At any one time in a nation, of course, various idologies—new and old—prevail and not all people, even within a region, accept the same ideology at the same time. Within a particular state for example, one group may be motivated by the greed of a political machine whereas another may be spurred by the public spirit of progressive reform. Nevertheless, an ideology usually exists that is accepted by a dominant group of citizens. As a result, politicians are able to condition their appeals to fit the beliefs treasured by their constituents.

The remainder of this chapter focuses on four ideological periods in American domestic politics. In the first, the Revolutionary period, the myths of the Founders were born. Despite differences in culture and economy, these myths have prevailed throughout American history and even today help people choose life-styles. In the *second* Ideological period, localism and frontier individualism were the dominant priorities in most states. For some Americans the movement westward took precedence; for the majority left behind, the organization of life in the towns, townships, or counties took top priority. In the third period, the seventy years following the Civil War, industrialization and urbanization dominated American life. Boss-and-machine ideologies ruled the city's ethnic ghettos. The myth of laissez-faire prevailed. The fourth period was characterized by the ideology of the social service state which emerged during the Great Depression. What at first was a response to the needs of the unemployed, soon became a reformer's creed that dominated government and affected all classes of people. In this period the national government has emerged to outspend states and localities through its superior power to raise money to serve the demands of public services consumers. Each period, really an amalgam of many ideologies uniquely combined, abounds with contradictions in logic. For instance, although strong economic individualism prevailed in the third ideological period, a great sense of kinship and neighborhood also could be found within ethnic ghettos. The Revolutionary period produced the sharply different views of Madison and Jefferson about government's capacity to serve the individual, yet they were long-time personal friends and later joined to work together in forming the Democratic party.

A final point about the nature of ideologies: Their relationship to the environment is always interactive. Existing ideologies condition emerging political, social, and economic circumstances; these circumstances in turn tend to modify the existing ideologies. Hence, ideologies and the environment in which they exist are interdependent, each affecting the other.

Ideological Roots: The Revolutionary Period

It was an agricultural nation that declared its independence from the mother country in 1776. Only about 3 percent of the people lived in nonrural communities, and not more than twenty-four incorporated municipalities existed in all thirteen new states. An important aristocracy existed. In the South, slave-owning planters concentrated along the coast and in the river valleys; in the rest of the nation, bankers, exporters-importers, shipowners, and manufacturers. Yet, at least outside the Deep South, most Americans were neither rich nor poor; rather they were yeomen farmers. Property requirements for voting were met easily in rural areas; nearly 90 percent of the adult white males of Massachusetts could vote at the time of the Revolution.[5]

> *Yeoman Farmer:* **A farmer, usually a husband-and-wife team, who owned, were buying, or hoped to buy their farm and operate it with or without hired hands. Their ideology differed sharply from that of the European peasant, who lacked both social and physical mobility and could never hope to own land.**

The American Revolution was premised on British *liberalism.* John Locke's *Second Treatise on Government* was the guiding principle of the Declaration of Independence. Independence was justified by the argument that the British had infringed on the colonists' natural "unalienable" rights of life, liberty, and property. The revolutionaries argued that without protection of individual rights, the social contract that bound them to obey the British was null and void. But of course the Revolution had to be won to establish these principles. The war brought together thirteen colonies that heretofore had little sense of commonality *and* little sense of commonality after the colonists (surprisingly) won the war. Many viewed the Confederacy as no more than a temporary alliance for the purpose of waging war.[6] Some of the more extreme revolutionaries were far more concerned with the abolition of governmental power than with the subsequent formation of a better system.

> *Liberalism:* **Liberalism, developed from the slowly emerging Renaissance emphasis on individualism, has always focused on individual freedom. Liberalism came to stress natural rights, human rationality and potential for improving one's lot, limitations on government, and freedom of the individual from external restraints. In the late seventeenth century, John Locke advocated classical liberalism, whereas early nineteenth-century liberals sought maximum freedom from government. In the late nineteenth century, T. H. Green of Oxford University held that liberalism could allow government to advance the welfare of individuals and prevent oppression. It was from this positive aspect of the concept that modern American liberalism developed.**

The Articles of Confederation affirmed the wishes of those who feared centralization of power. Beyond providing the limited power to declare war and coin money, the document is more important in terms of the powers it did *not* give the new central government—the power to tax, any executive or judicial power, or the power to regulate commerce. Laws could be passed only by two-thirds vote of the Congress (each state having one vote), and amendment required unanimous approval. With the exception of the few rights of Congress made explicit in the Articles, each state retained its "sovereignty, freedom and independence, and every power, jurisdiction, and right. . ."[7] Clearly, the choice of new governments would not be made collectively at first; rather it would be left to the individual states in the creation of their own constitutions and in the practices of each community.

In the states, political battles raged for a decade between those fearful of state power who advocated bills of rights, and proponents of state power as delineated in state constitutions. Those advocating bills of rights eventually won out, but it took more than a decade after the Revolution ended to decide the issue.

The Green Years of State and Local Governments

State legislatures, which championed the colonists against the royalist governors who represented British rule, became the dominant agencies in state government. The governors, on the other hand, were burdened by the unfavorable image of the executive branch—an image created when their prerevolutionary counterparts sided against the resident population. Each legislature usually chose the state officials, including a governor who was limited to a one-year term, had no veto power except in Massachusetts, and could not succeed himself. It also selected the judiciary.[8]

In these early days of the Republic, the values of thrift and hard work were already firmly established. But neither these values nor the importance of property had as yet produced the doctrine of laissez-faire, which called for the government to keep its hands off business. As a matter of fact:

> The colonists were accustomed to the mercantile system of intensive state regulation of economic affairs. Their argument with England had not been that the system was evil but that it was being used to colonial disadvantage.
> . . .State governments followed the practices that they knew and in which they believed. They fixed prices for transportation services, licensed inn-keepers and peddlers, constructed and operated turnpikes, and began issuing special charters to businesses.[9]

In New England, the typical form of local government was the town meeting. In the middle and southern states, where formal town meetings were less common, ad hoc public meetings registered protest or occasionally acted as governments.[10] All eligible voters (most adult males) could participate in town meetings, and most did. The meetings had few rules, although participants usually followed accepted precedents. They elected many officials (the unusually high number of eighty-four in Windham, Connecticut, ranged from the part-time moderator to the leather sealer).[11] Decisions made at the meetings were often carried out directly by the participants, rather than relying on the elected officials who would serve when the meetings were not in session. But as the new century dawned, the meetings more frequently began to serve primarily to elect large numbers of public officials. Although the more important officials came from a relatively small group, their decisions were subject to the consensus of the town meeting.[12] It would be some time before the average citizen abdicated most of the policy-making function at the town level to an elected elite.

In the cities, the pattern of organization also reflected the belief and disillusionments of the times. The urban structure, modeled on a British system that was familiar to the colonists had no separation of powers between the legislative and executive branches; the council possessed virtually all authority. It was headed by the mayor, who had no *veto* power and practically no executive power. His task was to preside over council meetings as one of its members and to perform civic ceremonial functions. Full-time jobs in city government were rare before the 1840s.

> *Veto:* **The act of the chief executive in disapproving a proposed ordinance or statute. Usually, a veto must be indicated within a given period of time and the proposal (together with objections) must be returned to the legislative house of origin. Normally, the legislative body can enact the ordinance or statute over the veto by repassing it with some specified extraordinary majority.**

Jeffersonian Localism and Madisonian Federalism

Jefferson and Madison worked together throughout the early decades of American politics. Nevertheless, they represented different views of the proper relationship between individual and government and the proper structure of government created to reflect that relationship. These views can be seen as differing ideologies of state and, particularly, local government.

Jeffersonian Antiurbanism and Localism

It is through the following quotation that Jeffersonian and subsequent American antiurbanism are traced.

> The mobs of great cities add just so much to the support of pure government, as sores do to the strength of the human body. It is the manners and spirit of a people which preserve a republic in vigor. A degeneracy in these is a canker which soon eats to the heart of its laws and constitutions.[13]

The quotation, however, frequently is overstated. Jefferson did not wholly reject city life in favor of the life-style of the yeoman farmer; he calculated the virtues of each. In Paris, his major experience with city life, he saw the positive aspects of the Enlightenment—philosophical discussion and the arts which reinforced his lifelong commitment to public education. Nevertheless, he believed that the city also produced the ''mobs.'' For Jefferson, mob rule was the opposite of the ultimate political goal, that of individual freedom. Mob rule involved people out of control, caught up in the spirit of the group. Jefferson believed that individual freedom existed when a person had resources and education to act wisely in his or her own interest. Jefferson did not reject cities; he rejected mobs in favor of individual freedom.

Jefferson further believed that the new political system needed direction in weaving a new social fabric and in forming a new government, and he offered advice in both areas. The city's virtues were calculated more negatively than the farm's, and Jefferson therefore overstated the virtues of yeoman life. In describing the ''manner and spirit'' of the new country in *Notes on the State of Virginia,* he concluded that wherever the choice arises, Americans should opt for the yeoman's life-style, where each relatively equal family could work unencumbered by the dependence on others that prevailed in the city.[14] The Louisiana Purchase can be viewed as Jefferson's intent to ensure that farmland would remain abundant. Not until his last years did he recognize the inevitability of urban and industrial development in the United States.

The social freedom produced by farm life did not mean political isolation. It produced localism, the participation Jefferson envisaged when he proposed a system whereby ruralites could participate actively in the new state. Some of the principles of localism dated back to the compacts made by the earliest American settlers, but in his letters Jefferson proposed these structures and combined them with the seemingly contradictory concerns for individuality. He described a ward system of ''little republics'' in which the people in a five- or six-square-mile area could come together to handle all matters they could accomplish for themselves. Anwar Syed compiled the following list from Jefferson's writings of duties for the ward:

- care of the poor
- building of roads
- policing

- administration of justice
- exercise of the militia
- education
- election of judges and police
- selection of jurors
- keeping election records.[15]

A task would be passed up to a higher level of government only if it could not be accomplished successfully in the ward, and only then to the next higher level of government—county first, then state, and finally nation. Surely with the New England town meeting in mind, Jefferson believed that each man should participate in political affairs locally. By so doing, not only would each participant protest against, even prevent, the harm government might do, he could also do good things and achieve individual happiness. The tasks of the farm would remain individual and largely private, but political action would play a prominent role in life.

> *Localism:* **An ideology holding that government is best when it is perceived as being close to individuals so they can participate directly and thereby check the possibility of individual harm.**

Jefferson's philosophical tenets were not achieved in the way he hoped. Care for the poor and policing would not become standard provisions by any level of government, let alone a local ward, until well into the twentieth century. The seeming contradiction between Jefferson's call for individual freedom and his desire for reasoned collective action lent credence to claims that Jefferson believed in practices that he almost certainly would have rejected. Nevertheless, two myths certainly can be traced to Jefferson: (1) that city life is dangerous and small-town and rural life inherently better; (antiurbanism) and (2) that government closest to the people is inherently good and government far away undoubtedly will do harm (localism). The ideology formed from these myths would have less to do with the structure of American government than those ideologies of Madison. But they probably explain as much about American life-style choices as any myths regarding American state and local politics.

Madisonian Federalism

James Madison, known as the Father of the Constitution, initiated the arguments most responsible for the structure given the new government. His philosophy of *federalism* is best represented in the *Federalist Papers,* the series of newspaper articles written by Madison, Alexander Hamilton, and John Jay in support of the proposed U.S. Constitution. In *Federalist 10,* which remains the best argument for the multiplicity of governments in the United States, Madison argued that the political harm government does is an extension of individual harm. Self-interest cannot be checked by checking its causes (both good—freedom and reason), but by checking its effects. Luckily, the United States is a vast land in which many governments, each with many units, can be formed. Each unit of government will naturally represent different interests and will inevitably be checked by other self-interested units. Madison thus saw *interest* as the inherent threat to government but also the solution to that threat. A government that cannot achieve its goals and is frustrated by other competing governments, is a good government. Rather than viewing a frustrating stalemate as failure, Madison suggests that this might just be the most individuals should hope for when acting collectively.

Far more than Jefferson, Madison was skeptical of government's capacity to act collectively for some common purpose. Even though Jefferson certainly feared the mob, the tyrant, or even the unenlightened, he had great faith in the free individual who with his neighbors acted reasonably for some common end. Madison lost faith in such solutions when he considered the actual mechanics of government. He argued that free governments *without exception* are tainted by factionalism, the "common impulse of passion or of interest adverse to the interests of other citizens, or the permanent and aggregate interests of the community." Such passion "is sown in the nature of man"; it destroys the capacity for a small well-knit community. He referred inconsistently to the enlightened statesmanship of the virtuous, but in character found reliance on such statesmanship to be impractical, if not impossible[16]

> It is vain to say that enlightened statesmen will be able to adjust these clashing interests and render them all subservient to the public good. Enlightened statesmen will not always be at the helm. Nor, in many cases, can such an adjustment be made at all without taking into view indirect and remote considerations, which will rarely prevail over the immediate interest which one party may find in disregarding the rights of another or the good of the whole.[17]

The conclusion, although somewhat bothersome to Madison, was inevitable: People cannot be trusted. They will tend to pursue self-interest. This view of human beings produced a kind of anti-localism in Madison that conflicts with the faith in localism expressed by Jefferson. Madison feared the mischief of someone in control of his or her own political power more than he worried about that person's freedom.

This negative view of people and distrust of the local community might have led Madison to a negative view of public participation; but participation was unavoidable, given his view of people. Government became a public forum in which an individual would pursue self-interest. The genius of Madison's theory of federalism was his harnessing of participation as both an expression of self-interest and the clue to its suppression. *Federalist 10* and *Federalist 51* argue that, with a large number of citizens participating in diverse ways, there will be a check on the ability of a self-interested majority to form, and a secondary check on the ability of a minority to take undue advantage of another minority. Unlike Jefferson, Madison questioned whether participation was good in its own right. Instead, he saw it as a mechanism to suppress the evil inclination of people. It was necessary as a check; it was not an inherent good.

Madison, like Jefferson, viewed the distribution of power in government as the clue to individual liberty. But rather than relying on the emerging virtuous citizen to demonstrate his virtue by participating locally, Madison put his faith in the superior power of the self-interested participant. This in turn was checked by expecting every self-interested individual to participate. Without stating it explicitly, Madison assumed that the self-interested individual would always pursue self-interest (by participating) *if allowed to do so.* The federal system established at the Constitutional Convention was the American form of that permission. It opened diverse avenues of government participation with each new unit of state, local, even national government. To the extent that each would be filled, each would be checked by the overwhelming number of competing avenues.

> *Federalism:* **A political ideology holding that government exists to protect the individual, and that that protection comes from dividing governments into a number of distinctly powerful parts so that no one part becomes sovereign over the others.**

The Founders thus provided two competing ideologies in support of the labyrinth of state and local governments and in support of widespread participation in these governments. Jefferson sought safe local government that would maximize the good individduals could accomplish together. Madison sought safe state and local government that would minimize the harm individuals could cause. Both provided reasons for the expansion of government controlled by individual participation. The egalitarian mood of the Jackson age of the 1820s and 1830s characterized a people seemingly willing to test both philosophies.

The Ideology of Frontier Individualism and Its Small Towns

Throughout American history the ideologies that dominate our politics have regularly alternated about every one and one-half generations between two themes. In one, the spirit of populism reigns, when some common folk become involved fairly actively and exert influence by virtue of that participation. The other is dominated by much more passiveness, when participation by common folk is greatly reduced or ineffective. The Revolutionary War signaled the first participatory period (well summarized in the writings of Jefferson), followed by the decline in participation during the period when the Constitution was written.

The Jeffersonian Period

The second cycle saw the decline of the Federalist party and the election of Thomas Jefferson as President in 1800. The Federalist party, which never had a chance for long life, was a class party in a nation increasingly subjected to the egalitarian influences of the frontier. While Federalists were looking to the advancement of commerce, industry, and the plantations, Thomas Jefferson, with the help of others, "had steadily gathered behind him the great mass of small farmers, mechanics [skilled tradesmen], shopkeepers, and other workers."[18] These were gradually molded into a party of the common people, the development of which was a bud that was to flower completely in the age of Andrew Jackson.

The party formed was the first truly American party, designed more to win elections by combining diverse interest groups than to organize legislatures or the Congress. Since 1800, American parties have been more interested in garnering votes for candidates than in promoting ideology. In that sense, it was Jefferson's election that saw the birth of the American two-party system, although the nominating convention and the development of a ''campaign'' would not emerge until challenges to the Jacksonians some thirty to forty years later.

In the early nineteenth century, changes took place in state government. Almost all of the new state constitutions omitted property ownership as a qualification for suffrage. In the 1820s and 1830s, the older states dropped their property requirements for voting—requirements that might otherwise have had important connotations for the expanding urban proletariat. Because of behavior that caused a decline in public confidence, state legislators who had been the heroes of the day during and immediately after the Revolution fell into disfavor and constitutional restrictions began to be placed on their powers.[19] The most common restrictions were those prohibiting the chartering of banks, except for a single state bank (the yeoman farmer, chronically in debt, was already in conflict with those who controlled the credit, as farmers were to remain throughout American history). Legislatures were also prohibited from granting individual divorces by special acts, formerly a common practice when no general divorce laws existed, available primarily to those of wealth and political influence. Finally, salaries of major officials were written into the state constitutions and the legislatures were prohibited from raising them.

Governors

The governorship also changed during the first two decades of the nineteenth century. The changes are a good example of how attitudes of a group in society change according to whether its friends currently hold political power. During the forming of the new U. S. Constitution, the conservative Federalists favored a strong chief executive. After they lost power, however, they came to oppose such an institution, whereas opponents who earlier had wanted a weak executive were now generally triumphant and (especially along the frontier) wanted to strengthen the executive.

The conservatives resorted to the Whig theory of the executive, so called for the party in England that opposed a strong monarch. This view held that presidents or governors should not play a part in policy making; that they should have few administrative powers; and, if they had a veto at all, that veto should be used only against unconstitutional legislation, not against proposals that disagree with personal ideology or political interests. The Jeffersonians did not offer an adequate theory to counter this. Their view was largely empirical; that is, executives could rightly exercise power if they did so in the interests of constituents. But the Jeffersonians prevailed as the legislative power was checked. Governors (and, a little later, mayors) began to acquire power to veto legislation, and the beginnings of administrative power came to them through a right to require reports in writing from other state officers. (Both these provisions had been written into the national Constitution.) *Judical review* increased in importance in the states (Jefferson opposed it on the national level—the federal judiciary had become the last refuge of the Federalists).

> *Judicial Review:* **Action by a court to rule on the question of whether a statute, ordinance, or administrative order is constitutional.**

Internal Improvements

During this period, the states were actively seeking to break down the obstacles preventing the westward movement of the frontier. They sought to connect the frontier with the established East and its ports, business firms, and institutions of credit. The Missouri Constitution of 1820 stated the case: "Internal improvements shall forever be encouraged by the government of this State, and it shall be the duty of the general assembly, as soon as may be, to make provision by law for ascertaining the most proper objects of improvement. . ." Between 1800 and 1820, Pennsylvania encouraged the development of business by issuing three hundred franchises (charters) to manufacturing corporations.[20] New York constructed a great 400-mile highway to the West, completed in 1825, in the Erie Canal.

Public Education

During the early years of the nation, Jefferson insisted that the states assume responsibility for education. Led by examples set in New England and New York education became public. But resistance continued for the first half of the century. In the South, resistance to the ideal of free public education was somewhat more ideological. Furthermore, blacks, routinely denied the benefits of what public education did exist, would not be provided even segregated facilities until the twentieth century. Until the Civil War, many states continued charging much of the cost of public education to the parent directly, with some provision for "free" education for the poor.[21] Beginning with the admission of Ohio (1803), the Democrats in Congress sought to prod the new states by requiring, as a condition of statehood, that the sixteenth section in each township be reserved for schools. In contrast to the usual pattern of establishing institutions first along the edge of civilization, however, the frontier states were somewhat slower in providing free public education than were the eastern states. The frontier practice of charging back part of the costs to parents was probably more an indication of their relative poverty than of lack of sympathy toward the principle. When public education took hold it was "public" in two senses. First, education was increasingly funded by the property tax. Along with rooting decision making in the locality, this move kept church influence to a minimum. Second, the peculiar American tradition of the school district was developed. School districts are limited-purpose governments created by state legislatures to provide education. The districts are therefore usually independent of city or county government and have their own taxing powers. Their creation demonstrated many of the American values of localism and federalism by being locally controlled and dominated, independent (in most decisions) of states and other localities, but ultimately legally dependent on the states. Gradually, state legislatures expanded the number and types of rules they made concerning education, but the principle of local control had become deeply established (more on school districts in chapter 7).

The Jacksonians

The difference between the philosophy of Jefferson, the man of reflection, and the ideology of the Jacksonians, men of action, has been described as one in which the former sought the ideal of equality in order to develop individuality, whereas the latter sought the same ideal as a means to provide opportunity for ambition and a chance to climb the ladder of wealth and power.[22] Note should be made that the terminology here is a bit misleading. Just as the ideals of Jefferson the revolutionary disagreed often with the tenets of the Jeffersonian period decades later, "Jacksonians" commonly stood far from the beliefs of Andrew Jackson, the man. Few of the ideas that took his name can be traced to the unlettered Jackson himself. Nevertheless, a political image emerged during this period. Unlike Jefferson, who had little contact with the common folk he championed intellectually, the Jacksonian politician, whose political environment included white male suffrage, concentrated on contacting his constituents and exploiting their commonly shared values. He did not seek to make philosophers out of them or to teach the alleged splendor of individualism. In this sense, the Jacksonian became the prototype of nearly all American politicians.

Two somewhat different threads were woven into the ideology of the Jacksonian period. The first was colored by the movement to the frontier, the second (best described by Alexis de Tocqueville) by the majority of people left behind in the small towns and farms of the original states. Together they created the myths that produced the growth of America from the rural society of the green years to the world industrial leader of the twentieth century. It was the ideology of a people constantly in debt yet perennially optimistic about the future; of common people who were now on their own, who now relized that they no longer belonged to an oligarchy of propertied aristocrats. As commonly occurs with ideologies, contradictory ideas were brought together; the two threads often lacked rational connection, but they worked together in political practice. Both threads would have influence well into future generations, where the ideals of the Jacksonian form of localism would become the basis for the myth of the superiority of small-town life (for example, supporting suburbia) and the movement to the frontier would give rise to the ideals of individualism that fueled the rapid growth of cities and, eventually, metropolitan areas.

The Frontier

Frontier values came out of everyday experiences in the struggle for survival, for success, and for wealth. The outlook on life—pragmatic rather than introspective and functional rather than universal—was applied to state, county, township, village, and city governments alike. An excellent statement of these beliefs may be found in the novel *Raintree County* by Ross Lockridge, Jr.

> It was the code of the early Hoosier, the backwoodsman or river man, a type already [in 1859] becoming extinct in Indiana. The code of Flash Perkins was the code of a people who had become great fighters and talkers in a wilderness where there was not much else a man could do for diversion except fight and talk. It was the code of the tellers of tall tales who tried to live up to their tales. It was the code of a competitive people, who had fought the Indian and a still greater antagonist, the wilderness itself, the stubborn, root-filled pioneer earth, the beautiful and deadly river, the sheer space of the West. It was the code of breezy, cocky men, who had no fear in heaven or earth they would admit to. The code involved never hitting a man who was down, never turning down a drink, never refusing to take a dare, never backing out of a fight—except with a woman. The code involved contempt for city folks,

redskins, varmints of all kinds, atheists, scholars, aristocrats, and the enemies of the United States of America.

Actually, every Raintree County man had a little of the code in him. It was simply the Code of the West, and though the West had already passed over Raintree County and left it far behind, nevertheless the County had once been and would always be a part of the West. As Professor Jerusalem Webster Stiles was wont to say, "To the true Easterner, everything on the other side of the Alleghenies is the West. And in a way that's right. . . ."[23]

The Small Town

Whereas Jefferson had hoped for the development of American localism, the brilliant French writer Alexis de Tocqueville found its fruition in the small towns of New England in the Jacksonian age. Tocqueville wandered New England wondering why this part of America had apparently succeeded with its democratic experiment so much better than had France. He concluded that the town had mastered the union between self-interest and community interest.[24] People participated in New England town meetings because they hoped to benefit from a partnership with their neighbors. But once that participation took hold, the activity itself became satisfying and mysteriously linked to the optimism so prevalent in the Jacksonian period. The New Englander enjoyed self-government, taking satisfaction in making decisions in town meetings and then carrying them out. Few complaints about services could be made by people who themselves were the providers. Little danger existed from a government that comprised the town people themselves.

Tocqueville nevertheless realized that the New England experiement would have many opportunities for failure. One was the possible threat to outsiders of "different" people who would feel ostracized, even tyrannized, by an active majority.[25] A second danger was that people would lose interest in the rather routine business of the meetings. By staying home and tending the farm a few extra hours, the hardworking farmer or merchant might produce a slightly greater profit but lose the satisfaction that came from participation in community affairs.[26] Most dangerous of all was the possibility that apathy would become endemic, creating a centralized democracy that would lose sight altogether of the interests of the people but would remain powerful by virtue of its election by an apathetic mass of voters.[27]

Indications of these dangers were to be seen in Tocqueville's time. In 1821, Boston, having grown to about 45,000 people, was experiencing poor attendance at town meetings. But the town employees were motivated to come—especially the lamplighters who, considering themselves underpaid, altered the budget to give themselves a generous pay increase. At the 1822 town meeting (much better attended), the majority present, rather than expecting the protection of well-attended meetings in the future, voted to abolish the town meeting and ask the legislature to create a city. Boston thus became the first city (in the legal sense, to be explained further in the next chapter) in New England.

Each of Tocqueville's dangers would be realized to some extent in subsequent state and local developments. When immigrants came to small American cities, their differing ways caused constant conflict with the old majorities. The tendency toward apathy, to let government provide for some of one's needs, would indeed become epidemic in the welfare state of the twentieth century. Nevertheless, that overstated ideal of small-town self-government would remain throughout American history, finding particular glorification in the suburban movement. The Jacksonian town came closest to that ideal.

Jacksonian Principles

Probably antecedent to all other Jacksonian principles was the concept of government by the common man (remember, women could not vote). Government existed not for a privileged class but for the general citizen. Any one man was equal to any other man. Jefferson had said so in 1776, when the country was controlled by an aristocracy; now the words were to be taken literally, even though only the visionary extended the concept beyond the white male in the 1820s. If this were the case, then it followed that any man was as good as any other in public office—no special qualifications were needed, no special training, nothing other than willingness to serve the community.

Out of this concept came the principle of universal manhood suffrage. It followed logically from egalitarianism, was necessary to the development of Jacksonian thought, and furthermore was the natural effect of inertia on the already existing tendency to broaden the electorate—a tendency that had begun even before the Revolution. Change in this respect accelerated dramatically during the 1830s especially; and by 1850, virtually all property restrictions had disappeared from voting requirements and universal white manhood suffrage had been achieved. A large component of the general public now possessed the potential to control government in its own interests. Universal manhood suffrage made it possible for any man to run for office, get support from all kinds of people, and be elected. Jacksonians were not greatly concerned with the education, experience, or private calling of a candidate. This viewpoint, incidentally, legitimized a career as a *professional politician* or even as a *political hack*.

> *Political Hacks:* **Individuals who are perennial office seekers and who depend for a livelihood on scraps from the political table. Their competence and degree of public faith are questionable. As politics has shifted from labor-intensive to technology-intensive, the role of the hack has diminished.**

> *Professional Politicians:* **Persons who make a living in the political arena and whose competence in a public job is assumed or has been demonstrated, even though they are not trusted by some members of the public.**

Following from the above, Jacksonians believed that public officeholders, as servants of the people, should hold their mandates directly from "the people." Therefore it was desirable to elect, rather than appoint, public officials. Gradually this came to mean the election of many officers, thus imposing on Americans the unique institution of the long, or "bedsheet," ballot. To further ensure proximity to the voters, short terms of one or two years in office and rapid turnover of personnel were advocated. In rural and small urban communities, government could be per-

sonal; the long ballot was therefore less of a handicap to the casual voter, who probably knew all or most of the candidates personally or by reputation. Similarly, whereas
rapid turnover meant inexperienced officeholders, this was no real problem where
government was on a neighborly basis and administration was nontechnical. The
public thought it more important that the bureaucracy be representative of the interests of the common people than that it be skilled and neutral.[28]

Administrative Trends

The trends begun during the early nineteenth century continued through the period
preceding the Civil War. The chief executive officer continued to gain back some of
the ground lost during and after the Revolution. Terms of office were lengthened in
some instances, restrictions against succeeding oneself were eased, and impeachment became more difficult. But governors and mayors, though given some appointive powers previously vested in the legislative body, had little administrative authority because of the prevalence of the long ballot. Oregon went so far as to make the
state printer an elective office—state printing contracts were lucrative and thus subject to abuse. It was assumed that direct public control over the printer through election would help eliminate the threat of corruption.

Party organization developed during the Jacksonian period. Through organization the party controlled patronage, and through the use of conventions and caucuses
(the primary election appeared much later) it controlled nominations. Parties tended
to be alliances of sectional interests, but the Democratic party, which had sponsored
the expansion of the suffrage and with which the ideology of frontier individualism
was associated in the popular mind, was much stronger than its opponents, who had
gathered together in the Whig party.

State constitutions were lengthened as the public, distrustful of legislatures that
often were corrupt, wrote a good deal of statutary law into them. Some lawyers and
political reformers have argued subsequently that the constitution should be retained
as fundamental law only, setting forth the structure of government and providing basic rules of the political process (particularly because it is often difficult to amend).
But the practice of adding statutory language to state constitutions has continued to
the present day (as will be discussed further in the next chapter).

Legislative corruption—bribery, blackmail, the shakedown, outright theft—
began before the Civil War and grew worse immediately afterward; nearly all states
were affected. In its early history, the Southern Pacific Railroad virtually bought control of the California legislature. The copper-mine owners did the same in Montana.
A party boss in Georgia used state money to buy into a railroad-car company, had the
legislature appropriate funds to buy cars from him, and then did not deliver the cars.
Reconstruction legislatures of the South reached the lowest ebb. Northern visitors
organized slumming expeditions to monitor the Louisiana legislature of carpetbag-
gers and recently freed slaves, none of whom were acquainted with the task for which
they were elected.[29]

Some state constitutions had sections written in providing that the question of holding a constitutional convention be submitted to the voters periodically, generally every
twenty years. The provision, still a feature of a few state constitutions heralded a trend

toward submitting constitutional amendments directly to the voters, who had to approve them before changes went into effect. This practice eventually became almost universal. Constitutions continued to have increasingly long lists of *don'ts* added to them with a view toward limiting the legislature's discretionary powers. The use of state credit for internal improvements had been greeted enthusiastically in the early years of the century, but road and canal building by state governments ran into a series of misfortunes. Some routes were poorly chosen or cost so much to develop that subsequent traffic did not liquidate the debt; the panic of 1837 had disastrous consequences for state finances; building was sometimes done inefficiently with political patronage a factor; and, as the final blow, while canals and turnpikes were still being built or before they were paid for, the railroad came along as a more efficient form of transportation. The result was a spate of constitutional provisions prohibiting the use of state credit in such undertakings. (The pragmatic frontier people, though they believed individuals could best depend on themselves, did not oppose state activity in the transportation field; but the failures in this area later were cited as "proof" that government was too inefficient to engage in activities that might be best performed by private enterprise.)

The Case of Ohio
Ohio offers an example of the trends of the day. The constitution of 1851 (with amendments still in effect) hemmed in the almost unrestricted legislature by limiting the amount of debt that might be contracted by the state and by establishing biennial sessions to replace the annual sessions provided for in the constitution of 1802—the less often a legislature met, the less damage it might do. The state was prohibited from buying stock in, or loaning its credit to, private business; and no debt was permitted for making internal improvements.

The judiciary was made elective (the legislature previously had selected judges). Only the governorship did not fit the fashion of the day, that is no provision was made for a veto, and no veto was made until 1874. In other respects, however, Ohio followed the prevailing style in writing a new constitution, and the style settled on was pragmatically determined from the ideology and life-styles of the day.

The Lasting Effects of Jacksonian Democracy

Ideologies probably never die entirely. "They depart farther and farther from reality with the passing of time, thus representing the original truth less and less perfectly. At the same time they tend to command even greater strength and ever wider acceptance partly because, since they have little to do with reality, no interest can be injured by protestations of platitude."[30] Thus, frontier values continue to influence the symbolism of politics. In particular, Americans still believe that "small" government is better than "big" government; that officeholders are more responsible to the people and likely to be more honest if they are directly elected; that rural government is more democratic and probably of a higher type than urban government; that a local government of neighbors is more efficient and more effective than a local government in the hands of a professional bureaucracy; and so on. At the same time, the individuals who accept these beliefs also hold other views resulting from their modern-day wants, so that *an individual's political attitudes are always of an ambiv-*

alent character. The citizen who believes that rural life is ''better'' than city life and thus rural government is more democratic than city government may also believe that all rural justices of the peace are incompetents who should be replaced by professional lawyer-judges at the county seat. A person who believes that small government is better than big government also wants services of various kinds from government, each of which contributes toward making government bigger. The suburbanite who wants a government of neighbors may also think that the village public works department would operate much better if it were headed by a fully qualified engineer.

Today's frontier ideology then, is a minority ideology, but nonetheless an important one. Centered in the American small town and the nostalgic urbanite, it is increasingly a reflection of frustration rather than a symbol of the good life.

States' Rights

One ideological movement that has never prevailed but has nonetheless persisted throughout American history is states' rights. For its advocates, states' rights is the legal principle that the states are soverign entities over, or at least alongside, the national government. It has been used both to challenge the supremacy of the national government and to limit its implied powers. For opponents, the doctrine of states' rights has no legal standing; it is viewed as an obstructionist ideology used to weaken the national government or prevent it from being innovative. When a legal principle is challenged, the tests of its validity are more clear and certain than with other ideological principles, the principle is tested in court. As a legal principle, states' rights arguments almost always fail that test. Furthermore although some states' rights principles have prevailed in other contexts (for example, segregationists and advocates of local control have been fairly successful in preventing the desegregation of American schools through a policy of busing), success rarely has come under the banner of states' rights. Nevertheless, states' rights is an argument that will not go away; it has continued to be used in varying forms throughout American history.

The Claims for States' Rights

The *Tenth Amendment* to the U. S. Constitution was written to clarify the sovereign relationship between state and national governments.

> **Tenth Amendment: ''The powers not delegated to the United States by the Constitution nor prohibited by it to the States, are reserved to the States respectively, or to the people.''**

Its authors sought to distinguish between those sovereign powers given the national government in the Constitution and those not given. Strict constructionists of the Constitution have used this amendment to argue for a type of dual federalism in which national sovereignty would be limited to those powers expressly delegated to the national government in the Constitution, whereas all others would remain within the sovereign purview of the states.

As early as 1798, the Kentucky and Virginia Resolutions restated the anti-

Federalist position that the nation was a compact among sovereign states, as had been the case under the Articles of Confederation, and not one established by the people directly. The resolutions (those from Kentucky drafted by Jefferson and those from Virginia by Madison) held that the states might take steps to veto any legislation they held to be unconstitutional. In these cases, the objection was to the Alien and Sedition Laws of the Federalists. Typically for states' rights arguments, the success of these arguments relied on the personal success of its adherents (in this case the Republican victory in 1800) rather than the legal enforcement of the principle.

In 1828, the South Carolina legislature passed a resolution of "Exposition and Protest" against the protective tariff adopted that year—the agricultural South opposed a high tariff that would encourage the development of industry in the North but would raise the cost of finished products to the consumer. The legislature attempted to nullify the tariff, ran into strong opposition from President Jackson, was forced to retreat when the rest of the South did not give it full support, and finally achieved some measure of success by winning a downward revision of the tariff. The principle expressed in the Constitution held, however, and neither South Carolina in this instance nor any state at a later time has succeeded in nullifying a national law by its own action.

Calhoun's View

Perhaps the doctrine of states' rights found its most eloquent spokesman in John C. Calhoun of South Carolina. To Calhoun, it has been said, states' rights became "an instrumentality primarily for the protection of property rights, with the protection of slavery foremost in his consideration."[31] Calhoun continued the classic struggle of the agrarian against the vested financial interests, but his agrarians were the *Bourbon aristocracy* of the Deep South. Calhoun's arguments for the preservation of the southern way of life as he knew it centered on the view that the Constitution was a compact among the states and that the national government, through its Supreme Court or otherwise, could not be the judge of its own powers. Rather, he argued, the states should properly resolve for themselves all conflicts.[32]

Bourbon Aristocracy: **The plantation-owning elite of the South and their descendants.**

Legal Claims

Despite the massive defeat of states' rights philosophies in the Civil War, the intervening century of decision making—from the death of John Marshall in 1835 to the late 1930s—had a decidedly states' rights bent in Supreme Court cases involving state and national disputes. These cases limited the national government's power in two important areas: authority to tax the states[33] and authority to regulate commerce.[34] These cases were subsequently reversed, but despite the expansion of implied powers of the national government since the New Deal, conservative Court decisions of recent decades have kept alive the terminology of state sovereignty.[35]

The Integration Issue

States' rights became a part of the arsenal of those southerners opposed to integration of schools before and after the 1954 United States Supreme Court decision in

Brown v. *Board of Education,* which favored a single national policy on this delicate but basic question.[36] States' rights is an argument well suited for the protection of regional attitudes against a contrary national policy.

In a similar vein governors, including liberal governors strongly committed to vigorous national government action, have not hesitated to use the states' rights argument if it was in their interests to do so. For example, Governor Franklin D. Roosevelt (New York) once denounced a federal court decision favorable to the utilities of that state as an invasion of a state's right to regulate such businesses within its border.[37] (The decision had not been helpful to Roosevelt's personal political plans.)

The states' rights argument, running as it does throughout American history, is thus a fine example of how values held dear by a people are verbalized into an ideology, told and retold until they become virtual folktales, and finally become instruments for the manipulation of attitudes and for the achievement of desired political goals by the manipulators.[38]

The Failure of States' Rights

Victories in states' rights questions have come more often by *not* testing the question in court. A long held tradition of reserving for their localities policy making in the areas of policing and education has proved far more successful than challenging federal interference in court. The Supreme Court set the pattern for federal supremacy in states' rights cases in the Marshall Court.[39] Although the national government limited itself until the New Deal, the doctrine of implied powers made the Tenth Amendment all but obsolete. As national power has greatly expanded in this century, the courts have rarely accepted states' rights arguments that a power is reserved to the states and not also held by the national government.

Less clear is the question of who shall prevail in specific conflicts between state and national government. In the greatest test, of course, the national government prevailed in the Civil War. In specific court cases since Franklin Roosevelt's failed attempt to pack the Supreme Court, the Court has been reluctant to limit the national government in conflicts with the states. Nevertheless, some justices have taken exception and occasionally have mustered a majority. Justice Rehnquist, for instance, argued that "This Court has never doubted there are limits upon the power of Congress to override state sovereignty. . . ."[40] But such limitations rarely are applied. Most recent examples in the Rehnquist Court have favored the national government (see chapters 3 and 4). Therefore states' rights should be viewed more in the context of ideology than in the context of legal principle (although advocates of any ideology attempt to win the courts over and to speak in legalistic language).

States' Rights in Modern Times

The trend toward bigger government increased the confidence of many citizens in the trustworthiness of government as an instrument for social action. The concept of cooperative federalism, that is, governments working together rather than in separate or competing spheres, met with wide acceptance. But the older idea of states' rights retained much of its vitality, as did that of individualism.

States' rights was used as an argument for those who, like many owners of small businesses, remained unreconciled to the concept of the social service state. It was used, but failed, as an argument by the oil companies seeking to deprive the national government of control over offshore oil reserves. It was also a principal weapon of many opponents of desegregation in the struggle for equal facilities. States' rights was used as a rallying cry by President Carter and President Reagan in their attempts to portray themselves as men "of the people," not beholden to the established powers in Washington. President Reagan in his first years in office, was especially successful in continuing to use states' rights rhetoric when arguing for limitations in national spending or regulation.

Watching government grow, many a conservative has complained of a continuing march on Washington. For the person seeking to preserve the status quo, state governments, which cynical ancestors had bribed or ignored, became objects of admiration. This point of view was nicely expressed by the best-known protagonist for the social service state. In a 1929 complaint, Franklin D. Roosevelt, the governor of New York, said:

> If there is a failure on the part of a State to provide adequate educational facilities for its boys and girls, an immediate cry goes up that a department of education should be established in Washington. If a State fails to keep abreast with modern [health] provisions, immediately the enthusiasts turn to the creation of a department of health in Washington. If a state fails adequately to regulate its public service corporations, the easiest course is to ask the Interstate Commerce Commission or the Federal Trade Commission to take jurisdiction.[41]

But the facts do not support the charge that state and local governments are vacating their policy making responsibilities, and the doctrine of states' rights remains essentially a weapon of ideological warfare.

The Ideology of Industrial Individualism

America industrialized rapidly in the decades following the Civil War. It became increasingly an urban nation, and big business with its large capital investments, intense mechanization, and impersonalized labor, became the order of the day. Industrial individualism, the dominant ideology of the times, was a modified and modernized version of frontier individualism, moved into the city and made to fit a new pattern of life. In place of the frontiersman, the new hero was the self-made man of industry in the Horatio Alger tradition. In place of the long-dominant Democratic party, the new Republican party emerged from the war—except in the South—as the strongest political coalition, the one that successfully associated itself with the new ideology. In place of a dominant legislative or executive branch of government, the judical branch ascended, becoming the energetic protector of the new myth. Through the Fourteenth Amendment to the U. S. Constitution (ensuring due process of law in connection with property rights), economic individualism was written into the fundamental law of the land.

The urbanization of America following the Civil War can be explained by a variety of factors. The displacement caused by the war led some Americans to the big cities. But the South would be perceived as rural for another century and the black population, which would be so important to later urban growth, remained in the rural South until the migration to the city began shortly before World War I. Yet the Civil War (like wars generally) produced extraordinary technological advancement. Expanding railroad lines provided greater food supplies and ready transportation within the cities. Increased capacities of piping systems to pump in fresh water and pump out sewage made the concentration of people possible. But technological capacity alone does not explain the movement of people; more important are the myths that drive them. Millions of European immigrants, fleeing the economic, social, political, or religious oppressions of their homelands, came to America. Frequently they found different but nevertheless oppressive conditions in the United States; yet, few returned home despite the fact that most would die poor, with moderate income deferred for their children or grandchildren. Despite riots in the streets, low wages, poor working conditions, and an unsympathetic political system, the myth prevailed, in part because the alternatives seemed even worse. More and more the population concentrated in the larger cities, partly because these locations cost the least, partly because jobs were most plentiful there, and partly because the political systems that helped people find jobs and housing were concentrated in these cities.

The period between the Civil War and the Great Depression, which began in the fall of 1929, was marked by disillusionment with universal suffrage among intellectuals and business leaders; the popularity of corrupt political machines; the development of the "efficiency and economy" reform movement, which sought to reestablish government dominated by middle-class values; and agrarian radicalism as a protest against laissez-faire extremism.

Poor Boy on the Road to Success

Horatio Alger wrote more than one hundred stories telling the nineteenth-century boy (they were not directed at girls) that opportunity was his for the taking and that success, measured in terms of material accomplishments results from virtue and hard work. Perhaps not every boy believed that by this simple formula he could become another Vanderbilt or Carnegie, but he was constantly bombarded with similar propaganda from all the media of communication, controlled as they were by persons whose interests coincided with those of the newly created titans of business and industry.[42] Undoubtedly these teachings profoundly affected Americans— urban and rural, rich and poor—and had much to do both with conditioning their own behavior and with the way they permitted the new giant corporations to create "clusters of private government which first neutralized state powers and then overcame them."[43]

The new ideology included the idea that business and industry were the nation's most important institutions; that what was good for business was good for the nation; that other institutions, social or political, should play a secondary role and not interfere with the activities of business. As free enterprise and laissez-faire became key symbols, government was regarded as inefficient, its control over business held to be not only a threat to the nation's progress but in fact immoral.

The Intellectual Is Not Impressed

During the decades following the Civil War, *The Nation,* the *Atlantic* and other periodicals carried the protests of intellectuals (people interested primarily in ideas) and business leaders, who commented unfavorably on the rise of the ignorant and poor to political power. They saw the demagogue and city boss as the effect of the common person's demand for a controlling voice in social and economic questions, which heretofore had been settled "rationally" by sophisticated responsible persons. The people now wanted *not* "great minds" in political office to lead them but obedient agents to help them meet "their overpowering anxiety about their daily bread."[44]

Yet, even as intellectuals defended free enterprise as a system of economics, they came to disapprove of its social results. Eventually, multimillionaires were seen by editors of *The Nation* as an even greater threat to America than was the common person. Both were regarded as self-seeking and self-centered, but the former, because of the power of their money, were thought to be more dangerous. This period of our history, then, saw a disenchantment with common people—they were not to be romanticized again until the days of the New Deal—and an embracing of the business leader, thought to be on the right track. But this viewpoint lasted only until the business leaders' own selfishness caused them to teeter on the pedestal where earlier they had been placed by the intellectual, the farmer, even the worker. They were eventually to lose the support of all except the growing middle class. However, the business leaders of the days of industrialism had two advantages over their pre-1860 counterparts that gave them enormous advantage in the political arena: They were now incomparablly wealthier, and business was far better organized with a better set of internal communications. Both advantages did much to give business leaders a strong voice in state and local governments.

Boss and Machine Politics

Little room was left for moral principles unconnected with the immediate business at hand in an age when tycoons were piling up fortunes, exploiting the consumer, seeking to destroy one another, and doing whatever was necessary to make money. Corruption existed in state and local government and reached into Congress itself, even to the Speaker's chair and to the cabinet. If bribery and spying existed in private business, why should the business leader not apply the same methods in getting governmental obstacles out of the way?

The machines succeeded at both the state and local levels, but even more in the growing urban centers of the Atlantic coast and the Midwest. Cities usually were ruled by weak-mayor-council systems, which put maximum power into the hands of city councils. Council members, elected by wards, represented different ethnic groups. Madisonian federalism undoubtedly would have created city governments incapable of unified action had not the machines been privately organized to overcome the system of checks and balances. City machines, which were hierarchical private organizations centered in political party organizations, came to rule the city by controlling nominations to council and executive offices (including the mayor) and offering city council members benefits and special privileges in return for unified action.[45]

Typically, the machine would work at three levels. At the top were the bosses and their lieutenants, skilled at organization. In the middle were government officials made wealthy by the kickback contract and other benefits. The machine received payments for granting licenses, jobs, permits, franchises, inside information, contracts and other benefits to business and industry that the city government controlled. It also dominated some of the hiring in industries associated with city projects and the distribution of welfare to the needy. These in turn would be traded for votes to those in greatest need of jobs and welfare. At the bottom of the machine, the distribution would be handled by block workers, often firefighters, police officers, and bartenders, who kept their jobs by delivering the vote for the machine. It appears that the average slum dweller gladly voted for the machine regardless of corruption as long as the machine delivered something in return. By offering something, machine governments by necessity became highly responsive and involved governments. But those of the middle class who had less need for such favors saw only what was, by their values, crass corruption: voter fraud (usually not strong-arm tactics but use of ineligible voters or multiple voting by individuals to inflate the machine's totals), bribes, extortion, and insider information—particularly in the sale of land and the granting of franchises and contracts. As the common person came to be viewed with suspicion, machines came to be vilified in print as America's shame or conspicuous failure, regardless of their success and their democratic qualities. It nevertheless should be remembered that boss and machine politics at the local level survived for nearly a century, largely because of their popularity with people whose plight was commonly ignored by most other social institutions.

The machines at the state level were less successful than local machines mainly because they rarely involved the voter in day-to-day decision making. In Wisconsin, the Republican machine rose to power in the last decades of the nineteenth century by controlling the sale of land, railroad rates, and the party nomination process in a state where opposing Democrats stood little chance of success. Insider deals allowed politicians to buy land at low prices and then resell it to unsuspecting immigrants on land contracts, which would require the farmer to turn over much of the profit to the machine. Few farmers, in deals they made before they came to Wisconsin, realized that the land had been cleared of timber but not of stumps, which had to be removed before farming could begin. But once the land was cleared, much of the profits were turned over to the machine as payment for the land. This process gave the machine the wealth necessary to control the nomination process at state conventions and retain control over the governorship and state legislature.

In a one-party state the initial battleground for political control was the nomination process in the majority party. In Wisconsin, after repeated failures, Robert LaFollette, Sr., won the governorship in 1900 at the Republican state convention and easily won the general election. His task then was to institutionalize the challenge to the machine. LaFollette did this successfully with a number of reforms, including outlawing the sale of Wisconsin land outside the state, establishing independent commissions and boards to set railroad rates and sell land, and, perhaps most important, by establishing an open primary system where the voter rather than the party bosses would decide nominations.[46]

Other states also had bosses and machines from both political parties. There was the Republican Southern Pacific Railroad machine which ran California from the 1880s until the election of Republican Hiram Johnson in 1910; the highly conservative rural-oriented Democratic Byrd machine in Virginia during the first half of this century; and the populistic Long machine begun by Huey (under the banner of "every man a king") in the 1920s, which continued until Huey's son Russell Long's retirement from the Senate in the 1980s.[47]

The Efficiency and Economy Movement

Reform of local governments came in two waves, each with its own goals. During the heyday of boss and machine politics, the efficiency and economy reformers led a haphazard attack on the machine. Their primary goal was to destroy machine corruption, regardless of the consequences should they succeed and have to run the cities themselves. They had little success in defeating machines. The later reform movement, which began with the demise of machines during and just after the Great Depression, has proceeded to the present day. It accepted many of the proposals of the earlier reformers, but the new reformer had the far more challenging task of establishing mechanisms to govern the new suburbs and other cities showing phenomenal growth after World War II. Even though the two movements sounded the same call for honest, businesslike government, they had different tasks.[48]

The efficiency and economy reformers began to organize as early as the 1870s. The movement, like its Jacksonian predecessor, was pragmatic, unsystematic, and loosely coordinated. It had no single intellectual leader and was not part of a general philosophy, although it did have definite Hamiltonian overtones. Its strength was centered in the upper-middle-class business leaders, with additional aid coming from a handful of academicians.

The difficulties that confronted reformers at first were almost overpowering. Political machines, often headed by well-known bosses, resisted by using any technique that would destroy or discourage the neophytes. The machine usually was well organized, with an army of workers and large numbers of voters who were obligated to it, and hence generally was able to defeat any attempts at reform. The minority of business leaders who turned reformers were in a particularly vulnerable position. A strong political machine in control of the state and city had many weapons against those who dared oppose it. It could, for example, increase the assessment on their properties, refuse them permits and licenses, or harass them through overenforcement of health, fire, building, and other codes.

Many industrialists and businessmen, convinced that it was cheaper and more effective to buy off the machine, refused to cooperate with reformers. The general public was almost completely cynical regarding the efforts of do-gooders, and in the slums of the burgeoning cities, a great many people found the machine a helpful crutch in time of need. To slum dwellers, the destruction of the machine would not be triumph but tragedy.

Reforms and Renovations

The principal slogans of the reformers centered on the beliefs (1) that "all politics is crooked," and (2) that state and local government is essentially a matter of "efficient business administration." Disillusionment with the mechanics proposed by Jacksonians to bring America truly democratic government resulted in a skepticism of unbridled majority rule, of legislative supremacy, of the spoils system, of the practice of electing versus appointing public officials. Reflecting the views of the times, *The Nation* took a series of editorial positions urging change. To strengthen executive leadership and restrict incompetent, irresponsible legislatures, it endorsed an executive budget (1882), administrative reorganization with the governor or mayor responsible for the actions of department heads (1885), the item veto, and the establishment of legislative staff agencies to provide professional advice to legislators (both in 1886). Eventually the lexicon of reform mechanics also included the Australian secret ballot, corrupt-practices legislation, publicity for campaign receipts and expenditures, proportional representation to give the minority some voice, the direct-primary election to overcome machine control of caucuses and conventions and to permit persons outside the machine to propose candidates, and the appointment of judges to remove them as far as possible from politics.[49]

Dozens of organizations were created as reformers became more skillful in political techniques. These included the National Short Ballot Organization, the National Popular Government League, the Proportional Representation League, the National Municipal League, the Bureau of Municipal Research of New York, and dozens of local reform clubs, taxpayers' leagues, local government committees of chambers of commerce, and various research agencies.

Reform—An Appraisal

The reform movement contributed to local self-government by reestablishing a certain amount of local responsibility, replacing the checks and balances of Jacksonian democracy with a more modern system of centralized leadership, and reestablishing at least a modicum of public respect and confidence in state and local government. However, it did some damage, too. It placed misleading overemphasis on forms and structures of government. It led people astray with its preachings to the effect that government was principally a matter of "efficient business management"—which it was not and never can be in a democracy that seeks to be responsive to voter demands.

The reform movement failed, for the most part, to make state and local government more representative of a cross section of society.[50] The old-style politician was thoroughly repudiated, but the balance of power in government was not fundamentally altered. Business leaders continued to dominate, whereas formerly they had to do so indirectly, through the state and city machines. As a new type of control developed, business leaders began to participate directly in government. Voter influence was now achieved *not* through traditional devices but through the media of mass communication.

Agrarian Radicalism

As America matured, changing from a frontier nation of farmers to an industrial nation of urbanites, emphasis gradually shifted from opportunity to security, from individual to collective activity. It is perhaps ironic, though certainly understandable, that the first significant efforts at collective action came from the farmers, the very people who were thought to represent, in Charles Beard's overworked phrase, "rugged individualism."

Farmers, in neglecting politics as a medium for protecting their interests, had gradually fallen into an impossible economic position and by the end of the nineteenth century had lost their political dominance. Theirs "was the only considerable economic group that exerted no organized pressure to control the price [they] sold for or the price [they] paid."[51] They had voted away the public domain to the railroads in a desperate need for transportation facilities—and the railroads were now repaying them with excessive freight charges.[52]

Political Action

In the decades after 1870, farmers began to protest against "ten cent corn and ten percent interest." They were told to "raise less corn and more hell." But they had determined to become politically active at a time when "legislatures were bought and sold like corner lots; senatorships went to the highest bidder; judges were more responsive to the wishes of bankers than to those of farmers."[53] The road to political success was as rutfilled and full of obstacles as the one that ran past their deteriorating farmhouses.

William Jennings Bryan told farmers (city dwellers were listening) that social problems were essentially moral questions and that their moral solutions required equal rights for all and special privileges for none. The urban worker, faced with job competition from immigrants and from southern sharecroppers who were leaving the farm, was slow to respond. Farmers, however, took action. They seized control of several state legislatures, in some cases elected a farmer to sit in the governor's chair, and demanded state action to replace the free enterprise system they had temporarily accepted. They returned to the old demand for cheaper currency; they sought, among other things, control over transportation, banking policies more helpful to the debtor, a standard system of grain grading, the construction of publicly owned grain elevators, and state crop insurance.[54]

Both the farmers and the business corporations, especially the railroads, established professional lobbies in the state capitals and in Washington. The conflict between farmers and their historic business enemies came about in the years after the Civil War, when the railroads developed rapidly and came virtually to monopolize control over the transportation of the farmers' products. Grain elevators, also essential to farmers' welfare because they controlled the sale price of grain and the conditions under which it could be sold, were owned by the railroads or absentee landlords in cities miles from the farmers who used them. Bankers controlled credit, and their policies permitted a continuing deflation of the currency, which forced on the farmer unbearable long-term debts. At the same time, the great industrial trusts began to control the productive and consumptive goods the farmers needed.

Granger Legislation

The *Granger movement* (the National Grange carried much of the farmer's political burden) was not a success. It flourished for a few years in a few states but failed to secure enactment of the legislation it wanted, or its laws were set aside by the courts. The farmers elected to legislatures repeatedly were unable to deliver on their promises. Yet the movement greatly affected subsequent legislation. Its principal proposals involved setting railroad rate charges; controlling the maximum charge for the storage of grain; and setting "dockage" rules which concerned the allowance made for weeds, straw, and waste before calculating the net weight of grain offered for sale at an elevator. Massachusetts established the first of the railroad and warehouse commissions in 1869, although it was only a fact-gathering agency. Greater control was vested in the Midwest commissions, where Illinois led the way (1871), followed closely by Minnesota, Iowa, and Wisconsin. The state Granger legislation, aimed as it was against the biggest of big business, was of course challenged in the conservative courts and ultimately in the United States Supreme Court, which at that time was regarded as the ultimate bastion of the doctrine of free enterprise. The Supreme Court, however, sided against unbridled laissez-faire, and, in a historic decision held that the state of Illinois (and by implication other states) could establish maximum charges for the storage of grain without depriving the granary owners of their property without due process of law.[55] Businesses, such as granaries or railroads, which were "clothed with the public interest," could be regulated. The precedent had thus been set, and although a few decades later the Court had some doubts about its decision—especially when faced with early labor legislation—the principle of regulation "in the public interest" had been established and the way opened for the social service state in the years following the onset of the Great Depression.[56]

> *Granger Movement:* **The agrarian radical movement of the 1870s and 1880s designed to raise agricultural profits and protect the farmer from exploitation by big business. So called because leadership was provided by The American Patrons of Husbandry, generally called the National Grange.**

The Social Service State

As the nation changed from an individualistic, rural society to one that was economically interdependent and urban, much social dislocation took place. When industrial individualism failed to meet social concerns, people turned to collective effort through government. The pattern first followed by the farmer was later taken up by organized labor and then even the business leader.

Challenging the Old Ideology

The Great Depression began in the fall of 1929 and lasted until the nation began to prepare for World War II a decade later. The depression convinced many that job security, guaranteed payments in the event of unemployment or industrial accident, government assistance in preparing for retirement, help in finding a job, and other hedges against starvation were more important than opportunity or the abstract principle of freedom from governmental control.

As *The Nation* noted in 1868. "If the doors of the future are once thrown open to what are called 'the masses,' and they catch even one glimpse of the splendid possibilities which lie within it, it is in vain to close them again. The vision never leaves their minds.''[57] And indeed, in a series of movements (the farmers' activities beginning in the 1870s, Theodore Roosevelt's Square Deal, Robert LaFollette's progressive movement, Woodrow Wilson's New Freedom, for example) the common folk came to realize that government potentially was a powerful weapon in their hands and that each of them had a vote equal to that of any banker or corporate president. The doors had been opened. When poverty was seen as a private problem, the poor were left to find their own solutions or rely on the private charities or the informal auspices of the machine. But the new poor in the Great Depression, who were not born poor as their ancestors had been, felt cheated by a system that had broken down, a system seemingly beyond individual control. If society was at least partially responsible for poverty, then government might be part of the solution.

It was not only the working class that sought government protection. For the first time farm organizations (if not all farmers) in the 1930s came to understand fully the techniques of political activity. Business people turned to government for credit when they could not get it elsewhere; home builders sought government aid; transportation industries sought government subsidies; even bankers, traditionally the most conservative business sector, accepted the idea of government insurance on bank deposits to stabilize business and build up public confidence. Whatever aspirations had been frustrated under industrial individualism, people now turned to government to bridge the gap between what they could provide for themselves and what they believed they needed to be psychologically secure. Even sincere believers in self-reliance recognized that most breadwinners worked for someone else who decided—almost arbitrarily it seemed—who was hired, fired, promoted, transferred, or raised in pay. Under these circumstances, the ideal life might lie beyond one's grasp, and governmental activity in some areas might be a necessary evil that could provide the individual protection lacking in the corporate system. The assumption in the 1930s and for decades afterwards was that government was benign; that is, it could be trusted to work on behalf of the common people. It was not until the 1960s and later that most people came to realize that ''government'' does not make decisions, that people working for the government do, that daily operations of government are handled by a bureaucracy that in a short time develops worrisome autonomy from the legislative branch of government and even from the executive and judiciary.

Rural versus Urban Social Systems

Another factor that made for collective action in the modern era was the trend toward an urban nation. Throughout American history, farmers and small-town dwellers provided most of their own household services. Room was always made for retired parents (physical disability was the only consideration in retirement, and it generally came gradually, without the shock that sudden retirement on a specified birthday later came to be) and for widowed or orphaned relatives. If farmers or merchants became ill, relatives and neighbors carried on their work. Involuntary unemployment was nonexistent. True, profitless years were common enough, but the garden and livestock provided food even during the worst depression, and the woodlot or corncrib supplied fuel.

An urban society however, was totally different. For example, not everyone could live on a hill, and only the government seemed able to provide the drainage needed on flat or low land. Where large numbers lived in close proximity, water and sewage were prime public health considerations. Ultimately, the only safe way to supply water and dispose of sewage was for government to develop carefully engineered—and expensive—physical plants. Houses became smaller, unable to accommodate retired parents or other dependents. Fewer people could provide adequately for retirement; yet their children often could afford neither to feed nor house them. The elderly who were willing to work found that no jobs were to be had—they were "too old."

An employee might be laid off at any time for any reason—too many sick days, superannuation, cyclic or seasonal business, a depression or financial panic, even a personality conflict. Urban society, therefore, produced economic interdependence where independence had once existed. It produced insecurities virtually unknown in an agrarian society. These circumstances caused people to look around for a social institution that could help them regain their poise and security. The most likely candidate—perhaps the only one available—was government. And when the call came, its leaders responded. The *machine*, the urban political system that had ruled the city, relied heavily on poor people who traded their votes for social services. Initially, as the New Deal spread, and then subsequently, as economic recovery followed World War II, the machines no longer were necessary. Formal governmental structures were now aided by a new desire to help and a new sharing relationship among the three levels of government; both factors allowed state and local governments to rely more heavily on the federal income tax. Government could now provide many services that the machines had provided before—*without* the electoral corruption. Author Harold Zink could find no case of a major machine being permanently destroyed by reformers at the local level before 1930.[58] But by the mid-1960s all of the great machines were dead, except those in Albany and Chicago; and they, too, would grind to a halt in another decade.

Machinelike Systems and Successful Reforms

The modified politics of today did not immediately replace the machines. Reform succeeded most directly in the new postwar suburbs and only slowly crept into the older central cities.

Former machine cities often exhibited machinelike attitudes. For example, the problem confronting Chicago Mayor Harold Washington in the mid-1980s was the result of a common circumstance, a city with a formal mayor-council system that emphasized checks and balances. Machine bosses avoided stalemates by relying on the collective greed of city council members and the ability of bosses to organize mutually advantageous actions. Once the service state ideology destroyed the machine structure, a reform-spirited mayor such as Washington faced a system designed to stymie collective decision making. The machinelike system that existed in Chicago after Mayor Richard J. Daley had a mayor, a council, and a county party organization each with its own agenda, each empowered to prevent one of the other entities from getting what it wanted. The result was a stalemated government with well-meaning but impotent leaders. It remains to be seen whether the current mayor, Richard M. Daley (son of Richard J.) can bring these parties back together. Although his denial of the machine mantel should be viewed skeptically (many bosses, the senior Daley included, claimed to be reformers), the experience of other machinelike cities suggests that such organization is not to be achieved in this century.

Often in machinelike cities the reforms mentioned in the following sections are adopted incrementally. Consequently, many cities that previously had machines today have many of the bureaucratic practices, business ethics, and reduced voter visibility that characterize successful reform. But the purest reform can be seen in the council-manager cities, particularly in middle-class suburbs where reform flourished from the outset.

Suburbia

The myths that drive people to relocate must be supported by technology and political action. The automobile, electric pump, and septic tank made the suburb possible. By the 1950s the upper middle class could afford to live far from where they worked and drive back and forth. With septic tanks and electronically driven pumps, suburbanites—no longer locked into municipal piping and water systems—did not have to await annexation to get services, as was the nineteenth-century pattern.

Socially, the central city came to be seen more and more as an inferior place to raise a family. The white middle class feared the movement of blacks from the farm to the city, a perception surely based on enduring racist stereotypes that date back to slavery and Reconstruction. When race was not a central issue, class, income or lifestyle could be. The civil rights movement led many whites, otherwise sympathetic to movement goals, to opt for the security of a homogeneous suburb where such matters could be left to intellectural debate rather than day-to-day decisions. Others simply pursued the myth of the virtues of the small town. Suburbs were perceived to fit this matrix, even though they would always be in close proximity to large population centers.[59] Indeed they were seen as combining the security of the small town with the opportunities of urban society.

Government did little to slow white flight, which the Supreme Court encouraged by requiring *intradistrict* busing of schoolchildren to accomplish desegregation[60] although not requiring *interdistrict* busing.[61] Consequently, whites seeking to avoid desegregation were encouraged to move to suburban areas where new school districts could remain segregated.

The Veterans Administration and the Federal Housing Authority provided low-cost mortgages to veterans and some "good-risk" poor, that is, those with steady jobs and sufficient wages. The so called good risks were disproportionately white. It can never be known whether those who took advantage of these programs turned out to be good risks largely because of the associated benefits of the particular life-style they found in the suburbs. Conversely, it can never be known whether the large number of poor left behind, generally more recently urbanized and disproportionately minority black and Hispanic, remained poor in part because of the inferior public housing and welfare programs that provided different life-styles from those found in the suburb. But widespread segregation followed these programs.

Metropolitan areas became fragmented, with different populations producing different styles of government. In the central city, machinelike governments slowly began to support an increasingly poor population with social services partially paid for with categorical grants-in-aid from the national and state governments. In the suburbs, the new reformers were given the best chance to test their assumptions in the council-manager form of government.

Reform Assumptions

Three assumptions stand behind the reform movement, which came to dominate government in the social service state:

Assumption 1: Democracy is successful if citizens are well served, regardless of their involvement in the process. It must be remembered that reformers today took many of their attitudes from the efficiency and economy reform movement, designed in the days of industrial individualism to kill the machines. The skepticism surrounding the virtues of the common person thus remains intact. Richard S. Childs, perhaps the most prominent theorist of civic reform, argued that democracy is "the concept of a government that will diligently cater to the sovereign people!"[62] But he then went on to attack the long ballot, ward elections, and political party organization. Perhaps his most telling comment is that government should "anticipate the popular wish." But reformers had little faith in placing responsibility in the hands of ordinary people, a process that had produced corruption. If the people are served, they need not be consulted.

Assumption 2: Administrators should determine the public interest. If the common person could not be trusted to make decisions, who could be? The corporate executive, a logical choice, had been discredited when the system of big business became suspect because of *its* corruption and failure to prevent the Great Depression. The choice instead came to be the technical expert, the scientist of government, the public administrator. It was assumed that if experts were properly trained, hired directly by government, and well paid so that corruption could be neutralized, government could serve the sovereign people without their interfering in decision making. Government thus comes to be bureaucracy.

This reform assumption is best illustrated in the council-manager form of government. In theory, the small city council elected at-large should determine public policy choices, whereas providing these choices (city services) should be left to the city manager—an expert. In practice, the managers often come to dominate the lay councils because they are on the job full time and have superior training, resources, and expertise. The distinction between the role of the council and that of the manager is lost. The public interest is mysteriously measured by expert guesses, rather than direct involvement by the common members of the public or their elected representatives.

Theorists writing about administrative behavior have used many words to develop a notion of what should be accepted as the public interest in the decision-making process.[63] It is accepted that administrators should serve a broad public, not a minority. But citizens do not define the interests they expect the government to serve. Certainly they are not likely to view government, as political scientists tend to, as serving a large number of clientele groups rather than a single public at large. And administrators similarly do not usually give the matter careful thought. Instead their assumptions concerning the public interest must be implied from their actions. From these actions, the following assumptions are found:[64]

- Administrators tend to identify the public interest with the expectations of their professional peers. A physician, a social work administrator, or a school superintendent, for example, is likely to think that the standards established and the administrative methods approved by the profession are right *and* in the public interest.
- Administrators tend to accept the expectations of their superiors and to view them as representative of the public interest. This is the road to convenience and security, and it is a simple and effective rationalization.
- Administrators tend to identify personal value systems with the public interest through a process psychologists call *projection*. One's views surely are held by a large number of persons in the general public, but individuals have no way of knowing what proportion of the public holds them. In any case, this approach minimizes personal psychological strain. Of course, administrators are often called on to do things that do not fit their personal values; in such cases, the more easily they can accept a superior's position as representing the public interest, the easier it is for them.
- Administrators tend to reach a decision—as do elective politicians—that will minimize interest group pressures on themselves and their agency. It is not difficult to identify in one's mind the views of the most interested persons or groups in relation to a particular policy or program with the general good. In this respect the tendency is to identify the public interest with the wishes of the interested publics.

Assumption 3. Government serves the public interest when it is rationally efficient. Ironically, after discrediting the democratic decision-making process during the period of industrial individualism, *process* again would determine priorities in reform government. Reformers assumed that the following administrative principles would produce efficient government.[65]

- Authority and responsibility should be concentrated in the chief executive officers by placing the heads of agencies under their authority and subject to their appointment, removal, and control. This was perhaps the most basic assumption and proved to be the most difficult to achieve, especially outside cities. Interest groups wishing to dominate the governmental administration of their interests have feared (probably with justification) that executive unity would increase the executive's power at the expense of their own. In cities, the dominant groups were more unified than at the county or state levels; and they wanted what they considered businesslike efficiency. As a result, strong mayors and city managers generally were given wide (but rarely complete) administrative powers where governors were not; and most counties remained without a chief executive of any kind.
- Related functions should be integrated into single departments, and the number of departments should be limited so that the executive can require direct ac-

countability from department heads. Reformers complained that often many agencies performed functions in the same general field with little coordination, effective planning, or responsibility.

- Boards and commissions might be used effectively for advisory, not administrative, purposes. Boards sometimes serve as quasi-legislative or quasi-judicial bodies. This type of activity arose, for example, in the case of public service commissions that establish rates for public utilities. In most states, and in cities with weak mayors, these boards were (and still are) common administrative devices.
- Budget control should be centralized under the direction of the chief executive with auditing under the legislative body. (Some characteristics of the executive budget will be discussed in chapter 9.) This administrative device has had widespread acceptance in principle and perhaps the greatest effect of any single development on executive control over agencies. Budget staffs, in the larger jurisdictions at least, have become the general management arm of the chief executive, not only reviewing the budget estimates of agencies but also aiding in coordinating their activities. Budget offices have become important agencies for administrative supervision, though they generally have only limited control over department expenditures. These offices apportion funds over the fiscal year and exercise certain minor controls, but they are not usually in a legal or political position to claim sweeping jurisdiction over the details of expenditures. The check-and-balance tradition has been maintained through the establishment of an independent audit—independent, that is, of the executive branch.
- Administrative staff services should be coordinated, usually through central agencies, to serve all operating departments. This principle has received more acceptance than the others because centralizing housekeeping functions has been thought to save money without losing policy control on the part of interest groups watching over the individual agency. Results have included a strong trend toward the central purchasing of materials and supplies (large-volume buying brings lower unit prices); the operation of central warehouses, records, archives, motor pools, printing, mailing, and telephone services; and the central maintenance of buildings and grounds. Personnel recruitment has also been centralized considerably.
- An executive cabinet should be established to coordinate governmental agencies. Cabinet members should be appointed by the chief executive rather than elected, so that they can be held responsible for their acts. Ironically, reformers view appointment as a greater safeguard for the public interest than election.

Who Benefits from Reform?

Two schools of thought address the question of who benefits from reform. The first comes mostly from the reformers and public administrators who argue that good intentions coupled with sound practice can be expected to produce democratic and efficient government. Theirs is primarily a deductive argument that asks rhetorically if the methods used are honest and good. Having abandoned the more direct methods of measuring individual satisfaction, they offer little evidence to support or deny the claim.

Many political scientists, a more skeptical lot, point to the ideological nature of the group that succeeded in reforming cities, and the frequent dissatisfaction found in social surveys of reform governments.[66] But regardless of who is served, most changes in state and local government structure since the Great Depression have been in the direction of reform.

The question of who benefits took somewhat different form when social scientists used the city as a convenient research site for the study of the nature of power. The community power structure debate raged for some time, principally in the 1950s and 1960s, over the function of interest groups in the political system and over who benefits from local public policy. *Pluralists* held that large numbers of interest groups rule in society.[67] Politics offers an arena in which the many groups struggle, bargain, and compromise to achieve temporary power over public policy. According to the pluralist view, however, no group dominates the policy-making process for very long because new groups form, new leaders are elected, and the process is always fluid. Those who rule in one policy area do not rule in others; those who rule at one time will not at another. *Elitists,* on the other hand, held that the political system is bipolar, divided between the single elite (disproportionately representing the higher socioeconomic groups) which rules and the masses which are ruled.[68] The political system is closed to the masses unless the governing elite incrementally accepts new members, admitting only the ones who accept the values of those already in power. Thus an election is a sham, between Tweedledum and Tweedledee—who already agree on the important things but may struggle between themselves for greater shares of power. Otherwise, only personality differences matter. And public policy always reflects the rather narrow values of the elite rather than the many, varying values of the masses.

Despite extensive study, the debate over power was never resolved, partly because no consensus existed about how to study community power and partly because much of the accepted evidence could support either theory, leaving analysts to accept whichever viewpoint fitted their ideology. This lack of resolution brought the community power structure debate to an end in the early 1970s. But the roles of groups are crucial to political action, and are addressed in a number of contexts throughout this book.

Social Movements

Frequently groups within the political system go beyond the prevailing ideologies or beyond the possibilities of contemporary structures to espouse change. The methods used may be conventional, such as voting, initiative and referendum, or even the legislative process; but in the period of the social service state occasionally radical change has been pursued through civil disobedience, demonstration, even violence. Certainly each method has been used in earlier periods of American history, but state and, particularly, local governments found themselves contending with these unconventional methods during the 1960s.

The New Deal raised the hopes of common people about the potential for government action, and the middle class succeeded in pursuing the suburban dream in the 1950s and 1960s. But the lower class, the racial minorities, and the middle-class liberal saw few of the promises fulfilled for society's have-nots. Government could not keep up with the aspirations of advocates of social change. Although the civil rights movement accomplished more change in racial attitudes in a decade than the century before had seen, it was not enough for those who wanted "now" the benefits lost during that century. Despite a "war" on poverty and a projected Great Society, which favored community action and stimulated governmental commitment to fight poverty (more than ever before in American history), it was not enough for those who wanted economic equality *"now."*

Just after 1960, New Left leaders also began to pressure state and local governments. In the past, local governments had been primarily record keepers, providers of consumer amenities, and executors of state criminal laws. State governments had established the basis for commercial and criminal law, commercial relationships, higher education, custody of felons, and care of the mentally ill. Their functions did not broaden much until the 1930s, when states began to provide financial aid from their more substantial tax base to local governments for health and welfare functions. In the 1960s, however, social reformers began to exert pressures on both state and local governments, which determined—for the most part—which laws were to be enforced and to what extent. In particular, state and local governments controlled fundamental decisions on the matters of greatest importance to the civil rights movement. In demanding equality in law enforcement, in employment opportunities, in housing, and in life's general amenities, the leaders tended to be as intolerant as were their counterparts on the right, unwilling to compromise and refusing to abide by traditional approaches to public policy making—negotiation and compromise. They borrowed many techniques from leaders of organized labor in the 1930s and from European reformers and student movements. The result was state and local governments that were more controversial, more dramatic, more newsworthy, and central to more significant decision making.

Because anyone can conceive of benefits that might be provided by government faster than government can actually provide them, any set of proposed policies is likely to be disappointing. (Social scientists call this the theory of rising expectations.) By the late 1960s, many in government were turning their attention from how to provide services to how to control those making the demands. Nevertheless, policies of fiscal federalism, which attempted to provide basic safety nets for the have-nots, were expanded and remain today.

After about the mid-1970s, movements for change became more benign, but they still complicated life for policy makers in state and local governments. Attention turned to two different considerations—the environment and equality of the sexes. Some demands could be met more easily than they had been in the 1960s, but it would require rethinking major assumptions about the extent to which the service state could solve social problems and the extent to which taxpayers would be willing to pay for social change. For example, governments now realized they could clean up a hazardous waste dump. But they did not find a way to assess accountability or distribute the costs between a public that wanted a clean environment and polluters (often major employers or local governments, many of which operate public dumps) who had gotten locked into dirty habits when population pressures were less, nonpolluting disposal sites were more available, and pollution was not considered to be a public problem.

Today governments accept the fairness of the principle of equal pay for equal work but cannot ensure it as large numbers of women enter the work force and large numbers of men claim the benefits of seniority and union pay scales guaranteed by contract.

The Conservatism of the 1980s and 1990s

The 1980s brought a period of conservatism that might herald the end of the social service state ideology or, more likely, produce a new pattern or trend in that ideology. More than a decade before this new wave of conservatism became popular, Edward Banfield suggested many of its themes in *The Unheavenly City.*[69] He argued that people of different social classes do not want the same things (they do not want equality); rather, they require different services to fit their different life-styles. Government could not solve problems successfully by spending more money because the solutions were too threatening to the middle class, or proposed approaches to problems simply did not work as solutions. Approaches chosen were often wasteful because they did not accomplish their goals. Social movements, so visible when Banfield was writing, were in effect dismissed as consisting of young boys having fun or making profit who would grow up and stop the commotion. A decade later, even key spokespersons for the New Deal, the War on Poverty and the Great Society philosophies were disillusioned by the capacities of government (Vietnam, the resignations of a president and a Speaker of the House, Three Mile Island, and Prince William Sound, for instance). The union movement, which had been at the heart of the Democratic party coalition and had provided many of the tools of protest, incurred a similar kind of disillusionment when it became unresponsive to individual demands and, like government, seemed to promise more than it could deliver. Union membership declined; by 1990, it was only about one-half the percentage of the work force it had been twenty years earlier. Around 1968, many veteran union members began to vote for conservatives, particularly in the highly visible presidential election. Conservatives, calling for government cutbacks and questioning the previously ''sacred'' entitlement of the have-nots, demanded some decentralization through a ''new federalism'' that would return programs to the states and localities and take them (and their costs) out of the hands of the less competent federal administrator. Leaders of the Democratic party, once the standard-bearers for the social service state ideology, found themselves on the defensive. Like their conservative critics, they began to argue for government cutbacks, controlled deficits, and limitations on compassion for the have-nots.

If all levels of government spending were combined, budgets during the 1980s remained among the highest in American history, as a percentage of gross national product, and within the average during the New Deal and the Great Society. In this light, the new conservatism suggests more a change in attitude than a change in spending practice. The immediate demand is to stop increases in expenditures, broadening of programs, or adoption of new programs. Less of a commitment has as yet been made to search for more effective approaches and hence more detailed understanding of programs that work to meet people's perceived needs.

Concluding Notes

The massive changes in political form in Europe as the 1980s drew to an end and the 1990s began suggest that international forces of revolution may challenge the tide of conservatism and bring on a period of worldwide change. Surely the social service state ideology in the United States will be further altered in the 1990s.

Each of the dominating ideologies discussed in this chapter has brought together contradictory ideas. For example, one major thread of the social service state ideology combined the rural interests of the South with the unionized urban Midwest and Northeast in the belief (best expressed by the Democratic party but also by the more unconventional movements of the 1960s) that the needy were entitled to government assistance. A second thread combined business concerns for profit and efficiency with the efficiency and economy reformers' concerns for the avoidance of political party and corruption. A third thread was most concerned with stemming the growth of government while still providing government benefits at levels unheard of prior to the social service state.

Understanding the place of the ideological movements of the present is almost impossible. Although it is clear that Europe is entering a new phase in its political history, whether the new ideas of the 1990s can be woven into the old ideology or whether a new ideology of state and local politics emerges in the United States remains for twenty-first-century philosophers to determine.

Notes

1. George H. Sabine, *History of Political Theory,* 4th ed. (New York: Holt, Rinehart, and Winston, 1973); Vernon L. Parrington, *Main Currents in American Thought* [first published in 1930] (New York: Harcourt Brace and World, three volumes, 1987).

2. Herbert McClosky, "Consensus and Ideology in American Politics," *American Political Science Review* 58 (June 1964):361–63.

3. Murray Edelman, *The Symbolic Uses of Politics* (Urbana, IL: The University of Illinois Press, 1964), 167.

4. Ross Lockridge, Jr., *Raintree County* (Boston: Houghton Mifflin, 1948), 776.

5. Robert E. Brown, *Middle-Class Democracy and the Revolution in Massachusetts* (Ithaca, NY: Cornell University Press, 1955), chapters 1–5 in particular.

6. Gordon S. Wood, *The Creation of The American Republic 1776–1787* (Chapel Hill: The University of North Carolina Press, 1969), 354–59. The view that the Declaration balances the competing view of the time can be seen in Donald S. Lutz, "The Declaration of Independence as Part of an American National Compact," *Publius* 19 (Winter 1989):41–58.

7. Ibid., 358.

8. Allan R. Richards, "The Traditions of Government in the States" in *The Forty-eight States: Their Tasks as Policy Makers and Administrators* (New York: The American Assembly, Graduate School of Business, Columbia University, 1955); Herbert Kaufman, "Emerging Conflicts in the Doctrines of Public Administration," *American Political Science Review* 50 (Dec. 1956):1057–73.

9. Richards, *Traditions of Government,* 42.

10. Philip Davidson, *Propaganda and the American Revolution 1763–1783* (Chapel Hill: The University of North Carolina Press, 1941), 54.

11. William F. Willingham, "Deference Democracy and Town Government in Windham, Connecticut, 1755 to 1786," *William and Mary Quarterly* 30 (Fall 1973):401–22.

12. Ibid., 421.

13. Thomas Perkins Abernathy, ed., *Notes on the State of Virginia by Thomas Jefferson* [first published in 1785, see Abernathy's Introduction, 4] (New York: Harper & Row, 1964), 158.

14. Ibid.

15. Anwar Syed, *The Political Theory of American Local Government* (New York: Random House, 1966), 38–39.

16. Clinton Rossiter, ed., *The Federalist Papers by Alexander Hamilton, James Madison and John Jay* [originally published in 1787 and 1788] (New York: The New American Library of World Literarure, 1961), 77–78.

17. Ibid., 80

18. Allan Nevins and Henry Steele Commager, *The Pocket History of the United States,* rev. ed. (New York: Pocket Books, 1951), 144.

19. Richards, *Traditions of Government,* 42–44.

20. Ibid., 44.

21. Charles R. Adrian and Ernest S. Griffith, *A History of American City Government: The Formulation of Tradition, 1775–1870* (New York: Praeger, 1976; Washington, DC: University Press of America, 1983), 76–81.

22. J. C. Livingston, "Alexander Hamilton and the American Tradition," *Midwest Journal of Political Science* 1 (Nov. 1957): 209–24.

23. From *Raintree County* by Ross Lockridge, Jr. Copyright 1947 and 1948 by Ross F. Lockridge. Copyright © renewed 1975 by Vernice Lockridge Noyes. Reprinted by permission of Houghton Mifflin Company. Quotation is from p. 174.

24. Alexis de Tocqueville, *Democracy in America* [originally published in 1835 and 1840] V. P. Mayer, ed., George Lawrence, trans. (Garden City, NY: Doubleday, 1969), 66–67.

25. Ibid., 254–56.

26. Ibid., 533–34.

27. Ibid., 674–79.

28. This point is made by Kaufman, "Emerging Conflicts," 1058–59.

29. C. G. Bowers, *The Tragic Era* (Boston: Houghton Mifflin, 1929); James Brycc, *Modern Democracies* (New York: Macmillan, 1921, volume 2); Richards, *Traditions of Government,* 40–64.

30. Roscoe C. Martin, *Grass Roots* (University, AL: University of Alabama Press, 1957), 87, which discusses the fact that the Jacksonian value of small government close to the people has come "to be associated with everything good and virtuous in American life."

31. Robert J. Harris, "States' Rights and Vested Interests," *Journal of Politics* 15 (Nov. 1954): 457–71.

32. See John C. Calhoun, *Disquisition on Government* [1851] (New York: The Liberal Arts Press, Inc., 1953). For a vigorous contemporary defense of states' rights, see J. J. Kilpatrick, *The Sovereign States: Notes of a Citizen of Virginia* (Chicago: Henry Regnery, 1957).

33. 11 Wall. 113 (1871)

34. See the Harold W. Chase and Craig R. Ducat edition of Edward S. Corwin, *The Constitution and What It Means Today,* 14th ed. (Princeton, NJ: Princeton University Press, 1978), 444–45.

35. See *National League of Cities* v. *Usery,* 426 U.S. 833 (1976), among others.

36. *Brown* v. *Board of Education of Topeka,* 347 U.S. (1954).

37. Frank Freidel, *Franklin D. Roosevelt: The Triumph,* (Boston: Little, Brown, 1956), chapter 8.

38. For a balanced appraisal of the function of the states, see Daniel J. Elazar, *American Federalism: A View From the States,* 3d ed. (New York: Thomas Y. Crowell, 1984).

39. *McCulloch* v. *Maryland,* 4 Wheat. 316 (1819).

40. *National League of Cities* v. *Usery,* 426 U.S. 833 (1976).

41. Quoted in Freidel, *Franklin D. Roosevelt,* 71–72.

42. For the impact of the Industrial Age on Americans, see Samuel P. Hays, *The Response to Industrialism* (Chicago: The University of Chicago Press, 1957).

43. Harris, "States' Rights," 461.

44. Alan P. Grimes, *The Political Liberalism of the New York Nation* (Chapel Hill: The University of North Carolina Press, 1953), chapter 3; also Parrington, *Main Currents in American Thought,* volume 3, 58–59.

45. For the best statement of machine values from a boss's point of view, see William L. Riordan, *Plunkett of Tammany Hall* [originally published in 1930] (New York: Dutton, 1963). To understand the variations in boss and machine politics, see Harold Zink, *City Bosses in the United States* [originally published in 1930] (New York: AMS Press, 1968). A history of the machine at the local level is provided by Ernest S. Griffith, *A History of American City Government, The Conspicuous Failure 1870–1900,* (New York: Praeger, 1974). The series continues into the reform period in *A History of American City Government: The Progressive Years and Their Aftermath 1900–1920* (New York: Praeger 1974), and Charles R. Adrian, *A History of American City Government, The Emergence of the Metropolis 1920–1945* (Lanham, MD: University Press of America, 1987).

46. See Robert M. LaFollette, *LaFollette's Autobiography* [first published in 1911] (Madison: University of Wisconsin Press, 1960).

47. T. Harry Williams, *Huey Long* (Baton Rouge: Louisiana State University Press, 1977). *All the King's Men* by Robert Penn Warren (New York: Harcourt Brace and World, 1946) is a novel based on Long's career. Also see V. O. Key, Jr. and Alexander Heard, *Southern Politics in State and Nation* (New York: Alfred A. Knopf, 1959).

48. For classic statements on the efficiency and economy movement positions, see Robert C. Brooks, "Bibliography of Municipal Problems and Conditions of City Life," *Municipal Affairs* (1903); Alfred Willoughby, "The Involved Citizen," *National Civic Review* 58 (Dec. 1969): 519–64.

49. Grimes, *Political Liberalism,* 44–51.

50. The failure of the movement to include a "solid basis in mass support" was pointed out long ago in John A. Vieg, "Advice for Municipal Reformers," *Public Opinion Quarterly* 1 (Oct. 1937): 87–92.

51. Parrington, *Main Currents,* 262.

52. Ibid., 262.

53. Ibid., 287.

54. Ibid., 262–87; Richard Hofstadter, *The American Political Tradition* (New York: Alfred A. Knopf, 1948), chapter 8.

55. *Munn* v. *Illinois,* 94 U.S. 113 (1876).

56. For a brief summary of Court decisions that finally cleared away legal obstacles to the social service state, see Harris "States' Rights," 461–71; and J. W. Hurst, *Law and the Conditions of Freedom in the Nineteenth Century United States* (Madison: The University of Wisconsin Press 1956).

57. Quoted in Grimes, *Political Liberalism,* 40.

58. Zink, *City Bosses.*

59. Among numerous descriptions of the suburban movement, still one of the best is Robert C. Wood, *Suburbia* (Boston: Houghton Mifflin, 1958). One of the best texts relating suburbs to the rest of the metropolitan area is John C. Bollens and Henry J. Schmandt, *The Metropolis,* 4th ed. (New York: Harper & Row, 1982).

60. *Brown* v. *Board of Education of Topeka,* 347 U.S. 483 (1954).

61. *Milliken* v. *Bradley* 418 U.S. 717 (1974).

62. Richard S. Childs, *Civic Victories* (New York: Harper & Row, 1952), xv.

63. A summary is provided in Glendon A. Schubert, Jr., *The Public Interest* (New York: The Free Press, 1960).

64. See Avery Leiserson, *Administrative Regulation* (Chicago: The University of Chicago Press, 1942), 14.

65. See Arthur E. Buck, *The Reorganization of State Governments in the United States* (New York: Columbia University Press, 1938) for a complete statement of the orthodox view.

66. See Michael Fine, "A Community Development Mind Set: The Ideological Roots of Reform and Public Choice Theory," *The Small City and Regional Community* 7 (1987): 78–85; and Part I of Harlan Hahn and Charles H. Levine, eds., *Readings in Urban Politics,* 2d ed. (New York: Longman, 1984). The article in Hahn by Samuel P. Hays, "The Politics of Reform in the Progressive Era," particularly makes the point that reformers benefit from relatively narrow interests. Note the distinction between cities in which the reformers' creed is found and others in which it is not, as shown in Oliver P. Williams and Charles R. Adrian, *Four Cities* (Philadephia: University of Pennsylvania Press, 1963).

67. Among the many pluralist works, an early influential study was Robert A. Dahl, *Who Governs? Democracy and Power in an American City* (New Haven, CT: Yale University Press, 1961). The likelihood that different cities will produce different power structures is shown in Williams and Adrian, *Four Cities.* A collection of articles from the many sides of this debate is Willis D. Hawley and Frederick M. Wirt, eds., *The Search for Community Power* (Englewood Cliffs, NJ: Prentice-Hall, 1968). The ideological nature of the debate can be found in Peter Bachrach and Morton S. Baratz, "Two Faces of Power," *American Political Science Review* 56 (Dec. 1962): 947–52.

68. One finds many "elitist" works; at the national level an early influential study was C. Wright Mills, *The Power Elite,* (Fair Lawn, NJ: Oxford University Press, 1956). An implicit conspiracy hypothesis seems to underlie the work by Floyd Hunter, *Community Power Structure* (Chapel Hill: The University of North Carolina Press, 1953), a study of Atlanta.

69. See Edward C. Banfield, *The Unheavenly City* (Boston: Little, Brown, 1968).

Drawing by Ed Fisher; © 1990 The New Yorker Magazine, Inc.

3

Rules for Rule Making

A constitution is a set of rules about rule making. Its principal purposes are to describe the basic structure and decision-making processes of government and to allocate political power. Allocation must be made among levels of government, among branches of government, and between government and the individual or private organization. Each constitution establishes state government and various local governments by a statement of their general powers and relationships to one another. Every state government is established with the familiar distribution of authority according to the principle of the separation of powers among the executive, legislative, and judicial branches. Some powers are given to government, whereas others, known as civil rights, are withheld from it and reserved for individuals. This preserves the principle that governments are limited.

In addition to the state constitutions, the legal setting of state and local government includes charters and statutes spelling out in greater detail the powers of cities, counties, school districts, and other local units. It also includes rules that govern government relationships at coordinate levels—intercity or interstate relations, for example—and between general and regional or local governments. This chapter will spell out some of the legal rules that condition the actions of national, state, and local governments.[1]

The Content of Constitutions

"We the people of Alaska, grateful to God. . . ."
"We the people of Puerto Rico, in order to organize ourselves politically on a fully democratic basis. . . ."

Thus begin two original American attempts at constitution writing.[2] And so begin almost all state and commonwealth constitutions now in effect. A preamble seems essential to each constitution. Most constitution writers tend to imitate the language of Gouverneur Morris, chairman of the famous Committee on Style, which in 1787

69

gave the final polish to the U. S. Constitution. Some state constitution writers also throw in a few twisted lines from Thomas Jefferson's Declaration of Independence. The preamble, however, is chiefly a collection of glittering generalities; it conveys no legal powers. Sometimes such generalizations go beyond the preamble and work their way into the body of the constitution. Rarely do they have any legal meaning. For example, Wisconsin, the state that is known for its breweries, has included the following statement in its bill of rights: "The blessings of a free government can only be maintained by a firm adherence to . . . temperance."

As Americans moved westward, they tended to become more equalitarian in outlook, and new constitutions reflected this fact.[3] This pattern continued all the way to the westernmost and newest states, Alaska and Hawaii. Each of these state constitutions contained the most liberal provisions concerning civil rights, and each provided for a minimum voting age lower than that prevailing before the Twenty-Sixth Amendment set a national norm.[4] This spirit is further illustrated by the adoption of the initiative method of amending constitutions, by the expansion of the bill of rights in some states, and by other features that have been adopted in recent years.

States have borrowed freely from one another in writing their constitutions. In 1777, Vermont relied heavily on the Pennsylvania constitution. The original Illinois constitution (1818) made generous use of the Kentucky, Ohio, New York, and Indiana constitutions. Almost one-half of the original California constitution was borrowed from the Iowa constitution and many other sections came from the New York constitution. In fact, five other state constitutions borrowed from the California convention delegates.[5]

Four features commonly are found in each state constitution:

1. A bill of rights
2. Provision for the basic structure of state government that follows the separation of powers doctrine, which distributes power among the executive, legislative, and judicial branches and further, in some states, among independent bureaucratic agencies (see chapters 4 and 7)
3. Specification of the powers of the branches of government (see chapters 8 and 13)
4. Provision for amending the constitution

The Bill of Rights

Each constitution contains a bill of rights, drawing the line between the power of the state and the power of an individual to act at will. Most bills of rights, *modeled* on the first ten amendments to the national Constitution, go beyond the rights listed there. State practices vary widely.[6] Furthermore, many provisions of the U. S. Bill of Rights apply only to the national government, not to the states. A bill of rights may be of general importance to show the liberal or democratic nature of the state. Specific application, however, becomes critical if an individual is in conflict with government. For example, it serves little purpose to protect freedom of speech for the individual who chooses not to speak or for the individual who speaks loudly in support of an idea that no one in power would challenge. Given American localism and federalism, those police powers of states that bring individuals and governments into conflict usually are powers exercised by state and local governments. Thus, in protecting an individual from the power of government, one must almost always look to the guarantees of the particular state—not national—constitution.

Because many community traditions run counter to principles laid down in the bill of rights, if those in power challenge a right, an individual must almost always go to court to uphold that right. Litigation is costly and intimidating; thus the forum for the clash is crucial. The bill of rights usually prevails in the courtroom, whereas outside the court process, tradition more often prevails. For example, the national courts have ruled frequently that school desegregation is mandatory in local school districts because of provisions in the national and state constitutions. But these protections have done little to desegregate schools that are never challenged in court and thus are maintained under the tradition of segregated neighborhood schooling.

The concern for a bill of rights dates back to the time when the first constitutions were ratified by the states during the revolutionary period. Few states have changed their bills of rights significantly over time. Although most of the first constitutions were not voted on by the people, but rather were ratified directly by conventions or existing state legislatures, even those in government who potentially would be limited by a bill of rights recognized the need.[7] Recent years have seen some important amendments, particularly in light of the widening national government role in civil rights for minorities and rights of those accused of crimes. Many states have amended their constitutions to add protections that otherwise would require action by the federal courts. On the other hand, some state courts have interpreted their bills of rights more broadly than has the U. S. Supreme Court in the federal case. For example, in *Serrano v. Priest* (1971), the California Supreme Court accepted the argument that the state's "equal protection of the laws" clause could be interpreted more liberally than the federal clause had been, even though the wording was identical.[8] It was argued that this was so because the traditions of the two sets of courts were not the same.[9] In other cases, added protections simply reflect the new-found powers of particular interest groups or changing social mores in regard to certain groups. For example, about one-third of the states have added provisions for equal rights for women, most coming as amendments since 1970.[10]

Specification of State Power

The U.S. Constitution is a relatively short document, but the Madisonian principles of extended governmental power and checks and balances have worked their way into most state constitutions. The constitutions provide for the institutional checks of separation of powers, and then go on to specify in detail the functions and powers of government. Early constitutions were brief; in 1880, the longest was that of Massachusetts, which contained about 12,000 words. Recent constitutions have increased in length, reaching a peak in Louisiana, for instance, of some 200,000 words before major revision in 1973. Most of each document contains provisions for specifying the powers of the three branches of state government and the accompanying bureaucracy designed to implement those powers.

Author Daniel J. Elazar suggests that although the national Constitution demonstrated the Madisonian principle of checks and balances, two other early principles are evident in state constitutions—the Whig and the managerial principles. The Whig tradition "placed great emphasis on direct, active, continuous, and well-nigh complete popular control over the legislature and government in general," through a variety of mechanisms for direct intervention by the individual.[11] The managerial perspective took the somewhat opposite view that professional decision making was possible in lawmaking and its administration. All three views contribute to voluminous state constitutions: The Madisonian view requires expanded institutional mechanisms to check the power of government, the Whig view requires expanded mechanisms for individual action, and the managerial view requires specification of bureaucratic power.

The fact that American legislatures have never been trusted fully by citizens has encouraged the writing of many rules circumscribing legislative powers. Constitutional provisions are devised to control the legislature or to prevent it from acting in certain areas. However, in recent decades this long-standing public attitude has tended to come into conflict with the general desire for expanded governmental functions. The federal government launched the scores of new programs of the New Deal and the Fair Deal without once amending the U. S. Constitution, but a similar feat was not possible in most states where restrictions on governmental powers required changes in the fundamental law before new programs could be established. Thus, constitutions grew in length initially in order to limit governmental power and later to ease existing restrictions.

Many state constitutions are relatively easy to amend—at least compared with the federal constitution—although a few (Illinois and Tennessee for example) are very difficult to amend. It is thus more possible at the state level than at the federal to appeal an unpopular judicial interpretation or legislative action by amending fundamental law.

Interest groups are always tempted to write their most favored policies into the constitution itself. Because a constitution is fundamental law, it would logically contain only enabling and prohibiting authority, in addition to a description of governmental structure. Upon this base, statute law (i.e., law formally enacted by a legislative body) would be built. In practice, however, groups within society learned in the nineteenth century that nothing except custom prevented the inclusion of statute law in the constitutions themselves. With this understood, they began using constitutions for their own ends. Because these bodies of law normally are more difficult to amend than are statutes, they gave added protection to the pet interests of certain groups. The fact that any constitutional provision enjoys special legitimacy and sanctity makes it more difficult for another group to mount a counterattack than if the provision were mere statute law.

It should not be assumed that an interest group, in putting one of its favorite pieces of legislation into the constitution, is seeking to achieve its goals by devious and deceptive means. In many cases, the group believes strongly in the particular piece of legislation and sincerely regards it as having a proper place in the fundamental law. A spokesperson for one interest group, in justifying a New York constitutional amendment in 1931 that involved statute law, put it simply: He agreed that constitutions should deal with fundamental law, but "in view of the importance [of the particular measure] it seems as if we were justified in making this exception.''[12]

The Amending Process

A state constitution can be amended in a variety of ways:[13]

1. Like the U.S. Constitution, it can be changed through executive, legislative, and judicial interpretation. This is, in fact, probably the most common means of changing it. For example, governors may interpret a vague provision concerning their powers; legislative leaders often give on-the-spot interpretations of the constitution during debates; attorneys general as a normal part of their jobs interpret the constitutions, and their views carry the force and effect of law unless overruled by higher authority; courts apply the constitution frequently through judicial review. Other levels of government indirectly amend the constitution by requiring state action that significantly changes the spirit of the constitution. For example, states have by statute changed their drinking age to remain eligible for federal highway funds regardless of the lower ages found in their constitutions. Unlike most of the formal methods that follow, amendment by interpretation does not require ratification by the voters.

2. A constitutional convention may recommend changes in the existing constitution or it may recommend an entirely new document. Some two hundred conventions have been called in America, and over half of these have led to new constitutions. Conventions may be called four different ways: (a) The most common form allows the legislature to refer the question to the voters; (b) The existing constitution may require the question to be put to the voters at regular intervals (e.g., every twenty years in Illinois); (c) The existing constitution may allow the legislature to call a convention without voter approval (e.g., Louisiana); (d) A petition of the people may call the convention, bypassing the legislature (at present, only in Florida, although all states that allow amendment by initiative could conceivably create a convention through this process). The existing constitution may not specify the way, but in these instances the courts have held that the legislature may submit the question to the voters (e.g., Arkansas).

At present, many states that provide for calling a convention do not specify how the document will be ratified. Once a convention is called, rules concerning adoption might be altered. This was the case when the national Constitution was created. Today, those states that specify ratification leave the question to the voters. Given the historical development of faith in the voter to decide fundamental questions, it is likely that the conventions will specify that the people must ratify the decisions of the convention. Ratification processes can be complicated. Some states require a simple majority of those voting on the question, some a majority of those voting at that election, and some an extraordinary majority (e.g., two-thirds in New Jersey).

Initiative: **A procedure permitting a specified number of voters to petition for proposed changes in a constitution, municipal charter, laws, or ordinances. These proposals are then accepted or rejected by voters at the polls.**

> *Referendum:* **A procedure permitting voters to accept or reject at the polls changes in a constitution, municipal charter, laws, or ordinances proposed by a legislative body. A referendum follows favorable action by a legislative body; the initiative is designed to operate independently of the legislature.**

3. Seventeen states allow voters to propose constitutional amendments through use of the *initiative.* No action is required by a convention or by the legislature. A petition is circulated stating the proposal. If enough signatures are obtained to satisfy the law, the proposal is placed on the ballot at the next election. Ratification is usually by a majority vote on the amendment, although Nevada requires two votes in general elections; Massachusetts and Nebraska require, in addition, approval by a percentage of the total vote in the election; and Illinois requires either a majority vote in the election or three-fifths vote on the amendment.

4. The most common formal means of proposing amendments to state constitutions is the *referendum*—submission by the legislature; every state authorizes this method. The referendum usually involves a resolution by the legislature and commonly requires two-thirds or three-fifths of the membership to vote in favor. This requirement, of course, makes passage difficult. A few states allow an amendment to be submitted by the vote of a simple majority in each house; but thirteen states require votes in two successive sessions, and this is often a major obstacle to change. In states with biennial sessions, it may delay amendment for as long as three years.

Again, voter ratification takes a variety of forms. Most states require a simple majority on the amendment, but nine states make passage more difficult by requiring additional stipulations. Only Delaware does not require a popular vote. Furthermore, after balloting, the constitution in a number of states requires additional acts of the legislature to implement or interpret the amendment.

5. A number of states use commissions in the amending process, although only Florida's constitution provides for direct submission by such a body. Commissions in other states take two forms—either as a permanent group designed to report recommendations to the legislature as a preliminary step in the referendum process (e.g., Utah), or as an ad hoc body called to aid special interest groups in their quest for constitutional change (often to shed pressure building for a constitutional convention or to prepare for such an event). Members of the commissions are appointed, usually by the governor or legislative leaders. The unique Florida Constitution Revision Commission can directly submit items to the voters, although most such proposals have failed since the creation of the commission in 1977.[14] Roughly one-half of the study commissions in this century were created in the 1960s, reflecting the expansion of state legislation and the growing demands put on state government by the national government during this period, primarily in the area of legislative reapportionment.[15]

The Politics of Constitution Writing

Constitutions are political documents. The fact that they help determine the rules of politics would in itself make them the object of manipulation by the various interests of society. Their content is constantly a matter of concern to groups and individuals, and the very fact that constitutions are more difficult to change than are statutes makes them attractive tools for interest groups to use in protecting their favorite legislation.

Major Revision: The Politics of Conventions

Twenty-three constitutional conventions met in seventeen states between 1960 and 1980.[16] But only three constitutional conventions were convened in the 1980s. More frequently, calls for conventions were defeated. New Hampshire's seventeenth constitutional convention was convened in 1984, after four hundred delegates were selected, one from each of the four hundred state House of Representative districts. In all, 175 proposals were considered; only 10 were approved for submission to the voters, and only 6 passed.[17] Rhode Island's convention, which met for most of 1986, produced 288 proposals, whittled down to fourteen ballot questions, of which eight passed.[18] Whereas these conventions were unlimited—they could tackle any issues permitted by the U. S. Constitution—they demonstrate the tendency toward piecemeal constitutional change. Major parts of the old constitutions remained. The originals date back to 1842 in the case of Rhode Island and 1784 in New Hampshire. Only Georgia's constitution (effective July 1, 1983), which eliminated the practice of incorporating hundreds of local amendments, is considered new since 1975. The older practice of rewriting an entire constitution is best illustrated by the constitution written by the 1984 convention in the District of Columbia, proposing Columbia as the fifty-first state.[19]

When writers of a constitution for New Mexico, which was about to be admitted to the Union, gathered in 1910, they were faced with many of the same practical considerations that their counterparts in other states had known.[20] Their approach to the job was probably not atypical. The convention was organized along strict party lines, even the clerical positions being distributed by the patronage machinery of the Republican party. The rules under which the convention would proceed were designed to minimize the potential influence of the Democratic minority. In doing their work, the members used earlier drafts of proposed New Mexico constitutions as they referred to the existing constitutions of all other states. Many committees simply copied sections that appealed to them from state constitutions. Partisan conflict revolved around the desire of the majority Republicans to write a conservative constitution tailored to the dominant economic elements of the area, including the owners of large ranches. The Democratic leader was a progressive who wanted to include in the constitution provisions for the initiative and referendum, strict regulation of railroads, the direct primary election, and an easy amending procedure—a typical progressive–reform platform of that day. The minority urged that judges be chosen on a nonpartisan ballot, a proposal designed to remove control from the powerful economic leaders who dominated the majority party.

The chief conflict was over the initiative and referendum. It is not easy today to realize how seriously this conflict was taken. Many liberals saw the initiative and referendum as the only device that would free the common people from domination by the few. In a sparsely settled area and with property ownership concentrated in a few hands, this seemed like a very real danger. Some conservatives, on the other hand, regarded the initiative and referendum as subversive of the principle of representative government and viewed the proposal with genuine alarm. The issue was finally compromised. The leaders recognized that popular support was strongly behind initiative and referendum and that any proposed constitution probably would not be adopted if it did not include a provision for it. They therefore included the initiative and referendum, but tied it up with a procedural process they believed—correctly, as it turned out—would be difficult to put to use. The issues before the constitutional convention in this case, as in most (or perhaps all) cases, involved a conflict of political, social, and economic interests that were compromised through much the same procedure as they are before any representative body.

More recent studies of conventions suggest that convention goers do treat a constitutional convention differently from other law-making modes. Delegates seem to show a particular tendency to come into a convention with an "above-politics" attitude.[21] For example, despite the use of partisan legislative districts as the basis for selecting delegates to the conventions in the 1980s, the convention delegates were selected on nonpartisan ballots. Nevertheless, studies of other recent conventions show the process of decision making will bring those in attendance into conventional decision-making patterns.[22] It was found that regardless of the election to the Illinois convention on a nonpartisan ballot, partisan concerns dominated the decision-making process, as they do in the Illinois legislature. The Republican majority in the Michigan convention of 1961–1962 was divided among moderates, who wanted to use the opportunities to boost George Romney's chances of becoming governor and conservatives who opposed him, while Democrats sought to exploit the division to their own advantage. Despite the political pulling and hauling, people generally agreed that a good constitution resulted.

Prior to 1920, rewriting state constitutions was part of the American way of life. From time to time, as ecological patterns of economic elites changed or political values evolved, new state constitutions were written. Over 230 state constitutional conventions have met in our history, with certain periods of intense constitution writing, particularly in the 1850s, when the values of frontier individualism were written into state fundamental law; again after the Civil War; and finally during the reform period between the 1890s and World War I. The sacrosanctity that came to be attached to the U. S. Constitution never has been applied to state constitutions. In some states, however, a related phenomenon arose. Thus although Massachusetts adopted a new constitution in 1919, the folklore of the commonwealth regards this relatively new document as the constitution of 1780.

Generally, citizens have been pragmatic toward their state constitutions. Yet, after World War I, the old pattern of periodic rewriting of fundamental law was interrupted. Between 1920 and 1960, only seven constitutions were adopted, excluding those of Alaska and Hawaii. Why this change? The answer probably is to be found in the rapid urbanization of the nation and in the clustering of urban populations around relatively few metropolitan areas. Residents of rural areas, villages, and small cities, who were overrepresented as a result of old apportionment rules, recognized that a complete reappraisal of state government by a constitutional convention selected on the basis of population would result in a considerable loss to them of influence in state government. To preserve the disproportionate power they possessed through the accident of shifting populations, persons in these areas opposed constitutional revision. It is also likely that as statute law accumulated in state constitutions over time, a growing number of groups came to possess a vested interest in retaining the existing document and in not risking the unknown in a convention.

After the one-person, one-vote doctrine was developed by Court rulings in the early 1960s, the basic reason for avoiding constitutional conventions no longer existed. Legislatures were reapportioned by court order, opening the door for change. Interest groups that had been underrepresented before took the reigns of power; their popular strength came to be reflected in state legislatures. Legislators, governors, and reformers began to call for conventions. Fourteen conventions were held in the 1960s and eight more in the 1970s. Fourteen states have passed provisions requiring periodic submission of the question of holding a convention to the voters, typically every twenty years. But when used, the opportunity usually is rejected. The rarity of conventions in the 1980s and the piecemeal nature of their products suggest that the revival of conventions after the one-person, one-vote rulings has subsided. Once again, the convention appears to be seen as more of a threat to groups in power than an opportunity for change.[23] When a proposed new constitution is on the ballot, it does not bring out huge numbers of voters unless particularly controversial material is included. A proposed constitution, stated in general terms authorizing powers, is one step short of bringing together the contestants in a specific and emotion-driven issue that attracts droves of voters in a hard-fought referendum. A proposed new constitution giving the legislature general taxing powers can be a ho-hum matter; calling for an amendment to provide a specific increase in the retail sales tax is likely to be quite another. Advisory commissions and a phasing process that adopts parts of the constitution by referendums have prevented the greater use of conventions. Interest groups focusing on more narrow changes to suit their needs found the referendum to be a more successful tool. The piecemeal approach led to over fourteen hundred proposed referendums in the 1970s, and over two hundred in the 1980s. It also produced greater interest at the polls, where the voter can concentrate more easily on the issues of special interest than on the whole constitution.

Piecemeal Politics

Despite difficulties in changing a state constitution, most such change involves relatively narrow matters, pressing concerns of the moment that rarely have been considered in terms of long-range implications. The referendum process has become a convenient mechanism by which those in government afford special benefits to groups that supported them. About 90 percent of constitutional changes have been proposed by referendum—almost eight thousand submitted to the voters—with over 65 percent passing. But many amendments have little substance. A study of Wisconsin, one of nineteen states to retain its original constitution, found over one hundred proposed referenda with 75 percent adopted. However, less than one-third of these involved major changes in state government that affected much of the citizenry—these passed particularly in the progressive era—whereas the most common single category of proposals involved the lesser question of legislative pay raises.[24]

The constitutional initiative appears to have an important function where it is authorized. Its critics contend that the device provides a method whereby well-financed special interest groups can change the basic rules of the game to fit their goals. Nevertheless, of the more than five hundred initiatives proposed by states that allow this method, only about one-third have been passed by the voters. In a forty-five-year period of Michigan's history, no extremist or crackpot amendment was ever approved by the voters (although several that might be so classified were submitted).

In June 1978, California voters passed Proposition 13, a constitutional initiative that restricted the local government's ability to raise property taxes. This was the linchpin for the tax-revolt movement that began at the state level in the mid-1970s and contributed to the electoral success of Ronald Reagan at the national level. Proposition 13 demonstrates the potential of an initiative to bypass the normal legislative process. Although most elected officials originally opposed the plan, voters overwhelmingly approved it. Indeed, a major factor promoting passage was the legislature's refusal, over about two decades, to respond to a swelling demand for local tax reform. High property taxes, reflecting soaring housing prices, kept many people out of the home-ownership market. Voters undoubtedly were swayed by the promise of lower taxes. Few could foresee the serious curtailment of local services that resulted.[25]

Constitutional initiatives represent legitimate parts of the ideological spectrum. But more than other methods of constitutional change, initiatives do not require the coalition building among groups typical of the legislative process or of conventions. The initiative today can be a product of media campaigning, therefore, and of those groups that can afford the high costs involved with this approach.[26] Therefore, limited interests will dominate the piecemeal process of constitutional change most common today.

Substantive changes in state constitutions involve a number of areas. Few summary studies have been done, but one covering the years 1970–1985 found that finance and taxation proposals topped the list with 500 proposals and over 300 adoptions, followed by between 200 and 300 proposals and over 140 adoptions each for the legislative, administrative, executive, and judicial branches of government, usually expanding the powers of government. Some 100 proposals and 90 adoptions each were in the areas of suffrage and elections, local government, state and local debt, and the bill of rights.[27]

Changes in the relationship between state and local government during the rapid expansion of governmental spending have demonstrated the states' willingness to exert their constitutional power over the localities by passing a variety of measures to restrict the local government's taxing and bonding powers. Furthermore, the expansion of state power has led to a number of structural changes in the branches of state government, most notably in the legislature (longer sessions, greater compensation, expanded staffs).

Changes in bills of rights have diminished the rights of those accused of crimes, but other areas of rights reflect an expansion. Many states have passed equal rights amendments for women and language modifications that make the constitution gender neutral.[28] As the rights of many groups have expanded in the past generation (e.g., women, blacks, Hispanics, the handicapped, and veterans), a corresponding increase has occurred in the administrative processes designed to expedite the protections, and so has expansion and unification of court systems to accommodate the growing judicial role. Further development has come in the areas of privacy, right-to-know legislation, and environmental protection.[29]

The Fourteenth Amendment

The national Constitution affects the states in numerous ways. As discussed in chapter 2, the Tenth Amendment reserves to the states those powers not given to the national government or denied to the states. Specification of these powers will be considered in the following chapter. More indirectly but with far greater impact, the national courts have interpreted the *Fourteenth Amendment* to place a number of limitations on state constitutions. In effect, the Fourteenth Amendment became a mechanism for changing state constitutions.

> *Fourteenth Amendment, Section One:* **. . . No State shall make or enforce any law which shall abridge the privileges or immunities of citizens of the United States; nor shall any State deprive any person of life, liberty, or property, without due process of law; nor deny to any person within its jurisdiction the equal protection of the laws.**

The Fourteenth Amendment was one of three passed after the Civil War to free slaves and ensure their full range of rights. But it had little effect for most of the century following its passage. Groups later protected by the amendment were not yet successful in applying it. Jim Crow laws in the South prevailed despite the amendment. The women's rights movement concentrated on gaining the vote, culminating in the passage of the Nineteenth Amendment in 1920. But this did little to widen the legal rights of women beyond the vote. The rights of the accused were protected in variable fashion by each state constitution. But the Supreme Court rarely extended to individuals in state courts the rights of the accused guaranteed in national courts by the national Constitution. Apportionment of state legislatures was considered a partisan matter, beyond the scope of constitutional interpretation by courts. Furthermore, when the amendment was applied, it was thought to apply only to racial issues and only narrowly.[30]

As early as 1925, the Supreme Court would recognize that First Amendment rights applied to the states by virtue of the due process clause of the Fourteenth Amendment.[31] But it was not until the Warren Court that use of the Fourteenth Amendment would become widespread. Beginning with *Brown v. Board of Education of Topeka*, 349 U.S. 294 (1954), the change would be dramatic. In *Brown*, the equal protection clause of the Fourteenth Amendment was used to require the states to desegregate public schools. In the 1960s the floodgates were opened. The amendment would be used in 1961 to protect the accused against the use in court of evidence illegally obtained,[32] in 1962 to reapportion state legislatures,[33] and in 1963 to extend the rights of counsel to the accused in state courts for major crimes.[34] Those who wanted to extend to the states the limitations found in the Fourth through Eighth Amendments, talked of "incorporating" the Bill of Rights in state constitutions by virtue of the due process clause of the Fourteenth Amendment. Although no blanket incorporation of the rights of the accused was to occur, the following were selectively incorporated: protection against self-incrimination (1964),[35] the right to confront witnesses,[36] the right to be warned of other rights (1966),[37] and the right to a speedy trial (1967).[38]

Although the Burger and Rehnquist courts technically limited some restrictions on the states in regard to the rights of the accused, they did not reverse the incorporation decisions of the Warren Court. They have shied away from further applying the Fourteenth Amendment to the states in four important areas: statewide financing of public schools (1973),[39] interdistrict busing of school children (1974),[40] zoning regulations that have the effect of restricting on the basis of social class (1977),[41] and affirmative action (1984, 1986 and 1989).[42] Yet, the Burger Court used the Fourteenth Amendment to restrict the states' control of abortions (1973)—thus extending the rights of privacy. A narrowly split Rehnquist Court returned parts of this controversial issue to the states in the *Webster* case (1989) by restricting some state-supported abortions.[43]

Once again, note that we are in a period in which the prevailing American ideologies are changing. The next few years will tell whether use of the Fourteenth Amendment to restrict state powers and make state bills of rights more similar was a temporary or a long-lasting phenomenon. Yet, it is unlikely that the courts will fully reverse the widespread change in state law brought on by Warren Court use of the Fourteenth Amendment. Little such change occurred in the 1970s or 1980s.

Fundamental Law for Local Government

Each state has a constitution and is, under our federal system, formally supreme in every field where it is not limited by the powers of the U. S. Constitution. Local government powers, on the other hand, are much more circumscribed. Each unit of local government is essentially an agent of the state government, and its powers are derived either from a charter or from statutory enabling legislation.

The Municipal Corporation

The municipality—the city, village, or borough—is, legally speaking, a corporation, that is, an artificial person created by the state. The powers of the municipality therefore are derived from the state just as are those of any other corporation, and they are expressed in a charter. A charter, the fundamental law of a corporation, establishes four things: (1) the physical boundaries of the municipality, (2) the structure of local government, (3) the powers that may be exercised by it, and (4) the general manner in which the powers granted may be exercised. The charter is almost never a single document and includes all state laws and judicial opinions that affect the structure, powers, or manner of exercising the powers of the corporation.

The city, in some respects, has a legal position not unlike that of a private corporation. In fact, only in the past two centuries or so has a distinction developed. The two remain similar in that each exists independently of members of the corporation; each may own property, make contracts, exist normally in perpetuity, and sue as well as be sued. They possess very important differences, too. A *private* corporation is created entirely by the voluntary request of a group of people who wish to form a corporation. They know the corporation law in advance and the conditions under which they will operate. Furthermore, once the corporate charter is granted it becomes a contract that cannot be altered or taken away (except under the rarest circumstances involving public interest). A *public* corporation, on the other hand, may be created with or without the consent of its membership (the persons living in the area); the terms of its charter may be quite different from what the people of the locality desire; even more important, the charter is not a contract and hence is subject to constant, involuntary, and sometimes arbitrary changes. It can even be taken away without advance notice unless the state constitution specifically prohibits this.

Two other important differences exist between public and private corporations. A public corporation can act only in the public interest and for a public purpose. A private corporation must always have the public interest in mind (one could not long exist, for example, if it were organized for the purpose of robbing banks), but it may also have private interests (such as profit making for the individual owners). The two also differ in the degree of control the state exercises over them. A private corporation can carry on any activities it wishes so long as it does not violate law; a public corporation can do only those things it is authorized to do. A corporation producing cigarettes, for example, could take on a sideline of producing plowshares, for example, without seeking an amendment to its charter or other permission from the state. (It could not, however, create a sideline manufacturing marijuana cigarettes, because this would not be in the public interest and could be curbed by the state under its police powers.) A municipal or public corporation, on the other hand, could not enter into a sideline such as municipal parking lots or a municipal theater, or adopt a new form of taxation without first having the state's authorization to do so.[44]

The Quasi Corporation

Cities, villages, and boroughs (in a few states) and a few counties, townships, and school districts operate under written charters and are therefore municipal corporations. Many other local units of government are not, however, including most of the counties, townships, unincorporated New England towns, and the so-called special districts (school, sewage-disposal, airport, environmental protection, rapid transit, drainage, mosquito-abatement, fire, and irrigation districts). These are known at law as *quasi corporations,* that is, bodies that resemble corporations. So far as the lay citizen is concerned, the principal distinction between corporations and quasi corporations is that a quasi corporation serves only as an administrative agent of the state, whereas the true public corporation serves a dual purpose. It acts not only as a local agent for the state but also performs certain local functions exclusively in the interests of the people living within the boundaries of the corporation.

In legal theory, the city (or other public corporation) acts as an agent of the state whenever it performs a function in which the state as a whole has a certain interest; for example, when it enforces the law or maintains public health standards or collects taxes. On the other hand, the city may perform some tasks purely for the comfort and convenience of the local inhabitants; for example, the operation of a water supply or public transportation system. Quasi corporations, in contrast, perform only those functions of statewide interest such as maintaining records, organizing elections, prosecuting crimes, maintaining roads, and educating children. Or so it used to be.

As will be further explained in later chapters, these political distinctions are losing both their meaning and their importance with the proliferation of special districts, which are formed frequently to comply with federal laws. The national government cannot mandate the formation of local laws, but it can give both state and local officials reason to form new quasi corporations to administer a national service. For example, metropolitan air pollution control districts are formed by state governments. Without these districts a variety of transportation-related benefits might be denied a state. Furthermore, the creation of special districts has become a common tool of interest groups that cannot control a particular resource through existing multipurpose municipalities. Frequently, the enabling legislation creating the special district blurs the distinction between corporation and quasi corporation.

Three Rules: The Judge as Umpire

Legal principles are rarely as persuasive as they appear in statute or following the announcement of a precedent. As stated before, legal principles often are challenged by traditions of greater force. Furthermore, judges are not bound to follow legal precedent. Although subject to being overruled by higher courts, judges recognize that decisions rarely will be appealed. When convinced of the arguments that run counter to the prevailing precedent, those judges therefore may accept a different rule or precedent based on tradition or local practice. This point is of particular importance in regard to the legal relationship between state and local government. A prevailing rule is established in precedent, but it is challenged by two minority rules found in some court decisions and strong traditions. This conflict often makes it necessary to question whether a particular unit of government has the power to perform a particular function in a particular way to be decided by the courts. The prevailing rule, known as Dillon's rule, holds that the city is merely a creature of the state, whereas the state itself is a sovereign body. Dillon's rule calls for a narrow construction of local powers and broad construction of state powers. To put it another way, the courts say that cities have only those powers expressly granted by, reasonably implied in, or necessary to carry out, state law.[45] In 1964, for example, the city of Louisville, Kentucky, was tied up for at least two months in a council proposal to construct a municipal zoo. After the city announced its plans, two lawsuits were filed. One challenged the city's right to purchase the proposed zoo site on the technical ground that the city proposed to buy only surface rights and that it could not do so without also buying the mineral rights. Another lawsuit was based on the argument that the city had no authority to establish a zoo. Both suits were lost and the city proceeded with its plans but only after considerable delay and some additional cost. The original plan was for the zoo to be opened to the public early in the summer of 1964, but the legal actions delayed opening until almost the end of the summer season.[46]

In 1965, the New York City Transit Authority faced a typical interest-group ploy, using legal means in an attempt to prevent the execution of policies the group disapproved of. The Transit Authority proposed to construct a tunnel under the East River at 63rd Street. The Citizen's Budget Commission, a middle-class reform group, preferred a tunnel at 61st Street, arguing that this would permit free transfers for passengers from Queens and the Bronx to two Manhattan subway lines. The interest group, unable to convince the Transit Authority, challenged its legal right to construct the tunnel at the proposed location, using the legal argument that due process of law had not been observed.[47]

In chapter 14 we will discuss a number of recent fiscal restraints placed on the localities by the states. During the financial problems of New York City in 1975, Dillon's rule ironically became a threat to the State of New York, which felt pressured to take greater control of the deteriorating city situation and seek national government help because state officials recognized that should New York declare bankruptcy, the state would be responsible for the debts incurred by the municipality it had created. On the other hand, California's 1978 Proposition 13 demonstrates how state power can be used to severely limit the fiscal power of localities.

Even in cities with home rule, supposedly broadening the powers of local government to choose their own options, Dillon's rule applies. When the city of Eau Claire, Wisconsin, wanted to combine some of the functions of police and fire protection in a public safety office, never defined in state law and therefore, never denied the locality, police and fire unions challenged the matter in court arguing that state laws governing the personnel practices of police and fire services prohibited the city from creating a public safety office. The state courts agreed with the argument of the unions against the city in 1988:

> If the legislature intends municipalities to be empowered to establish PSO [public safety office] programs and combine the police and fire functions, it should expressly act. However, in the absence of any legislative action, we conclude that the legislature has implicitly withdrawn the municipalities' authority to establish PSO programs such as the one proposed by Eau Claire.[48]

Dillon's rule explains why city officials may have to spend weeks and thousands of dollars in actions before the state courts seeking to justify a decision to finance a municipal parking lot from the parking meter fund rather than from the general revenue fund; seeking to find some theoretical justification for an antidiscrimination ordinance or for no smoking areas in restaurants or public buildings. That a majority of voters in the locality should demand them and that they should be adopted according to democratic procedures is not sufficient. Dillon's rule says, in effect, "if in doubt, you do not have the power." Local government officials routinely arrange for a friendly lawsuit in the early stages of any new undertaking. This involves expense and delay, but it allows the judges to make their decisions at a time when a negative finding will do less harm and cost less (usually) than would be the case if a disgruntled taxpayer brought a suit when a dam or bridge or parking lot was well under way. But in some cases, because of Dillon's rule courts may subject the city to obligations otherwise not borne by governments. In the 1980s this proved to be the case in personal liability suits, greatly expanding cities' insurance costs and leading to an insurance crisis for local governments.[49]

The two rules that challenge Dillon's by questioning whether states actually control the power of localities are known as Cooley's rule and Fordham's rule.[50] Cooley's rule is more extreme; it holds that the locality is legally sovereign, at least as much so as the state or national government in a federal system where no one sovereign exists.[51] Using no lesser authorities than Thomas Jefferson and Alexis de Tocqueville, Judge Cooley asserted that the powers of local government are as inherent as other natural principles found in American law. He asserted that the long history of local government demonstrates its sovereign nature. The rules of Judges Dillon and Cooley were both formed in the latter part of the nineteenth century. Even though Dillon's rule came to prevail, Cooley's rule has expressed a sentiment for localism rather than legal authority, but it has been used by some courts.

Fordham's rule is a middle ground.[52] It uses the spirit and principle of home rule; that is, it accepts the sovereignty of the state but holds that cities have powers not denied by constitution or statute. Judges who follow this principle may tend to interpret more liberally the powers delegated to localities. Whereas the rule has been used in more than ten states since 1960 and seems to be generous in spirit, it is still in essence Dillon's rule because, as the Eau Claire example demonstrates, courts can still apply whatever legislative restrictions or mandates, expressed or implied, they wish against local governments and they continue to control much local policy, especially relative to financial matters. Fordham's rule is important, nevertheless, because when it is accepted by judges it suggests that home rule exists in places where it may not be expressly granted.

Types of Charters

In the United States, local governments may operate under special-act or general-act charters, a system of classified general-act charters, optional general-act charters, or home-rule charters. The degree of local control increases roughly in the order listed here. Both corporations and quasi corporations may be found operating under any of these systems. Quasi corporations, however, do not refer to their enabling legislation as charters, although the legal effect and status is the same. A city clerk will say, "According to our charter, the city. . . ," but a county clerk will say, "According to state law, the county. . . ." The difference is one of tradition and point of view, not of substance. Home-rule cities have a document adopted by the voters and called the *city charter,* but in all other cities, all state laws governing the structure and powers of the city may be loosely called the *charter.*

Special-Act Charters

The oldest, and at one time the universal, method of granting charters was by legislative act bestowing a specific charter upon a municipality named in the act. This charter could be amended only by the legislature itself. Although quasi corporations customarily were provided for under general acts or the constitution, they often were modified as to detail of organization or powers by special legislation.

Beginning in 1851, when Ohio and Indiana by constitutional provision outlawed all special legislation, attempts have been made to limit its use elsewhere. Legislatures need not necessarily choose to abuse their potential powers of supervision over local government, and they have by no means always done so. Yet, reformers for over a century have argued that local governments should not be constantly subjected to legislative control in such a manner that the state governing body could substitute its own judgment anytime for that of the local governing body. Undoubtedly, special legislation simplified interference by the legislature with matters regarded as strictly local. However, various attempts to prevent the de facto enactment of special legislation have been unsuccessful. The extent of legislative activity in dealing with minute details of local government seems to depend more on tradition in the individual state than on any other factor. Despite its unpopularity in urban communities, special legislation continues in use. It is to be found especially in New England and the South.

General-Act Charters
The general-act charter, designed to provide for uniform powers, privileges, and structures for every *city* in the sate, has not met with much success except where it has been modified by home rule or local option. Because American municipalities vary from hamlets to empires of millions of people, it is unrealistic to expect that every city government should be exactly like every other in powers and structure; variation is needed. Quasi corporations often are established with uniform structure and powers, but again the vast differences in size and population commonly impel the legislature to modify the general pattern to fit local needs.

City: **An urban area of indeterminate population, size, and density with its own government. In this book, the term is interchangeable with *municipality*. Legal definitions of a city differ from one state to another, as do those for a village, town, borough, or other municipal corporation.**

No state has a single general-act charter to apply to all cities; all bear in mind the need for recognizing local requirements. Furthermore, most states make some provision for variation in the structure and powers of quasi corporations, although this is less likely the case than with municipalities.

Classification—Modified General Legislation
After states prohibited special legislation, they began to recognize that local governments of all sizes and populations could not be treated identically. As a result, some states began to classify these units of government, usually by population groupings, but also by other methods, such as form of government (e.g., council-manager or mayor-council). In some states, the constitution established the classifications; in others, it authorized the legislatures to do so; and in a third group of states, where the constitution was silent, the courts permitted the legislature to classify, holding this to be general legislation. Under this system, an act could not be made to apply to a specific city. Instead, it could be no more limiting than to all cities of the first class, for example. Villages, counties, townships, and school districts, as well as cities, are sometimes classified.

In some states, for example in Wisconsin since World War II, classification legislation has been used sparingly and for intended purposes, usually to bestow some benefit on Milwaukee, which is the only "City of the First Class."[53] In other states, however, legislators have sought deliberately to use the classification device to disguise frequent special legislation. California, for example, once classified each of its fifty-eight counties separately, thus allowing the legislature to retain complete control over each one. The legislature has since become too busy for this type of oversight, but it still retains virtually complete power. Sometimes the courts have insisted that classifications be reasonable, but in most cases they have been tolerant when the legislators have resorted to subterfuge.

General-Act Charters—Cafeteria Style

In those states without home-rule or special-act charters, it has been necessary to devise some way of meeting the particular needs of particular cities. To do this, optional-charter laws have been adopted. More than one-half of the states make use of this device, with about one-third of them using it as the principal method of providing city charters. (Counties and other units of local government can also operate under an optional-charter plan if a state legislature makes provision for them to do so.)

Under this plan, upon petition of a prescribed number of voters or by resolution of the governing body, a unit of local government may adopt a particular charter. Choice is limited to the options the legislature authorizes: perhaps only two or three charters, perhaps many. New Jersey offers its cities a choice from among fourteen possibilities; the people of the community may go through the cafeteria line, picking from the offerings set out by the state. They may take only those things offered, however, and without variations or alterations. This plan, which is convenient for the state and offers local citizens some choice, is gaining in popularity for cities, if not for other local units of government. Of course, the legislature still determines the structure of government to be permitted, and all amendments to charters must be obtained from the state.

Home Rule

Home rule, an indigenous Americanism, is the power granted to local units of government to frame, adopt, and amend charters for their government and to exercise powers of local self-government, subject to the constitution and general laws of the state. Home rule may be provided for in the state constitution or by enabling acts of the state legislature. It may be available to all cities and villages or only to those over a certain population. It may be a self-executing provision of the state constitution or it may require legislation before a city can avail itself of the authorization. In a few states, some counties have home-rule charters. For example, Ramsey County (in which St. Paul is located) was the first Minnesota county to adopt home rule. But the provision, passed in November 1990, meant little change until a variety of enabling legislation is passed; and even then court tests will be likely.

The adoption of home rule made an important difference in the procedure for securing charters and their subsequent amendments. Under the older system of special- and general-act municipal charters, a charter is secured through lobbying before the legislature, and every amendment to the charter must be through the method of sending city officials and other interested persons to the state capital to bargain with legislators. Under home rule, this is not necessary: The amendment is proposed (usually) by the local governing body and is voted on by eligible voters. If adopted, the new provision goes into effect, provided the courts find it does not violate the constitution or (except in a very few states) the general laws of the state. The rules for drawing up a new charter or making major revisions in an old one vary from state to state. The common procedure is for the voters of the city to elect a charter commission, which is usually given a certain amount of time in which to draft a charter for submission to the voters, who must then approve (usually by a simple majority vote).[54]

Home rule has been "helpful but not of great importance in enlarging the zone of municipal activity."[55] Although home-rule governments often enjoy greater powers than do non–home-rule units of government, most of them are potentially just as subject to state control over their affairs. In most home-rule states, the legislature enjoys concurrent or superior power to the local government in matters of local concern. And the legislature is, of course, supreme in those areas that the courts deem to be of state, rather than local, concern. Normally, general acts of the legislature—or what purport to be general acts—take precedence over local ordinances or charter provisions. Under these circumstances, the question of whether home rule will work and the extent to which it will work is a question not of law, but of public policy determined by the legislature, at whose sufferance home rule actually exists. Home rule is hence more often an attitude toward local government than it is a legal injunction against legislative action.

Local politicians (who wish to maximize their own autonomy from state control), good-government groups (which believe that efficiency and economy are furthered by local control of government), chambers of commerce (which have similar views), and other interests continue to press for home rule. They are especially anxious, in many cases, to have the idea applied to county government as well as to cities.[56]

Local Government Law: An Appraisal

Efforts to prevent or reduce legislative intervention in local decision making have been made through such devices as the constitutional prohibition of special legislation, constitutional control of classification, and the use of the optional-charter plan. These efforts have met with only limited success. The legislature remains paramount, and its members have found it relatively easy to legislate for specific communities whenever they have desired to do so (see table 3–1).

In seeking to grant independence to local government, advocates of general legislation have tended to minimize the fact that local units of government do have unique requirements that must be met by specific legislation. The result is that general legislation must always be modified to meet local needs to one degree or another. The legislatures of an increasing number of states, as a matter of public policy, have given the people a good deal of autonomy in local affairs. In some states, home rule has helped movements in this direction.

Some types of state control and supervision may have been helpful and not restrictive to local governments. Furthermore, in many cases local officials, instead of

TABLE 3–1   States Ranked by Degree of Local Government Discretionary Authority

Composite (All Types of Local Units)	Cities Only**	Counties Only**
1. Oregon	Texas	Oregon
2. Maine	Maine	Alaska
3. North Carolina	Michigan	North Carolina
4. Connecticut	Connecticut	Pennsylvania
5. Alaska	North Carolina	Delaware
6. Maryland	Oregon	Arkansas
7. Pennsylvania	Maryland	South Carolina
8. Virginia	Missouri	Louisiana
9. Delaware	Virginia	Maryland
10. Louisiana	Illinois	Utah
11. Texas	Ohio	Kansas
12. Illinois	Oklahoma	Minnesota
13. Oklahoma	Alaska	Virginia
14. Kansas	Arizona	Florida
15. South Carolina	Kansas	Wisconsin
16. Michigan	Louisiana	Kentucky
17. Minnesota	California	California
18. California	Georgia	Montana
19. Missouri	Minnesota	Illinois
20. Utah	Pennsylvania	Maine
21. Arkansas	South Carolina	North Dakota
22. New Hampshire	Wisconsin	Hawaii
23. Wisconsin	Alabama	New Mexico
24. North Dakota	Nebraska	Indiana
25. Arizona	North Dakota	New York
26. Florida	Delaware	Wyoming
27. Ohio	New Hampshire	Oklahoma
28. Alabama	Utah	Michigan
29. Kentucky	Wyoming	Washington
30. Georgia	Florida	Iowa
31. Montana	Mississippi	New Jersey
32. Washington	Tennessee	Georgia
33. Wyoming	Washington	Nevada
34. Tennessee	Arkansas	Tennessee
35. New York	New Jersey	Mississippi
36. New Jersey	Kentucky	New Hampshire
37. Indiana	Colorado	Alabama
38. Rhode Island	Montana	Arizona
39. Vermont	Iowa	South Dakota
40. Hawaii	Indiana	West Virginia
41. Nebraska	Massachusetts	Nebraska
42. Colorado	Rhode Island	Ohio
43. Massachusetts	South Dakota	Texas
44. Iowa	New York	Idaho
45. Mississippi	Nevada	Colorado
46. Nevada	West Virginia	Vermont
47. South Dakota	Idaho	Missouri
48. New Mexico	Vermont	Massachusetts
49. West Virginia	New Mexico	—
50. Idaho	—	—

Source: ACIR survey and staff calculation, as presented in ACIR, Measuring Local Government Discretionary Authority (Report M-131). Washington, DC, U.S. Government Printing Office, 1981.
*Because only one city, Honolulu, was found in Hawaii, the state was excluded.
**There were no counties in Connecticut or Rhode Island at the time of study.

chafing under the existing degree of state controls, approve of this control or are unconcerned with it. Local units of government inevitably will be subject to a great deal of legislative control. Nearly every function performed by them affects other people of the state. In a day of large economic units and rapid transportation and communication, it is impossible for local governments to isolate themselves. Furthermore, no natural cleavage is to be found between state and local interests and functions. Because one tends to grow out of the other gradually, the state and its subdivisions must work together.

Concluding Note

This chapter has provided a skeletal view of state and local government, the bones upon which the body of law and policy can be built. Subsequent chapters will develop the political institutions and processes of politics.

Notes

1. For statistical analysis on state constitutions see the constitution chapter of the most recent copy of *The Book of the States* (Lexington, KY: Council on State Governments). Copies of individual state constitutions can be found in legislative handbooks or manuals for each state. For a general review of the changes in constitutional design, including a fifty-year review of state constitutions, see ''Part One'' of *Publius* 12 (Winter 1982): 1. Subsequent review can be found in the edition devoted to ''New Developments in State Constitutional Law, *Publius* 17 (Winter 1987): 1; and also *State Constitutions in the Federal System* (Washington, D.C.: ACIR, 1989).

2. *Constitution* of the State of Alaska (1958) and *Constitution* of the Commonwealth of Puerto Rico (1952).

3. The historical development of constitutions is outlined by Albert L. Sturm, ''The Development of American State Constitutions,'' *Publius* 12 (Winter 1982): 57–97; for a comparison of the U.S. Constitution and state constitutions, see Janice C. May, ''Constitutional Amendment and Revision Revisited,'' *Publius* 17 (Winter 1987): 153–79.

4. Paul C. Bartholomew, ''A Comparative Analysis of the Constitutions of the States of Hawaii and Alaska,'' *Federal Bar Journal* 22 (Winter 1962): 44–48.

5. Robert B. Dishman, *The Constitutional Document as a Constitutional Problem* (New York: National Municipal League, 1961).

6. For a review of an extensive bill of rights, see Michael Fine, ''The Wisconsin Constitution and Constitutional Development'' in Wilder Crane, A. Clarke Hagensick et al., eds., *Wisconsin Government and Politics*, 4th ed. (Milwaukee: Department of Governmental Affairs, University of Wisconsin-Milwaukee, 1987).

7. Sturm, ''American State Constitutions,'' 60.

8. *Serrano* v. *Priest*, 5 Cal. 3d 584 (1971).

9. See the discussion of court jurisdictions in chapter 13.

10. Albert L. Sturm and Janice C. May, ''State Constitutions and Constitutional Revision: 1980–81 and the Past 50 Years,'' *1982–1983 Book of the States,* 126.

11. Daniel J. Elazar, ''The Principles and Traditions Underlying State Constitutions,'' *Publius* 12 (Winter 1982): 12–13.

12. Bernard Bellush, *Franklin D. Roosevelt as Governor of New York* (New York: Columbia University Press, 1955), 96–97.

13. For specification of each state's use of these forms, see the most recent edition of the *Book of the States*. The specific references in this section were taken from *1988–1989 Book of the States*, 19–20, and the *1990–1991 Book of the States*, 20–37.

14. Sturm, "American State Constitution," 85–86; and May, "Constitutional Amendment," 161.

15. On the issue of apportionment, see chapter 11.

16. May, "Constitutional Amendment," 155–56.

17. Albert L. Sturm and Janice C. May, "State Constitutions and Constitutional Revision, 1984–85," *1986–1987 Book of the States*, 5.

18. Albert L. Sturm and Janice C. May, "State Constitutions and Constitutional Revision, 1986–87," *1988–1989 Book of the States*, 3.

19. The Columbia proposal was not approved by Congress as of the date of this publication. A discussion of the convention is in Sturm and May, *1988–1989 Book of the States*, 3–4.

20. Thomas C. Donnelly, *The Governments of New Mexico*, (Albuquerque: The University of New Mexico Press, 1953), chapter 2, the basis for this section on New Mexico.

21. Wayne R. Swanson, Sean A. Kelleher, Arthur English, "Socialization of Constitution Makers: Political Experience, Role, Conflict, and Attitudinal Change," *Journal of Politics* 34 (Feb. 1972): 1.

22. Jack Van der Slik, Samuel J. Pernacciaro, David Kenney, "Patterns of Partisanship in a Nonpartisan Representational Setting: The Illinois Constitutional Convention," *American Journal of Political Science* 18 (Feb. 1974): 95–116.

23. May, "Constitutional Amendment," 168–70; and Sturm and May, *1988–1989 Book of the States*.

24. See Fine, "Wisconsin Constitution," 19–29.

25. For example, "236,000 Calls to Police Go Unanswered—Prop. 13 Cited," *Los Angeles Times*, January 1, 1979.

26. See chapter 6 for a description of this technique.

27. May, "Constitutional Amendment," 172.

28. See Sturm, "American State Constitution."

29. May, "Constitutional Amendment," 170–79.

30. See the *Slaughterhouse cases*, 16 Wall. 36 (1873).

31. *Gitlow* v. *New York*, 268 U.S. 652 (1925).

32. *Mapp* v. *Ohio*, 367 U.S. 643 (1961).

33. *Baker* v. *Carr*, 369 U.S. 186 (1962).

34. *Gideon* v. *Wainwright*, 372 U.S. 335 (1963).

35. *Malloy* v. *Hogan*, 378 U.S. 1 (1964).

36. *Pointer* v. *Texas*, 380 U.S. 400 (1965).

37. *Miranda* v. *Arizona*, 384 U.S. 456 (1966).

38. *Klopfer* v. *North Carolina*, 386 U.S. 371 (1967).

39. *San Antonio* v. *Rodriguez*, 411 U.S. 1 (1973).

40. *Milliken* v. *Bradley*, 418 U.S. 717 (1974).

41. *Village of Arlington Heights* v. *Metro Housing Development*, 429 U.S. 252 (1977).

42. The Court has split on questions of affirmative action since *University of California* v. *Bakke* 438 U.S. 265 (1978). The tide seems to be against its permissibility. See *Firefighters* v. *Stotts* 467 U.S. 561 (1984); *Wygant* v. *Jackson Board of Education* 476 U.S.

267 (1986); *Wards Cove Packing* v. *Antonio* (1989); and a partial reversal in 1989 of the 1971 *Griggs* v. *Duke Power Co.* in a case of the same name, see *StarTribune,* June 7, 1989, p.1; and *Martin* v. *Wilks,* see *StarTribune*, June 13, 1989, p.1.

43. *Roe* v. *Wade,* 410 U.S. 113 (1973), and *Webster* v. *Reproductive Health Services* 88–605 (1989).

44. See Eugene McQuillin, *The Law of Municipal Corporations,* 3d ed. (Chicago: Callaghan, Callaghan & Co., Inc., 1949).

45. John F. Dillon, *Commentaries on the Law of Municipal Corporations,* 5th ed. (Boston: Little, Brown, 1911), volume I, sec. 237. Although Dillon's rule applies specifically to municipal corporations, the same principle applies to the powers of quasi corporations.

46. *Louisville Times,* Oct. 8, 1964.

47. Citizens' Budget Commission, Inc., New York, press release, Aug. 2, 1965.

48. Michael Fine, "The Independence of the City: The Legal Constraints on the Tradition of Home Rule," *The Small City and Regional Community,* 8 (1989):96–7. The state supreme court upheld in *Local Union No. 487* v. *City of Eau Claire,* 86–1637 (1987). Quotation at pp. 96–97.

49. James Alexander, "Dillon's Rule Under the Burger Court: Municipal Liability Cases," *Publius* 18 (Winter 1988):127–40.

50. The contrast between the Dillon and Cooley positions is best explained in Anwar Syed, *The Political Theory of American Local Governments* (New York: Random House, 1966), chapter 3.

51. Thomas Cooley, *General Principles of Constitutional Law in the United States* (Boston: Little, Brown, 1880).

52. See William N. Casella, Jr., "A Century of Home Rule," *National Civic Review* 64 (Oct. 1975): 441–50. The original statement of the rule can be found in J. B. Fordham, *Model Constitutional Provisions for Municipal Home Rule,* (Chicago: American Municipal Association, 1953).

53. See Ed Miller, "Local Government," in Crane, Hagensick et al., *Wisconsin Government*, 31–49.

54. W. Brooke Graves, *American Intergovernmental Relations,* (New York: Charles Scribner's Sons, 1964), 700–10.

55. George C. S. Benson, "Sources of Municipal Powers," *Municipal Year Book* (Chicago: International City Managers' Association [ICMA], 1938), 149–65.

56. The number of states permitting home rule at the county or city level varies by the degree of autonomy permitted. The best estimates and updates can be found in the latest edition of the *Municipal Year Book,* (Washington: ICMA). The International City Management Association (formerly the International City Managers' Association), the professional organization of city managers and chief administrative officers, is a leading good-government organization of local administrators and a long-time advocate and lobbyist for home rule.

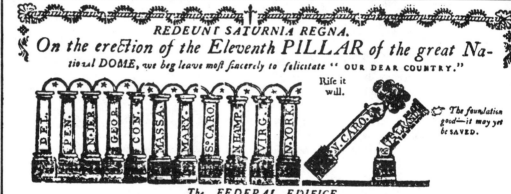

REDEUNT SATURNIA REGNA.

On the erection of the Eleventh PILLAR of the great Na-
tional DOME, we beg leave moſt ſincerely to felicitate " OUR DEAR COUNTRY. "

Riſe it
will.

The foundation
good—it may yet
be SAVED.

DEL. | PEN. | N. JER. | GEOR. | CON. | MASSA. | MARY. | S°. CARO. | N HAMP. | VIRG. | N. YORK. | N. CARO. | ELEVEN

The FEDERAL EDIFICE.
ELEVEN STARS, in quick ſucceſſion riſe—
ELEVEN COLUMNS ſtrike our wond'ring eyes,
Soon o'er the *whole*, ſhall ſwell the beauteous DOME,
COLUMBIA's boaſt—and FREEDOM's hallow'd home.
  Here ſhall the ARTS in glorious ſplendour ſhine !
And AGRICULTURE give her ſtores divine !
COMMERCE refin'd, diſpenſe us more than gold,
And this new world, teach WISDOM to the old—
RELIGION here ſhall fix her bleſt abode,
Array'd in *mildneſs*, like its parent GOD !
JUSTICE and LAW, ſhall endleſs PEACE maintain,
And *the* " SATURNIAN AGE," *return again.*

4

Federalism and Intergovernmental Relations

Government as we know it in the United States is based on the principle of *federalism* and organized in a *federal system*. It is characterized by a decentralization of power that was strongly favored in the early days of the Republic, when transportation and communication were slow, regional patterns of life and cultural values differed widely, and frontier commitment to individualism included support of grass-roots government and skepticism of any sovereign power.

Americans remain attached to the early principles of federalism and localism, but modern transportation and communication, growth of a nationwide economic system, and nomadic tendencies of contemporary Americans have contributed to the psychological breakdown of political barriers and the increasing desire for governments powerful enough to deliver services. Nevertheless, the federal system prevails and American commitments to decentralized government with many legally distinct jurisdictions remain intact.

Following the abandonment of the *confederate system* with the passage of the Constitution, the eighteenth-century concept of government, with each sector existing principally to check another, in turn gave way after the Civil War to having each level of government serve a specialized purpose and operate independently of other levels. In turn, during the Great Depression this approach had to be severely modified to fit the demands for cooperation and interdependence of governments in the modern social service state. In the 1990s, a new relationship among levels of government once again may be emerging. Decades of shared responsibilities are under attack for being bureaucratically burdensome and nationally meddlesome.

> *Confederate System:* **A political association of independent states brought together for certain purposes, usually foreign diplomacy and mutual defense. Power relationships between levels are determined by agreements among the states, and the central unit possesses only those powers delegated from and by the states.**

   This chapter will examine the values of federalism and the organization of the
federal system. Fiscal concerns have come to dominate political discussion regarding
the provision of services, but we should not forget that Americans have a rich tradition of federal politics that has always existed outside money matters. Accordingly,
this chapter will look at the power relationships among governments (chapter 14 will
explore their fiscal relationships). Of course, the division is artificial — fiscal concerns are questions of political power and in nearly all cases it requires varying
amounts of money to apply power. But we hope that through such a division the student may recognize that the processes of the federal system, initially unconcerned
with crass practicality, ultimately may determine the boundaries within which services will be distributed.

   **Federalism: A political ideology that holds that government exists to pro-
   tect the individual, which protection comes from dividing government into
   a number of distinctly powerful parts so that no one part becomes sovereign over the others.**

   **Federal System: A system in which power is divided between a central gov-
   ernment and regional governments, each constitutionally authoritative in
   its own area of jurisdiction.**

Federalism and the Federal System

As discussed in chapter 2, Americans developed unique forms of localism and federalism in fulfilling the goals of the British liberals to use government to protect the
individual. As a federal system evolved with a multitude of governments and separation of powers in most of them, the question became whether to protect the individual
by weakening one government with another so none would threaten individual rights,
or to promote government cooperation so that the individual could be better served.
As a result of these different, often opposite, concerns, relationships among governments have taken three prominent forms: Madisonian federalism, dual federalism,
and cooperative federalism.[1] Other forms are possible, but these demonstrate the historical variations.[2] Note, however, that some authors would argue that only one of the
three is historically accurate.[3]

Madisonian Federalism

Chapter 2 explored the intellectual roots of federalism in James Madison's defense of
a Constitution that protected the individual through multiplication of governmental
units, and through the states' rights view that one government's gains in power
should best be thought of as another government's power losses. In practice, Madison's view of constant checking through federalism has often been of secondary concern to the needs of individuals that have been met by strong rather than checked
governmental power. When particular conflicts threaten a government's power, they
rarely have persisted without legal resolution. In these cases, "lower" levels of government rarely have won the legal battles. But conflicts among governments persist

today and remain part of American political practice. Invariably a particular conflict prevents interest groups from getting everything they want through government; to that extent, *Madisonian federalism* is still an active theory in American politics.

> *Madisonian Federalism:* **A theory of federalism holding that the principal purpose of a federal system is to protect the individual from government and that the best way to do that is for the many units and parts of government to compete with each other so that no one becomes sovereign.**

The first century of American history often brought the conflicts among governments to court. *McCulloch* v. *Maryland* (1819) demonstrates how the Supreme Court under Chief Justice John Marshall (1801–1835) resolved the conflicts in favor of the national government.[4] By declaring unconstitutional Maryland's attempt to tax the national bank, two important precedents were established. First, the Court widened the powers of the national government by holding that powers delegated to the national government were very broad because of the "necessary and proper" clause of the Constitution.[5] Second, the Court held that the national "supreme law of the land" clause[6] made a national government power superior to a state power when the two were in conflict.

This Marshall Court ruling reduced considerably the impact of the Tenth Amendment's reservation of power to the states. But the tradition of state power went back to the Articles of Confederation, and the states refused to be reduced to a weaker partner without a fight. In the area of expenditure they remained most prominent despite the superior money-raising power of the national government. And although national government expenditure generally has increased as a percentage of total government expenditure, as recently as 1932 the states and their localities were raising 87.3 percent of total governmental taxes. It is only in the period of the welfare state ideology that the national government took the lead in raising and spending government money.[7]

Similar conflicts between state and local governments were ongoing but were resolved legally in favor of the "higher" government (in this context the state) by Dillon's rule and, more recently, Fordham's rule.

Dual Federalism

As we saw in the earlier discussion of states' rights, one defense of state sovereignty is a strict interpretation of the Constitution's Tenth Amendment, the argument that the national government should be absolutely limited to those powers delegated by the Constitution. Strictly speaking, the national government has only those powers delegated to it by the Constitution, whereas others reside in the states or are retained by the people. Nevertheless, the Marshall Court showed in *McCulloch* v. *Maryland* that such delegated powers could be interpreted through the "necessary and proper" clause to mean a variety of powers not specified but rather implied. The Court, under Chief Justice Roger B. Taney (1835–1863), reversed this broad trend. In theory, *dual federalism* emerged as the legal principle that both state and national governments are sovereign and thus each is equal in its own realm; they perform different functions and therefore do not conflict or cooperate and hence the national government's powers will be limited to those enumerated rather than those implied. On the one hand, the principle emerged as a legal victory for the states insofar as when conflicts emerged, limitations consequently were placed more often on the national government than on the states. On the other hand, in terms of policy making, the principle emerged as a victory neither for state nor national government as the two tended increasingly to perform different duties.

> *Dual Federalism:* **A political ideology that holds that government exists to protect the individual, which protection comes from dividing government into a number of distinctly powerful parts so that no one part becomes sovereign over the others.**

Dual federalism flourished from the 1830s until the Great Depression a century later. Before the Civil War,

> [I]n terms of governmental functions and services, the states exercised an almost exclusive role [sometimes shared with the localities] in the areas of elections and apportionment, civil and property rights, education, family and criminal law, business organization, local governmental organization and powers, as well as labor and race relations [including slavery]. During the last three decades of this period, the states also dominated banking. . . .
> National functions, on the other hand were still relatively few and became fewer as the decades passed.[8]

After the Civil War, the national government grew even stronger in foreign affairs, monetary and banking policy, interstate commerce, and direct regulation of railroads and other industries. The states similarly expanded in their traditional functions. A small but significant shared grant process was also emerging. And the national government was taking a far more active role in regulating functions still provided by states. Yet in 1930, state and national government functions still differed. The national government essentially was a regulatory, diplomatic, and military protector of the nation, whereas the states and localities were service providers.[9] Not until the New Deal did the principle of dual federalism become obsolete.

Two efforts to demonstrate greater separation between state and national governments have been hailed by some as the dawning of a contemporary period of dual federalism, but both failed. The first occurred early in President Ronald Reagan's administration when he advocated a swap of social welfare programs with the states, which would become wholly responsible for a variety of programs that currently were shared with the national government. In return, the latter would become wholly responsible for medical care. The president talked of returning these programs to their "rightful" governments,[10] but the plan gained little support from state and local officials, who feared its financial inadequacy. The plan was virtually ignored by Congress.[11]

The second occurred when William H. Rehnquist while still an associate justice, wrote in *National League of Cities* v. *Usery* (1975):

This Court has never doubted that there are limits upon the power of Congress to override state sovereignty, even when exercising its otherwise plenary powers to tax or to regulate commerce which are conferred by Art. I of the Constitution. . . . [W]e have reaffirmed today that the States as States stand on a quite different footing from an individual or a corporation when challenging the exercise of Congress' power to regulate commerce.[12]

For a decade it was argued that state governments could exercise powers over certain functions that traditionally had been within their purview as states, that the national government could not interfere. One example was the establishment of a minimum wage for local government employees (the states had created both the local governments and the wage laws).

Yet, distinguishing these special functions proved to be impossible in practice. The Court therefore overturned this move toward dual federalism in *Garcia* v. *San Antonio Transit Authority* (1985).[13] There it was argued that the people could be protected through the political process rather than through some attempt to distinguish separate, unique functions for each level of government. The Court argued that Congress, as the elected representatives of the people, and not the Court through an interpretation of the Tenth Amendment, could best define the national government's range of functions. Although this case was a 5–4 decision, it adhered to the conventional wisdom that prevailed in the social welfare state ideology before *National League of Cities,* holding that many functions of government would be shared by the national and subnational governments because of broad interpretation of the national government's implied and regulatory powers. State and local governments therefore would be partners—but not equal partners, given the national government's superior financial capacities in a time that emphasized service delivery by the bureaucracies of each level of government. *Garcia* was reaffirmed and the swing from dual federalism toward enhanced national government power was extended in *South Carolina* v. *Baker* (1988). Here the Court ruled that the states and localities were no longer exempt from national taxes (as they had been for one hundred years).[14] (Of course, as discussed earlier, the national government is exempt from state and local taxes since the ruling in *McCulloch* v. *Maryland.*)

Cooperative Federalism

The Great Depression of the 1930s changed our approach to the functions of government first in contending with poverty (the flurry of entitlement programs) and then with a variety of other programs for the middle classes (and the wealthy). Not only did the national government become protector of the nation but also a principal revenue source for these state and local programs. This brought a new sense of the relationship among governments described alternately as *marble-cake, picket-fence, creative,* and *rowboat* federalism. No longer was the national government to leave service provision to the states; it became the principal priority setter as multiple governments extended their service provision into a variety of new functional areas.

Cooperative Federalism: **A theory of federalism holding that the individual can best be protected by the services that the many governments may pro-**

vide. Therefore, governments are encouraged to cooperate to provide those services more easily and efficiently.

Many arguments for cooperative federalism hold that function of government is now the defining characteristic of relationships among levels. Principal divisions within the decision-making system are not among *levels* of government but among different *functions* of government. The picket-fence analogy suggests that each function encompasses a bureaucracy reaching from national to local government, paralleling other functional areas. A variation of the picket fence, the bamboo fence, adds horizontal links among bureaucratic specialists at each level of government.[15] In either case, the emphasis is on bureaucracy because functional specialists at all levels share the same values, standards, goals, procedures, and group memberships. For example, public health workers at one level of government have more in common with public health workers at another level of government than they do with highway engineers or education officials at their own level of government. They share common values that they believe point to desirable public policy. Consequently they do not regard themselves as being exploited or dominated by bureaucrats at a higher level of government.

Friction is seen as taking place primarily between professionals and nonprofessionals and between the bureaucracy and the legislative branch. Professionals, chosen for their competence based on training and experience, may clash with persons in a particular functional area who hold their jobs as a result of a patronage personnel policy. The conflict between bureaucracy and legislature stems from the fact that the former seeks to defend professional values and standards, whereas the latter sees its social function as that of defending and furthering grass-roots values and goals. Of course, the legislature also must find the funds.[16]

The "creative" nature of the cooperative "marble cake" is noted by one specialist on the subject:

> Because of the present pervasiveness of government in the United States, this means that every level of government is involved in virtually every governmental activity. Intergovernmental relations may involve informal cooperation, contracts for simple sharing, interchange of personnel, interdependent activities, grants-in-aid, tax offsets, and shared revenues.[17]

The extreme cooperative model argues that the three levels of government are linked like three passengers in a rowboat, each required to row in the same direction for the boat to get to its destination. But we should emphasize that such models tend to overstate cooperation among governments (the federal system will always retain some of Madison's hoped-for conflict among the levels). They also tend to understate the importance and unique value structure of each level of government.

***Grants-In-Aid:* Payments made by voluntary appropriation from one level of government to another. Such grants were common from lower to higher levels before adoption of the Constitution. They have been common from**

higher to lower levels since the New Deal began in 1933, but they originated much earlier.

Entitlement: **A governmental grant to an individual, usually provided by the national government as a matter of policy and supplemented and administered by state or local governments. Although American values change as to** *which* **entitlements should be provided, most of those eligible probably regard an entitlement as a right.**

The pattern of intergovernmental cooperation has always been characteristic of American federalism, but marked expansion of these governmental functions during the Great Depression further expanded that pattern. Earlier cooperation was influential in improving rivers and harbors, higher education, agricultural capabilities, and, after the coming of the auto, highway construction. The New Deal devised a variety of programs to alleviate the poverty of the depression by using the national government's power to raise money and prodding states and localities to spend more of their own dwindling funds to provide relief. The programs often involved *grants-in-aid* or *entitlement*. At first, the Supreme Court was a major impediment, striking down several of the early programs in 1935. But following Franklin Roosevelt's failed attempt to pack the Court after the 1936 election, the Court (with no change in membership but a revised perspective by one justice) began to accept New Deal legislation. As David Walker summarizes:

> In rapid succession, the Farm Mortgage Act of 1935, the amended Railway Labor Act of 1934, and the National Labor Relations Act and the Social Security Act of 1935 were upheld between March and June [1937].
> Thus, a new era of judicial construction was launched. The [interstate] commerce power was given broad interpretation. . . . [18]

After World War II, what once had been cooperation to aid the most needy and to care for the elderly became a process of widespread government grant dispersal for all classes of people. The biggest expansion to involve the national government came in the form of shared grants in the Great Society programs of the Johnson administration in the 1960s and the incrementally increasing entitlement programs (principally in Social Security and medical care) in the 1970s and 1980s. Most domestic programs of the national government are now administered—at least in part—by state or local governments; many also leave room for state and local policy making. From state to local governments, the largest increases have come in an ever-expanding education system and in proliferating state policies of property tax relief and other aids to cities, especially in the areas of health (including mental health), welfare for the poor, and roads.

Judicial Activism

Passage of the Fourteenth Amendment after the Civil War made possible the national government's frequent intervention into state affairs to protect individual rights. First Amendment rights were incorporated early in the century and most of the rest of the Bill of Rights was incorporated selectively by the Warren Court in the 1950s and 1960s. The Warren Court first intervened in race relations (school desegregation, voting rights, and the striking down of Jim Crow laws), but eventually the expansion frequently was to protect the rights of those accused of criminal activity.

Court intervention in state police powers mainly was a reaction to twentieth-century expansion of local government policing under the authority of state criminal statutes and charter expansions. The relative insignificance of the crime control function of police in the nineteenth century gave way in the twentieth century to increased concern for individual safety and protection by the state, which reached a peak in the late 1960s but has not been significantly reduced since. Police gained power through more laws against criminals, better internal organizations, better technology, and infinitely better communications systems. When the public—particularly the middle class—became more aware of the conditions and problems of those accused of crimes, the Warren Court acted. It used the national Bill of Rights through the Fourteenth Amendment's equal protection and due process clauses to move toward standardization in exercising police powers by state and local governments. Although the Burger and Rehnquist courts slowed this process down a bit, fundamental expansion through the exclusionary rule and *Miranda* warnings made local police wary of intervention either by federal judges or state judges using federal precedents.

Judicial intervention in local government affairs has proved to be similarly obtrusive to many local officials, as state legislatures have broadened civil codes to allow individuals to sue governments, particularly for personal injuries (torts).[19] Lawsuits have become particularly prominent in the traditional local functions of education, police and fire protection, and trash collection. Directly or indirectly, state and local insurance costs have risen dramatically. Governments must therefore insure themselves against such suits as well as pay increased labor costs for insurance to protect employees who fear liability incurred for violations. So far the states have not been able to avoid these Fourteenth Amendment–based costs by limiting liability for such violations. Furthermore, juries routinely make substantial awards in lawsuits against government. The cost of local government in the next decade may be set more by this indirect effect of federalism than by any other factor.

In education and policing, intervention by one government into the affairs of another has blossomed. Tocqueville noted the legalistic nature of Americans a century and a half ago, but it only has been since 1960 or so that local officials constantly look over their shoulders, expecting judicial intervention. An arrest, once a simple procedure done by a police officer, now requires strict obedience to rules set down by the Supreme Court that if disobeyed might subject the officer to career and financial ruin. Busing a child to school, once a simple matter of transportation, now is one of racial justice and spiraling insurance cost. To the citizen who feels wronged, the federal system that subjects lower government to the rules of higher government is long overdue. To the lower governments and their employees who must suffer the costs, this phenomenon is becoming a financial nightmare.

The Balance of Federalism

In a modern age of cooperation, competition, and judicial activism, the balance of federalism continues to be debated. The controversy encompasses actual trends in the balance and the desirability of trends. Some writers describe a constant decline of the states and their subdivisions; others see some changes, but with the lower units retaining their vitality and importance. Yet, some critics would applaud the end of any state independence as a supposedly necessary prelude to a more effective American government under a central authority.

Local government self-sufficiency, the rule before World War I, gave way to new procedures in the social service state. Under the old system (see the chapter 2 discussion of community power structure), community politics were the product of actions by a hierarchy of local decision makers that might be broad or narrow, depending on local custom; but however organized, these people often had considerable powers that appear rarely to have been challenged. When the decision base spread to include other units of government, decision making became more complex and spilled over to persons outside the community—often to distant state capitals and even to the nation's capital. Today, the burden of decision making has shifted away not only from the locality, but also from amateurs expressing local values and traditions, and to career persons, that is, specialists, in the field under consideration. Decision making now, compared to the idealized practice of yesteryear, is less personal, less local, less focused as to responsibility, less tailored to a particular locality, more efficient, more professional, more bureaucratized, more elaborate, and more costly.

Even before the Constitutional Convention met in Philadelphia in 1787, maintaining the balance of federalism was a matter of public discussion. Many ideologies bear on the continuing controversy, and predictions concerning the future of federalism have been varied. Will state and local governments retain their policy-making powers in the future? Or are they gradually being made into administrative units that depend on the national government for financing and, more and more, are subject to basic *and* detailed policy decisions of Congress and the national bureaucracy?

Types of Grants

Grants-in-aid from higher levels of government to lower ones have become a prominent part of our federal system, tipping the balance of federalism toward higher governments since cooperative federalism became the rule during the New Deal. (These will be addressed in chapter 14.) Since the Great Society, the biggest question regarding grants has been the allocation of discretion between the receiving government and the sending government. One type of grant, categorical, provides the least discretion by the receiving government; another type, revenue sharing, provides the greatest. The tendency at both national and state levels since the late 1960s has been to combine types of grants. Ultimately, the sending government always retains the power of discretion; but as "anti-Washington" presidents have been elected, the attitude of the sending government has increasingly supported greater discretion by the receiving government. Furthermore, as localism remains popular, states continue to give local governments some discretion on how to spend grants-in-aid, usually passing along with the grants responsibility for political outcomes.

Perspectives about the methods to exercise control also change over time. For example, until about the mid-1960s, improving the quality of state bureaucracies was a principal reason for developing categorical grants-in-aid.[20] It was clear that national administrators believed the states were often incapable of high-quality performance of duties. During the Reagan administration, however, these rules imposed by the national government would be viewed *at the national level* as cumbersome, costly, and meddling. Questions about these perspectives will be addressed more fully in chapter 14, but the fact that the fiscal balance of federalism in recent decades has been in constant flux should be noted here.

The Influence of Lower Levels of Governments

Shared decision making offers an opportunity for influence to flow upward as well as downward. Public officeholders and bureaucrats at one level of government influence decision making at higher levels of government in at least four different ways.

The first of these influences is lobbying. Individual states and populous cities and counties sometimes have their own lobbyists in Washington and local units in the state capital. Many special-purpose organizations permit various groups to lobby collectively. The Council of State Governments, which speaks for many state positions in Washington, has spawned other lobbying organizations. The National Governors' Association, the National Conference of State Legislatures, the National Conference of Chief State School Officers, and the National Association of Attorneys General are key examples. At the local level, similar agencies exist for collective lobbying of state and national governments including, for example, the United States Conference of Mayors and the National League of Cities; also state educational associations (which have their national counterpart in the National Educational Association), state leagues of cities, and such specialized organizations as the state association of justices of the peace. Since the early 1970s, election finance laws have generated political action committees (PACs) to allow interest groups to work around contribution limits for public elections. As private interest groups, PACs contribute and lobby across the three levels of government.

Second, and somewhat related to the first influence, is the continuous interaction through common interests, often a common political party of officeholders at all levels. When reapportioning, legislators have attempted to conform their districts to local political boundaries as much as permitted within the rules laid down by the Supreme Court. This often has led to close working relationships between county officers and state legislators where the county officer who favors or opposes a particular piece of legislation has direct access to the critical decision makers. They share a set of interests that provide the basis for understanding relationships. Governors are in ongoing contact with members of Congress relative to legislation affecting their states. A member from a dairy district has more concern for national dairy supports than for the policy of his or her party's president, who might support cutbacks in such supports. Mayors, particularly those of the largest cities in the state, have similar congressional contacts.

Third, persons in offices at higher levels of government may be sympathetic to the policy demands of lower levels of government and may well carry to the higher office a set of experiences and policy preferences they accumulated in the lower office. For example, many legislators are former county or municipal officeholders. Of 825 elected governors between 1900 and 1980, only 9.1 percent had held no prior public office.[21] Furthermore, between 1950 and 1980, thirty-five governors went on to the U.S. Senate and four to the House of Representatives[22]; and between 1950 and 1990, nine became party nominees for president or vice president, including President Carter and President Reagan. For example, the national workfare program, which requires welfare recipients to seek employment in return for their welfare checks, was a program first tested when President Reagan was governor of California. The massive tax revision passed in 1986 at the national level was based on a variety of state income tax assumptions about the wisdom of fewer categories of taxation and fewer deductions.

Fourth, a lower level of government influences policy at higher levels through imitation. Much of the domestic policy enacted by Congress reflects—in part at least—experiences in particular states that pioneer legislation on the subject. Furthermore state legislation can modify practices developed at the local level; in particular, the larger cities and counties seem to be outstanding innovators of policies that are later applied statewide. In addition to these vertical patterns of influence, states often pattern their own legislation on that already adopted in other states, and local governments tend to imitate other local governments.

Finally, localism cannot be discounted, even in the media age. Politicians, and to a lesser degree bureaucrats, respond to public opinion. By being closer to the people, local (and to some extent, state) governments can generate public attitudes to which higher governments must respond in policy making.

The Functions of States

The states have found a place for themselves today in the American federal system. It is not a highly dramatic position, but it is one of singular importance in a nation that is large both in population and area.

In general, the states now have primary responsibility for the following areas:

1. Their traditional functions of control (basic criminal and civil codes, the law of contract, higher education, custody of felons, policies for the mentally disturbed, chartering of local governments, overall health responsibilities, policing outside municipalities).
2. More recent activities that tie together urban and rural areas by providing for roads and welfare.
3. Their service as a metropolitan unit of government for many service functions that cannot be dealt with adequately by local governments (water sources, sewage disposal, metropolitan planning, school district reorganization, welfare regulations, air and water pollution).
4. Their service as a collection agency for taxes and other funds used by various

local governments through subsequent distribution by way of grants-in-aid or shared taxes.

5. Their role in organizing elections and apportioning national and state legislative districts.

At times, the states have appeared to be relatively weak in the overall balance of federalism. For instance, in the nineteenth century they performed few functions that citizens actually could observe. Also, they were the last level of government (except for rural counties) to professionalize administration. Finally, since the 1930s they frequently have been treated by the national government as administrative units for carrying out policies and funds provided "from above." But to a great extent, the appearance is misleading. For example, states have made considerable impact in their traditional areas of responsibility (such as higher education, which the national government has affected minimally except as to allied research policies). Furthermore, states took the lead in some new areas of government, creating innovative solutions before the national government provided much of the monies to achieve policy objectives (such as programs deinstitutionalizing the mentally ill and programs for environmental protection). States have appeared weak in the federal system not so much because they *are* weak but because they have not generated the positive public opinion that localities always have enjoyed because of their closeness to their constituencies. In recent decades, the national government has enjoyed such public favor because media focus on the site of dramatic military and diplomatic policy and of the primary shape of perhaps most domestic policy as well. However, in the 1980s governors became more aggressive at seeking that media attention, through forums such as the National Governors' Association, to demonstrate their willingness to seek innovative solutions to policy questions[23]; even state legislatures—traditionally the *least* innovative of governmental branches—have demonstrated greater visibility through the National Conference of State Legislatures.

National Government Relations with State and Locality

For much of the twentieth century, federalism has presumed a means of communication and of planned cooperation among levels of government. Just how these best can be institutionalized has been a pragmatic question subjected to much experimentation.

The Advisory Commission on Intergovernmental Relations

A Senate Subcommittee on Intergovernmental Relations was established in 1947, but four years later it was allowed to lapse. In 1949, the Commission on the Organization of the Executive Branch of the Government (the first Hoover Commission) dealt briefly with the subject of intergovernmental relations. In 1955 a Commission on Intergovernmental Relations, established in 1953 by President Eisenhower, issued a report. In 1959, a permanent Advisory Commission on Intergovernmental (ACIR) was created.

The commission was established by statute as a permanent, bipartisan agency of twenty-six members, "to give continuing study to the relationships among local, state, and national levels of government." The commission is composed of three persons each from the executive branch of the national government, the U.S. Senate, the House, county officials, state legislators, and private citizens; in addition the commission has four governors and four mayors. Members serve two-year terms. Even though its assigned task is to solve problems of intergovernmental relations, in practice the ACIR has become a principal source of government-funded studies on relations among governments. The commission takes policy stands on issues and recommendations are published and draft bills and executive orders developed to assist in implementing ACIR policies.

The Department of Housing and Urban Development

In 1965, Congress established the eleventh cabinet post with the creation of the Department of Housing and Urban Development (HUD). HUD absorbed functions from a number of existing agencies, with the Housing and Home Finance Administration becoming the core of the new department.

Opposition to cabinet status had centered in the House of Representatives, where many members from rural and small-town districts opposed the measure, probably because the effect of the creation of the agency would be to spend more federal funds in central-city areas. Indeed, proponents of the measure urged the change for the same reason. Opposition also came from conservatives who thought that cabinet status would give the agency greater bargaining power in seeking funds for urban programs, thought to be the bastion of liberalism. But the department has not been among the most visible; and the secretary has never enjoyed a closeness or "insider" status to the president. Furthermore, the creation of HUD demonstrates the more general change in the status of the cabinet in recent decades from an advisory group to the president to an enlarged collection of department heads, each lobbying the president for their own department (see chapter 9). And the feared overstatement of central-city concerns has not been realized. Although rural and small-town districts have not been the focus of the department, the central-city concerns have been offset to some degree by those of the suburbs (see chapter 8); and housing for both middle and lower classes (rather than urban development) has been the department's focus.

During the Reagan years, HUD largely was neglected as a focus for policy development or for mass media attention. But in 1989, after a change in administration, a major scandal emerged from the agency involving undue influence in securing housing loans and other benefits for localities and private business firms—not only by Republican leaders but also by members of Congress of both parties. In addition, huge personal profits appear to have been banked by some participants. Once again, the old questions arose of how to intermix the public and private sectors properly and to assert proper guidance to the intensely localized pressures thrust upon politicians. But the overarching question was how to serve the interests of the common person when large sums of public money are available for use in the private sector. (Testimony indicated that distribution of much of the money was poorly planned and that funds were not well protected.)

National Government Advice and Assistance to the States

State and local governments increasingly are finding it to their advantage to locate ambassadors at the nation's capital. Governors and mayors are called to do a great deal of entrepreneurial work, making frequent trips to Washington to try for qualification under some aid program; to seek a defense contract or a dam or other engineering project; to keep open an Air Force base, and the like. The Council of State Governments and the national government provide an information service to state and local governments concerning available assistance and the newest regulations.

The national government has many nonfinancial contacts with the states and their subdivisions in administration of governmental programs. Some of these contacts result from strings attached to grants-in-aid; others do not. Collectively they reflect the present-day trend toward the cooperation of administrative officers at all levels of government.

The national government has strongly encouraged local governments to cooperate with one another and with other units of government through a variety of techniques. It has sought to encourage local units to coordinate their applications for national grants-in-aid and otherwise to seek unified metropolitan-area goals, at least at the planning stage. These have been especially encouraged relative to economic development, public health, training for job skills, and policies toward convicted criminals.[24]

The national government has even encouraged local jurisdictions to rely occasionally on volunteerism for the administration of the last link in a chain of service to individuals. For example, although most federally owned stored food, when distributed, is made part of the food-stamps welfare program, some of it is distributed to counties that consign it to be prepared by volunteers for consumption; the volunteers also distribute it to home shut-ins as noon meals, even though the recipients may not be eligible for a welfare program. The emphasis on volunteerism has increased with President Bush's "points of light" program.

The day-to-day relationships between the national government and the states are so numerous they cannot be described fully. Within a given functional area, the national government frequently provides advice and assistance to state and local governments because of the greater expertise of the national government's bureaucrats or because the national government's task is different from that of states and localities. For example, in law enforcement, the national government has no conventional police force. But since the 1970s, the Federal Bureau of Investigation (FBI) has become responsible for policing a variety of crimes for which state and local governments rarely have expertise or resources (such as political corruption and organized crime). In addition, the FBI can concentrate on assisting local governments in training experts (the FBI Academy), keeping records (the FBI indexes of crime), or analyzing physical evidence (the National Crime Laboratory). Despite popular myths, however, the FBI rarely makes arrests for any of the eight types of major crimes on which it keeps records in the Uniform Crime Reports (murder, rape, assault, robbery, burglary, arson, larceny, and auto theft).

In a variety of functional areas, national grants-in-aid provide funds that allow the states and localities to study problems of their own. In others, especially the use of the National Guard for disaster relief or in coping with civil unrest, the national government's assistance pays virtually the full cost of the state program. Other forms of disaster relief directly to individuals, states, or localities from the national government in 1986 alone came to almost $1 billion.[25] These funds and services are immensely varied. They include assistance in the clearance of debris and wreckage; emergency health and sanitation measures; emergency repairs for streets, roads, bridges, dikes, levees, drainage facilities, public buildings, public utilities; temporary housing and emergency shelter; and a variety of other financial aids and services, including low-interest loans to individuals. Although such relief is controlled by the national government, it is rarely controversial and has come to be expected as part of the process by which state and local governments cope with natural disasters. Usually national government assistance is welcomed, but in areas where there may be some duplication of service (for example, local, state, and national governments provide governmental parks), the national government's "way" may appear paternalistic. As one author describes it:

> The availability of technical assistance does not assure that it will be used. Officials may feel perfectly competent to handle a problem without seeking assistance from another level of government. Even if they feel a need for assistance, considerations of ego may make them reluctant to ask for help. In addition, the price of technical assistance may be revealing sensitive information or complying with conditions imposed by the level of government providing assistance. . . . In either case, in some instances the price may appear too high.[26]

Unintended National Influences

National policy makers frequently exert unintended influences on state and local governments. Such influences usually are concentrated in relatively small areas; but for those locations, the national government's influence on policies can be extreme.

Revisiting Muncie, Indiana, home of a famous early study of community power, a research team found that, whereas the national government back in 1924 was represented "by the post office and the American flag," between 1968 and 1977, "$679,375,000 in national aid and direct payments flowed into Muncie from twenty-nine agencies through 976 programs—a dollar figure four times what the local leadership thought it was."[27]

An ACIR study, "Federal Influence on State and Local Roles in the Federal System," found that the national government had a variety of unintended influences on state and local governments. Four findings are of particular importance:

1. National government policy tends to keep states out of certain functions (for example, disaster relief).
2. Mandates from the national government are pushing local governments into certain functional areas (for example, community development) but not others

(for example, transportation). As a result, the distribution of local government functions is not left to the local governments.

3. National programs produce interest group support, which is difficult or impossible to forgo once the national government reduces its role. As a result, despite national government cutbacks in some areas, those earlier national priorities that created the interest group support continue to flourish at the state and local levels. Although not noted by the study cited, this took on added importance when the national government under the Reagan administration reduced its spending levels in some areas.

4. In general, the national government has respected traditional state and local government structure. But national grants-in-aid have given added vitality to some governmental units that otherwise might have never been created (special districts), died (townships), or diminished in importance (counties).[28]

National Approval of State and Local Activities

Whenever states or any of their subdivisions are involved in activities over which the national government has final jurisdiction, they must conform to national regulations. Similarly, they must agree to the strings that customarily are attached whenever a grant-in-aid is accepted, for technically a grant is a gift.

Thus, whenever national funds are involved in the construction of highways, the plans and technical specifications must be approved before a grant is made, which, in effect, may leave final approval of routes as well as types of materials and standards of construction to the national government. Before a state can receive national aid for public welfare programs, it must establish a merit system for the selection of professional caseworkers and administrators. If the state university operates a radio or television station, it must hold a Federal Communications Commission license; if the city or county builds a bridge over a navigable stream, it must have the plans approved by the Corps of Engineers; if a local housing authority accepts a Community Development Block Grant, it must agree to follow antidiscriminatory policies; before a hospital can receive national funds, the state must prepare an overall state plan that divides the state into hospital service areas (only a hospital fitting the plan may receive national aid).

The list of national supervisory controls is long. However, the easy conclusion that the national government makes all of the rules in modern American society is wrong. Areas of national control are of great importance but are relatively few, and it is not politically expedient for Congress or the national administration to seek to impose many effective policy controls on the states or their subdivisions. Where they do exist, however, national controls often are essential. State and local radio stations, for example, could not operate effectively without being coordinated with commercial stations. Other rules are not viewed with alarm by state and local administrators because their sense of professional standards agrees with the professional standards of the national employees with whom they deal. Therefore, they see themselves as involved in a cooperative venture to apply professional standards and do not feel coerced. Furthermore, despite the impression often created, national administrators usually try to be reasonable in administering the law and seek to work out problems jointly rather than by fiat. Still, in the event of an unresolved difference between a national agency and the state or local government with which it is dealing, the national requirements must be met if the state and local governments wish to qualify for national monies, and often they conclude they have little choice.

Interstate Relations

The Founders, writing the Constitution for a nation that was to become "one and indivisible," recognized in the eighteenth century that not all people would remain within their native states. Some would want to travel; they would want to do business in other states; criminals would seek to escape across state lines to try to avoid arrest. All of these possibilities were anticipated and planned for so well that the same basic arrangements provided for in the original Constitution are in effect today.

The Constitution, written not only to give structure to the new national government but also to solve some problems among the states, established the federal system. Article IV, which deals with interstate relations, contains four sections: a full faith and credit clause, a privileges and immunities clause, a provision for the admission of new states, and a provision guaranteeing a "republican" form of government in each state.

Full Faith and Credit

This clause of the Constitutional has been interpreted to mean that the court records, official documents, and vital statistical records of one state must be accepted in all other states. For example, if New Hampshire vital statistics show that Ann Torkelson was born in that state on a certain date, Oregon officials must accept that record in determining, for instance Ann's eligibility for old-age assistance.

Privileges and Immunities

The U.S. Constitution guarantees citizens of one state the privilege of traveling freely about the country, of moving from one state to another. While away from their state of residence, they actually may reside and live in another state, use its courts, make contracts, marry, own property, or engage in business. They also are entitled to tax equity and may not be discriminated against on state welfare rolls.

Some effective limits have been placed on the privileges and immunities clause by the courts. It does not, for example, prevent states from distinguishing between domestic and out-of-state corporations in making regulations or determining fees. Within limits set by the courts, a state can give favored treatment to firms incorporated in the state over those incorporated in other states. It does not guarantee that a person licensed in a trade or profession can practice in any other state. That is, a physician or lawyer moving from one state to another must meet the requirements of the second state before entering practice. Unskilled persons or persons whose occupations are not deemed closely connected with the health or welfare of the public are not subject to this kind of limitation, however. A third area of restrictive interpretation of privileges and immunities deals with property of the state. Because state universities are maintained in part by tax monies paid by state residents, and because the state's fish and game are protected by conservation officers, nonresident fees may be—and often are—substantially higher than resident fees.

Extradition

The Constitution provides for the return of fugitives from justice who have crossed state lines.

> A person charged in any state with treason, felony or other crime, who shall flee from justice, and be found in another state, shall on demand of the executive authority of the state from which he fled, be delivered up, to be removed to the state having jurisdiction of the crime.[29]

The Supreme Court has ruled, however, that "shall" is permissive in character, contrary to normal legal usage. The result is that the question of return is settled by the governor of the state in which the person is apprehended. Normally, fugitives are returned as a matter of routine, and frequently governors waive extradition. If the governor insists on extradition, however, the fugitive is entitled to a hearing. For this purpose, the governor may appoint a legal adviser to hold a hearing at which accused persons can state why they think they should not be returned for trial or imprisonment. In some cases, the state issuing the extradition request also offers testimony, usually in the form of a deposition, a written statement. Based on the hearing, the governor decides whether the person is to be returned, a decision not subject to appeal.

In unusual circumstances, a governor may grant asylum to a fugitive. This is most likely if the person is charged with an offense that is not a crime in the state of refuge, if the governor is convinced that the accused will not get a fair trial if returned, or if the accused has a long record of good citizenship in the state of refuge. In such cases, asylum may not be forever and applies only within the state of asylum. For example, a new governor might reverse a predecessor's decision, and crossing boundaries exposes the individual to arrest and another governor, who may reach a different conclusion. One example of the complexity of extradition began in 1975 with Dennis Banks, a leader of the American Indiana Movement. Convicted of robbery and assault in South Dakota, Banks fled a charge of rioting and assault from an incident outside a courthouse in Custer County, South Dakota. He was arrested in California in January 1976 but was granted asylum in California by Governor Edmund G. "Jerry" Brown, Jr. New Governor George Deukmegian threatened to end the asylum in 1983, precipitating Banks's flight to New York, where he sought asylum on the Onandoga Nation reservation and subsequently from Governor Mario Cuomo. A plea bargain eventually returned Banks to South Dakota, where he served a year of a three-year prison sentence.[30] Bill Janklow, attorney general of South Dakota at the time of the original incident and later governor, clearly saw the issue in terms of the crimes that had been committed and threats to the state police force. Governor Brown believed this was a question of Indian rights and the potential injustices of South Dakota's legal system. Although little was done or said on the matter by

Governors Deukmegian and Cuomo, undoubtedly they saw the issue as one now governed more by their partisan attitudes toward the earlier actors in the story than to the merits of the issues involved.

In the 1980s, some American states and cities offered asylum to foreign refugees refused haven by the national government. Usually this involved governors who disagreed with American foreign policy regarding Central America. The granting of such refuge has no legal force; no state can legally instruct its police forces to disobey national law. Nevertheless, this offering of asylum can reduce the cooperation between state and national governments, and such cooperation often is necessary for the national government to enforce its laws.

In most cases, of course, governors return the accused persons to the national government or state seeking extradition because they cannot afford to risk their reputations. If governors refuse extradition in but a few cases, their opponents will accuse them of turning the state into a haven for criminals. Politicians do not look forward to defending themselves against such charges.

Interstate Competition

One of the major factors motivating the Founders at Philadelphia in 1787 was a desire to make the United States into a single nation economically. They recognized that the future development of America depended on the encouragement rather than the restriction of trade. Yet, economic competition among states has caused them to seek control through means that violate the intent if not the letter—according to the courts—of the Constitution. State trade barriers have become especially common since the days of intense competition in the depressed 1930s.[31]

Trade restrictions that have been upheld in the courts include some such as these:

- A state may have rigid rules on the sale of sausage that in effect will outlaw products made in another state.
- A state may have rigid rules on the inspection of cattle coming into the state; the rules allegedly may be for the purpose of combating Bang's disease in herds within its own state. Local stock raisers benefit, but the disease continues.
- Another state may have rules that virtually prevent out-of-state nurseries from sending in their stock, even though those nurseries may have better reputations and their plants be less diseased than some locally grown stock.
- A state may tax wine produced locally at a rate lower than wine made in other states.

The defense presented in these cases is that the state legislature has a responsibility to aid its businesses and farmers. The effect of such rules is that the consumer pays more for the products affected. Furthermore, restrictive legislation in one state encourages other states to retaliate, which causes a breakdown in realizing a single economic nation.

Tax competition has become the most direct way in which a state government can affect economic competition among bordering states. Taxes can be so hidden or packaged as to make a place appear attractive to new industry. In 1986, competition to attract General Motors to build its planned Saturn automobile led a number of governors to go on a national talk show to pitch their states. Beyond the claims of lower taxes and better business climates, discussion revolved around the singing of state songs and each governor's TV image. A more mundane but effective incentive is for a state to require city property tax exemption for a certain number of years to new manufacturing or service establishments in the city. The idea is to attract industry, especially from other states, thus providing more jobs and ultimately a stronger tax base. Such practices are regarded by economists as unsound, but they are commonplace today and the encourage retaliation. Furthermore, these efforts are largely ineffective, because businesses are more interested in the availability of ample, low-cost labor and in proximity to markets than they are in tax patterns. Sometimes they are chiefly interested in raw material, such as timber, minerals, or a supply of high-quality water. As for GM's Saturn, when other factors were similar from one state to the next, the decision to locate in Tennessee may have been based finally on the southern climate, which allowed an earlier construction start. Two years after the project was given to Spring Lake, considerable anguish was expressed that the six-thousand-job, $5 billion plant may have come at too high a cost, perhaps bursting the bubble for local speculators.[32]

Interstate Cooperation

Although fears of an eroding economic base cause states to compete with one another, other pressures encourage cooperation. The Constitution permits states, with the consent of Congress, to enter into agreements with one another. The general practice of Congress appears to be to approve these compacts if they do not threaten to reduce the power of the national government and if other states do not object strenuously.

Perhaps the principal reason for interstate agreements has come from professional administrators anxious to apply to their activities the standards they and their peers regard as desirable. Thus, the Crime Compact of 1934 is now subscribed to by all states, and parole officers are able to cooperate with one another, little hindered by state lines. Ex-convicts are freer, therefore, to move to a new area where they may be better received while still subject to parole supervision. Regional reciprocity agreements among some states allow students from one state to attend professional schools in another when the first state finds it impossible to build such schools for a limited population or when it might simply be more economical to "farm out" their students.

A second major reason for such increased cooperation is that it is encouraged by the national government through grants-in-aid. Thus, Wisconsin in 1987 reluctantly agreed to raise the drinking age to 21, partially because it feared the cutoff of some national highway monies, but more importantly because it feared that the incidence of drunk driving would go up dramatically from border-hopping youths from neighboring states with a 21-year-old drinking age. The loss of highway monies probably would have been offset by higher tax revenues from the sale of liquor to 18–21-year-olds, but the fear of increased traffic deaths became persuasive when neighboring states raised their drinking age. Thus, the term *cooperation* once again may be misleading. States agree to work together to solve some common problems only because intervening forces make such cooperation necessary.

Uniform State Laws

In 1982, the National Conference of Commissioners on Uniform State Laws was established. Since that time, the conference has agreed on hundreds of proposed laws, the purpose of which is to simplify conduct of business across state lines. Conference activities have been supported by businesses and by the American Bar Association, which helps finance it.

Recommendations of the conference require action by each legislature to be effective. All the states have adopted the uniform laws on negotiable instruments, warehouse receipts, and stock transfer; other uniform laws have been adopted by at least some of the states. In certain cases, a legislature has adopted one of the uniform laws but modified some portions of it to fit local circumstances, thus making it non-uniform. Furthermore, the same law has not always been interpreted in the same manner by the courts in various states. Still, the work of the conference has helped simplify interstate relations.

Organizations of State Governments

To help state officials share experiences related to common problems, the Council of State Governments was formed in 1925. Its staff conducts and publishes research valuable to administrators and to persons drafting legislative bills. It sponsors a variety of affiliate organizations—the National Governors' Association, the National Conference of State Legislatures, the Conference of Chief Justices, the National Association of Attorneys General, and others. President Theodore Roosevelt sponsored the first National Governors' Conference in 1908. These have since become media events, frequently designed to give governors a sounding board to challenge or prod the national government into action supportive of the states.

The National Conference of State Legislatures similarly strives to help "lawmakers and their staffs meet the challenge of today's complex federal system." They publish *State Legislatures,* a magazine that keeps officials and other interested people abreast of developments in other states. Such interstate organizations have become lobbyists for the interests of state governments, more often seeking a common ground among the states than attempting to resolve the differences that will continue to be part of a federal system.

State Relations with Local Government

Local governments are the children of the state, and the state has been most unwilling to allow its children to grow up. A theory of perpetual infancy was adopted by nineteenth-century legislatures. Efforts at achieving independence for local governments through the legal device of constitutional limitations on states have been largely unsuccessful. Cities in most states achieved more independence and experienced less legislative supervision after the first decade or so of the twentieth century, but this seems to have resulted principally from a changing climate of opinion toward cities that accompanied the nation's urbanization, together with a slight increase of public trust in the politician—both state and local—following the demise of machine politics. Other local units of government have been given little additional freedom from state control in recent decades. For example, the demand for higher educational standards and the fact that the states pay an expanding share of the operating costs have resulted in increased state supervision over local school district activities.

State Judicial Oversight of Local Governments

Standing behind all local officials, looking over their shoulders as the baseball umpire looks over the shoulder of the catcher, is a judge. The judge settles all disputes between local government and the state, a taxpaper and the local unit, one local unit and another. Although judges make a determination only when asked to do so and then on the basis of laws and ordinances made by others, they are lawmakers, for they must decide ultimately what the law *means* and hence what the local government can and cannot do. Dillon's rule forces local governments constantly to prove in court that they have the powers to do what they seek to do.

State Administrative Oversight of Local Governments

The administrative branch of state government follows the typically Jacksonian pattern of decentralization. Because of the influence of this frontier ideology, departments of local government, such as the Ministry of the Interior in France or the Ministry of Local Government in Great Britain, seldom are found in the United States, although some states have departments (with varying jurisdictions) to coordinate state and local affairs and to oversee local finance. Administrative contacts between city and state characteristically are on a *functional* basis. That is, members of the state department of education oversee the activities of the local school district; the state department of health watches the activities of the local department of health; and so on.

Most of these relationships are informal, casual, day-to-day contacts in which professionally trained personnel interact on a knowledgeable and cooperative basis. But the law often allows draconian measures where necessary. Near the beginning of the 1989–1990 school year, for example, New Jersey seized the Jersey City school system after finding it academically bankrupt, politically corrupt, and administratively incompetent. It dismissed the school board and all the top administrative officers, appointing a caretaker head. Kentucky and New Mexico have also taken over districts in the past, though they were of smaller size. A number of state legislatures have passed laws allowing similar actions, and others can act if they so choose. At various times in the past, almost every local function has been taken over for a time by a state for one reason or another.

Legislative Oversight of Local Governments

The traditional pattern of direct legislative supervision of local government administration has declined in the twentieth century. This has happened not through accident but for two very good reasons. First, as the twentieth century advanced, government became too complicated for legislators, most of whom lack expertise and all of whom face increasingly lengthy and more complex agendas. Local government, except in the rural and urban-fringe areas, became professionalized and technical, its complex details understandable only to the professional full-time technician. Flexibility, which legislatures do not possess, was needed; so was continuous, rather than sporadic, oversight. The twentieth century thus represented a period during which state legislators are somewhat reluctantly but inexorably forced to transfer increased supervision over local government to the career bureaucracies of the administrative branch of state and local government.

Second, local units have successfully fought off new efforts at state legislative oversight in the twentieth century. This has been accomplished by methods such as appealing to localism, instilling fear that state-level direction will come with too high a price tag, and hard lobbying by local elected officials. Nonetheless a varying degree of legislative oversight is found in the states today particularly in those in which legislatures became more professionalized and took on more career staffs (akin to the national Congress. These are usually states where the legislature is more willing to pay the price of interference with local government. For example, in Minnesota enacting state guidelines for cities and counties for the placement of troubled children in local residential treatment facilities called for two expensive studies to be done by the state legislature to collect statewide data on these placements.[33] Before, these counties had collected their data using different methods and different definitions for the same information, so no statewide data were available. With data in hand, the legislature has proposed additional funds for counties to begin pilot projects on intensive in-home services for such children.

Mandates and Limitations

Which local government functions are subject to state oversight today? "Most", might be a brief answer. But beyond oversight stands the mandate (a requirement that something be done) or prohibition (the opposite of a mandate, a limitation on what may be done). The ACIR found five general categories of mandates and prohibitions:[34]

1. *Rules of the game.* These mandate the organization or procedures of local governments. In Wisconsin, for example, home rule allows cities and villages to organize in a variety of ways, but law mandates that towns have a "board composed of 3 supervisors, who are elected biennially at the town meeting."[35]
2. *Spillover mandates.* These set requirements when localities spend in functional areas of both state and local importance. In Florida, which has a growing AIDS problem, the legislature has mandated that Medicaid-eligible, indigent clients must be served by county hospitals.[36] Texas requires school districts to administer and certify that students have passed a state competency examination before granting a high school diploma.[37] In Wisconsin, each city is required to provide a solid-waste dump, even though the state has mandated the closing of a number of dumps to alleviate ground-water pollution.[38]
3. *Interlocal equities.* These regulate the effects that one locality will have on another. Most important is the matter of annexation and consolidation of land (see

chapter 8). California requires approval by the Local Agency Formation Commission before a vote can be taken on annexation.

4. *Losses of local tax base.* These regulate the revenue raised by local governments by exempting items from sales or property tax. For example, Minnesota exempts clothing from the local (and state) sales tax.

5. *Personnel benefits.* These involve instances in which the state sets working conditions or wage benefits for local employees. In Florida, state mandates to increase retirees' monthly benefits were estimated to cost $4.3 million in fiscal year 1988.[39] In Wisconsin, a variety of personnel statutes were ruled to limit the local government's home-rule powers. As a result, a city could not create a new department of public safety, and thereby replace some of the functions of the regulated police and fire departments.[40] Many states require local governments to hold elections allowing employees to decide whether they want a particular union as exclusive bargaining agent.

Four state constitutions (California, Massachusetts, New Hampshire, and New Mexico) require reimbursement from the state to local government for mandated services; a number of other states require some degree of reimbursement.[41] Often, such constitutional provision is only an unenforceable statement of intent. For example, in November 1990, Wisconsin voters passed a nonbinding referendum requiring the funding of local mandates, but legislators and political scientists alike could not determine what would be covered by the referendum. The California legislature ignored the obligation to pay in the very year of its adoption. "Sneaky" mandates skirt the law by requiring practices that states then find ways not to fund. For example, in Georgia the state refuses to incarcerate many state prisoners, leaving the counties with much of the cost of housing them in overcrowded jails, despite provision in law for the state to pick up the prisoners and pay county costs. (The state averages paying less than half the cost when prisoners stay in jail, compared to the total cost of imprisonment.)[42] Such actions have led states in recent years to create, and interested groups to form, a number of mandate study task forces.[43]

Techniques of Supervision

One popular perception of local government is that it is controlled by heavy-handed bureaucrats at the state capital, armed with court decrees and administrative orders. Although these devices do play a part, most state agencies try persuasion, education, and other noncoercive techniques wherever possible. The big stick is brought into play principally whenever the state overseers find evidence of incompetence, irresponsibility, or corruption.

Supervising state agencies usually start by requiring reports from local communities. These reports serve to warn the agency when trouble spots appear and tend to channel local activity, because the reporting officials—knowing they will be judged by their peers—will want a good record. But because reports do not necessarily require action, the problem is to ensure that they continue to perform a useful function. Computers and word processors allow this process to provide volumes of information today, sometimes more data than can be digested. Nevertheless, volume alone is not the problem. Some years ago in Minnesota, for example, state board of health regulations required the health officer of each city and village to make an annual sanitation inspection of the locality and to send a copy of the report to the state board. Actually, however, the state agency had no idea of how many inspections were being made and no one seemed to know why the information was filed with the state; no action ever resulted from the reports, and the state had no power to abate nuisances or to force local governments to do so. Still, bureaucracy is more self-correcting than the popular stereotype would hold—very few of the local health officers ever bothered to send in the report.

State agencies can furnish advice and information. In the larger states, these services may be nearly as varied as those available from the national government. They are especially important for smaller communities, where amateurs may be struggling to do an adequate job or where overworked professionals may not have time to keep up with the latest techniques in their fields. The relationship between the state and the technical specialists from the large city or populous county may become strained when local functionaries think themselves more competent than nominal state supervisors (in fact, they may be). Is the manager of a large city airport able to get along without advice from the state airports commissioner? The manager is likely to think so. Sometimes a long-running feud may color relationships between a department of a large city and the corresponding state agency. Usually, however, relations are friendly and cooperative. Smaller cities and counties have technicians who are likely to recognize their genuine need for advice and seek it.

One step beyond advice is technical aid. State agencies with (perhaps) larger budgets and more specialized personnel are in a position to help out the local amateur or semiprofessional. How effective can the chief of police be in a village or suburb of 1,500 against the professional criminal? And how much experience or forensic equipment can be used in the rare event of a murder in the town? One measure of such cooperation was found in the following report:

> A U.S. General Accounting Office survey reported. . . . 50% of local officials responding never asked the state for technical assistance. At the same time state officials are contacted more often than any other outside organizations to meet local technical assistance needs. Apparently local officials perceived fewer programs and less paperwork in dealing with state officials than with federal agencies.
>
> All States now have state agencies specifically designated to assist local governments. . . .
>
> The agencies offer a wide variety of services to local governments and try to promote intergovernmental cooperation, upgrade local management and planning capabilities, and facilitate administration of programs in such areas as economic development and housing. Some provide assistance for small jurisdictions in such matters as application for federal grants. Few exercise control functions, emphasizing their assistance capabilities.[44]

Other approaches failing, the state may also make use of its coercive power (remember, once again, Dillon's rule). Among other things, its agencies can grant or withhold permits; issue orders or rules; or withhold grants-in-aid if standards prescribed by state or sometimes federal law are not complied with. Particularly important are various rules restricting local government borrowing practices. The power of local government to do something is greatly reduced if the state government denies it the power to raise the necessary resources. It even is possible in most states, as a last resort, to apply substitute administration. When New York City was on the brink of bankruptcy in 1975, the ''bail-out'' plan finally provided involved guarantees from the national government but also required formation of the Emergency Financial Control Board and the Municipal Assistance Corporation, which, by state order, took much of the budget-making power away from the city council.[45]

There are two areas in which states emphasize uniform practice by local governments: apportionment and accounting. Most states today audit municipal accounts and require municipalities to submit financial reports to the state periodically. As we will discuss in chapter 11, when the national courts began to govern the practice of dividing legislative districts, it became commonplace for states to review and standardize the apportionment practices of local governments to prevent court action.

Organization of Supervision

The growing tendency to turn over state supervision to the administrative rather than the legislative branch of government probably has changed considerably the pattern of state–local relationships. Local professional technicians feel more at ease and less anxiety that they will be exploited when they deal with state professionals rather than with the politicians of the state legislature. Even contact with the legislature is frequently with specialized staff members, resulting in smoother, more confident relationship. The motivation of the professional administrator is different from that of the politician. Professional administrators stake their pride and reputation in everything they do, and success is measured by acceptance of their work by peers not only within the state but within the professional group to which they belong. Politicians stake their jobs in everything they do, and their success is measured by the number of votes they get compared with their opponents. Hence administrators are interested in doing the best possible job in accord with accepted professional standards and techniques. Politicians meet problems with the question: What approach will produce the most votes? If they wish to stay in office, they have little choice but to appeal to popular attitudes, although they will modify their behavior according to their own personal ideology. Their goals often dictate a different approach from that of administrator.

Interlocal Relations

The frequency of contracts between local units of government are increasing. This is so because local boundaries are not expanding; in fact, some are contracting as speed of transportation and of communication increase. The swelling complexity of government, together with an expanding population, has also created circumstances that encourage local governments to work out their problems together. The American system compounds these arrangements with the proliferation of special districts, creating a multitude of governments at the local level in any given place.

One study, inquiring into the means by which local governments have met service needs that transcend legal boundaries, has reported:

Informal cooperation among municipalities is one of the least tangible, but undoubtedly one of the most basic approaches to the solution of intermunicipal problems. It requires a language of standard definitions and a setting in which officials and citizens can meet to discuss common problems.

The most significant part of informal cooperation consists of personal contacts among operating officials. State associations of municipal officers, many of which have regional subdivisions, are of great importance. Among others, important are state associations of mayors, managers, selectmen [council members], finance personnel and law officers; and officials concerned with the functions of police and fire protection, public works, planning, health, welfare, education and libraries.[46]

Just as the Council of State Governments helps bring state officials together to discuss their common problems and to seek bases for cooperation, so do these regional and state associations of local government officers and professional employees help do the same thing on the local level. In addition to cooperative work on an informal basis, local units frequently make contractual arrangements with one another. These arrangements are not likely found between core city and suburb, but they also exist in semiurban and rural areas and between counties and the local governments within their boundaries.

Conflicts among local governments most often are generated by competition over the location of tax base. Suburbs often were formed, and resistance to annexation and consolidation often has been generated by the desire of residents on the metropolitan fringe to avoid paying core-city property tax rates while enjoying many of the benefits of those core cities. Special districts sometimes compound these conflicts, but sometimes they alleviate the competition in a given functional area (particularly schooling).

The relationships among the thousands of local governments, one of the unique characteristics of the American political system, will be the focus of chapter 8.

Concluding Note

It is true more and more that the major functions of government can be performed only through the joint activity and cooperation of national, state, and local governments. It is not a question of which level is to carry on these functions but rather how all three may aid and participate effectively. This is true in education, health, welfare, streets and highways, housing, airports, environmental control, law enforcement, and other functions. The pattern of the future undoubtedly will see more, rather than less, cooperation among the three levels of government in the United States.

Notes

1. A variety of books review the history of federalism. Two recommendations are Deil S. Wright, *Understanding Intergovernmental Relations,* 3d ed., (Monterey, CA: Brooks/Cole Publishing, 1988), chapter 3; and David B. Walker, *Toward a Functioning Federalism* (Cambridge, MA: Winthrop, 1981), part II.

2. Donald B. Rosenthal and James M. Hoefler, ''Competing Approaches to the

Study of American Federalism and Intergovernmental Relations, *Publius* 19 (Winter, 1989): 1–23, demonstrates five "schools" of federalism: dual, cooperative, pragmatic, non-centralized, and nation-centered; Wright, *Intergovernmental Relations,* argues for seven phases: conflict (1930s and before), cooperative (1030s–1950s), concentrated (1940s–1960s), creative (1950s–1960s),competitive (1960s–1970s), calculative (1970s–1980s), and contractive (1980s–1990s); Walker, *Towards a Functioning Federalism,* prefers two phases of dual federalism and two phases of cooperative. The purpose here is to show the many types of federalism. Every period in American history has shown some separation, some conflict, some creativity, and some cooperation.

3. Morton Grodzins argued that cooperative federalism has been continuous throughout American history. See Morton Grodzins, *The American System, A New View of Government in the United States,* (Chicago: Rand McNally, 1966). This view is challenged by Harry N. Schreiber, "The Condition of American Federalism: An Historian's View" in Lawrence J. O'Toole, Jr., *American Intergovernmental Relations* (Washington, DC: Congressional Quarterly Press, 1985), 51–57.

4. *McCulloch* v. *State of Maryland,* 4 Wheat. 316 (1819).

5. Article I, Section 8 of the U.S. Constitution. See also *Gibbons* v. *Ogden,* 9 Wheat. 1 (1824).

6. Article VI, Section 2 of the U.S. Constitution.

7. Wright, *Intergovernmental Relations,* 126.

8. Walker, *Towards a Functioning Federalism,* 52.

9. Ibid., 64–65.

10. See *Publius* 16:1 (Winter 1986), which is devoted to this issue; and John Kincaid, "The State of American Federalism—1987," *Publius* 18:3 (Summer 1988):1–15.

11. See Timothy Conlan, "Federalism and Competing Values in the Reagan Administration," *Publius* 16:1 (Winter 1986): 29–48.

12. *National League of Cities* v *Usery,* 426 U.S. 833 (1976).

13. *Garcia* v. *San Antonio Metropolitan Transit Authority,* 469 U.S. 528 (1985).

14. *South Carolina* v. *Baker,* 108 S.CT. 1355 (1988). For discussion of the changing Court opinion, see James R. Alexander, "State Sovereignty in the Federal System," *Publius* 16:2 (Spring 1986): 1–15; and Kincaid "The State of American Federalism."

15. David C. Nice, *Federalism: The Politics of Intergovernmental Relations* (New York: St. Martin's Press, 1987), 10–11.

16. Charles R. Adrian, "State and Local Government Participation in the Design and Administration of Intergovernmental Programs," *Annals* 359 (May 1965): 35–43.

17. Daniel J. Elazar, "The Shaping of Intergovernmental Relations in the Twentieth Century," *Annals* 359 (May 1965): 10–22.

18. Walker, *Toward a Functioning Federalism,* 69.

19. See Gary W. Copeland and Kenneth J. Meier, "Tort Reform and Regulation of the Insurance Industry: Medical Malpractice Liability Proposals in 1986," *Publius* 17:3 (Summer 1987): 163–78.

20. Michael D. Reagan and John G. Sanzone, *The New Federalism,* 2d ed. (New York: Oxford University Press, 1981).

21. Total determined by data taken from tables in Larry Sabato, *Goodbye to Goodtime Charlie* (Washington, DC: C Q Press, 1983), 36–39.

22. Ibid., 46.

23. See Thad L. Beyle, "The Governor as Innovator in the Federal System," *Publius* 18:3 (Summer 1988):131–52.

24. Melvin Mogulof, "Federally Encouraged Multijurisdictional Agencies," *Urban Affairs Quarterly* 9 (September 1973):113–32.

25. Information provided to the authors by Deborah Schilling of the Office of Disaster Assistance Programs, Washington, D.C.

26. Nice, *Federalism,* 106. The author cites Parris Glendening and Mavis Reeves, *Pragmatic Federalism,* 2d ed. (Pacific Palisades, CA: Palisades Publishers, 1984).

27. See chapter 2 for a discussion of community power structure. The early community power studies mentioned are Robert S. Lynd and Helen M. Lynd, *Middletown* (New York: Harcourt, Brace and World, 1929); and Robert S. Lynd and Helen M. Lynd, *Middletown in Transition* (New York: Harcourt, Brace and World, 1937). The quotations are taken from Walker, *Toward a Functioning Federalism,* 3.

28. "Federal Influence on State and Local Roles in the Federal System." A commission report of the Advisory Commission on Intergovernmental Relations, Washington, D.C., November 1981, chapter 3.

29. Article IV, Section 2 of the U.S. Constitution.

30. This story was pieced together from a variety of stories in the *Sioux Falls Argus Leader,* as reported by *Newsbank.*

31. F. E. Melder, *State and Local Barriers to Interstate Commerce* (Orono, ME: The University Press, 1937).

32. See the column by Larry Batson, "Spring Hill 'Winds Down' to 'Gear Up' for Saturn," *Minneapolis Star and Tribune,* March 22, 1987, sec. A, 1, 90.

33. Kerry Kinney Fine, "Out of Home Placement of Children" (St. Paul: Research Department, Minnesota House of Representatives, 1983); and Kerry Kinney Fine and Mary Jane Lehnertz, "Out of Home Placement 1981 and 1984: A Comparison" (St. Paul: Research Department, Minnesota House of Representatives, 1986).

34. "State and Local Roles in the Federal System." A commission report of the Advisory Commission on Intergovernmental Relations, Washington, D.C., 1982, 157. For a case study: Gerald Benjamin and Charles Brecher, eds., *The Two New Yorks: State-City Relations in the Changing Federal System* (New York: Russell Sage Foundation, 1989).

35. 1989–90 State of Wisconsin *Blue Book*, Madison, 1989, 274.

36. Joseph Zimmerman, "Changing State-Local Relationships," *1988–1989 Book of the States* (Lexington, KY: Council of State Governments, 1988), 448.

37. Neal Tannahill and Wendell M. Bedichek, *Texas Government*, 3d ed. (Glenview, IL: Scott, Foresman, 1989), 361.

38. David M. Jones, "Other State Functions" in Wilder Crane, A. Clarke Hagensick et al., eds., *Wisconsin Government and Politics,* 4th ed. (Milwaukee: Department of Governmental Affairs, University of Wisconsin-Milwaukee, 1987).

39. Zimmerman, "Changing . . . Relationships," 448.

40. Michael R. Fine, "The Independence of the City: The Legal Constraints of Home Rule," *The Small City and Regional Community* 8 (1989):91–98.

41. Joseph Zimmerman, "Developments in State-Local Relations: 84–85," *1986–1987 Book of States* (Lexington, KY: Council of State Governments, 1986), 433–37.

42. Zimmerman, *1988–1989 Book of the States,* 448–49.

43. Ibid.

44. "State and Local Roles in the Federal Systems," 153.

45. See Terry Nichols Clark and Lorna Crowley Ferguson, *City Money* (New York: Columbia University Press, 1983), 196; and the collection of articles in parts 2 and 3 of Charles Brecher and Raymond D. Horton, eds., *Setting Municipal Priorities* (New York and London: New York University Press, 1984).

46. George Goodwin, *Intermunicipal Relations in Massachusetts* (Amherst: The Bureau of Government Research, University of Massachusetts, 1956), 3–4, by permission of the publisher.

5

The Electorate and Interest Groups

A quality that distinguishes the American political system from others is its ability to find a role for the common individual in a federal system. In chapter 2, we discussed this in the context of localism; in this chapter and the next, we will look at the electoral process and those groups and political parties that organize that process. This chapter will begin by looking at some of the participants—the electorate and interest groups. Chapter 6 will examine the process—the crucial part played by the political party and the organization of elections, followed by a note on experiments in direct democracy today; that is the recall, referendum, and initiative.

The Electorate

It is likely that more data have been generated about the electorate than any other phenomenon in politics. We know that middle-class people vote more often than do those in the lower class, urbanites more than farmers, men more than women, the middle-aged more than the young, and whites more than blacks. For a number of reasons, however, these factors may be overstated. "Easy" relationships often also are measures of unstated relationships. The statistical technique of multivariate analysis suggests that much conventional wisdom about who votes is misleading. For example, even though whites vote more than blacks, a number of studies have shown that middle-class blacks in fact may vote in higher proportions than middle-class whites in some elections.[1] (Voting is a matter of motivation, and conditions leading any group to the polls vary through time and circumstance.) Despite the conclusion that men are more likely to vote than women, more detailed study shows that "to the age of forty, men and women vote at virtually the same rate" and nearly all the differences in turnout between older men and women is "accounted for by differences in other demographics."[2] Furthermore, given the variation in federalism, a particular state or local election often raises an issue or involves a candidate that challenges even the general predictors. Although in the 1960s legislation was necessary to protect blacks' right to vote, by the 1980s blacks were being elected mayors in many large cities. The election of black mayors in New York, Los Angeles, Chicago, Philadelphia, Detroit, Cleveland, Baltimore, Atlanta, New Orleans, Oakland, St. Louis, and many medium-sized cities has produced high black voter turnout in those cities.

Although little study has been done to isolate demographic differences between national, state, and local elections, the relevance of level cannot be overlooked. Those demographics that support low voter turnout are more likely to have greater effect in state and local elections, where turnout generally is low. But the behavior found in elections, as in other institutions in the federal system, are better understood in terms of the organization and processes of day-to-day activity than in conclusions based on demographic correlations. Voter turnout ultimately will depend on the role of the political party in the particular election, on whether an incumbent runs, what kind of campaign is generated in a particular election, or even on the issues involved. A study of gubernatorial elections showed that when two models of elections are compared, one a socioeconomic model based on the demographics above, and the other a political mobilization model based on such things as campaign spending and partisan competitiveness, the political mobilization model predicts more of the voter turnout.[3] It is to these concerns we will turn in the next chapter.

This chapter also will look at the voters and interest groups in democratic processes. Voters are all of the people who do not fall into any of the categories of nonvoters. Stated another way, political scientists refer to *structural* and *preferential* nonvoters. Structural nonvoters are prevented from voting because of the structure of legal requirements. These may deal with citizenship, age, sex, race, legal sanity, ability to read, ownership of property, and other formal provisions of law. In quite different fashion, preferential nonvoting may involve apathy or personal attitudes toward voting. These types of nonparticipation will be examined in the later sections.

Structural Nonvoting

Twentieth-century America is a nation committed to the concept of universal suffrage and, save for blacks in the South prior to the civil rights movement of midcentury and persons disfranchised as a result of changing their residence shortly before an election, this goal has been substantially realized. The U.S. Constitution prevents states from prohibiting the vote based on race (Thirteenth Amendment), gender (Nineteenth Amendment), failure to pay a poll tax (Twenty-Fourth Amendment), or age for those 18 or over (Twenty-Sixth Amendment). On most matters, voting eligibility is left to the states. However, under constitutional provisions, Congress has passed a variety of voting rights provisions that allow the federal courts to become involved with eligibility. Voter regulation not controlled by federal law or court rulings is left to the states. Although property ownership was a common prerequisite in early American history, today's eligibility requirements in a general election usually include citizenship; a minimum age of 18; a minimum period of in the state residence, county, and polling district; and registration.

Meeting these criteria, does not guarantee freedom to vote. For example, some states disfranchise persons for a number of reasons, including:

- Being under guardianship
- Being declared legally insane (in Wisconsin, *non compos mentis;* in Texas, *idiots and lunatics*)
- Severe mental deficiency or imprisonment
- Dishonorable discharge from military service
- Conviction of defrauding the United States or any of the states or having offered or accepted bribes
- Voluntarily aiding or abetting an attempted overthrow of the U.S. government
- Voluntarily bearing arms against the United States

High population mobility, which makes residence requirements especially significant, probably disqualifies many people from voting. Residence requirements are, to a degree, vestiges of an earlier theory of voting and are not in accord with universal suffrage. But this has not been a high-priority issue for those in power (who are usually long-term residents of an area) or for such interest groups as the League of Women Voters, who champion high voter turnout; nor does the general public seem much concerned about it.

Literacy requirements
In an effort to reduce the political influence of the foreign-born, some states imposed English literacy requirements. With immigrants often concentrated in cities and belonging to one political party and the legislature under the control of the opposite party, this requirement might be expected in the struggle for political control of the state. The same type of literacy test once was used to discourage blacks from voting.

The Voting Rights Act of 1965 provided that persons could not be denied the right to vote if they had successfully completed six grades of education (or more, if applied to all voters in the state) in a school under the American flag even though teaching in that school was not conducted in the English language. This provision protected Puerto Ricans in New York, which had a literacy test. (In 1966, the United States Supreme Court ruled that the New York literacy test could be taken in Spanish as well as English.) At first, the act suspended literacy requirements in any political subdivision in which the director of the census certified that under 50 percent of the persons of voting age were registered to vote. By virtue of 1970 amendments, the law (made permanent in 1975) was expanded to apply to all places, effectively eliminating literacy tests.[4]

Restrictions on the Institutionalized
In general, inmates of state or local institutions may not vote. Although states vary, usually the rule applies to the mentally ill and to inmates in jails or prisons. A widespread misconception is that persons convicted of felonies lose their citizenship. However, in some states such persons lose certain civil rights, including the right to vote. In other states, under certain circumstances individuals may permanently regain their right to vote—even their right to hold public office—if they are not actually incarcerated. For example, the Texas legislature passed a law in 1983 restoring voter

eligibility to felons after a five-year waiting period. Restriction on holding public office remains, unless a pardon is granted by the governor.[5]

Taxpaying Requirements

During the Great Depression, several states provided that only property owners could vote on questions on direct appropriation of public money or issuance of bonds. This move was dictated by homeowners, who wanted to save their property in a day of increased demands for governmental services (especially public welfare) and of evaporating taxpaying ability.

Payment of the poll tax, long a requirement in southern states as a prerequisite for state and local voting, was a controversial subject for many years. Tied in with eligibility to vote, the tax served to retain control of governments for the prosperous because it disfranchised low income whites and blacks alike. The tax was simple enough in concept—a head tax of a few dollars on each adult (or male) within specified age groups. Through various devices—requiring payment of all past-due taxes to be eligible to vote, deliberate failure to send out tax bills or notices, making tax payments due long before elections, for example—the less literate and less politically conscious easily were disfranchised. In the years following World War II, the tax developed a special notoriety that was probably responsible for its repeal in ten states. The passage of the Twenty-Fourth Amendment in 1964 outlawed the poll tax in national elections, but some states prepared separate ballots distinguishing the level of election and continuing the tax. It took a Supreme Court decision in 1966 to outlaw its use in state elections.[6] These and other cases striking down restrictions based on property ownership have made the courts the major force in determining voter eligibility and in creating a system in which property or ability to pay no longer restricts voting eligibility.

Registration

Requiring individuals to register before they may vote is a nearly universal practice in today's urban areas. Chapter 6 will discuss the use of registration as a device to restrict voting in party primaries. Registration is not, in the legal sense, an additional qualification for voting but only a mechanism for determining that those who cast ballots actually are qualified. The device was begun as a means of reducing fraudulent voting and was especially supported in earlier decades by reformers seeking to control the freewheeling activities of big-city machines. In the South, registration was an effective device for controlling access to the polls and could be used for example, to argue that a black person (not infrequently a poor white, too) could not meet the literacy requirement or "correctly interpret" a portion of the state constitution.

An urban, industrial society is also a mobile society. Yet, our election laws are based largely on the more stable population patterns of landowners in the nineteenth century. Some states dictate the amount of time one must have lived in the county or precinct. Even a thirty-day residency period may disfranchise a large number of people. The Michigan constitution attempts to overcome this by eliminating residency requirements for presidential elections and allowing persons who have moved within the state within thirty days of an election to vote in their former precincts. A number of other states have adopted similar provisions.[7]

Actually registration often involves anticipation and action. Most states require registration ten to thirty days before the election (Arizona requires registration fifty days before). Maine, Minnesota, Oregon, and Wisconsin, however, allow registration at the polls. Most states continue to permit the purging from the rolls persons who do not vote, although many places do not practice this because of the cost or because it is advantageous to the party in charge not to do so. Because states have periodic rather than permanent registration, it is likely that many voters do not know they must reregister and therefore are turned away on election day. In California, however, anyone about to be dropped from the rolls is notified by mail and need only return an enclosed postcard to remain registered.

Low voter turnout undoubtedly results in small part from the difficulty of registration, although attitudinal factors are more significant. One study concluded that turnout would be improved in national elections if closing dates were eliminated; registration offices were open evenings and Saturdays; and if absentee registration was permitted.[8] Twenty-two states and then the national government (1984) passed laws making polling places and registration more accessible to the handicapped and elderly.[9] For many years, most Californians have registered not at permanent offices (frequently inconveniently located) but at temporary offices located in shopping centers. But registration and access rules are limited factors, often overstated by interest groups advocating such rule changes.

Preferential Nonvoting

Political scientists have collected enough data concerning voter participation both in the United States and abroad to develop some fairly clear concepts as to the kinds of people who vote, who do not, and why they do not.[10] People who prefer not to vote— now about one-half of those eligible in presidential elections and far more at the state and local levels—generally are apathetic, bored, skeptical, frustrated, or disillusioned with the electoral process. Many of these people, whether poorly or well educated, are aware that the individual act of voting in strict payoff terms is irrational; that is, that voting outcomes almost never depend on the single vote but rather are meaningful only in groups or categories of voters shifting in a consistent fashion (the aged, homeowners, commercial farmers, automobile drivers, blacks, right-to-lifers, skilled workers, for example). Many people believe "my vote won't count anyway." Others believe "no matter how I vote, the country will be run about the same." Such people are discussed in the following section.

The individual, in making choices, frequently encounters three kinds of costs: decision-making costs, responsibility costs, and costs of errors. Any one of these costs may be high, low, or moderate, depending on the choice made. The difference between many everyday choices and those affecting a person as a citizen in a democracy may be dramatized by comparing choices involved in buying clothes with choices faced in the voting booth. For the clothes shopper, the decision-making choices are notoriously high—at least according to the American stereotype. For example, much time, energy, and thought go into making a decision. Responsibility costs are high, for the shopper will be blamed if the clothes are considered unattractive by those whose opinions matter to him or her. The costs of errors in this case are equal to the responsibility costs and hence are also high. As a voter, on the other hand, this same person finds that decision-making costs are low. Information cost, one kind of decision-making cost, is high, but so far as the typical voter is concerned, one need not learn very much either about issues or about candidates. A number of guidelines can be followed in deciding how to vote; these include personal experiences, habits, and the views of friends or opinion leaders. Responsibility costs are low for voters; that is, they are broadly socialized (spread widely among citizens), and individuals risk little criticism if their candidate proves to be incompetent. Costs of errors by voters are potentially very high, for a "bad" public official can do much damage to society, but these costs are also highly socialized. So the typical voter finds the personal value of citizenship as measured by the costs of voting to be low, much lower than the value of clothing as measured by the costs involved in the purchase. The result, except when public concern is extremely high, is the frequent decision *not* to vote.

Low Voter Turnout

The pattern of voter turnout varies widely from one state or locality to another, but one statistic stands out: In state and local elections, a majority of eligible voters consistently choose not to vote. Generally (with many exceptions), voter turnout is highest when state or local elections accompany a presidential election; turnout is higher in statewide elections than in local elections; in general elections when contested than in contested primaries; and when elections are more competitive than when they are less competitive. Comparing percentages of voter turnout over time is always misleading because percentage measures are based on eligibility, a standard that changes with time. Recently enfranchised voters, who usually must grow accustomed to participation, are among the lowest in turnout. We therefore will concentrate on voter turnout by comparing groups with similar eligibility.

Between 1960 and 1986, turnout for governor's races in nonpresidential years varied from an average of 64 percent in North Dakota to a 26 percent average in Georgia.[11] The West has the highest national election voter turnout and the South, traditionally with less competitive races in general elections and a population less accustomed to voting, has the lowest turnout in general elections. Participation in primaries often proves to be highest in one-party states where the primary election in effect chooses the public official. But only in the South, where one-party state politics had been common since 1868, did the primary election totals approach general election turnout between 1960 and 1986. Outside the South, primary turnout averages only slightly above one-half of general election turnout.[12]

Studies indicate that about one-third of eligible voters go to the polls regularly in local elections. The extent of voting varies in different sections of the country, and between different governmental units in the same section; that is, each locality has its own tradition of participation or nonparticipation. Sometimes a matter of particular interest will bring out a larger vote for a local election than was the case in the preceding presidential vote. The degree to which the electorate is organized or to which organized groups are active in campaigns influences the size of the turnout.

Voter turnout for special elections relative to constitutional amendments, the question of calling a constitutional convention, or the voting on delegates to constitutional conventions typically has been especially light. Some observers have concluded that this scant attention is a result of the relative unimportance of state government in the mind of the voter. This explanation seems unlikely, however, considering that similar light turnouts are found in nearly all special elections. The relative lack of public concern is probably related, instead, to two factors: one is the low visibility of almost every election at any level of government except that involving the chief executive; the other is that a constitutional convention or a proposed amendment to the state constitution does not in itself serve to allocate resources—instead, it only establishes the rules under which resources are to be allocated. The fact that this is one step more removed from the making of public policy that directly influences the voter is probably significant.

Many factors influence turnout. In city elections in twenty years preceding 1989, for example, Los Angeles varied between 64 percent in 1973 and 8.6 percent a decade later. During that time, the issue of school busing came and went, much of the middle class moved out of the city or sent their children to private schools, thousands of immigrants became citizens but had backgrounds of experience in nondemocratic nations of Asia and Latin America, and the big decisions increasingly were perceived to have been made by the state and national courts or the state legislature. In city council elections, incumbents have so much control over elections that close contests are rare (see chapter 6). In the 1989 city general election in Los Angeles, the turnout of eligible voters was 11 percent.

Voter Indifference

One scholar, surveying local elections, has concluded the following:

> Despite high levels of popular education, economic stability, a fair degree of social mobility, a marvelously efficient communications system, and related advantages usually assumed to provide sufficient conditions for democratic pluralism, the vast majority of citizens remain apathetic, uninterested, and inactive in political affairs at the community level.[13]

In state and local elections, turnout varies with the emotional appeal of issues and the degree to which they provoke anxieties. For example, in the Los Angeles Unified School District, the nation's second largest, turnout during the 1950s and early 1960s totaled 35 percent to 45 percent of the eligible voters. During this time, the city was still growing rapidly, parents wanted to vote for school construction bonds, and the population was still largely middle class. Later busing and curriculum issues encouraged turnout. But by the 1980s, many middle-class families had moved to the suburbs, others sent their children to private schools, the proportion of noncitizen immigrant parents had increased sharply, dramatic issues declined in number, and voter participation shrank. In some elections, a mere 7 percent to 15 percent of eligible voters participated. Only two groups consistently voted: The elderly, alway a high-turnout group and teachers, who in some elections made up 10 percent of the active electorate. Teachers are very much parties at interest in school board decisions. Their trade unions sharply influence school board membership, but their power is limited because about 80 percent of school board funds in California come from the state rather than being raised locally. Nevertheless, the perception of power led to very high teacher turnout.[14]

Although the ideal of grass-roots democracy calls for vigorous participation in the political process, beyond the ballot box the indifference extends to getting public positions filled. For instance, not only is there no competition for some jobs; sometimes no one can even be drafted for a position.

Voter Fatigue

Another factor reducing voter participation in state and local elections is voter fatigue. People simply grow weary of trudging off to elections. In no other nation in the world do so many candidates challenge for each position. Furthermore, unlike other nations, we usually have primaries (and sometimes runoffs) preceding general elections, which more than doubles the number. Dozens of offices are placed on the ballot, many virtually unknown to the voters. The public wants the *right* to vote for fence viewers, drain commissioners, and water district board members—not because they actually vote for them but as a check, *just in case.* Few nations ask policy questions of voters, but in the United States, especially west of the Missouri, every voter, asked to vote on countless ballot propositions becomes his or her own policy maker. What is more, it is easy for a voter to get on the ballot; in some mayoral primaries, for example, more than fifty persons may file for candidacy. After working through all the offices and ballot proposals, voters going to the polls can become mentally exhausted. Much of the ballot often goes unmarked. Even so, today's electorate will not support shortening the ballot.

Dull Elections

Ballot results show that the cure to voter apathy and fatigue is not so much learning good citizenship as it is holding exciting elections. However, for at least two reasons, the trend is toward less interesting local elections. The first is the pattern of shared decision making and intergovernmental relations by which no one person or legislative body can be held responsible for solving a particular problem. Even poorly informed citizens know that the mayor, the county board, or the school board cannot make the policy and carry it out. As discussed in the last chapter, one major project may require the cooperation of several local governments, many state departments, and numerous federal agencies. Putting the pieces together may take many fiscal years and elections. Those who want to give credit or blame are frustrated; many simply decide not to vote.

A second factor contributing to dull elections is an unintentional effect of the one-person, one-vote judicial rule, and that is to make all representative districts virtually identical in population size (see chapter 11). The nineteenth-century practice of drawing boundaries along social lines (such as ethnic makeup or annexed old towns) was abandoned. Contemporary boundaries, although of equal population, often have no meaning to voters; they may have fantastic, senseless shapes, and may have populations of such diverse and conflicting interests that no one can conscientiously claim to represent them adequately. Such districts are increasing in number because many local governments are shifting from at-large to district elections (see chapter 7). Meaningless or uninteresting local elections were not the goals of reformers but have been the result of at least some of their accomplishments.

Attitudinal Nonvoting

Finally, a low voter turnout may be a measure either of voter satisfaction or, more likely, of voter futility. At one time, almost all preferential nonvoters seemed apathetic (for whatever reason). They were characteristically poorly educated, had low incomes, were usually young, and had low information and interest levels. In the past several decades however, a new nonvoter has appeared, representing perhaps 15 percent of the total. These people, well educated with good incomes and *not* necessarily youthful, know that governmental decisions affect them. They are well informed about issues, and they pay taxes—some pay quite heavy taxes. But they deliberately choose not to vote. Studies indicate that they believe voting does not make any difference to their welfare; that they cannot change things by voting; that important governmental policies, although wrong, will not be changed by their vote, that the wrong choices are being offered on either domestic or foreign policy outcomes, or both. Such people, not likely to change their attitudes or behavior in the immediate future, may be increasing in number. They raise serious questions about the validity of a democratic system that relies on the election process to articulate policy demands, or even to satisfactorily check public policy makers.

Interest Groups in the Political Process

As Madison realized at the creation of the Constitution, although interest groups are necessary to preserving democratic principles in a federalist system, they also threaten the freedom of individuals (see chapter 2). Recent decades have seen an expansion of the number of interest groups in America.[15] We can therefore test Madison's observation that the greater the number of factions, the greater the likelihood that no single group will gain extraordinary power.

The political process is a by-product of the struggle for individual power, prestige, and security. Some people, in their search, become part of the relatively small group of the politically active.[16] The general public, politically passive though it may be, becomes a collection of groups seeking services from government to help themselves in turn achieve these same ends. Or they seek to prevent government from launching certain services if they believe their goals can be reached by some alternative nongovernmental activity.

To achieve desired objectives in public policy, individuals may choose to work through a political party. If the party stands for a defined set of principles, (common in European democracies) this approach is worthwhile. In the United States, however, major political parties are loose coalitions, each covering a variety of political viewpoints; this often is the case, even at the local level. Individuals belong to a political party for many reasons—for example economic status, geographic location, and family tradition. Seldom, however, can they go to the polls and vote for a set of policies. So they may choose to become active in a political party and seek to influence its policies. But the simple act of voting for the slate of a particular party will not guarantee selection of public officials with whom they are ideologically compatible. Persons wishing to influence public policy, usually will find it more expedient and fruitful to join forces with like-minded persons in an interest group. In fact, one individual may belong to a number of such groups, not all of which express like views toward the same policy questions. It is this overlap of membership in groups that helps mitigate conflicts and enables a stable system to develop.

Interests and Interest Groups

Philosophers and social scientists have long debated whether interests are derived from the individual or from the society. The subjective view holds that interests are preferences that individuals state for themselves. The objective view holds that what is in one's interest is determined by a consensus in society about the logical outcomes of one's actions. Both notions of interest are important to politics. The decision to vote rests on our faith in democracies that the subjective view is valuable; but public policy rests on the assumption that policy makers can determine what is in the interests of a "interest" greater than the voter. Use of the term *objective* should not be misconstrued. For example; all interests involve values; all politics involves values. The terms *objective interest* and *subjective interest* are used only to distinguish whether the interests are presumed to be from the viewpoint of the political actor or from the viewpoint of some greater number of people who agree that their logic dictates that something is valuable to someone else.[17]

In this book, a political interest is assumed to be either economic or ideological. Furthermore, an interest may be conceived of in either short- or long-run terms. The importance of ideology may vary from one socioeconomic group to another. This also may be true of willingness to consider long-term factors; that is, the rate at which the future is discounted. Similarly, an interest may be viewed in parochial or neighborhood terms, or it may be viewed in a socially and spatially broader context. Thus, subcultures form in the society that combine different group values, different demands on the political process, and different reactions to public policy. It seems probable that each subculture "has a more or less distinctive notion of how much a citizen ought to sacrifice for the sake of the community as well as of what the welfare of the community is constituted; in a word, each has its own idea of what justice requires and of the importance of acting justly."[18]

An interest group differs from a political party chiefly in that an interest group does not seek to capture offices for its members; instead, it *attempts* to influence public policy. It also differs from most U.S. political parties in that it is made up of persons with closely related interests and viewpoints—it is normally much more ideologically cohesive than a political party. Much has been said of the evil influences and danger of political pressure groups; some critics even suggest they be abolished or stringently controlled. Most such suggestions however, are, naive. After all, if we had a system of two or more political parties, each with a definite platform of proposed action to which the parties could be held, interest group *lobbying* would take place largely within the party structures, because it would be important to control platforms and policy directives. Such is not the case in the United States, however. Neither is it practical to say that a public official can determine the viewpoints of a cross section of the citizenry simply by noting the comments of those who contact him or her personally—not in any but the smallest villages, at any rate. And only the naive or foolhardy would suggest that officeholders should be elected with no promises to the public and then be entrusted to use their own free will and best judgment ''for all the people'' while in office. They must constantly be reminded of the nature of the shifting viewpoints of their constituents.

> *Lobbying:* **Various acts, often performed by full-time specialists, that seek to influence legislative and administrative officials so their actions in turn will be favorable to the lobbying group. Lobbyists also are frequently in charge of communicating opinions and information to legislators and the general public.**

Interest groups are a necessity in a modern democracy. They marshall individual opinions, organize them, and present them skillfully to governmental decision makers. Individual pressure groups no doubt sometimes go beyond the bounds of society's mores failing to portray accurately the interests, desires, and aspirations of their individual members and otherwise acting irresponsibly. But most are kept in check by the counterpart pressure group. That is, a watcher usually is also watched. In fact, public policy is, to some degree, the end result of the interaction among the various interest groups. Public policy in this sense is the total force and direction of each group as determined by its age, respectability, size of membership, wealth, ability of leadership, skill at lobbying, inside connections, intensity of interest, and other pertinent factors. But, as will become clear later in this chapter, all groups are not equal; nor should they be. The political system, understood in this way, should not be seen as inherently fair or good. We look at groups to understand some of the internal dynamics of politics.

Characteristics of Interest Groups and Those Who Join Them

Social scientists continue to debate why interest groups form.[19] Not everyone chooses to join groups, and not all groups are created for the same reasons. Some are created especially for the purpose of lobbying, whereas for others lobbying is only a sideline. Some are temporary organizations created to address a special problem, whereas others are permanent groups. Some, in large cities and at the state and national level, always actively lobby at the seat of government, but others lobby only when a matter of particular interest is under consideration. The National Rifle Association, for example, was created for the specific purpose of minimizing governmental control over private ownership and use of guns; lobbying, on the other hand, is only *one* of the many activities of the AFL-CIO. Temporary organizations often are created to campaign on a single matter (for example, a school bond issue). A manufacturers association or a part of government itself (for example, a state university) would have enough interests involved to be on hand constantly, at least when the legislative body is in session; but a group such as the motion-picture–theater operators might not engage in lobbying except when a measure is under consideration that affects its members.

Despite the plethora of groups, the role of the common individual should not be understated. Even though Americans are joiners, it is easy to exaggerate the extent to which they belong to organized interest groups that can represent them. Fewer than one-half of all adult Americans belong to voluntary organizations.[20] Of those who do, relatively few belong to more than one. In at least one case where middle-sized communities were to be studied, it was necessary to abandon an original attempt to observe their politics from the perspective of group participation because the groups were too few, too ephemeral, and too vague as to membership and strength of support in the area.[21]

The ability to influence government through membership in interest groups reflects the advantages of higher-income (and usually of higher-educated) persons. About 70 percent of persons in lower-income brackets do not belong to any groups, as compared with about one-third of high-income persons. Furthermore, about two-thirds of those with grade school educations do not belong to any organization, as compared with about 40 percent of college graduates and 20 percent of those with graduate degrees.[22]

Groups constantly realign their forces as expediency demands. It should not be assumed that politics is simply business versus labor—though that is a part of it—or that business executives always work together or that various groups operate in fairly permanent alignments.[23] Fluidity is one characteristic of the interest-group system. To take an example, we might find the National Education Association, a teachers union, in coalition with the Association of Towns in lobbying for more state spending on local governments. Once the percentage of shared revenue is more or less determined, however, the two groups might be lined up in bitter opposition over which local governments should get more of the shared revenue.[24] Business executives often line up on opposite sides of an issue. For example, downtown merchants might lobby before a city council for one-way streets, because this would channel traffic to their stores, but neighborhood shopping-area merchants might oppose one-way streets because of reduced accessibility to their locations. Downtown and neighborhood shopping-area merchants alike may favor municipally owned parking lots, whereas realtors are likely to oppose them. Labor unions frequently come into conflict with one another before legislative or administrative bodies. Business executives and labor leaders work together on many matters, as do upper-middle-class reformers and welfare recipients. Ours is a dynamic system.

Organized and Unorganized Groups

If all groups in society were organized and competent to present their sides of issues, the process of determining public policy through compromise among the various interests would be highly effective. It happens, however, that not all group interests are well protected. Less-articulate members of the working class are not so likely to have their views expressed before legislative bodies as are members of society's most prestigious groups. Group power varies in terms of status, inside connections, funds for distributing information on their positions, and other factors. It should not be assumed, however, that a group is strong because it is well organized or weak because it is unorganized. A well-organized and vigorously active group may, for example,

have its relative strength reduced through the gerrymandering of city councils or legislative bodies.[25] Organized labor, with its strength concentrated in small geographic
areas, is subject to this kind of limitation. In a democracy, virtually all groups are free
to organize and to lobby, but the ability of the members of a group to understand the
techniques of doing this varies greatly; even those who know how the process works
do not necessarily succeed. The result is a weakening of the representativeness of a
politics based on the summation of forces.

The relative strength of an interest group, in terms of numbers or by any other
single measure of power, is not necessarily proportional when compared with other
groups. The ability to use potential political resources depends to some extent on the
ideological acceptability of the particular interest as well as of its particular potential
resources. Those resources may include cash on hand, but may also be a measure of
"[q]uality leadership, access to political decision makers, a favorable public image," and "a hard working and knowledgeable staff . . . ."[26] Some critics dismiss
the American system as unduly biased toward the status quo and against the poor or
poorly organized persons of so-called low status. An example of a large group that is
highly restricted in political influence in relation to its size is the Hispanic population
in New Mexico (over one-third of the population). The Hispanic organization

> . . . has never been transformed into more modern forms of interest articulation such as
> those existing among women's groups, Indians, Blacks, labor unions and the like. Rea-
> sons include the heterogeneity of the Hispanic population; competition for access to
> government by more sophisticated Anglos in the women's movement and organized
> labor [older Hispanic leaders have adapted slowly to learn media requirements]; low
> levels of education among Hispanics; social tolerance of gerrymandering techniques in
> certain areas; and an extraordinary reluctance to air ethnic grievances, especially
> among Hispanic elites. For all these reasons, the state's Hispanic population cannot be
> considered to behave as an interest group, at least not to the same extent as Indians or
> feminists.[27]

Group Technique and Motivation

Groups vary according to their degree of organization, the techniques they use, and
the level to which they are motivated to participate in politics.

Techniques might be said to vary according to the way in which the group fits
into the system of cultural values. One group may be able to "get away with" something that would produce unfavorable publicity for another. For example, a medical
association may feel impelled to act within the public image of dignity it has created
for itself; a labor union can safely be more free-swinging in its behavior. A conservative group, with press approval may make recommendations concerning the election
of nonpartisan judges, a liberal group may be criticized by the same press for "interfering" if it does the same thing. Groups' political motivation has many bases. Some
organizations, for example, seek the sanctions or resources of the state to support
their own battles against other interests. Labor or management can benefit in their
struggles by having governmental officials or legal provisions that support one side.
Public employees have become such effective lobbyists that some state legislatures

have passed laws expressly prohibiting lobbying by them. For example, in 1989 an interpretation of a Wisconsin law prohibiting public employee lobbying resulted in a memo from the University of Wisconsin's lawyer admonishing all employees to take care not to represent themselves as speaking for a university department when contacting a state legislator about pending legislation. Such a lobbying effort, despite the protections of Wisconsin's Declaration of Rights (broader protection than in most states), could be a violation of the law.

As noted earlier, groups realign through time. One motivation for this is a change in status. Northern blacks who once thought they could not make economic or social progress through political action later found that they could. As a result, they have changed their behavior pattern from almost total political apathy to intense activity. Southern blacks, prevented from participating as recently as the 1960s in many areas, are now highly active and play major roles in determining the outcome of many southern elections. Even a prominent segregationist such as Governor George Wallace of Alabama eventually had to recognize the importance of appealing to the black vote in winning his last terms as governor in 1978 and 1982.

In other cases, one might make the generalization that the political activity of any group is proportional to its stake in the marginal definition of legality and of law-enforcement levels. The closer the group is to the line between legal and illegal, the more politically involved it becomes. Thus, middle-management bureaucrats in private industry are not intensely involved in politics, except by choice, because their jobs and life-styles are well within the bounds of accepted behavior. They are not likely to be in trouble with the law or find their welfare very dependent on its decisions. Similarly, professional bank robbers are not politically active because their job is so far outside the law that they cannot possibly hope to secure government sanction of their activities. But those on the edge of legality, where economic survival depends on marginal definitions, are the ones with the greatest stake in public policies and decisions, and they make the maximum investment in the political process. Thus, those groups advocating casino gambling in Atlantic City had to be politically active because this business is just barely acceptable as legitimate by American values.[28] And activism had to remain vitally important after the legalization, when it became clear that the casino operations would not be the solution to very many of Atlantic City's problems.

Americans vote, lobby, or otherwise take part in the political process according to their level of motivation. This, in turn, varies according to whether the individual's activities are well within the norms of society and of established public policy, or whether decisions on public policy that may affect the individual are unpredictable.

Groups and the Public Interest

When any group announces a policy position, it seeks explicitly or implicitly to associate its stand with the public interest. In fact, virtually every politically active individual or group claims to be acting in the name of public interest. Critics of the stand taken by a particular group, on the other hand, commonly complain that pressure groups are selfish and that they ought to act in the public interest. With everyone thus using the term *public interest*, it becomes useless as an analytical tool. Yes, it is a basic part of the myth of democracy to say that public policies are adopted—or ought to be—in the public interest. As such, the concept may serve a useful function in encouraging compliance with the law, which in turn is an important device for achieving a stable society. It is also useful as a symbol to remind legislators and administrators that no matter how many groups they may have listened to before making a decision, other groups and citizens who are unrepresented or underrepresented before them also will be affected by the decision. As one writer on the subject has said:

> Instead of being associated with substantive goals or policies, the public interest better survives identification with the process of group accommodation. The public interest rests not in some policy emerging from the settlement of conflict, but with the method of that settlement itself, with compromising in a peaceful, orderly, predictable way the demands put upon society.[29]

The Complexity of Interests—An Illustration

"There are two sides to every question," a teaching we all learn at an early age. Actually, this worthy proverb is quite untrue, as there are *many* sides to every question. The following description of the diversity of interests found in the Minnesota legislative session of 1931 relative to a single economic activity is still relevant.

> The [motoring] public wanted to reduce highway hazards by putting specific limitation on the length, width, height, and load capacities of motor vehicles. The large trucking firms wanted legislation to curb wildcat operators engaged in cutthroat competition. The railroads professed to work for the reduction of truck competition and the recapture of less than carload business, although they are actually playing a deeper game. Organized labor was chiefly interested in regulation of the wages, hours, and working conditions of truck drivers, while [unions representing] railroad workers carefully checked all proposed transportation legislation to determine its possible effects on the security of their jobs.[30]

This variety of viewpoints toward the same governmental activity, the regulation of the trucking industry, must be multiplied by the number of potential and actual governmental activities considered by a legislative body to approximate the staggering complexity of the total forces operating in the political process.

Types of Interest Groups

Interest groups operate in basically the same pattern whether on the national, state, or local level. To be sure, there may be differences in the relative balance of power of the various groups. On the national and state levels, for example, agricultural groups tend to be powerful, whereas in the cities they have but a small support group. Liquor lobbyists tend to be more powerful before state and local bodies than before the national government. Real estate groups and merchants tend to be extraordinarily powerful in city politics.

The relative strength of any lobby probably varies over time. Thus, in prosperous times, people may accept much leadership from, and make many concessions to, business leaders. In a recession, business groups fall into lower esteem and, hence, lower political strength. The pattern of interest group strengths varies from state to state. In some places, a single group seems to dominate the scene, but the group may be different in each state. In others, two very strong groups may be closely balanced and the pattern of conflict on many issues may reflect the struggle between these groups. In still others, many groups may be closely balanced with hegemony depending on the nature of the issue. Sugar interests and agricultural unions, which once dominated Hawaii's politics, now must compete with a variety of interest groups including, particularly, "small business, the tourist industry, development and environmental interests, native Hawaiians, and some public interest groups . . . ."[31]

So many business groups exert pressure on the government that they probably would overshadow and overpower all others were it not that they spend so much of their time opposing one another. An organization is equipped to lobby for every business interest in the city, county, or state. The pattern is so complex that a particular business may be represented by an elaborate combination of groups, some with broad interests that include those of a specific calling and others dealing with a particular type of business; the individual business executive may lobby before council or legislature. For example, a supermarket chain may have its interests represented generally by the state chamber of commerce but may also belong to an association of chain stores (which parries the thrusts of the convenience-store lobby), a retail food dealers organization, or package liquor dealers association (if some of the stores have permits to sell it); and the company itself may register a lobbyist. In addition, if the chain is encountering labor problems, it may contribute to a right-to-work committee that lobbies against the union shop, and the executives of the company may choose to help support the state taxpayers league.

Business groups that appear to have the same interests often are in competition with one another for governmental support and public opinion. A city may become an interest group that significantly affects the private interests of those within the metropolitan area outside the city borders. When Bloomington, the largest suburb of Minneapolis, granted permits and a good deal of support services for the building of a "megamall" (touted as the "largest mall in America," including an amusement park), stores at other malls around the metropolitan area feared for their own survival.[32]

Labor unions, once seen as illegitimate interest groups, fell on hard times in the 1980s, only a few decades after being accepted as part of the "establishment." The decline began with the loss to foreign economies of the "smokestack industries," which had been the bedrock of the labor union movement. The labor force grew rapidly in the 1980s with the expansion of service industries, but because members of these groups were little interested in organization, union membership stagnated. In 1989, 16.8 percent of American workers were unionized, down from 30 percent twenty years earlier. Ironically, given his experience as a labor leader in the Screen Actors' Guild, President Reagan's attack on labor, illustrated by his appointment of nontraditional labor people in the Department of Labor and the dispute with the air-traffic controllers, furthered the reduction of labor influence in politics at all levels.

Perhaps the labor groups of greatest recent importance to state and local governments have been the public employee unions, whose strengths vary widely from state to state. In Wisconsin, for example, the successful passage of no-strike, mandatory arbitration for teachers and local government employees contributed to relatively high wage settlements and likelihood that Democratic candidates for statewide office must court the public employee unions for statewide success.[33] When Democratic Governor Tony Earl lost favor with university employees, the largest employee group, he lost his reelection bid to Republican Tommy Thompson. In neighboring Minnesota, the state Democratic party, known as the DFL (Democratic Farmer Labor party), owes its name to a merger of interest groups—including labor—in 1944. In California, unions of the state government, local governments and teachers are among the most powerful in politics. In Florida, one study concludes unions have become a major influence on cities and school districts.[34] In contrast, labor unions in Texas are relatively unimportant and play a small role in either state or local politics.[35]

Major interests that usually are represented before state and local governments would include the following:

- Chambers of commerce or manufacturers associations
- Banks
- Downtown merchants associations
- Public utilities
- Railroads, truckers, taxicab companies
- Insurance companies
- General contractors
- Lawyers, physicians, dentists, teachers, and other professions
- Realtors
- Liquor and race track interests
- Newspapers
- General labor union organizations and their subdivisions
- Racial, ethnic, and religious organizations
- Public employees, government officials, veterans
- Agricultural and conservation groups
- Highway interests
- Good-government and reform groups

Protest groups are a common phenomenon in American society. Although the issue that generates them changes through time, such groups usually share reluctance to use conventional interest group politics to produce what they want. Violence, either by them or toward them, has been a common occurrence. Angry farmers from Massachusetts who joined in what came to be known as Shays's Rebellion contributed to a call for a stronger national government that lead to the Constitution. The burning of the Charleston Convent in Boston in 1834, followed by the attack on a Catholic funeral procession by firemen in 1837 (known as the Broad Street riot), illustrates the level of religious conflict in that period. The civil rights movement of the 1950s and 1960s borrowed heavily from the unconventional tactics developed by labor unions earlier in this century. In recent decades, fundamentalist religious groups have favored similar tactics to protest government policy on abortion. Groups that employ protest tactics almost always require response on the part of governmental agencies, mostly local police forces, who themselves may become active participants in the conflict. Whether protest group demands are legitimate or not, they place extraordinary pressures on the resources of local governments in the short run and often change the ways in which local government resources are distributed in the long run.

In addition to the groups representing the major pressures, legislative bodies are intermittently subjected to the idiosyncratic behavior of the extreme left and right fringes of the political continuum and to the loud and insisted demands of crackpots, faddists, zealots, headline grabbers, representatives of unusual businesses, and inventors of schemes and machines. California has had colorful lobbies, such as the Antivivisection League, the Dancing Masters of California, the Dog Defenders League, the Pines to Palms Wildlife Committee, the State Council of Trail Hound Clubs, and the Western Nudist Conference.[36]

Concluding Note

Even though the tendency of the electorate seems to be toward greater inactivity, America demonstrates an inexhaustible supply of active voluntary groups, each of which shows an interest in affecting public policy. The next chapter will examine groups in the election process, principally as they coalesce into political parties. Later chapters will return to the task of groups in the institutions and political processes of state and local governments.

Notes

1. See Sidney Verba and Norman H. Nie, *Participation in America* (New York: Harper & Row, 1972), 156.

2. Raymond Wolfinger, *Who Votes?* (New Haven, CT: Yale University Press, 1980), 42.

3. Samuel C. Patterson and Gregory A. Caldeira, "Getting Out the Vote: Participation in Gubernatorial Elections," *American Political Science Review* 77 (1983): 675–89. See also Norman R. Luttbeg, "Differential Voting Turnout Decline in the American States, 1960–82," *Social Science Quarterly* 65 (March 1984): 60–73.

4. See Sarah McCally Morehouse, *State Politics, Parties and Policy* (New York: Holt, Rinehart and Winston 1981), 83.

5. Wilbourn E. Benton, *Texas Politics, Constraints and Opportunities*, 5th ed. (Chicago: Nelson-Hall Publishers, 1984), 64

6. *Harper* v. *Virginia State Board of Elections*, 383 U.S. 663 (1966).

7. The registration and requirements for a particular state can be found in the latest edition of *Book of the States* (Lexington, KY: Council of State Governments).

8. Wolfinger, *Who Votes?*, 73.

9. *1986–1987 Book of the States*, 177–178; *1988–1989 Book of the States*, 180.

10. Most of the study has been at the national level. It is presumed that the conclusions about the national government generally apply to the states.

11. Malcolm E. Jewell and David M. Olson, *Political Parties and Elections in American States*, 3d ed. (Chicago: The Dorsey Press, 1988), 208.

12. Ibid., 108–20.

13. Robert V. Presthus, *Men at the Top,* (Fair Lawn, NJ: Open University Press, 1964), 432–33.

14. Rich Connell, "Senior Citizens May Have Big Say in School Elections," *Los Angeles Times,* April 6,1989, part II, pp. 1, 8; also, W. W. Crouch et al., *California Government and Politics,* 7th ed. (Englewood Cliffs, NJ: Prentice-Hall 1981), 218–21.

15. Kay Lehman Schlozman and John T. Tierney, *Organized Interests and American Democracy* (New York: Harper & Row, 1986), chapter 4. Although the authors studied the nation's capital, the same conclusions apply to a state capital or to a major city.

16. See the writings of Harold Lasswell, especially *Psychopathology and Politics* (Chicago: University of Chicago Press, 1930), and *Power and Personality* (New York: W. W. Norton, 1948).

17. Schlozman and Tierney, *Organized Interests,* 16–35.

18. James Q. Wilson and Edward C. Banfield, "Public Regardingness as a Value Premise in Voting Behavior," *American Political Science Review* 58 (Dec. 1964): 885. Banfield also attempts to identify and define these classes in *The Unheavenly City Revisited* (Boston: Little, Brown, 1974).

19. Schlozman and Tierney, *Organized Interests,* chapter 6.

20. As noted in Schlozman and Tierney, *Organized Interests,* 59, footnote 6. We have no recent national poll material and therefore accept the continued validity of the older studies. Further substantiation can be found in Ronald J. Hrebenar and Ruth K. Scott, *Interest Group Politics in America* (Englewood Cliffs, NJ: Prentice-Hall, 1982), chapter 2. Two of the older studies that measured this are Verba and Nie, *Participation in America,* and Charles R. Wright and Herbert H. Hyman, "Voluntary Association Membership of American Adults," *American Sociological Review* 23 (June 1958): 284–94.

21. Oliver P. Williams and Charles R. Adrian, *Four Cities* (Philadelphia: University of Pennsylvania Press, 1963).

22. "A National Metropolitan Work Force Survey," April 1976, as cited by Schlozman and Tierney, *Organized Interests,* 59–63.

23. Jeffrey M. Berry, *The Interest Group Society,* 2d ed. (Glenview, IL: Scott, Foresman/Little Brown, 1989), chapter 10.

24. See the discussion of this conflict, Michael Fine and Mort Sipress, "Budget and Finance," in Wilder Crane, A. Clarke Hagensick et al., eds., *Wisconsin Government and Politics,* 4th ed. (Milwaukee: Department of Governmental Affairs, University of Wisconsin-Milwaukee, 1987), 245-48.

25. For a discussion of gerrymandering, see chapters 7 and 11.

26. Hrebenar and Scott, *Interest Group Politics in America,* 62.

27. Jose Garcia with Clive S. Thomas, "New Mexico: Traditional Interests in a Traditional State" in Ronald J. Hrebenar and Clive S. Thomas, eds., *Interest Group Politics in the American West* (Salt Lake City: University of Utah Press, 1987), 940.

28. George Sternlieb and James Hughes, *Atlantic City Gamble* (Cambridge, MA: Harvard University Press, 1984).

29. Frank J. Sorauf, "The Public Interest Reconsidered," *Journal of Politics* 19 (Nov. 1957) :638. See also Glendon A. Schubert, Jr., *The Public Interest* (New York: The Free Press, 1960); and E. P. Herring, *Public Administration and the Public Interest* (New York: McGraw-Hill, 1936). The way in which administrators and judges view the public interest is discussed in chapters 10 and 13 herein.

30. George H. Mayer, *The Political Career of Floyd B. Olson* (Minneapolis: University of Minnesota Press, 1951), 74. Olson was governor of Minnesota from 1931 to 1936. Used by permission of, and copyright 1951 by, The University of Minnesota Press.

31. Anne F. Lee, "Hawaii: Planters, Public Employees, and the Public Interest," in Hrebenar and Thomas, eds., *Interest Group Politics,* 62.

32. *StarTribune,* June 11, 1989, p.1.

33. Mordecai Lee, "Interest Groups," in Crane, Hagensick et al., *Wisconsin Government . . . ,* 84.

34. Robert Benedetti and Manning J. Dauer, "Cities and Counties," in Manning J. Dauer, ed., *Florida's Politics and Government,* 2d ed. (Gainesville: University Press of Florida, 1984), 210.

35. Benton, *Texas Politics,* 30.

36. Most states, including California, require lobbies to register with the state (see chapter 12), and many states also compile lists of interest groups whether or not they lobby. Such a list usually can be found in a state legislative manual.

The American Way

6

Parties, Elections, and Direct Democracy

Individuals may participate in the American political system in a variety of ways. Despite widespread apathy and futility, participation commonly involves interest groups or the decision to vote. Some *individuals* become involved in campaign activities, elections, or voting on issues.[1] Although other commitments prevent most citizens from running for office at the national level, bringing in a few hundred to a few thousand votes and working a few nights a month are sufficient to be elected as a city council member or county board member. Our attraction to direct democracy receded as we became a more industrialized country with a large population, but the occasional town meeting, recall petition, or initiative or referendum vote still allows for direct participation. This chapter therefore will look at the election process, beginning with the political party and following with a discussion of election mechanisms for candidates and issues. Because emphasis on general theories of parties and elections requires more detail than is possible here, we will concentrate instead on those election aspects that distinguish state and local patterns from national ones. Furthermore, it should be remembered that the political party plays many roles outside the election process. These will be considered in later chapters, particularly in the context of state and local legislatures.

Political Parties

A political party is a coalition that persists over time for the purpose of gaining elective public offices, organizing legislatures, or promoting political platforms. As such, a party differs from an interest group (or pressure group), which is a group of people banded together for the purpose of promoting social or economic interests. Of course, a political party may be ideologically cohesive—the members may all have the same basic values and attitudes toward issues of public policy—which generally is true in most European democracies. But it is not true for mainstream parties in America. Today, American candidates have become self-starters who choose the party; rarely does the party actually recruit the candidate for election. Nevertheless, regardless of ideological commitments, a candidate's affiliation with the party and success in party nomination procedures usually are prerequisites to success in partisan general elections.

Party Organization

Party structure, like election machinery, is determined in large measure by the desires of the party or faction in power at the time the laws or rules are adopted or modified. Seldom are basic theoretical questions regarding what is democratically desirable or the total political picture considered in making laws or rules to deal with these matters. Until the reform movement, which began at the end of the nineteenth century, and demanded legal requirements for party organization, the structure of each group was determined by its own leadership and varied according to time and party. Today, parties are controlled (as to organizational pattern) by detailed state law and formal rules as well as informal arrangements established to meet the needs of the moment. The latter may be far different from the former, and detailed rules and laws probably have not been of much importance in shaping political patterns. They are most predominant with regard to the nomination processes.

The meaning of party membership in the United States is vague, for very few individuals participate actively in partisan campaigning. The term *party membership* is most useful if we say that a member of a party is someone who identifies with a particular party label. No one is elected to membership and, except for a few doctrinaire parties, no one carries a party card or is subject to expulsion. Membership varies from confirmed partisans, who always vote the straight party or faction line, to the independent, who reluctantly registers as a party member only because it is necessary in order to vote in the primary election.

Ironically, the pronounced decline of party discipline came with the defeat of machines by earlier reformers, especially following World War I and during the Great Depression.[2] After World War II, a wave of interest swept through party organizations, with reformers and political scientists calling for increased party discipline. These later reformers assumed that discipline would produce a higher level of party responsibility—that parties with a high degree of internal control over membership would also become programmatic parties. If this assumption was correct, the two major parties presumably would take different positions, which would permit a real choice of public policies by voters. On the other hand, said reformers, opponents of party responsibility "conjure up visions of polarized parties, downtrodden minorities, and multipartyism as the fruits of party responsibility. They are able to make these improbable references by working with an exceedingly simple model, by ignoring the functions of party competition and the complex of factors that seem to shape party systems."[3]

Even in the few states where political parties have reasonably identifiable positions on current issues many party members do not agree with the party position; and probably even more members do not vote for the party because of its stand on issues. Members tend to vote for a party for traditional reasons or as a result of symbolic appeals or dramatic candidates rather than in response to rational arguments. Studies of delegates to state party conventions (one measure of party regularity) find that the party regulars are more often "people of accomplishment (as shown by education and income)'' and usually people of greater ideological intensity than those who simply vote for the party. But the party organization is designed to win elections not to worry about ideological consistency, even among delegates. In the electoral process, the party often can provide some modest funding for those seeking statewide office; coordinate or initiate the production of poll data; and coordinate efforts to get out the vote, though this always has been more true in the East than in the West.[4]

Local parties usually are more disorganized than organized. Gone in most places is the familiar machine structure that characterized local parties in the days between the Civil War and World War II. Even in the average local majority party, leaders "often lack the incentives with which to staff and maintain the most active party organization" and "the political culture of the locale does not recognize the propriety of the politics of reward and sanction on which machine organization rests."[5] In the more disorganized parties,

> . . . most of the committee positions in the party's county unit are unfilled or are held by completely inactive incumbents. A chairman and a handful of loyal party officials may meet occasionally to carry out the most essential affairs of the party. Their main activity occurs shortly before the primary elections, as they plead with members of the party to become candidates or step in themselves as candidates to "fill the party ticket." They are largely without influence or following, for theirs is often a chronic minority party. They meet infrequently, raise little money for election campaigns, and create little or no public attention.[6]

Some analysts, however, cling to the idea that state and local parties thrive. Whether this notion is valid depends partly on what is used to measure party strength. For example, some evidence suggests that even though parties declined in terms of their traditional ability to affect voters, they actually strengthened some aspects of organization, such as the activism of those most involved and the efforts to sustain organization during nonelection periods.[7] Yet the same studies show that state parties are not coordinated efforts from national to state to local level. "Local party organizational strength is relatively independent of the strength of the state party organizations, despite the fact that state party organizations give substantial quantities of assistance to the local parties."[8]

Party Competition

The influence of party competition on voting and policy making has never been fully assessed, but a number of theories are supported. Although electoral party influence is on the wane in the mass media age, we are entering a period of widespread party competition that is new to the twentieth century. From the Civil War to the New Deal, the Republicans prevailed in northern states and the Democrats in the South. During this period, the opposition stood little chance of winning the legislature or governorship in these states.[9] Party realignment in the 1930s produced some competitive states in the North, whereas the South remained Democratic. As recently as the 1970s, only one-fourth of the states had genuine competition between the two major parties for state offices. In the others, factions within the dominant party predominated more than the party itself.

Party competition changed dramatically in the 1980s. Following the 1990 election, only 20 of 49 states with partisan legislatures (Nebraska is nonpartisan) had one party in control of both the legislature and the governorship; in 17 states the Democrats controlled, and the Republicans controlled in the other 3. Nine of these states, however, showed other types of party splits in statewide elections; for example, Democratic Mississippi had two Republican U.S. senators, and seven Democratic states had one. The Republican state of South Dakota had one Democratic U.S. senator. In only eleven (22 percent) of the states were the governor, U.S. senators and the state legislature controlled by one party (see table 6–1).

An earlier generation of political scientists had great faith in party competition's effect on the rationality of the voter—greater choice would mean greater clarity of issue and policy—but few present-day analysts see increased voter rationality during the period of increased competition. Increases in party competition have come during a period of continued decline in voter turnout (for the reasons outlined in the last chapter), increased influence of media-oriented campaigning, and declining party importance. Ironically, as the minority party becomes more competitive, the candidates rely less on the party and more on the image-making methods of electioneering.

Voting patterns and party allegiance seem to grow more complicated, as does American life. When the election is over, the balance of power may shift in a state; a minority party may become the majority party in government, bringing a new type of politics and a new style of political leadership. The effects on the party preparing for the next election are often as great as the effects on those governing. In the usual state system (single-member district representation), losing district elections provides minimal reward—no seats in the legislature.[10] But even the party that loses an election will remain better organized and more active when both parties have a real chance to win statewide, or even legislative, races. Although individual races may seem out of reach because of well-entrenched incumbents, the party can set its sights on keeping or recapturing a majority by winning the more competitive statewide elections or zeroing in on the few seats that might change hands and swing the balance in the legislature.

Even though the Madisonian system of checks and balances (discussed in chapter 2) was not originally designed with political parties in mind, today's parties provide some of the best opportunities for such checking. After the election is over, parties play a crucial role in government, particularly in organizing the legislative branch. Most governors find what Republican presidents have found since World War II: Winning office is easier than governing. Party division between the legislative and executive branch means greater emphasis on compromise and greater likelihood that changes in public policy will be incremental. Such party deadlock among policy makers may give even more power to the bureaucrats who must implement political decisions.

When a district is not competitive, the political process works differently. Legislators elected from noncompetitive districts usually are assured renomination and therefore are free from much concern with reelection; the nomination is tantamount to election. As will be shown later in the chapter, the nomination process is different from the general election in a number of important respects, particularly in terms of

TABLE 6–1   Party Competition, 1990–1991

State	Governor	State Legislature	U.S. Senate
Alabama	R	D	D
Alaska	I	S	R
Arizona	D	S	S
Arkansas	D	D	D
California	R	D	S
Colorado	D	R	S
Connecticut	I	D	D
Delaware	R	S	S
Florida	D	D	S
Georgia	D	D	D
Hawaii	D	D	D
Idaho	D	R	R
Illinois	R	D	D
Indiana	D	S	R
Iowa	R	D	S
Kansas	D	S	R
Kentucky	D	D	S
Louisiana	D	D	D
Maine	R	D	S
Maryland	D	D	D
Massachusetts	R	D	D
Michigan	R	S	D
Minnesota	R	D	S
Mississippi	D	D	R
Missouri	R	D	R
Montana	R	D	S
Nebraska	D	Nonpartisan	D
Nevada	D	D	D
New Hampshire	R	R	R
New Jersey	D	D	D
New Mexico	D	D	S
New York	D	S	S
North Carolina	R	D	S
North Dakota	D	S	D
Ohio	R	S	D
Oklahoma	D	D	S
Oregon	D	S	R
Pennsylvania	D	S	R
Rhode Island	D	D	S
South Carolina	R	D	S
South Dakota	R	R	S
Tennessee	D	D	D
Texas	D	D	S
Utah	R	R	R
Vermont	R	S	S
Virginia	D	D	S
Washington	D	D	S
West Virginia	D	D	D
Wisconsin	R	D	S
Wyoming	D	R	R
Total	29D,19R,2I	31D,6R,12S	17D,11R,26S
			(56D,44R)

Key: D-Democrat, R-Republican, S-Split, I-Independent; legislative houses with even splits are listed as S.

149

who participates in the process. When the campaign experience of such legislators is different from those from competitive districts, they may be allowed to campaign for others (often securing enduring friendships) and may therefore increase their prospects for legislative leadership roles.

When lack of competition extends beyond a few districts to the whole state or local government, factions often arise. Two or more groups or factions in these governments (even in some competitive states) use the same party label, although groups may be as competitive with one another for public office as if they bore different labels. Thus, many Southern and border states are made up of factions, each a political party within the definition given above but all calling themselves the "Democrats."[11] Similar factions are found in both major parties in all parts of the nation. For example, in New York and California in the 1960s, Democrats split between liberal reformers and party regulars, and Indiana and Minnesota in the 1980s have seen Republicans split between the usual party participants and religious fundamentalists. Since the death of the elder Mayor Daley in 1976, Chicago has been split into factions in every mayor's race.

The primary election process has tended to encourage factionalism, with the result that the United States does not have two parties but rather dozens perhaps hundreds of them. Yet we think of only two parties because nearly all factions call themselves either Republicans or Democrats. (In this book, "party" will refer specifically to all factions grouped under a single label.)

Nonpartisan Elections: The Prevailing Urban Pattern

Early in the twentieth century, reformers began to advocate nonpartisan elections. Today, the nonpartisan ballot is used widely and is particularly popular in the Midwest and the area west of the Mississippi, especially in municipal elections. The device is also found in school, township, judicial, county, and other elections.[12] For example, all municipal, town, and village elections, county supervisor elections, and judicial elections in Wisconsin are nonpartisan by law, as are all local and judicial elections in California.

The term *nonpartisanship* has various meanings. Sometimes it is used, especially in newspapers, when *bipartisanship* is meant; sometimes in connection with elections in areas so overwhelmingly dominated by a single party that the party label in effect becomes meaningless; sometimes as part of the political ideology of the middle-class suburbanite, which emphasizes rational discussion toward consensus on the best person for the job. Finally, the term is used to refer to an election system in which no party labels appear on the ballot, although political parties may in fact be involved in the election campaign. Because the ballot generally is a long one, with many candidates to be selected; nonpartisan elections in the United States are to be distinguished from ordinary partisan elections in most of the British Commonwealth countries, where the party of the candidate does not appear on the ballot either, but party identification is easy to determine because the ballot is brief.

When progressivism and urban reform were at a peak, many states adopted the nonpartisan ballot for municipal, judicial, and school elections. Three states—California, Minnesota, and North Dakota—made county offices nonpartisan. Others elect most county officials on the partisan ballot. (In Wisconsin, for example, the county board members are elected on the nonpartisan ballot, but the sheriff and county clerk remain on a partisan ballot.) The Nebraska legislature was placed on the nonpartisan ballot in 1935 (following the lead of Minnesota which, after sixty year's of nonpartisanship, returned to a partisan legislature in 1972) and is the only nonpartisan state today. Probably more than one-half of all elections to public office in the United States now use the nonpartisan ballot. The ballot is used for most school elections and over 70 percent of municipal elections (see table 6-2), including almost all of suburbia and wherever reform governments prevail unless state law does not permit it.[13]

Evidence indicates that partisan and nonpartisan politicians are not insulated into separate compartments, as they once tended to be. In an era of self-starting candidates who raise their own campaign funds and organize their own campaigns or hire managers, this is in no way unusual. Sometimes those who begin their careers in the nonpartisan arena later run for partisan office. In fewer cases, the opposite career pattern has appeared (probably because fewer more important jobs are found in that direction). But as we will discuss in later chapters, different career patterns are followed for executives and legislators at the state and local levels. Although local officials are more likely to have other vocations, reducing the likelihood of their running for higher office, state politicians—usually elected initially on a partisan ballot—more often view politics as their craft.

The Election Process

Elections involve two processes: nomination, or the selection of candidates; and the general elections proper, where candidates actually are chosen. In each process voters may decide issues of public policy through the devices of "direct democracy" (see discussion later in this chapter). The basic machinery of elections, which is controlled by law in all states, has evolved gradually. The machinery has been manipulated to benefit the groups that happen to dominate state constitutional conventions,

TABLE 6–2 Partisan and Nonpartisan Elections

	Total Cities Reporting	Partisan	Nonpartisan
All Cities	3,927	1,076 (27.4%)	2,851 (72.6%)
Forms of Government			
Mayor-Council	1,707	666 (39.0%)	1,041 (61.0%)
Council Manager	2,102	380 (18.1%)	1,722 (81.9%)
Commission	118	30 (25.4%)	88 (74.6%)

Source: Charles R. Adrian, "Forms of City Government in American History," *Municipal Year Book, 1988* (Washington, D.C.: International City Management Association, 1988), 8.

legislatures, and other institutions through which the election procedures can be controlled. Because this is the case, election law varies greatly from one state to another and even from one locality to another within a state.

Methods of Nomination

Before there can be an election, the nominees must be selected and numerous ways exist for placing candidates in nomination. The large majority of nominations today are either by the partisan or the nonpartisan direct primary election. Other techniques include caucus or convention, sponsorship, and petition.

Early Nomination Devices

The caucus, the oldest form of nomination in the United States, consisted originally of an informal meeting to choose candidates for the various public offices becoming vacant. But with the growth of cities, the caucus became too large and eventually declined. To overcome the problem of unwieldiness, the convention method came into use. Under this approach nominations were made at formal meetings with the membership in the convention made up of delegates chosen by caucus at the precinct—or smallest political subdivision—level. But the widespread development of citywide or statewide political machines in the nineteenth century made this method subject to corruption.

The machine controlled the precinct caucus by excluding unwanted persons. This could be done by keeping secret the time and place of meetings, by threats, by better strategic planning, and by other devices. Whoever controlled the precinct caucuses controlled the convention. Because one party was dominant in most cities, counties, and states and a balanced two-party system was the exception, the machines often controlled the elective office simply by controlling the nomination process.

Reforms in Nomination

Beginning early this century, the reform movement produced a change in nomination procedure. The direct *primary election* was substituted for the caucus and convention. It is now almost universal in the United States although for some offices a few states use it in combination with the convention.

Primary Election: **A method for nominating candidates for public office by which voters have a direct choice from among those who wish to be considered for nomination.**

A primary election is a nonassembled caucus. When the conventions proved unrepresentative and class- or boss-ridden, the primary election was devised to return nominations "to the people." In large measure the plan transfers control of the nomination machinery from the party to the state, with all parties choosing their candidates on the same day under the supervision of public election officials through secret ballots that were standardized and usually printed at public expense (in contrast to many caucus and convention systems).

Since Connecticut adopted the direct primary as its principal nominating device in 1955, every state has used some form of the primary for certain offices. The method, first used under Democratic party control in Pennsylvania in the 1840s gradually spread. By the 1870s it was used for statewide nominations, with Wisconsin becoming the first (in 1903) to adopt compulsory statewide primary elections. Despite the leadership of Wisconsin, which probably can be attributed to the reform zeal generated by "Fightin' Bob" LaFollette, it was in the South that the primary system first came into general use. This appears to have resulted from efforts on the part of excluded groups and classes to overcome the oligarchical nature of one-partyism.[14] The primary was adopted first in the one-party states and later in the competitive two-party states. After the South, the West picked up the plan, then the Midwest, and finally the East, where old and well-established party systems delayed acceptance.

As recently as the 1970s, Indiana, New York, and Delaware used conventions as the only method of nominating gubernatorial candidates. Virginia still uses the method for both party's gubernatorial candidates.[15] Numerous local candidates are nominated through caucuses. Some California cities as well as school districts in some states make use of nomination by petition directly onto the final ballot, with the candidate who receives a plurality being declared elected. This method saves the expense of primary elections and usually has satisfactory results in small cities, but when the plan was in effect in Boston, it created controversy because the mayor was sometimes a plurality, rather than majority, choice. Some California cities use the sponsor system, which requires a petition signed by only a few persons, the "sponsors" of the candidate. A sum of money must be paid as a filing fee (unless the candidate takes a pauper's oath), and it is returned under certain conditions. More often in other states these petition procedures are used to determine eligibility for the primary ballot, reducing the clutter of superfluous candidates.

In a number of states, conventions are held prior to primaries for a variety of party organizational reasons, to draft platforms, and to select delegates to national nominating conventions. Furthermore, they often endorse candidates who run in the primaries. In a few states convention endorsement is legally necessary to get on the ballot. In others, the informal endorsement process affects the primary, often heading off challenge at the polls. For years, Minnesotans have taken such informal endorsement seriously. The experience of Governor Rudy Perpich demonstrates the possibilities. Perpich first assumed the vacant governorship from his office as lieutenant governor in 1976, then lost the general election despite party endorsement in 1978. Four years later, he won election without endorsement after successfully challenging the party's endorsed candidate in a primary, and then won reelection in 1986 with party endorsement. In 1990 he lost his reelection bid with endorsement to the unendorsed Republican, Arne Carlson.

A survey of twenty states with endorsing conventions found the endorsement so decisive that challengers are almost nonexistent in six state parties, endorsees rarely are beaten in another ten state parties, and only four state parties produce endorsements that are usually challenged and occasionally upset.[16]

Types of Primaries
Primary elections may be nonpartisan or partisan. In both types, candidates for nomination usually qualify for a place on the primary ballot by securing a required number of signatures of qualified voters on a petition.

The nonpartisan primary is actually an elimination contest. Names appear on the ballot without party designation. The first election, popularly and sometimes legally called a primary, serves to eliminate all candidates except twice the number to be elected. Hence, if seven candidates file for the office of mayor, only two will survive the primary, the two with the highest number of votes. If seven members of the council are to be elected, the fourteen highest in the primary are nominated. In some cases, such as in many California cities and in elections for the Chicago city council, if any candidate receives a majority of the vote cast in the primary, that candidate is declared elected. this plan serves to avoid the cost of placing such a candidate on the final ballot, even though in the absence of such a rule, it would be possible for a candidate to receive a majority of votes in the primary and still lose the final election. (This rule is based on the assumption that the distribution of the vote is about the same in the low-turnout primary as in the regular election, but as is well known, this is manifestly not the case.)

In practice, primary rules are mechanisms of potential advantage. For some candidates, winning in the general election is a far simpler task than winning the primary. In 1975, Louisiana, traditionally one of the most Democratic states, adopted the nonpartisan primary for statewide and congressional races. It apparently was a ploy by the Democrats to head off the resurgence of the Republican party by forcing Republicans to compete against Democrats early in the election process, rather than waiting for the primary-worn Democratic nominee in a general election. Apparently it has succeeded in protecting incumbents, mostly Democrats.[17] In recent elections for mayor of Chicago, long-time machine Democrats, fearing a wave of reform and antimachine minority strength, considered running as independents or even Republicans, similarly to sidestep the problem of winning the primary.

Partisan primaries are usually referred to as *open* or *closed* although in actuality degrees of each exist. The most open primary, the *blanket primary* (used statewide in Alaska and Washington), allows voters to choose candidates from either party for each office, although they may vote for only one candidate for each office. Less open primaries allow the voter to choose party ballots on the day of the election but require that the voter stay within one party's choices at that primary. This form of primary either requires the voter to state publicly the choice of party at the polls by requesting a ballot of that party (eleven states), or it allows the voter to choose inside the voting booth (nine states). In the most closed primaries, the voter must designate the party of choice by registration at some designated time prior to the election, and record is kept of that registration (seventeen states). At election time, the voter is allowed to choose only names on the ballot of the party he or she is registered with. Semiclosed primaries exist in the remaining ten states, either allowing new voters to choose at election time or allowing voters to switch affiliation at the time of election, despite the written registration requirement. Two such states have special rules allowing registered independents to vote in a party primary, even though separate registration for independents exists.[18]

Debate about how open the partisan primary should be centers on the question of whether the primary is seen as an integral part of the election or a party tool used prior to the election. Those who see the primary as an integral part of the election process argue that closing the primary diminishes the right to vote; opponents argue that logic dictates a closed system of election. They ask, "Why should members of the opposition be allowed to interfere in 'our' party?" With voter loyalty to the party declining, however, a more open door seems highly likely in the future.

Open primaries do allow the mischief of crossover voting, when voters choose the opposition party ballot deliberately to select a weak opponent for the general election or simply because their own party offers no "real" choices. The practice is less common when many important races take place in one election. Then, with the exception of the blanket primary process, crossing over eliminates the opportunity to vote for other offices in the party of registration. Of course, a voter may cross over even in the closed primary, but this requires advance planning and some degree of dishonesty (rarely illegality) when registering. In 1948, using procedures no longer allowed, Republican Earl Warren won both Democratic and Republican nominations for governor of California. More recently, the national Democratic party has insisted on closing the primary system for choice of delegates to the national convention. This led to a 1981 Supreme Court case compelling Wisconsin Democrats to abide by Democratic National Committee rules.[19] But the national parties rarely use this legal hold over states in national elections because they fear that angering potential supporters in the nomination process by challenging parochial concerns will come back to haunt them in the general election. Although, they could have compelled compliance with the rules, Wisconsin was allowed to use the open primary to select Democratic delegates in 1988.

The Runoff Primary

The tendency in all states is for popular interest to concentrate in the primary of the stronger party. As chances diminish for the minority party to win elections, popular participation in that party's primary also decreases—but at a faster rate. In the South, the advantage of the Democratic party has been so great that ten states (including Louisiana, mentioned earlier) have tried to ensure majority choice for public office by requiring a *runoff primary* in cases where no candidate wins a majority in the first primary. The runoff, which usually is conducted between the two candidates getting the most votes in the first primary, is used to prevent the manipulation of the results by flooding the ballot with a multiplicity of candidates. The runoff ensures that the candidate who finally wins is acceptable to a majority of those voting, though not necessarily a first choice. (Under these rules, *A* defeats *B*, but it is easy to demonstrate mathematically that if more candidates and "exhaustive" voting were permitted in the runoff, either or both might lose.) Minority group members (particularly blacks) who have had success at heading off primary challenges within their group have described the runoff election as an institutional tool to discourage their election. (The runoff was not devised for this purpose, however. It was in use long before blacks would vote in force in the South.)

Public Attitude

Because in many parts of the nation nomination is tantamount to election—even in two-party states and many one-party areas—the ordinary citizen regards the primary as an integral part of the election process, the part where very often the *real* decisions are made. Americans resent that they usually must reveal their party preference in order to vote; and even when the open primary is used, they are incensed to discover that splitting the ticket is not permitted (except where the blanket primary is used). Yet the primary symbolizes popular participation in the political process, and the device undoubtedly has helped to restore genuine popular competition in the process of selecting public officers after that competition had all but disappeared in many parts of the country as a result of the rise of one-partyism and bossism in the years following the Civil War.

The primary election has always had its critics. They have pointed out, for example, that the primary produces extra elections and a long ballot, at least in those areas where nominations are genuinely competitive. The long ballot confuses, frustrates, and discourages the voter. The primary election has never enjoyed a large measure of popular participation, if long-run averages are considered. As noted in the previous chapter, nonvoting has become more common than voting; typically just over one-half of those who vote in the general election also vote in the primary. The exception is where one party dominates the general election, making the primary election the "real" election. In the South between 1969 and the off-presidential gubernatorial elections in 1986, more people voted in the Democratic primaries than in the general election. But this pattern is fading.[20]

The need to conduct a campaign for the nomination discourages many individuals from entering the race or even from indicating that they are available for nomination. The primary is expensive for those who must campaign against competition for a nomination, and the goal of making all interested and qualified persons easily available for the public to nominate is thus frustrated by the fact that only the wealthy or those financed by party or interest group can afford to enter. Rarely will a party help finance a candidate in a contested primary.

The primary has not greatly changed the kinds of persons nominated for office, as its originators hoped it would, though it may contribute to the nomination of publicity lovers and demagogues and discourage less exhibitionistic types. It contributes to the selection of persons with recognizable political names, names that sound like those of persons already well known in the locality, and of persons who happen to have a position at or near the top of a long ballot.[21] It discourages party responsibility or the development of slates of candidates who collectively take positions on the issues of the day. It encourages intraparty rather than interparty conflict, thus contributing to the tendency toward factionalism that is so incomprehensible to the typical voter.

Despite these drawbacks, the primary is an entrenched part of Americana. It is, and probably will long remain, the mechanism through which a preponderance of actual decisions is made in selecting persons for public office. Perhaps changes in it can be devised to make it a more effective contributor to the democratic process, but election "reforms" usually come about because a party or faction embraces a rule change (such as the Louisiana case cited above), seeing in it immediate advantage. The differences in party structure and election machinery from one state to another are in part, at least, a function of the desire of those in power to strengthen their chances of staying in power. If changes in the nomination process are to be made, they must be made within the political environment as it exists in each state.

The Advantage of Incumbents

In American elections, partisan *and* nonpartisan, incumbents enjoy a huge advantage. This is so for the following reasons:

- They gain more publicity than others.
- They usually have greater claims on party support (whether this support exists or not).
- They can raise campaign funds more easily (most contributors like to bet on a probable winner).
- They usually have better access to information and knowledge about the current political scene.
- They may be able to frighten off opposition for the nomination in many ways, (for example, by demanding financial support early from big-time givers or by quickly approaching well known politicians or celebrities and wrapping up endorsements before potential opponents can even get organized).

Their tactics may produce short-term advantages for the campaign—and all previous trends have been intensified since about 1970 by the skillful use of political action committees (PACs), discussed below.

Even in the office presenting the greatest statewide opportunity for officeholders to lose—the governorship—incumbency is an enormous advantage. A study of governors elected between 1963 and 1986 found that whereas about one-fourth of the incumbents lost reelection, over half the races without an incumbent produced a change of party in power. Thus, incumbents were twice as likely as nonincumbents to hold a governorship for their party.[22] In 1988 and 1990 combined, only seven of the thirty incumbent governors lost reelection. In the state legislatures, the totals were even more dramatic. For example, in 1986 in Wisconsin, 106 of 107 incumbent legislators won in the primary, and 103 of 107 won the general election.[23] In 1988 and 1990, only three incumbents lost reelection in each election. Governors are more vulnerable, as all executives are, because they can be seen as individually responsible for mismanagement. While voters may dislike legislative bodies, they rarely blame their own legislator. Thus governors are more vulnerable than legislators, but incumbents in both cases win most of the time. Circumstances tend to be similar in local government. In Los Angeles County, the nation's most populous county, according to the California Commission on Campaign Financing (1989): "Year-round fund raising and enormous campaign war chests have eliminated nearly all serious challenges to incumbents, resulting in incumbent dominance that protects [county] supervisors from criticism and controversy." In another study by the commission, this of California local government generally, incumbents outspent challengers by a margin of nine to one. Of all contributions raised, incumbents received 83 percent. Furthermore, incumbents received 60 percent of their funds in nonelection years when challengers were dormant; 99 percent of the money challengers were able to find was located in election years. The best key to political success, by far, is incumbency. This pattern has become so dominant since the early 1970s that would-be challengers and excluded interest groups were earnestly looking for remedies by the late 1980s. A favorite item of inquiry was limitation of the number of consecutive terms an incumbent could serve. This approach used to be a hardy perennial for governorships in the South but does not appear to have had a major effect on political behavior where it was in effect. In 1990, voters in Colorado, California, Oklahoma, and Kansas City, Missouri, approved limits on the terms of public officials.

The General Election Campaign

The structure of political parties is becoming less and less important in state and local politics. This is so because a very large percentage of offices are now filled by non-partisan elections and because the political parties, as such, have sunk to the position of serving primarily as symbols in the general election, once they have organized the nomination process. They are still important but are no longer the active organizations that once dominated American politics at all levels.

The old-style political machines are all nearly dead today. They were operated from top to bottom by career workers. Today, no party could afford the salaries required for such a structure. Amateurs, although of some value to candidates, cannot take the careerists' place. And the hope that very many members of the middle or working classes want to spend their leisure hours in political activities does not stand the test of reality. With few exceptions, the formal party organizations are skeletal blueprints made up of a few eager devotees to whom politics is a hobby or a vehicle for wealth and fame as the rewards of loyal and hard work. Most candidates today find their own sources of campaign financing and receive little or nothing from their parties. Campaign organizations are now ad hoc in nature, created by the candidate for a single campaign.

In some elections, particularly at the local level, where few votes are cast, voting by ''friends and neighbors'' still prevails.[24] A candidate can be elected by virtue of direct appeal to the voter; for example, knocking on doors, holding public forums, using yard signs and bumper stickers, and relying on word-of-mouth about the candidates. In other elections, incumbents run unopposed, or party affiliation is so strong for one party that the general election is simply a formality—the outcome already has been determined in the primary. Candidates today, however, especially for the higher offices but increasingly for all competitive races, have to look beyond the party for help. Campaigning through the mass media has become a substitute for personal contact through the party organization. The *image* of the candidate, rather than the candidate, is what the voter now sees; therefore candidates know they need the assistance of a new kind of specialist—the professional campaign manager or the expert in commercial advertising and public relations. These persons must create a salable image for a single candidate in a single campaign. Contemporary campaign management firms have demonstrated to candidates that it is cheaper and more efficient to let them handle media problems than it is to turn the money over to party amateurs or to try to make all the decisions themselves; that it is more effective to emphasize style and image than it is to sell content—that is, issues and policy positions; and that an attractive personality generally will bring in more votes than will a candidate who subjects voters to lengthy and weighty discussions of issues. Candidates, social problems, political issues, and economic difficulties all are translated—seemingly without effort—into catchy slogans and effective symbols.

This media system of raising funds and campaigning for office has greatly changed the nature of the campaign. In small state and local governments, the effect has not been significant but in more populous areas, such as Los Angeles County, incumbent politicians of a new breed have been the result:[25] They isolate themselves from the voters, rely on phalanxes of paid political advisors, raise contributions around the clock, accumulate huge war chests in non-election years, scare off challengers, solicit contributions from persons with financial interests pending before them, spend large sums on entertainment, fund raising and travel, and communicate with the public through orchestrated media campaigns.

Campaign management firms have become big business in the United States, having borrowed extensively from what political scientists know about voter behavior—which is a good deal. They poll the voters in advance to plan campaigns, pretest strategies, study responses to themes in key precincts, and test all their assumptions against actual voting patterns after election day. For more and more offices, the problems of the candidate are not party approval and availability of party workers; the problem now is to get past the primary election with the help of campaign management firms (after which they can often virtually ignore the party organization).

Money and the Political Action Committee

To campaign effectively using the methods discussed above, a candidate must find the large amounts of money needed to hire these firms. If the funds can be raised, candidates have no need for the party (although the party as a *symbol* remains). They do not even need campaign managers; all their requirements are provided for as a complete package by the campaign firm. Raising money is a process that restricts successful candidates to those who are rich enough to draw on their own resources or who have mastered the techniques of raising money. After the Watergate scandals of the national government, governments at all levels became more conscious of limitations on fund-raising. Some governments did little. Most commonly, state governments (and often local governments under state mandate) adopted some form of regulation of the bookkeeping of campaign funds, often coupled with the requirement that candidates disclose the source of campaign contributions.[26]

Fund-raising is costly work and the huge sums one might expect to be used to court voters actually are expended as overhead in seeking campaign funds. A study of eighteen local government jurisdictions in California found that on the average, politicians spent only 38 percent of the funds they raised in actually contacting potential voters.[27] Practices varied by size of city, however (California has no villages or towns). Overhead amounted to a substantial 43 percent in small cities but increased to a massive 67 percent in the largest cities. Candidates in smaller cities spent relatively more on conducting surveys, whereas those in large cities used more for consulting and spent four times more on funds transferred to other candidates. In actual contacts, large-city campaigners spent more than three times as much on voter handouts as on radio or television, a sharp contrast to state or national elections. Those in small cities

also relied on handouts but spent virtually nothing on broadcasting in a giant metropolitan area, where TV is far too expensive and even radio is spread over too many
voters who cannot vote in the city of the candidate paying the bill.

Attempts have been made to adopt some form of public financing.[28] For example, Wisconsin candidates for statewide office and for the legislature who demonstrate their viability by raising a certain amount of money (in small increments) on
their own qualify for public financing.[29]

The Political Action Committee (PAC) has come to be the principal source of
campaign funding outside the candidates' personal wealth. PACs are interest groups
that serve a variety of lobbying roles, but their most important function is to raise
money for candidates.[30] In terms of variety, one typology found six PAC types: the
single corporation, the labor union, the ideological, the individual candidate, the professional association, and the "superpac," which distributes the funds of a number of
PACs at once.[31] As mentioned in the previous chapter, many commentators see the
PAC, lobby, or any interest group as inherently evil. But politics always involves
interest, and few would hold that their own interests are evil.[32]

There was much thrashing about in the 1980s in searching for more propitious
ways of financing campaigns in the face of runaway costs. Prospects did not prove to
be very favorable. The amateurism that dominated much of even state and congressional levels in the nineteenth century continued to fade. And the new-style incumbents were prepared to raise what money they could and spend as much as was
needed—or far more. Some reformers have urged limits on candidate spending, but
this is not easy to enforce because friends can pick up the slack when the limit is
reached; not as efficient a system, but it bypasses the limit. In return for the restriction, public financing is sometimes suggested to make up the difference. But, some
fear, this could lead to treasury raids largely to the benefit of incumbents. As a result
of this view, in 1988 California (where over 90 percent of legislators running for
reelection are successful) prohibited by initiative all public financing of state and local races. However, those who pursue public financing assert that it would reduce,
even eliminate, the use of PACs; yet Wisconsin's experience shows little evidence of
this. In that state, despite a public financing scheme, the system still expects a good
deal of personal fund-raising in order to demonstrate a candidate's viability. This
allows for continued use of PACs, albeit with somewhat different procedures to
channel PAC money around restrictive rules.[33] In any event, except for those that
were authorized and given specific rules by initiative, PACs are the products of
legislators—and sitting members are not deserving of the name *politician* if they cannot devise ways for public financing to benefit incumbents. Legislators make nearly
all of the election rules; most of them want to keep their jobs; *and virtually all election
rules are designed accordingly.*

Does money determine who wins or loses campaigns? Competitive races usually involve competitive financing. Thus in many races other factors are of greater
importance in the final analysis. But surely without PAC money, independent
wealth, or generous rules on public financing, few challengers can expect to win public office. PACs usually are more than willing to contribute to the incumbents, often
even when they are not challenged. The contribution is designed to gain access and to
influence public policy; it rarely is intended as an overt bribe, but rather as a mecha-

nism to have the interest group's views heard prior to legislation or executive action that is of interest to the PAC. In studying one year's primaries, Malcolm Jewell's findings well summarize the influence of money:

> (1) In races that are won in a landslide, the winner usually spends a very high propor-
> tion of the total, much more than is necessary to win. . . . (The incumbent, for example,
> today often collects far more dollars than are needed, spends them lavishly, and fright-
> ens off challengers, or simply inundates the opponent's meager funds.)
> (2) Money is particularly important for candidates who lack a record in politics and are
> not well known but are able to finance very expensive campaigns. (This is, for example,
> the rich or well-connected non-incumbent syndrome.)
> (3) In races among well known, strong candidates, money is seldom decisive. Both
> candidates usually have substantial funds, and where a significant imbalance exists in
> funding, the underdog sometimes wins. (This situation sometimes obtains, for example,
> when two incumbents are thrown into the same district after reapportionment.)[34]

Still, to Jewell's summary we could perhaps add that the underdog's prospects decline and the incumbent's become ever greater as the jurisdiction becomes more populous and the legislative body becomes more professionalized.

Experiments in Direct Democracy

The Initiative and Referendum

The rise of the boss and machine system and the decline in the prestige of governing bodies in the last half of the nineteenth century was accompanied by a decline in faith in representative democracy. As a consequence, middle-class reformers proposed what were then considered radical solutions. They renovated and reorganized some old American institutions, introduced some new ones, and offered techniques for di-rect democracy as a check on excesses and incompetence. As discussed earlier in chapter 3, the idea of permitting the electorate to vote on constitutions and amend-ments dates almost from the beginnings of state government, and referendums on bond issues also were established at an early date. The innovation of the reformers was to extend the referendum to ordinary legislation and to authorize the initiative. The discussion that follows pertains to legislative initiatives and referenda.

> *Initiative:* **A procedure permitting a specified number of voters to propose by petition changes in a constitution, municipal charter, laws, or ordi-nances. The initiative permits legislation to be effected with no reliance on the legislative body. These proposals are then accepted or rejected by vot-ers at the polls.**

> *Referendum:* **A procedure permitting voters to accept or reject at the polls changes in a constitution, municipal charter, laws, or ordinances proposed by a legislative body. A referendum *follows* favorable action by a legisla-tive body.**

The Procedure

An initiated proposal usually is drafted by the attorneys for the particular interest group seeking the legislation. Petitions to put the proposal on the ballot are then circulated, either by volunteers or by persons hired for the purpose, often at the price of a certain amount per signature. The total signatures required may be a specific number or a certain percentage of voters (registered or voting for a certain office at the last general election or some other formula). Where such a percentage is used, it is generally from 5 to 10 percent but may be higher. In most instances the proposal is adopted if supported by a majority of those voting on it, although in some cases a majority of those voting in the *election* is required (this means that voters who ignore the proposal, in effect vote no), or some special formula may be used. Extraordinary majorities may reduce significantly the chances of passage. Often, an initiated item may not be amended or repealed by the legislative body, at least within a certain prescribed time limit.

Antecedents for the initiative and referendum, particularly the latter, are to be found in the direct democracy of ancient Greece, the ancient tribal governments of Germany, the right to petition the monarch in medieval England, the town meeting of colonial New England, and the direct democracy of Switzerland.[35] As early as 1825, the Maryland legislature provided for a referendum on the question of establishing a public school system. It later became commonplace to hold referendums on liquor questions, charter amendments, public utility franchises, bond issues, and other matters. California, Iowa, and Nebraska in the late nineteenth century authorized the use of the initiative and referendum by cities. The San Francisco home-rule charter of 1898 was the first such document to provide for them. The movement then spread rapidly and is today widely authorized.

Around the beginning of this century, when many governments accepted the initiative and referendum, proponents made exaggerated claims for their merits. Opponents were alarmed that these devices might be used to hamstring the governmental process. The results have not borne out the claims of either side. The first state to adopt the initiative and referendum was South Dakota. It was only slightly ahead of other states where members of the progressive movement advocated it. The initiative and referendum resulted from a lack of trust in state legislatures and a popular view that legislatures were either too conservative to meet the demands of the times or were corrupt, or both.[36] Within ten years or so, about twenty states adopted the processes; then the drive seems to have spent itself. After 1917, only Alaska, upon its admission to statehood, made constitutional provision for the initiative and referendum.

Several types of initiatives are to be found. Under the *direct initiative,* if the required number of signatures are obtained on a petition, the proposed law is placed on the ballot for a vote. Under the *indirect initiative,* petitions with the required number of signatures must be submitted to the legislature to give it an opportunity to enact the proposed measure, or a substantially similar substitute. If the legislature fails to act within a stipulated period of time, the question of the adoption of the proposed law is placed before the voters. Thirteen states and the District of Columbia use the direct method solely; five states use the indirect method solely; and Ohio, Washington, and Utah allow either.

Three types of referendums are in use. One, the *petition referendum* (used in twenty-four states and the District of Columbia), provides that before a proposed law goes into effect, it must be approved by voters according to some formula if a petition containing a specified number of signatures asks for such a vote. The *optional referendum* (used in fourteen states) is one in which the legislature itself may order a referendum on any measure it has passed, requiring that a specified majority of voters approve before the proposed law goes into effect. Nineteen states constitutionally require referendums for certain types of debt authorization.

Arguments Concerning the Initiative and Referendum

Proponents of direct democracy argued that corrupt and incompetent governing bodies made it necessary for voters to have a check on the government. Reformers also took note of the trend toward a concentration of authority in government and a breakdown of the traditional check-and-balance system. The initiative and referendum could serve to replace some of these disappearing checks. It was argued that the use of such devices strengthened popular control over government by giving voters "a gun behind the door," which could serve as a means of requiring greater alertness, honesty, and responsiveness on the part of legislators.

Reformers believed that the initiative and referendum would protect the people from political tricks and thefts from the public treasury. Some argued that both would encourage voters to become better informed on issues because they would have to vote on so many of them directly and they could influence policy making directly. The processes were adopted at a time when *populism* was in vogue and its leaders demanded more democracy so that the people could govern themselves. Opponents argued that the initiative and referendum confused legislative responsibility, lengthened an already long ballot, had a bad psychological effect on governing bodies, expected more than was reasonable from an uninformed and interested electorate, promoted radicalism and disrespect for property rights, opposed the principles of Americanism (because the Constitution is based on representative, not direct, democracy), and allowed well-organized pressure groups representing a minority of the population to exercise an inordinate advantage.[37]

Beyond procedure, the initiative and referendum differ importantly from the ordinary legislative process in that a proposal must be accepted or rejected in its entirety. They do not permit "compromises between the initial demands of groups of varying size and intensity."[38] The vote on each measure counts equally irrespective of intensity of interest. In the legislature, a member sometimes will think it more important to support the desires of a highly motivated minority than those of an apathetic majority. In such delicate areas as civil rights and race relations, where negotiation and compromise are essential, the initiative and referendum are particularly ill suited.[39]

The debate over the use of the initiative and referendum has subsided in recent years, though the use of these devices is, if anything, increasing. Perhaps it is necessary here to make only two points without discussing the merits of the arguments briefly outlined above. First, the processes seem to carry the implicit assumption that the individual voter is always informed and rational in all choices. Actually, of course, this assumption is false. Voters in a democracy are not asked to rule, but merely to choose those who are to rule. They are not asked to vote rationally, but only according to their state of satisfactions. However, the initiative and referendum ask more than this of voters. The devices ask voters to help rule themselves and to make policy decisions on questions that are often complex, technical, and minutely detailed. They are even more susceptible to the image maker's abilities to manipulate symbols than are candidates. Political parties may enter the debate, but rarely are they clearly identified as being for or against a ballot issue. Interest groups and political factions, however, may be highly involved.

Second, opponents of the initiative and referendum are wont to overlook the fact that the American political structure is pluralistic and not neatly integrated and that the political process typically is based on the interaction of organized groups. Political subdivisions, for the most part, do not have responsible political party structures; cities, for example, seldom have two-party systems regularly competing for voter support. When governing bodies are neither responsible to nor representative of a cross section of the population, the initiative and referendum may well be used as a check. They continue to be used extensively and, since the 1960s, the initiative in particular seems to have gained a resurgence of interest. Although most elections contain only a handful of initiatives, some, particularly in California, where the initiative is most popular, may overburden even the most committed and rational voter. For example, in the 1988 general election in California, nine bond measures, eight referenda, and twelve initiatives, as well as a number of local measures appeared on the ballot. Five partly conflicting measures applied to auto insurance alone.

For some special-interest groups the initiative and referendum may well have become easier tools to accomplish limited goals than the more conventional legislative process, but this is not clear. In the auto-insurance issue, the legislature, subject to enormous pressures from insurance companies, the California Trial Lawyers' Association, and consumer groups led by Ralph Nader, had not been able to adopt any bill over several sessions. The insurance companies then tried a "no-fault" initiative, which promptly provoked competing measures from other groups. A total of more than $100 million was spent on the five propositions and $29 million more on the other measures on the same ballot—the most ever spent on an initiative and referendum election anywhere. Only one of the measures passed, the one that was promoted by Nader and seemed to promise the most to the voters, not the one on which the most money had been spent in support. The essential features of the surviving measure did not go into effect but were promptly plunged into what promised to be a lengthy court battle.

What this experience seemed to indicate is that legislatures in the most populous states at least have, like Congress, encountered impasses in relation to crucial issues involving powerful interests or sharp ideological differences. In addition, the measures in this case point to an obvious or necessarily effective alternative means of making public policy. (California's Proposition 13 also resulted from an impasse, but the initiative process in that case served to resolve the immediate issues.) How critical legislation can be adopted effectively may become an increasingly serious problem in the near future.

The Recall

A third reform practice that was to produce popular control of government was the *recall*. It was used extensively by reformers, who argued that a faithless or incompetent public servant should not be inflicted on the people for the duration of the term but removed as soon as shortcomings are discovered. Jacksonians, displeased with the increasing popularity of the four-year term over the traditional two-year term found it easier to accept the longer term if "continuous responsibility" were maintained through the availability of the recall. The mechanism probably was first provided for in the Los Angeles home-rule charter of 1903 and on the state level in Oregon in 1908.

> *Recall:* **A device allowing any elective officer to be removed from office by popular vote prior to the expiration of the term.**

The Procedure

A petition must be circulated to recall an official. Because a large number of signatures usually is required (from 15 to 55 percent of the vote cast for the office of the individual under attack or for some other office, such as that of mayor or governor in the last election) an organized group with high motivation and a sizable treasury usually is necessary to initiate a recall. After sufficient signatures are procured and certified by the appropriate official, an election becomes obligatory. Several variants of the recall ballot exist, and its form may serve either to aid or discourage the prospects for removal of the official.

Arguments Pro and Con

The principal argument for the recall is that it ensures continuous responsibility, so that the public need not wait in exasperation and frustration until an official's term comes to an end. It is also argued that with a sword hanging over their heads, public officials will try to remain alert at all times.

Opponents of the recall point to its costliness; A special election is imperative because it would be unfair to conduct such an election in connection with other questions (although this is sometimes done). A second objection is that it does not attempt to prove charges against an officeholder but merely attempts to persuade the electorate, by whatever means, to remove the incumbent. A third objection is that the recall is unnecessary; in all states, improper conduct by public officials is grounds for removal by judicial, legislative, or sometimes gubernatorial action. A final objection centers on the assertion that the recall serves as a tool for well-organized groups and for political recrimination. Similarly, it is said that the threat of recall is a legal means for constant intimidation, public whims, and sentimentality.

For example, two years of controversy in 1989–1990 over a court ruling permitting Indian tribes to spear fish under treaty rights in Wisconsin led to attempts to recall a state legislator (and to remove a member of Congress who, by the Constitution, cannot be recalled) for supporting those rights and for not sufficiently championing the threatened recreation industry. The effort at recall failed even though many voters apparently sympathized with the recall sponsors. They seemed to believe that recall was not a proper penalty for disagreement over one issue. Nevertheless, strong leaders with a positive program may find some interest group standing in their path and threatening a recall action if they seek to carry out a program, even if it is the program that elected them to office.

A trend away from the recall continues. It has never been widely used, though it does appear in connection with specific issues, such as school busing or curriculum as mentioned above. Few new adoptions of it have taken place since 1920, but it is authorized for some or all state officers in fifteen states—none of them in the Northeast—and for one or all local officers in over one-half of the nation's cities, particularly those with council-manager (reform) governments.[40]

The Public Hearing

Another device that involves the citizen in decision making is the public hearing. This institution is unusual in Europe, but dates from colonial times in America, where tradition requires the general public to be consulted, or at least informed, about almost every public policy decision. Public hearings generally involve an informal procedure at which all persons present are allowed to speak. Public hearings commonly are held prior to making decisions concerning land zoning, the location of bars or "half-way houses," highways, changing public utility rates, property tax exemptions (for example, granting a variance for a cemetery), the location of a new school, and dozens of other matters. Frequently, public hearings are required by the national government prior to the distribution by local governments of certain types of national grants.

Political neophytes sometimes find the hearing procedure puzzling because nearly everyone is opposed to the proposal that is the subject of the hearing. The official or public body conducting the hearing does not, of course, take a spot vote solely on the basis of the hearing. Instead, the hearing is a safety valve for allowing disapproving persons to gain a feeling of having had their "day in court"; opponents may even succeed in having the proposed policy modified somewhat. The hearing also allows officials to judge the political climate prior to decisions, thereby possibly learning how to minimize unfavorable responses to their final decision.

The Advisory Group

Citizens' advisory groups provide some of the same functions for the political system as do public hearings. They began as informal calls for public discussions but gradually became more institutionalized in the late nineteenth century as administration emerged as a one-person job. To replace the former governing boards and commissions, advisory committees with individual terms of office appeared. In some cases, legislation today requires that these be established for example, for urban renewal activities. Advisory bodies may be constituted of representatives of various interest groups, or they may be appointed for the special purpose of ratifying and hence legitimizing policies desired by a governor, mayor, or manager; or they may be used for the actual purpose of developing a public policy in relation to some specific problem.

Advisory groups are characterized by slow action and lack of innovation; that is, a general acceptance of administrative goals, established and accepted methods, and reliance on the advice of experts, as well as a lack of realism concerning the financial and political aspects of the problem they are considering. Although these groups improve the communications network between the decision makers and affected citizens, they do not resolve the sense of alienation on the part of the citizen; nor do they represent a cross section of the community, for they usually are chosen from higher-status persons, representatives of interest groups, and persons who are particularly concerned about the problem or function involved.

As is discussed in chapter 10, membership in advisory groups has become a modern form of patronage, for appointment to such groups, though unpaid, is often eagerly sought for the status and access to decision makers it accords. Such groups have been rapidly expanding in numbers for many years.

Concluding Note

This chapter has examined the nature of the process of nomination, the machinery of election, and the structure of political parties in American government. We turn next to the forms and structures of governmental institutions and the processes of politics that take place within them.

Notes

1. For the relationship between voting and other conventional forms of participation, see Sidney Verba and Norman Nie, *Participation in America* (New York: Harper & Row, 1972).

2. See chapter 2.

3. Thomas Flinn, "Party Responsibility in the States," *American Political Science Review* 58 (Mar. 1961): 60–71. For an example of party structure in a state that has long rejected "party responsibility," see Michael J. Ross, *California, Its Government and Politics*, 3d ed. (Monterey, CA: Brooks/Cole Publishing Co., 1988), especially the section titled "Antipartyism," 48–53.

4. Malcolm E. Jewell and David M. Olson, *Political Parties and Elections in American States*, 3d ed. (Chicago: The Dorsey Press, 1986), chapter 3, quotation at 56.

5. Frank J. Sorauf and Paul Allen Beck, *Party Politics in America*, 6th ed. (Glenview, IL: Scott, Foresman and Company, 1988), 91.

6. Ibid, 9.

7. James J. Gibson, Cornelius P. Cotter, John F. Bibby, and Robert J. Huckshorn, "Assessing Party Organizational Strength," *American Journal of Political Science* 27 (May 1983) :193–222; and James L. Gibson, Cornelius P. Cotter, John F. Bibby, and Robert J. Huckshorn, "Whither State and Local Parties?: A Cross-Sectional and Longitudinal Analysis of the Strength of Party Organization," *American Journal of Political Science* 29 (Feb. 1985): 139–60.

8. Gibson, et al., "Whither State. . . Parties?" 155.

9. Jewell and Olson, *Political Parties*, chapter 2. The theory of realignment was first delineated in V. O. Key, Jr., "A Theory of Critical Elections," *Journal of Politics* 17 (Jan. 1955):3–18. It was further spelled out in Walter Dean Burnham, *Critical Elections and the*

Mainsprings of American Politics (New York: W. W. Norton, 1970); and James L. Sundquist, *Dynamics of the Party System* (Washington, D.C.: Brookings Institution, 1973). For a state study, Michael P. Rogin and John L. Shover, *Political Change in California* (Westport, CT: Greenwood Publishing Corporation, 1969).

10. For more detail, see the extended discussion of apportionment in chapter 11.

11. The patterns in the South have changed, but the best understanding of the traditional relationships remains V. O. Key, Jr., and Alexander Heard, *Southern Politics* (New York: Alfred A. Knopf, 1949). On trends, see Robert P. Steed, L. W. Moreland, and Tod A. Baker, *The Disappearing South? Studies in Regional Change and Continuity* (Tuscaloosa: The University of Alabama Press, 1990).

12. For the effects of nonpartisanship, see Charles R. Adrian, "A Typology for Nonpartisan Elections," *Western Political Quarterly* 12 (June 1959):449–58, and citations there; J. Leiper Freeman, "Local Party Systems," *American Journal of Sociology* 64 (Nov. 1958):282–89. On the nonpartisan legislature in Minnesota, see Charles R. Adrian, "The Origin of Minnesota's Nonpartisan Legislature," *Minnesota History* 33 (Winter 1952):155–63. On the repeal in Minnesota, see The *Minnesota Legislative Manual, 1987–1988,* St. Paul, 1987, 16.

13. For a discussion of the relationship between nonpartisanship and city structure, see Charles R. Adrian, "Forms of City Government in American History," *The Municipal Year Book, 1988* (Washington, D.C.: International City Management Association, 1988).

14. Key and Heard, *Southern Politics*, 87–97.

15. Jewell and Olson, *Political Parties*, chapter 4.

16. Ibid, 96.

17. Charles D. Hadley, "The Impact of the Louisiana Open Elections System Reform, *State Governments* 58 (No. 4 1986):152–56.

18. The material in this paragraph relies on Jewell and Olson, *Political Parties,* 89–95. Also see Craig L. Carr and Gary L. Scott, "The Logic of State Primary Classification Schemes," *American Politics Quarterly* 12 (Oct. 1984):465–76.

19. *Democratic Party of U.S.* v. *La Follette,* 449 U.S. 897 (1981). For a discussion of the issues surrounding this debate, see Gary D. Wekkin, *Democrat vs. Democrat: The National Party's Campaign to Close the Wisconsin Primary* (Columbia: University of Missouri Press, 1984).

20. Jewell and Olson, *Political Parties*, 111, Figure 4–2.

21. H. M. Bain and Donald S. Hecock, *Ballot Position and Voter's Choice* (Detroit, MI: Wayne State University Press, 1957).

22. Jewell and Olson, *Political Parties,* 187–90.

23. John F. Bibby, "Political Parties and Elections in Wisconsin" in Wilder Crane, A. Clark Hagensick, et al., eds., *Wisconsin Government and Politics,* 4th ed. (Milwaukee: Department of Governmental Affairs, University of Wisconsin, 1987), 54.

24. Key and Heard, *Southern Politics*, 37–41; for the persistence of this pattern in low-population areas, see the Report of the California Commission on Campaign Financing, summarized in detail in the *Los Angeles Times,* August 27, 1989, part I.

25. Dan Nimmo, *The Political Persuaders* (Englewood Cliffs, NJ: Prentice-Hall, 1970); and Edwin Diamond and Stephen Bates, *The Spot: The Rise of Political Advertising on Television* (Cambridge, MA: The MIT Press, 1984). The quotation is from the California Commission *Report* cited in the preceding note.

26. For a collection of essays on experiences in a number of states, see Herbert Alexander, ed., *Campaign Money: Reform and Reality in the States* (New York: The Free Press, 1976) and the appendix: "The Citizen Research Foundation's Model State Statute on Politics, Elections, and Public Office."

27. *Los Angeles Times,* September 3, 1989, part I. The study was done by the California Commission on Campaign Financing, a nonprofit, private commission, and was financed by five private foundations.

28. See the collection of case studies in Herbert Alexander and Jennifer W. Frutig, *Public Financing of State Elections* (Los Angeles: Citizens Research Foundation, 1982).

29. Bibby, "Political Parties. . . Wisconsin," 66–67.

30. The study of PACs has been at the national level, but their use at the state and even local level is also significant. For a general statement, see Larry J. Sabato, *PAC Power: Inside the World of Political Action Committees* (New York: W. W. Norton, 1984).

31. Jewell and Olson, *Political Parties,* 162–64.

32. An excellent case study of interest groups at the local level is Bernard Bellush and Jewel Bellush, "Participation in Local Politics: District Council 37 in New York," *National Civic Review* 74 (May 1985):5, 213–30. District Council 37's membership consists of employees of New York City.

33. Bibby "Political Parties . . . Wisconsin," 66–67.

34. Malcolm E. Jewell, "Political Money and Gubernatorial Primaries," *State Government* 56 (1983):1, 72.

35. See William B. Munro, ed., *The Initiative, Referendum and Recall* (New York: Macmillan, 1913); Hugh A. Bone, *The Initiative and Referendum* (New York: National Municipal League, 1959).

36. For the particulars of any given state, consult the latest edition of the *Book of the States* (Lexington, KY: Council of State Governments).

37. Extensive arguments on the pros and cons are presented in Munro, *The Initiative*, chapters 1–11.

38. Raymond E. Wolfinger and Fred I. Greenstein, "The Repeal of Fair Housing in California: An Analysis of Referendum Voting," *American Political Science Review* 62 (Sept. 1968): 753–69.

39. Ibid.

40. See the *Book of the States* for state totals; for local, Adrian, the *Municipal Year Book, 1988,* 10.

The Library of Congress

7

Forms of Government

Forms of government are important because they affect the pattern of influence of various groups on government. Yet, Americans have been obsessed with the idea of a relationship between structure and the effectiveness of government. Many advocates of reform have been guilty of overstatement concerning this. Much literature exists urging the council-manager form of city government or the strong governor type of state government, for example, on the ground that these plans follow the organizational form of the business world—the corporation. The assumption is that the success of the one should ensure the success of the other.

The "one grand solution" approach contrasts with the views of such persons as the Minneapolis alderman who once said that forms of government have nothing at all to do with the effectiveness or honesty of government. He believed that Minneapolis, which had a nineteenth-century form of government when he made the comment in the middle of the twentieth century, operated as well as it would under any of the newer forms often advocated by reformers. This viewpoint was not new, however; similar expressions have come from Alexander Pope, Edmund Burke, and Lincoln Steffens.

Structural arrangements have an effect on the quality of government, but they neither guarantee good government nor prevent it. The structure of government helps to establish behavior patterns and attitudes toward power and the exercise of power that definitely affect the decision-making process. In a weak-governor state, a department head may present a program to the legislature without clearing it with the governor, his nominal boss—in fact, the governor may first learn of it in the press. This program may be pushed with a vigor at least equal to that behind the governor's own competing program. Such behavior would be considered contemptuous—and probably would have disastrous consequences for the department head—in a strong-governor state. But in a weak-governor state, department heads not only can get away with it, but the fact that they do further weakens the governor's position as an administrative leader by creating a climate of opinion that discourages consultation or coordination between agency heads and the governor. A study of the relationship of attitudes of officeholders toward one another probably would reveal considerable variation, depending on the structure of government.

In the general parlance of social science, governmental structure is more often a dependent variable than an independent variable. As we saw in chapter 5, the more likely independent variable is the political process of group demands and interaction. Others have asserted that even those processes are dependent on ideologies (discussed in chapter 2). In a widely accepted study of police behavior, it is shown that ideologies govern the general process that structures and organizes the local political behavior of police forces. Another study concludes that structure is the leading factor in making the council-manager form of city government more cooperative than the mayor-council form.[1]

Different organizational contexts are produced by different political value structures. The differences in organization that are studied in this chapter therefore should not be overstated. Such differences, which frequently determine day-to-day decisions in a given state or locality, also reflect differences in value structure that cannot easily be studied directly. As a result, they become good clues to the variation in political behavior in the American federal system but should not be thought of as the great cause of such variation.

This chapter will concentrate on the formal structures of government. Even so, remember that power also is organized in other ways; for example, as it was in the political party in the period roughly between the Civil War and the Great Depression and today through political action committees. Political scientists usually talk about the ''informal'' powers of the old political boss, but it would be more accurate to speak of alternative power sources. Usually these come from a formal position within the *political party*, and these powers were dominant and hence more important than those of public office because they were more flexible in tying together and directing the economic and social forces of the area; the party had the effective political clout. In the old boss-and-machine system, each ward had a boss who held a powerful party position. The ward leaders would elect a citywide boss, typically one who could effect compromise among various ethnic values and who had impressive administrative skills. Richard J. Daley of Chicago, the last of the great city bosses, held some of his power as mayor, but most of it came as head of the Cook County Democratic Committee and the rest because the first two allowed him to name the chair of the finance committee of the board of aldermen (the city council). To this power he applied brilliant administrative skills. Similarly, many of the strongest state chief executives have come from weak-governor states; such was the case with Huey P. Long of Louisiana in the 1930s. The boss system in city, state, or even rural county depended primarily on the power of patronage; the granting or withholding of permits, licenses, franchises; favorable legislative action, intimidation, corruption; and the ability to persuade or lead—all carried out through the party machinery.[2]

State Government Organization

Distrust of the colonial chief executive during Revolutionary times helped to establish a general climate of opinion toward state government that was favorable to the legislature and less favorable to the governor. As was seen in chapter 2, the conservative interests that provided for strong administrative powers in the presidency were less powerful in the states, and the same philosophy was not applied in these areas.

Indeed, the Jacksonian movement took hold in state government before the governorship was restored to its prewar dignity and power. As a result, certain values of that period were established in state constitutions—particularly during the excess of constitution writing of the 1850s—and these values became the basis of persistent attitudes toward state government that still prevail in many states today.

The Weak-Governor System

The pattern of state government organization that arose in the nineteenth century and that remains influential today is analogous to the weak-mayor system (discussed below), which is also a product of the Jacksonian period of frontier individualism. It called for:

- Many elective officers, each independent of the others
- A constitution that provided much of the detail of government organization
- The control of many agencies by boards and commissions with overlapping terms of office and with members who are virtually unremovable by the governor or anyone else
- A governor with few administrative powers of any kind
- A personnel system based on patronage or, later, on a civil service commission wholly independent of the governor
- A legislative budget

In classifying states as weak-governor or strong-governor, a variety of criteria can measure the power of a chief executive in relation to the power of other executives and the legislative branch. One study combined five measures: tenure potential (length of term and constraints on the ability to run for reelection), appointive power, budget-making power, organizational power over the bureaucracy, and veto power.[3] The results can be seen in table 7–1. Although many other factors might be involved, it might be argued that the states with moderate and weak scores fit the weak-governor model, represented in twenty-seven states. The other twenty-three might constitute strong-governor systems.

The Strong-Governor System

Several states have adopted forms of government that could be classified as strong-governor types; that is, those in which the governor has extensive administrative powers and control over the various agencies of state government through the power of appointment and removal of agency heads. This form came with the reform movement, which placed heavy emphasis on the application of business principles to governmental administration. The efficiency-and-economy reorganization drive, centering in cities where business leaders lived and paid most of the taxes, did not affect state government significantly until 1909 in Oregon—and then it came from a populistic reform group, the People's Power League. In New York the next year, however, the contemporary business view was presented by Governor Charles Evans Hughes in his inaugural address. In 1917, Governor Frank O. Lowden led the way

Figure 7-1: Organizational Chart of Kansas State Government

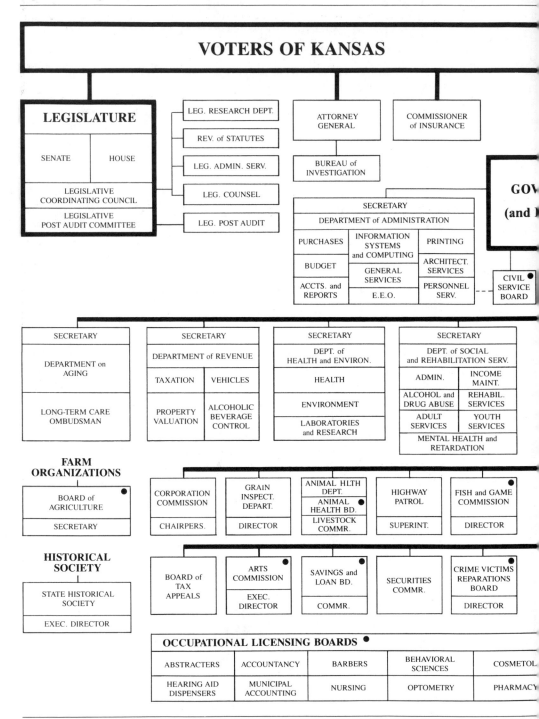

VOTERS OF KANSAS

LEGISLATURE

SENATE | HOUSE

LEGISLATIVE COORDINATING COUNCIL

LEGISLATIVE POST AUDIT COMMITTEE

LEG. RESEARCH DEPT.

REV. of STATUTES

LEG. ADMIN. SERV.

LEG. COUNSEL

LEG. POST AUDIT

ATTORNEY GENERAL

BUREAU of INVESTIGATION

COMMISSIONER of INSURANCE

GOV
(and

SECRETARY
DEPARTMENT of ADMINISTRATION

PURCHASES	INFORMATION SYSTEMS and COMPUTING	PRINTING
BUDGET	GENERAL SERVICES	ARCHITECT. SERVICES
ACCTS. and REPORTS	E.E.O.	PERSONNEL SERV.

CIVIL SERVICE BOARD

SECRETARY

DEPARTMENT on AGING

LONG-TERM CARE OMBUDSMAN

SECRETARY
DEPARTMENT of REVENUE

| TAXATION | VEHICLES |
| PROPERTY VALUATION | ALCOHOLIC BEVERAGE CONTROL |

SECRETARY
DEPT. of HEALTH and ENVIRON.

HEALTH

ENVIRONMENT

LABORATORIES and RESEARCH

SECRETARY
DEPT. of SOCIAL and REHABILITATION SERV.

ADMIN.	INCOME MAINT.
ALCOHOL and DRUG ABUSE	REHABIL. SERVICES
ADULT SERVICES	YOUTH SERVICES
MENTAL HEALTH and RETARDATION	

FARM ORGANIZATIONS

BOARD of AGRICULTURE

SECRETARY

CORPORATION COMMISSION

CHAIRPERS.

GRAIN INSPECT. DEPART.

DIRECTOR

ANIMAL HLTH DEPT.

ANIMAL HEALTH BD.

LIVESTOCK COMMR.

HIGHWAY PATROL

SUPERINT.

FISH and GAME COMMISSION

DIRECTOR

HISTORICAL SOCIETY

STATE HISTORICAL SOCIETY

EXEC. DIRECTOR

BOARD of TAX APPEALS

ARTS COMMISSION

EXEC. DIRECTOR

SAVINGS and LOAN BD.

COMMR.

SECURITIES COMMR.

CRIME VICTIMS REPARATIONS BOARD

DIRECTOR

OCCUPATIONAL LICENSING BOARDS

| ABSTRACTERS | ACCOUNTANCY | BARBERS | BEHAVIORAL SCIENCES | COSMETOL |
| HEARING AID DISPENSERS | MUNICIPAL ACCOUNTING | NURSING | OPTOMETRY | PHARMACY |

Source: Kansas Directory, State of Kansas, Topeka, pp. 138–139.

174

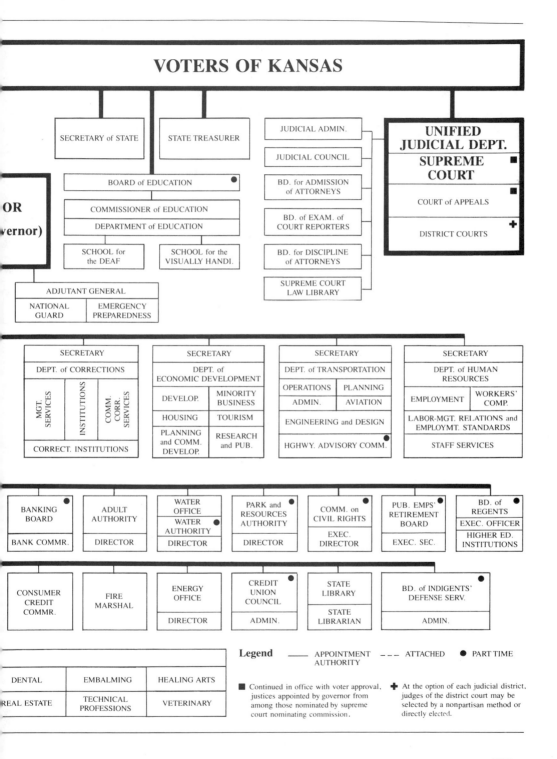

VOTERS OF KANSAS

SECRETARY of STATE

STATE TREASURER

JUDICIAL ADMIN.

JUDICIAL COUNCIL

BD. for ADMISSION of ATTORNEYS

BD. of EXAM. of COURT REPORTERS

BD. for DISCIPLINE of ATTORNEYS

SUPREME COURT LAW LIBRARY

UNIFIED JUDICIAL DEPT. SUPREME COURT ■

COURT of APPEALS ■

DISTRICT COURTS ✚

OR (ernor)

BOARD of EDUCATION ●

COMMISSIONER of EDUCATION

DEPARTMENT of EDUCATION

SCHOOL for the DEAF

SCHOOL for the VISUALLY HANDI.

ADJUTANT GENERAL

NATIONAL GUARD

EMERGENCY PREPAREDNESS

SECRETARY

DEPT. of CORRECTIONS

MGT. SERVICES | INSTITUTIONS | COMM. CORR. SERVICES

CORRECT. INSTITUTIONS

SECRETARY

DEPT. of ECONOMIC DEVELOPMENT

DEVELOP.	MINORITY BUSINESS
HOUSING	TOURISM
PLANNING and COMM. DEVELOP.	RESEARCH and PUB.

SECRETARY

DEPT. of TRANSPORTATION

| OPERATIONS | PLANNING |
| ADMIN. | AVIATION |

ENGINEERING and DESIGN

HGHWY. ADVISORY COMM. ●

SECRETARY

DEPT. of HUMAN RESOURCES

| EMPLOYMENT | WORKERS' COMP. |

LABOR-MGT. RELATIONS and EMPLOYMT. STANDARDS

STAFF SERVICES

BANKING BOARD ●

BANK COMMR.

ADULT AUTHORITY

DIRECTOR

WATER OFFICE

WATER AUTHORITY ●

DIRECTOR

PARK and RESOURCES AUTHORITY ●

DIRECTOR

COMM. on CIVIL RIGHTS ●

EXEC. DIRECTOR

PUB. EMPS' RETIREMENT BOARD ●

EXEC. SEC.

BD. of REGENTS ●

EXEC. OFFICER

HIGHER ED. INSTITUTIONS

CONSUMER CREDIT COMMR.

FIRE MARSHAL

ENERGY OFFICE

DIRECTOR

CREDIT UNION COUNCIL ●

ADMIN.

STATE LIBRARY

STATE LIBRARIAN

BD. of INDIGENTS' DEFENSE SERV. ●

ADMIN.

| DENTAL | EMBALMING | HEALING ARTS |
| REAL ESTATE | TECHNICAL PROFESSIONS | VETERINARY |

Legend   —— APPOINTMENT AUTHORITY   --- ATTACHED   ● PART TIME

■ Continued in office with voter approval, justices appointed by governor from among those nominated by supreme court nominating commission.

✚ At the option of each judicial district, judges of the district court may be selected by a nonpartisan method or directly elected.

TABLE 7-1   Formal Powers of Governors

Very Strong	Strong	Moderate	Weak
New Jersey	Alaska	Indiana	Mississippi
Pennsylvania	Maine	Oregon	Texas
Utah	Montana	Rhode Island	South Carolina
Hawaii	Tennessee	Vermont	New Hampshire
Maryland	Arizona	Alabama	North Carolina
Massachusetts	Colorado	Arkansas	Nevada
Minnesota	Delaware	New Mexico	
New York	Idaho	Oklahoma	
	Iowa	Washington	
	California	Florida	
	Connecticut	Georgia	
	Illinois	Kansas	
	Michigan	Kentucky	
	South Dakota	Louisiana	
	Wyoming	North Dakota	
		West Virginia	
		Missouri	
		Nebraska	
		Ohio	
		Virginia	
		Wisconsin	

Source: Thad L. Beyle, "Governors," in Virginia Gray, Herbert Jacob, and Kenneth N. Vines, eds., *Politics in the American States: A Comparative Analysis*, 4th ed. (Boston: Little, Brown and Company, 1983), 202.
States listed in rank order of power within category.

for Illinois to adopt a state administrative reorganization plan. Others followed in three waves, first during the Great Depression; second, around 1950 when the vogue called for the appointment of "Little Hoover" commissions that imitated the national government's Commission on Organization of the Executive Branch of the Government headed by former President Herbert Hoover; and third, when

> an unprecedented number of states [23] including Michigan [effective 1965]] underwent major reorganization in a decade and half [1965–1979]: Wisconsin [1967], California and Colorado [1968], Massachusetts and Florida [1969], Delaware and Maryland [1969–1970], Arkansas, Georgia, Maine, Montana, and North Carolina [1971], Virginia [1972], Kentucky [1972–1973], South Dakota [1973], Missouri and Idaho [1974], Arizona [1971–1975], Louisiana [1975–1976], New Mexico and West Virginia [1977] and Connecticut [1977–1979].[4]

The aims of reformers were described by one of them as including the following:

1. Use of the short ballot and concentration of authority and responsibility in the governors, giving them administrative control over all state agencies.
2. Reduction of the number of departments from the scores that commonly existed to a "manageable" number—perhaps a dozen or so.

3. Elimination of boards and commissions from administrative responsibilities.
4. Development of a cabinet and personal staff for the governors.
5. Provision for an independent audit of state funds made to the legislature.
6. Development of a personnel system based on merit.
7. Preparation of a budget and controlled expenditure of funds under the supervision of the governor.[5]

The more recent reorganizational trend suggests:

8. Giving the governor the power to reorganize the branch of government subject only to legislative veto.[6]

The constant complaint of the reformers was that "neither the governor nor any other state officer was in a position to exercise managerial power with reference to state business. The various agencies of administration had no common head and recognized little responsibility to any high executive officer."[7] Most of the reforms proposed were, and remain, unproved as to their effectiveness as a means of providing either better administration or more representative government. However, the need for effective executive leadership in an age of big government, with all of its complexities, is seldom seriously questioned today. The effectiveness of reform on representative government, on the other hand, is still uncertain.

The Function of the Legislature

Under the traditional weak-governor organization, not only are department heads powerful and independent of the governor but the legislature is also a powerful organization, not only making policy for state government but also having a considerable hand in the detailed operations of each agency. Committee leaders are quite apt to have a good deal to say about even the smallest details of day-to-day operation in the departments whose legislative authorizations must go through the committee. In some cases, committee leaders influence the number of job positions authorized in a particular agency, and they have a voice in deciding who is to fill them. Through the appropriation of funds in a highly detailed budget, they also are able to control how funds are spent, leaving relatively little more administrative discretion to the department head and even less to the governor. In many of the weakest-governor states, the legislature still dominates the budget process.

The reformers sought to change the legislature principally in two ways: (1) make it more representative of the public in the *apportionment* process by reducing the effects of *gerrymandering*, and (2) restrict its functions to policy making, leaving day-to-day operations in the hands of a professional bureaucracy responsible to a competent department head who in turn is responsible to the governor. The ideal role was thought to be one in which the legislators would consider only broad policy questions, leaving personalities and details out of their area of oversight. It was also held that the legislature should employ an auditor who would check on the efficiency and honesty of the administrative branch and report directly to the legislature, thus serving as a check on the governor and the governor's appointees without interfering with their work.

Apportionment: **The process of dividing a population into legislative districts.**

Gerrymandering: **The process of apportioning for political gain. All apportionment involves gerrymandering, usually for partisan reasons. But opponents of gerrymandering generally have advocated less overt partisanship and strict adherence to a one-person, one-vote principle.**

In many states, the legislature became more professional after the relationship between legislature and executive was modified as described in chapters 11 and 12. The legislature took back part of its lost power by strengthening its oversight of the executive branch. Oversight involved investigation of the bureaucracy through the extensive use of professional staffs and committee hearings, often when the legislature was not in session. A second step involved the development of professional staffs in the legislature to do legal research before passage of new legislation. Few states went so far as the U.S. Congress did in either of these changes, but the modifications suggest a third variation to the more traditional strong legislature–weak governor, and strong governor–weak legislature patterns. This legislative pattern is rarely found except where the executive branch has previously gone through extensive reorganization and reform.

State government remains much more traditional in form and character than do municipal governments. Furthermore, most of the changes that have taken place at the state level have been compromise changes, based on making minimal concessions in an unsystematic fashion. It is therefore difficult to classify states by form of government, as many that follow similar patterns are quite different in specifics.

The Patchwork of Local Government

Much has been written over many years concerning the irrational pattern—or lack of pattern—to be found in American local government. Most of these criticisms center on two points: that local government boundaries drawn up to suit a nineteenth-century pattern of transportation and communication are inappropriate for the twentieth century; and that technological and social change—as well as changes in the task of various units of government—make the traditional units and their structural form unsuited for contemporary government, especially in terms of costs. Both criticisms seem plausible. It is possible—though by no means certain—that local government areas would have been much larger in size and population if America had been settled under conditions including present-day technology. It is rather intriguing to observe that New Jersey, organized in the 1600s and 1700s, has 21 counties and hundreds of townships; Georgia, organized at about the same time, has 158 counties but no townships; Kansas, developed in the mid-1800s, has 105 counties and 1,360 townships. Yet, California, which is physically large and immensely populous, has only 57 counties with no townships; and gigantic (but sparsely populated) Alaska has only twelve state-designated boroughs (actually three city-boroughs, nine boroughs that the Census Bureau designates as county equivalents, and one nongovernmental, unorganized borough that the Census Bureau divided into eleven statistical areas), which provide all local governmental services.[8]

People on the frontier not only distrusted controls from a remote city and preferred grass-roots controls but also treated the local unit of government as a social community. Its problems and activities helped create a set of common interests and goals for the area and reduced some of the chronic psychological problems of frontier isolation. But the ideologies of the eighteenth and nineteenth centuries governed the structure of American cities. Even today, many Jeffersonian and Madisonian values prevail in producing fractured metropolitan areas despite modern technologies. In cities, boundaries were drawn according to the limits of the built-up area, for technology did not permit urban services to be offered outside the city limits. In rural America, the local governing unit encompassed an area not greater than that which would place the town hall within approximately one hour's buggy ride from the farthest corner; the county was an area where (east of the Missouri) no one was more than one day's buggy or horesback ride from the county seat. It was thus not illogical for the six-by-six-mile congressional township originally established for survey purposes to become the unit of local government in the Midwest. And ninety-two counties were not "too many" in Indiana in the 1840s; nor, following the older tradition, are eighty-seven too many in Minnesota at the end of the twentieth century.

Yet, in the final quarter of the twentieth century, a township can be traversed in ten minutes by an automobile traveling at a side-road pace. A county courthouse 20 miles away can be reached in less than half an hour. Local services, once supported by a sparse population existing at a low standard of living, now are backed by greater earning capacity and more people. Are the old boundaries still appropriate? Many students of government say they are not. They seem inefficiently small by modern standards, certainly not structured with modern service requirements in mind. Nor do they meet the needs of today's technical administration or of larger units of government required for adequate service by today's standards. The loyalties that supposedly exist toward traditional units are not proved and may well be exaggerated in the claims made by local politicians. Nonetheless, efficiency cannot be the only criterion used in drawing boundaries. It seems likely that most citizens also are concerned with psychological identification with the local unit of government—especially with the representative character of government; and the citizens are especially interested in the question of whether they have access to the decision-making personnel of local government that seem to represent their interests and values. In this sense, drawing anew "logical" or "efficient" local boundaries may seem to local citizens both illogical and unreasonable. In a society in which a sense of isolation from the rest of humanity is strong and a sense of togetherness is weak, people want to believe in something; they need, among other things, a sense of political community.

The Number of Local Units

Local government changes "have occurred on the basis of step-by-step, incremental, ad hoc adjustments made to answer specific needs and forces and demands, and not on the basis of adherence of any general doctrine.''[9] Nationwide, local units of government are declining in number. About half the units in existence in 1942 had disappeared by 1987. Most of the decline occurred as a result of the consolidation of school districts in the postwar years to 1970, but quite a few towns and townships were abolished, too (see table 7–2). Special districts (e.g., for sewage disposal, fire protection, or mosquito abatement) have continued to increase in number, almost making up for the decline of school districts. This proliferation will be a major theme of the next chapter.

The largest number of local units of government are in the midwestern states (topped by 6,628 governments in Illinois in the 1987 *Census of Governments*), with its traditional townships and tiny school districts. An exception is Pennsylvania (4,957 governments), which uses the township system and also has the largest number of school districts outside the Midwest.

The fewest governmental units are to be found in the geographically small states—Hawaii (19), Rhode Island (126), Delaware (282), and Maryland (402)—and in sparsely settled Alaska (173), Nevada (198), and New Mexico (332). In the South and West, where the township system never was established and where school districts always have covered more territory than in the Midwest, governments are relatively few in number.

TABLE 7–2   Number and Change of Governments in the United States, by Type

Number	1942	1957*	1967	1977	1987
U.S.	1	1	1	1	1
States	48	50	50	50	50
Local					
Counties	3,050	3,050	3,049	3,042	3,042
Cities	16,220	17,215	18,048	18,862	19,200
Towns	18,919	17,198	17,105	16,822	16,691
School Districts	108,579	50,454	21,782	15,174	14,721
Special Districts	8,299	14,424	21,264	25,962	29,532
All Governments	155,116	102,392	81,299	79,913	83,237

Percent Change**	1942– 1957	1957– 1967	1967– 1977	1977– 1987	1942– 1987
U.S.	—	—	—	—	—
States	4.17%	—	—	—	4.17%
Local					
Counties	—	−0.03%	−0.23%	—	−0.26%
Cities	6.13%	4.84%	4.51%	1.79%	18.37%
Towns	−9.10%	−0.54%	−1.65%	−0.78%	−11.78%
School Districts	−53.53%	−56.83%	−30.34%	−2.99%	−86.44%
Special Districts	73.80%	47.42%	22.09%	13.75%	255.85%
All Governments	−33.99%	−20.60%	−1.70%	4.16%	−46.34%

Source: U.S. Bureau of the Census, *Statistical Abstract of the United States*, 1989, p. 266. The percent changes are calculated by the authors.
*The 1952 figures on local governments are adjusted to include units in Alaska and Hawaii that became states in 1959.
**The Census of Governments was first taken in 1942 and has been taken every five years since 1952.

TABLE 7-3   Location of U.S. Counties

Geographical Area	Percent of Counties	Percent of Population
Northeast	6.4%	20.7%
North Central	34.6%	24.5%
South	45.1%	34.5%
West	13.8%	20.4%

Source: *Municipal Year Book, 1988* for counties; 1989 *Statistical Abstract of the United States* for population.

The County

Counties—in Louisiana they are called parishes—are to be found in every state except tiny Rhode Island and Connecticut and sparsely populated Alaska. The average state has sixty-one counties, but the pattern varies according to region. In the South, where townships were never established to aid with administration, the county is relatively small in size. But in the Midwest, where townships flourish in some states, large numbers of counties are kept as representative units of government. In the West, where distances are vast, the county is quite large (see table 7-3).

With a few exceptions, county boundaries are drawn irrespective of whether the area enclosed is rural or urban territory or a combination of the two. As a result, America's population is distributed unevenly over the 3,042 counties of the nation. As shown in table 7-4, over one-fifth of the population resides in the twenty-five most populous counties, about one-third in the most populous fifty, and over one-half resides in one-fifth of the counties. On the other hand, nearly one-fourth of the nation's counties are organized to serve less than 5 percent of the population. It may be assumed that these counties provide only minimal services and receive a fairly large amount of state financial aid.

But, once again, efficiency may not be the prime consideration in evaluating a unit of government. Except in New England, where it has never been important, the county has served from earliest times as a basic unit of grass-roots government. Until the advent of the auto and telephone, it was the largest government with which the citizen could hope to have direct, personal contact. Especially in rural areas, a legion of social organizations used the county as the area of focus for numerous functions, including the following:

- Administering health, welfare, and educational programs
- Dispensing justice
- Paying taxes (even state taxes)
- Electing legislative representatives
- Coordinating agricultural extension programs
- Supporting voluntary social agencies
- Running the county fair
- Keeping vital statistics and land-ownership and debt records
- Maintaining roads

Designation as county seat was a prize sought, sometimes in bitter contest, by every locality. The winning locality became a trade center, the seat of the local bureaucracy, the home of governmental hangers-on such as lawyers and members of abstract companies (today perhaps title insurance companies), the location for the county fair (usually), the recreation and business center, and the home of retired farmers. The county was not an impersonal administrative unit of the state with arbitrary boundaries but rather a real and important social and political center. In most of the United States, despite changes in our way of life, it remains such today.[10]

In response to local values and needs, county governments developed organizational variety (see table 7–4). As people moved westward, they brought with them to the new territories traditions already established in the East. But mutations of structure, of nomenclature, of powers took place everywhere.

County government is, in general, organized around a governing board and a varied and often complex array of individual officers, boards, commissions, and ex-officio bodies. The pattern ordinarily is not uniform, even within a state. Part of the structure and even many details of organization may be set out in the state constitution, with the remainder usually determined by state law. As we discussed in chapter 3, in most instances counties do not operate with charters or with home rule. More so than municipalities, they exercise directed powers in regard to service delivery by administering state services following state rules. Yet, as representative bodies in some states, particularly in rural counties, service delivery is secondary to the role played by the county board as a representative and responsive body to day-to-day concerns of the vocal publics.

The variation in county government is reflected in the variety of names given to governing bodies. Although most were referred to by titles similar to either board of commissioners or board of supervisors, those in Delaware were called levy courts; in several states, county courts; in Kentucky, fiscal courts; in Texas, commissioner's courts; in most of Georgia, commissioners of roads and revenue; and in Louisiana, parish police juries. Their names provide guideposts throughout the nation's history: colonists, frontier heroes, presidents, Native American chiefs and tribes, war heros, local politicians, British, Dutch, French, German, Spanish, and other place names in nostalgia for the Old Country and places reluctantly abandoned "back East." Countless other names survive, some still filled with meaning, others half forgotten, all once important to groups with the political clout to have them stamped on our maps.

The Commission Form

The most common form of county organization has a small governing board made up of persons elected specifically to serve on those bodies and with no duties at other than the county level. The board of county commissioners (in some states—such as Iowa—called the board of county supervisors) is usually small in size, commonly having three or five members. (Because of this tradition, each of the five supervisors in Los Angeles County in the 1990s represented about as many people as do three U.S. representatives.) The board is elected by districts or at-large, or nominated by district and elected at-large.[11] The area from which commissioners are chosen (called districts usually, but beats in Mississippi and wards in Louisiana) is commonly much

TABLE 7-4 Population Characteristics of American Counties

Distribution of U.S. Counties		
Population Category	Number of Counties	Percentage of Population
250,000 or more	167	52.1%
100,000–249,999	231	16.4%
50,000–99,999	387	12.6%
25,000–49,999	616	10.0%
10,000–24,999	943	7.2%
under 5,000	698	1.9%
County Total	3,042	100.0%

Source: *Statistical Abstract of the United States*, 1989.

Largest Counties					
In order of size:	1986 Rank	1986 Population	1980 Rank	1980 Population	Change 1980–1986
Los Angeles, CA	1	8,295,900	1	7,447,503	10.23%
Cook, IL	2	5,297,900	2	5,253,655	0.84%
Harris, TX	3	2,798,300	3	2,409,547	13.89%
Kings, NY	4	2,293,200	5	2,230,936	2.72%
San Diego, CA	5	2,201,300	8	1,861,864	15.42%
Orange, CA	6	2,168,800	6	1,932,709	10.89%
Wayne, MI	7	2,164,300	4	2,337,891	−8.02%
Queens, NY	8	1,923,300	7	1,891,325	1.66%
Maricopa, AZ	9	1,900,200	12	1,509,052	20.58%
Dallas, TX	10	1,833,100	11	1,556,390	15.10%
Dade, FL	11	1,769,500	10	1,625,781	8.12%
Philadelphia, PA	12	1,642,900	9	1,688,210	−2.76%
New York, NY	13	1,478,000	15	1,428,285	3.36%
Cuyahoga, OH	14	1,445,400	13	1,498,400	−3.67%
Santa Clara, CA	15	1,401,600	18	1,295,071	7.60%
Allegheny, PA	16	1,373,600	14	1,450,085	−5.57%
Middlesex, MA	17	1,367,000	16	1,367,034	−0.00%
King, WA	18	1,362,300	20	1,269,749	6.79%
Nassau, NY	19	1,323,000	17	1,321,582	0.11%
Suffolk, NY	20	1,312,000	19	1,284,231	2.12%
Alameda, CA	21	1,208,700	22	1,105,379	8.55%
Bronx, NY	22	1,193,600	21	1,168,972	2.06%
Bexar, TX	23	1,170,000	26	988,800	15.49%
Broward, FL	24	1,142,400	23	1,018,200	10.87%
San Bernardino, CA	25	1,139,100	30	895,016	21.43%
Top 25 Total		51,205,400		47,835,667	6.58%
*Percent of total U.S. Population		1986 21.24%		1980 19.04%	

Source: *1988 County and City Data Book*, Census Bureau. (These are published every five years; no estimates are made except in these data books and the dicennial census.)
*Computed by authors.

183

larger than a town or township. Typically, the board has both legislative and administrative powers. In the nineteenth century, some judicial powers were also given the board, although these were generally given to separately elected judges in the twentieth century. The commissioner form was developed in Pennsylvania and spread westward, along the lines of parallel, as was typical of American frontier migration. Thus Ohio, Indiana, southern Illinois, Iowa, and the western states generally followed the Pennsylvania tradition. These areas continue to have small boards and are more likely to have county executives as discussed below.

The Supervisor Form

The State of New York, which adopted some of the tradition of the New England town but modified it and gave greater emphasis to the county, served as the breeding ground for another kind of county government, the supervisor form. Again, the migrants carried the old form of government with them in westerly fashion, so that, in addition to New Jersey, the supervisor form is found in Michigan, Wisconsin, and northern Illinois. The pattern of settlement ended there, however, and Minnesota adopted the commissioner plan (its sparsely populated northern areas were not divided into townships). The supervisor form is characterized by a governing body made up of persons originally elected as township supervisors and who sat on the county governing board in an ex-officio capacity. Prior to the one-person, one-vote rulings discussed below, the size of the board was determined by the number of townships in the county, although in most states the cities were also entitled to representation on the board according to a formula determined in state law. The largest such governing body was in Wayne County (Detroit), Michigan, which once had a membership of 117. A more typical board of supervisors would have around twenty members, although quite a few were larger than that; some had fewer than ten.

Because of the traditional ex-officio character of board membership under the supervisor form, citizens of these states seem to be less aware of county government than are citizens in commissioner states. Furthermore, large boards of supervisors encourage the use of the committee system for getting the board's work done, and this removes county government still more from citizen oversight. On the other hand, as large boards came to represent the population more closely, the county supervisor became more closely tuned to neighborhood or local concerns, particularly in rural counties. In some urban counties, the county supervisor has come to represent fewer people than a city council member, particularly if the city elects members-at-large. Thus, there is wide variation in patterns of responsiveness in counties that approximate the supervisor form.

In addition to the conventional (New York–type) supervisor structure of county government, several variations might be subsumed under this form, for they depend on ex-officio governing boards. In some states a judge, usually a judge of probate, serves both as chairperson of the county and as judicial officer. Other members of the board, usually called commissioners, function primarily as members of that body. Patterns are changing in most of Kentucky and Tennessee, but the other members used to be the justices of the peace of the county, an arrangement that made for large governing boards. In Arkansas and in a few counties elsewhere, a single judge acts both in a judicial capacity and as the line legislative officer of the county.

County Boards after the One-Person, One-Vote Ruling

The traditional method of selecting supervisors resulted in gross inequities of representation based on population. When the equal population (one-person, one-vote,) rule was applied to some counties in the 1960s, the states began to adopt new methods of choosing the county governing board before they were forced to act by Supreme Court rule. The supervisorial tradition of rather large boards was preserved, but they were made more manageable in size for the more urban counties, while still permitting a high degree of representativeness. In the more common commission states, the boards remained small, though they were redistricted to improve their representativeness where necessary. Eventually, the Supreme Court rulings required one-person, one-vote put an end to the inequities of population representation, although gerrymandering preserved the flavor of township representation on boards (where it had been strong) as efforts were made to abide as much as possible to traditional political boundaries. As a result, a township of greater population would get more members on the board than had previously been the case, but the supervisor's self-perception still is often as a representative of that neighborhood or area of the county rather than as a spokesperson for common concerns.

It should not be assumed that the one-person, one-vote mandate of the Supreme Court ended problems of county representation. At least two major concerns remain. First, many counties retain very small governing boards at a time of continued population growth in urban areas; for example, a number of counties still have fewer than five board members. A single county judge acting as legislator provides perfect apportionment, but distant representation. By 1990 each of the five board members in Los Angeles County, which has a population larger than that of New York City, represented over 1.5 million people. Today, districts are of equal size, but they are scarcely part of a "local" government. In contrast, in states with the supervisorial tradition, large, cumbersome boards and disjointed governments continue to be the practice in many counties. Second, the drawing of boundaries to produce almost equal population for each district, despite the local efforts mentioned earlier, often has resulted in socially or ethnically meaningless districts, in effect depriving otherwise cohesive groups of effective representation. This practice stands in contrast to nineteenth-century tradition, which emphasized ethnic or class representation over district head counts. Yet, it is difficult theoretically to defend any concept in preference to equal population by district. We will return to such questions in greater detail in chapter 11.

Executive and Administrative Trends in County Government

The most important changes in county structure have come in provision for administrative and executive practice. As recently as 1970, county executives were rare in all but a few large urban counties, but today over one-fifth of American counties have

Figure 7–2: County Government Usually Is Not Centrally Controlled

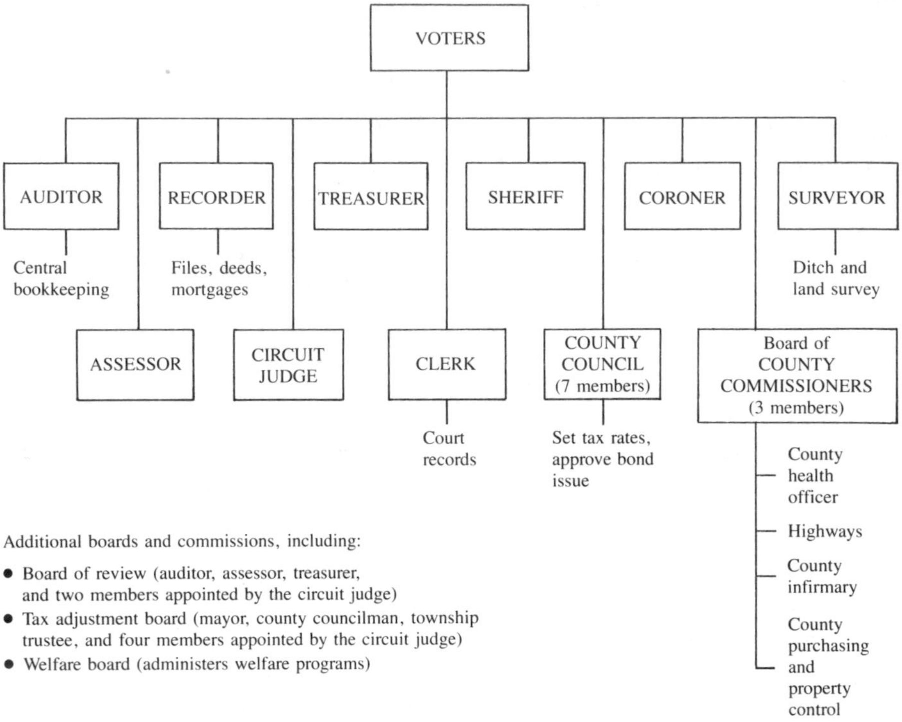

Source: Bureau of Government Research, Indiana University, Bloomington, IN.

appointed (or in few cases elected) county executives.[12] Nevertheless, the traditional form prevails, that is, with a variety of elected executives and no chief executive.

Traditionally, the long ballot was used widely and, where used, each of the elected officials is independent (by and large) of the county board. The original Jacksonian theory called for coordination through the political party, but current party practice does not result in effective performance of this function in the typical county. The legislative body usually has few, if any, coordinating powers over elective officials. The powers of each officer and board are carefully described in state law, and no person could be classified as the chief executive officer in these counties.

The American county is descended from the English county, which in turn stems from the Anglo-Saxon shire. Thus, county offices have a great deal of tradition behind them. Sheriffs' offices stem from the shire-reeve, which originated in the ninth century as the king's law officer in the shire. Similarly, a long history stands behind the offices of clerk, coroner, and treasurer. In addition to those named above, more than one-half of the states have elective county officials in the following posts: recorder or register of deeds, superintendent of county schools (an office of declining importance in most states), assessor, attorney or solicitor, and surveyor or engineer. Although no county actually elects a dog catcher, some do elect public weighers, drain commissioners, and officers with such strange-sounding titles as surrogate (in

New York, an officer who probates wills) and prothonotary (in Pennsylvania and Delaware, the clerk of the court of common pleas).

In addition to elective officers, many officers, boards, and commissions are appointive or ex-officio in their makeup. Unlike the elected county board, these have resisted the one-person, one-vote rule. The right of appointment usually rests with the county boards, and they many be found for a great variety of functions: for the county fair, airports, elections, roads, health, welfare, hospitals, libraries, schools, and dozens of others. It is through the use of these boards that county government achieves the ultimate in decentralized and uncoordinated operation. Even the county governing board is likely to lose effective supervision over its own boards and commissions. Each function of government operates without any necessary relationship to other functions and far below the level of perception of the average citizen.[13]

One current trend in county government is toward a county chief executive (see figure 7–3). The goal of an elected or appointed chief executive has been to coordinate the varied functions of county business, allowing the board to act as the legislature does in the strong-governor or national governmental form. In many of these instances, exceptions are still found in regard to independent executives, such as an independent sheriff. Except for Arkansas, where every county elects an executive, most chief executives are not elected; instead they are appointed chief administrators. The counties with appointed administrators reached one-fifth of the total in the mid-1980s, and there is reason to believe that the number will increase steadily in the 1990s, where reform subcultures prevail.[14]

Figure 7–3: Executive Leadership Proposed for Urban Counties

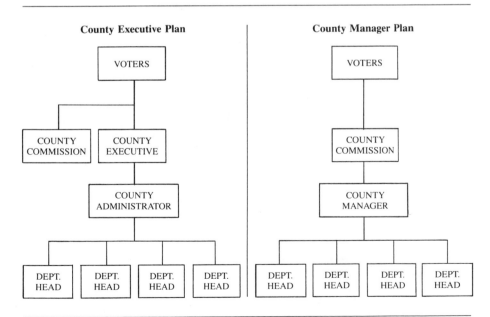

Source: C.J. Hein, *The Stake of Rural People in Metropolitan Government*, U.S. Department of Agriculture, 1961, 7.

A second trend is for counties to perform an increasing number of government functions, particularly counties with a large proportion of urban residents. The traditional function—law enforcement, judicial administration, road construction and maintenance, public welfare, record keeping, and, in some states, school administration—have been augmented both through the assumption of new services and through the transfer to the county of services once provided by other local governments, particularly the townships.[15] Many functions once considered properly those of municipal corporations are now performed by counties, even in rural areas. In fact, some counties in some states perform all functions of the municipality, although the number and assortment vary. A diversity of federal and state services must be administered by counties that wish to receive certain grants-in-aid. Perhaps the most costly and time consuming is the public welfare function for the poor, often taken on grudgingly, but required in all states (except Alaska and in New England) by federal and state law.

A third trend is the cost increases of county government, even allowing for increased returns to citizens in the form of more and better services. This is so because in some urbanized areas the county government now partially duplicates urban services, with core-city taxpayers often being called on to help pay for elaborate services provided by both the city and the county. At the same time, many rural counties that have undergone significant population losses find residents absorbing the cost burden of modern service levels, professional personnel, an eroding tax base, and a declining farm economy.

As American counties increasingly become responsible for administering the services for national and state governments, they remain the governments with least discretion under state law and least visibility to the average urbanite. Furthermore, they are least representative of the traditional American safeguard of separation of powers.

Towns and Townships

The county is an intermediate unit of government for the most part. In the East and Midwest, as well as in some other regions, a local unit of government (in addition to cities), is closer to the people than is the county. The oldest of these local units is the New England town, a unit unique to that region. Despite having been admired by Thomas Jefferson and other serious thinkers as the ideal form of direct democracy, town government did not spread to other parts of America, although some elements were adopted when New Englanders left their rocky, forested lands and moved westward.

The Town

Faced with severe winters and potentially hostile Indians, New England colonists settled in small villages and farmed the land surrounding them. These self-contained units, each of which constituted a church congregation, was a natural governmental area. The term *town* came to mean the entire community, rural and urban alike. Although the towns were not incorporated, they were recognized by the legislature as having a right to exercise certain powers, which elsewhere came to be associated with the municipal corporation. Later, when New England counties were established, they served principally as judicial districts. As some areas became increasingly urbanized, the town continued to serve as the basic unit of local government. During the War of Independence, not a single municipal corporation was to be found in New England. Even today, the town remains the area's common unit of local government, though some modification is taking place. (In Maine, a similar unit is called the *plantation*, but its government is now essentially the same as that of the town.)

Town Government

At a meeting of all qualified voters, town government is carried out. Voters choose officers-and make basic policy at an annual meeting (traditionally held in March), with as many other meetings as may be necessary. After making basic policy, the people choose a town board, usually three in number but in some places as many as nine. An important duty of the board members is to set the agenda for the next meeting by issuing a *warrant* stating that agenda. Some have complained that this allows a relatively small number of people to dominate the town meeting, a complaint that recognizes the importance of agenda setting in governments of *any* type or size.

A fairly large number of other officers—a clerk, treasurer, assessor, constable, and school committee—are either elected or appointed by the board. The members and elective officers are then entrusted with carrying out the basic policies established by community action.[16]

Town urbanization has been accompanied by a sharp decrease in attendance at town meetings and a consequent decline in the democratic effectiveness of this form of government. Even in rural towns attendance is often poor, so that finding persons willing to serve in town offices is likely to be a problem. A survey found attendance to go up dramatically as the size of the town *decreased* in size. Nevertheless, few towns meetings had average attendance of over 10 percent. Special-interest proponents turn out in relatively high numbers when issues affect them directly. But overall, it appears today that attending a town meeting is not a high priority to the average New Englander. (Were our nineteenth-century predecessors any more diligent in protecting their privileges? The answer appears to be no. The pattern in Boston in the early 1820s was the same as is reported today. See our description of the incorporation of Boston in chapter 2.)[17]

In many areas of New England, a representative town meeting plan allows voters to choose a large number of citizens, perhaps one hundred or more, to attend the meeting, represent them, and vote. Other citizens can take part in debates, but they no longer have direct votes. This plan is used in large urban places such as Brookline, Massachusetts (population over 50,000), where one Alfred D. Chandler is said to have invented the plan in 1915. In a 1984 study, forty-five Massachusetts towns were found to use the representative meeting, with seven in Connecticut, one each in Maine and Vermont, and none in New Hampshire or Rhode Island.[18]

Before the one-person, one-vote ruling, it was common for all New England towns to have representation in state legislatures, thus also strengthening their communal sense. Today, activities following meeting adjournment are largely administrative. Rarely is there separation of powers in representative towns, but it is becoming more and more common for the board to choose a manager to handle actual administration. This is particularly the case in Maine and Vermont but is to be found in all New England states. The New England legislatures have been under constant pressure to alter the traditional town government to help meet contemporary needs. For example, they have created new offices and commissions (aviation commissioner, planning boards, civil service commissions, library trustees, and finance committees—the last in order to provide better planning in budget making so that the budget is not pieced together haphazardly at the public meeting). Titles vary by states and even towns, of course.

Townships

In the Middle Atlantic states and in the Midwest, townships (confusingly, in some states, officially called towns) developed as primary units of rural government. In the East, townships were irregularly shaped, as they were in New England, but the tendency in the Midwest was to follow the lines established by the surveyors who laid out this vast area on congressional order (beginning in 1787), using a six-by-six-mile basic unit of measure called the *congressional township*. A great many townships therefore are square in shape and enclose an area of thirty-six square miles.

Township Government

Township government is organized along the lines of the New England town, some of the states even retaining the town meeting brought along by the early settlers. The annual meeting, which is poorly attended today unless an unusually important issue is on the agenda, has fewer powers than is the case in New England; but it usually does have the right to levy taxes, approve a budget, adopt such ordinances as state law permits, and, to a lessening degree today, elect officers. Often a principal function is zoning, particularly on urban fringes, where some residents seek the services that support suburban life-styles, and older residents often are fighting the influx of "outsiders." Planning also is a major function.

The states that follow the New York plan of organization generally adopted the annual meeting (New York itself abolished it in the 1930s), whereas those following the Pennsylvania pattern of local government never have had annual meetings. Details of organization vary widely.

The Decline of the Rural Township

The township was designed to suit the needs of a society that featured slow communications, primary social relationships, and the general property tax. Additionally, it became the representative district for the state legislature. In today's society, with its high labor and operations costs and with a great deal of specialization in personnel and equipment, the township is less suitable as a unit of government, and it is now too small to be a legislative district in compliance with the one-person, one-vote rule. The decline of the township may be noted both in the transfer of its traditional functions to the county and in the failure of residents of townships (and New England towns) to fill many of their offices. Nevertheless, in many parts of the nation, the township remains largely because it serves as a district for election administration or performs the tax assessment function. A number of the other traditional functions may soon disappear.

Wisconsin divides all of its unincorporated area into towns and then permits residents to incorporate the township. (The term *town* is used in the Wisconsin constitution, but *township* is used in many town ordinances and sometimes—but not always—to distinguish the incorporated town from the unincorporated town.) Such incorporation allows the township some degree of independence from the county and tax-base–hungry neighboring municipalities, which might desire annexation of the town or portions of it. Nevertheless, the incorporated town differs from the municipality in that the former does not have home rule and has its own limitations on the structure of its government. The *Wisconsin Blue Book* describes this variation on the midwestern town:

> [t]own governments are found in all areas of Wisconsin except within the corporate boundaries of cities and villages. Wisconsin has 1267 towns (including the county of Menominee, which is also designated a town). Towns have no powers other than those granted by Wisconsin statutes. In addition to local road maintenance, Wisconsin town governments carry out a variety of functions and, in some instances, even undertake urban-type services, usually through town-established sanitary and utility districts. The governing body is the town board composed of three supervisors, who are elected biennially at the town meeting. If a board is authorized to exercise village powers, it may have up to 5 members with staggered terms. The position of town supervisor is largely administrative; supervisors carry out the policies set at the annual meeting held on the second Tuesday of April or another date set by the electors. The town chairperson has a number of executive powers and duties. The town board may also create the position town administrator.[19]

The pattern of township change is different on the fringes of some larger cities. In several states, urbanized townships increasingly perform urban functions. In New Jersey, townships serve as municipal corporations and in that highly urbanized state are virtually indistinguishable from cities—except as to flexibility of governmental organization. The same is true of first-class townships in Pennsylvania (those with a density of over three hundred persons per square mile) and to a lessor degree in New York. In various mid-Atlantic states, attempts have been made to fit the township form of government, which was designed for rural government on the frontier, to modern urban society.

Michigan townships have nearly all the powers of cities, and many suburban areas are satisfied to remain organized in this fashion even though it gives them little flexibility in organizational structure. The only important local service, in terms of potential policy controversies, that is not controlled by Michigan townships is roads. The state-shared tax system makes it financially advantageous for urbanizing areas not to incorporate as cities. But, as is true in Wisconsin, some townships can vote to adopt charters. In Michigan, this gives them a degree of home rule and allows the hiring of managers. Townships so organized are officially called *charter townships*. In fringe areas, where the township remains a vital social force and performs mainly urban services, it is in essence a special type of city government, existing through

TABLE 7–5 Distribution of U.S. Municipalities by Population Groups and Type of Governments

Population	Mayor-Council	Council-Manager	Commission	Town Meeting
Over 1,000,000	6			
500,000–999,999	13	5		
250,000–499,999	16	22	2	
100,000–249,999	40	72	6	
50,000–99,999	106	179	9	5
25,000–49,999	236	365	30	21
10,000–24,999	735	673	54	125
5,000–9,999	1,000	579	33	136
2,000–4,999	1,532	466	39	164
under 2,500	132	220	3	50
Total*	3,815	2,576	176	501

Source: Compiled by the authors from *Municipal Year Book, 1988*, International City Management Association, p. xiv.
*Limited to cities surveyed by the ICMA in this category.

historical accident. The township and town remain part of the uniquely American preference for governmental fragmentation and for providing avenues that allow citizen input.

Forms of Municipal Government

Three basic forms of city government are used in the United States: mayor-council, commission, and council-manager. Many variations of the mayor-council plan exist, and important differences are found between so-called strong-mayor and weak-mayor plans of this type (see table 7–5).

Even though the structure of city government has been more deliberately planned than state, county, town, or township government, few cities fit the ideal of the general plan they follow. Probably no two cities in the United States have exactly the same structure. Nearly every charter commission or state legislature, in considering structure, finds it politically expedient to add its own improvisations on the given theme. For example, the strong-mayor-council system calls for the appointment of department heads by the mayor, yet many such cities have elective clerks and treasurers. Similarly, at-large election of council members is the strong-mayor-council rule, but increasing numbers of larger cities with this form have adopted ward elections. Although what follows in this section distinguishes one form from another by concentrating on the differences among structures, recent study indicates that the trend in the 1990s is for cities to drift toward one another in structural pattern. Reasons for this include the following: the coordination of functions among bureaucrats at the three levels of government, the expanding role of appointed chief administrative officers in cities with elected mayors, the clearer distinction of roles between mayor and city manager in cities with both officials, and greater recognition of the need to represent a wider variety of interest groups in cities with traditionally small councils.[20] These once again caution against overstating the importance of political structure.

The Mayor-Council Form

During most of the nineteenth century, American cities operated with the weak-mayor-council (or weak-mayor) system. Near the end of that century, what is now called the strong-mayor system gradually evolved. In recent years a third principal derivative—the strong-mayor-council plan with chief administrative officer plan—has been developed to correct a perceived weakness of the strong-mayor system in large cities.

The various types of mayor-council cities collectively make up over one-half of all cities of the nation under any form of government. In America, 47.9 percent of cities of over five thousand population have mayor-councils. So do most smaller cities, except in New England, where the town remains the governing body in smaller urban areas. Of the twenty-three American cities of over 500,000 inhabitants, eighteen use the mayor-council plan, usually a strong-mayor type. Of the small cities of five thousand to ten thousand people, 56 percent have the mayor-council form, usually a weak-mayor type; 70 percent either have this mayor-council plan or the town form, which resembles the weak-mayor-council system in these municipalities.

The Weak-Mayor-Council Plan

In the early 1800s, America's budding cities borrowed from rural government certain essential concepts. Today we call these concepts the weak-mayor-council plan.

Characteristics. The weak-mayor plan is a product of Jacksonian democracy. It reflects the spirit of the frontier, with a skepticism both of politicians and of government itself. It grew out of a time when the functions of city government were few, when local officials were coordinated through the political party, and when people were afraid to give powers to a single executive. Implicit in the weak-mayor plan are the beliefs that if politicians have few powers and many checks on them, they can do relatively little damage, and that if one politician becomes corrupt, this will not necessarily corrupt the whole government. As discussed in chapter 2, the form was frequently adapted to the informal organization of the political machine.

The council is both a legislative and an executive organization under the weak-mayor plan. In small cities, the council consists of five or seven members, but in larger cities it is usually a fairly large body of perhaps eleven to fifty members; at one time, councils might have been as large as two hundred. Except in small cities, members usually are elected by wards on a partisan ballot.

In addition to making policy, the council appoints several administrative officers, such as the city engineer and the city attorney. Council members (sometimes called aldermen if they represent wards) may serve on several ex-officio boards and commissions. A committee of the council usually prepares the budget and may even appoint the controller, who administers the expenditure of the budget. Mayors are not "weak" because they lack policy-making power—often they have a veto, can recommend legislation, and may even preside over the council—but because they lack administrative power. In fact, no single individual is charged with ensuring that the laws and ordinances are properly carried out or that the city administration proceeds in accord with an overall plan. Mayors have highly restricted appointive powers; even when they are allowed to make appointments, they may not be able to remove those they place in office, which deprives mayors of any real control over or responsibility for appointees.

Ordinarily, several of the principal city offices are filled by direct election—the long ballot is characteristic of the weak-mayor plan. A large number of boards and commissions also are likely, some filled by appointment by the council or the mayor, some ex-officio, some elected.

Appraisal. The weak-mayor plan was never intended to serve large, impersonal urban communities. The arguments for the plan are based on the precepts of Jacksonianism, ideas still popular with a large number of American people. For example, Americans may not know which officers are elected and which are appointed or what the qualifications are for a good city clerk or city controller, or even what their duties are; but they are likely to insist that those elected should continue to be elected. They will also argue that elective officials, no matter what their duties, are more responsible to the public than are appointive officials. The strongest argument for the weak-mayor plan is that, with many elective officers and with a fairly large council elected by wards, it offers the ordinary, noninfluential citizen the best chance for access to the decision-making centers of government. Yet, ironically, the very clumsiness and lack of coordination of the plan in an impersonal urban society makes it the least likely to be visible to citizens who want to know what it is doing. Therefore, it also provides the best chance for corruption to creep in unnoticed, as demonstrated during the days of the political machine.

The plan is problematic for any but small communities, where government is on a neighborly basis, because of the lack of provision for political and administrative leadership. In larger cities, no officer is authorized to coordinate the multifold activities of a complex, modern city; and no one can balance the demands of the parks department against those of public works. Each functional agency gallops off in its own direction, spending money with little oversight and causing an excess of wealth in one department while another struggles in poverty. The political party, which was well coordinated and organized diverse interests in the 1800s, today is weakened in this area by public concern for honesty and general distaste for strong partisanship.

The weak-mayor system characteristically is found in small cities and villages. In villages, there is no separation of powers and the mayor or president merely presides over the council, without veto power. In this form, the weak-mayor plan is close to the townships, towns, and traditional English forms of local government. Many cities of considerable size still have relatively weak mayors, especially in the South, though they may be found in all parts of the nation (Los Angeles, Chicago, Atlanta, and San Francisco are examples). In areas where the simple, primary relationships of rural society are replaced by the impersonal urban way of life, the weak-mayor system definitely has been found wanting, as its one great advantage is the opportunity for citizen participation.

The Strong-Mayor-Council Plan

The development of the strong-mayor system of government in the last two decades of the nineteenth century was gradual. The plan differed only in degree from that of the weak-mayor system. It was not conceived of as a distinctly new form of government, nor was it one. Actually, the weak-mayor form resembled the structure of most state governments then and now. The strong-mayor system, on the other hand, was modeled on the national government with its *integrated administrative structure* under the control of the president.

> *Integrated Administrative Structure:* **A structure in which all administrative authority and responsibility theoretically is in the hands of a single individual or body. The administrative structure is arranged so that each employee or officer is formally responsible to a superior who in turn must answer to another superior, until ultimately department heads each are responsible to a single chief executive. This structure is called a** *hierarchy.*

Characteristics. Most mayor-council cities represent a compromise between the very weak- and the very stong-mayor plan. This should be kept in mind in considering the description below.

In the strong-mayor-council city, administrative responsibility is concentrated in the hands of the mayor, whereas policy making is a joint function of the mayor and the council. The plan calls for a short ballot with the mayor as the only elected administrative officer. The mayor in turn appoints and dismisses departments heads, preferably (according to reformers) without approval of the council. The mayor thus becomes the officer responsible for carrying out established policy and for coordinating the efforts of the various departments. The mayor also is responsible for the preparation of the annual budget and the administration of the budget once it is adopted by the council. This allows for the whole financial picture and the needs of the various departments to be compared in policy making and is in contrast to the piecemeal methods by which these issues are approached under the weak-mayor plan.

The mayor's legal position allows for both powerful political and administrative leadership. Not only does the mayor have the veto power and the right to recommend legislative policy to the council, as is usual under the weak-mayor system, but complete control over administration also allows for constant oversight of the needs of the city as a whole and furnishes a vantage point from which to recommend policy. This strong position puts the mayor constantly in the limelight, with actions and recommendations getting generous media coverage, and a budget that normally is so conspicuously tied to day-to-day knowledge of governmental affairs that the burden of proof for any change rests on the council.

The council plays a definitely subordiante role in the strong-mayor city and does not, as in the weak-mayor city, share in the performance of administrative duties. Its functions are limited to the exercise of legislative policy making, and even this role must be shared with the mayor. The council is likely to be small (typically seven or nine members) and elected at-large on either a partisan or, more common today, a nonpartisan ballot. Unless the city is very large, members usually serve on a part-time basis, with four-year terms for mayor and council members alike. This term, longer than on the frontier, is the result of the reform belief that public officials should be given enough time in office to prove themselves.

Appraisal. Because of its provision for vigorous political leadership, the strong-mayor plan seems especially adaptable for use in large cities, where the complexities of government require firm leadership and direction. Most of the nation's largest cities, in fact, do have versions of this plan, which allows for the pinpointing of responsibility and for overall policy planning and coordination of administration.

A disadvantage is that the plan seems to expect too much of the mayor. When problems for central cities mounted in the 1960s and 1970s, few people of the caliber the job required were willing to run for the office. When central cities began to re-emerge in the 1980s and 1990s because of factors such as increased revenue bases, changing demographics, and gentrification—as well as the fact that big-city problems are now also found in suburbs—pressures on the mayor have been somewhat allevi-ated. But other disadvantages persist. Few persons combine the talents of the adroit politician with those of the expert administrator that the plan expects. Furthermore, the plan permits deadlocks between a strong mayor and council that occasionally may refuse to allow itself to be dominated—particularly where large cities have strong mayors with ward elections of council members. Battle often is waged between a mayor who represents downtown business growth and council members who prefer small ward businesses and a greater dispersal of the city's resources among the wards. Should the mayor be the victor in such battle, downtown growth may become evident in the changing skyline of the central city. Should the council members win, however, the city's tax base may suffer. In a stalemate, the strong leadership ex-pected in this form will be a disappointment to the city's hopeful residents.

The Strong-Mayor-Council Plan with Chief Administrative Officer

As an administrator, the chief executive in a strong-mayor city may well recog-nize the shortcomings of the office and attempt to do something about them. The most common method of buttressing the mayoral position is to appoint an able, profession-ally experienced administrator as chief fiscal officer, usually called the *controller*. This person may act as something of a deputy mayor and attend to many details of administration. But the typical politician-mayor does not always want a professional technician as a deputy, following instead a trend toward establishing by charter or ordinance an official known by various titles but perhaps most commonly called a *chief administrative officer* (CAO). The CAO's powers vary considerably from one city to another, and sometimes the position can scarcely be differentiated from the chief budget or fiscal officer. The CAO is appointed by the mayor (theoretically at least) and should generally carry out the same tasks performed in a private corpora-tion by the chief operations officer, including, for example, the following:

- Supervising heads of various departments
- Preparing the budget
- Directing personnel
- Coordinating various departments in routine day-to-day administration
- Providing technical and professional advice to the mayor

The goal then, is to free the mayor to perform activities that are equivalent to those performed by a chief executive officer in the private sector—serving as ceremonial head of the city (e.g., greeting the governor, laying cornerstones, serving on *ad hoc* committees, and presenting the Citizen of the Year award), and devising, proposing, and launching broad overall policy. Of course, the mayor retains overall responsibility for the work of the CAO.

The CAO plan probably originated in San Fransisco in 1931, although other cities have some claim to it. In the period after World War II, it spread to many of the nation's largest cities, including New York, Los Angeles, Philadelphia, Honolulu, and New Orleans. CAOs may come to be seen as being similar to the city manager by those in state and national bureaucracies; in effect, as fellow "experts." Thus, the growing popularity of this form highlights the tendency toward the merging of forms mentioned above.[21]

The Commission Plan

During the rebuilding of Galveston, Texas, after it was devastated by a hurricane in September 1900, the legislature suspended local self-government in the city and substituted a temporary government of five local businessmen—the Galveston Commission, from which the plan derives its name. The commission, working with great zeal under extraordinary conditions accomplished much more at less cost than had its almost bankrupt predecessor government.

After the emergency the plan, now with elected commissioners, was retained permanently in Galveston, and the publicity it had received attracted much interest. Hailed as a "businessman's government," the plan—ten years after its accidental creation—had been installed in 108 cities, and at least 500 cities by 1917. Then, in a reversal, municipal reformers lost interest in the commission plan and instead began to advocate the new council-manager plan as the true embodiment of a business form of organization. The number of cities using the commission plan (135 plans in cities of over 5,000 population in 1986) has declined steadily since World War I.

Characteristics. The commission plan's outstanding feature is the dual role of the commissioners. Each serves individually as the head of one of the city's administrative departments, and collectively they serve as the policy-making council for the city, with no separation of powers. The commission performs legislative *and* executive functions.

The commission is always small, usually consisting of five members, but varying from three to seven. The mayor has no powers beyond those of the other commissioners, except to perform ceremonial duties for the city and preside over council meetings (with no veto power). The mayor usually is specifically elected to the office, but in a few places, the candidate who happens to receive the highest number of votes becomes mayor. Commissioners usually are elected on a nonpartisan ticket, at-large, for four-year terms. The ballot is short, especially because terms of office of the commissioners are staggered with only two or three members of a five-member commission elected at one time.

Appraisal. The commission plan provided for a more modern approach to administration than did the weak-mayor systems at the turn of the century. Its short ballot concentrated responsibility in the hands of a few persons so that the interested citizen could assess credit or blame for municipal activities. The plan shortened the ballot and allowed voters a chance to learn something about the character and qualifications of the candidates. Furthermore, only the principal officers of the city were chosen by election.

The plan, however, had too many disadvantages to be workable. For one thing, it was not possible to get the high quality of personnel needed through election, especially in smaller cities. Qualified citizens were not willing to give up their businesses or professions to run for an office that paid relatively low salary and offered no job security. The plan encouraged amateur administration, for many chosen to the commission had little or no administrative experience. In this respect, there was little change from traditional Jacksonian practice.

Other weaknesses were more serious. The commission was so small that no provision was made for the function of criticism. The mayor-council plan at least allowed the council to react critically to the mayor's actions. Under the commission plan, a fraternity of tolerance was more likely the custom, where a mutual hands-off policy meant that several different city governments really operated independently of each other, with an occasional five-power conference to satisfy the demands of the charter. Finally, the plan provided no overall policy for administrative leadership. For example, with each commissioner jealously guarding control over a particular department, the top of the administrative pyramid was sawed off, so that each department moved in its own direction. The plan was quickly outmoded with the development of the council-manager plan and the modern strong-mayor plan. Inherent weaknesses in the commission plan have made it more anachronistic than some older forms of government that still thrive in America. Nevertheless, it is still used in modified form in some cities. Thus, Fargo, North Dakota, uses a "portfolio" system in which each commissioner supervises a group of departments, each with its own department head. Other cities have a professional as the permanent deputy commissioner to handle routine administration within the department. Still others use a budget or personnel officer under the joint control of all commissioners. But the plan is slowly dying.

The Council-Manager Plan

The origin of the council-manager plan is unknown. One of the first known instances in which it was urged was in an editorial in the August 1899 issue of *California Municipalities*. Haven A. Mason, editor of the magazine, urged that there should be "a distinct profession of municipal managers."[22] In 1908, Staunton, Virginia, by ordinance hired a general manager to serve as a full-time administrator under a weak-mayor and bicameral (two-house)-council system. A few years later, Richard S. Childs, a businessman who was at that time secretary of the National Short Ballot Organization and who later became president of the National Municipal League, drew up a plan that embodied the basic characteristics of the council-manager plan as we know it today. His plan, adopted first by Sumter, South Carolina (1912), and then by Dayton, Ohio (1913), triggered the rapid spread of the form thereafter. By 1915, forty-nine manager cities had been created; by 1920 there were 158. The number has increased uninterrupted ever since.[23]

By 1990, over 2,500 council-manager cities existed; nearly 50 percent of the cities with 10,000 to 500,000 in population have managers. Of the twenty-four cities estimated to have a population of more than 500,000, five have the council-manager plan: Dallas, Phoenix, San Antonio, San Jose, and San Diego. In addition, metropolitan Dade County, Florida, with a population of over 1.7 million, has a manager. Los Angeles County with a population greater than 8 million, has a chief administrative officer with many of the powers of a manager. But the system thrives in *mid-size* cities (see table 7-5).

The council-manager form of government was most likely to be used in cities having a young, mobile, white, middle-class, rapidly growing population,[24] often the characteristics of the homogeneous population of the growing suburbs in the 1920s and in the two decades after World War II. Working-class cities usually have some version of the mayor-council form. A 1986 study of Colorado cities suggests that size, age of the city, and state mandates at the time of charter issue are also crucial to predicting form.[25]

The political difficulty in changing form of government is significant, so much so that cities usually maintain their council-manager or mayor-council form, regardless of demographic changes after the original chartering. The changes that do take place are more often *within* a form (for example from at-large to ward election or from weak-mayor to strong-mayor). The council-manager plan, however, is frequently challenged, even in cities that have long used the plan. For instance, fifty years after it went into effect in Dayton, Ohio (1913), a referendum vote on abandonment was held but defeated by a margin of 6 to 1. In 1931, Cleveland became the largest city to discontinue the plan. Albuquerque gave up the form in 1974 after many years of assault.[26] Some smaller cities have changed more recently, finding the council-manager form unsuitable for isolated small cities, in contrast to those in the large metropolis. In the 1980s two smaller cities in western Wisconsin held referendums to change from a council-manager to a mayor-council form. One, Menomonie, changed; the other Eau Claire, rejected an overall change but did support modification from at-large to ward elections. At about the same time, Long Beach and several other California cities also went from at-large to ward elections. These changes suggest some dissatisfaction with the reduction in input from citizens and neighborhoods afforded by the form; however, many such changes reflect in part the large growth in population since the cities first adopted the plan, in some cases as much as forty to sixty years earlier. Economically and socially complex San Diego, the second-largest city in California, is vastly different from the modest-sized, sleepy navy town it was when it first adopted the plan in 1925, for example. Managership in general is now sometimes viciously attacked as unsuitable, but form of government is not of principal concern to most voters, and so in every city the decision may be about the personality or competence of the manager of the moment, or some secondary issue identified with the major proponents of change, or the manager may simply be caught between rival power factions on the council.

Characteristics. Outstanding features of the council-manager plan include a lay council that is responsible for policy and a professional administration under a chief administrator that is responsible to the council. In theory, the structure rivals that of the British parliamentary system in its simplicity.

The council is small, five to nine members, and usually is elected at-large, on a nonpartisan ballot, often for four-year staggered terms. In theory, it is responsible to the public for all policy making and ultimately for the overall character of administration. Under the model charter, members of the council are the only officers who are popularly elected.[27] The intent of the short ballot is to concentrate responsibility on these people and to ask voters to fill only those positions in which they can reasonably be expected to take an interest.

No separation of powers or checks and balances exists. The mayor (the title used in only some council-manager cities) or president of the city or village council, who normally performs only ceremonial functions and presides over council meetings, has no administrative powers except in an emergency, and no veto. In more than one-half of the council-manager cities with over five thousand population, the council chooses the mayor from its own membership. Most other cities use direct election, and a few give the post to the person with the most votes in the council race. Administration of the city is integrated under the control of a professional manager, who is hired by the council and, in the model plan, serves for no defined term but rather at the pleasure of a council majority. The manager, a professional administrator, is expected to hire professionally competent technicians to run the various city departments. The lower administrative positions, roughly those below the department heads, also are filled with technically competent individuals usually chosen by civil service merit examination.

Appraisal. Municipal reformers have tended to accord to this plan inordinate praise, often attributing to it miraculous powers to bring about efficient and economical city administration regardless of the traditions of city government, the kind of personnel it employs, and the existence or lack of public understanding and support of the basic principles of the plan. These exaggerated claims for the plan, as well as some of the specious arguments against it, should be discounted by the sophisticated student of government.

The general political climate in which the council-manager plan exists and the tradition against more than token pay for members of the council, help ensure a lay council of amateur politicians uninterested in making a living out of the job. (This is quite different from the style of the old-fashioned machine politician.) The council-manager plan emphasizes professional and technical competence, from the manager down to the lowest-paid position, an appropriate characteristic in a complex modern society. Criticism is allowed because the legislative branch has no reason *not* to be free to comment on the quality of the work of the manager. Even so, council members being intimidated by the very professionalism of the administrators, may be reluctant to exercise this freedom.

Although the manager plan is simple in mechanism, it is sometimes misunderstood. It has been called "dictatorial" or "un-American," but the argument is exaggerated, for responsibility for administration is quite clear. Some argue that the plan costs too much for smaller cities, but it is used successfully in a number of cities with fewer than five thousand. A frequently cited study of the 1960s found that council-manager cities actually spent less than the mayor-council cities,[28] although it is very difficult to hold constant the multitude of variables other than governmental form. For example, regionalism, not form of government, may account for higher costs.[29] The higher salaries demanded by experts in the council-manager form might be offset by the kinds of efficiency that middle-class people seek, particularly when coupled with the degree of honesty generally associated with reform governments (see chapter 2).

A more valid criticism of the plan centers on the question of the competence of some managers, a problem that has been complicated by the number of adoptions of the plan outrunning the supply of trained and experienced persons to serve. Some cities have adopted the plan but have not been able or willing to hire qualified managers. In cities where the plan is not trusted, managers have had the status of errand runners. But the council cannot lead collectively; therefore, lay and part-time as it is, it looks to the professional, full-time manager for policy recommendations. The manager is nearly always in a better position to make recommendations than is the council.[30] Yet, a council that regularly accepts the manager's recommendations is not necessarily a rubber-stamp council; it may simply be a council that has hired a competent manager who is sensitive to local values. The function of the council has emerged not so much as the ideal of the original plan but a reviewing and vetoing agency, checking on the manager more than leading in policy making. But lack of regular policy making by elected officials or widespread citizen input allows the plan to succeed very differently in different places.

In theory, the manager is administrator and the council is policymaker. In practice, this sharp separation is difficult to achieve. Frequently, managers serve a period of probation during which they are under close scrutiny and probably suspect as outsiders; therefore they may try to appear as ''nonpolitical'' as possible. Of course, all decisions of a chief executive are political. The manager, then, must learn to integrate the professional training received into the particular political culture of the city. After the council becomes comfortable with the manager's competence and public attitudes, it usually will come to rely on his or her advice in regard to policy decisions. Thus the budget, the most important policy statement, eventually will be prepared by the manager and supported by technical studies. Lay council members, often themselves professionals in other areas, come to be comfortable with manager decisions *or* intimidated by manager expertise.

Other failures in carrying out the original council-manager plan arise if the mayor challenges the manager for control of policy; or if the council tries to continue the traditional practice of entering into administrative oversight at the lower levels, bypassing the manager and undermining the confidence of subordinates. Opinion leaders and voters who are oriented along ethnic and class lines believe the councils are too small to be representative of a cross section of the population and conclude that electing persons to councils by the at-large system results in ''an overrepresentation of business and professional interests and an underrepresentation of labor, ethnic, and other lower-class interests.''[31] Some voters resent managers who are not directly accountable to them—the old Jacksonian syndrome.

The council-manager plan will continue to be the choice of new suburban governments and of most cities desiring change. Its success may require that it change somewhat, much as the mayor-council form did over time. Two changes suggest some middle ground between advocates and opponents of the form: the incorporation of ward elections into the system and an expanded role for the mayor (or council president) in representing the city beyond its borders.[32]

Special Districts

A special district is an organized unit of government that has its own governing body and taxing power, autonomy from other governments, and, usually, its own bonding authority. It is thus a separate unit of government that performs one or more public services. Special districts exist for varied purposes, including:

- Water distribution
- Community colleges
- Public health
- Libraries
- Recreation
- Sewage disposal
- Airports
- Planning
- Parking
- Fire protection
- Mosquito abatement

However, the most common and important use is as school districts to provide primary and secondary education, the highest local government priority. They may have boundaries coterminous with (or overlapping) another unit of government (such as a city or county). They exist in both rural and urban areas and are to be found in every state.

The use of special districts typically is defended with one or more of the following arguments:

1. It makes it possible—or at least easier—to finance a particular governmental function because bonds can be floated and taxes levied in the name of the special district rather than of some county or municipality already heavily burdened.
2. Persons involved in a single function regarded as important in the locality will draw greater support from professionals in the field and higher-status members of the locality if separately organized.
3. Special districts, being wholly dependent on their own resources, must be "businesslike" and must avoid "politics" by (in part) ignoring parochial demands of a narrow constituency and concentrating on efficiency.
4. Greater flexibility is possible concerning boundaries; that is, a district is better able than other units of local government to fit its boundaries to the area actually in need of the particular service.

Although these arguments have been valid in some districts, particularly school districts, where high-quality education is often justified without much argument, they often fail in districts that provide services that the middle class considers to be of marginal importance (e.g., rapid transit districts). The presumption that politics somehow can be eliminated from government organization and administration is never correct. Those who use such rhetoric of course mean that certain political processes (such as reliance on public opinion as measured by frequent elections) should be replaced with others (such as merit systems to select public officials and policy making by such professionals). Special districts historically have been defended with such rhetoric, more so than other types of government.

An ad hoc district may be governed by a state-appointed body; one appointed by officials from the local governments overlaid by the district, with members being either appointed especially for the position or in ex-officio capacities; one appointed by a judge; or one elected by the voters of the area. The latter possibility is atypical (though common enough west of the Missouri), so that nonschool special-purpose districts ordinarily do not come within the direct oversight of the voting public. School districts generally are governed by a school board, which is elected by voters. The district is similar to council-manager government in that the board then usually hires a chief executive (the superintendent) who is a trained administrator who in turn will hire other administrators (such as school principals).

Growth of Special Districts

Special districts account for over one-half of all governments in the United States. Three trends in their growth since World War II are of importance: the enormous growth of nonschool special districts, the steady decline in the number of school districts, and the emergence of metropolitanwide special districts. (For convenience, the term *special district* will be used for nonschool special districts and *school district* for school districts. Both are special districts and exist for essentially the same purposes except as to function).

The general trend of special districts has been one of steady increase in number since the end of World War II. In 1952, four times as many special districts existed as did counties; but by 1987, there were almost ten times as many. By 1987, special districts were by far the most common form of government in the United States, having almost tripled in number since World War II and accounting for over one-third of all governments. In the two decades after the war, most special districts were to be found in rural areas or on the fringe of metropolitan areas where services were demanded, but residents did not want the high cost of incorporating general-purpose governments. Since 1972, however, the increase in special districts has been concentrated in metropolitan areas, particularly within California, Illinois, and Pennsylvania, which now have the greatest number of such districts. Special districts in rural areas are commonly those for fire protection, soil conservation, and drainage, and in urban areas for housing, which together make up about one-half the total districts.[33]

Several factors account for the trend toward special districts. Some are created to meet national grant-in-aid conditions, especially those for soil conservation and housing. Often special districts are the only practical means of supplying added services in a metropolitan area. The pattern of use seems to depend on local customs and perhaps on the accident of the gradual accumulation of rigid constitutional and statutory restrictions controlling general governments and discouraging the use of the existing units for newer services. For example, one might expect special districts to be used especially in states not having townships, but that has not proved to be the case. Special districts are very popular in the West, where they are used especially for the procurement, distribution, and allocation of scarce water supplies. But they are found in every part of the land.

Whenever a specific problem needs the simplest, least-expensive accommodation, the special district approach usually has strong appeal. Citizens do not resist this approach (as they do attempts at governmental consolidation), because they expect it to be less expensive and to preserve the independence of their local government. Interest groups that may want services performed by government (amateur pilots wanting an airport, physicians wanting a hospital), together with the professional administrators of particular functions, characteristically want their special problems handled in a special way by a special organization.[34]

Special districts tend to have higher debts than general purpose governments—evidence that functions generally assigned to special districts are of a high-cost, capital-outlay type. This does not discourage their use.

School administrators long ago convinced the American public that they should be independent of the rest of local government, and the school district is at once the most common and the best-known special district. Others have followed the lead of educators and pressure groups supporting them. The special district also has had great appeal to the wistful who would take their pet governmental function "out of politics." But the school district *is* a government and serves the same functions as any American political system; it raises taxes and is expected to provide services checked by the public and special interests and a forum for response to the public. In fact, a report of the ACIR suggests that school districts might even be thought of as multipurpose governments, even though technically they serve one function:

> Although the school district is a special-purpose entity, its activities are closely related to, if not seemingly duplicative of those performed by general purpose units of local government. The education function itself—particularly vocational education—is an integral part of training programs [formerly] covered by the Comprehensive Employment and Training Act [of the national government] administered by cities and counties as prime sponsors. Similarly, activities of city park and recreation departments frequently parallel activities conducted by schools. In large cities, moreover, efforts to establish neighborhood subunits for purposes of representation and service can vie with, or complement, similar efforts for strictly school purposes.[35]

The decline in the number of school districts can be seen in table 7-2: 108,579 districts in 1942 were cut to 14,721 in 1987, although the decline in numbers had largely been completed by 1970. But these figures can be misleading. Consolidation occurred almost entirely in rural areas as part of the high school movement following World War I, as society changed its concept of a normal education from eight years to twelve. It took place in the face of high capital costs for building new schools, for costs would otherwise be spread over too small a tax base. Rural areas also faced problems of declining enrollment and inability to afford some of the programs expected in urban areas, mandated by state laws, or made conditions of national grants. At first districts tried to avoid consolidation by use of interdistrict tuition payments and other techniques, but after World War II, often stimulated by state grants and mandates, consolidation became the standard approach. Bollens and Schmandt make this observation:

> Although the era of large-scale school consolidation has now passed, the reasons for the success of the merger drive remain of interest. Two factors stand out prominently in this connection. One is the willingness shown by state legislatures to foster such action, a readiness prompted by rising educational costs and increasing pressure on the states to assume a greater share of school financing. The other is the strong advocacy of consolidation demonstrated by professional educators and civic leaders who see merger of the smaller districts as imperative to quality education.[36]

In urban areas, the formation of new suburban school districts allows suburbanites to continue to avoid metropolitan desegregation or integration with lower-class areas that have taxable property of less value. Although the Supreme Court has ruled that a district cannot be formed for the purpose of segregating, a district is virtually free from desegregation plans if it is not formed to segregate and happens to be largely of one race, making intradistrict desegregation impossible.[37] If racial issues were not involved, the consolidation of school districts in some metropolitan areas would be far more likely.

The need for an areawide approach to problems exists in rural areas, as in the case of drains that cross township and county lines, as well as in urban areas. Problems requiring such an approach have increased as urban populations have increased. With other solutions failing or seeming to be politically impossible, the special district has been turned to. It has been very popular in many rapidly urbanizing states and has served, as in California, as a substitute for incorporation or for a fringe government of less area than the county. In most metropolitan areas, the special district is the only exclusively metropolitanwide government. About one-half of the MSAs in the United States have them. Part of their attraction lies in the fact that it is easier to create them than it is to consolidate existing governments.[38] By leaving the political status quo undisturbed, jobs are not threatened, property taxpayers need have little fear of being assessed for someone else's benefit, and conversely, in the metropolitan district, it is more likely a taxpayer will pay his or her fair share of the cost. Usually, the debts and costs of special districts do not count in determining debt and tax limits of regular local governments, and the bonds of such districts are sometimes more easily marketed than those of other local governments. Furthermore, the metropolitan special district may be mandated by a higher government if the area is to receive higher government grants, particularly for environmental protection. Many metropolitan pollution control districts exist simply to protect the outside revenue source, not because the people or municipalities involved are particularly concerned with metropolitan pollution control.

Pros and Cons of Districts

Special districts make possible the provision of governmental services when and where they are most needed, and they limit the financial burden to residents who benefit most directly, while at the same time they skip lightly over the myriad local government boundaries that otherwise stand in the way of making these services available. Other units of government frequently cannot or will not supply these services.

Disadvantages of special districts include the fact that the behind-the-scenes way in which they generally operate helps to make them especially profitable for lawyers, engineers, bankers, bonding houses, and sellers of equipment, services, and real estate. Often designed to meet short-range needs, they fail to consider more permanent solutions, and, because they downplay the urgency of a situation (for a considerable portion of a locality), they serve to forestall efforts toward long-range, rational governmental organization.

Special districts often have done very good jobs in construction and engineering and sometimes in management. However, they do not necessarily eliminate political patronage, guarantee professional administration of functions, and remove from the arena of politics governmental functions that involve issues of policy. Special districts often result in increased total cost of local governments because of duplication of personnel, inefficient utilization of equipment, and inability to save through centralized purchasing and other centralized housekeeping activities. They do not (1) balance the various needs for services of a locality; (2) recognize the interdependence of various functions; and (3) coordinate their activities and budget with those of the other governments in their areas.

If the governing board of a district is elective, the ballot is made longer and voters are asked to fill offices in which they may have little interest. If the governing board is indirectly chosen, as is usually the case, no real responsibility is owed the public for the function performed. On this point, Victor Jones has concluded the following in regard to metropolitanwide special districts:

> A corporate form of metropolitan government in which the selection of the authority or district commission members is once more removed from the electoral controls may give us efficient and effective government but it cannot give us good government. It is not necessary, nor is it desirable, for all policy-making officials to be directly elected by popular vote. They should, however, be subject to the budgetary control of popularly elected legislators and their policies should be subject to debate and discussion.[39]

The relationship among governments in metropolitan areas are the subject of the next chapter.

Concluding Note

Structures of government are tools. They are important, but, like other machinery, they may be modern or antiquated and hence are not all equally suited for present-day government. A tool will not operate itself, nor will the same one be equally effective in different tasks. Local cultural circumstances will influence the type of structure that is needed and the quality of government that will be produced from any chosen form.

Notes

1. James Q. Wilson, *Varieties of Police Behavior* (New York: Atheneum, 1970), 233; James H. Svara, *Official Leadership in the City* (New York: Oxford University Press, 1989).

2. See chapter 2. The discussion of southern governors in the mid-twentieth century can be found in V. O. Key, Jr., and Alexander Heard, *Southern Politics* (New York: Vintage, 1949).

3. Thad L. Beyle, "Governors," in Virginia Gray, Herbert Jacob, and Kenneth N. Vines, eds., *Politics in the American States: A Comparative Analysis*, 4th ed. (Boston: Little, Brown, 1983), 180–222. On the powers of executives and legislators, see chapters 9 and 12, respectively; also Thad L. Beyle, "The Governors, 1988–89," *1990–1991 Book of the States* (Lexington, KY: Council of State Governments), 50–61; and Thad L. Beyle, "The Institutionalized Powers of the Governorship; 1965–1985," *Comparative State Politics Newsletter* 9:1 (Feb. 1987): 26–27.

4. Larry Sabato, *Goodbye to Good-time Charlie: The American Governorship Transformed*, 2d ed. (Washington D.C.: CQ Press, 1983), 61–62.

5. Arthur E. Buck, *The Reorganization of State Governments in the United States* (New York: Columbia University Press, 1938).

6. Sabato, *Good-time Charlie*, 62.

7. Leonard D. White, *Trends in Public Administration* (New York: McGraw-Hill, 1933), 176.

8. *The Census of Governments, 1987*, vol. 1 (U.S. Census Bureau, Washington, D.C., issued in September 1988), 4 and A-9. The census of governments has been similarly done every five years since 1957. Smaller censuses were done in 1942 and 1952.

9. York Willbern, *The Withering Away of the City* (Tuscaloosa: University of Alabama Press, 1964), 106

10. For details on county government and its history, see Lane W. Lancaster, *Government in Rural America*, 2d ed. (New York: Van Nostrand Reinhold, 1952); or Clyde F. Snider, *Local Government in Rural America* (New York: Appleton-Century-Crofts, 1957). The county as an urban unit is discussed in John C. Bollens et al., eds., *American County Government* (Beverly Hills, CA: Sage Publications, 1969). One measure of the neglect given counties by urban scholars is seen in that the most recent book known on the topic (Bollens et al.) is more than two decades old.

11. On the political significance of commissions, see Bertil Hanson, "County Commissioners of Oklahoma," *Midwest Journal of Political Science* 9 (Nov. 1965):388–400.

12 *Municipal Year Book, 1988* (Washington, D.C.: International City Management Association, 1988), xvi.

13. See Edward W. Weidner, *The American County: Patchwork of Boards* (National Municipal League, 1946).

14. *Municipal Year Book, 1988*, xviii.

15. See Clyde F. Snider, "American County Government: A Mid-Century Review," *American Political Science Review* 46 (Mar. 1952): 66–70, William N. Cassella, "County Government in Transistion," *Public Administration Review* 16 (Summer 1956): 223–31; "Improving County Government," *Public Management* 53 (Apr. 1971).

16. On the historical evolution of "plantations," see Snider, *Local Government*, chapter 8.

17. See also Joseph F. Zimmerman, "The New England Town Meeting: Pure Democracy in Action?," *The Municipal Year Book, 1984*, 102–6; and Roscoe C. Martin, *Grass Roots* (Tuscaloosa: University of Alabama Press, 1957), 60–62.

18. Zimmerman, ibid.

19. State of Wisconsin, *Blue Book, 1985–86* (Madison: Wisconsin Legislative Reference Bureau, 1985) 274.

20. Charles R. Adrian, "Forms of City Government in American History," *Municipal Year Book, 1988*, 9.

21. Ibid.

22. The editorial is reprinted in John C. Bollens, *Appointed Executive Local Government: The California Experience* (Los Angeles: Haynes Foundation, 1952), appendix III.

23. For the history of city management, see Charles R. Adrian, *A History of American City Government: The Emergence of the Metropolis, 1920–1945* (Lanham, MD: University Press of America, 1987), 324–38; and Richard J. Stillman II, *The Rise of the City Manager* (Albuquerque: University of New Mexico Press, 1974). An updated count of council-manager cities can be found in the latest edition of the *Municipal Year Book*.

24. Leo F. Schnore and Robert R. Alford, "Forms of Government and Socioeconomic Characteristics of Suburbs," *Administrative Science Quarterly* 8 (June 1963): 1–17.

25. Rodney E. Hero, "Understanding Urban Governmental Structures," *Publius* 16:2 (Spring 1986): 133–40.

26. Adrian, *History*, 228–29.

27. See the most recent *Model City Charter* (New York: National Municipal League). The council-manager plan has been endorsed by the league, a good-government organization, since 1916.

28. Robert L. Lineberry and Edmund P. Fowler, "Reformism and Public Policy in American Cities," *American Political Science Review* 61 (Dec. 1967): 701–16.

29. Naomi Bailin Wish, "The Cost and Quality of Urban Life: A Matter of Governmental Structure or Regional Variation?," *Municipal Year Book, 1986*, 17–23.

30. Clarence E. Ridley, *The Role of the City Manger in Policy Formulation* (Chicago: International City Managers' Association, 1958); and Charles R. Adrian, "Leadership and Decision-making in Manger Cities: A Study of Three Communities," *Public Administration Review* 18 (Summer 1958): 208–13.

31. See Samuel P. Hays, "The Politics of Reform in the Progressive Era," in Harlan Hahn and Charles H. Levine, eds., *Readings in Urban Politics*, 2d ed. (New York: Longman, 1984). The quotation is from Charles D. Goff, "The Politics of Council-Manager Plan Adoption and Abandonment in Wisconsin," a paper presented at the Midwest Conference of Political Scientists, Ann Arbor, MI, 1958.

32. Charles R. Adrian and James F. Sullivan, "The Urban Appointed Chief Executive, Past and Emergent: From Technician and Voice of Consensus to Expert Resource Person and Bargaining Agent," *The Urban Interest* 1 (Spring 1979): 3–9.

33. *Census of Governments, 1987*.

34. Victor Jones, "Local Government Organization in Metropolitan Areas," in Coleman Woodbury, ed., *The Future of Cities and Urban Redevelopment* (Chicago: University of Chicago Press, 1953), 527–28.

35. "State and Local Roles in the Federal System," A Commission *Report* of the Advisory Commission on Intergovernmental Relations (Washington, D.C., April 1982), 256–57.

36. John C. Bollens and Henry J. Schmandt, *The Metropolis*, 4th ed. (New York: Harper & Row, 1982), 323.

37. *Milliken* v. *Bradley*, 418 U.S. 717 (1974).

38. Bollens and Schmandt, *The Metropolis*, 361.

39. Jones, "Local Government," 585–86.

The Bettmann Archive

Government in Metropolitan Areas

A favorite European stereotype sees Americans as holding efficiency to be a value second in importance only to the possession of material things. Metropolitan organization in this country effectively refutes that notion, however. Our metropolitan areas are inefficient in dozens of ways, particularly in land usage and in governmental organization and operation, if measured in terms of costs alone. Furthermore, fragmentation of the metropolitan area is not a result of accident or apathy (although both are contributing factors) so much as it is of deliberate choice by many contemporary urban dwellers.[1]

Fragmentation: **The peculiarly American phenomenon of dividing natural metropolitan communities into many, sometimes overlapping, political jurisdictions.**

The urban area in which most Americans live today is more than a legal entity existing within carefully prescribed boundaries and headed by a single government. It is actually a sociological complex consisting of a downtown sector, a blighted and decaying older portion, newer sections that are principally residential in character, gentrified residential sections, new business centers outside the core (malls and industrial parks), and, most important, the *suburbs*, where the majority of metropolitan dwellers live. The pattern of movement—from the center toward the periphery (even during the *gentrification* movement of the 1980s—applies to residences, businesses, and industries. But the problems of government stretch across the whole metropolis.

Suburb: **An identifiable area beyond the legal boundaries of the core city but lying within its economic and sociological limits and having a population at least partially dependent for a livelihood on the core city. The suburb often is incorporated as a separate city, in part because its residents wish to avoid the risk of becoming legally attached to the core city.**

211

Gentrification: **The renewal of core-city neighborhoods by people (in Britain, the** *gentry*) **who remain in or move to decaying neighborhoods and revitalize them. Gentrification reduces the availability of low-cost housing for the poor but tends to be favored by city council members and city planners seeking a higher tax base and retention of some middle-class residents within the city limits.**

The Pattern of Metropolitan Growth

Prior to the twentieth century, American cities were transportation centers, first at natural ocean harbors, then on the shores of the great rivers and lakes, later along the canals built by human toil, and later yet along railway lines:

> The relatively early founding of the cities that were to grow large is a testimonial to the importance of transportation not only as a factor in access, which helps determine when a suitable area is to be settled as an urban place, but also as a factor in the growth rate of the community. While a number of factors contributed to the continuing growth of our largest cities, all of them were major points requiring a break in transportation. That is, they were located where land travel ended and water travel began, or where one type of land travel was substituted for another, or one type of water travel for another.[2]

By the middle of the nineteenth century, incorporation was common practice. Usually a city would build out from the transportation hub. Governmental leaders would incorporate enough land to grow into or, when growth spilled over those borders, would annex enough unsettled land for further growth. This practice stopped in most places only when a natural border or a political one (for example, a state line or an incorporated suburb) prevented further annexation.

From its earliest days, the United States was a metropolitan country. For most of our history more people lived in the diversified core city than in the suburbs. But when technology allowed, some people have always "lived apart," choosing to settle beyond the city border.[3] Whereas natural resource limitations prevented some suburbanization, American laws of incorporation made other suburbs possible early in the nineteenth century. For those who could afford to settle beyond the core-city boundary, the psychological flavor of a frontier or rural environment could be maintained. In addition, the benefits could be satisfying in terms of reduced taxes and living apart from people with different life-styles and values. The conventional wisdom that suburbanization in the United States is a post–World War II phenomenon is challenged by the fact that metropolitan areas outside the core city were growing rapidly in the nineteenth and early twentieth centuries. Occasionally, the suburbs grew more rapidly than the core city (see chapter 1 for a discussion of the distribution of the metropolitan population in the 1980s).

> Between 1820 and the outbreak of the Civil War the urban population increased ninefold. The fastest rate of growth was in the metropolitan areas. As early as the 1840's, the suburbs of large cities had the highest growth rate of all:

City	Core City (percentage of growth) 1840–1850	Suburbs (percentage of growth) 1840–1850
Boston	61.0%	84.7%
New York	64.9%	130.3%*
Philadelphia	29.6%	74.8%

*Includes Brooklyn, then a separate city.[4]

Historian Kenneth Jackson argues that it was the fragmentation of American metropolises that most characterized American urbanization:

> In 1920, when the Census Bureau announced that more than half the American population lived in urban areas, what was really unique about the United States was not the size of its huge cities, but the extent of their suburban sprawl; not the numbers of its workers, but the number of its commuters; not the height of its skyscrapers, but the proportion of its homeowners. Suburbanization had become a demographic phenomenon as important as the movement of eastern and southern Europeans to Ellis Island or the migration of American blacks to northern cities.[5]

But before World War II, the characteristics of later suburbs were often found in the newer areas of the core city. It was the core city that usually was linked to the water supply, which made food delivery and sewage disposal possible. The majority within the metropolitan area could not afford to move to the suburbs. The railroad made suburban living possible for the rich.[6] But working people needed the model T and governments willing both to build the roads on which to ride the new car and to underwrite the cost of suburban home-building through easily accessible mortgages. "As late as 1920 two-thirds of the metropolitan population lived in central cities. In 1960 the distribution was nearly equal between city and fringe area; by 1980 the suburban proportion had risen to almost 60 percent."[7] The trend continues into the 1990s, surpassing 60 percent by 1985.

> *Annexation:* **The method, provided under law, to incorporate new land into an existing city. Laws of annexation vary widely by state, but more often they favor opponents in the area being annexed over those in the city doing the annexing.**

The Core City

Cities that lack a reason for being become ghost towns. Those that thrive reflect successfully the demands of the economy, effectively assisted by the political system. Every city, within its boundaries or close by, must have a commercial or industrial base from which to provide jobs and build. It must have a supply of acceptable housing for all classes and a transportation and communication system that allows it to keep in touch with other people both within and outside the urban area. It must have a set of systems to allow it to supply its residents with the goods and services expected by the culture. There are many ways by which all this can be done, some more pleasing than others. American cities evolved in a fully integrated fashion in the nineteenth century, but in the twentieth century the familiar contemporary pattern developed: The core cities aged, suburbia grew, the middle class, then the working class, industry, commerce and the shopping center, and much else trekked outward, but government no longer could push its boundaries in equal measure. Serious social problems arose, but with them hope survived.

Gentrification, the proliferation of skyscrapers, the restoration of deteriorated homes, and the renewed spirit of residences in cities once in decline (such as Pittsburgh or Baltimore), led to the hope in the early 1980s for a renaissance of core cities, reversing decades of deterioration. The difficulty, however, is that American core cities differ considerably and social patterns indicating recovery are often modest in scope and short-lived, thus eluding assessment.[8]

Core cities, by their very definition, are heterogeneous, usually containing neighborhoods and subcultures that vary widely as to their social, political, and economic health. Thus for the ghetto dweller, a dramatic increase in tax base or renewed interest in the core by the middle class may be seen as a personal threat rather than a boon to the city at large. Conversely, the displacement costs to the lower-class family during a period of neighborhood renovation may seem like a modest price to pay for a growing, "thriving" city to someone of the middle class who does not have to bear the cost.

Census projections show continued reduction in the growth rate of core-city population, compared with the suburbs. Although conventional nuclear families continue to move to the suburbs, the core has become a more acceptable choice for the increasing numbers of people living as unconventional families. The results of gentrification are apparently being offset by the continued movement of middle-class families to the suburbs.[9] The income gaps between suburb and central city continue.

The centrifugal movement of population and industry to the periphery of the urban area is causing a multitude of problems for both the core and the suburbs. Some of these problems are severe and others appear to be chronic. (We emphasize, however, that with an expansion of population and industry, serious problems would result whatever the direction or shape of the movement.)

Loss of the Tax Base

Although the cost of operating municipal governments has increased along with almost everything else, the movement toward the suburbs has seen the core cities lose some of their tax base. Industries tend to move to the suburbs when they build new plants, retail stores expand by building in suburban malls, and the families best able to pay property taxes on their homes are most likely to move to the newest suburbs. (It is always cheaper to build on raw land than in an area that must first be cleared of older buildings).

To pyramid the troubles, as the prosperous citizens move out, part of the population loss is made up by the rural-to-urban migration and the immigration from abroad that resupplies the work force of cities, but the newcomers to the core are likely initially to be a financial liability rather than an asset. The majority of migrants will settle first in the city, probably in the decaying zone of transition. For a variety of ideological reasons (see chapter 2), they are likely to create welfare, police, and juvenile problems. They are unlikely to be homeowners, and those who own their blighted dwellings do not pay as much in taxes as the city must spend in the area. Furthermore, as the density of population in the core city decreases, the value of homes also decreases because demand for them becomes less. The eroding of the tax base is therefore a cumulative phenomenon.[10]

Fragmentation and the Poor

The most chronic and pervasive problems of the core city involve the condition of the poor. Despite success in remedying many of the problems of the middle class, American democracy—itself a middle-class institution—has not succeeded in substantially eliminating poverty, most of which is concentrated in the core cities. As suburbs became more diversified, lower-class suburbs sprang up in the inner ring around the core; and rural poverty, more severe than any found in American cities, is still widespread. But difficult as it is to agree on measurements, by almost any of them, a majority of poverty-stricken families are still found in the core cities, as they have been for the past century. By offering a residence physically and politically independent from that of the lower classes, most suburbanites, through urban fragmentation, can avoid contact with the problems of poverty on a day-to-day basis. Although the gentrification movement post-dates most of the suburban shift, it too can be explained as a source of fragmentation and segregation based on social class. Gentrified neighborhoods are not examples of integrated social classes; as a neighborhood is gentrified, the poor must find residence elsewhere and therefore again are more likely to be segregated in areas with disproportionate social problems.

Chapter 1 addressed the relationship of poverty to family structure and race, and chapter 2 explored how poverty was viewed when different ideologies came to dominate American state and local politics. This section will look at the relationship between poverty and metropolitan fragmentation. A controversy has arisen over the propriety of government concentrating poverty in certain sections of the metropolitan area. Two principal views developed in the 1960s, when the urban (in most cases, read core-city) "crisis" was high on the American agenda. One held that the continued concentration of poverty in the core city was inevitable. (The poor have always lived in this location in the American city, starting with the early growth of industry when factories were located just outside the central business district and workers had to live within walking distance of the job. As the city grew, people moved outward, roughly in the order of their prosperity). Edward Banfield has argued that the pattern of metropolitan growth is "logical," driven by the "imperatives" of population increase, technological growth, income distribution, and, most important, social class.[11] According to his view, the kind of poverty experienced in American core cities (principally, relative deprivation) is a reflection of the historical pattern in which the newest poor immigrant settles in the core city. Banfield contends that government action did not produce this concentration of poverty (rather, the imperatives did), and it is unlikely that government action will significantly change it.[12] As long as poverty is inevitable, so are the problems associated with it in the core city. Of course non-lower-class persons who remain in the core city will have to bear an even greater tax and psychological burden for these problems. But little thought is given to them other than to assume that as they rise in social class, they too will leave the blighted core behind and seek comfort in suburbia.

This theory of inevitability has its critics. It is challenged by those who argue that the resulting fragmentation is unacceptable because it weakens the sense of metropolitan community, thus making problem solving more difficult. These critics attempt to show that government itself has played a major role in the fragmentation of the metropolitan area and the resulting concentration of the poor. One of them, Norton Long, holds that the suburbs act as walls, trapping the inner-city poor and obscuring more effective approaches to metropolitan problems. The unemployed central-city worker cannot commute to a suburban job even should one await.[13] Furthermore, the suburbanite may not recognize that by avoiding dealing with the inner-city poor, approaches to metropolitan problems remain segmented and unlikely to be pursued because no areawide government exists to attempt them. (This explanation, however, seems to assume that the average suburbanite is actually concerned about the poor and understates the fact that a workable approach to the problems of poverty are state and national in scope and responsibility.)

The suburb or any zoned area of a city is created through the chartering laws of state government. Thus, these must comply with the Fourteenth Amendment to the Constitution, which guarantees that no state shall deny the equal protection of the laws. Zoning rules, which create fragmented metropolitan areas, have been found not to violate equal protection.[14] Still, critics of metropolitan fragmentation contend that state and local action does violate that right. For example, they argue that a zoning regulation of a suburb requiring that building be limited to quarter-acre lots for single-family homes, would necessarily prevent the core-city poor from enjoying the benefits of the life-style found in the zone.[15] Of course, no one would suggest that the poor have a right to such benefits if they cannot afford them and if those who do enjoy them pay for them entirely. But the zoning regulation makes the creation of such a zone cheaper because the law prevents others from using the land. In effect, the government has subsidized the lifestyle of the persons living there by granting them exclusive right to use of the land within their financial capacity. (Ironically, the poor are criticized for being ''on welfare'' by suburbanites, many of whom would be shocked to learn that they too are being subsidized—though upon being so informed they would argue that *their* subsidy is more socially acceptable.) The argument concludes that core-city residents should recover some of the costs of living in the core from suburbanites, who indirectly impose these costs by moving outward with zoning ordinance assistance. (Suburbanites counter, of course, that they pay substantial taxes to the state and national governments, some of which are used for intergovernmental payments to core cities as well as to the poor directly.)

Opponents of the argument that the core-city ghetto is a product of deliberate government policy point out that no benefit of government is shared equally by everyone, that the poor would not put the suburban land to better use if the government posed no impediment to doing so, that middle- and upper-income people receive this benefit fairly because they have used the democratic political processes of government to create such benefits, and that they probably would use the land in similar fashion if government did not expedite the process. (This is, in fact, the pattern in

Houston, a city with no zoning ordinance. The same effect achieved by zoning is also possible through covenants in deeds of sale, which are enforceable under contract law, though this is a clumsier procedure.) In effect, critics return to the notion that the pattern of metropolitan growth is natural and logical.

Whatever the explanation for the concentration of poor in the core city, it is unlikely that the pattern will reverse in the foreseeable future. Regardless of where the poor reside, poverty will be handled in our federal system through an intergovernmental relations approach. Local governments may contribute to poverty, but they will not be principally responsible for handling it. Most antipoverty programs are designed by the national government and matched in part by the states and—with only few exceptions—not by the localities.

The Core City's Future

The "downtown" area was circumscribed in the nineteenth century and earlier (in the cities of the East and much of the Midwest) by two controlling factors: limitations on the distance people could travel by public transportation or, more commonly, by walking to work or shopping, and the location of a body of water over which heavy materials (coal, firewood, lumber, grain, metals) could be brought to the businesses and industries of the city and, often, which could provide a waterfall or rapids as a source of power. In the twentieth century, the internal combustion engine brought greater flexibility to transportation, as electricity did to power. This has freed business and industry from a single, dominant "downtown" and given a different shape to our core cities and metropolitan areas.

Over the years, the city's downtown business section has lost much of its retail trade to shopping centers. Two strategies battle against the ensuing deterioration. One is to compete with the mall by making downtown as convenient for shopping as the mall. In the 1970s, San Bernardino, California, was one of the first cities to cover a large section of downtown, in effect making it into a mall (though this did not hide the aging buildings, the renovation of which would have been extremely expensive). Similarly, with much ballyhoo, Atlanta "reopened" its underground shopping mall in June 1989, hailing the dawn of a new downtown retail market. But attempts to return today to a nineteenth-century approach to shopping are often undertaken too late or simply cannot be fitted to the current pattern of the metropolitan area. The other strategy is to recognize the failure of downtown as a contemporary retail trading center and redefine it as a banking, insurance, entertainment, government, or simply an office center. The skylines of many cities reflect this emphasis on office space. Only after large numbers of people again are commuting to downtown will retail trade return.

Core cities are finding a variety of ways to recover part of their lost tax base. A simple way is a highway toll tax imposed on suburbanites who commute into the city in the morning and out of the city in the evening. Such special taxation is justified by core-city leaders, who point out that the suburban commuter uses the roads or bridges the most, but the core taxpayer must maintain them. Not many other similar methods exist. One is when road maintenance is paid for through the state-shared fuel tax, but most suburban commuters probably buy their gasoline at home so the suburb gets the credit. Another is a requirement in some municipalities that municipal employees (usually of the middle class) live in the city in which they work. Municipal employees have challenged these rules in court, but usually to no avail.

Gentrification has increased the tax base of the core city slightly. But as long as the core remains the primary residence of the poor, who impose the greatest burden on the tax base, core cities will have to offset this burden by increased shared grants and taxes from higher governments, which rely more heavily than the city on progressive taxes. Nevertheless, suburbanites are in the plurality at the moment and are likely to be in the future, and suburban legislators, listening to their constituents, are not eager to earmark programs for the poor.

A ghetto renovation approach favored by conservatives in recent decades involves *enterprise zones*. These are used to attract new business to the core and thus provide local jobs. Enterprise zones have been underfunded, and claims abound that the monies made available for them are going to established entrepreneurs who pass little benefit along to the poor. (These claims were substantiated with the HUD scandal that unfolded in 1989.) Finding skilled labor, hiring middle-class people willing to work in the zone, meeting insurance costs, and finding security are some of the problems that create a need for substantial subsidies. Prospects for such zones have never appeared to be bright.

> *Enterprise Zone:* **A blighted city area selected to attract businesses that will hire area residents in exchange for special tax advantages and other incentives.**

To the extent that the core city is on its own, it may have to attract new taxpayers by changing its image. For example, middle-class families with children may be influenced by the image of the schools, even though schools are administered by special districts rather than city government. Metropolitan St. Louis developed a voucher school system in the early 1980s, and numerous other areas have experimented with this approach. Within certain guidelines, each student is given a voucher to choose a school anywhere in the area. The core-city schools compete by specializing in popular subjects to attract suburban middle-class students. Nevertheless this, like so many attempts to fight core-city–suburban disparities, has not been successful. One survey of the St. Louis area found that fifteen students from minority groups left the core to use suburban schools for each suburbanite who came to the core.[16] But schooling is a focus for state efforts to provide some degree of equalization between the core and suburban areas. In a voucherlike move, Minnesota mandated open enrollment in all of its schools in the late 1980s. Few students initially moved from their home districts, however.[17] Following Minnesota's lead, nearly a dozen states considered or passed some form of open enrollment legislation. As will be discussed below, beyond opening the schools some states have mandated greater equity in spending between core and suburban schools.

Projections for the next century indicate a still more flexible pattern of development for cities as they emerge (probably mostly in Texas and the Old South). The core cities will continue to be weaker partners to the suburbs in the metropolitan areas throughout the 1990s. More of the poor will remain in the core cities, particularly in those that attract immigrants. But the image of a core city destined for crisis will diminish. As we discussed in chapter 1 and will reexamine in the next section, many suburbs are becoming more like core cities. Years before its skyscrapers were built, Los Angeles was described (though not accurately) as a city without (someone said "in search of") a downtown. This image may become commonplace in the twenty-first century, when fragmented metropolitan areas defy our present distinctions between core city and suburb.

Suburbs

Founders of individual suburbs usually attempted to create small-town environments, and this included a desire to keep the population homogeneous. In some instances, controlling residential access has been accomplished by incorporating a separate city, but in other cases it has been done simply through leaving the core city and establishing a neighborhood of like people who are then governed by township or county. This, however, generally requires a satisfactory zoning ordinance in the urbanizing sector.

The suburbanization pattern within metropolitan areas differs markedly from one area and state to another, depending on local economic base, traditions, and statutes, past and present. The population characteristics of suburbanites also vary widely. Areas that before World War I had been inhabited almost entirely by the rich by 1970 housed a plurality of Americans, mostly middle-class and skilled or semi-skilled working-class families. However, large metropolitan areas generally have one or more suburbs consisting of poor people living under substandard conditions, such as Detroit's Royal Oak Township or Los Angeles's Compton.

Although some suburbs today are still homogeneous, they are becoming less so, and suburbia as a whole has become diversified. For example, one author speaks of "Exclusive Suburbs," "Middle-Class Suburbs," "Black Suburbs," and "Elderly Suburbs."[18] Another found that lower-class suburbs often depend on grants from higher governments to assist the lower-income population, much as is done in core cities, a pattern that may accelerate.[19] Although it could be said that suburban living is for everyone, the attraction is greater for the two-spouse family with children. The suburb is still best designed for raising families; and in many instances the possibility of the suburban lifestyle that most represents the values Robert Wood asserted decades ago is affordable only for those of moderate and above-moderate incomes and practical only for two-parent families. It is also true, however, that suburbs are often the cheapest and best source of available land for building as a city grows, though the core city remains the site for gentrification, high-rise apartments and condominiums, and public housing. Housing units for all but the poorest, new factories and warehouses, and new commercial areas are commonly located in suburbia. Indeed, many contemporary suburban leaders must choose between expanding the shopping mall (which will augment the tax base but increase noise, pollution, traffic, crime, and other problems) and controlling suburban growth (retaining its small-town flavor). As it continues to develop, the service economy can quite commonly be located in almost any part of the metropolis—including the suburbs—and function successfully.

The suburbs as we know them today became possible after World War II. Many factors contributed to their growth: suburban addresses gained high status. Technological developments and the availability of electrical power made possible the decentralization of industry. The growing importance of service industries with few employees followed. Together with prosperity after World War II, the national government's policy through the VA and FHA of loan guarantees to the mortgage holder made purchase possible for those who possessed only a small portion of the price of a home. Advances in water-supply and sewage-disposal technology and methods of communication also contributed to the flexibility of living patterns.

Postwar mass-produced housing in the suburbs proved to be best suited to American needs during a period characterized by high rates of marriage and birth. (When birth rates dropped in the 1960s and then leveled off after about 1972, the suburban pattern was already well established.) Finally, business and industry followed the crowd. They did so partly because by the end of World War II most downtown areas, built in the nineteenth century before the automobile, were obsolescent, but also in order to be nearer to customers and labor supply, and perhaps chiefly in order to build modern few-story plants with adjacent parking lots on land that was less expensive and better located than that in their older locations. The suburb, then, became a location for factory, branch stores, business headquarters of all sorts, and shopping centers.

Why Move to the Suburbs?

The postwar rush to the suburbs ranks with the move across the Appalachians (and the later migration to Oregon, Utah, and California) as one of the great mass migrations of a historically restless people. What forces continue to push the urban population toward the periphery of the metropolis? No doubt the swelling urban population is an important factor; after all, additional urban population is likely to require increasing area. But this alone does not explain the great suburban movement. Rather, we should ask, what do most American people want from life? Where and under what conditions can their desires best be fulfilled? The answers seem to rest in the fact that Americans wish to combine what they like about the large city with their attraction to the values of idealized small-town life. For example, people want the friendships and convenient access to economic and governmental establishments found in the small town; yet, at the same time they want recreational and artistic variety, wide choice of career or occupational opportunity, the chance to avoid close personal scrutiny by neighbors, and the potential for better income found in the large city.

The suburb seems to be widely regarded as the best available compromise. In addition to allowing the urbanite to keep some of the best of both the large city and the small town, other subjectively determined values held by Americans today add to the attractiveness of the suburb. Studies show that people want to own their homes. Those with families want single-family dwellings at a cost they can afford and more space than is available in built-up cities. They want to avoid, or at least reduce, dirt, noise, crime, congestion, traffic, and taxes. They want vegetable gardens and rose bushes and a private play yard for the children. Today many of the services found in the city are often found in neighboring suburbs as well. Most people would like the following nearby: a small grocery for last-minute shopping; a chain drugstore; a multiscreen movie theater; a video rental store; and a grade school. Other services—the supermarket, the high school, the sports stadium, and places of work—need only be within a reasonable driving distance.

People want better government than they think they get in the core city. They want "services without politics." A "better, more honest" government is something that many think is available in the suburb. The core city is regarded as politics-ridden with a great amount of chronic conflict. Many yearn for neighborliness and the reestablishment of some of the primary controls of rural and small-town society.

Eventually, some suburbs came to have many of the problems of core cities; for example, traffic congestion, crime (even ghetto gangs), and some political corruption. The problem suburb is seen as a place to leave behind, much as was the core. Once again, myth rather than reality may dominate. Many suburbanites know their neighbor only to wave to over the roar of power mower or snow blower. Although sociologists do not seem to have an accurate measure of what suburbanites desire most, it seems likely that what they value above all is being surrounded by families that share their life-style and social rules. In addition, a suburban address may carry more prestige than a core-city address, especially in a rapidly growing city; and this fact is important as a source of recognition in an impersonal society.

The Demand for Independence

Not only has the population of the fringe area grown rapidly, but the pace of suburban proliferation has stepped up. In 1911, eight incorporated municipalities existed in St. Louis County, Missouri. By 1935, the number had increased to twenty-five. The postwar expansion brought the total to ninety-six in 1956.[20] The 1987 *Census of Governments* showed the number had declined through consolidation to eight-nine, but by then (actually beginning in the postwar period) the metropolitan area stretched well beyond a single county. A similar pattern may be found around most metropolitan areas. Not only do these figures indicate population expansion in many directions from the core cities, but also a tendency toward governmental fragmentation of the fringe area. As each group of subdivisions becomes partially populated, it tends to seek incorporation for itself rather than annexation to another suburb or to the core city.

> *Consolidation:* **The method, under law, for incorporating two or more governments into one. This usually requires separate votes of the population of each of the governments doing the consolidating.**

Why do people want "their own little suburb"? A major reason is surely a desire to own their own homes (however heavily mortgaged). Because the cost of home ownership is increased by core-city taxes levied to provide urban services, suburbanites hope to afford a home by keeping taxes low. Because many suburbanites may fear losing access to home ownership, they will fight anything that threatens higher costs, including taxes. This attitude, therefore, produces hostility toward annexation. It also may produce opposition to incorporation, for that symbolizes increased taxes and the threat of being required to accept cost for urban services. But incorporation is also a mechanism for protecting against annexation, requiring instead that the more protective laws of *consolidation* be followed. Therefore suburban development follows different patterns to achieve a greater sense of local control.

The Desire for Access

A psychological factor that has contributed to suburban proliferation is the desire of citizens to have access to the decision-making centers of local government. As urban life became more impersonal with the growth of population and as the old-fashioned political machine declined, no longer serving as an access point to great numbers of citizens, the feeling of isolation and frustration on the part of the urbanite must have increased. The reform practice of electing all council members at-large contributed to the barrier between ordinary citizens and decision makers. But in the suburb, people found (or at least sought) a reestablishment of those close relationships that symbolized democracy on the frontier, and they regained the comfortable feeling of having influence over government decisions and of having officeholders who share their social values.

The concern that the sense of *community* is being lost is common in metropolitan America. One observer has seen three efforts to find it again. The first is to use planning and the power of the state to slow down the process of change. A second is to seek community in suburbia. A third is to find its modern equivalent in metropolitan government.[21] Yet the urbanite carries only the most tangential loyalties to the metropolitan area as a whole. Few regional institutions can be easily identified. To the typical citizen, the only reality is the family and the neighborhood, so "regional problems find no vehicle for their solution and the capacity to look ahead, to plan rationally, to awake a regional consciousness is lost."[22] Because of their narrow scope of vision and limited loyalties, most suburbanites know little of the structure or physical limits of their local government, to say nothing of the metropolitan area as a whole. They do not know what legal powers their suburb possesses, what it is prohibited from doing by state law, how services can be provided, what a reasonable cost for these services would be, or why they cost what they do. To them the local government is good, not because they possess an emotional loyalty to it but because through it they believe they have influence and access in relation to governmental services, whereas through any type of regional government they do not.[23]

Government in the suburbs is also likely to be more personal than it is in the core city. Anyone who wants to know their suburban officials personally can do so easily. The police officer, hired by a force that prides itself on honesty, who would not think of accepting a bribe, would be welcome as a neighbor for lunch or a coffee break in many suburban homes. The officer would "succeed" by doing the small, relatively personal services residents desire.[24]

Having easy access to government does not mean the suburbanite will use it very often. A small percentage of people actually do use access regularly; political participation beyond voting is always reserved for a small elite (along with a few hobbyists), which surely is easier to penetrate in suburbia than it is in the core city;

but few find it worthwhile to make the effort. Nevertheless, the myth of access and control attracts people to the suburb.

The Desire for Local Control

Over which governmental functions do suburbanites wish to retain control for themselves and their neighbors? In which service areas is diversity preferred over uniformity? An attitude study probably would show that suburbanites believe that some services are more important than others in terms of how they affect the character of their neighborhoods. The areas over which suburbanites most want local control probably would include land use, police protection, maintenance of residential streets, and schools.

Local wishes may call for luxury services, minimal services, or something in between. Wealthy people do not want to be forced into a single mold by the creation of one legal entity for the whole area, they can afford (and often wish to have) services that core-city government would not likely provide. (In one Cleveland suburb, for example, members of the police department once delivered the milk, and in a Los Angeles suburb the police directed traffic to private parties. But such actions are rare.) Paradoxically, wealthy suburbanites sometimes desire fewer services than they might have to accept from the core city. For example, they may not want their streets widened (the cost in an area of two-acre estates would be very high and the result would destroy the pristine rural charm of the area and encourage through traffic and the curious) or lighted (they prefer their own ornamental lighting, using carriage lights and flood lamps).

In contrast, some modest suburbs dislike and fear the core city. In these areas, residents can barely afford to own their homes. They want minimal services because they fear even a small increase in costs through "unnecessary" services that might force them out of the home-owning category with all its prestige and psychological satisfaction. To these people, joining the core city would mean buying a package of services they think they can do without and can ill afford. People falling between these two extremes recognize that additional services are symbols of prestige that cost money. Although they usually are willing to pay extra taxes for extra services, they generally believe these services can be secured more cheaply by incorporation rather than by annexation.

It should be clear why residents of different types of suburban areas would want to control the above functions. Low-income neighborhoods may want to haul their own rubbish. Well-to-do people may prefer twice-a-week collection from the back door, whereas the core city offers only once-a-week service from the front curb. Local control of educational services is desired because of its expense and because of the importance of a good school as a status symbol. Parents want to control the social environment of their children in grammar school and high school, just as they later may want them to go to the "right" college. They seek the safety of the school's childcare or a neighborhood latch-key program on a block where trusted friends are always home in the evening. Low-income and elderly people may want minimal services in education out of cost considerations. Higher-income areas use the school to indicate their relative status. Automobiles and stylish wardrobes are important devices for displaying "pecuniary emulation," but the size and luxury of the school auditorium and, especially perhaps, of the swimming pool or computer center (if any) have also become important symbols in contemporary suburbia. Leaving these decisions to the impersonal bureaucracy of a large-city school system would be undesirable to all suburbanites, regardless of income level. Land-use policies, which by the logic of the planning profession are the most regionwide in character of all policies, are vitally important to the suburbanite. The ethnic, industrial, and commercial balance also is of great concern to suburbanites. They may want social classes—even races—segregated. They want to be personally acquainted with, or believe they can influence, the planning commission so that the land use in their area will not change— unless to their advantage. The professional bureaucracy of the core city and its impersonal dedication to the principles of planning do not spell an improvement to the suburbanite; it means instead loss of control and potential disaster for the individual homeowner.

In certain areas the suburbanite might not object strongly to regionwide administration of services. These probably would include those functions in which specialists make key policy and the average citizen views the function as not involving policy making or "politics" at all. Examples include public health and welfare, sewage disposal, and water supply. In these areas suburbanites see no strong need to control policy, but they usually are not willing to spend more than a minimum amount for the service. With few disagreements over such things as innoculation policies, restaurant inspections, or water quality, they may think of public health as a routine matter for professionals and a rather distant countywide function. (But not all public health matters are without controversy and the difficult items may be increasing in number. Issues have gone from water fluoridation and birth control information in the 1950s to AIDS treatment, public smoking, and abortion policies in the 1990s.)

Suburbanites will insist that a well and an electric pump are cheaper than a municipal system, so long as the home system brings forth water. If it no longer does, they do not care how the water is obtained so long as it is not "too" expensive; but they do care about the rules of distribution, especially during dry years, when lawn watering or washing the car may be at stake. Those are seen as local policy matters.

Duplication of Services

The social waste of a fragmented metropolitan area is at a dangerous level. With the area broken up into a series of small units, it becomes difficult to make use of the advantages of specialization of personnel and mechanization of equipment. For example, sewage-disposal and water-filtration plants require such large capital investments that they are not economical unless they are in constant use. Small plants are expensive either because they are inefficient or because they do an inadequate job. Yet these plants are to be found in great numbers in any metropolitan area despite state and federal efforts to consolidate them. Suburbanites may favor them through deliberate choice ("We don't want to depend on the city for our water"), through ignorance, or because the cost of the inefficiency is widely socialized (as when a suburb dumps poorly treated sewage into a river, which then flows through other urban areas).[25]

Amateurism and Specialization

With so many specialists, some suburbs try to get along with ill-trained amateurs. Business executives who would hire nothing but qualified specialists in their own firms permit amateurs to furnish services to their suburban homes. On the other hand, the governmental operations of suburbs are simpler than those of large cities, and fewer skills are required. The suburbanite avoids some of the increasing costs of scale that characterize urban government and can "get by" with a few specialists if the service demands are limited as to functional areas requiring professionalism. One way to limit the need for professional workers is to split service functions, performing the complex tasks with properly qualified personnel at the regional level and using less-expensive personnel in the individual suburb. This can be done, for example, by separating water supply at distant sources (regional) from water distribution (local), police training from police patrol, school financing from school curriculum, or expressways from local streets.

Lack of Services

"Taxes are lower in Perambulator Park," the real estate advertisements proclaim. They are less likely to mention that taxes are lower because almost no services are provided. The absence of many services usually thought to characterize urban life may be accounted for in a variety of ways, some of which have been mentioned earlier in this chapter. Many services are more expensive in the suburbs than in the core city because of the reduced population density. This applies particularly to storm drainage, sidewalks, street paving and maintenance, street lighting, water supply, garbage collection, and sewage disposal. New suburbanites may balk at the costs of special assessments, but such protests fall on the deaf ears of long-time residents who have already paid the costs individually and do not now want to provide payments from which they will not benefit directly.

Suburban Schooling

Education is the governmental function of greatest interest to suburbanites and the one for which the tax rate increases most rapidly and the largest proportion of tax funds are spent. The mentality of suburbia is carried over into the special-district politics of suburban school districts. Even though these schools may be quite ordinary, access to them becomes a measure of distinction between living in a suburban area and living elsewhere.

The steady movement outward from the decaying core city has been the pattern now for nearly half a century. For the most part, the trend simply reflects where new homes are built. But the pattern also shows certain inconsistencies that have provoked considerable debate as to whether some white families move to the suburbs chiefly out of racial or class considerations or out of a desire for the supposedly superior school regardless of race; but whatever the reasons, "white flight" has become an American reality. Two Supreme Court cases effectively permitted segregated suburban schools. One protected suburban school districts from plans designed to achieve integration by busing children across district lines,[26] and the other protected suburban school districts from fiscal equalization formulas.[27] State governments, nevertheless, may (and often do) devise formulas for equalization.[28]

A major problem with contemporary education lies in the fact that we know so little about the effects of education and what makes it work or not work. Many studies, even elaborate ones, do not help much. The Kerner Commission report of 1968, for example, although widely cited for a number of years, never went beyond clichés and did not inquire into the prospects and limitations of learning. Furthermore, it attributed education's failures to causes cited in conventional wisdom, even though the earlier Coleman report of 1965 (discussed below) contained reams of fresh empirical data and implications so startling that at first they were not fully understood even by the chairman. Many reports do not distinguish clearly between learning, which is an individual task, and teaching or other educational activities, which are institutional undertakings. There is reason to believe that many critics of the schools tend to seek easy and quick solutions. But because learning is a result of *individual* effort, good schools are primarily a product of good students and, the Coleman report seems to suggest, very little else. Teachers, libraries, teaching devices, and the like, though important, are strictly secondary tools. If this is so, the task of improving the schools—especially in an era that downplays reading and writing and in which the television set is a far more powerful influence than the average teacher—is likely to be vastly more difficult than many reformers have yet admitted or perhaps even realized. Once again, existing conditions would seem to favor suburbia, but specifically the middle classes *wherever they live.* Yet the greatest need of the poor, in order to escape their condition, is marketable skills; and the schools still seem the institution most likely to provide them. The quality of a school is rarely measured solely on its financial support. The 1965 Coleman report—the most complete study yet of motivation and achievement in public schools—concludes the following: It is the positive or negative orientation toward learning by students, their peers, and their parents that shapes the quality of an individual school and how much its students learn, not dollars spent per pupil, not equipment, ability of teachers, size of classes, or any other factor. But students oriented toward learning do want good-quality schooling, and equality of financial support can be justified as fairness even if it does not directly affect learning. In a controversial study of the schools in 1983, the National Commission on Excellence in Education concluded that the nation was "at risk" unless the content of curricula was upgraded, students were subjected to higher expectations, and school time (particularly high school time) was better spent.[29] The weaknesses that were criticized, if they were weaknesses, were a product of a changing culture rather than of a deliberate failure of the schools; but by these measures, suburban schools generally continue to be of higher quality than core-city schools. Most important, children in suburban schools learn more, they are more likely to go to college, and they have access to more extracurricular activities.

Suburban schools can expect the variety of proposals from those living in core-city districts (vouchers, open enrollment, and so forth) that attempt to open up suburban schools to core pupils. Thus far, few proposals have been adopted by suburbanite-dominated legislatures. They are most successful, however, in metropolitan areas where race is not the overriding concern. Where proposals have been

adopted, the pattern of schooling has changed little, suggesting continued commitment to the neighborhood school for most parents. Nevertheless, the plans do provide
greater opportunity to the otherwise trapped core-city student seeking a better opportunity than that provided by the core school. Plans usually are opposed by suburbanites who want to retain their marks of distinction.

Lack of Cooperation

Suburbs tend to be intensely jealous of their independence and—egged on by local
officeholders—they attribute ulterior motives to all suggestions of cooperation with the
core city or even with other suburbs. This attitude, one likely to increase lack of coordination and inefficient use of equipment, was so strong when councils of governments
(COGs) were proposed in the 1960s that many suburban governments resisted joining,
even though COGs had no powers over them other than those helping to meet and discuss mutual problems (see the discussion of COGs later in this chapter). COGs have
since become routine and have aided somewhat in reducing hostilities.

Rising Costs

Fringe-area taxes may start at what appears to be a much lower level than those of the
core city, but the suburban buyer can be assured that they will increase at a rapid
pace. Suburbanites own larger parcels of land than their core-city counterparts. The
major portion of property taxes go toward the schools, and in contemporary suburbia
one school bond issue has followed another, with each issue raising taxes. As population density increases, the need for other urban services increases; that is, each new
service must be paid for by additional taxes. Inner circle suburbs are now facing renovation costs that previously were the lot of core cities, though usually the renovation
is less elaborate than in the core city.

     Water and sewage systems must be installed. Soon neighbors want to have their
streets paved and a storm sewer laid. Streetlights become desirable and fire and police
service may be expanded. The sewage-disposal problem, an enormous expense, must
be dealt with. All these problems fall on the mortgage- and debt-ridden suburbanite.
Many services now in demand were never faced by the subdivision developer who in
any case has long since disappeared from the area. Residents desperately seek solutions
through special districts, incorporation, new state legislation, or, in rare cases, annexation of new land or consolidation with another municipality. Thus, lower taxes in the
suburb—much like better government—may be a myth in the long run. Even so, myths
more than facts have to do with why people locate in an area, because myths are more
easily communicated and often more easily accepted (see chapter 2).

The Image of Suburbia

Suburbs have long been sharply taken to task by social critics. They have had to endure
the chronic hostility of intellectuals even though studies show they are, to the people who
typically occupy them, mostly pleasant places with responsible, satisfactory governments. Scott Donaldson found that some critics detest conformity. But middlle-class peo-

ple are notorious conformists, no matter where they live. Suburbia is said to produce excessive loneliness—but other critics denounce "too much" neighboring. Does either differ from the situation of many residents of the core city? Some critics express a grave disappointment in the failure of the suburbs to uphold Jeffersonian ideals. Yet suburbia has been seen by some as the medium for relocating the small town and the ideal local government in a modern setting. Suburbanites have not acted as intellectuals have wanted the children of Jefferson to act, however.[30] Most of all, suburbia probably became the object of intellectuals' scorn and distrust primarily because its occupants have been portrayed as philistines, Babbitts, boorish people leading dull lives, the *bourgeoisie* in their predictable, conformist, imitative, conservative behavior. Suburbanites, of course, do not see themselves as ignorant, unenlightened, or uncultured. Rather, they accept and enjoy their life-style, of which suburbia (and the brief attention given to its consensual governments) is a part. They are bemused by censure by those who are more interested in ideas than in material pleasures.

Donaldson thought criticism of suburbia reached a peak in the 1950s, but it flares up on occasion still today. The likely reason is that because the intellectuals' actual target is not suburbia as such, but rather is that traditional antagonist of intellectuals, the middle class and all those who emulate its behavior.

Metropolitan-Area Politics

The issues listed above generally are those of either the core city or the suburbs. But there are matters of concern to the metropolitan area as a whole that necessitate metropolitanwide government. For instance:

- Unsafe sewage-disposal practices in any part of the metropolitan area may endanger health in another part.
- Economics may dictate a collective effort to secure additional water supplies from a distant lake or mountain stream.
- Traffic-flow patterns for an entire area are necessarily interrelated.
- Land-use practices in any one section will affect those in another.
- Pollution and noise nuisances pay no more attention to legal boundaries than do germs.

Even when the issue of structural reorganization of the metropolitan area is placed on the local agenda, existing legal arrangements may make it unfeasible. For example, the core city may be completely surrounded by incorporated municipalities, and state law may be forbiddingly complex so far as consolidation of such areas is concerned. State law may facilitate the incorporation of small suburbs that have inadequate tax resources, suburbs that resist consolidation or other plans for metropolitan government. Outside the core, people have long accepted the reality of fragmentation.

Little agreement exists as to which problems are the most important for metropolitanwide government, and they probably differ from one metropolitan area to another according to local values and existing service levels. The greatest problem of all, perhaps, is "the inability of metropolitan residents to reach any substantial degree of consensus as to what should be done . . . about the generally recognized issues of their common life—government organization, finance, blight and redevelop-ment, schools, race relations, land use control, and so on.''[31]

Numerous proposals have been made over the years seeking to establish metropoli-tan government. Up to the present, however, each of these has nearly always proved to be either unsuccessful as a permanent policy or politically inexpedient. Currently, no trend toward the adoption of any one approach exists; neither has anyone devised a plan that proved practical and successful. Some isolated exceptions are to be found and some make shift and temporary devices have been put to use in various places.

Annexation

Reviewing from earlier chapters, the term *city* may be legally defined by incorpora-tion or it may be used to refer to a sociological community of urban people who think of themselves as living in the *same place,* even though they have not formed the legal city. As a metropolitan area grows, the most obvious way to keep the two identical would be for the core city to annex fringe areas as they become urbanized, or even in anticipation of such growth, or to consolidate the areas already separately incorpo-rated. Formerly, annexation was widely used but has become more and more unsatis-factory to those in the fringe. As industry, commerce, and higher-cost houses move outward to use undeveloped land, demands in the core city for annexation increase. Indeed, a considerable number of annexations take place each year, but they seldom succeed in equating the political with the sociological city, for three reasons:

1. Older and larger core cities (mainly in the Northeast and Midwest) are usually wholly surrounded by incorporated areas, leaving nothing to annex. By the 1920s, this was the case with most of the big cities of that time.[32]
2. Annexation is nearly always unpopular in the fringe areas.
3. State law usually makes it difficult to annex, requiring a separate referendum vote of the area being annexed. Only in a few states (notably Arizona, Mis-souri, Oklahoma, Texas, and Virginia) is the core city relatively free to expand its boundaries as the surrounding unincorporated area becomes urbanized.

Given these factors, most annexation has been in the South and the West with, not surprisingly, California and Texas usually in the lead in terms of area and population annexed.[33]

An analysis of census data shows that over one-half of incorporated places with 2,500 or more people reported changes in their borders during each decade since the 1940s (some with as many as one hundred changes in a decade). But most annexation is relatively small in area size (fewer than 100 acres) and population (many involving no people, on average fewer than 100). Major exceptions, however, include Bir-mingham, Alabama, which annexed over 36 square miles in 1986, (but involved fewer than 1,000 people); and Houston, which annexed areas occupied by 251,000 people in the 1970s. But western and southern core cities are also becoming sur-rounded by incorporated land and the trend has shown a decline in the number of residents in areas annexed in each postwar decade.[34]

Many cities are faced with a seemingly unending debate as to whether they should annex additional territory. Usually, as the city grows older or as industry begins to prefer the periphery to the central part of the city, the "expand-or-die" ideology of the chamber of commerce becomes dominant. The question of annexation also arises in relation to policy concerning the supplying of municipal services outside municipal boundaries. Some cities refuse to extend services to any area unless it is annexed. Such coercion is resented by suburbanites, but central-city administrators and residents have little sympathy for the plight of those already sapping their potential tax base. Refusal of services was upheld by the U.S. Supreme Court in 1985.[35] Large cities sometimes choose to supply services to suburbs in order to make their own utilities profitable.

In 1959 the Minnesota legislature began a trend when it established a municipal commission authorized to hear petitions for incorporation, detachment, and annexation of land within the state. Based on certain criteria, the commission was authorized to rule on questions of proposed incorporation of villages or cities within the three most populous counties. The status of counties elsewhere in the state was under jurisdiction of the county governing board. A similar law, also designed to provide a more rational and systematic procedure for incorporation and annexation, was adopted in Wisconsin that same year.[36] California has a Local Agencies Formation and Annexation Commission for each county. It attempts to provide a rational approach to incorporation and annexation. The commission consists of two county officers, appointed by the board of supervisors, and two city council members, appointed by all county mayors, meeting as a committee. These four choose a fifth member. On the basis of criteria prescribed by law, they decide whether to permit the creation of a new special district, the incorporation of a new city, or the annexation of territory to an existing city or special district.[37] Eleven states use some version of this approach.[38]

Occasionally, annexation may take unusual forms to prevent the incorporation of a suburban area or to deal with the limited unincorporated land around a city. For example, Texas allows its central cities to control subdivision practices in unincorporated territories on their borders, so-called territorial jurisdiction:

> The most dramatic use of these powers has been through "spoke" or "finger" annexation by cities such as San Antonio and Houston. By annexing highway rights of way, the central cities sent spokes or fingers out through the suburbs. This expanded the cities' zones of extraterritorial jurisdiction and prevented new suburban municipalities from incorporating. As parts of the extraterritorial zone urbanized, they were then annexed without referendum to the central city. These tactics enabled Texas central cities to keep growing and to capture the growing suburban tax base, while many northern and midwestern cities were increasingly surrounded by incorporated suburbs. If San Antonio, for example, were restricted to its 1950 boundaries, it would have lost 55,000 people between 1960 and 1975. Instead it grew by 169,000 and kept 80 percent of Bexar County's population within the city boundaries.[39]

When one effect of annexation is the dilution of minority representation in city government, the annexation may be challenged in federal courts as a violation of the Voting Rights Act. The courts have not been consistent in regard to this issue, but in a noteworthy case they struck down an annexation in Houston in 1979 on the ground that the annexation would have diluted the black and Hispanic population's power in city government. Houston adopted a citywide district representation scheme to allow its growth to continue.[40]

No trend exists in legislatures, with their powerful suburban representation, toward revising laws dating from the nineteenth century to make annexation or consolidation easier, and suburbanites show little inclination toward annexation. Therefore, annexation will be used almost entirely for small boundary changes of little significance to the overall governing of the metropolis.

Special Districts

If annexation becomes impossible, the next approach might be to create special districts for those particular functions that require metropolitanwide administration. This approach is an increasingly common one. Services might include park, sewerage, water, parking, pollution control, airport, or planning. In addition to their general characteristics (discussed in chapter 7), districts may be authorized to perform more than one function. They often are used for areas smaller than the total metropolitan area and, it should be remembered, special districts do not have power in the large number of functional areas that municipalities serve. Usually the metropolitanwide special district operates by agreement and suffers from the threat, usually implicit, that governments will pull out if the taxes become ominous or if policy is not reached by consensus. Some districts are formed by order of the state or are required to qualify for national government shared grants. Therefore, metropolitanwide special districts should be thought of as metropolitan governments; but they are not going to integrate most of the metropolitanwide problems or provide the approach that metropolitan government advocates are searching for, because they are always limited in scope and often are unpopular.

City-County Consolidation

Until recently, reformers believed that consolidating the city with the metropolitan county was desired second only to annexation and was a truer and more permanent solution than the special district. This plan (and its dozens of variations) calls for integrating the functions of the core city with those of the county. The county may retain a partial identity, and incorporated municipalities may remain independent for some purposes. New Orleans (1805), Boston (1822), Philadelphia (1854), and New York City (1898) were consolidated in the nineteenth century, but after Honolulu's incorporation (1907), the practice fell into disfavor for forty years, when reformers sought to try again.

Numerous attempts at city-county consolidation have been made since World War II, but few have succeeded. The following consolidation successes involved the largest populations: the combination of Baton Rouge with East Baton Rouge parish (1947), Nashville with Davidson County (1962), Jacksonville with Duval County (1967), Indianapolis with Marion County (1969), and Lexington and Fayette County (1972). When Alaska created counties (called boroughs), three separate consolidations (Anchorage, Juneau, and Sitka) followed, creating counties of enormous area but with little population.[41] In terms of area, Sitka is now the nation's largest municipality, with 2,938 square miles (about the area of Delaware and Rhode Island combined).

A case study of the Lexington, Kentucky, consolidation found that the most apparent benefits were precisely those hoped for by reformers: elimination of jurisdictional conflicts in the delivery of services and a greater sharing of the costs of metropolitanwide services, particularly (in this case) an areawide sewer service. Nevertheless, the city continued to be plagued by nonreformed partisan politics, including more than one controversial mayor's race, a firefighter's strike, and repeated efforts for demerger.[42]

Comprehensive consolidation usually requires statewide approval on a constitutional amendment referendum, legislative approval, or a majority vote on referendum both in the core city and in the portions of the county outside. Such approval is not easy to secure. Only by legislative fiat with no popular vote, for example, was the Indianapolis consolidation achieved. Only in few states would such action be thinkable, even if legal.[43] Not only is city-county consolidation almost impossible politically; in addition, it does not guarantee that the city-county will have sufficient powers to meet all metropolitan problems, and it causes even greater political difficulties if the metropolitan area expands beyond the county limits.[44] A single large metropolitan area usually extends over many counties, sometimes into several states (as is the case of Chicago, New York, and Philadelphia, for example). Most states have refused to consolidate their counties, and American federalism makes incorporation across state lines impossible. For these reasons and those discussed earlier, a legally consolidated, multipurpose metropolitan government is unlikely.

City-County Separation

Core-city dwellers, watching the county snowplows at work in the unincorporated reaches of suburbia and remembering that the city often bears much of the cost of county government but secures few services from it, are likely to be intrigued with the idea of separating the city from the rest of the county. This plan is not far different from city-county consolidation except that instead of integrating the offices and leaving the county boundaries as they are, separation would create a city-county of the core city and create a new county of the outlying areas. This, of course, would not create a metropolitanwide government.

San Francisco, Baltimore, St. Louis, Denver, and all cities of over 10,000 in Virginia are separate city-counties and have been for a long time. The plan encounters many of the same problems as does city-county consolidation and is no more practical politically. Furthermore, it is not likely to be satisfactory because it traps the city within its own walls (except in Virginia) instead of treating metropolitan problems on an areawide basis.

Metropolitan Federation

Strong arguments, based on efficiency, economy, and equity, call for functions of government to be integrated throughout the metropolitan area. At the same time, merit is seen in keeping government as close to the people as possible and a psychological value is apparent in retaining the spirit of the smaller suburb as against the impersonality of the core city. Because of the dilemma thus created, some students of the problem have suggested that federal plans of government be applied to the metropolitan area with two tiers of government, one areawide to perform functions fitting that classification and another for the immediate locality to handle functions of a more parochial interest. It is sometimes suggested, for example, that functions such as sewage disposal, water supply, police protection, and planning should be areawide, whereas garbage collection and local street maintenance might be appropriate for the lower-tier government.

This plan has been used in London, England, and Toronto, Ontario. Dade County (Miami), Florida, has come closest in the United States, with a lower tier of municipalities retaining their identities and some powers, and a higher tier—the county—governed by a council-manager form of government.[45] But the Miami plan clearly envisions the municipalities as junior partners in the arrangement. The county charter contains a "supremacy" clause that gives it power whenever conflicts arise with the municipalities and most services are provided by Dade County. The cities nevertheless continue to do some zoning and deliver a limited variety of services if they wish to (more likely trash collection and policing than transportation or housing), leaving them to the county if they do not. This has led to a complicated taxing system, which has led to repeated deficits for the county. Most important, the municipalities retain their own mayors and city councils, giving the appearance of retaining a distinct identity and providing the population with closer forums for political discourse. With these forums available, some of the most outspoken critics of the metropolitan government have been mayors of the larger municipalities.[46]

The County as a Metropolitan Unit

Because many metropolitan areas are located in single counties, it sometimes is suggested that the existing county governments might be used as a basis for forming supergovernments. However, several handicaps work against such a plan. First, the county may be a poor profile of the metropolitan area. That is, the core city may be tucked off in the corner of a county that is in large part rural (for example, San Diego), or the metropolitan area may extend over several counties. Second, in most states, many legal obstacles discourage the county's acting as a municipality. Third, the majority of counties will not have a chief executive officer, thus making efficiency a problem.

A few urban counties have been given powers and governmental structures that enable them to act as supergovernments. One early example is Los Angeles County, which has a chief administrative officer and furnishes many urban services to unincorporated areas as well as, by contract, to incorporated municipalities. Westchester County in New York has, in effect, the strong-mayor plan of government with an elective chief executive. Several urban counties that provide such services have the council manager form. But Westchester and Los Angeles point to the fact that even supergovernmental counties only encompass a portion of the metropolitan area.

Other Arrangements

To help meet the problems of furnishing services to a complex metropolitan area, some legislation short of "master-solution" proposals has been adopted. Sometimes cities are permitted to own or control land outside their boundaries. Extraterritorial powers may be given a city to help control nuisances, to secure a water supply, to operate an airport, to meet recreation needs, and to control subdividing of land, for example. The approach is helpful but of limited influence on metropolitan problems and is resented by the fringe areas. As noted earlier, Texas cities have used such powers to try to forestall suburban incorporation and provide greater opportunity for annexation.[47]

The most common means of attacking joint problems and needs is to make use of formal or informal devices of cooperation, including formal agreements. Examples include agreements for the disposal of sewage, garbage, and rubbish; for the sharing of facilities (e.g., police radio networks); and for the supplying of various services, especially water supply.

Metropolitan decision makers, under pressure from both national and state governments to face up to their problems, are showing more promise in doing so than they did decades ago. Increasingly, their intergovernmental financial assistance is coupled with requirements for planning and coordination. Local officials recognize the possibility that if they do not perform satisfactorily, more decisions will be taken out of their hands and moved to higher levels. In some instances, however, they look forward to losing some responsibility for functional areas that involve chronic problems (e.g., public welfare and air-pollution control). Furthermore, metropolitan decision makers know they can reduce pressure for drastic governmental reorganization by cooperating on the most pressing problems.

In every metropolitan area, a vast and complex communication network exists among the various professions. Formal organizations for highway engineers, public health officers, and sanitary engineers, for example, provide regular meeting opportunities at which mutual problems are discussed. In addition, countless informal contracts are made as occasions arise. Sometimes, leading politicians or professionals involved in a given function will call a meeting or conference, which will permit discussion by representatives of all interested communities.

Metropolitanwide action usually takes place only within a narrowly defined functional area. Such action arises in response to a particularly difficult problem related to dominant life-style and not as a result of a particular ideology. Furthermore, action usually comes only after extensive discussion and sometimes a number of failures to launch proposals. Skilled and experienced political leaders must convince the general public to accept a proposal that leaders have agreed on. "Outsiders" have little chance of success without the backing of the professionals. Although the public must be convinced of a need for change—or at least not to offer serious opposition— proposals for metropolitan action usually evoke relatively little citizen interest. Because they result from negotiations, proposals almost always reflect numerous compromises. They must be accomplished within the limits of state law and must have the acquiescence of important state decision makers. Finally, the national government has played an increasingly large part in the metropolitan decision-making process in recent years and is likely to become more involved in the future.[48]

Councils of Governments, exceeding three hundred in number, are made up of representatives of principal governments in an area. They "seek to identify area-wide problems and to arrive at negotiated agreements."[49] They are easy to create, partially because they have little legal power. Even so they are criticized—

particularly by minority groups—for their membership plans, which often represent *governments* equally rather than being based on *population*. Councils of Government (COGs) were not well funded in the 1980s but were widely used as metropolitanwide planning groups and they relied heavily on national grants for funding many of their study-group activities. Rarely are COGs empowered to do more than make recommendations to the existing municipalities, although in some areas they are given powers by the state to review plans that have areawide impact. (In the odd practice of metropolitan government, it is rarely specified what happens if a negative review is given.)

A step beyond the conventional COG is the Twin Cities Metropolitan Council in the Minneapolis–St. Paul metropolitan area. The council, created by the legislature in 1967, is not necessarily comprised of representatives of existing governments, but instead consists of appointees of the governor, confirmed by the state senate, who serve districts of equal size designed especially for the council. The council

> today is a planning and policy-making agency for guiding both the physical and social development of the metropolitan area as well as the delivery of regional public services. It is neither a general purpose regional government as in Nashville or Jacksonville nor a voluntary council of governments as exist in many other metropolises. It does not provide services nor does it zone land. Such impact as its actions have are conveyed by the 140 cities, 7 counties, and 26 special districts and metropolitan agencies in the area. The existence of the municipal and county governments has not been affected by the Council's emergence. Yet, in matters defined as having metropolitan impact, the Council can either compel or prevent actions by these other governments, and it has a broad though noncoercive sphere of influence beyond that. It also exerts some influence over metropolitan actions of state agencies such as the Department of Transportation.[50]

Reformers argue that this "COG with teeth" can reduce duplication and plan effectively, through bypassing the voters as most COGs do.[51] But the system is not without its faults. Insufficient public accountability continues, relatively little political leadership exists, and the inability to plan or to achieve long-range goals, a fault so typical of democracy and frustrating to reformers, continues.[52]

Occasionally methods are devised to frustrate metropolitanwide reform efforts. These are relatively rare because metropolitan fragmentation is the rule and such devices are unnecessary. Detachment is the opposite of annexation and involves the breaking off of part of a continuing city and allowing that parcel to become unincorporated again. These are very rare, but 33,000 people were separated from Little Rock, Arkansas, in 1973 and Lanett, Alabama, lost two-thirds of its population and 20 square miles in 1986. Disincorporation involves the dissolution of a city, reverting the entire city to the unincorporated area of the county or township. These have usually involved places very small in size; the largest in the 1970s was Bennington Village, Vermont with a population of 7,950; in the 1980s the largest was Willamantic, Connecticut (approximately 15,000 in population). Both represent the most likely cases in which disincorporation could occur, in New England, where such cities may choose to return to town government. But there most cases are in cities of fewer than one thousand.[53]

A number of incorporations in Los Angeles County in the late 1950s led to an experiment in providing services without requiring annexation or consolidation with surrounding large municipalities. This has come to be called the Lakewood Plan, after Lakewood, one of the first cities to try this approach. In the Lakewood Plan a city provides few if any services itself, instead relying on contractual agreements with the county, private companies, or other surrounding municipalities. In theory, the plan allows the city to shop around for the services that best suit its constituents, while also allowing potential savings by shopping for the most economical service. Critics of the plan point out that such an approach denies some accountability of the city itself, and, of course, the plan would work only if a sufficient number of larger governments existed to contract with. For this reason, the plan makes some sense for low-demand suburbs, but is impractical for large municipalities or as a form of municipal government.[54] It continues to work after thirty years because all desired services are available by contract with Los Angeles County. In many cases, the cities can contract for as much of a service as they desire (or is required by state law). For example, water-supply and sewage-treatment functions are charged by volume and each city chooses its police protection level by contracting for specific services and the number of deputy sheriffs desired.

The Failure of Integration

The value patterns of those who support plans for metropolitan supergovernments are not dominant, and the leaders of integration movements characteristically do not give adequate consideration to other values. The result is that proposals for reorganization of metropolitan governments rarely are implemented.[55]

A variety of upper-income business and professional people tend to favor metropolitan government for a number of reasons. Some are concerned that, as a result of the middle-class exodus to the suburbs, they will lose the political control of the core city to leaders of low-income groups. Some believe that governmental consolidation will reduce costs through economies of scale. Low-income groups tend to oppose metropolitan government for a number of reasons. Blacks fear that such a government will dilute their political power, because they are concentrated in the core city or more segregated suburbs of the metropolitan area. Labor leaders or working-class people sometimes also oppose metropolitan plans because they include proposals for a short ballot and professional leadership; that is, they fear loss of access and representation. Some low-income as well as middle-income persons fear that metropolitan government would be more expensive to them; that is, that it would result in more rapid tax increases than would otherwise be the case. Some middle-income suburbanites believe that not only would they pay most of the costs but that metropolitan government would be characterized by a high level of political conflict and visibility. This, they fear, would increase local discontent with government, divide people unnecessarily along class and perhaps racial lines, add costs, and create rising expectations that would fester unfulfilled. Therefore, the question of whether or not to have metropolitan government is not simply one of efficiency and economy, as most reformers believed, or even the ''solution'' to racial or class conflict as a minority of reformers believed, but is a political question closely related to costs and to perceived abilities to influence policy making.

Suburban officeholders and the entrenched bureaucracy of the area will almost always oppose metropolitan government, and reformers seldom pay enough attention to their values and interests or show any imagination in compromising with them. They fail to recognize that representativeness of government and access to the decision makers are likely to be more important considerations for the typical citizen than are questions of efficiency and economy. Rarely does a metropolitan study even mention these two psychologically important factors, to say nothing of adequately providing for them. Reformers tend to forget that the symbols—efficiency, a bigger and better ''Zilchville,'' and the like—that they respond to with enthusiasm ring no bells for the common citizen, who dominates the decision when a proposal is put to a popular referendum; ordinary citizens are characteristically apathetic. If water flows from the tap and the toilet flushes today, they are not likely to ask whether it will do so tomorrow. To them the ''fire brigade'' approach is adequate—wait until a fire is burning before you try to put it out. Even though our democracy's often-noted reluctance to plan for a more distant future will continue to be criticized by reformers, the best evidence suggests that societies that engage in extended planning are not better served by it; instead, they inefficiently engage in frequent revisions of the plan.

Perspectives on the Metropolis

A vast literature has accumulated on metropolitan areas and the difficulties of supplying urban services to them. Thousands of surveys have been conducted. Yet, despite the reams of paper devoted to the subject, little work has been done concerning the levels of awareness metropolitan residents have of their own area and its problems; no rank order of values has been worked out; few studies have been made as to why integration proposals fail. One of the least productive areas for empirical study is the study of what has *not* happened. Interpretations of metropolitan-area politics depend in part, therefore, on one's perspective of the metropolitan area. Several perspectives have been, or might be, used in interpreting this aspect of American politics:

1. The traditional, reform-movement stress was on a search for ''solution,'' with an emphasis on efficiency and economy goals rather than on securing access and representation. The emphasis was on structural reform, with the implicit assumption that, given metropolitanwide formal institutions, metropolitan areas would be well governed. These reformers generally assumed that other citizens in the area were as well informed as they, or at least adequately well informed to react favorably to their arguments. Because *they* had no problems with access and representation—being overwhelmingly upper-middle class—they failed to observe this central problem.[56]

2. The metropolitan area may be viewed as a problem in diplomacy. That is, decision making in the metropolitan area may be seen as resembling that of the diplomatic arena. When it is, relative size is not so important as securing the unanimity required for agreement in diplomatic negotiations. Viewing the area as a diplomatic problem also permits us to analyze it in terms of alliances of various groups. These alliances are not always so simple as one of the core city against the suburbs. They

may involve groups of suburbs against other groups, or alliances may be formed on the basis of particular functions, rather than for all purposes of negotiation.[57]

3. The metropolitan area may be viewed as a market for services. In this sense, it can be analyzed in economic terms.[58] In large metropolitan areas, several suppliers of services may exist. For example, the core city, plus the county government, plus some of the larger suburbs may all compete for customers among suburbs for the distribution of water, for sewage disposal, or some other function. Cooperative arrangements involving buying from the lowest bidder are possible where both the purveyor and the consumer of services believe they gain through the transaction—the fundamental requirement, in economic theory, for an exchange. The concept of the market also applies to the fact that residents of the area appear to choose their place of residence in terms of the amenities they desire and can afford. Critics of this popular explanation point out that many in the metropolitan area are not rational in their choice (a common characteristic of communities) and some others who are, are not given the choice to decide.

4. The dozens, sometimes hundreds, of governmental units in a metropolitan area make it sensible to view the metropolitan area as a part of the system of intergovernmental relations. Shared decision making involves not only the traditional three levels of government but also a great amount of interlocal cooperation. To the extent that this is the case, the emphasis on shared values and goals by professional administrators in various areas of government is especially appropriate. If the notion of cooperation is reasonably satisfactory as an explanation of how decisions are made relative to American domestic policy today, the implication is that metropolitan areas will be able to operate satisfactorily (though certainly not ideally) through the use of negotiation and shared decision making and financing. As shown in chapter 4, cooperation is a major element in new federalism, but conflict is probably more prominent.[59]

5. The metropolitan area may be viewed as a complex of local governments that, if combined into a single unit, would no longer be a local government, but that, through county and state governments, might be able to provide those services that strictly local governments cannot provide by themselves. Although many of the metropolitan areas cover more than one county—and these are generally the largest such areas—the others increasingly may find the county a useful unit of metropolitan government. In these areas as well as in those that cover more than a single county, the state is likely to provide metropolitanwide services in future years. In such areas as air and water pollution, highway systems, health services, welfare services, urban renewal, and areawide planning, the state is particularly likely to serve as a metropolitan unit of government. Thus, this perspective recognizes that a fully integrated metropolitan area is unlikely in American politics, but that metropolitan government, nevertheless, exists within the fragmented metropolis.[60]

6. The metropolitan area can also be viewed as a set of competing and sometimes conflicting ideologies. Perhaps this view has been least investigated, but in the future we may find research being done relative to its importance in developing public policy in metropolitan areas, where some residents are committed to the values of the welfare state, whereas a small but sometimes politically important minority remains committed to the small-town ideology of the nineteenth century, a more radical ideology of class struggle, or to some new, emerging ideology.[61]

Concluding Note

Each device tried so far for the areawide government of the metropolis either is basically unacceptable politically to groups powerful enough to block adoption or has proved inadequate as an approach. Any proposal that does not meet the requirement of responsibility and responsiveness to the general public must be dismissed—as it will be by the electorate—as lacking accord with our basic concepts of democratic theories. More often, the prevailing fragmentation is unconsciously supported by the prevailing ideologies discussed in chapter 2.

Notes

1. On this point, see Robert C. Wood, "Metropolitan Government, 1957: An Extrapolation of Trends," *American Political Science Review* 52 (Mar. 1958): 108–22; and his *Suburbia: Its People and Their Politics* (Boston: Houghton Mifflin, 1959). On the role of government in this choice, see Edward Banfield, *The Unheavenly City Revisited* (Boston: Little, Brown, 1974), particularly chapter 2; and Anthony Downs, *Opening Up the Suburbs* (New Haven, CT: Yale University Press, 1973).

2. Charles R. Adrian and Ernest S. Griffith, *A History of American City Government: The Formation of Traditions, 1775–1870* (New York: Praeger, 1976), 11.

3. This is discussed, for the period as early as 1800, in Kenneth T. Jackson, *Crabgrass Frontier, The Suburbanization of the United States* (New York: Oxford University Press, 1985), chapter 2.

4. Adrian and Griffith, *American City Government,* 19.

5. Jackson, *Crabgrass Frontier,* 190.

6. See Charles R. Adrian, *A History of American City Government: The Emergence of The Metropolis, 1920–1945* (Lanham, MD: University Press of America, 1987), especially chapter 3; and Charles R. Adrian and Charles Press, *Governing Urban America,* 5th ed. (New York: McGraw-Hill, 1977), 9.

7. John C. Bollens and Henry J. Schmandt, *The Metropolis: Its People, Politics, and Economic Life,* 4th ed. (New York: Harper & Row, 1982), 19. The 1990 estimate is from the Census Bureau (see chapter 1). Twenty-six essays on the meaning and characteristics of suburbia through time are offered in Barbara M. Kelly, *Suburbia Re-Examined,* (Westport, CT: Greenwood Press, 1989).

8. Larry H. Long and Donald C. Dahmann, *The City-Suburb Income Gap: Is It Being Narrowed by a Back-to-the-City Movement?* (Washington, DC: Census Bureau, Mar. 1980). A later study showed widespread disagreement on the definition of gentrification and explanation of the phenomenon. It seemed unlikely that consensus is to be forthcoming in the near future. See Bruce London, Barrett A. Lee, and S. Gregory Lipton, "The Determinants of Gentrification in the United States: A City Level Analysis," *Urban Affairs Quarterly* 21:3 (Mar. 1986): 369–87.

9. Ibid. Also see George Sternlieb and James W. Hughs, "The Uncertain Future of the Central City," *Urban Affairs Quarterly* 18:4 (June 1983): 455–72.

10. The phenomenon is most likely today in southern and western cities, where immigration is high, particularly from Asia and Latin America. For an older eastern account of a decaying core city and its relation to the suburb, see Clark Taylor, "Newark: Parasitic Suburb," *Society* (Sept.–Oct. 1972).

11. Banfield, *Unheavenly City,* particularly chapters 2 and 3. The effect of class,

and especially of gentrification, on school integration policy in Boston is described in J. Anthony Lucas, *Common Ground,* (New York: Vintage, 1985).

12. Banfield, *Unheavenly City,* 234–35.

13. Norton Long, *The Unwalled City* (New York: Basic Books, 1972), x.

14. *Village of Arlington Heights* vs. *Metro Housing Development,* 429 U.S. 252 (1977).

15. See Downs, *Opening Up Suburbs.*

16. The *New York Times,* Feb. 9, 1984, as reported in John J. Harrigan, *Political Change in the Metropolis,* 4th ed. (Glenview, IL.: Scott, Foresman, 1989), 297, 300. This (with Bollens and Schmandt, *The Metropolis*) is the other major text strictly on metropolitan government.

17. Minnesota Statutes, 1988, Sections 120.062 and 123.3515; Also see *Star Tribune,* Mar. 14, 1989, p. 1.

18. Harrigan, *Political Change,* 251–56.

19. Mark Schneider and John Logan, ''Suburban Municipalities: The Changing System of Intergovernmental Relations in the Mid-1970s,'' *Urban Affairs Quarterly* 21:1 (Sept. 1985): 87–105.

20. John C. Bollens et al., *Background for Action,* (St. Louis Metropolitan Survey, 1957), 99, 30–34.

21. York Willbern, *The Withering Away of the City* (Tuscaloosa: University of Alabama Press, 1964), 70.

22. Wood, ''Metropolitan Government,'' 111. On this section, see also his *Suburbia*; and Edward C. Banfield and Morton Grodzins, *Government and Housing* (New York: McGraw-Hill, 1958).

23. Basil G. Zimmer and Amos H. Hawley, ''Local Government as Viewed by Fringe Residents,'' *Rural Sociology* 28 (Dec. 1958):363–70. Provides partial verification. Even poorly informed suburbanites have elementary knowledge of their options in adjusting personal decisions to public policy, as is explained in Albert O. Hirschman's *Exit, Voice, and Loyalty* (Cambridge, MA: Harvard University Press, 1970). The resident can roughly calculate the costs of leaving the suburb (buying elsewhere), joining in active dissent, or going along with the public decision, however reluctantly.

24. Still the best study of suburban policing is found in James Q. Wilson, *Varieties of Police Behavior* (Cambridge, MA: Harvard University Press, 1968). On the general subject, see Wood, *Suburbia.*

25. Vincent Ostrom, Robert Bish, and Elinor Ostrom, *Local Government in the United States* (San Francisco: ICS Press, 1988), especially chapter 6.

26. *Milliken* v. *Bradley,* 418 U.S. 717 (1974).

27. *San Antonio* v. *Rodriquez,* 411 U.S. 1 (1973).

28. A number of court cases and studies concentrated principally on involuntary efforts in New Jersey and California. See Richard Lehne, *The Quest for Justice* (New York: Longman, 1978); and Richard F. Elmore and Milbrey Wallin McLaughlin, *Reform and Retrenchment: The Politics of California School Finance Reform,* (Cambridge, MA: Ballinger Publishing, 1982).

29. See *A Nation at Risk, The Imperative for Educational Reform,* 1983; and James S. Coleman, *Equal Educational Opportunity Survey* (Washington, DC: Government Printing Office, 1966).

30. The stereotyping and harsh criticism of suburbia are rejected in Scott Donaldson, *The Suburban Myth* (New York: Columbia University Press, 1969). On the benefits of specialization, see Robert L. Bish and Vincent Ostrom, *Understanding Urban Government* (Washington, DC: American Enterprise Institute for Public Policy Research, 1973).

31. Coleman Woodbury, "Great Cities, Great Problems, Great Possibilities?" *Public Administration Review* 18 (Autumn 1958):339.

32. Adrian, *A History of American Government,* 103.

33. Bollens and Schmandt, *The Metropolis,* 307–08.

34. The Census Bureau does an annual survey of boundary changes, reported in the *Municipal Year Book* (Washington, DC: International City Management Association). Trends reported in this section can be found in two reviews: for the 1980s, Joel C. Miller, "Municipal Annexation and Boundary Change," the *Municipal Year Book, 1988,* 57–68; and for the 1970s, Joel C. Miller and Richard L. Forstall, "Annexations and Corporate Changes: 1970–79 and 1980–83," the *Municipal Year Book, 1985,* 96–101.

35. *Town of Hallie et al.* v. *City of Eau Claire,* 471 U.S. 34 (1985).

36. Kenneth G. Bueche, *Incorporation Laws: One Aspect of the Urban Problem* (Boulder: Bureau of Governmental Research and Service, University of Colorado, 1963).

37. Ibid., 200–201; John Goldbach, *Boundary Change in California: The Local Agency Formation Commissions* (Davis: Institute of Governmental Affairs, University of California, 1970).

38. Anthony G. White, *Local Government Boundary Commissions* (Monticello, IL: Council of Planning Librarians,1973), 1–3; Orval Etter, "Boundary Control in Oregon," *National Civic Review* 62 (Nov. 1973):538*ff.* A review of the *Book of the States* (Lexington, KY: Council of State Governments) and *Municipal Year Book* finds only Kansas (1986) in addition to the ten reported by White.

39. Harrigan, *Political Change,* 312.

40. Ibid, 121–22, 313.

41. See the yearly reviews of boundary changes in Miller, "Municipal Annexation," in the *Municipal Year Book.* See also Miller and Forstall, the *Municipal Year Book, 1984,* 99; for the 1970s, for history, the *Municipal Year Book, 1986,* 77; and for 1980–1986, the *Municipal Year Book, 1987,* 70.

42. W. E. Lyons, *The Politics of City-County Merger* (Lexington: The University Press of Kentucky, 1977).

43. Robert D. Seltzer, "Indiana Passes 'UNIGOV' Law," *National Civic Review* 58 (June 1969):265; York Willbern, "Unigov: Local Reorganization in Indianapolis," in Advisory Commission on Intergovernmental Relations, *Regional Governance: Promise and Performance* (Washington, DC, 1973), 59–64.

44. For the Baton Rouge adoption, see Thomas H. Reed, "Progress in Metropolitan Integration," *Public Administration Review* 9 (Winter 1949) :1–10; R. G. Kean, "Consolidation That Works," *National Municipal Review* 45 (Nov. 1956):478–85. For the difficulties encountered in the early years of the Baton Rouge consolidation, E. Gordon Kean, Jr., "East Baton Rouge Parish," *Guide to County Organization and Management,* (Washington, DC: National Association of Counties, 1968), 31–35.

45. Gustave Serino, *Miami's Metropolitan Experiment* (Gainesville: Public Administration Clearing Service, University of Florida, 1958); Edward Sofen, *The Miami Metropolitan Experiment* (Bloomington: Indiana University Press, 1963), and Aileen Lotz, "Metropolitan Dade County," in *Regional Governance: Promise and Performance—Substate Regionalism and the Federal System* (Washington, DC: ACIR, 1973); and Ostrom, Bish, and Ostrom, *Local Government.*

46. See Harrigan, *Political Change;* James F. Horan and G. Thomas Taylor, Jr., *Experiments in Metropolitan Government* (New York: Praeger, 1977), chapter 4.

47. Harrigan, *Political Change,* 312.

48. See Charles R. Adrian, "Toward a Theory of Metropolitan Decision Making," a paper presented to the annual meeting of the American Political Science Association,

1972; and Roscoe C. Martin, *Metropolis in Transition* (Washington, DC: U.S. Housing and Home Finance Agency, 1963), which presents nine case studies.

49. Harrigan, *Political Change,* 343–47; Bollens and Schmandt, *The Metropolis,* 367–75; Nelson Wikstrom, *Councils of Governments, A Study of Political Incrementalism* (Chicago: Nelson-Hall, 1977); Walter A. Scheiber, "Councils of Government: An Assessment," *Public Management* 52 (Apr. 1970):24–25; and "Councils of Governments in the United States," *Municipal Year Book, 1970* (Washington, DC: International City Management Association, 1970), 39–45.

50. William Johnson, and John J. Harrigan, "Innovation by Increments: The Twin Cities as a Case Study in Metropolitan Reform," *Western Political Quarterly* 31 (June 1978):206.

51. Johnson and Harrigan, "Innovation by Increments . . . ," 206–18; and John J. Harrigan and William Johnson, *Governing the Twin Cities Region: The Metropolitan Council in Comparative Perspective* (Minneapolis: The University of Minnesota Press, 1978).

52. Tom Todd, "Metropolitan Governance Project," a series of papers produced by the Research Department, Minnesota House of Representatives, St. Paul, Nov. 1985.

53. Detachments and disincorporations are reviewed yearly in the *Municipal Year Book.* The examples in this paragraph were taken from a review of the 1970s by Miller and Forstall, the *Municipal Year Book, 1985;* and for the 1980s by Miller, the *Municipal Year Book, 1988.*

54. See Gary J. Miller, *Cities by Contract* (Cambridge, MA: The MIT Press, 1981).

55. For a summary of the values involved and the literature about them, see chapter 2; and Timothy Schlitz and William Moffitt, "Inner-City/Outer-City Relationships in Metropolitan Areas," *Urban Affairs Quarterly* 7 (Sept. 1971) :75–108.

56. See Paul Studenski, *Government of Metropolitan Areas* (New York: National Municipal League, 1930).

57. Matthew Holden, Jr., "The Governance of the Metropolis as a Problem in Diplomacy," *Journal of Politics* 26 (Aug. 1964) :627–47.

58. See Miller, "Municipal Annexation"; Robert L. Bish, *The Public Economy of Metropolitan Areas* (Chicago: Markham Publishing Company, 1971); and the review of the public choice–theory approach to metropolitan government in Bish and Ostrom, *Understanding Urban Governments;* and Ostrom, Bish, and Ostrom, *Local Government.*

59. See chapter 4; and Samuel A. Kirkpatrick and David R. Morgan, "Policy Support and Orientation toward Metropolitan Political Integration among Urban Officials," *Social Science Quarterly* 52 (Dec. 1971) :656–71. This provides empirical data showing that such cooperation is possible where consensual service activities (such as water supply or sewage disposal) are involved, but not where political conflict is generated.

60. Charles R. Adrian, "Public Attitudes and Metropolitan Decision Making," in Russell W. Maddox, Jr., ed., *Issues in State and Local Government* (New York: Van Nostrand Reinhold, 1965), 311–21.

61. See Michael R. Fine, "The Ideologies of Urban Politics," unpublished doctoral thesis, University of California, 1979.

"*Let's run through this once more—and, remember, you choke up at Paragraph Three and brush away the tear at Paragraph Five.*"

9

Executive Officers

I n colonial times, governors were distrusted by the people because they represented the Crown rather than the colonists. This same attitude of skepticism
lived on after the War of Independence was won, and it was reinforced by the individualism of the frontier. Throughout the nineteenth century, the powers of executives
in public office were circumscribed and balanced with a system of checks.

One characteristic of twentieth-century American government has been the
increasing authority and influence of the chief executive. This has not been true at
the national level alone. Through statutes, constitutional amendments, and new
state constitutions, the powers of the governor also have been increasing, as have
those of mayors and managers at the city level, and even in counties. For example,
many counties now have elected or appointed chief executive officers; in some
other counties, the clerk or another administrative officer has assumed these responsibilities. Often the executive powers exercised are established by informal
arrangement.

Of course, this shifting of authority and influence has caused some unrest.
Most political scientists, however, detect no sign that the executive at the state or
local level will move beyond the traditional functions in a democratic system. The
chief executive still is enormously hampered by the rules and customs of the system.
This has been pointed out by Richard Neustadt relative to the presidency and by practically all literature discussing the powers of state governors and local mayors and
managers.[1] Powers are further restricted by the growing fragmentation of government into special districts discussed in the preceding two chapters. As an executive's
power within a government rises, it usually is offset by the multiplicity of executives
in collegial governments who must be negotiated with, particularly when pursuing
shared grants. Even the last of the big-city bosses was significantly checked. Of
Mayor Richard J. Daley of Chicago in his heyday, Edward Banfield, commented that
"despite his great power as boss, [he] can do little even in the city proper without at
least tacit support from the governor."[2]

Chief executives at any level are fixers, negotiators, diplomats, or needlers.
They are the ones who must marshal public support or opposition, activate latent is-

sues, and focus public attention. They seldom give direct orders; they are expected to lead, not command.

The Conflict over Centralized Leadership

The question of how much power to give to the chief executive has historically been intertwined with the conflict between the elements of society, especially commercial interests, that stood to profit from central regulation, and others whose interests were best served by maximizing government at the local level. Yeoman farmers disliked central government whether it was in the hands of the king or of business leaders and correctly perceived that executive power may be an instrument for centralization. Only with the advent of the social service state did strengthening of executive power become a popular cause, and even then it was the result of desperation.

Although the Jacksonian period saw some increase in the status of chief executives, and a rise from the low esteem of the period just after the War of Independence, those who dominated politics during the first half of the nineteenth century kept executives weak. They did so by favoring rotation in office and advocating many elective positions. Because the Jacksonians represented the worker and the yeoman farmer, and not the commercial interests of the day, they reflected the values of these groups.

The responsible party following an election was supposed to continue to coordinate the activities of elective officers, but this party goal broke down. Nevertheless, in the years after the Civil War, most Jacksonian traditions—including rotation in office, amateurism, the long ballot, and others—remained intact. The result was a highly diffused executive power. During this period, the value preferences of business leaders in an era of rapidly accumulating wealth, the general sense of opportunities to advance economically in almost any line of activity, and the attitudes of boss-and-machine politicians that existed at the time permitted corruption to become widespread. When reformers made their influence felt beginning in the 1870s, they favored the establishment of many governmental activities outside the regular political structure. The result was an increase in the number of independent boards and commissions. By the beginning of the twentieth century, most state or local chief executives were administratively impotent, unless as boss or through the party machine they could achieve the powers the law denied them.

After about 1910, a move to increase chief executive powers began to have some effect in the states (somewhat earlier in cities). The reasons for this include the more complex nature of government, thus making coordination more necessary; a growing awareness of the existence of distinctive administrative skills; the high cost of modern government, which encouraged many citizens to grasp at any possibility for cutting down expenses; and an increase in executive prestige together with a growing conviction that the people could elect some who would act, not for the leaders of industry, but for the ordinary citizen.

The increased administrative and legislative influence of the governor in turn produced greater visibility, which helped attract more of a variety of persons to the job. This acted reciprocally to increase the status of governors. Modern techniques in the art of administration made it possible to bring the efforts of a vast number or people to a single focus in the office of the chief executive. Urbanization had an effect on the governor's office, for the incumbent increasingly became the voice of the people in the cities, protecting the urbanite from the potential hostility of rural-dominated legislatures. The Great Depression, finally, helped add to the prestige of government executives at all levels when citizens turned to firm leadership in a social-service state as the best hope for assistance with their personal economic problems and insecurities.[3] But as we noted in chapter 7, wide variation continues among the states and localities as to the centralization of executive power. A recent composite shows less than half the states with what might be called a strong-governor model.[4]

Of all executive officers, short of the president, perhaps the public pays most attention to its governors. This chapter will concentrate on that office, but not to the exclusion of other executive offices.

The Office of Governor

"The governor is not the executive; he is but a single piece of the executive," Woodrow Wilson, who was to become governor of New Jersey, once complained. He was quite correct, at least for the majority of states in his day and ours. But the governor is also more than the executive, and the office is more than a single individual. The governorship is an institution; to the people, it is a symbol of the unity of society within the state; to governors, their staffs and many advisers, it is an image to be carefully constructed and then disseminated through the mass media until it influences every politically conscious person in the state. The governorship is many things, as is the presidency, and the governor must play many roles and learn to help the public while at the same time keeping each role individually identifiable. The governor serves many roles: chief of state, voice of the people, chief executive, commander-in-chief of the state's armed forces, chief legislator, and party chief.[5] As chief executive the governor makes numerous appointments and creates an executive budget; as chief legislator the governor exercises more veto power than the president. No one person acting alone could play so many roles and exercise so much power.

There is a good deal of truth in the popular perception that those around the executive really run the state. The executive process in any large city or state is a collective process that produces a collective product, much as does management in big business.

Staff Composition

The governorship is an institution and its brain center is the governor's personal staff. In many states the staff is limited in size, although by the 1980s every governor's staff included a chief of staff, a legislative liaison, a legal counsel, a press secretary, and an appointment secretary, as well as receptionists, file clerks, mail clerks, police aides, and telephone operators.[6] (Each major staff position goes by different names depending on the conventions of the state.) Author Larry Sabato found:

> In 1956 the average staff size in a governor's office was 4.3 persons, and by 1966 the number had increased only slightly to 6.6. But since then the growth of gubernatorial

offices has been remarkable. In 1979 the average governor's office staff size was 34 and its budget approached $1.2 million.[7]

The trend continues; in 1990, the average staff size was over fifty. The governors of New York and Texas each have staffs of more than 175.[8] Furthermore, in most states the governor's staff is augmented by the person in charge of the executive budget (usually the controller, budget director, or commissioner of administration) and by political party leaders and the few paid members of the party staff.

Elected executives always want more staff, in effect invoking Parkinson's law (see chapter 10). They argue that the increases are justified because of the increasing complexity of government and the need to compete with experts in other branches of government and the private sector. Although exaggerated, this argument is shared by legislators who also are expanding their work and staffs. Elected chief executives usually are more experienced and interested in the attention-grabbing roles of chief of state or voice of the people than in the technical duties as chief executive, but they fear being outflanked by career bureaucrats. With like-minded legislators confirming these fears with expansion of their own staffs, augmentation of personnel (both exec-utive *and* legislative) has become a rule of bureaucracy beyond rational needs (mea-sured by better legislation or administration). This does not diminish the skill and competence of the many bright staff members, nor does it overlook the organiza-tional system-maintenance value of hiring staff for patronage purposes. The regular bureaucracy has jobs protected against arbitrary or political dismissals and individ-uals may work within it for a lifetime. The governor's staff, however, holds its posi-tions on a temporary basis subject to termination with the expiration of the governor's term. But its members enjoy many of the other advantages and characteristics of bu-reaucracy and they have become a sizable and specialized maze that is well en-trenched in American state and local governments.

In the process of assembling a governor's staff, we see dramatized one of the major difficulties of a political executive. One observer has written the following:

> Little, if any, advance planning normally goes into selection of top personnel for an administration prior to the day of the election. The press of the campaign usually re-quires that such matters be deferred until a later date, and that date never seems to arrive until the candidate finds himself a governor-elect. Then the impact of personnel recruit-ment becomes so sharp that the campaign staff—in moments of retrospection—wonders why adequate time was not spent during the campaign on this phase of the post-election requirements. This reason is apparent to any participant in the political process: total commitment is first to win the election and then to worry about forming an administra-tion.[9]

Most staff members are young, well educated, highly interested in politics and, often, persons who see the job as a stepping-stone in their own political, legal, aca-demic or other careers. But in some states, the top staff positions have so grown in importance that a prominent member of the legislature may resign to join the gover-nor's staff, recognizing that is where "real" decisions are made. Staff members must be highly capable and willing to serve as the governor's alter ego. Normally, they will be as anonymous—and just as important to the total effort—as offensive tackles on a football team. But, as we saw at the national level in both the Watergate and Iran-Contra scandals, it is these obscure actors who ultimately may determine the course of public affairs.

The extent to which the staff can project an image chosen by an executive is limited, as once noted by a staff member of former Governor Mark Hatfield of Oregon.[10] The staff cannot create strength where none exists, though members can provide helpful ideas. They cannot second-guess the boss. Statements of ''what the governor really meant to say'' will not be believed more than once, if then. The governor *is* the decision maker whose style and concept of the gubernatorial role must be accepted by the staff. Staff members have in common the fact that governors place trust in them and delegate to them a great deal of responsibility, for they must do things governors would do themselves if they had the time. This being the case, governors normally staff their offices without considering the patronage factors that usually are so important. They do not care about size of political contributions in the past, degree of party activity, geographical section of the state where the individual lives, for example. However, in recent years governors deliberately have sought women and minority staff members. The vital question is whether the person can fill the job with vigor, imagination, and a devotion to anonymity. Those wishing to place a personal stamp on what they do or unwilling to accept a governer's policy decision are not suited to this type of work. But they may nevertheless later run for office. It might be added that, as with the White House staff, opportunities and pressures to perform favors beyond what the public regards as proper may occur, so that corruption occasionally appears.

Open and Closed Staffs

Staffs vary widely from state to state and with individuals governors; the practices of no two staffs are entirely alike. Nevertheless, the practices range along a continuum from the extreme *open* staff to the extreme *closed* staff.

In the open staff, the chief executive purposely chooses top staff members who might disagree with one another within the range of choices the governor accepts. More than one top staff member has free access to the governor. The governor hopes to get the greatest range of policy advice so as to ultimately make the final major decisions, rather than leaving them to be made by the staff. This form of staffing does seem to give greater power to the elected official and, therefore, might be seen as more democratic. On the other hand, a governor may not be competent or well suited to make final decisions, and this form of decision making in such cases tends to take more time in crises and may give the appearance of a staff in disarray.

In the closed process, the governor chooses a chief of staff who is expected to choose subordinate staff members, forming a pyramid of responsibility and information flow. In this hierarchical staff, the most important role of the chief of staff is ''gatekeeper'' to the governor. That is, the chief executive will see only those people approved by the chief of staff. Appointments actually are made by the staff, and policy choices are narrowed down to those selected by the staff for ultimate approval by the governor. Most chief executives prefer this staffing process because it frees the governor from much of the day-to-day drudgery of administration and policy making and leaves more time for more informal roles involving public opinion, which most politicians relish. But this approach reduces the policy-making power of the governor, often turning decisions over to staff members who never undergo public scrutiny. And the process will break down if governors never hear attractive alternatives or if the governor is shut out of important decisions altogether by overzealous—albeit often well-intentioned—staff members.

Staff Roles

Perhaps the most important role of the staff is the development of policy recommendations to be presented to the voters during campaigns and the legislature during sessions. The governor must appear knowledgeable about issues and problems in the state and have a suggestion in response to every inquiry. At any time and in the name of the governor the staff can gather information from state agencies and private persons throughout the state; therefore, it usually can provide the governor with more information than is to be had by legislative leaders or the governor's opponents. Few governors have experience in all the policy areas they deal with, and even if they do, no single one can make all the policy decisions demanded by the office. Thus, the governor's actual policy-making role is one of priority setting. Even so, this does not lighten the load of an ''omniscient'' chief executive in the policy-making process. It is the staff's job to prevent the governor from appearing foolish or uninformed in regard to even the most obscure policy issue.

Although the press secretary—usually an experienced journalist—will frame the governor's words for major press releases, each staff member responsible for certain subject areas will watch for warning signs of possible political hot water as well as developments the governor can claim credit for. By the same token, staff will keep an eye open for pegs which to hang news stories favorable to the governor. The staff must act as liaison with the various state, local, and federal government agencies. It is their job to know any difficulties an agency is experiencing, what goals it is pursuing, who are its friends and enemies among the interest groups and lobbyists, what ideas for legislation agency staffs are developing that the governor might endorse (or quell), their budget situation, and any other information that the governor might ask for in staff meetings or the press secretary might need to frame a well-informed story.

The staff member's role is quite different from the head of an agency and ultimately more important in the budget process, even though that agency chief may be better known or more powerful politically. The staff member is not expected to be an advocate for the department of responsibility but instead to view the agency as part of the larger governmental puzzle and seek to make the part fit properly. Nevertheless, as staff sizes grow and the executive office of the governor becomes more complex, staff members may become advocates for policies they must investigate and prepare for the governor. This always has been expected of department heads but has increasingly become a tendency within staffs. The result is usually a hierarchy within the staff in which those in most frequent contact with the governor become (like the boss) involved less with detail and more with general priority setting and public opinion.

Thus, subordinate staff members become the true contacts between the elected executive and the bureaucracy that governors are expected to oversee.

Each governor will have a staff member assigned to work with the legislative members, although all staff members deal with legislators in their assigned areas. The governor's program, once developed, must be interpreted to members of the party in the legislature, and support from these members must be secured to the greatest extent possible. The legislative secretary provides information to legislators concerning the implications of pending legislation, keeps track of all pieces of major legislation as well as of all administration bills, and may attend party caucuses. The legislative secretary must be able to brief the governor at any time on the status of the administration program and of political assets and liabilities to be found in legislation presented by the opposition. This staff member must try to placate members of the governor's party in the legislature who may be sensitive about being "dictated to" and also must try to win over any wavering members. During critical times in a legislative session, the legislative secretary will be the busiest person on the staff.

The appointive powers of a governor vary widely and are treated differently, depending on whether the governor is permitted strong partisan patronage or faces more bureaucratic methods of appointment. In states with strong party structures, one staff member will be expected to keep in touch with party officials and their paid staffs (if any). The executive secretary most likely handles clearances for appointments to state offices, boards, commissions, and these assignments. Each proposed appointment must be cleared through party channels. Perhaps the executive secretary does not know, for example, that the candidate for appointment supported the governor's opponent. Because more than one person may be qualified, party workers will prefer that a party activist (or at least a supporter of the governor) gets the assignment. (But in weak party states, the governor may ignore or even defy the wishes of local party members.)

The staff member in charge of appointments will have another task, a difficult and almost thankless one—*almost,* because the governor will appreciate what is done. That is the job of informing candidates that the governor had had to pass them over. A person who is really skilled at this assignment can let persons down so gently that they scarcely know they have been refused. And if the disappointed person must blame someone, the staff member must see to it that is is *not* the governor. This job is not only difficult, but it also entails the expenditure of a great amount of time of the "hand holding" sort. Furthermore, this person will use up even more time talking with county party leaders and other important politicians who stop at the governor's office when they visit the capital. The use of this time may seem inefficient, but it is necessary to support the governor's role as party leader.

Contacting the Governor

Many personal callers—famous, obscure, important, psychotic, desperate, or curious—come to the office of every governor:

> In the office [of Governor Franklin D. Roosevelt of New York], day in and day out, there were streams of visitors, some on state business, some from other parts of the

> country . . . some who simply wished to see a governor and prominent political leader.
> [Personal Secretary, Guernsey Cross] turned away most of those whose business was
> not definite, and could not guarantee that many who came without appointments could
> get in. Usually when Roosevelt went home there were still ten or fifteen disappointed
> ones left in the anteroom. . . .[11]

The staff is responsible for answering most of the governor's mail and deciding
which pieces of it should go the governor personally. Governor Roosevelt "never
permitted a letter to go unanswered [thus] strengthening his contact with men and
women from all walks of life. . . ."[12] Every wise governor follows the same policy—
except for "crank" mail.

Today's governors receive over five-hundred pieces of mail a day.[13] The mail
includes the greatest possible variety. They are sent complimentary copies of periodicals, including everything from highbrow "little magazines" to scurrilous hate-
peddling tabloids, to such intriguing items as the *Pretzel Baker*. Staff members scan
them for possibly useful material. Governors receive letters from "crackpots," some
of whom are paranoid and blame public officials for all their troubles; others have the
world's greatest invention which, if the governor would lend assistance, would produce a fortune for both; some offer cures for the troubles of humanity; quite a few are
religious fanatics. Every governor's office has a list of these correspondents, whose
letters are *not* answered. Many letters of complaints are not answered over the governor's signature unless they come from prominent persons or the complaint can be
rectified. Others are answered over a staff member's signature or referred to a state
agency for reply. (The agency may be able to mollify the citizen, but if it cannot, this
technique allows the complainant's displeasure to be projected upon the anonymous
staff member or agency bureaucrat, thus often preserving undamaged the perception
of the governor held by the disturbed citizen.)

Most of the governor's mail comes from ordinary citizens in need of help. Typically, these are people who do not understand bureaucracy, who have been frustrated in other efforts to get satisfaction concerning some real or fancied problem,
and who do not have connections through the party organization, the government
bureaucracy, or the business world. Having nowhere else to go (they often state this
explicitly in their letters), they turn to the state's chief executive for help. The request
may deal with an agency over which the governor has jurisdiction, and the complaint
may be a valid, but more often it will concern a state agency over which the governor
has no control, or will involve a matter falling within the jurisdiction of some local or
federal agency. Every request is given consideration and a reply. Contrary to popular
impression, little attention is paid to party membership or activity, and the governor's
staff will ordinarily not seek preferred treatment but only fair treatment for those who
complain. In the majority of cases, the governor is helpless to act. For example, people write for jobs when none are to be had, seek the release of felons over whose
sentence the governor has no control, and ask for additional welfare aid even though
the eligibility requirements are spelled out in state and federal law and the governor
cannot modify them. People in trouble write to governors asking them to overrule the
workers' compensation board, to set aside the deliberations of the state supreme
court, or to waive legislation and ordinances set up to ensure equity. In their despera-

tion, they are not interested in justice or equity; often they seek neither. They want their personal problem taken care of, and nothing else matters. Governors may be able to help them—and daily they get hundreds of pieces of mail. Governors never see most of them, but the staff plods through them, seeking to avoid making enemies and, where possible, to make friends. Many an injustice has been avoided and many a piece of red tape cut in this way. Frequently, the problem is no more complicated than putting the individual in touch with the public or private agency that can be of help.

It is probably not much of an exaggeration to say that the governor's image and record are at the mercy of the staff. The real world to the governor's eye may well be that conveyed by the staff.[14]

Gubernatorial Roles and Powers

We have seen, then, that the governorship must be viewed as an institution. It is created through a formula, the individual ingredients of which become blended. During much of the official day, the governor loses an individual personality and becomes part of the total institution—the governorship—which, in addition to officeholder consists of personal staff, certain other high government officials (which may be organized as a cabinet), and principal members of the governor's political party. The governor may or may not be the actual leader of the team. Publicly, of course, the governor is the entire institution—constituents are unaware of most other members.[15]

Chief of State

Like the U.S. president, though in a much more modest way, governors serve as the living symbol of the state. Ironically, when we rejected the idea of a monarchy at the founding of the American system, we saddled chief executives with the role of ceremonial chief of state, today played elsewhere by the few remaining royal families. The intended check has made our presidents, governors, and mayors more powerful. In this role, governors are not representatives of political parties; they are not seen as the ones who control patronage or struggle with the legislature over a new state school-aid formula. Instead, they claim to be representatives of all the people of the state as they dedicate a new highway, open the state convention of the Sea League of America, throw out the first baseball of the season, attend the funeral of a prominent politician, send greetings to the Western Bohemian Fraternal Association, or proclaim February 16 as Lithuanian Independence Day.

They are called on to shake thousands of hands as they travel about the state. They allow thousands of school children to tour their offices each year, none of voting age but all anxious to get home to tell mother, father, uncle, and aunt—who *are* voting age—that they shook the hand of the governor. Coleman Ransone reports that, when asked, close to 70 percent of governors would generally accede to the request to appear at the state fair opening and 95 percent would generally accede to the request to address the state chamber of commerce. Three-fourths would accede to a highway ribbon-cutting request.[16] Though much of the work—the proclamations, the letters, the speeches—can be taken care of by the staff, the rituals governors are expected to take part in require a great deal of personal time. To avoid them jeopardizes their political careers; to accept them, perhaps with reluctance but more likely with considerable enthusiasm, is the rule, for most governors genuinely like people. Even those who do not, find that ceremonial functions allow them to make contact with constituents under very favorable conditions and with a minimum of the tension and conflict that accompany political appearances. Through these contacts, governors can keep their physician's finger on the public pulse while allaying suspicion by appearing in priestly garb.

Governors are asked to send letters of greeting to every kind of meeting, from the sheet-metal workers' anniversary ball to the state well drillers' association. Of course, governors cannot devote time to every such letters demand. In addition to letters of greeting, governors are asked to issue fifty to one-hundred proclamations each year. These vary from a proclamation to support a worthy charity drive to one supporting the bizarre and improbable. For example, when governors' staffs across the country were confronted with requests to issue National Laugh Week proclamations, they knew whom the laugh would be on if they obliged—journalists dislike handouts announcing yet another special day, week, or month even under the best of conditions. Yet, long-suffering members of the governor's staff must find nice things to say about Plumbing, Heating, or Cooling Week or Good Posture Month. The assignment may pain them, but the letters and proclamations are vitally important to the people requesting them, even though staff members may sometimes have to check to make sure that requests are legitimate. The job, furthermore, cannot be turned over to a clerk, for many requests involve subtle policy questions (Should the governor praise the state board of realtors just after it has helped to kill the administration's public housing bill?) Or the job easily could involve the governor in political hot water, such as taking sides in feuds among professional organizations.

Ordinarily, neither the governor nor the staff originates proclamations and greetings; they are requested by individuals or groups, and those making the requests frequently furnish a draft of what it is they want said. Sometimes people unknown to the governor or the party write to ask that they be publicly congratulated, perhaps on a fiftieth wedding anniversary or election to a lodge office. Governors, through their staffs, will oblige. The important thing in these time-consuming ceremonial functions is that the letter or proclamation appear to be drafted and signed by the governor personally. (Most governors authorize a staff member or two to sign their name to certain documents and letters.) Even persons who would never vote for the governor will seek a letter of greeting from the governor for their favorite organization's annual convention. The governor after all, is, the living symbol of the state. Ceremonial functions may involve a certain amount of adolescent horseplay. For example, the 1963 dedication of a municipal swimming pool in Boulder, Colorado, astronaut Scott Carpenter, was tossed into the pool by the mayor when Carpenter dedicated the pool; the mayor in turn was then tossed in by others. Even frivolous duties potentially can be politically harmful. For example, Governor Rudy Perpich of Minnesota saw little harm in declaring a special day for each member of the Minnesota Twins, who won the 1987 World Series, but complaints festered long after he advised (but did not *require*) a school holiday to celebrate the victory. Some parents were angered when their children were released, which for some necessitated arranging for child care, whereas others balked at their children being required to stay in school and miss the parade. Perhaps the angriest voters were the downtown merchants, who were forced to close their doors to protect against vandalism as thousands of teenagers, bent on celebrating both a Twins victory *and* a school holiday, crowded into stores with little intention of buying anything.

Even the state's first family must be on guard. Woe to one governor's wife who was quoted as referring to honey as "bee poop" at the meeting of the State Bee-keepers' Association.

Voice of the People

Just as "the President is the American people's one authentic trumpet,"[17] so are governors the voice for the morality, the higher aspirations, and the conscience of the citizens of the state. Although they are able to command only a small portion of the prestige and attention of the President, governors are still the only ones in a position to speak of the ideals of the people of the state in a sense that is accepted as being above politics. They can speak convincingly about the need for education for all, for the protection of young and old, the dependent mother, the mentally ill. Whatever their policies, they are expected to present the higher values of society and to defend them—even though their means of implementing specific programs may belie their true interest and their specific proposals may become items of intense controversy.

As an individual, the governor portrays not only the state government but the state itself. Politically speaking, however, this is a two-edged sword. The governor, rather than the legislature, is credited with almost everything perceived by the voters as an *advancement* in state government. This tendency has been capitalized on by all able and successful governors. For example, when he first became chief executive with a legislature controlled by the opposition party, Governor Franklin D. Roosevelt of New York announced that "about 90 percent of the legislation ought not to be taken up from a partisan point of view."[18] From such an approach, a governor goes on, aided by a favorable image as voice of the people, to create the impression that a program is the nonpartisan one symbolizing the higher aims of the state, and legislative opposition is a devilish thing designed to thwart the will of the people. Sometimes this gambit is successful. But unfortunately for many governors, the public *also* blames them for anything that goes wrong during their administration, no matter where the responsibility in fact lies. Thus, governors generally believe that any new taxes added during their tenure will be blamed on them, whether they favored them or not.

As the federal system becomes more and more complex, the governor must speak for the state outside its borders. Staying in favor with the administration in Washington may have a greater effect on the state's economy than any policy the governor can change. Thus, an early supporter of President Bush, Tommy Thompson of Wisconsin, can expect to have a "friend in the White House." Even a governor who is of the same party as the president may be disliked or perceived as a threat to run against the president in the future. It is impossible to measure, but it is likely that the feud Governor Jerry Brown of California had with President Carter reduced the likelihood of California receiving some discretionary federal grants-in-aid. Similarly, Minnesota Republic Governor Al Quie's standing in the early Reagan administration was far higher than was that of Wisconsin Republican Governor Lee Dreyfus, despite the fact that Dreyfus was doing far better than Quie in the polls back home in their respective states.

A "traveling" governor may be lambasted in the state press for not taking care of business at home, even though that governor is successful in bringing new jobs to the state from overseas. Governors who are not good spokespersons outside state borders frequently must leave the chore to someone else, but no one else is similarly viewed as the voice of the people of the state. The governor therefore must walk the mysterious line between becoming well know outside the state and appearing to be a national or international political figure who no longer is interested in the specific problems of the state.

Chief Executive

Although few governors have the legal powers necessary to give them control over the way in which state agencies are administered, they do have quite a few powers. Symbolically they are regarded as heads of administrations, and the governors' mail certainly indicates that they are so viewed by the public. As political leaders and as a voice of the people, governors may be able to exert influence over administration where their legal powers fail them. In many cases, however, governors lack both power and effective influence over the administration of some (perhaps many) departments, both because of the way department heads are selected and because of legislative provisions designed to insulate certain agencies from gubernatorial influence. Furthermore, few governors have had much executive experience prior to taking office, and fewer yet use such experience as the stepping-stone to the governorship. A study covering a thirty-year period showed that only 10 percent of the governors held an administrative post immediately prior to being elected, and only 20 percent had had any administrative experience.[19] The notion that "the buck stops here" is important in distinguishing executive from other types of decision making. Far more frequently than the top actors in the other branches of government, the state chief executive is expected to make what will be perceived of as a *final* decision. But without prior experience in the process, governors are reluctant to make final decisions on administrative questions. They realize that the potential for harm is greater than the potential for political good because the governor will be blamed when things go wrong—even though many will move decisively for a share of the credit when things go right.

Appointments

In the chief executive role, the powers of appointment shapes the administration. Gubernatorial appointments usually are subject to approval by the state senate (or less often by the whole legislature or a variety of boards or commissions, depending on the office and the state). Sometimes they can appoint, but cannot remove, an official—removal power being vested in the civil service commission, state supreme court, or some other agency. Some department heads are chosen by boards or commissions appointed for staggered terms, so that the department may remain in the hands of the political enemy unless the governor remains in office for many years. In a few instances, department heads are civil servants. The administrative structure is so complex and the eligibility pool so large that gubernatorial staffs have difficulty in keeping up with changes that take place. Thus governors have appointed dead people to office or living ones to commissions that no longer exist.

Some governors have power to remove local officials after notice and hearing, although this power is seldom exercised because it is likely that either a local politician who has violated the local mores will be removed through other means before the governor need act *or* removal of a local politician would be unpopular and hence politically damaging.

The governor's appointment role has always been greatest as the importance of the state office increases. Years ago, governors had thousands of appointments through patronage, but the number has been reduced as the percentage of full-time state employees under some form of civil service system jumped from 50 to 75 percent between 1958 and 1980 and as the patronage system came under attack by the courts in the 1990s.[20] As will be discussed in greater detail in the following chapter, patronage and merit systems are not opposites. Often the guise of merit is simply a legal mechanism of job protection measuring seniority or some other factor. Nevertheless, a merit system usually will weaken the power of the governor, turning decision making over to bureaucrats who are less concerned with partisan matters or legislatures who set the rules of merit. But governors usually retain control over those at the top of most agency hierarchies. Remembering that the bureaucratic maze of government will continue in power regardless of changes in political leadership, a successful governor (or the staff) will make appointments that will incrementally change a department in the direction the governor hopes to go. A chief executive who appoints someone unpopular within the bureaucracy may see that person cut off from the information flow within his or her own administration. As was shown in the Reagan administration, this may prove desirable if it is intended by the chief executive that a department favored by the legislature be reduced in power. Nevertheless, it is usually unavailing to "shake up" a bureaucracy from the top. Unfortunately for the governor who wants to change bureaucratic outcomes, it is at the top where their greatest power lies.

Finally, governors are aware that those who do not make appointments quickly or who cannot get their appointments approved may see the department come under greater control by bureaucrats. Government agencies do not stop working while awaiting a new leader. The power is generally exercised by the highest-ranking career bureaucrat until an appointment is made at the top. Failure to appoint successfully will weaken that governor's administrative power.

Budget Control

During the 1920s and 1930s, first reform and then economic pressures were so great that several state constitutions were amended to give governors the power of the item veto, and many legislatures surrendered part of their traditional control over the purse. They permitted the establishment of all or part of the executive-budget system, which divided up the financial process so that the executive branch recommend's revenues and expenditures in the form of a systematic, comprehensive statement of income and outgo. The legislature then adopts this budget, nearly always with some modification. The executive branch next oversees the expenditure of appropriations by the various departments, requiring them to spend at a rate that will not exhaust their appropriations prematurely and keeping expenditures within the requirements of the law. Finally, the legislative branch, through its auditors, ascertains whether its instructions have been carried out and whether appropriate provisions of the state law have been followed by the executive. The power of chief executives, through budget officers, is potentially broad, both in preparing the budget itself—the document is, of course, a major policy statement explaining how the governor would spend money— and in controlling its expenditure after the legislature votes the funds. Budget officers and their budget examiners serve to advise executives and legislators by reviewing appropriation requests and preparing evidence in support of the final policy position taken by the governors. Budget officers control the conditions under which appropriations may be spent.

One measure of a governor's budget-making power is the executive budget; forty-five states claim to have one, though powers differ. A second measure is whether a governor must share that power. In a few states it is shared by the governor with either a budget director or the legislature. Only in three states (Mississippi, South Carolina, and Texas) are budget-making powers of the governor considered weak, because budgets are prepared by a source wholly independent from the governor.[21] Over forty states leave the power wholly to the governor. Nevertheless, as will be discussed in chapters 11 and 12, the state legislatures are hiring increasingly larger staffs to assist them in responding to the governor's budget and to modify significant portions of the final budget. Even with the executive budget, the members of the legislature or their staffs may be instrumental in preliminary agency budget requests, which will be submitted to the governor in the earlier stages of the budgetary process. Yet, the governor's budget staff is almost always many times larger than the legislature's. The complexity of the budget often means that those who put in the most hours in the preparation process will have a significant advantage in the process.

Whenever budgets are discussed, they are almost always overrated in importance. They are an aspect of planning, blueprints for the unpredictable future, that state ways to raise money and spend it; as such, they are always built on some degree of shaky ground. Governors always can recommend supplemental appropriations contrary to the budget, and as long as a way can be found to raise the money, legislatures always can, and frequently do, change the blueprint when unforeseen factors arise or the balance of power between legislature and executive shifts. Bureaucrats modify budgets in countless subtle ways as they administer them (for more on budgets, see chapter 14).

Pardon and Extradition

Gubernatorial power to pardon originates from British sovereign authority. Under feudal theory, monarchs ultimately owned all land, and the law was theirs too. Therefore, they could pardon offenses against the law. Until shortly into the twentieth century, the pardon was almost the only device by which prisoners could be released before completing their full sentence. In some states, nearly 50 percent of all prisoners were pardoned before the expiration of their sentences, prior to the instituting of probation and parole.

Pardoning power sometimes has been abused. For example, Governor Len Small of Illinois was so generous with pardons that his 1924 opponents commissioned a song, "Oh, Pardon Me," which they used against him. Governor John C. Walton of Oklahoma freed 693 prisoners in eleven months and was impeached and convicted for having taken bribes for some of the pardons. Governor Miriam "Ma" Ferguson of Texas pardoned 3,700 prisoners in two years—and some of the state's newspapers derisively ran daily pardon columns. In 1979, the successor to Governor Ray Blanton of Tennessee was secretly sworn in three days early to negate proposed pardons by Blanton of fifty-two prisoners (including twenty-three murderers); he himself later served prison time for a variety of federal charges for related improprieties.[22] Today's federal mail fraud and racketeering statutes serve as checks against misuse of powers where state criminal justice systems are reluctant or inadequate to correct the corruption. In 1987, Governor Edwin Edwards of Louisiana lost his bid for reelection for an unprecedented fourth term after being acquitted on federal racketeering charges. But most governors probably have disliked the responsibility for acting on pardons and paroles and few have purposefully misused them in recent decades.

Today, few sentences are commuted and very few prisoners are pardoned, although some governors continue the tradition of granting Christmas pardons, a practice designed to help maintain the morale of long-termers. Executive clemency, usually administered by a board of specialists, now serves to correct miscarriages of justice and is given only rarely for other reasons.

As discussed in chapter 4, governors can use their extradition powers to assist other governors in pursuing felons and even, infrequently, can withhold it. But extradition too has become a bureaucratic process, usually administered by a board of assistant attorneys general without direct intervention by the governor, although the right of appeal remains intact.

The Executive Potential

A governor with considerable administrative skill can strongly influence how a state operates, even in the absence of complete statutory power to act as chief executive. In Kentucky, a study concluded that "the problem is to persuade governors to maximize for the general improvement of state administration the power governors often fail to realize they possess."[23] The observation would no doubt apply in other states.

Since the beginning of the century, presidents increasingly have used a powerful tool, the executive order, an instruction that has the force and effect of law. Governors are now showing interest in this power, too. Such orders may derive either from constitutional or statutory sources or the implied authorization when a state constitution defines the governor's responsibility to execute the law. Executive orders are used to respond to crisis situations (energy, civil defense, natural disaster, for example), to reorganize the executive branch, to respond to federal law, or to administer state business. In most states, little legislative power exists with which to counter such action.[24]

Commander-in-Chief

The governor serves as commander-in-chief of the National Guard when it is not called into national service, as it is in times of emergency or war. The guard, which is supported by national government funds, apparently has outlived its traditional function, but it is protected by powerful interests made up of members of the guard and veterans' organizations. Prior to World War II, the guard was available on call of the governor to handle large disturbances such as prison riots, race riots and strikes. On these occasions, the guard sometimes was used ruthlessly and brutally in putting down prison riots; it often served, especially in the 1930s, as a management tool in breaking up industrial strikes; and it sometimes added to, rather than relieved, tensions in race disturbances. Sometimes in cases of civil disturbance the assistance of the Guard was needed and was used with discretion, of course.

Since World War II, the guard often has been an instrument of rescue and relief, in addition to its role as an embodiment of force. Guard units have become community-service organizations. Instead of using them in emergencies, governors now prefer to rely on the state police or highway patrol to maintain order. This is possible as a result of the growth of these forces, from 8,400 in 1938 to over 35,000 in 1971, and a doubling to over 75,000 by 1990. The most effective activity of the National Guard since World War II has been in aid and rescue work in connection with disaster relief, particularly in the wake of tornadoes, hurricanes, and floods. But the guard is best known for its other roles. For example, difficulties arose in Little Rock, Arkansas, over school integration in 1957, federal troops were used during the period of greatest tension and the National Guard was called into federal service.[25] The guard continued to be used for emergency police work, especially in ghetto riots and on college campuses in the 1960s and 1970s, but almost every such use has provoked public controversy. The inadequacy of the guard was well demonstrated in the Detroit ghetto riot of 1967, when the area assigned to experienced U.S. Army troops suffered far fewer human casualties and less property damage than did that assigned to the Michigan National Guard. In May 1970, four students were killed and others injured during a student demonstration on the Kent State University campus when members of the Ohio National Guard fired directly into a crowd.

Controversies surrounding the nonrelief functions of the guard continued into the 1980s. A number of governors challenged President Reagan's order to send the state guard troops to train in Central America without nationalizing them, but in 1990 the Supreme Court upheld the president's power to do so.[26] Despite numerous examples of controversy, inefficiency, and incompetence, the National Guard is likely to survive because of its powerful support from interest groups and state governors and its ability to secure federal revenue.

Chief Legislator

The public has never paid much attention to the pleas of reformers for an integrated administrative structure under the governor. This is so not only because the public is well grounded in the Jacksonian myth holding that any office is more responsible if it is elective, but also because the public thinks of the governor primarily as a policy leader and not as an administrator. The governor has, in fact, become so important as a policy

leader that usually the legislature is left to veto, modify, or perhaps enlarge upon gubernatorial recommendations; but it is not likely to provide policy leadership or innovation. Most of the public does not seem to expect more than that from the legislature.

Governors are in a position to influence the legislature as well as the public and
to serve as leaders of policy as a result of their right to submit comprehensive executive budgets and messages to the legislature; their power to call or not call special
sessions of the legislature, thus somewhat limiting the legislature's ability to act; and
their power to veto bills. Legislative leaders often resist gubernatorial leadership,
regardless of whether the governor is of the same party. Yet, governors can rally
public opinion and attract a great deal of publicity in support of their recommendations. Their superior public relations power will be resented, however, as will their
imaginative, varied programs. Thus, the Republican majority early in this century in
the New York legislature "adopted the policy that anything desired by [Governor] Al
Smith was evil, extravagant, radical, or unscientific, despite the fact that many of the
views of the Tammany Governor had been evolved from studies made by eminent
Republicans."[27]

The approach was spectacularly unsuccessful. By the time Governor Smith left
office, he had accumulated one of the most impressive lists of accomplishments of
any governor in any state. Similarly, the persistent lack of political wisdom of the
legislative leadership in New York did much to enhance Governor Franklin D.
Roosevelt's public image as a man of creativity who developed workable ideas regarding public problems, a man of action. On many occasions Roosevelt's sails could
have been trimmed by imaginative action and effective reactions by legislative leaders.[28]

Governors have great resources. They can call on any of the state agencies for
ideas and data, and even those in enemy or neutral hands cannot afford to refuse information. Governors also can call knowledgeable private parties. For example, a
favorite device is the study commission, often made up of politically inactive persons
or members of the opposite party or faction, in addition to gubernatorial stalwarts.
The legislature sometimes will refuse to appropriate money for such groups, but because of the prestige of a governor's study commission and their interest in the subject matter, such individuals often will work hard without any compensation. The
ideas they develop are immensely valuable to the governors and their staffs in putting
programs together. Yet, although study commissions are expected to provide leadership in achieving policy goals, they often lack many of the powers of the president,
particularly those informal powers presidents have acquired in the postwar era
through the manipulation of the mass media.[29]

Since the mid-1960s, governors have replaced private-sector commissions
with publicly supported boards to plan beyond the immediate budget.

> Today there are state planning and policy development offices in all states but five.
> About half are located in the governors' offices as a part of their personal staff. About 42
> percent are located with the budget office in a planning and budget agency or a depart-
> ment of administration, while in four states the state planning is in a cabinet level depart-
> ment. In all cases today, directors of state planning and policy development and their
> staffs work for the governor who is their only client.[30]

In presenting programs to the legislature, governors may include some spectacular items too costly for the state without imposing additional taxes. They may well pass along to the legislatures the politically thankless task of telling this to the people. They may recommend items found in the party platform, knowing that the less practical ones will be killed in the legislature. The items they *really* want may be presented cloaked in moderation leaving the door open for compromise and allowing the legislators to save face by working out some of the details. But if the legislature is seriously out of step with the times, it may be stampeded by the governor's popular appeal and attention-getting ability.

Politicians may be forceful leaders on behalf of the demands of effective interests. They are not unwilling to make decisions where social conflict exists, as they are sometimes accused of being. Nearly all their policy decisions involve conflicts of interest among the public; some are happy with the proposals, some unhappy. The politicians' task is to assess the balance of interests revolving about issues. If they fail to act, it is because they do not feel confident of having adequately evaluated a situation. At this point they need help from staff, interest groups, appropriate department heads, and citizens who are specialists in a particular subject. Once a strong governor can evaluate the desires of those represented in society, action will follow, even on controversial proposals. One study found three types of issues presented by governors at their state-of-the-state addresses: perennial big-ticket items (education, highways, corrections, health care, law enforcement, and welfare); cyclical issues (''those which grow in concern, peak, and then steadily decline,'' such as government reorganization or tax changes); and transitory issues (often put on the agenda by outside events, e.g., the death penalty).[31] Perennial items constituted three-fourths of the state budgets, but they were not the key issues at election time. Party politics and taxes usually were key to a governor's defeat in recent decades.[32]

In addition to the pressures governors can exert through the use of the budget and messages to the legislature, they can invite key legislators to breakfast or afternoon conferences where they can channel the conversation into serious discussion of the topics and goals set for a session. Other pressure techniques also can be applied, such as using patronage or arranging for ''spontaneous'' public rallies on the capitol steps. Governors cannot expect to get all they ask for (many would be appalled if they did), but they do serve as major policy leaders. And by claiming credit for everything adopted by the legislature that they approve of and by chastising the legislature for not adopting the rest of the program, governors can advance their own careers. The balance of power between legislature and governor was addressed generally in chapter 7. But a 1987 study by the National Governors Association combined a variety of factors addressed both here and in Chapter 12—the governor's tenure potential, appointment powers, budget-making powers, party powers, veto powers, and the legislature's budget-adjusting power—and found that between 1965 and 1985 the governor's power over the executive branch had increased, while the governor's power over the legislature had decreased.[33]

The Veto

The power to veto is a potent weapon in the hands of governors, both as a threat and in actual use.[34] The veto is one of the few gubernatorial powers that are broader in scope than the equivalent power of the president, although the powers of state legislatures to override a veto is similar to that of Congress. The governor can veto entire bills being presented by the legislature, as can the president, but governors in forty-three states, unlike the president, also can veto single sections of appropriation bills, the so-called *item veto*. Unlike the general veto, the item veto allows the part of the bill that the governor accepts to be signed into law. This prevents some of the pork barreling that goes on at the national level—and that probably would be even more pronounced at the state level without an item veto, given the narrow concerns of state legislators. Republican Governor Tommy Tompson's use of Wisconsin's variation of the item veto, known as the partial veto, precipitated a state constitutional amendment in April 1990, known as the "Vanna White amendment" (named after the popular game show hostess). In a number of cases Tompson used the partial veto (upheld by the courts) to take zeros out of appropriation bills and in one case to remove the word "not" from a welfare stipulation. The amendment restricts the governor from removing individual letters (turning them around, as Vanna does), but Wisconsin's governor still retains substantial partial veto powers.[35] In all states that use the item veto, the provisions to override are similar to those for a general veto.

Governors in eleven states make use of a particularly powerful item veto (called the *California item veto*) by which they can reduce (not merely exclude) items in appropriation bills. The governor cannot increase the appropriation, however. Usually item vetoes can be overridden in the same fashion as general vetoes. This is of little use to a liberal governor, but a conservative can use it virtually to dictate the budget without risking veto. (In this context a conservative governor would be one who wants less than the legislature; a liberal, one who wants larger appropriations.)

In most states, the *pocket veto* (no action by the governor) exists as it does at the national level, although the number of days the governor is given before such a veto takes effect varies. The pocket veto automatically kills a bill if the legislature has meanwhile adjourned, but the bill automatically goes into effect if the legislature remains in session. This is a far more important veto at the state level than it is at the national. Legislatures usually meet for a shorter period than does Congress. Furthermore legislators, like students and textbook writers, procrastinate. Despite a three- or four-month session in which to complete a bill (the legislator's version of the term paper), most bills pass during the last week before adjournment. Therefore most bills are subject to the pocket veto, which cannot be overridden because the legislature is not in session to override. Some states avoid this situation by requiring the legislature to consider end-of-session vetoes in a special session held for that purpose only. In other states the legislatures control their own calendars and simply recess rather than adjourning—never creating the legal circumstance permitting the pocket veto.

North Carolina is the only state whose governor has no veto power; and even as late as 1985, the North Caroline legislature again refused to place a referendum before the voters to grant that power.[36] (Not surprisingly, legislators are reluctant to increase the governor's powers against the legislature's.)

The proper use of the gubernatorial veto on reapportionment bills has been questioned in several states. Because reapportionment so directly relates to the legislature and because the constituency of the governor is different from that of most legislators, rural legislators have often argued that apportionment bills should not be subject to veto. Nevertheless, the power of governors to shape reapportionment generally has been upheld, as exemplified by a 1965 Minnesota Supreme Court ruling that upheld the authority of the governor to veto reapportionment legislation. Furthermore, in 1983 the Wisconsin Supreme Court upheld the power of the governor to work with the legislature to reapportion a second time in a decade. The courts had reapportioned Wisconsin when a Republican governor vetoed the Democratic legislature's reapportionment effort in 1981, but the Democrats faced no such veto in 1983 after the election of a Democratic governor. States with at least one house of the legislature of one party and a governor of the other can expect reapportionment vetoes when the governor believes the courts will produce a better compromise than can be achieved with the legislature. Thus, after the 1970 census, California had a Democratic legislature and a Republican governor Ronald Reagan who vetoed the reapportionment bill. The state supreme court then appointed three *special masters* as its representatives, who did the redistricting. In 1980, with both governor and legislature of the same party, redistricting was accomplished with little difficulty. (Reapportionment will be discussed in greater detail in chapter 11.)

The rate of gubernatorial vetoes has remained relatively constant since World War II (about 5 percent), but the rate of legislative overrides has increased, although both vary widely from state to state and depend on tradition, partisan makeup of the state, and the perspective of the individual governor. A survey of thirty-seven legislative assistants to governors and twenty-five former governors showed a variety of reasons for the decision to veto. None of the assistants and only 14 percent of the former governors surveyed believed that governors should veto solely on the grounds of constitutionality or balancing the budget. Few, on the other hand, believed that governors should veto whenever they would have voted against the bill if they had been in the legislature (10 percent of the assistants and 29 percent of the former governors). The survey suggests that vetoes are to be taken very seriously. Fully 74 percent of the assistants and 92 percent of the former governors believed ''that the presumption should be that a bill should be signed unless the governor has a very strong objection to it.''[37]

Governors and legislators know that a veto can be fatal to a measure; and in many states, an override attempt is rarely successful. The governor therefore uses the *threat* of veto far more often, heading off the veto itself. The threat of veto, particularly the item veto, may be the strongest weapon a conservative governor uses in the art of negotiating with an ''unruly'' legislature. It is little wonder that President Reagan called so vehemently for the power of item veto; as governor, he had learned what mighty power the threat of a veto could be.

Chief of Party

Even after the drastic decline in the strength of political parties in the media age, governors are at least the nominal, and frequently the real, head of their party. Governors must spend a good deal of time attending party activities—barbecues, dances, picnics, rallies, and conventions. They try to iron out disputes between rival factions or rival members of the legislature. They dispense patronage in a manner that preserves a reasonable level of satisfaction among the party rank and file while at the same time securing persons sufficiently competent for public office.

In each election at the state and sometimes the local level, governors must campaign for party candidates whether or not they themselves are candidates. As they travel about their state, they must be sure to apprise the local party leaders and candidates of their plans, or those people may sit out the next campaign. When a U.S. senator dies or resigns, the governor must choose someone who will be honored by party workers but who will not become a Frankenstein's monster, that is stronger than the appointing governor. In some instances, governors must choose an interim senator who will *not* run for the full term should the governor want the job in the next election. They are expected to endorse party platforms, so their voices in sending messages to the legislatures are at once that of the governorship *and* of the party. Their role as party leader, in fact, becomes intertwined with virtually everything they do, either explicitly or implicitly, while they carry out other duties.

Governors in Crises

Although items of grave concern and importance to the welfare of citizens are everyday matters in the governor's office, certain situations call for emergency action. Governors and their staffs plan for such circumstances, often in cooperation with the state police and other officials. Conditions that create a state of emergency fall into two primary categories:

1. *Uncontrolled violence (natural or human).* In the event of a flood, tornado or other natural disaster, the governor probably would cancel everything else, go immediately to the scene, possibly call out the state police or National Guard, (and as a symbol of the state) seek to reassure people. It certainly would not hurt any politician to be photographed, tired and disheveled, gazing on the ruins. A race riot or serious labor disturbance could result in bloodshed and property damage as well serious deterioration of intergroup relations if prompt action is not taken. If the governor does not have a plan and does not act decisively in such a situation, a political career also could be ruined. This is especially true in the event of a prison riot or break out.

2. *Political crises.* An unexpected political maneuver by the opposition in the legislature, discovery that a trusted lieutenant is receiving kickbacks on contracts, a charge that a mental hospital patient has been abused, or dozens of other matters dealing with party morale or the governor's own political future, may require the cancellation of other plans and immediate work on the crises situation. If the afternoon papers carry headlines followed by television "details at eleven" of a particular stratagem by an opposition leader, or of some charge of misfeasance or failure to act, or a grand plan to solve the state's financial problems, the governor and staff immediately will have to go into damage-control operations to minimize the mass media advantage gained by the opposition and to regain the initiative as quickly as possible. The general rule is to decide first whether an overt defense is indicated (sometimes the best defense is silence). If it is, veteran politicians consider it advisable to release a partial answer as quickly as possible and then to develop the theme, preferably with new material, which will help distract the public from the opposition's main point and regain the initiative. Although the press secretary becomes a key person, only the governor can make the ultimate decisions. Frequently this must be done in the face of

conflicting advice from staff and party leaders, for veteran politicians by no means always agree on what should be done at such times.

The Big Decisions

In a sense every decision made in the governor's office has important implications, both for political futures and for citizens' welfare. The most innocent-appearing problems may suddenly become headline material; therefore, some decisions are of special importance to the governor *and* to the public. Basic changes in existing public policy, new state programs, major alterations in the tax structure—all are critical. How are such decisions made? The answer probably varies with the personality of governors, the political structure of the state, the alignment of interest groups, among other factors. Governors are likely to seek a wide range of opinions on such subjects. If time permits, a citizens' study group may be appointed to look into a specific matter and offer advice. The press secretary will spend a good deal of time considering the public relations implications of various alternatives and toying with various ways to release the final decision to the press. The budget officer will be asked to bring in detailed reports on the fiscal implications of various possibilities, and official figures may be checked against those from independent sources. The governor's staff will meet to discuss alternatives, and staff members will be encouraged to anticipate every possible argument from opponents and every possible question the governor can expect from the press. In states with strong party organization, the assistant in charge of patronage will evaluate possible alternatives in terms of rank-and-file party reaction. Department heads concerned with the policy, and their staffs, will be brought in for consultation.

The state party leader and other key party figures will be consulted and tipped off prior to the press release as to the decision. They will be told the public and private reasons behind the decision so they can back up the governor's position. Interest group leaders who were instrumental in the governor's nomination and election and who helped finance the last campaign either will be consulted or will volunteer suggestions, which will *not* be taken lightly.

Finally the governor, alone or perhaps with a very small group of advisers, will make the decision. It will be announced in a carefully timed and worded news release. Political supporters will maneuver for a spot, however brief, on the six o'clock news to be seen defending the governor. Lesser lights may be assisted in writing letters to the editor in defense of the decision. Legislative leaders will be briefed so that they may use the appropriate arguments. Reams of statistical evidence in support of the positions will come from the budget office. Party chieftains will publicly praise the "courageous, imaginative leadership" of the governor. Ultimately the results, or what appear to be the results, of the decision will help to determine the political fate of the governor and of the party or faction. Governors cannot afford to be wrong often on the big decisions.

Legal Considerations

Rules in every state constitution prescribe qualifications for the governor.[38] For example, a person must be a citizen of the United States and in most states at least age 30 (age 25 in Arizona and Illinois, age 18 in California and Washington; seven states have no formal age provision). In eleven states a candidate must have been a state citizen (usually defined by voter registration) for a certain period of time (usually at least five years); in the other states the candidate must have been a state resident (usually defined as a taxpayer or driver's license holder who resides in the state most of the year) for a certain number of years (usually five); and in a number of states the candidate must be a qualified voter, usually this simplifies the qualification process, but on occasion it may disqualify an otherwise qualified person, for example, a felon. These legal qualifications generally are far less important than are considerations of "availability"—the right person in the right place at the right time, politically speaking. With rare exceptions, someone barely meeting an age or residency requirement will be considered too young or too much the outsider.

Term of Office

Early state constitutions commonly provided a one-year term for governors, but the trend has been toward lengthening the tenure. Massachusetts was the last state (1920) to give up the one-year provision; and after the most recent change in Arkansas took effect (1986) only New Hampshire, Rhode Island, and Vermont had two-year terms, the others electing for four years. In four states (Kentucky, Mississippi, New Mexico, and Virginia) governors cannot succeed themselves; and in twenty-four others they can serve no more than two terms consecutively. Four-year terms with no restrictions on reelection is characteristic of party-competitive states.

Longer terms stem from late-nineteenth-century reform beliefs that this would reduce the time spent on campaigning, thus freeing more for work on policy leadership and administration. Jacksonians believed that shorter terms would give voters greater control over elected officials, drawing them "closer to the people." In fact, both assumptions are probably wrong: Elected persons spend every available moment campaigning, regardless of election schedules. For offices other than governor, the tendency also has been for longer terms, though with no consistency, especially at the local level.

Compensation and Perquisites

It was once thought—based on the British Tories, virtually all of whom had inherited wealth—that neither governors nor other public officeholders should be paid; or, they should receive only modest pay. The argument was that seeking public office for personal gain should not be encouraged. But the social functions the governor is expected to perform and the gubernatorial life-style are so costly that "hungry" governors may be tempted to accept gifts from favor seekers. That is, unless they are personally wealthy (as many governors have been). It was once argued that the pay for most elective offices should be high enough to attract capable people, but no evidence indicates that high pay raises the caliber of elected officials' performance. (Career civil service is another matter, however.) On the other hand, exceptionally low pay in today's market probably will discourage some people from staying in office, given the lucrative lobbying jobs available to ex-office holders.

Neither citizens nor legislators apparently have regarded high salary as important for recruiting competent persons to run for the office of governor, but compensation has risen steadily in most states, in 1990 ranging from $35,000 in Arkansas and Maine to $130,000 in New York. The additional benefits can be substantial. For example, in every state except Texas, the governor is provided with a state automobile; in thirty-nine states (including Texas) the governor has access to an airplane and governors in twenty-four states have access to a helicopter. Most are given a healthy travel allowance and an official residence that is free from state taxation; a few are furnished summer homes, too. But even *where* the governor lives is a political question, subject to dispute. For example, when California Governor Ronald Reagan decided that the Victorian-era state residence was a "firetrap" and refused to live in it, friends had built for him a gigantic modern home. Reagan's successor, Democrat Jerry Brown, a part-time populist, refused to set foot in the place. Brown's successor, George Deukmejian, though a conservative Republican without a large populist following, declared the place an anathema and settled for a housing allowance.

Controversy over gubernatorial salaries sometimes becomes the topic in the mass media, which occasionally tell voters who is the highest paid person on the state payroll; commonly a surgeon at the state hospital, a top highway engineer, or the state university football coach is paid several times the salary of the governor. Many state employees are better paid than the governor. Furthermore, the governor is paid less than most chief executive officers of corporations that compare in size to the state administration. On the other hand, the governor is paid more than the majority of state officials and certainly more than most state residents. Governors who today often may have to determine comparable worth for state officials have no measuring stick for their own salaries. But as was shown during the controversy over national government pay raises early in the Bush administration, average voters are suspicious of salaries higher than their own. In California, for example, Governor Jerry Brown gained much political mileage from refusing to let his pay rise above $50,000, despite higher pay in other large states. His successor, George Deukmejian, then had to face the political embarrassment of accepting almost double that salary (though this was more in line with the salary of governors of other large states at the time).

Paths to the Governorship

One study showed that between 1870 and 1950, 995 different individuals were elected governors, 45.8 percent of whom were lawyers. A second study showed that over the following thirty-years, 57 percent held law degrees.[39] One need not be a lawyer to win in politics, but it helps, principally because of the lawyer's "legal skills which give him a monopoly of offices related to the administration of law in the court system." Nearly all judges and prosecutors, in addition to principal law enforcement officers, are lawyers, and it is through these offices that most paths of advancement to higher political office, including the governorship, lie.[40] Lawyers have a more practical reason for entering politics: Large law firms usually will grant leave for service in public office (it connects the firm to those in power) and may even allow officeholders to enjoy profit-sharing plans. Others entering politics often will have to sacrifice career advancement. But it should be recognized that the career politician may have served very little time in practicing law prior to entering politics.

The pattern of advancement to the governorship varies. Since World War II, the most common path has been to begin in the state legislature and use legislative leadership as the stepping-stone to the governorship. However, almost an equal number went to the governorship directly from statewide elective office (slightly more than one-fifth), and many began in law enforcement and went to the governorship through the legislature, through statewide office, or directly. Yet, in the most populous states, the tendency is to recruit governors from career paths outside the legislature. About one in ten governors went there directly from Congress, with over half the states having at least one governor from Congress since 1950, and that path has been increasingly used.[41]

Removal and Succession

Other than by death, resignation, or removal from the state, governors may be removed by conviction on impeachment (except in Oregon). This has happened rarely, but it is a convenient political weapon, and almost every governor who attempts to provide legislative leadership will be threatened with its use. Ten governors have left office following impeachment (either through resignation or removal), five in this century—the latest being Evan Meecham of Arizona in 1988. Eight others were impeached but acquitted. The impeachment procedure is usually one of the lower house's instituting procedures on the basis of charges involving mis-, mal-, or nonfeasance in office. Impeachment technically is a positive vote on the indictment. The trial on the impeachment usually takes place in the senate, and penalty on conviction is removal from office. Additional penalties may be imposed.

Eight other governors were removed using other methods (resignation after indictment, recall, or removal by the courts). Only one governor, Lynn Frazier of North Dakota, was recalled from office (1922) by popular vote (a recall petition on J. Howard Pyle of Arizona was certified in 1955, but his term ended prior to the recall election). (An attempt to recall Evan Meecham was under way when he was impeached. The Arizona Supreme Court canceled the recall election and declared that his successor, Secretary of State Rose Mofford, "is not a 'stop-gap governor, but is the new chief executive who should finish Meecham's four-year term.") Recall is authorized in several states but is rarely attempted because the process is complicated and expensive because of the large number of petition signatures required.[42]

If the governor for any reason, leaves office the line of succession is as follows:

- the lieutenant governor (forty-two-states)
- the speaker or president of the senate (five states)
- the secretary of state (three states)

Unlike federal practice, the designated successor acts for the chief executive whenever the latter leaves the legal jurisdiction in most states. This can cause political mischief if the successor is from the opposition party or uses the post differently from the governor. The governor is elected on a ticket with his or her successor in only twenty-two states. The practice of permitting the governor to exercise the powers of office only when physically present within the state's borders is probably an anachronism in today's world of facsimile machines, telephones, and airplanes. On occasion, acting governors, capitalizing on the governor's absence, made appointments or vetoed bills knowing that their actions were antithetical to the governor's policy positions or career interests.

Other Executive Officers

Many states elect executive officers in addition to the governor (often a number on a long ballot). In Jacksonian theory, these persons were to work together as a team, with the party serving to coordinate their otherwise independent status. But with today's loose party arrangements, they are often of differing political parties or factions and thus may work against one another.

The office of lieutenant governor originated in colonial America. It has been supported through the popular preference for elective office and for having the governor be succeeded, if necessary, by someone elected for that purpose. It also reflects the example of the vice presidency at the national level. Lieutenant governors usually are given the power to preside over the state senate and *ex officio* on a variety of boards and commissions.[43] Most spend little time presiding, however; senate members generally prefer to have one of their own in the chair and do not encourage the lieutenant governor's presence.

Other elective offices include the secretary of state, attorney general, treasurer, auditor, and members of various boards and commissions (e.g., highways, public instruction, and higher education)[44] In addition to routine duties, these officeholders considerably influence policy making. Attorneys general can make headlines by investigating irregularities, graft, and corruption. They often decide what will be investigated and hence whose ''ox is to be gored.'' Secretaries of state may expedite or delay special elections as political considerations dictate or investigate possible violations of campaign expenditure laws.

If their staffs are large enough only to perform spot checks, auditors general may select the local governments whose books are to be inspected, and they may try harder to detect irregularities when inspecting opposition camps. Treasurers can decide which bankers are to profit from state bank deposits.

The secretaries of state, glorified county clerks who keep the official records, also keep election records and may have some supervisory powers over elections. Treasurers, although keepers of funds, normally pay out no money except on a warrant signed by the controller, the auditor, or both. They have no discretion in money matters and usually are bonded against theft. They may also administer the floating of state bond issues and influence where and how tax receipts are to be deposited until spent. Attorneys general are chief interpreters of the law and chief law enforcement officers of the state. Legislative acts cannot be wholly self-defining and state's chief attorneys spend a great deal of time preparing opinions concerning the powers of various state agencies and local units of government. Sometimes the resultant interpretations are quite favorable to the political interests of the attorneys general.

Auditors are charged with watching over the administrative branch of government. Sometimes they have only postaudit power; that is, they review expenditures after the fact to see if spending was according to "legislative intent" and without corruption or undue waste. At other times, they (or the controllers) may have the power of preaudit power to approve expenditures before they take place. This also enables them to interpret "legislative intent" and thus determine whether an agency is to be allowed to spend money for a certain purpose or in a certain way—a most influential power. Students of administration often bemoan the fact that the preaudit and postaudit frequently are intermingled in state government, for this confuses the control function of the executive budget with the audit function. In a few states, the auditor is selected by the legislature and performs only postaudit functions. Accounting and expenditure control (preauditing) is usually given to the executive in cities with the strong-mayor or council-manager plans, whereas postauditing is done by an auditor who is selected by the council or popularly elected. The distinction is important, for the preauditor determines whether any unusual expenditure or new or unique interpretations of the law are to be permitted. An unimaginative or reluctant auditor with preaudit powers can effectively block important parts of an executive's program. For this reason, a number of states and localities, particularly in places with recent constitutions or charters have separated the functions.

The offices of other elected executives should be thought of as institutions as is the case for the governorship (although on a smaller scale). For example, attorneys general rarely will make big decisions without their own staff help. And the day-to-day decisions often are made by scores of lawyers working for the justice departments, many of whom stay in office well beyond the terms of those elected, and many of whom take little direction from the attorney general (who commonly steals the big decision headline). As we will examine in the next chapter, the power in state and local government is shifting away from elected officials to the bureaucracy.

The Office of Mayor

The qualifications and success of mayors varies widely. Many are no more than amiable mediocrites, lacking ability and imagination and obligated to a few interest groups that put them in office. Small-town mayors usually have achieved some success in the small-business sector. Long active in local politics and civic affairs, most are well liked by their neighbors. Large cities seem to be producing an increasing number of capable chief executives, reversing the trend from the postwar period through the 1970s that saw the office as a dead-end job whose problems were beyond solution. The most important recent development in regard to mayors may be the effects on race relations of the emergence of black mayors (as we discussed in earlier chapters).

Mayors are dominant figures and chief negotiators among ideological and economic interests in the large cities.[45] They usually lead the coalitions of power that succeed in triggering action programs. Because of the visibility and role expectations that come with their jobs, mayors have a good deal of the informal power of persuasion. But the formal power may be limited by type of government (see chapter 7) and the inferior position the city may play in the intergovernmental system (see chapter 4).

The mayor who wants to be successful in policy making in any form must enter and negotiate throughout the process, particularly with the council:

A mayor who has the personal ability to become policy leader nevertheless must realize that councils control money and land use, the two essential ingredients of urban policy. Therefore, the most important site for evaluating a mayor's administration is in the linkage with the city council. . . . A mayor who does not sit in when the council is making major policy decisions is operating with a severe handicap, with one eye closed and one arm tied behind him.

The necessity for policy to emerge from a widespread process of debate and information exchange makes it essential for the mayor to be involved in the crucial final states of policy decision making in the council.[46]

Some mayors choose never to do more than act as custodian for the council, to see that the laws are properly exercised.[47] But this perception is rarely deemed adequate any longer outside small towns. Most mayors have little in the way of political organization behind them, and their offices are highly dependent for powers, finances, and problem solving on state and national governments, even county and regional decisions. Big city mayors have to depend primarily on public relations, mass media, diplomatic and exhortative skills, and vast networks among political, economic, ethnic, and "do-good" leaders.

Mayors continue to find themselves in much the same position as did Richard Lee in New Haven, who "was not the peak of a pyramid but rather at the center of intersecting circles. He rarely commanded. He negotiated, cajoled, exhorted, beguiled, charmed, pressed, appealed, reasoned, promised, insisted, demanded, even threatened, but he most needed support from other leaders who simply could not be commanded. Because the mayor did not dare to command, he had to bargain."[48] And this was a mayor—at least in his early days in office—of the older style: a product of a party machine.[49]

Much like the governor, the mayor may act as chief of state and in so doing enjoy the political rewards of many ceremonial functions of state. A study of Mayor Tom Bradley of Los Angeles showed that in a nonelection year:

Bradley devoted between 10 and 20 hours per week to pancake breakfasts, picnics, weddings, parades, cocktail receptions and other social engagements. In all Bradley attended 512 such events [in 1987], including 38 black-tie affairs, 29 anniversary celebrations, 26 cocktail receptions, 19 grand openings and 13 birthday parties. He was on hand for the opening of a Pioneer Chicken and a Best Western, the reopening of a Baskin-Robbins and a promotional ceremony unveiling Cherry 7-Up. The Mayor says he makes his extensive rounds for reasons other than picking up a contribution or a vote. He likes stepping out, mingling with people and showing up unexpectedly at an intimate social affair.[50]

In his fifth term, he still enjoyed these political benefits, even as the shine on his long career began to fade.

An impressive list of public servants can be compiled from names of persons who have served as mayors, especially since the early 1900s. The problem of securing able persons as mayors of large cities is complicated, however, by the fact that candidates are likely to have to obligate themselves to interest groups with specific political goals. This is so because someone must furnish the money for the expensive big-city campaign. Although mayors so obligated could represent a substantial portion of the population, be imaginative and aggressive in meeting problems, and be responsive to citizen demands, in practice it appears that often they (or some of their department heads, today called management teams) are not. In addition to pressures from interest group supporters, big-city mayors suffer another obstacle. Their department heads and other administrators involved in their own activities, and mayors may not be well versed on these projects. On occasion they learn about them only often painfully through headlines or the evening news. Mayor Ed Koch of New York long enjoyed a reputation as an opponent of dishonest behavior and was immensely popular. By 1988, however, corruption and criminal behavior within his administration had become so serious that he was hip-deep in political difficulties and was eliminated in a try for still another term the next year. In Los Angeles, Mayor Tom Bradley enjoyed a reputation as the very image of middle-class rectitude when in 1989, early in his fifth term, he encountered accusations of conflict of interest in accepting fees from banks that did business with the city. At least six public agencies—local, state, and national—inquired into his stock dealings and sought to know whether he had helped steer public money toward business associates. He was not accused of criminal intent, but his fine reputation was damaged.

Recent demands for controls over campaign expenditures are not likcly to free big-city mayors from the ties necessary for political advancement. As Ed Koch found in New York in 1982 and Tom Bradley in California in 1982 and 1986, being elected mayor of the largest city in a state may not be a wide enough political base upon which to be elected governor. Since World War II, few mayors have found success in elective politics beyond city hall. Hubert Humphrey, once mayor of Minneapolis, is the only former mayor among postwar presidential nominees, and few mayors have even succeeded to the governorship or U. S. Senate. (Only two presidents have served as mayors: Andrew Johnson in tiny Greeneville, Tennessee, in the 1830s and Grover Cleveland, who first gained fame as reform mayor of Buffalo, New York, in the 1880s.) Big-city mayors encounter not only the constant threat of corruption, but they face problems that are either intractable or cannot be solve without the involvement of higher levels of government. It is rare for a mayor to be able to document a record of real success in personally wrestling major problems to the ground.

To make matters worse, demographics have long worked against mayors. The core cities continue to shrink in size relative to the suburbs. Their great losses in the 1970s were slowed down and some reversed in the 1980s, but the suburbs still grew more than twice as fast. As a result, core cities have lost clout relative to the political parties of their states and of the nation. In addition to other problems, voter participation is declining in core cities, causing a still more disproportionate loss of influence. The largest cities are growing in part from noncitizen immigrants—who are nonvoters. Some large cities in the 1980s actually lost black residents, who increasingly *are* voters, to be replaced with Hispanics, who have a low turnout pattern.

As the 1990s began, mayors with their costly problems were not especially welcome at the White House, (where the intergovernmental relations adviser was from rural South Dakota). Many states, including liberal Massachusetts and New York, were cutting back on state aid to urban areas. National and state politicians, of course, respond to calls from where the votes are; and they are in the suburbs. It is no accident that the lobby of the U.S. Conference of Mayors' Washington headquarters features a large wall photograph of President Franklin D. Roosevelt—who died in 1945.[51] Big-city mayors could last "look good" in testifying in Washington during the administrations of Lyndon B. Johnson (the War on Poverty, from 1964) and Richard M. Nixon (Revenue Sharing, from 1972).

Roles and Powers of the Mayor

The roles and powers exercised by mayors vary widely throughout the United States. Persons called mayor (they may have different titles) in cities with a commission or a council-manager system normally have few formal powers other than those of presiding over the council and performing ceremonial functions. They might rarely use the prestige of the office for political gain. For example, Pete Wilson, former mayor of council-manager San Diego, still used the office as a stepping-stone to the U. S. Senate in 1982 and governorship of California in 1990. Mayors in mayor-council cities may have a great many powers, or they may be merely one of many members of the city administration—as is the case in a very weak-mayor city—except that such mayors nearly always have veto power.

In general, especially in large cities, mayoral powers and roles are similar to gubernatorial powers and roles. So are those of their respective staff. In mayor-council cities of large size, mayors tend to have greater administrative powers than those commonly given to governors. In smaller communities the values, interest, and personalities of the mayors are easily made known. The office is administered more as an individual than as a staff operation, as it would be in states or large cities. Mayoral and gubernatorial legislative powers are similar, as are administrative and ceremonial functions.[52] Mayors are so powerful in some strong-mayor cities that the council does not attempt to make policy independently of the mayor. In such cities, the mayor is *in fact* the chief administrative officer with supervisory and coordinative powers over the various departments, an authority that very few governors have been granted.

Legal Considerations

Mayors must be residents of their cities, but other generalizations cannot be made because of the great variety in size and form of government of cities spread over fifty states, each of which has its own laws. Statutes or charters may have rules concerning age, residency, citizenship, or other considerations. If the office is restricted to members of the council, as it often is under the council-manager plan, the charter may leave selection to the members, or it may prescribe the rules of rotation.

The method of choosing mayors varies greatly according to form of government (see table 9–1). Mayors may be selected by the voters directly, as they are in nearly all mayor-council cities, or they may be chosen by the council. In many council-manager and commission cities there is no mayor. In a few cities, the person who gets the largest number of votes in the election for council seats becomes mayor, and in some council-manager and commission cities this person may be referred to as mayor, although no such designation is provided for in the laws or charter.

TABLE 9-1   Method of Mayoral Selection

	Direct Election	Council Selection	Highest Vote Getter	Council Rotation	Other
Mayor-council	98.0%	1.9%	0.0%	0.1%	0.1%
Council-manager	61.8%	35.5%	0.6%	2.0%	0.1%
Commission	69.2%	29.1%	1.7%	0.0%	0.0%

Source: Charles R. Adrian, "Forms of City Government in American History," *Municipal Year Book, 1988,* (Washington, D.C.: International City Management Association, 1988) p. 10.

Mayoral salaries vary according to both the size of the city and the structure of its government. In general, salaries are highest in mayor-council cities.[53] The pay usually is modest, and one of the subordinate officers with professional skills (e.g., the health officer, city engineer, and especially the city manager if there is one) are likely to be better paid than the mayor. Although the trend is toward a four-year term, mayor tenure varies from one to six years and is likely to be shorter in weak-mayor-council cities. Removals and succession follow much the same pattern as for governors.

The City Manager

A basic part of the theory of council-manager government is that the entire city (or other unit) administration should be professionalized. Managers are supposed to be trained to use the tools of administration and, especially in smaller cities, to possess a technical skill, such as engineering, as well. Managers must be diplomats, for their jobs depend on an ability to get along with the councils and department heads. They must be politicians of a special sort, too, for they are called on to give advice on matters of public policy but to avoid involvement in controversial campaign issues.

Managers play important roles in policy innovation and leadership, in public relations, and, in a role secondary to that of mayors, in ceremonial functions.[54] They do many of the things an elected officeholder would do and act very much as politicians act in many of their roles. Managers, however, think of themselves (and are probably perceived by the public) as being professional administrators possessing special qualifications. Undoubtedly they enjoy widespread respect and higher prestige than would be accorded an elected official in a similar role.[55]

Selection and Tenure

Managers, like school superintendents, often are chosen from persons living and working outside the local unit that is doing the hiring. This usually is permitted by charter or state law because the governing body is looking not for a deserving local politician but for a professionally competent administrator. Legislators may glean candidates from the state league of cities, the International City Management Association (the managers' professional organization), the retiring manager, or universities where recent municipal administrators have studied. Sometimes a department head of the hiring city (or another one) is chosen. Most managers today are college graduates and often have advanced degrees in public administration, engineering, or some other appropriate field.

Normally selected by the governing body by majority vote, the manager is dismissable by that body at any time by the same method. Nevertheless, a few managers have been given contracts that require the city to pay them off in the event of removal. For the plan to work successfully, it is essential that the governing body be allowed to remove the manager at any time and for any reason deemed by a majority to be sufficient. Otherwise, the city's administration can become autonomous and irresponsible. Generally, the manager is paid a higher salary than an elective chief executive would receive for a similar position.[56]

In a statewide study of the office of city manager in Florida, the following findings were reported.[57]

- Wherever mayors were directly elected, they tended to develop a separate power base from that of the rest of the council. This tended to bring them into conflict with the city managers, and the tenure of managers in such cities was shortened.
- No relationship existed between the rate of population growth in a city and the tenure of the manager. However, if a city tended through growth to attract people of a different class or income level, this might have an effect on the tenure of the manager. In other words, a change in dominant life-style in the locality might produce a demand for a change in the manager.
- Local residents and amateur managers tended to have longer average tenure than did professional managers. Local amateurs may have had little formal education, but they frequently have acquired some "factional or clique ties that impart political strength." These kinds of persons are in a much stronger position as a rule to contend with council opponents than are professional managers brought in from the outside.[58]
- Manager tenure is longer in cities with little conflict within the local power complex and with a low level of interest conflict. In other words, manager tenure is longest in cities with a high level of political consensus.
- Manager usually play a major part in policy development and in the making of principal decisions in their cities. "Therefore, they were right in the heart of politics, in the broadest sense of that term, to the extent that certain interests might well be alienated as a result of actions taken by the council on manager recommendations. Such alienated persons might and sometimes did seek political retaliation."[59]

Duties

Whereas charters vary widely, the manager is the chief administrative officer of the city and has all or most of the following responsibilities:

1. Overseeing enforcement of all laws and ordinances
2. Controlling all departments, with power to appoint, supervise, and remove department heads and bureau chiefs

3. Making recommendations to the council as appropriate
4. Keeping the council advised of the financial condition of the city and future needs and trends
5. Preparing and submitting to the council the annual budget
6. Preparing and submitting to the council reports and memoranda as requested
7. Keeping the council, and indirectly the public, informed concerning the operations of all aspects of government
8. Performing such other duties as the governing body may legally assign

The manager thus has full responsibility to the governing body for the conduct of the administration of the city, county, or other unit of government.

In most cases, the manager presents significant matters to the governing body for consideration. Because such items are not initiated by legislators, these officials usually have no vested interest and are free to consider them on the merits of the question. New business coming before the governing body usually is first referred to the manager for a report at a future meeting. The manager, in making a report, is in a position to consider the effect of possible forms of action on all departments. No legislator making the report could do this so well. Furthermore, by leaving the report to the manager, the legislators remain free to criticize and judge it.

Managers, from the beginnings of the plan, have come under occasional attack by trade unions, which have feared plan bias toward business interests, emphasis of middle-class and small-town values, and minimization of political conflict and compromise. Since about 1970, the plan has also been under some attack by forces that perceive the manager plan to be unrepresentative. These critics have been successful in a few instances in changing the local charter to mayor-council (e.g., Albuquerque in 1974), or more often in reducing the powers of the manager by strengthening the mayor or the council. This has come by changing the council from at-large to district representation or by increasing the salaries of the elected officials or making their jobs full-time. In those cities, perceptions had developed that important social policy issues could best be dealt with by elected, representative leaders. This has led to redefinition of the manager's role in these cities, "with mayors and council members expecting them to be less the policy leader and much more the specialist in intergovernmental relations (especially as to the techniques of getting money from other governmental units) and the efficiency expert who can find ways of keeping taxes and size of the locally supported budget as low as possible."[60]

Managership is today an important profession in America. The attitudes of those who practice it have a profound effect on the kind of government that local communities experience.

Other Local Offices

For counties, townships, and cities, a variety of elective officials (the treasurer, clerk, assessor, auditor, attorney, controller, police chief, or public-works director) perform many functions that parallel those of state executive officers. Cities have shown a pronounced decline in the number of administrators who hold office by election. At the same time, a trend toward the development of a chief executive office in the nonmunicipal units of local government has been strong (as discussed in chapter 7). For these units of government the structure often is partially spelled out in the state constitution, making changes difficult, and it remains common for department heads and officers (as distinguished from employees) to be elected in local units of government outside cities.

Minor Officials as Policy Makers

Elected administrative officers perform many routine duties, such as recording titles to property, keeping the records of board meetings, paying out money as prescribed by law, and auditing expenditures. But they also have considerable policy-making influence. A county, township, or village clerk may become a veritable manager. The auditor, who knows how the money has been spent in the past, sometimes exercises considerable influence over county policies. The village attorney, perhaps by virtue of a monopoly on legal skills, may steer the policy-making activities of the council. The sheriff, who is elected and thus neither supervised by nor accountable to the county board or state officials in most cases may decide singlehandedly (within the constraints of state law) what the law enforcement policies in the county will be. The county prosecutor, in the same position, may be able to determine which cases are to be prosecuted, which are to be dropped after investigation, and which are to be ignored. The assessor may choose to reward friends and punish enemies, allow a large and profitable business firm to enjoy a low assessment, levy an assessment at more than market value, or underassess elderly persons who can barely pay the property tax.

Concluding Note

A state or local executive office is a number of things. It usually provides an opportunity for election, and the officer who serves may think of the role as one of representation. A chief executive is also a leader who shapes policy priorities. Soon after the Revolutionary War the distrust leveled against executive power began to wane and the people came to rely more and more on executive rather than legislative decision making to solve complex problems, particularly in times of perceived crisis. This chapter has concentrated on elected chief executives and their offices in the policy-making process. It should be remembered, however, that day-to-day state or local government usually is in the hands of bureaucrats who are far removed from the specific task of policy making and beyond the watchful eye of elected or even appointed chief executives. Bureaucracy is the subject of the next chapter.

Notes

1. Richard E. Neustadt, *Presidential Power* (New York: John Wiley & Sons, rev. ed., 1980).

2. Edward C. Banfield, *Political Influence* (New York: The Free Press, 1961), 325; see also his earlier work with Martin Meyerson, *Politics, Planning, and the Public Interest* (New York: The Free Press, 1955).

3. See, generally, chapter 2; Charles R. Adrian, *A History of American City Government: The Emergence of the Metropolis, 1920–1945* (Lanham, MD: University Press of America, 1987), chapter 3; Larry Sabato, *Goodbye to Good-time Charlie: The American Governorship Transformed,* 2d ed. (Washington, DC: CQ Press, 1983); Leslie Lipson, *The American Governor; From Figurehead to Leader* (Chicago: University of Chicago Press, 1939); and Richard S. Childs, *Civil Victories* (New York: Harper & Row, 1952).

4. Thad L. Beyle, "Governors," in Virginia Gray, Herbert Jacob, and Kenneth N. Vines, eds., *Politics in the American States*, 4th ed. (New York: Little, Brown, 1983), 180–222.

5. These categories follow those in Clinton Rossiter, *The American Presidency* [first published in 1956] (New York: Harcourt, Brace & World, 1987).

6. See Coleman B. Ransone, Jr., *The American Governorship* (Westport, CT: Greenwood Press, 1982), 109.

7. Sabato, *Good-time Charlie*, 85; the pre-1979 figures are from Donald P. Sprengel, *Gubernatorial Staffs: Functional and Political Profiles* (Iowa City: Institute of Public Affairs, University of Iowa, 1969), 308–30.

8. Computed by the authors from data on p. 88 of the *1988–1989 Book of the States* (Lexington, KY: Council of State Governments, 1988).

9. David J. Allen, *New Governor in Indiana* (Bloomington: Institute of Public Administration, Indiana University, 1965), 27.

10. Conrad Joyner, "The Governor's Staff: Its Role in Image Projection," a paper read at the 1961 meetings of the American Political Science Association, St. Louis.

11. Frank Freidel, *Franklin D. Roosevelt: The Triumph* (Boston: Little, Brown, 1956).

12. Bernard Bellush, *Franklin D. Roosevelt as Governor of New York* (New York: Columbia University Press, 1955), 33.

13. *Governing the American States: A Handbook for New Governors* (Washington, D.C.: Center for Policy Research, National Governors Association, 1978), 50 (as quoted in Ransone, *American Governorship,* 118).

14. Peter Tropp, "Governors' and Mayors' Offices: The Role of the States," *National Civic Review* 63 (May 1974):242ff.

15. For a typical day in the life of Governor Franklin D. Roosevelt of New York, see Bellush, *Roosevelt as Governor,* 34–35. Any good biography of a governor will help the reader gain an understanding of gubernatorial roles. For the parallel roles of mayors, see John P. Kotter and P. R. Lawrence, *Mayors in Action* (New York: Wiley-Interscience, 1974).

16. Ransone, *American Governorship,* 99.

17. Rossiter, *American Presidency,* 23.

18. Freidel, *Roosevelt: The Triumph,* 15.

19. Computed by the authors from the table presented by Sabato, *Good-time Charlie,* 38–39 for the years 1951–1981.

20. See Sabato, *Good-time Charlie,* 67, for the earlier data; for 1990, see "Court Limits Political Patronage," *Star Tribune,* June 22, 1990, 1.

21. Data taken from *1990–1991 Book of the States,* 67–68; *1988–1989 Book of the States,* 37; *1986–1987 Book of the States,* 39, 220–21; and Beyle, "Governors," 198–99 and Appendix 6.3.

22. Sabato, *Good-time Charlie,* 50.

23. Gladys M. Kammerer, "The Governor as Chief Administrator in Kentucky," *Journal of Politics* 16 (May 1954):236–56. See also Ransone, *American Governorship.*

24. The information in this paragraph was taken from E. Lee Bernick, "Discovering the Governor's Power: The Executive Order," *State Government* 57 (1984):97–101.

25. See *Cooper v. Aaron,* 358 U.S. 1 (1958).

26. *Star Tribune,* June 12, 1990, 1A.

27. Bellush, *Roosevelt as Governor,* 29.

28. See Freidel, *Roosevelt: The Triumph;* Bellush, *Roosevelt as Governor.* On Smith's accomplishments while in office, see Freidel, *Roosevelt: The Triumph,* 11.

29. J. Stephen Tyrett, "The Vulnerability of American Governors, 1900–1969," *Midwest Journal of Political Science* 15 (Feb. 1971):108–32.

30. Harold F. Wise and Bertram Wakely, "The Practice of State Planning and Policy Development," *State Government* 57 (1984), 85.

31. Beyle, "Governors," 203–204.

32. Sabato, *Good-time Charlie,* 109.

33. Thad L. Beyle, "The Institutionalized Powers of the Governorship, 1965–1985," *Comparative State Politics Newsletter* 9 (Feb. 1988):26–27; and Thad Beyle, "Governors 1986–1987," *1988–1989 Book of the States,* 30.

34. For specific veto powers in each state, consult the most recent edition of the *Book of the States.*

35. The Wisconsin partial veto is discussed by Edward J. Miller in Wilder S. Crane, A. Clarke Hagensick et al., eds., *Wisconsin Government and Politics,* 4th ed. (Milwaukee: Department of Government Affairs, University of Wisconsin-Milwaukee, 1987), 147. Its limits are discussed in the same work by Michael R. Fine, "Constitutions," *Wisconsin Government and Politics,* 5th ed. forthcoming.

36. Thad Beyle, "The Governors," the *1986–1988 Book of the States,* 27.

37. Thad L. Beyle, "The Governor as Chief Legislator," in Thad L. Beyle and Lynn R. Munchmore, *Being Governor: The View from the Office* (Durham, NC: Duke University Press, 1983), 131–43.

38. Unless otherwise noted, the data in this section were taken from the *1988-1989 Book of the States,* and current data can be found in the most recent edition of this work.

39. Sabato, *Good-time Charlie;* Joseph A. Schlesinger, "Lawyers and American Politics," *Midwest Journal of Politics* 1 (May 1957): 26–39.

40. Joseph A. Schlesinger, *Ambition and Politics: Political Careers in the United States* (Chicago: Rand McNally, 1966).

41. Sabato, *Good-time Charlie,* chapter 2; and Joseph A. Schlesinger, "The Politics of the Executive," in Herbert Jacobs and Kenneth Vines, eds., *Politics in the American States: A Comparative Análysis,* 2d ed. (Boston: Little, Brown, 1971).

42. This section relies on the review section of the history of gubernatorial removals, "Gubernatorial Investigations," in Beyle, *1988–1989 Book of the States,* 26–28. The quotation is on 28.

43. *The Lieutenant Governor: The Office and Its Powers* (Lexington, KY: The National Conference of Lieutenant Governors, The Council of State Governments, 1976); Thomas R. Morris, *Virginia's Lieutenant Governors* (Charlottesville: Institute of Government, University of Virginia, 1970); and Byron R. Abernethy, *Some Persisting Questions Concerning the Constitutional State Executive* (Lawrence: Governmental Research Center, University of Kansas, 1960), 18.

44. See the latest volume of the *Book of the States* for details.

45. John C. Bollens and Henry J. Schmandt, *The Metropolis,* 4th ed. (New York:

Harper & Row, 1985), 101; and Robert H. Salisbury, "Urban Politics: The New Convergence of Power," *Journal of Politics* 26 (Nov. 1964):775–97.

46. Alan Reed, "Chief Executives and Administrative Officers" in Jack Rabin and Don Dodd, eds., *State and Local Government Administration* (New York: Marcel Dekker, 1985), 49.

47. John P. Kotter and Paul R. Lawrence, *Mayors in Action* (New York: John Wiley & Sons, 1974).

48. Robert A. Dahl, *Who Governs?* (New Haven, CT: Yale University Press, 1966), 204.

49. See Norman I. Fainstein and Susan S. Fainstein, "New Haven: The Limits of the Local State," in Fainstein, et al., eds, *Restructuring the City* (New York: Longman, rev. ed., 1986), 27–79.

50. For a sense of the life-style and problems of a big-city mayor, see the series of articles on Mayor Bradley in the *Los Angeles Times,* week of June 12, 1988. The quotation is from the June 13 article, p.1.

51. On this paragraph, Dick Kirschten, "More Problems, Less Clout," *National Journal,* August 12, 1989, 2026–30.

52. For details, Charles R. Adrian and Charles Press, *Governing Urban America,* 5th ed. (New York: McGraw-Hill, 1977), chapter 8.

53. For details, see the most recent edition of the *Municipal Year Book* (Washington, D.C.: International City Management Association).

54. Ronald O. Loveridge, *The City Manager in Legislative Politics* (Indianapolis: Bobbs-Merrill, 1971); Clarence E. Ridley, *The Role of the Manager in Policy Formation* (Chicago: International City Management Association, 1958); and James H. Svara, *Official Leadership in the City* (New York: Oxford University Press, 1990).

55. On the relationship between managers and other officers, see James H. Svara, "The Complimentary Roles of Officials in Council Manager Government," the *Municipal Year Book, 1988,* 23–34. For the manager generally, see chapter 7; Harold A. Stone, Don K. Price, and Katharine H. Stone, *City Manager Government in the United States* (Chicago: Public Administration Service, 1940); and the periodical, *Public Management* (Washington, DC: International City Management Association).

56. Salary ranges are given in the most recent issue of the *Municipal Year Book.*

57. Gladys M. Kammerer et al., *City Managers in Politics* (Gainesville: University of Florida Press, 1962), chapter 5. These conclusions have not been successfully challenged.

58. Ibid., 81.

59. Ibid., 83.

60. This paragraph relies on Charles R. Adrian and James F. Sullivan, "The Urban Appointed Chief Executive, Past and Emergent: From Technician and Voice of Consensus to Expert Resource Person and Bargaining Agent," *The Urban Interest* 1 (Spring 1979):3–9. Also see chapter 7.

"*Under new business: Peterson, at Hammond Point Beach, reports that a person in the water is flailing about and calling for help. Peterson wants to know what action, if any, he should take.*"

10

Administration and the Bureaucracy

W hen a state legislature adopts a law or a code (a body of interrelated laws) designed to launch a governmental program—for example to provide for the physical safety of all workers in the state at their place of employment—an elaborate *administrative* structure to carry out the code must also be created. An organized group carries out these rules or regulations (technically known as administrative ordinances). The regulations cannot apply themselves; they must be *administered* by human beings, a *bureaucracy,* acting through a system of *organization* and management. This chapter will deal with how governments are organized to carry out their own rules and regulations. (At the local level, the pattern is similar except that the bureaucracy will be smaller and perhaps less skillfully trained unless the local unit is very populous, *and* local legislative bodies cannot enact laws, only ordinances. However, such enactments have the force and effect of law unless set aside by the courts or legislature.)

A modern bureaucracy carries on activities that a politically effective portion of the public expects of government or at least accepts from its legislative branch. The bureaucracy carries out the administration of governmental activities through its method of organization (the structure of the administrative system's authoritative and routine personal interrelations) and of management (which is designed to achieve rational cooperation).[1]

> *Bureaucracy:* **An organization whose personnel have specialized work assignments. Such assignments involve formal rules, essentially impersonal relationships among persons within the agency and with those in external clientele groups, and a formal hierarchical structure (one arranged in order of rank).**

> *Clientele Group:* **An interest group that works with a government agency that serves it and that may be able to help or harm it through use of certain powers, such as regulation or subsidy.**

Because of its complex nature modern society needs organization and management.—in both its private and public components—high-tech equipment and methods, complex public and private programs, and the general demand for highly trained
people pursuing specialized careers all contribute to that need. In addressing Congress in 1829, President Andrew Jackson could suggest that nearly any person "of
good will" could perform nearly any governmental task. Such a statement would be
unthinkable today. From Jackson's spoils system of personnel administration, in
which friends, especially those active in one's political party, were appointed to fill
vacancies, we have moved on to a merit system based on tests designed to determine
the ability of individuals to perform the thousands of specialized tasks now needed by
governments on each level of the federal system. Bureaucracies require trained competent people.

State governments, which remained oriented toward rural America for longer
than did the national government, were more reluctant to surrender the spoils system.
During the depression, however, the states began moving toward the merit system
and broadening their scope of services. Cities, pushed forward by requirements attached to federal grants and other programs during the 1930s, had already moved
toward a merit system. School districts, starting in the 1890s, had begun to professionalize sooner than other local governments (though many of them did not grow to
fit the requirements of the high school movement until the 1920s through the 1950s,
even later in some cases). Other local units—counties and townships, for example—
were perhaps the slowest of all, most having less need for technical skills than other
local units. But they, too, followed along after World War II. The reasons for these
changes were the expanded demands for governmental services, especially during
and after the Great Depression, and the new and more complex technologies. The
next section will discuss some of these developments.[2]

Developments in Administration

To understand the magnitude and influence of modern public management, it is necessary to compare the functions of state and local government today with those of
about two and a half generations ago (a generation is about twenty-five years). In
1913, except for higher education, states spent little money for schools. And relatively few persons went to college in those days. Local government provided much of
the education of the day through the one-room school, offering minimal programs
taught by poorly trained, largely inexperienced, and low-paid teachers. Roads, another major expenditure program today, were cared for largely by the local unit.
They were often unsurfaced and required little care in that preautomobile age. Most
states had little to do with highways before the beginnings of the good-roads movement and the adoption of the first Federal-Aid Highway Act in 1916. The mentally ill
received no rehabilitative treatment in those days; they were given custodial care in
ramshackle asylums run by untrained persons who received patronage appointments
from the city, county, or state. Some patients were housed in the local jail. Except for
the important work of the big-city machines, welfare was a private and, to some extent, a local government function provided reluctantly and barely at subsistence
level; the states kept out of the field except for some institutional care. Even the well-

known welfare of the big-city machines was formally provided through party organization rather than city government. In general, state government functions were minimal, centering on regulation of utilities and other businesses, control over state colleges and universities, enactment of laws governing business transactions and criminal statutes, and supervision over local government powers and activities. State government was distant and had few direct contacts with the ordinary citizen. Local government was more active and spent more—about 6.6 times as much—than state government but was a thin shadow of its present-day self as a supplier of services to the citizen. Even though the growth in state government activities has been more spectacular, both state and local governments have become vitally important social institutions affecting the daily lives of each citizen.

The Historical Trend

Some of the developments in administrative organization have been noted in chapter 2 of this book. The legislatures at first dominated government at both the state and local levels. As legislative bodies and city councils declined in prestige and importance during the nineteenth century, they were replaced both by the direct democracy of the initiative and referendum and by a large number of elective administrative officials. Both trends contributed to the development of the long ballot.

As governmental functions increased, the number of governmental agencies also increased. Each new function tended to be established as a separate agency, usually in order to protect it from the competing fiscal demands of the older, better-established functions. The interest groups that secured the adoption of new programs and policies generally preferred this arrangement. As a result, states typically have had dozens of separate agencies, and only in recent decades has there been a substantial decline in their number. The more populous cities had once been similarly departmentalized, though reorganizations resulting from the adoption of the strong-mayor, council-manager, or commission forms generally had decreased the number of separate municipal agencies. After a while, the rising number of agencies resulted in a problem of communication. It became difficult for the governor, the legislator, or the concerned citizen to determine what was being done in the agencies or who was responsible for specific activities.

One possible result of having a large number of agencies in state government is that the governor may be pressured into devoting time that is disproportionate to an agency's apparent social importance. This could happen because of low agency morale, a feud between two clientele groups, or simply the forceful and aggressive personality of the department head.

Administrative Developments

The municipal-reorganization began primarily in the 1890s. It was concerned with eradicating corruption and stopping administrative sprawl. Administrative reorganization of counties and other nonschool local units followed along at a much slower pace. At the state level, reform concentrated at first on the reshuffling of agencies so as to group them into a smaller number and to make them formally accountable to the

governor. This movement gained headway after about 1910. Although few comprehensive reorganizations have taken place since, there has been a gradual evolution in
state administration, highlighted by expanding staff services, greater professionalization of personnel, more effective administrative planning, the development of the
executive budget, and firmer executive leadership within departments and over departments.

The first state commission on administrative reorganization was appointed in
Wisconsin in 1911. It was followed by similar groups in Massachusetts and New Jersey the next year. The action in Wisconsin, a part of the progressive movement in that
state, took place in the the same year that President William Howard Taft appointed
the Commission on Economy and Efficiency for the national government. The movement gained great momentum with the general reorganization in Illinois in 1917 under Governor Frank Lowden. Reformers during the 1920s spent considerable time in
talking about and urging the administrative integration of state governments. Even
though a majority of the states took some kind of action, few came close to adopting
the set of recommendations reformers desired.

Following World War II, beginning with the first Hoover Commission at the
national level and spreading to the states, there was a revival of structural reorganization efforts. In all, thirty-five states eventually established ''Little Hoover'' commissions in the years following 1949. Some were appointed by the governor and some by
the legislature; some consisted partly of state officials and legislators and partly of
private citizens.[3] Although some changes resulted from the reports of these groups,
there was relatively little support for drastic overhauls of state structures. Administrative reorganization is, after all, a political question, and changes in it are likely to
take place in the same general fashion as do changes in substantive public policy.
That is, adjustments are made on the basis of small increments of change. The efficiency and economy movement did, however, establish a kind of liturgy for reform;
and this received or benefited from a certain sense of legitimacy accorded to it by
many educated, middle-class citizens interested in politics and government generally.

Following the adoption of the one-person, one-vote rule in the early 1960s and
the consequent redistricting of state legislatures, the movement for administrative
reorganization resumed. The change in the manner of selecting legislators both
shifted power toward the suburbs, where reform sentiment tended to concentrate,
and caused a break in the logjam in rural-oriented legislatures, which for a long time
had inhibited new constitution writing. Many of the new or altered constitutions of
the period either provided for administrative reform or cleared the way for it. Some
twenty states made major changes in administrative structures over the next two decades in a trend that still continues.[4]

As the burden increased state and local government, as urban and suburban
political power increased at the state level, as administration came increasingly under
the merit system, demands also increased for administrative reform. Department
heads favored hierarchical arrangements that clearly put them in charge, and they
wanted trained, well-qualified persons (''professionals'') throughout the staff. Members of reform organizations demanded action, whereas editors, looking at huge
budgets and many remaining patronage positions in the agencies (and perhaps eager

to show that they had ideas on how to improve state governments, now staggering under rapidly growing loads), urged reform. Yet, old opponents remained, often with viewpoints as strong as ever. The state medical association, the state bar association, and the state cosmetology association, among many such professional organizations, most certainly did not want their agencies reformed in any way but one they approved of. Lobbyists and legislators, perhaps unable to see what power shifts would result from change, might not be eager for reform. Employees of existing agencies, also unsure of the effects of change, might join the opponents.

Organizational reforms traditionally have had to bear the burden of proof if change is wanted. And for good reason. Proposed reforms always threaten power relationships, career patterns, and even one's job. Do they offer promise, too? Certainly reformers have genuinely believed so. In politics, it is often true that persons of every ideological perspective will substitute strong emotional feelings for evidence concerning cause and effect. After a century or more of reform it is still not clear what administrative changes result from it. This is in large part because any modification in political structure or process always produces many other changes, intended and unintended. In the most recent round of reorganization, from the 1950s, reformers relied less on what once was thought to be self-evident arguments and more on strategy. In particular, two approaches became popular. (Reform ideas and techniques become political myths, and during a reform period a large communications network may exist that serves to pass them along and integrate them.) One approach was to create a constitutional rule to require that all state agencies be collapsed into a specific number, for example fourteen departments as in Missouri, by a specified date. The legislature could decide how the consolidation was to be accomplished, subject to a governor's veto.[5] The other idea, used in the Georgia and Michigan constitutions, allowed the governor to reorganize the administration. If, within a specific period of time, one or both houses of the legislature or a majority of the constitutionally established elected officers—whatever was provided for in the constitution—did not disapprove, the proposal would go into effect.[6] The incentive to act was now much greater than it had been under previous rules for reorganization. In the first, the legislature could well be inspired to see a duty to act. The governor, with a powerful veto, could also have a considerable say. In the second approach, even a politically staunch governor would be likely to see reasons for modifying administrative arrangements that the governor's party had long defended.

Organization

State or local government agencies may be organized in a number of ways. Some are headed by an elective officer. Some have a single administrator appointed by and responsible to the chief executive. In other cases, the administrator may be chosen by the chief executive but may be removable only by a complicated process involving perhaps the civil service commission or the courts. In a fourth category are those agencies headed by boards or commissions (the two terms mean the same). Board members usually are appointed for long, staggered terms, and the chief executive may find members to be irremovable for practical purposes. When a board controls, an agency may be administered in a variety of ways. The chair of the board may also serve as the chief administrator of the agency; the board may choose an executive secretary or a director, with its own powers reserved in law or practice to broad policy making; the commission may be advisory only, with the chief executive appointing the administrative head; but the most common arrangement has been for the board to divide its work among its members, each exercising considerable autonomy. Each of these structures is likely to produce a different pattern of administration.

Organization and Ideology

Allowing always for some time lag, it seems that state administrative structures tend to reflect contemporary ideological concerns in society. In the period between 1915 and 1930, for example, road building was considered to be important by citizens who increasingly could afford automobiles. Highway agencies were established on a semiautonomous basis, and the highway departments were generally treated preferentially by legislators and governors. Today, because of their high levels of expenditures, highway departments are still important, but they have faded somewhat into the background. The emphasis is now likely to be on a separate department to deal with environmental issues.

Many governmental functions could be established in any one of a large number of departments. A current social problem, for example, is drug use. If this problem were viewed principally as a matter of public health, it could be administered in a department of health; if it were seen primarily as one of educating people about the characteristics and dangers of drugs, it could be administered in a department of education; if it were viewed principally as a problem that occurs in poverty, it might be addressed by a department of welfare; if it were thought of primarily as a crime problem, it could be addressed by state and local police departments; or if it were seen as being principally a disease related to certain emotional difficulties, it might be handled by a department of mental health.

The regular use of various illegal drugs ("chemical substance abuse" is the preferred euphemism) has become not just a problem for a few people in a few social categories, but has developed into an integral part of American culture, or at least of significant subcultures. One should not be misled by a mid-1989 Gallup poll that showed that the sample considered drug abuse to be the nation's most serious problem (27 percent selected it) and that "tougher" antidrug laws were needed. The public will not pay the price required for effective prevention of the importation of drugs (for example, the costs *in money* are astounding to those in the public who are more concerned with balancing the budget, but costs are similarly astounding in *foregoing civil liberties* to civil libertarians.) However, the public applauds gigantic police "drug busts," even though they have no lasting effect on the business. Similarly, the public is not willing to bear the cost of reducing violence between rival drug-dealing gangs (some in the public refuse higher taxes; others refuse to forego the considerable restrictions placed on police activity), even though they treat the violence as both media entertainment (witness the popularity of shows on television catering to the fascination with "news" about such violent activity) and with fear for personal safety (witness the number of people who modify their behavior in response to such publicity despite little scientific evidence that such altered behavior reduces individual risk).

Politics is always about values; politics cannot be divorced from moral questions. But on issues such as drugs there is greater public attention to the value-laden nature of politics. The FBI sting of Washington, D.C., Mayor Marion Barry reinforced the public perception of the matter as a moral *and* political question and demonstrated how moral questions are compounded in a political system (particularly as complicated as a federal one). Was the mayor entrapped? Should the mayor's obvious drug use be treated as a crime? Should a mayor be held to a different standard of justice? Are civil rights in jeopardy if people are required to deny criminal behavior under oath? (What mayor could possibly "take the Fifth"?)

Although almost every agency of government is affected by the illegal drug industry, it is seen as a problem that should be handled by the police (or a special police, such as the Federal Drug Enforcement Administration). This is not only an unfair and impossible task to be foisted upon the police, it also indicates a rather resigned acceptance of the situation. But it hints as well at at least an oblique recognition of the immense difficulties involved in attempting to change anything that has become a part of the culture itself. (By the early 1990s casual use of cocaine by the middle class appeared to be declining with the spread of knowledge concerning the damaging effects of addiction. Among poor, hard-core users, however, efforts to change attitudes appear to be far less successful.) The preferred organizational structure becomes one of a highly truncated approach, one of having the police control social excesses at the local level and far-reaching debate at the national level. Therefore our federal system, which had no capacity to coordinate actions (even if there were some consensus on what actions were warranted), produces a "national drug policy" without an organizational system to enforce one. It is reminiscent of the organizational approach during the national government's last experiment with law enforcement—Prohibition.

The Choice of Organization: A Problem

Beginning in the 1950s, many state officials became interested in the establishment of programs for the aged. These cut across traditional department lines, for they dealt with housing, welfare, health, and employment, among other areas. How should the program be established in order to minimize conflict with existing programs and organizational patterns? What kind of organization would best fit the needs of the aged and be most acceptable to their interest groups?

It is difficult to determine the most effective agency structure or the best allocation of functions within agencies. The pattern of organization, in fact, tends somewhat to shape the emphasis given a particular activity. When functions are lumped together, they may lose some of their public visibility. If a function of government operates under conditions that involve substantial social consensus, this creates no particular political problem (for example, in the case of public health). On the other hand, the political leader who wants to increase public interest in and the visibility of a particular function will tend to want to place that function in a separate agency. For example, former Governor Rudy Perpich of Minnesota, who was from a small city, successfully pushed for creation of the Greater Minnesota Corporation to fund business development outside the Twin Cities. To establish new programs as separate organizations usually best suits the interests involved and seems to give them their best chance for survival under the protection of the chief executive.

The values, standards, and goals of various professions—as well as the allocation of a function to a particular agency—may have an important bearing on how that function is administered. For example, persons convicted under the criminal statutes are likely to be treated differently in a separate department of corrections if that department is dominated chiefly by the custodial values of the professional peace officer. On the other hand, prisoners who are extremely disturbed psychologically will be treated differently if they are in institutions subject to rehabilitative values of mental health professionals.

As compared with other types of organizations, where an individual serves as head of an agency and is appointed by the governor, the agency programs are likely to be:

- More diversified
- More related to the overall balance of needs in the annual budget
- Less able to avoid cuts during an economy drive
- More involved in decisions that are important to the political future of the governor
- Less dominated by a single interest group
- More easily shaken out of bureaucratic lethargy by a chief executive who must be concerned with public reactions to governmental programs

When the heads of agencies are independent of the chief executive (because they are elected to office, because they cannot easily be removed, or because they are civil servants) the agency is likely to develop a strong in-group sense against the rest of the government; professional standards are likely to be the criteria used for making decisions; and bureaucratic inertia, if it becomes very great, cannot easily be overcome because of the difficulty of exerting pressure from outside. The agency becomes largely insulated from ordinary controls, although it usually will have to seek to maintain good relations with the legislative body unless it can obtain an independent budget. Agencies with independent heads may include (among others) state or city police and social welfare or public health departments. Except for the police, the trend is away from this type of organization. There is little enough accountability in government; this approach minimizes it.

Boards and Commissions

The use of boards and commissions, which became widespread after the Civil War, marked a transition from control of departments by legislative committees to control by the chief executive. The approach also reflected a desire to take government ''out of politics.'' Boards were either bipartisan or, later, nonpartisan in structure; members usually were appointed for long and overlapping terms, and their removal from office usually was difficult.

Librarians, educators, physicians, and other professionals often strongly favor independent boards over their agencies. Almost always an attempt is made to create an autonomous agency in the cases of public health, public transportation, airports, parks and recreation, art galleries, and museums. Education has long enjoyed considerable independence.

Boards and commissions seem inappropriate for the direct administration of any agency, and the tendency to organize in this fashion is declining. On the other hand, a board chair with administrative skill can sometimes serve adequately as the agency head. It is not uncommon in agencies that have boards as policy-making bodies for most of the policies ultimately adopted to be generated within the agency bureaucracy and to be adopted by the commission. In some cases, as with the various examining boards that control qualification for licensure (such as boards of cosmetology, medicine, dentistry, law), boards view their principal tasks to be preserving orthodoxy and preventing administrative heads, who may be lay people, from doing something the profession would not like.

Many boards and commissions are established by law in such a way as to require interest-group representation. In other cases, it is a firmly established custom for certain groups to be included in the membership. The idea of group representation seems antithetical to the traditional American skepticism about "special interests" and "special privilege," but it is very much in harmony with the concept of a pluralistic society that is a basic part of our culture.

The Importance of Professionals

The question of how agencies are structured has declined in importance since the Great Depression because of the overwhelming ascendancy of professional employees of government—the bureaucracy.

> The more complex the governmental arrangements, the greater the influence and [importance] of governmental professionals, of experts, of career bureaucrats, whether within government or as staff members of interest groups. The more complicated the maze, the more expertness, the more experience, the more constant attention is required to thread a path through it. The involvement, for example, of several levels of government in public welfare programs or in urban renewal programs has helped produce a system of regulations and policies and understandings which can be negotiated only by professionals, or by those whose interests are so directly involved that they must invest the time and effort necessary to learn their way around.[7]

Civil Service and the Merit System

The term *civil service* refers to civilian employees of government. In practice it is often used to indicate some kind of job security or interchangeably with *merit system*. The latter term refers to a method of choosing government employees on the basis of examinations demonstrating the technical or professional competence of the applicant. The former term is used for a variety of purposes, especially to imply job protection. The beginnings of state and local civil service based in part on the merit system appeared in 1884, but the principle did not become widely accepted until the 1930s. The national government, through its insistence on professional competence of administrators for some programs receiving federal grants-in-aid, has prodded many cities and states along in this direction.

The Patronage–Merit Dichotomy

Since reformers began to campaign for a merit principle of hiring administered by a civil service commission, the American public has been bombarded with propaganda seeking to establish a dichotomy between the merit system and the patronage system of personnel administration. This painting of simple contrasts was originally an attention-getting device designed to help eliminate corrupt patronage practices. But the campaign, which played on our well-rooted skepticism concerning government, was so successful that a great many Americans apparently believe that the friends of every politician are either thieves or idiots. Furthermore, the merit plan in its early days was always based on the control by a civil service commission of factors such as detailed examinations, promotions, and dismissals. This was thought necessary in order to prevent sabotage.

The patronage system flourished in a time when many government positions required little or no skill. The system successfully linked politics and administration. Jobs could be allocated proportionately among ethnic groups and political machines waxed in part on assessments on wages and salaries. But greater and greater skills came to be needed in almost every agency of government—backhoe operators replaced ditchdiggers, electricians replaced gas lamplighters, career teachers with five years of higher education replaced the ill-educated farmer's daughter in the primary school. Two or three levels of government joined to finance and shape policy in increasing numbers of activities that once were local or private functions—even the building inspector was required to be a college graduate. State and local governments turned to the merit system; the most reluctant of them compromised between patronage and merit. Even Chicago, with the remains of a big-city machine, was making concessions rapidly in the late 1980s by reducing the number or patronage positions, many of which were redundant and a luxury the city could no longer afford. Whereas, some patronage remains in most jurisdictions, it goes in large measure to persons with marketable skills. For example:

- Probate judges appoint—and determine the pay for—estate appraisers (e.g., land, buildings, jewels).
- Anthropologists with the right connections promote a cottage industry by preparing environmental impact reports for local agencies as required by the federal Environmental Protection Agency.
- Consulting firms—for a fat fee—tell city governments how they should reorganize or departments what kind of computer system to install; or they prepare new master plans for agencies that want to cite outside ''authority,'' or develop a complete package for a departmental grant-in-aid application.
- City councils and county boards appoint citizens to sundry advisory commissions, positions that are eagerly sought for their prestige and influence, even though most of them are unpaid.

And there is one other major difference between current and traditional patronage: Current patronage beneficiaries generally have a working relationship with individual officeholders, not with the political party organization. It is but another sign of the shift of the significant role of the parties from organization to symbols. Indeed, many local patronage dispensers have no important connection with any political party; they are elected on nonpartisan ballots.

Those who do use old-style party patronage come under broad attack for blatant partisanship, even suffering defeat in court challenges in 1990.[8] (The skillful mayor or governor may survive such an attack by arguing that his or her practice is traditional and would be used by the opponents if they had a chance or if they could use some other practice that is given less scrutiny by the mass media, such as noncompetitive bid contracts.)

Today, an informal system of personnel administration may produce a competent civil service or a corrupt one, just as is the case with a formal system. Conditions vary in government employment according to social and economic conditions and to the prevailing political value system.

The Civil Service Commission

The acts establishing civil service merit systems in 1883 (federal) and 1884 (New York and Massachusetts) provided for a semi-independent civil service commission and began a pattern that is still typical. It is common to have a three-member civil service commission appointed (usually by the chief executive) for overlapping terms, with not more than two of the members from the same political party. An executive secretary, normally hired to handle the actual administration may be highly influential in the determination of policies.

The commission:

- Makes rules regarding examinations
- Classifies positions
- Administers service (quality-of-performance) rating plans
- Conducts examinations
- Keeps a list of eligible appointees
- Sometimes establishes uniform wages, hours, and conditions of labor (so that two clerks doing approximately the same job but in different departments will receive the same pay)
- Makes rules on transfers and promotions
- May review cases involving the disciplining or dismissal of employees
- May, especially in larger systems, conduct training programs
- Certifies the payrolls so as to discourage payroll padding

Today there is a trend toward establishing personnel departments under a single head, the personnel director, who is responsible to the chief executive (there may be an *advisory* civil service commission). Personnel administration thus becomes an executive function and responsibility, as it always is in the private sector.

The Merit System and the Culture

Many artificial safeguards have been established in the past in attempts to require use of the merit system. These have included the independent commission, elaborate rules concerning tenure and dismissal, detailed examinations, complex position-classification systems, and the like. All are inadequate protection, and there are many devices for evasion of the merit principle if that is the officeholder's desire. Yet, the career approach to personnel administration works in many circumstances because it has become a part of the local political style.

The spirit, rather than the letter, of the merit system is the important thing. Many small and middle-sized local units of government cannot afford to employ professional personnel directors and staffs. The mayor, manager, clerk, department head, or other official may act as personnel officer. Yet, in many places with no organized merit system, policy is to get the best available person for the job. It should also be remembered that in state and local government the major personnel problem is likely to be *not* spoils but relatively low pay, particularly in smaller towns and within the higher ranks everywhere.

The Merit System and Representativeness

As the work of state and local employees became more complex in a technological society, reformers emphasized the need for a merit system to recognize proper qualifications irrespective of any other considerations. This ideal was certain to encounter political factors, however, with which personnel organizations would have to seek compromises. Indeed, one could argue that their ideal encountered other ideals considered by their supporters to be equally important, namely a bureaucracy free of bias with regard to race, religion, national origin, or sex, and in a more general sense, one representative of a cross section of the population at large.

The idea of a representative bureaucracy had been a theme of the Jacksonian reformers in the 1820s and 1830s, as well as of the big-city bosses in their heyday (between the 1880s and the 1940s); indeed, the goal was popular even earlier during the French Revolution. But it was irrelevant in the view of "efficiency and economy" civil service reformers early in the twentieth century. As the idea regained favor in the 1960s, the question was how to implement policies leading to such a goal. As employment discrimination became an issue in the civil rights movement, the national government pressured state and local agencies to adopt fair employment practices. Local units set up commissions toward this end and at the federal level the Equal Employment Opportunity Commission threatened to withhold federal grants and loans when discrimination against minority groups (later including women) was practiced. This ideal became a part of the Intergovernmental Personnel Act of 1970. Changes did not come rapidly, however, and groups organized to press for more action. Women's groups joined with those of minority groups, even though their problems were basically different. A considerable and fast-growing pool of educated and skilled women were discriminated against; ethnic (especially racial) minorities were discriminated against, too, but their pool of available skilled persons was generally smaller. In trying to deal with both issues—racial discrimination and sex discrimination—a controversial affirmative action plan, with goals and timetables for eradicating discrimination, was established under the eye of the federal Office of Civil Rights.

By 1990, large numbers of blacks and Hispanics (as well as other minority groups) were employed in state and local positions but overwhelmingly in lower-level positions. Women were approaching equality but not in the highest positions. At that time, two issues were important on the political agenda of relevant interest groups. From women there was pressure for governments to accept the concept of comparable worth to prevent jobs typically filled overwhelmingly by women (nurses, cafeteria workers, stenographers) from being underpaid in relation to jobs of similar skill levels occupied primarily by men. In its early years, this approach encountered heavy weather. Not only did it assume that apples and oranges could be compared as to worth, but many objections arose to its application, including the fact that it would be certain to increase the size of the state personnel budget, a matter of great concern in the money-tight 1980s and 1990s. There could be no doubt, however, that "women's jobs" were underpaid compared to men's.

For blacks, especially, an issue was raised as to whether the merit examinations have a white middle-class bias built into them. The charge of white bias most often centers on the use of standard English in examinations, with no allowance for black idioms. But, personnel officers object, knowledge of mainstream English is expected in government employment. The "middle-class" objection, similarly, is related to the fact that the educated and skilled primarily are middle-class people (except for the relatively small number of skilled blue-collar workers). The opportunity for advancement to and through the higher levels realistically is predicated on an acceptance and understanding of middle-class ways. This creates a significant problem that is too complicated to be addressed here but must somehow be dealt with, not just by the employer but, even more, in the home and school. Many problems remain to be managed before our governments have personnel systems that hire only those fully qualified for the job while in no way discriminating unfairly against anyone.

Position Classification

In the establishment of a merit system of civil service, the various jobs are categorized. Objective position classification consists of determining the duties and responsibilities of individual jobs, whether occupied or vacant, and the assignment of each position to a class category together with other positions of similar or related duties and responsibilities. Thus positions may be classified, for example, as junior clerk-typist, senior budget analyst, patrol officer, chauffeur, or personnel director. According accurate and meaningful classifications to positions is a technical and difficult job and can be done properly only by persons with training in personnel administration techniques. Furthermore, we now know that it cannot be done in so scientific a fashion as was once hoped and believed.

After the duties of each job position have been described, the number and types of classes needed (such as beginning surveyor, intermediate glassblower) are determined and are given descriptive titles. Positions are then assigned to classes (such as that of confidential recordkeeper in the department's northern field office). This last activity may create a good deal of controversy. Because it is a part of the supervisor's duty to look after the welfare of subordinates, a bureau chief may well engage in bitter controversy with the personnel agency over the proper rating of a valued employee, one who may seem far more valuable to the supervisor than to the personnel office.

A position-classification plan performs many useful functions when it works as intended. Classification raises employee morale by standardizing job titles. It permits the use of a uniform pay plan so that all persons doing approximately the same work receive the same pay. In an earlier day, employee pay depended largely on the ability of the department head as a lobbyist before the chief executive, the controller, or the legislative body. Still today, of course, much pressure may be brought to bear against standardization of salaries, and legislators may refuse to base salaries on the position classifications established by the personnel agency. If salaries are standardized, classification permits periodic uniform pay raises and allows for the transfer of employees among departments on the basis of their job descriptions. It improves the efficiency of selection programs and simplifies recruitment, for a single standard examination may be given for a class (e.g., clerk-typist), even though many positions in that class are to be filled.[9] Nevertheless, abuse exists. Frequently changes in position or title are used to gain pay increases for often worthy employees who do nothing different in their ''new'' jobs from what they did in their ''old'' ones. Department heads realize that this may be the only way to get pay increases from reluctant legislatures or higher executives.

Public Employee Unions

Most public employees perform jobs similar or identical to those in private enterprise, so it is not surprising that many employees desire membership in a trade union. The largest cities are the most unionized, but other local governments and many state governments are unionized, too. Employees may belong to AFL-CIO unions, to national unions of public employees, or to statewide or local unions. An increasing number of states require either state or local governments, or both, to bargain collectively with employee unions if employees so desire. A common complaint of local officials is that legislatures (whose members gain politically through this action) commonly leave it to local units to find the additional dollars this policy is certain to cost.

Union employees represent powerful lobbies and major voting blocs. They work at both state and local levels for higher pay and better fringe benefits. Occasionally they become involved in substantive matters, especially those that might affect the existing bureaucracy. They also support or oppose candidates for public office and raise funds for favored candidates. Public employees are the most dependable voting category because of their immediate and overwhelming direct interest in the election. In characteristically low-turnout local elections, employees may sway the outcome if they are in agreement—and the union makes every effort to guarantee that the bulk of them are. In a very light turnout for a nevertheless important school district election in Los Angeles in 1989, it was estimated that 10 percent of the voters were teachers—and many others probably included their spouses, relatives, or close friends.

The Concept of Adequate Standards

The political process would be much simpler if we had objective criteria for measuring adequate standards of service and of performance levels in government. But we do not. These standards are culturally determined and as such vary through time and geographic location. In large cities and populous states the merit system typically is in effect, probably modified by pressures from trade unions, ethnic groups, professional organizations, and others with political clout and particular demands. Thus, merit system professionals will want people hired and promoted on the basis of standardized tests, unions will want to modify the rules to emphasize job security and the importance of seniority over test scores, black leaders will want to see more blacks hired under affirmative action, the state medical society will want M.D. status for certain positions. People in small rural counties, on the other hand, may not— probably *will* not—expect the civil servants in the courthouse to be selected by a merit system, and they probably do not expect them to have a great deal of training for their jobs. In most cases, public employees probably meet community expectations as to standards. Similarly, the level of services wanted or expected will vary according to economic conditions, local values, population density, and other considerations.

Because of their vested interest, professional organizations set standards for their areas of governmental activity. These standards often are spoken of as being *optimum*—a word that somehow has come to be used in the journalistic and political milieu as if it meant "minimum acceptable" instead of "best." Psychiatrists prescribe standards both for service levels and for administrative organization of mental hospitals; educators, for public schools; social workers, for public welfare; and so on. The goal usually is set so high that few governmental units can claim to meet them.

Politicians use the optimal goals of professional organizations for their own political propaganda. So do nonelective administrators, who themselves are frequently members of such groups. Legislators find it difficult to defend themselves if they do not provide a full program or meet the standards, because neither the politicians nor the public can judge the fairness of the criteria used or whether they provide for minimal or ideal goals. Furthermore, each professional organization deals only with goals in its own area of governmental service whereas the beleaguered legislator must balance one such demand against another, and all of them against what the public seems willing to pay.

The Chief Executive

One scholar has seen the "most essential and characteristic functions" of executives to be the following: First, they must make value judgments. They translate the overall mission of the organization into specific goals and redivide these in turn into immediate objectives and targets. They also decide what kinds of compromises are acceptable if compromises must be made. Second, they make moral judgments, shaping the organizational image, deciding what the fundamental duties of the organization are and how activities must relate to what society regards as right and legitimate. Third, they make estimates about probability through medium- to long-range plans concerning what the organization should be doing in the probable future. They estimate how the public will react to various possible developments and concerning the capability of the organization and its members. Finally, they engage in long-range planning and the limited encouragement of innovation, the development of ideas concerning future courses of action, and the means of dealing with problems.[10]

Chief executives are important in the administrative process, not only because they may have power to hire and fire department heads, but also because they coordinate a variety of different programs and interests. They are the principal architects of policy and the liaison between agencies that provide services and clientele groups that receive them. This role is so crucial that a portion of chapter 9 is devoted to it.

The Agency Head

Subordinate to the chief executives but above middle management and clerical and minor employees are the principal administrators—the agency heads or heads of large divisions. They play vital roles in policy formulation because they are likely to know particular governmental activities better than the chief executive or legislators. They have easy access to experts, and they advise the chief executive on ideas for a program. Department heads testify before legislative bodies or committees, demonstrating great skill at withholding information unfavorable to their own points of view.

Agency Heads as Symbols

Agency heads, like the chief executive and members of the legislative body, spend a great deal of time in symbolic activities. Even though matters requiring decision pile up on their desks, they trudge from one meeting to another, often spending an afternoon in the governor's office, in an interdepartmental meeting; as an ex-officio member of some board; or at a convention of a professional group with which the agency has important relations, making a comment here and there or perhaps a platitudinous speech of welcome. In this way their activities follow much the same pattern as do those of principal executives in large private corporations.

From a rational or "efficiency" point of view, this activity may seem enormously wasteful. Yet it is very important, for at the top level, administrators (who often have worked their way up through the agency ranks) leave to trusted aides much of the actual work that goes out over their signatures. Such administrators spend most of their time molding agency members into effective working units, reassuring them of their importance by expressing their values in public speeches, and giving awards to employees who have completed many years of service. They seek to maintain smooth relationships between the agency and its clientele groups, its interest-group support, the chief executive, the legislative body, and all potential friends and enemies. Their principal task is to understand and to communicate to others the values, loyalties, and goals of their organizations.

The informed citizen should understand, too, that in the process of seeking to placate their various publics, the personnel in the various departments often come into conflict with one another by competing over budgetary matters and seeking status. Some department heads feud publicly with other department heads with resultant damage to all of government, because citizens are likely to believe the worst of what officials say about one another.

Because the status and even the survival of a government agency may depend on how it is perceived by the public, state and local agencies maintain their own public relations staffs. These are not always large—the legislative body may see to that— but they are important.

Bureaucracy and Democratic Government

The problem with contemporary American bureaucracy is that whereas citizens want many services from their government, cultural values imply a danger of losing democratic control over policy making if professional bureaucracies grow large.

About fifty years ago, Leonard D. White, an early American student of bureaucracy, thought he saw a new shape in the democracy that was then evolving. He said that although he expected the formal task of declaring the law to remain with legislative bodies, the determination of how power would be used and the purposes of its use would ''continue to shift from directly elected representative bodies to authorities chiefly characterized by expertness and official responsibility rather than by representative qualities.''[11]

What White anticipated has been realized. The daily operations of the U.S. governments at all levels today are performed by modern mature bureaucracies that function according to the rules anticipated by the German social scientist Max Weber (1864-1920)[12] and later scholars. We continue to teach politics and democracy much as we did when government performed few functions, most of which were carried out by amateur or semiprofessional employees who lacked the institutional organization that could give them great power bases. However, much governmental policy today is made and carried out by politically autonomous organizations staffed by specialized bureaucrats chosen by other experienced bureaucrats and who operate according to their own rules, only loosely guided by legislative or executive policy. A working knowledge of contemporary state and local government depends on an understanding of this fourth (or fifth) branch of government,[13] hence this brief sketch, which incorporates the conclusions of many scholars.

A bureaucracy operates within a permanent organization—for every bureaucracy has a strong in-group, out-group feeling. Its members are trained in specialized tasks or are general but professional administrators. In nearly all bureaucracies, it is paradoxical that the farther removed from the actual work of the agency one is, the higher one's pay becomes. For example, the highway commissioner, not the engineer who designed that beautiful bridge over the Green River, receives and expects to have the largest paycheck in the department. Administrators, not teachers who actually work with children, are the highest paid bureaucrats in a school system. Although the explanation for this is that pay is based on specialized knowledge or scarcity of skills, one suspects that power is also a factor. Administrators are notorious for overestimating the social worth of their own contribution.

Bureaucrats are employed and promoted on the basis of examination according to abilities valued within the agency. (In the United States, this process is modified

somewhat by the goals and values of the separate personnel staff serving all departments. As a result, substantive agencies sometimes seek autonomy from the general
personnel office. City police, for example, claim they should have their own hiring
and promotion systems because their work is highly specialized and particularly vital
to society.)

Hierarchy

Each agency is organized as a hierarchy with its own set of values, standards, goals,
and procedures. It operates by applying uniform rules and regulations. Maximum
performance is not an agency objective, though lip service may be paid to it. Instead,
the actual goal is to do what's "good enough"—good enough to placate clientele,
legislators, and significant interest-group leaders. It engages in *satisficing,* to use
Herbert Simon's ugly but distinctive term,[14] and it also invokes Parkinson's two laws
and the Peter principle, even though these were first offered to us somewhat tongue in
cheek.

According to Parkinson's law of work, work within a bureaucracy simply expands to fill the amount of time available. His law of triviality argues that the amount
of time spent on any bureaucratic problem varies inversely with the importance or
cost of the problem. The former is based on the fact that no project involves a set
amount of time and so tends to be worked on until the interval available expires. The
latter is based on the reality that the simpler the problem, the more people there will
be who have opinions about it. For example, everyone has an opinion on whether
coffee should be served at the next committee meeting, but few will have a knowledgeable opinion concerning a staff recommendation to purchase one multimillion-
dollar piece of high-tech equipment in preference to another. Under the Peter principle, bureaucrats continue to rise in job assignments until they reach one step beyond
their capabilities—their level of incompetence. The finest and most popular teacher
in the school may be a real bomb as principal. The best technician in the laboratory
may be embarrassingly incompetent as laboratory administrator. That fine number-
two person in the state highway department may have to be removed from the top
spot. One job does not necessarily serve as preparation for the next higher one,
though bureaucracies tend to promote as if it does.[15]

Life Cycle

A bureaucracy has a life cycle of its own. New functions of government may be given
separate organizations of their own by interested politicians in order to keep old-line
agencies from cannibalizing what is seen as worth taking and destroying the rest. As a
bureaucracy matures it becomes independent of other groups and makes survival its
first law. Every agency has supporters, starting with its own employees, who want to
keep their jobs. It forms its own "iron triangle" with interest groups and legislative
committees and staffs that provide mutual support. Simple inertia favors its continued existence, as does its own propaganda about its value. Even agencies that are
conceived as temporary tend to live to a ripe old age.

Survival is ensured and criticism is insulated by certain defense strategies by agencies of which three predominate. The first capitalizes on the fact that many governmental activities have no measure for success or failure and often no ultimate agency goal; instead they have only a continuous process. Are the state parks well run? Is the state drug enforcement administration an effective agency? The second strategy argues that the agency performed effectively but its knowledge, information, or procedures were misused by others. The house burned to the ground even though the fire department functioned properly because the alarm was turned in too late. The public health service performed properly relative to a flu threat that never materalized; overeager politicians made a fiasco of the affair. The bureaucrats may be right, or partly right, in their explanations but the citizen or the legislator is left to guess at the full story. The third strategy, an ''explanation'' for all seasons, is that the agency could have done a good job if it had been properly financed. This is the standard explanation for any idea that does not work. Defenders of various welfare programs use ''inadequate funding'' to rationalize failure of their programs. AIDS could be conquered with more vigorous and better-financed state and local programs. Both the strengths and the weaknesses of these three defensive strategies rest on the fact that in any given case any of them could be wholly true, wholly false, or somewhere in between. Who knows? Sometimes only the agency fully knows and it will not provide a clear answer.

Innovation is a concept alien to any burcaucracy, except for incremental changes compatible with its values, standards, and goals. Major changes therefore must be imposed from outside the agency, perhaps with some assistance from an internal dissenter or self-seeker. Long-valued equipment and procedures persist, for every organization is inherently conservative.

Organizational Loyalty

When individuals join a bureaucratic organization they are expected immediately to begin to learn the values, goals, standards, and procedures of their new home. More important, they are expected to accept and abide by them. Failure to do so can be very costly to one's career. The most despised person from the organizational point of view is the whistle-blower, the individual who reveals weaknesses or improprieties within the agency to the auditors, mass media, or legislators. Testifying before a legislative committee concerning such things as waste of resources, systematic evasion of a legislative mandate to perform a task, failure to keep up with the agency's assigned job, or advocacy of a technique or responsibility not wanted by agency leaders does happen, but it is almost certain to result in ostracism of the individual. No appeal to consideration for the taxpayer, fairness to clientele, or need to modernize the agency, for instance, will overcome the whistle-blower's gross act of disloyalty. Not even the protection of a powerful legislator will do much good, for the bureaucrats have a thousand ways, subtle and obvious, of inflicting revenge, and they can afford to bide their time. The whistler ordinarily has little choice but to resign.

Institutionalized Complaints

To aid and protect agency clients or any citizens who are having difficulties with public officials and employees, many local governments and a few states (such as Alaska,

Hawaii, Iowa, Nebraska) have created the office of ombudsman, a position and concept borrowed from Sweden. This officer, located outside any regular agency, seeks to protect individual rights, preserve fairness, negotiate compromises when appropriate, see that the law is enforced, overcome callous neglect, and do whatever else can be done to penetrate the defenses of a bureaucracy when someone believes he or she has been wronged. Often legislators at the state and local levels, who traditionally have sought to aid individual constituents (an important support-building activity), see themselves as possessing and deserving the ombudsman role and hence may oppose setting up a separate office for this purpose. But legislators may encounter a lack of staff and possible conflicts of interest that are not problems to the professional ombudsman. In one form or another, however, the office to bridge the gap between the common person and the impersonal bureaucracy is well and widely established.

Means as Ends

An agency's rules not only become sacrosanct, they become ends in themselves. Often the reason for a rule is lost in the mists of memory, but it continues in force. The rules are secured by red tape, its use serving to leave a carefully marked trail that protects both the individual bureaucrat and the agency (even though it may not do much for the client). Similarly, gobbledygook saves time and effort and separates the insiders from the others, the priesthood from the laity.

Each agency having identifiable clients tends to treat them impersonally and routinely as cases, not individuals. The bureaucrat often sees justice in treating everyone the same. The client does not seek justice but wants a problem solved to his or her personal satisfaction. When a complaint to the contrary is made, "the rules" inevitably are cited. Furthermore, passing the buck for failure to satisfy an outsider is easy and a routine tactic. The result is the infinite regression of bureaucratic responsibility.

Although a bureaucracy customarily is made up of highly competent individuals, pressures to conform result in devotion to rules and resistance to innovation. Hence a bureaucracy sometimes is said to be the only human organization in which the whole is less than the sum of the parts. Of course, there is some room for individual behavior within the group. Organizational constraints are powerful, but they are not perfect. And bureaucracies, their behavior patterns, and the meaning of this for society and democracy are variously interpreted by researchers and textbook writers.

Rule-Making Power

The most important characteristic of bureaucracy in relation to democracy, beyond its independence and permanence, is its authority to make rules, which that same bureaucracy then enforces. No legislative body could provide all the rules needed to cover every circumstance or exigency. The bureaucracy is allowed, indeed expected, to fill the gap. These rules, which may have enormous impact on the individual citizen, have the force and effect of law. An external appeal can be taken from them only to the courts (another bureaucracy that claims superiority through seniority) or the legislative body, which for the ordinary citizen often is too expensive, time consuming, or difficult. The importance of the rules made and enforced by the bureaucracy can scarcely be overstated. The "workable plan for affirmative action" required of almost every organization was devised by the federal Office of Civil Rights with only the most tenuous basis in statute or executive order. An individual taxpayer may claim a deduction based on a rule made by the state tax agency. If the deduction is disallowed, it may cost the taxpayer thousands of dollars, with only the barest chance of getting the ruling reversed, no matter how picayune or hair splitting the decision may seem. (The agency will quickly point out, however, that it has much of the law on its side: Unless you can prove you do not owe the money, you do.) The decision of a district attorney to prosecute or not can sometimes mean to an individual the difference between a happy life and years in state prison.

Interbranch Friction

The bureaucracy not only faces conflict with other bureaucracies (including the courts), but also with the executive. The skills, knowledge, and experience of the bureaucracy is, however, often useful to the chief executive in meeting public concerns and expectations and in framing programs for elections and for presentation to the legislature. The greatest friction and potential conflict for the bureaucracy, however, is with the legislative branch, the controllers of the purse. It is here that professional knowledge and procedures contest with grass-roots expectations. To the legislator, a problem of great importance in his or her district must be "solved" by the next election or there is no tomorrow. His or her constituents are the key reference group. The bureaucrat, on the other hand, views policy development over a much longer time span, is committed to a set of values, standards, goals, and procedures that may admit of little grass-roots consideration, and receives status recognition from professional peers rather than from elected officials. The resulting tension between the two branches is continuous and permanent. At times—not always—it may be constructive.

Bureaucracy as Essential

Professional administration remains the key to modern government and to maintaining the service levels the public expects. The bureaucracy is literally indispensable at all levels of government because of what it does, not because of what it is. What does it do? It provides competence, stability, predictability, and continuity to the everyday work of governments. And it is the branch of each government with which the ordinary individual is most likely to come into direct contact. That contact often is not reassuring. As the power and scope of the bureaucracy expands, it seems to nibble away at the public's sense of the efficacy of democracy.

Bureaucracy as Antithesis

Keeping in mind the ideologies that have guided Americans in evaluating politics, it is understandable that bureaucracy should come to be regarded as the antithesis of democracy. Several decades ago, when the proponents of a professional bureaucracy also gave support to the concept of integrated administrative control under the chief executive, they reinforced one popular fear with another. There also has been a tendency, both in conventional wisdom and in some academic writing, to romanticize the representative character of legislative bodies—national, state, and local. Furthermore, this same combination of forces has been lined up at times in support of the idea that "whatever the people want is right, and they should have it." Hence, if the people want a chaotic pattern of government, it must be right; if they prefer amateur legislative opinion to that of professional bureaucratic opinion, the former must be better. These ideas are reflected in the Latin inscription found in most capitols, though usually beyond the ken of tourists and legislators alike: *vox populi, vox Dei*— the voice of the people is the voice of God. The difficulty with this self-congratulatory notion is that the *vox populi* can be interpreted in a great many ways by legislators, bureaucrats, chief executives, and editors. And what seems to be the voice of the people today is viewed by those same people tomorrow as a bad mistake. The legislator who must take the short view and the bureaucrat who is sometimes permitted the luxury of the long view, may both speak the voice of the people— if the problem is viewed from the vantage of the historian.

Bureaucracy and the Individual

The problems of bureaucracy in a modern society are more complex than the question of public acceptance of the bureaucrat or the problem of retaining democratic control over a bureaucracy. It is possible that the bureaucratic system, in itself, contributes to current personality problems, and conflict may exist between expected bureaucratic behavior and expected behavior of the individual as a citizen.

One study, for example, has found conflicts between the needs of mentally healthy individuals and the demands of formal organization. Mental health in our society is dependent in part on a degree of creativity in and independent activity by individuals. The culture, furthermore, urges us to make the fullest use of whatever abilities we have. But at the lower echelons in a bureaucracy, the work situation calls for individuals to be dependent on their supervisors, to accept orders passively, and to use few and relatively unimportant skills. The incongruence between, on the one hand, psychological needs (which, of course, vary with the individual) and social expectations and, on the other hand, bureaucratic expectations may cause lower-echelon bureaucrats to feel frustrated and defeated, to emphasize short-term considerations rather than broader organizational or social problems, and to experience a sense of conflict. As members of the lower reaches of the bureaucracy attempt to advance, they find fewer positions available at each higher level and themselves in mutual competition, which adds to the sense of conflict. Hostility toward the supervisor, or "boss," may also develop and individuals may tend to focus only on some small part of the function of the organization and never take an interest in the total operation.

In sum, "this dilemma between individual needs and organization demands is a basic, continual problem imposing an eternal challenge to the leader. How is it possible to create an organization in which the individuals may obtain optimum expression and, simultaneously, in which the organization itself may obtain optimum satisfaction of its demands?''[16] Bureaucracy is essential in our society, but it poses problems both to the democratic system of government and to the emotional well-being of members of society.

Concluding Note

We may assume that it is difficult at times to turn the bureaucratic troops around or to divert their path, that red tape and literal interpretations of the rules are endemic to bureaucracy, that mature bureaucracies tend to resist innovation and lack initiative, and that trained specialists are sometimes impatient with unknowing laymen, without assuming that bureaucrats wish to destroy the system in which, as citizens, they too live.

Americans probably have reason to be on guard against an irresponsible, autocratic, muscle-bound bureaucracy. But there is no evidence to indicate that the danger from this direction is any greater than is the danger from an irresponsible legislative body, an autocratic chief executive, or a muscle-bound court system. Each contains its dangers; each must be watched.

Notes

1. Dwight Waldo, *The Enterprise of Public Administration* (Novato, CA: Chandler and Sharp, 1980), chapters 1 and 3.

2. Ibid., chapters 2 and 3.

3. Roscoe C. Martin, *The Cities and the Federal System* (New York; Atherton Press, 1965), chapter 3.

4. Karl A. Bosworth, "The Politics of Management Improvement in the States," *American Political Science Review* 47 (March 1953): 88–99; York Willbern, "Administrative Organization," in James W. Fesler, ed., *The 50 States and Their Local Governments* (New York: Alfred A. Knopf, 1967). The trends in recent decades are discussed in chapters 2 and 4.

5. R. P. Knuth, "Reorganization Bill Enacted in Missouri," *National Civic Review* 63 (April 1974): 195–96.

6. Albert B. Saye, "Georgia Revamps State Agencies," *National Civic Review* 61 (March 1972): 136–37.

7. York Willbern, *The Withering Away of the City* (University: University of Alabama Press, 1964), p. 218.

8. "Court Limits Political Patronage," *Star Tribune,* June 22, 1990, 1A.

9. Ismar Baruch, *Position-classification in the Public Service* (Chicago: Civil Service Assembly, 1942), still a standard reference.

10. Edward C. Banfield, "The Training of the Executive," in Carl J. Friedrich and Seymour E. Harris, eds., *Public Policy* (Cambridge, MA: Graduate School of Public Administration, Harvard University, 1960), 27–28.

11. Leonard D. White, *The Future of Government in the United States* (Chicago: University of Chicago Press, 1942).

12. E. M. Henderson and Talcott Parsons, trans. and eds., Max Weber, *The Theory of Social and Economic Organization* (New York: The Free Press, 1947).

13. The legislative, executive, and judicial branches are the traditional three, but this

theory is based on an eighteenth-century concept. The fourth branch, the mass media of communication, is sometimes informally added. The bureaucracy, which in its modern form scarcely extends back more than a century, is then the fifth branch, but not in order of importance.

14. Herbert Simon, *Administrative Behavior,* 2d ed. (New York: Macmillan, 1957).

15. C. Northcote Parkinson, *Parkinson's Law and Other Essays in Administration* (Boston: Houghton Mifflin, 1957); Laurence Peter and Raymond Hull, *The Peter Principle* (New York: William Morrow, 1969).

16. Chris Argyris, ''The Individual and Organization: Some Problems of Mutual Adjustment,'' *Administrative Science Quarterly* 2 (June 1957):1–24.

The Library of Congress

11

Legislative Organization, Functions, and Membership

"**A** member of the legislature," said one who was serving in Oregon, "assumes reality in the eyes of a constituent when he [or she] does something which touches that constituent personally."[1] Because this is so, a legislator is given little room to strive for greatness, to look at the larger picture, or to apply broad general principles to the major issues of the day. Constituents do not expect their legislators to be geniuses or authorities on the law. They do expect them to care for the little, individual problems that confront citizens in their day-to-day living.

Legislative bodies at all levels, from the state on down, spend most of their time dealing with subjects that indirectly affect all people, but directly affect relatively few. Thus, when the legislator quoted above was first elected, he stated:

> I arrived at our new marble Capitol expecting to spend most of my time considering momentous issues—social security, taxes, conservation, civil liberties. Instead we have devoted long hours to the discussion of regulations for the labeling of eggs. We have argued about the alignment of irrigation ditches, the speed of motorboats on mountain lakes, the salaries of justices of the peace, and whether or not barbers and beauty parlor attendants should be high school graduates. For two days we wrangled about a bill specifying the proper scales for weighing logs and lumber.
>
> None of these questions concerns large numbers of people. Yet each question concerns a few people vitally. Two or three poultry raisers told me that a change in the labeling of fresh and cold storage eggs would put them out of business. . . .[2]

It is because most legislative bills do not concern many people directly and because they do concern a few vitally that the legislative climate described above is what it is. This situation is in fact an important consideration in the determination of the caliber of legislative personnel, in the tendency of interest groups to bypass the legislature on the most important issues, in the general lack of policy leadership among legislators, and in the general status of legislatures as social institutions.

Two developments in recent decades have greatly changed the place of legislatures in the state political process: the tendency toward professionalization in legislatures (mirroring the national Congress) in some states and the changes in all state legislatures because of the landmark 1960s apportionment cases of the United States Supreme Court. By virtue of court rulings, each state must now follow the one-person, one-vote rule when apportioning. This creates bicameral legislatures whose houses are more alike than in the decades preceding this kind of reapportionment; the checks and balances of bicameralism are reduced.

The state legislative body, once viewed as the very symbol of representative democracy, gradually has lost status through the last century or so as the judicial, executive, and administrative branches have increased in importance and as national government policy has increasingly influenced state policy. But where the trend toward modernization is to be found, legislative business is also expanding greatly.[3] As recently as World War II, only four state legislatures met every year; in 1988 the number had risen to forty-one, and seven of the nine—which had only one session—also held special sessions during the biennium.[4] As recently as the 1950–1951 biennium, only 47,000 bills were considered by state legislatures of which 15,000 were enacted (31 percent); by comparison in the 1986–87 biennium, almost 185,000 bills were introduced and over 47,000 (25 percent) passed.[5] Many of those that passed were a good deal longer than those of three decades earlier.

The legislatures at the state and local levels will be the subject of this chapter and the next. This chapter will describe the general functions, structures, and membership of the legislatures. We will focus on reapportionment in light of the 1990 census. Chapter 12 will focus on the legislative process and representation.

Legislative Structure

States show their individuality in the varied nomenclature of their legislative bodies. What is called the legislature in most states is called the general assembly in others and is known by a variety of other terms, including the general court in Massachusetts and New Hampshire. But in quite a few states, the term *assembly* applies to the lower house, which may also be called the house of delegates or house of representatives. In New Jersey, for example, the lower house is called the general assembly, but in North Carolina this term refers to the entire legislature. Every upper house is called the senate—a symbol of prestige since Roman times and dearly loved by all who can claim membership in such a body.

Bicameralism

Several colonial legislatures consisted of but one house, although most were *bicameral*. In the nineteenth century, however, the two-house system became the norm in the states, partly in imitation of the national government, partly because it permitted the constituencies to be divided according to two different methods. It fitted in well with the politician's constant desire to please everyone to some degree, to strike a compromise. The chances are that representation under a two-house system will reflect the demands of more groups, and this is more important politically than pleasing relatively few groups completely through a unicameral system. Even after the one-person, one-vote rulings, district size differs from house to house and the corresponding opportunities for serving constituencies expand with bicameralism. Of course, opportunities for preventing the passage of legislation and for checks on interest groups also expand with bicameralism.

> *Bicameral Legislature:* **A two-house legislature. this is the norm of the states, whereas** *Unicameralism*, **one-house legislatures (councils and boards), are the norm of localities in the twentieth century.**

Several decades ago, some reformers called for the adoption of unicameral legislatures. They argued that the two-house system allows for passing the buck, that it obscures responsibility for legislative decisions, encourages deadlocks, and offers an additional excuse for gerrymandering because there will be efforts to find a basis other than population for representation in one house to help justify the existence of bicameralism.

Under the leadership of a prominent reformer, Senator George Norris, Nebraska adopted unicameralism in 1934. In this one-party, overwhelmingly rural and socially homogeneous state, the plan appears to have worked satisfactorily.[6] Relatively little interest in unicameralism has developed elsewhere, however, though it is still strongly supported by some reformers. Advocacy was revived after the courts required all apportionment to be population-based and some observers mistakenly believed this would eliminate any benefit of a two-house perspective. Opinion-leading newspapers, including the *New York Times* and the *St. Louis Post-Dispatch*, have endorsed unicameralism, but public support and interest are lacking. Multiple referendum attempts to adopt unicameral systems in recent decades have been rejected.[7] Buckpassing, the obscuring of responsibility, and other alleged weaknesses in the bicameral system could easily be transferred to unicameralism by willful legislators. Reformers who look to structural change as a means for overcoming "offensive" behavior patterns give too little credit to the imaginativeness and creative ability of the American politician.

Size of Legislative Membership

The size of legislative houses in the United States seems to have depended on considerations of expediency when each was determined.[8] It is significant that a reapportionment is likely to result in an increase in the size of at least one house unless size is determined in the state constitution. Membership in the upper houses of legislatures varies from twenty in Alaska and twenty-one in Delaware and Nevada to sixty-one in New York and sixty-seven in Minnesota (see table 11–1). The lower houses have an even greater range: from forty in Alaska and forty-one in Delaware to four hundred in New Hampshire. Approximately half the states divide their senate districts equally to form lower-house districts; the other half separately apportion house and senate. The ratio of lower- to upper-house seats in most states varies little—with the exception of New Hampshire, which has a ratio of almost 17:1. Sixteen states evenly divided 2:1 and six evenly divide 3:1. The enormous size of the lower houses in New England relative to population results from the fact that the town is used there as the representative unit. As we discussed in chapters 2 and 7, the towns were formed with the Jef-

TABLE 11-1   Sizes of Legislative Bodies (1990)

State	Senate	House	Total
Alabama	35	105	140
Alaska	20	40	60
Arizona	30	60	90
Arkansas	35	100	135
California	40	80	120
Colorado	35	65	100
Connecticut	36	151	187
Delaware	21	41	62
Florida	40	120	160
Georgia	56	180	236
Hawaii	25	51	76
Idaho	42	84	126
Illinois	59	118	177
Indiana	50	100	150
Iowa	50	100	150
Kansas	40	125	165
Kentucky	38	100	138
Louisiana	39	105	144
Maine	35	151	186
Maryland	47	141	188
Massachusetts	40	160	200
Michigan	38	110	148
Minnesota	67	134	201
Mississippi	52	122	174
Missouri	34	163	197
Montana	50	100	150
Nebraska	49	—	49
Nevada	21	42	63
New Hampshire	24	400	424
New Jersey	40	80	120
New Mexico	42	70	112
New York	61	150	211
North Carolina	50	120	170
North Dakota	53	106	159
Ohio	33	99	132
Oklahoma	48	101	149
Oregon	30	60	90
Pennsylvania	50	203	253
Rhode Island	50	100	150
South Carolina	46	124	170
South Dakota	35	70	105
Tennessee	33	99	132
Texas	31	150	181
Utah	29	75	104
Vermont	30	150	180
Virginia	40	100	140
Washington	49	98	147
West Virginia	34	100	134
Wisconsin	33	99	132
Wyoming	30	64	94
Total	1995	5466	7461

Source: National Conference of State Legislatures.

fersonian hope of providing direct democracy. As population grew and representative democracy replaced direct democracy, the town's retention as the unit of apportionment, created extremely large legislative houses in the eighteenth century. The tradition of using the town for lower-house apportionment has been kept even in recent decades, with some states guaranteeing one seat to the least populous towns, despite the constraints of the equal population requirement (discussed below). Legislative houses tend to be quite small in the West, commonly under one hundred members. California has only forty members in its senate to represent about 30 million people, so that each one represents more people than does a representative in the United States Congress.

Terms of Office

No consensus exists in America on the preferred term of office for legislators. Many local councils and boards elect for one-year terms, lower houses elect typically for two-year terms, upper houses for four years; but, of course, the U.S. Senate elects its members for six years. The solution we have chosen to this inability to determine a uniform term of office—experimentation with a variety of terms—typifies how a variety of problems are solved in a pluralist society. Legislators are said to need longer terms of office to plan and to be free from the demands of the election process. Short terms are seen as an important check on unpopular legislators. Frequent elections are said to make legislators more responsible to the people who elect them. However, the vast majority of legislators today are reelected. The electoral process serves the variety of purposes discussed in chapter 6, but with rare exceptions, turning out incumbents is not one of them. Incumbents have had an advantage throughout the history of American legislative bodies, but long tenure was not a characteristic of the frontier. It advanced with urbanism, the political machine, and the career legislator.

In the absence of consensus, the term of office for legislators seems about as haphazard as the size of legislative bodies. Generally, members of the senate enjoy a longer term than do those in the lower house. About three-fourths of the senates have four-year terms, whereas the others have two-year terms. The overwhelming majority of lower houses have two-year terms (forty-five of forty-nine in 1990). In some legislatures, the four-year terms are staggered so that part of the membership is elected every two years. In others, senators are elected with their governors, usually in the off year from presidential elections. The timing is important, because voter turnout is higher in presidential election years, and the characteristics of the electorate are different from the off-year election.

Prerequisites and Perquisites

As with governors, certain qualifications usually are required of legislators. They must be citizens, have resided in the state a certain length of time, have reached a certain age (senators usually have a higher minimum-age requirement than representatives), and must be registered or eligible voters.

The pay for legislators at one time was small, but with modernization has come demand for a career salary. Some state constitutions permit legislators to raise their salaries and to vote themselves increased expense and travel allowances. Because of public resistance to a highly paid vocational legislature, much legislative compensation is in the form of unvouchered expense accounts, generous retirement benefits, travel allowances, use of state-owned automobiles, state-provided district offices, and extra pay and staff for legislative leaders.

In 1990, California, Pennsylvania, Michigan, and New York had base annual salaries of over $40,000. As legislators pressed for higher salaries, the pay restrictions once common in state constitutions gradually have been removed. Up to World War II, legislators frequently were limited to $3 or $4 a day for a limited number of days. The argument was that these rules made legislators easy victims of the old-fashioned lobbyist whose little black bag carried such tempting items as bourbon whiskey and unmarked $20 bills. On the other hand, no evidence shows that increased pay has improved the caliber of legislators. Overt bribery has declined, but whether this is the result of better pay or of changing values and social conditions is not known.

In addition to base pay, legislators receive extra compensation for special sessions and for travel and other allowances. In addition to salary, per diem living expenses are becoming common. Such expenses can be as high as $100 for those who do not normally reside in the capital; $140 per day may be granted for special committee meetings and special session. In contrast, Maine offered salaries ranging from $7,500 in odd years to $4,400 in even years in the 1980s, with only $26 for meals and $24 for lodging; New Hampshire offers a $100 salary and $3 per diem for the biennium.[9]

Some reformers have argued that the only way to raise the quality of the legislative body is to provide salaries that will attract persons from a higher-income bracket—presumably more capable persons. This argument probably misses the point. Whereas it is difficult to know who might choose a legislative career if the benefits were greater, no evidence exists that increases in salaries within practical amounts have any substantial effect on the recruitment process, except perhaps to encourage more candidates to enter the primaries. The question of quality—which means different things to different people—in a legislative body is a relatively unimportant one. Forces affecting legislative voting patterns are the same irrespective of education or ability of legislators. The strongest argument for raising legislative salaries is not related to quality or whether legislators indeed earn more than they receive. Rather, it is that unless legislative salaries are increased from time to time, legislators will be reluctant to increase bureaucratic salaries. And it is in the area of competition with the private sector for qualified personnel that state governments are most vulnerable.

Sessions

After the corn was picked, Christmas reverently observed, and the New Year boisterously brought in, nineteenth-century rural American squires took off for the state capital where often they remained until spring planting time—after which they would stay with great reluctance. In those simpler days, legislative sessions were brief.

(Most people wanted it that way, as was indicated by the frontier proverb: ''The legislature is in session and no man's life or property is safe.'')

The length of sessions is still constitutionally limited, to sixty or ninety days in some states, but the demands of contemporary government are such that in practice the work of the legislature usually cannot be completed in that time. Several devices have been developed to circumvent this limitation. Georgia, for example, ''covers the clock,'' thereby pretending that the legislators are not aware that the time limit has expired. In this fashion, it is possible to extend the session to a time equal to the legal session plus the number of days the governor (who cannot use this subterfuge) had to consider a bill before signing or vetoing it. Another device is to adjourn and go immediately into special session. Some state constitutions have been amended to extend the time limit or do away with it. Some legislatures recess rather than adjourn, providing leaders the opportunity to come back into session at any time and ensuring that a governor cannot pocket veto a bill.

Traditionally, regular sessions met in odd-numbered years only, but this pattern is changing along with the trend toward longer sessions. Quite a few states have formally amended their constitutions to provide for annual sessions. In some states, the governor alone can determine the subject matter that may be considered at a special session; in others, the rules of the legislature alone control the agenda.

Legislative Functions

The modern legislative function in the governmental process, that of declaring and thus legitimatizing the law, is a relatively recent one in Western civilization; traditionally, it belonged to the courts. The oldest functions of legislative bodies are debate, criticism, modification, information, and investigation.

Development of Assemblies

To understand the trend in the use of legislative bodies as a part of the total process of policy making, it is necessary to place these institutions in their historical context. Representative assemblies originated in Europe in about the thirteenth century out of the feudal obligation of vassals to provide counsel to the sovereign. At first, these early parliamentarians served chiefly to petition the crown and to enter formal complaints against the sovereign and the incipient bureaucracy. (The term *parliament* is descended from the French for ''talking place.'') Later, especially in England, they developed the right, on behalf of the influential classes, to give or withhold consent when the sovereign proposed unusual expenditures or risky undertakings.

American legislatures, even before the War of Independence, began to develop a positive voice in decision making, although in most colonies the governor was much more powerful than they were. With the fall from favor of executives during that war, the new state legislatures became powerful, as did city councils. The frontier influence of egalitarianism encouraged this trend, and for much of the nineteenth century governors and mayors were in eclipse as molders of policy. The same period also was the golden age of parliamentary power in the European democracies.

With the rise of a complicated, technological society and the increase in governmental functions that accompanied urbanization, individuals and interest groups turned to the executive for policy leadership.[10] The popular assembly then began to retreat to its historic reactive function. But because Americans do not remember this change in that role, there has been much criticism of executive "usurpation" and of the "bureaucracy's taking over." The essentially negative function of the legislature as a check on the executive represents, then, the reestablishment of the traditional pattern rather than relegation of the legislature to a lesser role.

Lawgiving Function

The central struggle between modern legislatures and executives has been concerned with control over policies in the raising and spending of money, just as it was in the Middle Ages. As a logical and perhaps necessary part of the increasing power of the executive, fiscal policy making has shifted from the legislature to the executive. As a result of the change, responsibility for the innovation of taxation and appropriation proposals is placed with the executive, with the legislative body serving to review and (usually) modify them.

In the days of legislative supremacy, members of the tax, appropriation, and budget committees in each house made up the budget, informally working out differences among themselves. Today, these committees continue to work, dissecting the executive budget, listening to interest-group representatives and agency personnel, imposing their own (often considerable) interest and store of information, and helping to center the spotlight on the process that determines the public's tax load. The policy-making initiative has been lost by the representative assemblies and nothing is more indicative of this than the dominance of the executive budget. But through actions in reviewing the tax and spending proposals of executives and administrators, of modifying them, and of withholding approval, the assemblies continue to perform an ancient function. The legislators' role is changing from innovator to modifier and, sometimes, refiner. History notwithstanding, being a legislator is becoming a fulltime occupation. Legislators may develop into specialists in particular areas of policy for which their modifications of executive proposals can be quite specific. Fulltime nonpartisan staffs of lawyers and social scientists now commonly assist in bill preparation. The process is further expanded today by word processing and paper duplication, which allow more material to be handled more quickly.

The Oversight Function

Oversight, a function that actually combines a variety of functions (considering new legislation, modifying old legislation, and investigating policy that is suspected to be contrary to legislative intent), in some states is conducted by committees when the legislature is not in session; it is of growing importance. Frequently reports produced by such committees or revelations during public testimony are contrary to executive or bureaucratic claims and place the legislators (particularly the committee chairs) into the center of public controversies.

Although investigation is a traditional legislative function, legislatures do not ordinarily use their powers to the extent that Congress does. However, investigations may deal with the need for new laws, suspected corruption, mismanagement in an agency, or improprieties in the behavior of employees. Potential headlines can tempt and motivate the legislator beyond ordinary efforts. For example, if the governor or other elected official is not of the same party or faction as the majority in one house, an election year can produce a rash of investigations of the administration. Sometimes these fishing expeditions find cases of popularly unacceptable behavior; at other times they only appear to do so. In either event, the material is generally useful against the incumbent and will gain a "bite" on the television news.

Quite a few committee investigations are aimed at exploring areas where new legislation may be needed. In the hectic sessions characteristic of most legislatures, little opportunity exists for careful study or extensive hearings. Between-session investigations help to overcome this deficiency, particularly as some legislators have reduced the time devoted to their other professions. The legislative investigation is intended to make it more difficult for the executive and judicial branches to become dishonest, lazy, autocratic, or unresponsive to social values and wants. Most serve these intentions, but the exceptions are probably more visible and better remembered.

Ceremonial Function

Although the legislative body acting collectively, or the members individually, are not called upon as often as is the governor to perform ritualistic functions, they do spend much of their time on this sort of thing. Some states pass more resolutions declaring the will of the legislature than they pass statutes. As with the governor, such activity is important to the legislator's political future. For example, legislative houses invite famous guests of the state to address it. The California legislature has invited astronauts, returning military heroes, distinguished foreign visitors, and others to appear before it. To be photographed with these superstars for one's newsletter and the local press does the legislator's political standing no harm.

Constituent Function

The legislator is not simply a lawmaker but also a representative and *ombudsman*. Solving problems for individuals endears legislators to their constituents and may be an effective source of information as well. Legislators will be contacted to handle a constituent problem with the bureaucracy, to offer advice on the passage of legislation, and to trouble shoot where some other public official has failed. Citizens easily can be overwhelmed by the complexity of modern government. The legislator or a member of the staff may be nothing more than a traffic cop who directs the constituent to the right department to handle a problem. Although few bureaucrats sit in fear of legislators, it is in their interest, given their dependence on legislative funding for departments, to expedite the citizen request that comes via the legislator's office rather than from the citizen directly. Some legislatures have nonpartisan offices specifically designed to handle constituent services; others reserve this as a major staff task. Legislators recognize the political benefit in performing the role of ombudsman, of serving as vital connecting links between citizen and bureaucrat.

Remember, legislatures can submit proposals for constitutional amendments to the voters. This, together with the power to submit the question of calling a constitutional convention, is known as the *constituent power* of the legislature.

Executive Function

A great many appointments to administrative positions, to boards and commissions, and in some states to judicial posts are made by governors. These appointments generally are subject to the consent of the state senate. That body, in this action, is exercising a function that stems from the days when some colonial upper houses served as the executive council, advising the governor. In a few states in New England and in the South, the legislature selects some judges as well as some state administrative officers. In Minnesota, the board of regents of the University of Minnesota is "elected" by the legislature. Candidates mount campaigns to win a majority vote of both houses meeting in joint session. These appointments are not subject to the governor's veto. Legislatures also commonly prescribe detailed organizational structure for each public agency and may state quite specifically the administrative procedures that they are to follow in performing their functions.

Judicial Function

As in the case of Congress, legislatures judge the qualifications of their own members. Usually, members can determine whether they will seat a member whose claim by right of election is clouded for some reason. They can also sit in judgment of members accused of wrongdoing and may expel them. The impeachment powers possessed by legislatures are also judicial in nature. Common practice is for one house of the legislature to indict (thus "impeach") the accused officer and the other house to sit as jury to decide guilt or innocence of the impeached officer.

Apportionment

The number of seats in each house of the legislature is usually, but not always, determined by the constitution or by constitutional formula. With the exception of Nebraska, American legislatures are bicameral, with the members of each house representing different constituents. Unlike legislatures in many nations, most state legislatures are elected from single-member districts, and seldom is a legislator elected from a district larger than a county.

In all states it is necessary to create legislative districts and assign seats to them by *apportionment* and it is over this issue that numerous political battles continue to be fought. The most important quarrels over reapportionment resulted from the fact that the nation has urbanized rapidly, whereas states continued to be governed by apportionment practice from the days when we were a rural, small-town country. If we consider population as the basis of representation, rural areas for about seventy years beginning in the 1890s were disproportionately strong in at least one house of legislative bodies; the urban voice was far weaker than its numbers of people suggest in the *malapportioned* houses. Legislatures in most states developed such a reputation for being rural-oriented that they scarcely were thought of in connection with urban problems. (At one time—in Florida, Kansas, New Mexico, Oklahoma, and Tennessee—districts with less than 30 percent of the population could elect a majority in *both* houses of the legislature.) The courts eventually acted to remedy the imbalance, rather than leaving it to be corrected (if at all) by the checks and balances of bicameralism. Reapportionment has therefore become not only a most important legislative decision but also one of principal concern to the judicial branch.

> *Apportionment:* **The process of dividing a population into legislative districts.**

> *Malapportionment:* **A situation that exists wherever the one-person, one-vote rule is not followed. Underrepresentation exists in the malapportioned districts of a legislative house that have more people than do other districts. Overrepresentation exists in the malapportioned districts of a legislative house that have fewer people than do other districts.**

The Role of the Judiciary

The court case that began the process of changing to a different rule of apportionment was *Baker* v. *Carr* (1962).[11] The United States Supreme Court accepted jurisdiction in a reapportionment case, rejecting the older precedent that apportionment was a "political question" containing no justiciable question (one that could be settled as a matter of law). The Court then went on to rule that lower courts should consider whether the Tennessee legislature had violated the equal protection clause of the Fourteenth Amendment by failing to reapportion itself as required by the Constitution. Although this did not settle the matter, the direction in which the Court would move had been established. The next year, it ruled that the Georgia county-unit system of voting in primary elections for the governorship and for members of Congress, a system under which the person who carried a majority of counties would win irrespective of the cumulative vote, also deprived citizens of their right to equal protection.[12] This case made it clear that by equal protection the court was talking about total population or total potential votes—in other words, one-person, one-vote.[13] (Each state legislature must apportion its congressional districts as well as its own districts; hence, the Fourteenth Amendment would apply to the apportionment of the U.S. House of Representatives within the limitations of those provisions of the Constitution that specifically dictate the apportionment of that body.)

In 1964, the Court went the full distance to the logical conclusion by ruling that when state legislatures determine the boundaries of congressional districts they must make sure "as nearly as practical, one person's vote in a Congressional election must be worth as much as another's"[14] And in June 1964 in *Reynolds v. Sims,* the Court ruled that both houses of a state legislature must be apportioned as strictly as possible according to population.[15] The Court did not indicate how much of a margin of variation it would permit, but it held again that the equal protection clause applied to apportionment. In this historic case, the Court also dealt with two touchy arguments on which the opponents of straight population representation had based their hopes. It ruled that the pattern of representation in the United States Congress, in which every state is given two senators regardless of population, did not apply to the House of Representatives or to state legislatures. The Court specifically pointed out that the Senate apportionment was the result not of the estimate by the Founders of what was equitable, but of a political deal necessary in order for the Constitution to be politically acceptable to the less populous states. The Court also ruled that popular votes relative to apportionment plans were not relevant to the case. The majority opinion in Reynolds, written by Chief Justice Earl Warren, said that "a citizen's constitutional rights can hardly be infringed upon because a majority of the people choose to do so." In a companion case—*Lucas* v.*Colorado General Assembly*—the Court would expressly reject a 2–1 vote of the Colorado electorate, which chose an apportionment plan based on factors other than providing one-person, one-vote.[16]

In the reapportionment cases, the Supreme Court moved from a pragmatic approach to apportionment to a dogmatic social theory, which holds that one-person, one-vote provides for political equality. This conclusion is not proved either in the Court's decisions or in the arguments before the Court. The arguments centered on the fact of uneven apportionment. Because of its logic, the idea of equality that is implicit in one-person, one-vote was assumed to be desirable and to further democracy. The Constitution required a far more complicated notion of equality ("equal protection").[17] Some might argue that if the Madisonian principle of protection through checks and balances is to be maintained, legislative houses *must* represent different constituencies to produce such protection. Although legislative houses still differ in size, thus representing different majorities after one-person, one-vote, the likelihood of widely different constituencies is reduced by following the same principle of apportionment in each house. In dissenting, Justice John Marshall Harlan went so far as to argue that the founders specifically rejected the one-person, one-vote principle. But these questions carried little weight with the majority of the Court, which was bent on a particular measure of protection.

A number of other legal questions arose. The Court seemingly ignored the point that equal totals by population (the census is used to measure population) may be quite different from equal numbers by qualified voters. For example, a household of two adults with four minor children will be counted as six votes in determining the number of legislative seats but be eligible for only two votes for those legislators. In this example, one person may equal one vote, but six people equal only two votes, which when considered, gives rise to complex problems of equity.[18] The Court chose to deal with the question of what is an acceptable deviation from one-person, one-vote, but has not done so with great clarity. Although the states apportion both, the state legislative apportionment is allowed to depart from the one-person, one-vote rule more than the apportionment of the national House of Representatives. Long-held traditions of respecting existing political boundaries such as counties or even townships when apportioning could produce great deviation from the one-person, one-vote rate. The Court has finessed this issue by permitting additional seats in the legislature for a few small counties as long as the overall effect of the apportionment (aside from the few deviating units) was still to respect one-person, one-vote. Thus in 1983, advocates of departure from one-person, one-vote could claim victory when the Court let stand the creation of a Wyoming legislative district that deviated 89 percent from the norm so that a small county could remain represented as a county in the state house of representatives.[19] But dogmatic adherents to one-person, one-vote downplayed the deviation, arguing as did the Court dissenters that despite the mistake of the majority of the Court, the permitted district was an isolated example and the overall effect of the apportionment for most residents of Wyoming respected one-person, one-vote. But a decade earlier, the Court had similarly shown respect for a plan that deviated as much as 16 percent to respect political jurisdictions.[20]

The Court's involvement extended to the apportionment of seats on local councils and boards.[21] Minority groups had long held that at-large systems of election reduce the likelihood of minority-group representation in legislatures at any level. A group that might be a majority in a district frequently is in a minority areawide. But the courts refused to strike down the multimember apportionment plans in state legislatures or in local governments unless it could be shown that the apportionment was expressly designed to discriminate on the basis of race.[22] The argument once again rests on discriminatory intent versus discriminatory effect. The effect of many apportionments may be to diminish the strength of some minority-group members, but as a general rule such effect alone without demonstrated intent is not reason to strike down apportionment plans.

Whereas the Court ruled in 1968 that local governments that performed normal governmental functions are required to adhere to the *Reynolds* rules, some exception is made for the variety of local boards that act as governments but do not perform ''normal governmental activities.'' Thus the Court permitted the granting of 37,825 votes to a private company and only one vote to a small landowner when apportioning the votes for a water district in California in 1973,[23] using water appropriation rights rather than number of residents as a basis. It also permitted malapportionment of a water district, which handled the touchy political question of nuclear power in Arizona in 1981.[24]

In 1989, the U. S. Supreme Court found that the New York City Board of Estimate and Taxation was established unconstitutionally because borough representation was not based on population. The board had had a powerful voice in budget making, zoning, land use, and city contracts, serving in these areas as a second house of the city council. Opponents of the ruling in the smallest borough, Staten Island (Richmond), immediately sought to secede from the city, with leaders arguing that Staten Island residents would lose all influence in city politics without the special allocation of representatives on the board.

> *Gerrymandering:* **The process of apportioning for political gain. All apportionment involves gerrymandering usually for partisan reasons. But opponents of gerrymandering generally have advocated less overt partisanship and adherence to a one-person, one-vote principle.**

The Process of Reapportionment

The law that reapportions a state is passed like any other; it is therefore the legislators themselves who apportion, subject to the governor's veto. (Strictly speaking, it is residents who are apportioned or distributed apportionally. It is the precise drawing

of districts for each of the portions, or redistricting, that is of major political significance.) The Court's role in dealing with apportionment has not extended to the most
important force involved, which is partisan political gain. The courts assumed jurisdiction over reapportionment reluctantly and only after a number of cases in which
jurisdiction was refused. But once the Court's decisions were clear, state legislators
began adopting processes that would comply with the new rules but still protect their
incumbency and partisan concerns. Not only is *gerrymandering* still permitted, but it
continues to be an inherent factor in all reapportionment. The question is not *whether*
political gain for some and loss for others exist is apportionment, but *who* will gain or
lose. Gerrymandering for strictly political gain is not reason enough for Court interference. The express desire to gain partisan advantage or protect incumbents is not
treated with the same degree of scrutiny as racial bias. Thus the Court would permit
Connecticut to consider party strength in its reapportionment after the 1970 census,[25]
whereas Indiana Republicans were permitted to apportion so as to maintain their majority despite a Democratic majority of the population after the 1980 census.[26] Some
have heralded the Indiana case as a departure from past precedent in that the Court
agreed that some forms of gerrymandering for partisan purposes were subject to the
Fourteenth Amendment tests, although they failed to strike down the particular plan.
Thus as the Court agrees to hear more cases involving gerrymandering, it may be
more likely to strike down more of them after the 1990 reapportionments; but the
ground rules as to what is judicially acceptable are not yet clear.

Because political considerations are always high priorities most states now follow similar processes of reapportionment. Initially, the legislature must comply with
the following rules garnered from the Court cases (assuming the usual case of single-
member districts):

1. Each legislative district for a given house must represent the same number of
   people (within acceptable deviation guidelines).
2. Each legislative district must have one line around it; that is, it must be contigu-
   ous territory.
3. The legislature must be reapportioned after each census, before the next legislative election, or at least a serious attempt must be made and efforts continued
   until success is achieved (a court retains jurisdiction over an incomplete case
   before it).

(Multimember districts will challenge rule 1 by allowing different-sized districts with
different numbers of representatives as long as the one-person, one-vote rule is followed.)

Additional rules for whatever political or practical reasons may legally bind
those doing the redistricting as long as they do not violate Court rules in regard to the
national Constitution. For example, many states require the legislative districts to be
"compact," preventing some forms of gerrymandering. Wisconsin typifies many
such state rules by adding three in its constitution:

1. The legislative districts must be "bounded by county, precinct, town, or ward
   lines."

2. The districts must be "as compact as practicable."
3. No assembly district may be divided in creating a senate district.

As long as the rules are followed, other practices may be used to seek political gain. When the federal courts reapportioned Wisconsin after a Republican governor and a Democratic legislature could not agree on a plan, the courts upheld a second reapportionment after a Democratic governor was elected. The rules noted above did not prohibit repeated reapportionments within a ten-year period.

Each state must differ because of its unique circumstances. Wisconsin's rules 1 and 3 above could not possibly be applied in California. The role of the courts is only a last resort, and a court will interfere only when challenge is brought by an offended party who has standing (that is, it is the legally correct court in which to bring the case). As a result, *numerous violations of the rules can be found; which the courts have never been asked to correct* or which have been upheld by lower courts departing from precedent, confident that no appeal will be taken. Usually the Court's role is simply to set the initial parameters of reapportionment; the process is almost always controlled by the legislature. The demands of reformers have led a few states to turn over the reapportionment process to nonpartisan commissions.

Decisions about precisely where boundary lines are drawn can drastically affect the distribution of power of each party, as figure 11-1 shows. Usually it is the legislature most remote from the last census, the one sitting at the time of the new census, that does the reapportionment. As a result, the legislators come from districts that might be badly malapportioned after a decade of population shifts. As the law moves through the legislative process, legislators must therefore consider which priorities will be maximized in the process. Past voting records are studied to identify concentrations of party voters. In some respects the legislators' decisions are based on conventional political concerns, but because reapportionment will determine their likelihood of reelection, the partisanship of reapportionment is intense and the legislators' interest in reapportionment is usually unmatched. Whereas each legislator is concerned with reelection, as illustrated in simplified example (see figure 11-1), an apportionment plan that maximizes the likelihood of reelection does not necessarily maximize the benefit to the majority party. In an area apportioned into three districts and five parts Democratic to four Republican, plan 1 probably would produce a 3–0 Democratic victory, whereas plan 2 probably would produce a 2–1 Democratic victory. Plan 2 would be safer for incumbent Democrats in the top part of the area but less beneficial to the party areawide. Plan 1 would be better to the party as a whole, though more risky to each Democrat running. A legislator must decide which priorities take precedence when voting for a reapportionment plan.

Usually, when the same party controls both houses of the legislature as well as the governorship, the first concern is protecting incumbents of both parties. But equally important may be increasing party control of the legislature. Ironically, this may be done by creating districts that are safest for the minority party, thus concentrating their votes in a few districts and allowing the majority vote to spread to the maximum number of districts. Frequently care is taken to protect incumbents of both parties so that, for example, no two incumbent legislators will find themselves running in the same district. With the knowledge that some members of both parties will

Figure 11–1: How the Shape and Boundaries of Districts Affect the Power of Political
                Parties

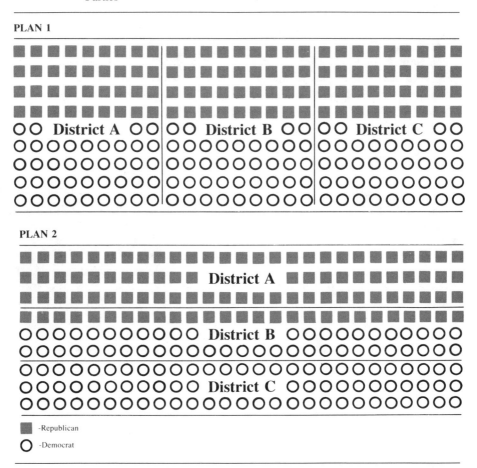

PLAN 1

PLAN 2

■ -Republican

○ -Democrat

win, long-held friendships with the minority party members may be served in this
process. Furthermore, minority party incumbents may be protected to lessen the ac-
cusation of gerrymandering. Voters cannot complain easily when "their" legislator
has won, the process has obeyed the law, but alas the other party wins control.

  If the majority party has declined in size since the last apportionment, it may be
necessary to apportion in a way that likely will give some seats to the opposition at the
expense of the majority. Volunteers might be produced by appointing the likely losers
to judgeships or other attractive posts. Those with proven strength in winning votes in
marginal districts also may be gerrymandered into such districts. But why put successful politicians at risk? Ultimately, this scenario involves the nasty business of deciding
who has been less faithful to the party and therefore is more expendable. Even though
the American party system is in decline, as discussed earlier, the prospect of a difficult
reapportionment may strengthen the legislative parties by giving the legislator incen-

tive to obey party dictates so that he or she will be well treated in the apportionment process, at least in those years just before and just after the end of a decade.

When different parties control different parts of the apportionment process, political deals must be struck to reach a compromise. Without such deals, the courts will be forced to apportion in response to suits brought by people who have become un- derrepresented since the last census. For example, a Republican governor in a state whose legislature is Democratic will have to decide not simply whether the plan that comes from the legislature benefits Republicans, but whether a court will likely pro- duce a better or worse plan. If the matter goes to court, as it almost assuredly will, the court (federal if the national Constitution is alleged to be violated, state if the state rules are involved) will pay less concern to incumbency than the legislators do. As a result, if at all possible the court will not be allowed to apportion. The courts can be involved only when the legislative process breaks down either because of a refusal to act or a violation of the law.

The Effects of Reapportionment

In theory, the reapportionment decisions of the Supreme Court were designed to ben- efit the growing urban and suburban populations and reduce the impact of rural legis- lators. Advocates of the decisions believed that anyone from underrepresented dis- tricts should benefit by an apportionment plan, which followed the one-person, one-vote principle.

In practice, the result is unclear. Gerrymandering by incumbent legislators has produced legal plans that maintain control by groups expected to decline in power. Concern for protecting incumbency and increasing majority party power continues to abound. Belief that gerrymandering somehow can be eliminated is unfounded. Parti- sanship is inherent in the process, even when nonpartisan commissions or judges do the apportioning. A California case study concludes that reformers' attempts to take the process out of politics reduces the fairness of the process by reducing the number of groups represented in the process, and "it is doubtful that any reapportioner would ever be above partisan suspicion, regardless of the stringency of the selection criteria applied."[27]

From a study of six states, Timothy O'Rourke suggests different levels of ef- fects of reapportionment. Predictably, in states with greater malapportionment be- fore the reapportionment rulings, changes were more pronounced in favor of urban representation. For example in New Jersey and Delaware, greater suburban repre- sentation was found after reapportionment; in Tennessee, Kansas, and New Jersey, greater black representation. But institutional factors reduced the likelihood that such changes would carry over into the leadership of the legislature. Leadership changes in houses and committees did occur, but at a lower rate than the turnover of the legis- lature as a whole. Most important, O'Rourke concludes that "the overall influence of reapportionment on policy has been rather limited and immeasurable."[28]

As the rest of this chapter and the next will attest, other major changes are oc- curring in state legislatures. For example, the professionalization of legislators seems to be occurring at a faster pace than are policy changes in response to appor- tionment. Further, party power continues to decline. The effects of these other factors are often easy to measure and may be so intricately mixed with apportionment that it would be impossible to recognize the real effects of apportionment. The function of state governments in the American political system is based on tradition and ideology. Urbanites have neglected state government as a possible source of assistance with their problems in both well-apportioned and malapportioned states. If the attitudes of political leaders and opinion molders in society toward state governments were to change, the result might be a substantial increase in the importance of state government and the extent of apportionment on the basis of population could become more significant. Finally, it is possible that reapportionment will have reduced effects as the population continues to shift from central city to suburb and as regional and central city demographic differences with suburbs continue to decrease. If districts in a state become more alike, they will likely elect similar-minded legislators. The apportionment of districts is only as significant as the differences in the legislators elected from differing constituencies.

Apportionment of local boards may become more important than the apportionment of the state legislatures. The possibility of at-large apportionment at the local level makes the options greater. Minority groups are far more often potential majorities in the small local districts elected by wards than in larger legislative districts created by at-large systems. At-large districts are therefore more likely to come under the scrutiny of those who would use the courts to protect against the diminishment of electoral power through reapportionment plans. Legal or political battles to keep district apportionment and to fight at-large or discriminatory apportionment plans will be the most likely apportionment issues of the next decade.

Members of the Legislatures

Given the state preference for district representation, legislature membership varies, depending to some extent on district demographics. Information about membership may be available only by consulting the particular legislature in question, and even then records may not be kept beyond the measure of the present pattern.

Career or Traditional State Legislator?

For most of America's history, the task of representing friends and neighbors by serving in the legislature was thought to be a citizen's duty. Pay was low, rarely an acceptable living wage. The legislative session was a short part of the year. Seats were usually occupied, in pre-1850 America, either by well-to-do persons with a sense of social obligation (and a desire to protect their wealth) or by farmers who had a minimum of chores between harvest and spring planting. Social changes brought demands for change. Working-class representatives could ill afford to become legislators unless the pay was good or they were paid by a trade union or other source while attending sessions. Even today, the general emphasis on getting ahead makes legislative service a liability rather than an asset for all but a few, such as members of the legal profession. Most lawyers, especially young ones, like the contacts they make and find that serving a few terms at the state capital can be a means of good and ethical advertising. Similarly, some business leaders are encouraged by their firms to seek legislative seats. Some businesses have a policy of granting a leave of absence during sessions to any salaried employee who is elected to the legislature. And the increasing number of public employees who run for the legislature—particularly teachers—enjoy job protection in many states or localities.

The conflict between legislative and other careers however, depends greatly on where a particular legislature stands on the continuum from traditional to professional. Patterns vary widely from the traditional to the career legislator.[29] Many states have characteristics of both, but here we will describe the extremes. The traditional legislator serves in a state with a legislature of normal size but a small population, where sessions are short and few bills of a general nature pass, where staff support is highly partisan and limited, and where the election process is relatively easy for incumbents who depend on party organization. The members are unlikely to think of politics as a career. Professional legislators, on the other hand, are similar to members of Congress in that they work on legislative business beyond the formal legislative sessions, their states have relatively long legislative sessions, and the legislators see themselves principally as politicians who can do the job properly only with the support of a professional staff. The "other" job, which most continue to maintain at least minimally is seen by the legislator as something to go back to after the legislative career ends or as a secondary source of income. Legislators in many districts must muster sizable funds for election campaigns and may have to organize or pay professional campaign staffs if the party is weak. Conflicts with their other careers may force the politico to choose between a full-time legislative career or leaving the legislature. The professional usually is younger and better educated than the traditional legislator. If politics is to be a career, the legislature may turn out to be the first step on the way to higher office. Many political hopefuls may not yet recognize this, but the perspective is changing as legislative salaries and perquisites change.[30]

A 1986 study found that "more than 60 percent of the legislators in New York and Pennsylvania define their occupation as legislator." In total "eleven percent of all state lawmakers consider themselves full-time legislators."[31] Furthermore, professional legislatures are more likely found in states where legislative sessions are lengthy. "The legislatures in nine states are generally considered full-time: California, Illinois, Massachusetts, Michigan, New Jersey, New York, Ohio, Pennsylvania and Wisconsin."[32] In these and other states, extended sessions mean career legislators.

The effects of vocation, a relatively new phenomenon, are not yet very well documented, but at least one effect is likely to be important: Those with a career at stake will care more than amateurs about reelection. The positive side of this may be that legislators are more concerned with the needs of their constituents but will probably have fewer contacts with them; instead, lobbyists will reflect demands. This may also increase the costs of government—legislative careerists want full-time salaries and the support devices to do a "better job," to impress constituents, and perhaps to pass more legislation. Furthermore the election process may become more costly as modern techniques are employed in elections where the stakes of losing have increased and the use of PACs is expanding. Although incumbency is a strong advantage in all state legislatures, it has become almost insurmountable where careers are at stake. As career emphasis widens, some backlash may occur. Representative Vic

Krouse of Michigan, in an effort to return to traditionalism through cutting legislative salaries by more than half, concluded: "When you spend all your time in Lansing, you're more influenced by the lobbyists than by your constituents." Taking this a step farther, he concluded that full-time legislators tried to give to their constituents the appearance of being traditionalists. "They're afraid that people will say, 'you're the kind of guy we don't want. You're one of the reasons we are one of the most heavily taxed states in the nation.' "[33]

Rich Jones, director of legislative programs for the National Conference of State Legislatures, began a series of articles on the legislature in the twenty-first century by noting the tension between tradition and professionalism felt by legislators and the degree to which forces in the process will decide the issue in the future:

> . . . current and former legislators, political scientists and media representatives—generally agreed that legislatures should try to avoid becoming highly professional bodies like the U.S. Congress. These observers thought the inability of congressional leaders to forge consensus on important issues such as the budget deficit, sky-high campaign costs, a heavy reliance on staff, and career members who become entrenched incumbents, make Congress a less than enviable model to follow. . .
>
> Because of the strong emotional and philosophical commitment to the traditional part-time model, it is likely that legislatures will resist the trends pushing them toward full-time status. . . . .
>
> But legislatures can only squeeze so much wasted time from the current process. The trends pushing legislatures toward becoming full-time institutions are strong and, as issues become more complex, are likely to get stronger. . . .
>
> When sessions convene in the year 2011 there are likely to be more full-time legislatures than in 1990, and fewer purely part-time bodies. The states in the middle of these two extremes, while not yet full-time will likely be headed in that direction.[34]

Prior to 1970, about two-thirds of all legislators were lawyers, farmers, or business persons, but this figure declined to about one-half by the late 1980s. Very few skilled craftsmen or hourly employees of any kind are members. But many legislators have several occupations. A favorite device is for persons who own farms to list themselves as farmers, though a tenant may do the work and the "farmer" live in the city. Furthermore, the full-time legislator may list the occupation he or she hopes to go back to, rather than the current occupation. Lawyers, traditionally the mainstay of legislatures, are on the decline in numbers. Lawyers have tended to be younger than others when first elected to the legislature and were also younger at retirement. They were more likely than others to retire voluntarily but more likely to remain in politics afterwards. As legislators, lawyers had many interests and did not usually vote as a bloc on policy matters.[35] Even though legislative service is still helpful to young lawyers, advertising now allows them to publicize services more directly and makes the years in the state capital less important to them, though the personal contacts can still be significant.

Nationwide occupation totals may be misleading. Regional or state variations may differ immensely from the national trend. The National Conference of State Legislatures' 1986 study reported that the number of farmers remained constant, but it found that the number declined by 12 percent in South Dakota while increasing almost 5 percent in both Iowa and Kansas (see table 11–2).[36] Rule changes affecting a particular occupation (for example, limitations on session length) may permit some the time necessary to go to the legislature and not others. The attractiveness of the legislative career, the social mores in regard to a given occupation, or altered economic circumstances, may produce a changing pattern of occupations. The legislatures, once dominated by businesspeople, farmers, and lawyers, are now more open to others—especially, in an increasing number of states, to the occupation called *legislator*.

The civil rights movement of the 1950s and 1960s greatly affected membership in the legislatures, resulting in a dramatic increase in the number of black legislators elected. Earlier, black and Hispanic members were so few nationwide that national percentages were not reported. The increase has resulted from judicial reapportionment rulings creating districts of concentrated black population, switching from multimember districts to the smaller single-member districts, the continuing urbanization of blacks and Hispanics (and hence their concentration in identifiable areas rather than their dispersion in rural areas), and their increasing propensity to vote and run for public office, particularly blacks in the South. White voters are also increasingly voting for black candidates, although this phenomenon is manifested more in mayoral rather than legislative races. In 1985, blacks held 385 (5.2 percent) legislative seats and Hispanics 108 (1.4 percent). Although apportionment changes increased minority representation, the concentration of minority-group members in some districts also contributes to the likelihood that they will be underrepresented in legislatures.

In recent years, the legislative milieu has been modified by more women members (see table 11–3). The overall number of women has quadrupled since 1969; ranging in 1987 from 32.5 percent in New Hampshire to 2.3 percent in Mississippi.[37] It is difficult to measure the effects of women legislators in terms of public policy, although other effects, especially personal effects on those involved, are significant. For example, Minnesota's Mary Forsythe noted that she was seen as an oddity when first elected in 1973. Up to the time of her election, only seventeen women had been elected to the Minnesota legislature. ''When we first came, lobbyists used to address

TABLE 11–2   Occupations of Legislators

	1976	1986
Lawyers	22%	16%
Business owners	16%	14%
Legislators	n.a.	11%
Farmers	10%	10%
Business managers/employees	9%	9%
Retired/homemakers/students	n.a.	9%
Educators	8%	8%

Source: Andrea Paterson, ''Is the Citizen Legislator Becoming Extinct?'' *State Legislatures* 12 (July 1986):6. The 1986 figures are from a survey conducted by the National Conference of State Legislatures. The 1976 figures are from a survey conducted by the Insurance Information Institute.
N.a.: not available.

TABLE 11-3   Women in State Legislatures

1969	4%
1975	8%
1979	10%
1987	16%

Source: National Information Bank on Women in Public Office.

[the members of] committees as 'gentlemen.' They don't do that anymore.''[38] In the 1980s, women from both political parties were chosen majority leader of the Minnesota House of Representative. One legislator concludes that the ''woman's approach to legislative leadership is likely to favor consensus building and collaboration over confrontation. Moreover women leaders are likely to be sympathetic to women in need and to education.''[39] This was substantiated in a 1987 study of women office-holders, which found that ''78% of women but only 47% of men think the Equal Rights Amendment should be ratified; 57% of the men and 80% of the women oppose a Constitutional amendment to prohibit abortion; and 39% of the women and 26% of the men disagree with the statement, 'If left alone, except for essential federal regulations, the private sector can find ways to solve our economic problems.' ''[40] Because women are three times more likely to hold seats in state legislatures than in Congress, it is likely that the state legislatures will become a battleground for those few policy areas where men and women differ greatly.

County and Township Boards

Some attention already has been given in chapters 7 and 8 to the size and patterns of local governing boards. The detail concerning these various bodies is too complicated to summarize here. An inquiry at the county, town, or township clerk's office should produce detailed information concerning any specific local unit of government.

Virtually all local governing bodies are now unicameral. The meeting pattern is different from that of the state legislature in that local bodies usually meet once a week or once a month, rather than in the periodic long session that is dictated for legislatures by the distances some members live from the capital. Governing bodies with large memberships, especially county boards under the supervisor system, are likely to allow important decisions to be made by small committees of the board, with the full body simply voting for or against the committee's recommendations. Such committees may also perform administrative tasks. For example, a police and fire committee may interview candidates for the police department and choose the chief. Some smaller boards use the committee system too, but these are likely to operate even more informally than does the state legislature; and the close in group relationship that springs up in bodies of fewer than ten persons (for example) is likely to be the dominant consideration in law making. Relationships are personal rather than party or constituency oriented and pressures for unanimity are great.

Some board members, especially in counties under the commissioner system, are likely to make a career of membership. Otherwise, members may be drawn from almost any walk of life. Most members are of good standing in their neighborhood, performing a task they interpret as a civic responsibility. They seek to carry to board deliberations what they believe to be the consensus in the neighborhood.

City Councils

No comprehensive studies of city councils or county boards have ever been made. No institution—neither private foundations concerned about democracy, the U.S. Bureau of the Census, nor national organizations of cities and city officials—has ever developed a profile of councils by size of city, form of government, occupation of council members, relationship to the political process, organizational structure, agendas through time, patterns of leadership, and other information that has been collected on Congress and many state legislatures. Although certainly not complete, the most extensive and valuable information is to be found in the survey of cities of over five thousand in population shown in the *Municipal Year Book*, published by the International City Management Association.

The pattern of functions of members of the council varies with the forms of city government. In weak-mayor cities, for example, each member, in addition to sharing the policy-making duties, commonly serves as a ward supervisor handling administrative functions. On the other hand, in council-manager cities, a council member normally has only policy-making duties.

Council salaries are generally fixed at a low rate, perhaps a few hundred dollars a year (or nothing at all), to discourage candidates motivated by salary. In largest cities, council members may be paid a full salary, though this is highly unusual. Washington, D.C.; Los Angeles; and Portland, Oregon, paid their members top salaries, over $43,000, in 1983.[41] Pay is likely to be highest, other conditions being equal, in commission-type cities, where council members are also administrators.[42] A 1981 survey found that 86 percent of councils paid their members.[43]

Terms of council members range from one year to six years. The four-year term has become the most common and is more likely to be found in larger than in smaller cities. The size of councils ranges from two members in several cities to Chicago's fifty. The size of the council roughly increases with the city's population, though form of government is also a factor. Small cities are likely to have councils of five or fewer members; large cities commonly have no more than nine, however. Weak-mayor cities have larger councils than other types. Councils that elect all members at once may have serious orientation problems, although many members will be incumbents. As a result; about three-fourths of the cities stagger the election of members so that terms overlap and some members will always be accustomed to the local rules of the game.[44]

All councils are now unicameral, although at the beginning of the century, about one-third of cities of over 25,000 had bicameral councils. With the successes of the efficiency and economy reform movement, the emphasis on the council as a *representative* body declined as illustrated in Philadelphia. Prior to a 1919 charter change, it had an upper house with 20 members and a lower one with 120. Six lower-house council members and one upper-house member were elected from each council

TABLE 11–4   Women and Minority-group Council Members

White	Black	Hispanic	Male	Female
94.8%	3.5%	1.3%	87.2%	12.8%

Source: Mary Schellinger, "Council Profile," *Baseline Data Reports* 15:1–13, International City Management Association, Washington, May 1983. Although 6,761 cities were surveyed, varying numbers were reported for each question.

district. After the change, only one board of twenty members remained to represent a city whose population approached 2 million in 1920. The reformulation is indicative of the much greater rate of change that has taken place in city as compared with state government.[45]

Nineteenth-century city council members usually were elected by wards, but 60 percent of the cities of more than five thousand population now elect members at-large, another one-fourth of the cities elect members with a mixed system of at least some at-large members, and a much greater percentage of the smaller cities elect members at-large. In large cities, serious questions of representativeness have been raised by the practice of electing but a few council members, and all of them at-large.[46] Individual citizens have, in these cities, lost their traditional direct contact with representatives. Almost three-fourths of American cities now elect council members on a ballot without party designation. This practice, especially common in council-manager cities, again reduces the supports for direct representation of citizen demands.[47]

The election of black council members has increased significantly in recent years, but the percentage of blacks elected suggests continued underrepresentation. The survey reported in table 11–4 found 3.5 percent black and 1.3 percent Hispanic representation on councils.[48] Blacks, of course, may choose to vote for white council members challenged by blacks, and it is difficult to say whether underrepresentation of blacks based on their percentage of the city's population produces significantly different public policy favorable to black interest groups. It is also difficult to say whether policy discrimination has been greater against poor blacks than against other poor persons. Certainly, public bodies characteristically have given priority consideration to the more affluent members of society.

A number of factors appear to be related to black underrepresentation on councils, but the likelihood that a black will be elected is most importantly related to the method of council election used. A recent study of all American cities of over five thousand in population, finds that cities with large black populations that use district representation are more than twice as likely to elect black council members than are such cities that use at-large representation.[49] These kinds of conclusions have supported the lawsuits challenging at-large representation. As discussed earlier the debate continues in the courts over whether discriminatory *intent* on the part of charter makers must be shown in this regard, or only discriminatory *effect*.

The pattern of women representation on councils follows the patterns and ef-

TABLE 11–5   Occupations of Council Members

Lawyers	Other Professionals	Business Executives	Business Employees	Homemakers	Teachers	Retired
3.9%	7.9%	31.0%	24.3%	5.1%	8.4%	11.7%

Source: Mary Schellinger, "Council Profile," *Baseline Data Reports* 15:1–13, International City Management Association, Washington, May 1983. Although 6,761 cities were surveyed, varying numbers were reported for each question.

fects found in regard to state legislatures. According to the most recent data available, shown in table 11-4, 12.8 percent of council members surveyed were women.

In most American cities, council members typically are local merchants—well respected, active in civic organizations, and college graduates (see table 11–5). Some run for the council because of the prestige and publicity the position affords, or because they believe the prominence of the position will help business; but many act from a sense of community responsibility. They usually are not among the top of the business leadership in earnings and standing. Typically, they are above-average in intelligence, but it is not necessary for the council members to be leading members of the city; if it has a few able leaders, that is enough, for the plodding type who will accept and follow that leadership is also needed.

Generally, as cities increase in size, the prominence of council members tends to decrease. In the largest cities, they may well work full-time at city hall and may have run for the office partly because of the salary involved or as an initial step in a political career. Although venal and corrupt council members were once commonly found in these large cities, they are now a rarity. Today council members can look forward to good jobs as lobbyists if they wish to leave public office or to other positions in firms that want reliable access to city decision makers. The greatest sins of the council members in the metropolis today are likely to be in their allegiance to particular interest groups—real estate boards, labor unions, builders and contractors, liquor dealers, downtown merchants. The council members are likely to view their function as that of protecting these particular pressure groups, although they invariably claim to act "for all the people." In differing degrees, this same pattern may be found as cities decrease in size, but the value consensus that generally exists in smaller communities makes loyalty to interest groups a less-important factor: nearly everyone agrees on what is right and wrong and on the general limits within which public policy should be established.

Concluding Note

We have examined how a legislature is put together, what it does, and how its membership is chosen. In the next chapter, we will move from the *what* of a legislature to the *how* of it—from what a legislature *is* to how it *works*. We will delineate the process of law creation and look at how people and organizations are represented and to what degree.

Notes

1. Richard L. Neuberger, "I Go to the Legislature," *Survey Graphic* 30 (July 1941):373*ff*

2. Ibid., 374.

3. William T. Pound, "The State Legislatures," *1988–1989 Book of the States* (Lexington, KY: Council of State Governments, 1988), 76–83.

4. Ibid.

5. 1950–1951 totals from Thomas R. Dye, "State Legislative Politics," in Herbert Jacob and Kenneth N. Vines, eds., *Politics in the American States: A Comparative Analysis* (Boston: Little, Brown, 1965), 152; 1980's totals computed by the authors from the *1988–1989 Book of the States,* 114–17.

6. See Adam C. Breckenridge, *One House for Two* (Washington, DC: Public Affairs Press, 1958); George S. Blair, *American Legislatures* (New York: Harper & Row 1967), 141–45.

7. Lloyd B. Omdahl, "Drive for Unicameralism Needs National Support," *National Civic Review* 63 (Nov. 1974):526–30.

8. Specific totals for particular states can be found in the latest edition of the *Book of the States.*

9. Ibid.

10. See chapters 7 and 8.

11. *Baker* v. *Carr,* 369 U.S. 186 (1962). Earlier significant cases were *Fergus* v. *Marks,* 321 III. 510 (1926); *Magraw* v. *Donovan,* 163 F. Supp. 1589 (1958), dismissed after legislature reapportioned, 177 F. Supp. 803 (1959); and *Colegrove* v. *Green,* 328 U.S. 549 (1946).

12. *Gray* v. *Sanders,* 371 U.S. 821 (1963).

13. The court used the term *one-man, one-vote* in the early apportionment cases; it would change to *one-person, one-vote* by the early 1970s cases. We use the contemporary term throughout the discussion.

14. *Westberry* v. *Sanders,* 376 U.S. 1 (1964).

15. *Reynolds* v. *Sims,* 377 U.S. 533 (1964).

16. *Lucas* v. *Colorado General Assembly,* 377 U.S. 713 (1964).

17. A. Spencer Hill, "The Reapportionment Decisions: A Return to Dogma?" *Journal of Politics* 31 (Feb. 1969):186–213. See also the dissenting opinions of Justice John Marshall Harlan in the apportionment cases.

18. Ruth C. Silva, "One Man, One Vote and the Population Base," in R. A. Goldwin, ed., *Representation and Misrepresentation* (Chicago: Rand McNally 1968), 53–70.

19. *Brown* v. *Thomson,* 462 U.S. 835 (1983).

20. *Mahan* v. *Howell,* 410 U.S. 315 (1973).

21. *Avery* v. *Midland County,* 390 U.S. 374 (1968).

22. For the state ruling, see *Whitcome* v. *Chavis,* 403 U.S. 123 (1971).

23. *Salyer Land Co.* v. *Tulare Water District,* 410 U.S. 719 (1973). Involved here was the western "appropriation doctrine," in which water rights are bought and sold, and not the more common "riparian doctrine," in which abutting landowners are entitled to reasonable use.

24. *Ball* v. *James,* 451 U.S. 355 (1981).

25. *Gaffney* v. *Cummings,* 412 U.S. 735 (1971)

26. *Davis* v. *Bandemener,* 106 S. Ct. 2797 (1986).

27. Bruce E. Cain, *The Reapportionment Puzzle* (Berkeley: University of California Press, 1984), 182–83.

28. Information in the paragraph is taken from Timothy G. O'Rourke, *The Impact of Reapportionment* (New Brunswick, NJ: Transaction Books, 1980), chapter 7; the quotation is at 151.

29. Alan Rosenthal, *Legislative Life: People, Process, and Performance in the States* (New York: Harper & Row, 1981), particularly 57–60.

30. Ibid., 58. Also see *State Legislators' Occupations: A Decade of Change* (Denver: National Conference of State Legislatures, 1987).

31. Andrea Paterson, "Is the Citizen Legislator Becoming Extinct?" *State Legislatures* 12 (July, 1986):22–25; the quotation is at 23.

32. Ibid.

33. Ibid., 24.

34. Rich Jones, "The Legislatures 2010: Which Direction?" *State Legislatures* 16 (July 1990):22–25.

35. David R. Derge, "The Lawyer in the Indiana Assembly," *Midwest Journal of Political Science* 6 (Feb. 1962):19–53; Leon D. Epstein, *Politics in Wisconsin* (Madison: University of Wisconsin Press, 1958), 111–15.

36. Paterson, "Is the Citizen Extinct?", 22.

37. "Number of Women in State Legislatures Increases Yearly," *State Legislatures* 13 (Oct. 1987):7.

38. *Minneapolis Star and Tribune*, Feb. 2, 1987, 15A.

39. Reported in "Women in State Legislatures and Local Office," *State Policy Reports* 54 (June 1988):21, from data collected by The Center for the American Woman and Politics, Eagleton Institute of Politics, Rutgers University, New Brunswick, N.J.

40. Vera Katz, "Women Chart New Legislative Course," *The Journal of State Government* (Sept./Oct. 1987):213.

41. Mary Schellinger, "Council Profile," *Baseline Data Reports* 15 (May 1983):12 (Washington, D.C.: International City Management Association).

42. For pay in specific cities, see the most recent issue of the *Municipal Year Book* (Washington, D.C.: International City Management Association).

43. Schellinger, "Council Profile," 12.

44. Ibid., 4.

45. See Charles R. Adrian, *A History of American City Government, 1920–1945* (Lanham MD: University Press of America, 1987) chapter 2.

46. Charles R. Adrian, "Forms of City Government in American History," *Municipal Year Book, 1988*, 8.

47. Tari Renner, "Municipal Election Processes: The Impact on Minority Representation," *Municipal Year Book, 1988*, 14.

48. Schellinger "Council Profile," 7.

49. Renner, "Municipal Election Processes," 19. The findings are similar to those found a decade earlier by Albert K. Karnig, "Black Representation on City Councils," *Urban Affairs Quarterly* 12 (Dec. 1976):223–43; and by Thomas R. Dye and Theodore P. Robinson, "Reformism and Black Representation on City Councils," *Social Science Quarterly* 59 (June 1978): 133–41. The findings are also substantiated by Richard L. Engstrom and Michael D. McDonald, "The Election of Blacks to City Councils: Clarifying the Impact of Electoral Arrangements on the Seats/Population Relationship," *American Political Science Review* 75 (June 1981):344–54. Here the claim of black underrepresentation is not established, but rather a measure of a different variable such as socioeconomic status is challenged.

Reprinted with permission of the Rocky Mountain News

12

The Legislative Process and Representation

E xcept for the limited use of the initiative and referendum, modern democracy is of the representative type (see chapter 5). We therefore should understand what is meant by representation. One authority has described it as "primarily a frame of mind, reflecting a process of social communication that often changes in important respects without disturbing the outward appearance of political institutions . . . [it is] the agreement prevailing between the ruler and the ruled."[1]

How does the legislature do its job in order to preserve that agreement between the rulers and the ruled? In this chapter we will look at some meanings of representation and the legislative process that seeks to provide it.

Representation

Who represents the individual in the making of public policy? It is possible for someone to vote for a liberal governor from one party, a middle-of-the-road representative for the lower house of the legislature from another party, and a conservative member of the state senate from the governor's party. Can all these represent one individual? Suppose that one belongs to a powerful labor union that lobbies for a particular program regarding state grants in aid to public schools but that one's representatives on the local school board oppose this program, the governor (for whom the individual also voted) has another plan, and one's favorite radio station urges legislators to abandon grants-in-aid altogether. Just who is representing this individual's interests?[2]

Society and its governments are able to operate because, although within each individual there is a degree of antagonism, conflict, and competition with every other individual, there is also a degree of common purpose. In relation to every other individual, therefore, a combination of shared interests and potential conflicts exists. The intensity of the relationship varies greatly, and in modern society each of us is handicapped because we do not know all the others with whom we are in agreement or conflict. To make the situation even more complex, within each individual is a perceived conflict between personal interests and the

337

community's interests. One's representatives must try to reflect both of these interests.

Two Sets of Roles

The role of the legislator in representing the interests of the constituent will be governed by a number of factors. A widely used study of Congress can be applied to the
state legislatures.[3] That study measured the use of three different models of representation: the responsible-party model, the instructed-delegate model, and the Burkean
model. The *responsible-party model* holds that legislators look to their political party
for leadership and statement of legislative principles. The party leaders generate
some consensus on a given issue among members and the legislator votes with the
party, expecting sanction if they disobey. The model predicts that the legislator will
determine the party position and vote accordingly. In the *instructed-delegate model*
the legislator's obligation is to vote in the legislature the way a majority of the constituents want. The model predicts that the legislator will determine the voter's demand
and vote accordingly. The *Burkean model*, following the thought of British philoso-
pher Edmund Burke (1729–1797), holds that when legislators believe an action is in
the best interest of their constituents, they should act according to that judgment, if
necessary ignoring constituent preferences.

Each of these models has fundamental flaws. The party model *assumes* that the
party can control its members and that it can reach policy decisions. The American
system provides few mechanisms for such control. The instructed-delegate model
assumes that the legislator can determine the view of the voter and that voters have
clear views. In practice this is difficult for most issues. The Burkean model *assumes*
that the legislator has the capacity to decide complex and technical issues. In reality,
even the best-educated and best-informed legislators can be expert on only a few issues, relying more often on the advice of the "experts in the field," either through the
interplay between legislators and members of the executive and administrative
branches of government or through the intervention of lobbyists. Nevertheless, each
of the three models explains the behavior of some legislators on some issues. The
model that best explains a vote of the legislature may differ depending on the issue or
process or circumstance of the particular issue.

Some legislators may not be concerned with their proper role. In a Connecticut
study by James Barber, four roles were identified, each of which suggests different
types of representation by the activity of state legislators. Some legislators were categorized as "spectators." In general, these persons attended sessions regularly but did
not introduce many bills or participate in debate. They found the legislative sessions
"fascinating and entertaining" and appeared to regard it as a diversion from the hum-
drum of everyday life.[4] Spectators tended to differ from other legislators in a number
of ways: they had made considerably less personal effort to get nominated, attended
far fewer meetings during the campaign, were less sought after for advice, had a
lower opinion of their ability as legislators, viewed themselves less as "politicians,"
were less interested in leadership positions, had fewer relatives who were active in
politics, and were less likely to be under 40 years of age, to have education beyond

high school, to have high incomes, to come from larger communities, or to expect income to increase in the following decade. Spectators were more willing to run for reelection than were other legislators and, in fact, did run for reelection more often than others in the two elections following the study.[5]

A second group of legislators, the "advertisers," seeks to make contacts and to publicize their businesses. About one-half of the advertisers among freshmen legislators were lawyers. Almost all others, however, were in occupations that depended on individual advisory or sales relationships with clients and customers.[6] Unlike the spectator, who is looking for entertainment and fellowship, the advertiser sees the job of legislator as a stepping-stone in a professional career. Advertisers, as a group, were more likely than the average legislator to have sought their nomination, to seek to become well known to other legislators, to offer and be sought after for advice, to secure important committee assignments, and to consider themselves superior legislators. In general, advertisers expect enough publicity in one or two terms in the legislature to satisfy their purposes.

A third type of legislator, the somewhat unusual "reluctants," serve out of a sense of obligation to society. They may be older persons who have achieved considerable success in a nonpolitical calling. They are not highly aggressive but bring to the legislature a great deal of experience. The position is not particularly prestigious, so far as they are concerned, and offers no direct economic payoffs in terms of career advancement.

Most reluctants liked campaigning more than they had expected and more than the typical freshman legislator; but once in the legislature, they quite certainly did not assume leadership positions or accept important committee posts. Having held in the past, positions of social importance, they realistically tended to consider themselves as less influential than the average legislator and graded themselves as less effective than the average.[7]

A fourth category, called "lawmakers," concentrates on the work of the legislature itself. They, "in comparison with other new members. . . appear to devote an unusual amount of attention and energy to the formulation and production of legislation. . .. On both sides of the aisle, these were the new members who came to grips with the substantive problems of the legislature and contributed considerably more than their share, proportionately, to the final result."[8] Most lawmakers were responsible for originating action that led to their nomination; they campaigned hard and attended many meetings during the campaign. They were anxious to become known to other members of the legislature, were sought out by members seeking advice, and had a high opinion of themselves as legislators. They regarded themselves as "politicians," for the most part, and were far more interested in seeking leadership positions than were typical legislators. They were also more willing to run for three or more future sessions of the legislature, and a disproportionate number of them did in fact run for reelection to a third term. However, this was in part a result of their having moved into other governmental positions; indeed 94 percent sought some governmental office, including that of legislator, after their first session. In some cases, lawmakers did not run for reelection because they were promoted to more important and more time-consuming positions in their own (nonpolitical) occupations.

Legislators and Their Constituencies

According to political scientist Heinz Eulau,[9] legislators sense a need to consider the welfare of the state as a whole, but they concentrate on their own districts, where they can see three possible roles for themselves.

In their role as "errand runners," legislators regard their tasks as those of helping constituents with their particular problems and defending the interests of the district. This role probably applies to local government as well as to state legislators.

Some members see their principal job as keeping people informed. Like errand runners, "communicators" are oriented chiefly toward their own districts. To them their most important activities are answering all mail promptly, making frequent speeches in their own districts, and appearing in the media whenever possible.

"Mentors" view their job mainly in terms of their responsibility to explain events and policies to constituents. They tend to be oriented toward the problems of the state as a whole, as they see them, rather than toward those of a particular district. They see the job as one of explaining to constituents why "what is good for the state is good for the district."

Lobbying

The old-style professional lobbyist, carrying a black bag filled with temptation, is a passing character on the political scene.[10] Today, the most effective lobbyists generally are officers of influential organized groups, respected citizens who do careful research and whose sense of ethics are in accord with the society in which they live. A 1986 study of the states found 33,000 such lobbyists at the state level, with 3,500 in Florida alone.[11] The term *lobbyist* continues to carry the old *negative* connotation, but influence is now exerted on a different plane, and inducements are usually much more subtle. As described in earlier chapters, Madison warned of the influence of interest groups at the founding of the Republic (see chapter 2). Whereas many have sought to reduce the influence of the lobbyist through disclosure laws, campaign spending limitations, public financing of elections, or outright banning of certain lobbying practices, no solution has proven more successful than Madison's novel suggestion that control of interest groups comes principally from other interest groups.

Nonmonetary enticements still have their place when lobbyists seek to explain their positions to members of a committee. Overt bribery is uncommon today (although it does exist), and the post–Watergate spending control laws of the 1970s are not likely to change the general pattern much. Lobbyists must be more creative today. For example, on important legislation, pressure groups may offer—or *imply* the offer of—campaign contributions for the next election. Sometimes they do something that reluctant legislators respond to even more surely: They threaten to finance the campaign of the legislator's opponent in the next election. For this purpose, a PAC is an effective weapon.

Who Are the Lobbyists?

Definitions of lobbyists in state statutes vary widely. Forty-three states define a lobbyist as "anyone receiving compensation to influence legislative action." Twenty-three states define a lobbyist as "anyone spending money to influence legislation."

Nineteen states define a lobbyist as "anyone representing someone else's interests," and thirteen states add "anyone attempting to influence legislation." (A number of states use more than one of these phrases in their definition.) These definitions are so difficult to pin down that most states specify what a lobbyist is *not* from a list that includes "public officials acting in an official capacity, anyone who speaks only before committees or boards, anyone with professional knowledge acting as a professional witness, members of the media, representatives of religious organizations, anyone performing professional bill drafting services," and others.[12]

Lobbyists are likely to be lawyers or executive secretaries or some other officer of interest groups. A growing number are ex-legislators who know the informal rules of the legislative process, the subtle ways to capitalize on timing and thought patterns of key legislators.

They are likely to have been frequenting legislative sessions for a longer time than have most of the members of the body. And some lobbyists also are members of the legislature; some see their interest group's agenda as equal or superior to the interests of constituents. And some lobbying firms have been established that must distinguish themselves from those in Washington in order to be effective at the state and local level. This lobbying has become big business:

> An example of the sophistication legislators face today is the complex coordinating service offered by Multistate Associates, headquartered in Great Neck, N.Y., and Washington, D.C. Multistate maintains a network of approximately 1000 state and local lobbyists across the country and matches clients with appropriate lobbyists as needed. It provides a range of services from simply reporting what is happening on particular issues in a state to strategy to direct lobbying. It also helps companies market goods to state governments. With $3 million in lobbying services last year, [the owner] says, his company is the largest single purchaser and provider of state lobbying services in the country. . . .
>
> State and Federal Associates of Alexandria, Va., is another Washington-area firm that offers to coordinate the work of state lobbyists. Bob Raven, a partner in the company, explains that his emphasis is on building unusual coalitions to work on a particular issue, then coordinating the strategy for the campaign. In promoting interstate banking, for example, he has enlisted economic development, labor, consumer and business groups, and coordinated their efforts through lobbyists for each of those groups.[13]

Raven explains further that states provide 70 percent and the localities a "growing" 10 percent of his business because they are much more likely to pass legislation than the national government.

The typical lobbyist receives a salary that is equivalent to that of a junior executive officer—and this will usually be in payment for many activities in addition to working at the capitol. But lobbyists, particularly members of lobbying firms, are becoming more sophisticated in their billing methods, often billing multiple clients for one action if it can be shown that more than one client benefited.[14]

Methods of Lobbying

Lobbyists do much of their work by giving formal testimony before legislative committees and by deluging legislators with propaganda or with letters that they outline and arrange to have mailed to legislators by the membership of their interest groups. They write bills or suggested amendments to bills and hold dinners at which they can discuss their position on matters. Lobbyists spend most of their time in the capitol or a hotel lobby engaging in light banter with legislators and other lobbyists. In the course of some of these conversations, the point of view of the lobbyist's employer will be presented—often fleetingly and unsystematically. The object of lobbying is to use the technique of projection; by creating a favorable image, lobbyists hope to encourage a similar one for their employer. The goal is to monopolize the conversation or at least to minimize the similar effort of the opposing view. At the same time, they engage in as much serious talk as the patience and interest of the particular legislator will permit. Lobbying is a subtle art, the influence of which is difficult to measure systematically.[15] But with the added enticement of PAC money in recent years, few legislators can refuse to listen.

Although some states attempt to limit the lobbying activities of state bureaucrats, the difficulty often lies in the definition of *lobbyist*. Whereas a state may legally prohibit lobbying by state employees, a vice president of the state university may spend more than half his or her time at the capitol (virtually full-time during the legislative session) to be "on call" for legislators who need information that is necessary for university legislation. The university official also is available to make a call to a favorite restaurant to bring in late dinners for staff members during the end-of-session crunch. Although not registered or called lobbyist, this individual may prove to be the most effective lobbyist in what may be the area of greatest state expenditure.

A study of lobbyists in Oklahoma concluded that the lobbyist role was not perceived in the same way by all persons performing that function. They were classified as "contractors," "informants," or "watchdogs."[16] The contracter sees the job as one of building personal acquaintanceships with legislators and serving as a communication link between interest groups and legislators. The informant sees the task as that of effectively presenting the case to a group through carefully prepared information for legislators, including frequent formal presentations to legislative committees. To this lobbyist, lobbying is likely to be public rather than private and to concentrate more on formal testimony than on light chatter over a cup of coffee or a highball. The watchdog sees the job as being one of keeping a careful eye on the legislative calendar and floor debates. This representative wants to tell a group when danger or opportunity is observed, so that it may bring pressure on legislators by whatever approaches are appropriate. A Colorado legislator, critical of the growing number of public service watchdogs, states:

> They want to have a different set of rules for the rest of the world than the ones under which they operate. They think they should receive greater standing than lobbyists for, say, a spaceship company in Colorado, that a legislator should immediately jump to respond to whatever their group brings.[17]

Ralph Haben, a lobbyist who was Speaker of the House in Florida, found considerable change in the 1980s in the number of informants:

> As a lobbyist, 10 years ago there was nobody on the other side, and now you can assume 90 percent of the time some other lobbyist will object to what you want to do.

You can work with them, compromise it out, or try to run over them. And that's not all bad.[18]

Lobby Registration and Control

In efforts to regulate lobbying, the states once again present the enigmatic character that has so long puzzled observers. Although little systematic evidence exists, it is widely believed that the states frequently are the scene of flagrant abuses of lobbying, with many tactics commonly employed that would not be tolerated if they were attempted in relation to Congress. Yet the states, or some of them, began an attempt to regulate lobbying more than a century ago, whereas lobby regulation at the national level first occurred in 1946. One observer has commented on the most widespread practice, that of disclosure:

> In the strictest sense, [lobby regulation laws] are not solutions at all. At bottom, state lobbying laws involve no more than the casual application of a wholesome general principle to some of the more visible aspects of group-legislative relationships—primarily those that can be described as ''lobbying.'' This principle has been called ''disclosure.'' It rests on the old-fashioned belief that, in a democracy, the public interest is always served by the widest possible diffusion of information about matters of public consequence or interest. It further holds that when such information is wanting, withheld, or otherwise unavailable, government should require that it be disclosed. The disclosure principle is as simple as that. It assumes no benefits or uses in advance. It assumes only that if men had access to the facts, they will seek them out and put them to whatever use their preference and needs dictate.[19]

Although lobby control laws date from 1792, Massachusetts was the first state (1890) to require systematic disclosure of activities by lobbyists. This became the most common form of lobby legislation. By 1990, every state required some form of disclosure, forty-one states requiring disclosure of gifts to individual legislators or staff, twenty-seven requiring disclosure of the total amount spent by a lobbyist, and twelve requiring lobbyists to disclose their sources of income. Legislation requiring disclosure generally was written hastily, borrowed from a neighboring state usually when charges were being made that legislators had been unduly influenced by lobbyists or were in danger of being subverted.[20] Some states are shifting the burden to the public official, requiring legislators and staff members to file a form disclosing any expenditure made for their benefit over a specified (relatively small) amount. Although legislators—under scrutiny of the media during campaigns—might give the requirement some attention, staff members generally see the form as a nuisance to be signed quickly and returned to the appropriate commission.

In 1974, at the height of public demands for lobby restrictions, California passed a law that proved to be the model for other states wanting to publicize their opposition to prevailing lobbying practice. The law focuses on so-called social lobbying,—the cocktail party or elaborate lunch, for example. The law

> not only provides for lobby registration and a complete listing of lobbyists' clients, but also requires monthly reports on each meal or drink that a lobbyist purchases for a legis-

lator. The overall impact of the law is not yet clear. In the view of a former Speaker of the California Assembly, Jesse Unruh, "it means nothing." In contrast, the chairman of the Fair Political Practices Commission, the agency charged with the administration of the law observes, "The whole way of doing business has changed. . . . We've really opened up and equalized the system so that every interest gets a fair shake."[21]

Both Unruh and the chair of the Fair Political Practices Commission exaggerated. The 1974 act did affect relationships, but it did not produce much equity. It was a nuisance to all concerned but scarcely affected the overall role of interest groups in the political process. It has made relationships more distant and more related to campaign contributions that pass the stringent tests of the law. At least the Sacramento restaurant lobby can be said to have suffered from the passage of this legislation.

Control over indirect influence of the lobbyist at election time was discussed earlier in chapter 5. Once again, the most common practice is disclosure of campaign contributions, but some states have gone the extra step by limiting campaign contributions from lobbyists or forgoing private contributions altogether through some form of public financing of legislative elections.

Lobbying is a natural part of the legislative process. It can never be eliminated and would greatly increase the staffing costs of the legislature if it were seriously cut back. Disclosure laws may increase public knowledge of lobbyists' activity, but most of what is disclosed demonstrates behavior that remains unchanged by the "control." Other forms of lobbying controls will be circumvented by the legislator who is so inclined; but although impossible to measure, such inclination seems on the decline. Unfortunately, the volume of lobbying control legislation increases the number of technical violations of the law and therefore may create the appearance of increased corruption. Ultimately, control of the lobbyists' unwarranted influence depends on the quality of the legislators themselves.

Parties and Process

State legislatures generally follow the organizational and procedural patterns of Congress. Though states differ as to detail, the pattern of decentralized policy making through the committee system is characteristic.

Presiding Officers

In the lower house, the Speaker presides. This officer is, in form, elected by the entire membership, but in practice the choice normally is made in a caucus of members of the majority party or faction. Sometimes actual selection is by a few top leaders. The vote on the speakership commonly is a formality, but it usually is the one test of party loyalty that must not be failed. Legislators may defect on an important roll call later in the session without losing status as party members. But if they do not support the party candidate for Speaker, they will not get majority party assignments to committees and may not be invited to caucuses. In this sense, it is the key vote of the session. The actual power of the Speaker varies from being principal leader to being merely the spokesperson for the leadership group.

Prior to 1970, in states with a lieutenant governor, it was that official who usually was authorized to preside over the senate and who had powers similar to the U.S. vice president. But a movement to strip the lieutenant governor of this power has existed for about the past two decades. Of the forty-three states with lieutenant governors, fourteen have taken the legislative power away.[22] Patterned on the vice president, the lieutenant governor is never a member of the senate, does not have a vote except sometimes in case of a tie, and usually has little influence over policy formulation. Legislators characteristically have a strong in-group sense and do not want to be ruled by outsiders. A noteworthy exception is Texas, where in the 1940s Lieutenant Governor Allan Shivers (who later became governor) exercised "dictatorial" powers over the senate, and where lieutenant governors in recent decades have maintained extraordinary powers of office to punish members who disagree with them (for example, by denying cherished committee assignments).[23] In states with no lieutenant governor, the senate chooses its own presiding officer. A caucus leader, having a title like majority leader or senate president *pro tem*, is in reality the most influential member of the senate in most states. A variety of other leadership positions may be chosen by both legislative houses. Practices vary widely, from the single senate leader in Alabama, Mississippi, South Carolina, and Texas to the more than twenty leadership positions in Hawaii, Michigan, Rhode Island, and Washington.[24] The Speaker of the lower house appoints the standing committees in all but three states. Committee members in the upper house usually are named by a committee on committees, which normally consists of the most powerful members of the majority group in the senate.[25] This power goes to the lieutenant governor in eight states.

The practices of legislative leaders vary widely. One state legislative expert classifies the leaders' activities into six roles:

1. *Organizing for work* involves control of the committee system, choosing the right people to lead the committees and the right mix of members to make committees work predictably.
2. *Processing legislation* involves "moving the bills through the multiple stages of the legislative process."
3. *Negotiating agreements* is done among members.
4. *Dispensing benefits* is a traditional task, most important in the appointment of lesser leaders and committee chairs.
5. *Handling the press* requires delicate balance.
6. *Maintaining the institution* is done by dealing with day-to-day and longer-term problems of administering a large institution.[26]

Legislative leaders now serve less time in the role than in years past. From 1975 to 1985, about one-third of the leaders left the legislature following each biennial election, and in 1987 over one-half of the states elected new presiding officers in at least one chamber. A 1987 survey found only 8 of the ninety-nine presiding officers having served ten or more years, the longest for fourteen years:

Most leave voluntarily either to seek higher office, pursue other career paths or retire. They are motivated by political ambition and circumstances, a need to make more money than legislative salaries often provide, a sense of accomplishment about their legislative goals or, in some instances, by fatigue or burnout. A few leave involuntarily because of electoral defeat, ouster by leadership challenge or changes in party control.[27]

This rapid turnover contributes to the declining power of party leaders and increases the power of the ecletic committee system in the legislative process.

The Committee System

Because legislative houses normally are made up of a large number of persons and because the floor of such houses is not the most effective place for serious decision making or for political horse trading, American legislatures traditionally do most of their work through committees. The committee system seems to be necessary where the deliberative body is large, but the approach used in state legislatures has been widely criticized because the system obscures the nature of the legislature's work, confuses responsibility to the public, and frequently allows the committee majority (a small percentage of the overall house) to determine policy.

A 1987 survey found that over half of the more than four thousand local governments surveyed also used *standing committees*, averaging seven in number with a normal size of four or five members, but with at least one example of a committee of over fifty members.[28]

The committee system in state and local legislatures works basically the same as it does in Congress. The legislative house as a whole becomes chiefly a ratifying body for the actions of the committees. Even if the house can override a committee recommendation or relieve the committee of further consideration of a bill, these actions are not likely, because each legislator—like each member of Congress—will tacitly agree to allow other legislators to be supreme in their committee areas if they will extend the same privilege to colleagues. The committee is the key group in the legislature.[29]

The committee system has some advantages. For instance, legislative bodies, to provide adequately for representativeness, must be fairly large. If they are to get their work done, the committee system is a logical means by which to expedite the job. Members of committees are advised to become specialists in their fields, to know much more about a specific subject than does the average legislator. They may learn enough to make knowledgeable recommendations to their colleagues concerning programs and budgets. Also, the committee system provides a means of specialization of effort within the legislature (similar policies of specialization are followed in the executive and judicial branches). In our complicated contemporary world, we need highly capable persons in the legislature to serve as general overseers of those who carry out policy. The committee system, therefore, permits the legislature to carry on one of its most vital democratic functions, that of criticism and review.

In many legislatures, two committees often are more important than the presiding officers. One is the committee on committees, mentioned above. The other, the *rules committee*, is powerful, not because the permanent rules of a legislative body are changed very often, but because it is the group that can grant a bill a special order on the calendar of the house or a special rule to be handled in an unconventional way.

In the rush of bills toward the end of the session, sometimes the only way a bill can get before the house is through such action by the rules committee. This group practically may decide what is to become law, a question that in theory belongs to the house as a whole. Some states traditionally permit only members of the majority party or faction to sit on the rules committee, thus permitting the inner circle to keep its tactical plans secret.

Usually a large number of committees are used in each house—North Carolina had the largest number of standing committees in 1989, with thirty-four in the house and fifty-three in the senate.[30] Standing committees range in size from fewer than ten members to more than fifty in various legislatures around the country. Exceptions to this general pattern are to be found in Connecticut and Maine, which depend wholly or partly on *joint committees*, with membership from both houses sitting together. Similarly in Wisconsin, the most important committee, the *joint finance committee*, handles all appropriations and taxes. Although reform efforts in recent decades have aimed at reducing the number of committees so as to encourage more concentration on the important bills, legislators like the prestige of serving on many committees. Having a large number of committees also is convenient because it provides handy places into which to shunt new members as well as potentially influential members of the minority party or faction. Thus, committees were once so specialized in the Minnesota House of Representatives that it had a committee on binding twine and another on (railroad) sleeping cars.

Committees are also useful as places in which to bury legislation that political pressure demands to be introduced but that most legislators think should not become law. Some legislatures have impressive-sounding committees—such as a committee on government operations—that exist primarily as burial grounds for such legislation.

Although not observed so rigidly in most legislatures as it once was in Congress, the seniority system of assigning committee seats is important. Perhaps it is less observed because until recent decades, legislative turnover was very high; but the idea of "wait your turn" is an important one in many of our social institutions, beginning with children's play groups. Thus, it is common for ranking members to want, and to receive, the most desirable assignments. Committee chairs often are assigned exclusively on the basis of seniority, and it is virtually impossible to remove an incompetent senior member from such a position. But practices vary widely, and the influence of senior members may be more that of informal persuader than formal power.

The Formation of Law

The pattern of introduction, hearings, floor debate, and rules on passing legislation varies somewhat from state to state, but in general it follows that used in Congress. Figure 12–1 outlines the passage of a bill according to the rules in Illinois. Bills may be drafted by the attorney general's office at the request of a state agency or on request of the governor; they may be written by a lobbyist or by an attorney for an interest group; or they may be drawn up, in some states, by the legislative billdrafting service or appropriate staff member at the request of a legislator.

Figure 12-1: Life or Death of a Bill: The Illinois Pattern

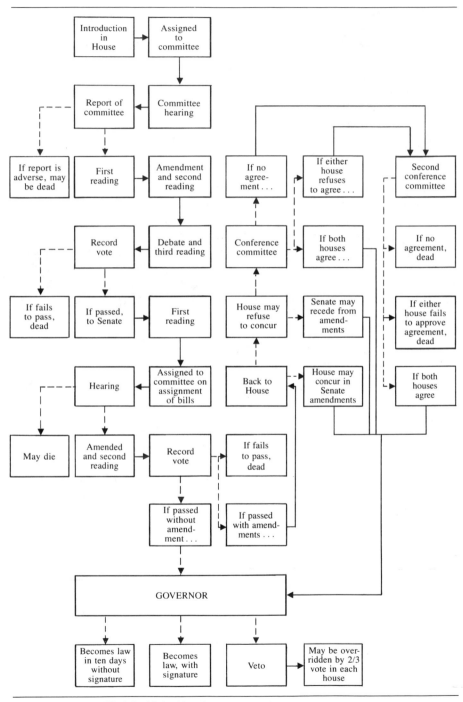

Source: Compiled from Illinois Legislative Manual.
Dotted lines indicates alternative possibilities.

The number of bills introduced annually in each legislature and the trend in the number introduced seem to vary greatly from one state to another and probably depend not so much on the importance and complexity of issues of public policy confronting state decision makers as on differing political styles and formal rules. In some states, the political realities of the moment make it easier to produce ''garbage'' bills, hundreds of pages long, covering what would normally be divided into many separate bills. As noted earlier, the incidence of lengthening sessions of some legislatures increases the volume of legislation, but this may be partially offset by a disinclination to introduce local bills. In a two-year period, a medium-population state, Massachusetts for example, can therefore be found to introduce over 17,000 bills, whereas Missouri, with similar population introduced fewer than 2,800.[31]

The fate of a bill may rest with the committee to which it is assigned. The committee having power to decide which committee should receive the bill may sometimes, by the decision made, determine the fate of the measure. One committee chairperson may view the bill with definite favor; another, determined to kill it, may be influential enough to do so even though the bill probably would pass if it reached the floor of the house.

Public hearing procedures vary from state to state and according to the assumed importance of a bill. Some state capitols include a few hearing rooms to accommodate public hearings. Some state traditions do not support the demand for public hearings and few are held, even on matters of great moment. In some of the more professional legislatures, the practice of holding hearings away from the capital to give distant constituents better opportunity to participate—also a useful reminder at election time—has become frequent practice, particularly when the legislature is not in session.

If bills pass the two houses in even slightly different form, they must go to a *conference committee,* usually made up of equal representation from the two houses. However, once again the presiding officer or committee empowered to decide who sits on the conference committee is often in a position to expedite or to impede passage of the bill (it is easy to stack the conference committee with friends or enemies of the bill). In some states, however, it is customary for the originating house to accept the amendments of the second house without holding a conference.

Once a bill is passed, some kind of waiting period is common before it goes into effect. For example, New Mexico's waiting period is ninety days after the adjournment of the legislature, except for general appropriation bills, which apply as soon as approved by the governor or when passed over the veto. Any act ''necessary for the preservation of the public peace, health, or safety'' also takes immediate effect, provided that two-thirds of the members of each house agree to it.

In a sense, a new law must go through a further process of refinement before it becomes binding as a part of the rules that control the actions of society. The legislature could not be specific enough in its language, no matter how it tried, to make the meaning of every part of the law completely clear. Therefore, a new act must be ''interpreted'' by rulings of the attorney general; such rulings have the force and effect of law unless overruled by the courts. Important laws, especially if they venture into new areas of governmental activity or prescribe new procedures, are tested finally in the supreme court of the state before their full content is clarified. Occasionally, a state law will go to the United States Supreme Court for interpretation if it is claimed that it conflicts with federal law or the United States Constitution. Even after the statutes are so interpreted, a body of administrative law often is necessary to implement the law passed. These administrative rules further refine the meaning, perhaps directing the law away from the intent of its framers. And the persons who execute the provisions of the law also interpret it by the way they carry it out.

One problem facing state legislatures that has received much media attention stems from legislators who attempt to determine how to vote on issues raised in bills presented to them in a final, last-minute rush. Some kind of Parkinson's law has probably always applied to legislatures; that is, they tend to take up the amount of time available, irrespective of the number or importance of issues before them. Then, in a desperate lurch to meet a constitutional deadline or one established by the leadership, or to get home to campaign, they pass most of the major acts of a session in a short period of time. For example, during seven regular sessions, the Kansas legislature passed, on the average, 41 percent of its legislation during the first *three months* of the session and 59 percent during the last *three days*[32] Given the increased complexity of issues facing legislatures and the increased conflict in the political arena, it is perhaps understandable that most legislative sessions have grown longer. But this overall pattern of end-of-season rush has not changed.

The Threat of Deadlock

Legislatures in the most populous states (and some others as well) have, like Congress, encountered impasses in recent years in relation to critical issues involving the countervailing forces of powerful interest groups. The issue becomes not what bill should be passed but whether any bill at all can be adopted. For example, after years of the legislature considering and then failing to act on local tax reform in California, the impasse was finally resolved in 1979, at least in the near term, outside the legislature through the initiative process and Proposition 13. Another major issue was the high cost and method of determining premiums for motor vehicle insurance. Rates had been driven up by excessive jury awards on lawsuits, more vehicles on the road and hence more accidents, rising theft and insurance fraud, and runaway medical costs. Even so, many drivers believed the cause to be greedy insurance companies (most of which, no doubt, did carve out comfortable profits).

The legislature was placed under enormous pressure from insurance companies, the California Trial Lawyers' Association, and consumer groups led by Ralph Nader. For several sessions it could pass no bill, but demands for rate reductions did not diminish. As noted in chapter 6, the insurance companies then decided to abandon the legislative route and try a ''no fault'' initiative, which promptly provoked competing measures from other groups. The one measure that passed was taken to court and was altered substantially by the state supreme court and then became bogged down in both legislative and bureaucratic conflicts. One year after the election, an opinion poll showed that a large majority of the voters expected never to receive a reduction in premiums. Legislators, who had failed over many years to resolve the issue, were not about to try again. More was involved here than the greed of voters and insurance executives. Premiums assessed by ZIP code and based on driver experience produced relatively lower premiums for the prosperous and, in some areas, fearfully heavy costs for persons with low incomes. This introduced dozens of questions about, for example, social equity, social responsibility, the "right" to drive an automobile, and the requirement of insurance. The means by which highly visible or important legislation can be adopted in effective form may become an increasingly serious problem in our ever-more-complex society.

Party Organization and Discipline

In the typical legislative session, few issues are decided along party lines, but in many legislatures, the most important issues tend to be shaped by party differences. Pressures to vote a party line appear to be declining, however, as the legislator becomes less dependent on party officials for political survival. The role of party may be most important today in the choice of leaders and the organization of committees, as well as in the discipline that seems to exist during battles over reapportionment. This is true in California, for example, where parties usually come alive for these purposes only, even though they hardly exist as organizations any longer, except in the legislature.

The function of the political party in state legislatures varies a great deal. A number of studies in the 1950s showed patterns that have held up to the present when conditions mirror those of that period. Whereas party is in decline everywhere (as discussed in chapter 6), the processes of party influence have been maintained.[33] Lobbyists could achieve great power in California with its weak-party system,[34] but would find this much more difficult in New York, where party discipline in the legislature has always been strong.[35] One measure of the party's decline in importance in the mind of the voter is the frequency of ticket splitting. Some period of mixed government—control of the governorship by one party and the legislature by the other—has been experienced in every state except Mississippi, Georgia, and Hawaii (Nebraska is nonpartisan) between 1965 and 1992.[36]

The pattern of party control is not to be found in many legislatures. In states with the one-party system, Democratic Louisiana for example, party caucuses would be meaningless, and the quasi nonpartisanship of the legislature in such states results in turn in encouraging party breakup into factions.[37] In states with strong two-party systems, considerable voting along party lines exists, to a degree that "appears to be significantly higher in those two-party states which are larger and more urban." In large two-party industrial states, "a high level of party voting in the legislature results from party alignments which have largely followed the liberal-conservative, urban-rural pattern of national politics."[38] In such states, however, each party tends to move toward a moderate position, and representatives from districts that are atypical of the party frequently show independence of party discipline, as they do in Congress. A great many legislative roll calls are unanimous, and the number of cases of clear alignment of one party against another is relatively small.

The strength of the party can be measured by the activity of the party caucus. No example of routine caucus votes that bind members to vote accordingly on legislation is found in the states today, although Wisconsin and Colorado do have such votes on their budgets. In New York and Pennsylvania the caucus is used by strong leaders to affect selected policy. Where party leadership is weaker, the caucus may meet in an attempt to create party cohesion (e.g., Iowa) or to gauge the opinion of members in the policy-making process (e.g., Kentucky). The caucus may serve primarily to keep the membership informed (e.g., Montana) or to give members opportunity to control the leaders (e.g., Massachusetts).[39] Even in states with highly competitive two-party systems, most legislative districts are not two-party competitive, and the degree of competition changes only slightly through time. In the majority of legislative constituencies in the United States, competition for the office takes place within a single political party. Furthermore, the incumbent has a considerable advantage; and even in those districts with a relatively high degree of competitiveness in the primary election, the incumbent seldom loses. Most state legislators are quite secure in their jobs for as long as they want them.

The party influences the interpersonal relations and friendship patterns within the individual's own party. Furthermore, the legislators with the most "friends" are the party leaders, although such a conclusion hinges on the chicken-and-egg or cause-and-effect debate that plagues the social sciences. That is, are legislative leaders in their position because they have many friends? Or do they have many so-called friends because they are leaders?

The Unwritten Rules

The formal organization of a legislature may have little meaning. Thus, "there is often a paper caucus that meets only biennially. There are. . . committees that do not receive bills on the subjects implied by their titles or that rubber stamp those bills they do receive. A lieutenant-governor may be powerful in one state and a figurehead in the next."[40]

The institutional structure of a legislature is such that actual leaders are also likely to occupy the formal positions of power, but with no necessary rank ordering of their relative power. For example, in one state the Speaker of the House may be the most powerful leader, whereas in another state the Speaker may be someone who has been "kicked upstairs," and the majority floor leader or some other person may be the dominant leader. Leaders gain power through control over procedure, committee assignments, and their influence with the governor. They may use various techniques—the caucus, a rules committee, or the standing committees (bills may be arbitrarily assigned to committees controlled by dependable legislators).

Malcolm Jewell, a specialist on state legislatures, has observed that although most bodies are organized for strong leadership, they are not usually organized "to provide careful deliberation on legislation. Usually the sessions are too short, and the legislatures too poorly staffed, to permit that." Because of their weaknesses as innovative bodies, leadership often comes not from within the body, but from the governor's office. The unwritten rules of the legislative process are important to the maintenance of the political system and to the legislative institution itself; such rules add support to and often modify the formal rules. In this sense, unwritten rules fill in the chinks in the structure that is the legislative institution. Indeed, "they are directly relevant to and supportive of the purposes and functions of the legislature as these are conceived of by legislators: They maintain the working consensus essential to legislative performance."[41]

As is the case with formal rules, unwritten rules are enforced through sanctions, which are understood and can be anticipated by members. Both formal and informal rules are enforced primarily, of course, not through threat of punishment but rather through consensus. Legislators are judged by colleagues in part by their understanding and acceptance of the unwritten rules of the game. Legislators are more effective to the extent that they demonstrate such understanding, not only to the leaders of the body but also to the rank-and-file members:

> The maintenance of group norms which constitute the working consensus appears to be independent of the power or influence acquired through holding formal office. Rules of the game are the property and the creature of the group membership at large, not a reflection of requirements set by either personal or formal leadership. Formal leadership operates within the working consensus provided, in large part, by legislators playing their consensual roles.[42]

Ahead of almost every other consideration is the fact that each house of the legislature is a rather exclusive club. That fact, rather than party or even constituency, determines, for all but a few mavericks, behavior patterns. For the club, traditions preserve and protect the group and train new members for acceptable roles. This is less the case in state legislatures than it is in Congress, but it is important and tends to move legislatures toward moderation and away from high-risk policy proposals.[43]

A study of four legislatures (California, New Jersey, Ohio, and Tennessee) found a variety of informal rules, stated here in the words of the legislators themselves:

1. Rules to promote group cohesion and solidarity—
    "Support another member's bill if it doesn't affect you or your district"
    "Don't steal another member's bill"
    "Accept the author's amendments to a bill"
    "Don't make personal attacks on other members"
    "Oppose the bill, not the man"
    "Don't be a *prima donna,* an individualist, an extremist or a publicity hound"
    "Don't be overambitious"
    "Don't divulge confidential information"
    "Defend the legislature and its members against outsiders."
2. Rules to promote predictability of behavior—
    "Keep your word"
    "Abide by your commitments"
    "Notify in advance if you can't keep your commitment."
    "Don't engage in parliamentary chicanery"
3. Rules to channel and limit conflict—
    "Be willing to compromise"
    "Accept half a loaf"
    "Go along with the majority of the party"
    "Respect the seniority system"

"Respect older members"
"Don't try to accomplish too much too soon"
"Respect committee jurisdiction"
"Don't vote to discharge a committee"
4. Rules to expedite legislative business—
"Don't talk too much"
"Don't fight unnecessarily"
"Don't introduce too many bills and amendments"
"Be punctual and regular"
"Take the job seriously"
"Don't be too political"
"Don't call attention to the absence of a quorum."[44]

Legislative Staff Assistance

A legislative resolution in Texas submitting a constitutional amendment proposed to provide state aid for the permanently disabled was carelessly worded to provide for a referendum by the voters to be held on "the second Tuesday in November," when it should have been worded "the Tuesday after the first Monday." As a result, a special election had to be held to vote on the amendment, even though a general election had been held a week earlier. The cost to the taxpayers for this blunder amounted to about $250,000. Nebraska once passed a new weed-abatement act, designed principally to reduce the number of noxious weeds in rural areas. The act made elaborate provision for the administration of the program, even including the election of weed commissioners. But apparently no one thought to exempt Douglas County (the Omaha area), where the ground is covered mostly with concrete, asphalt, and well-tended, if not entirely weed-free, lawns. The county was faced with a mandatory requirement of providing an unneeded and ineffective service. The California Senate carelessly passed a bill that would have made it a felony to conceive a child by sexual intercourse, though this was not the intent of the bill. The bill actually was intended to limit "human conception outside the womb." These incidents illustrate the need for careful bill drafting and the expensive or ridiculous results of its absence.

Legislators in an increasing number of states, in an attempt to improve their work and reduce their dependence on lobbyists and the administrative bureaucracy, have employed staffs to assist them. In other states, however, they have persistently refused to do this, even though the result could considerably improve their public image. It is likely that many legislators do not understand the nature of staff work or conceive of the benefits it can produce. In the many states where the governor may be of a different party from that of the legislative leadership, the leadership would be in a much stronger position to fend off the governor's criticisms and to improve the party's chances on the next election if a staff were available to do research and to generate ideas. The use of legislative reference bureaus is expanding; and in a large state, such a bureau is likely to consist of at least fifty persons, including attorneys, researchers, and clerical employees. Because a variety of staffs are found in a single legislature, the houses and members may become more distant from one another. "An effect of these trends is to reduce the sense of the legislature as an institution and

to reduce the opportunities and the need for two houses to work jointly and coopera-
tively together.''[45]

With few exceptions, staff is provided to most standing committees today.
Two-thirds of the states provide a joint central staff agency, usually nonpartisan in
nature, for the two legislative houses. Clerical staff usually is provided each member
of professional legislatures, and in some states this extends to members both in the
capital and in the home district. Political parties often hire a variety of staff members
in patronage jobs to provide work for party faithful around the legislature to serve the
caucus, its members, or even committees. In legislatures with both partisan and career nonpartisan staffs, these partisan jobs are usually low paying, being the least
prestigious of staff jobs. Nevertheless, they are a good place for future politicians to
begin learning the rules of the political game. And they tend to handle the services
that help the constituent at any time, and are vital credits to members come election
time.[46] California, with one of the best-staffed legislatures, demonstrates the trend in
staff work and provides the following:

1. A legislative counsel, with over ninety lawyers who draft most legislation
2. A legislative analyst's office, which advises the legislature on anything with
   fiscal implications—often in reaction to the executive budget
3. An auditor general, a certified public accountant with staff, who does the postaudit reports with evaluation of the administration for each program passed
4. A committee staff
5. A partisan staff for each party
6. A personal staff for each member

Legislative assistance is centered in a legislative reference bureau or a billdrafting service, sometimes both. Most states have legislative councils of selected
legislators together with (sometimes) a research staff. This group works between sessions, investigating or drawing up legislation and perhaps preparing programs and
making recommendations for their colleague's consideration at the next session.
Generally these councils have greatly improved the spadework done prior to the enactment of legislation, and they have freed the legislator from an otherwise total dependence on the interest groups and the administration. Increasingly, the quality of
the professional staff defines the professionalism of the legislature. Top staff
members—lawyers and Ph.D.s—may be making high public-sector salaries, sometimes even more than full-time legislators. A legislature with its own professional
staff, can begin to reassert itself and challenge the notion of a governor being the chief
legislator. But frequently the top staff members are experts in a field, much like department policy makers in the executive branch. Because staff members have more in
common with their fellow bureaucrats in the executive branch than elected members
of either executive or legislative branch, their interaction may come to dominate the
policy-making process. Today's lobbyists may have to be as skilled in lobbying staff
as they are with legislators, although patterns vary widely. Some states continue to
provide limited professional staff support, particularly the less populated and less
wealthy states.

Committee staffs are of particular importance in the oversight function of the legislature. Much like Congress, some legislators may be best known for their work on such committees when the legislature is not in session. Whereas legislators may have to tend to their other jobs or to reelection concerns during interim periods, the success of this oversight function is particularly dependent on the staff members who prepare the legislators on such committees for the formal committee hearings. Staff lawyers do some of the public interviewing of witnesses. But usually, when the spotlight is on the committee hearing, the staff members must be satisfied that their influence be measured by the success of the committee's work; the publicity will be reserved for the elected politician.

Concluding Note

Legislative bodies represent a basic part of the process of public policy formulation— but only a part. Along with the chief executive, interest groups, the administrative hierarchy, and the courts, they share the central task of changing, within achievable limits, *wants* into *policy*. Chapter 14 will add to the ongoing discussion in seeking to show that policy making is a continuous, many-faceted process. Yet the adequacy of the law in meeting social needs and the quality of its enforcement cannot be expected to be better than that of the legislative body, for in a democracy, it is said to speak for "the people." The changes in the legislature brought on by the reapportionment decisions of the courts, the declining role of political parties, and the move to full-time legislators and abundant staff, are among the major ingredients in the more general changes being experienced by state governments.

Notes

1. Alfred De Grazia, *Public and Republic* (New York: Alfred A. Knopf, 1951), 3.

2. Discussion of the relationship of the individual and the locality to public representation may be found in John Dewey, *The Public and Its Problems* (New York: Holt, Rinehart and Winston, 1927); and David Truman, *The Governmental Process* (New York: Alfred A. Knopf, 1951).

3. Warren E. Miller and Donald E. Stokes, "Constituency Influence in Congress," reprinted in Stephen V. Monsma and Jack R. VanDer Slik, *American Politics: Research and Readings* [first published in 1963] (New York: Holt, Rinehart and Winston, 1970).

4. James D. Barber, *The Lawmakers* (New Haven, CT: Yale University Press, 1980), chapter 1.

5. Ibid., chapter 2.

6. Ibid., chapter 3.

7. Ibid., chapter 4.

8. Ibid., chapter 5. Quotation at 164.

9. Heinz Eulau, "The Legislator and His District: Areal Roles," in John C. Wahlke, Heinz Eulau, William Buchanan, and LeRoy C. Ferguson, eds., *The Legislative System: Explorations in Legislative Behavior* (New York: John Wiley and Sons, 1962), chapter 13. Also see the essays edited by Heinz Eulau and John C. Wahlke, *The Politics of Representation: Continuities in Theory and Research* (Beverly Hills, CA: Sage Publications, 1978).

10. For the reminiscenses of an old-time lobbyist, see Arthur H. Samish and Bob Thomas, *The Secret Boss of California* (New York: Crown Publishers, 1971).

11. *Campaign Finance, Ethics, and Lobby Law Blue Book,* (Lexington, KY: Council of State Governments, 1987).

12. *1990–1991 Book of the States,* 189–90.

13. Randy Welch, "Lobbyists, Lobbyists All Over the Lot," *State Legislatures* 15:2 (Feb. 1989):18–22, quotation at 21.

14. Ibid., 20.

15. For a discussion of interest group influence, see Malcolm Jewell, "Legislators and Constituents in the Representative Process," in Gerhard Loewenberg, Samuel C. Patterson, and Malcolm E. Jewell, eds., *Handbook of Legislative Research* (Cambridge, MA: Harvard University Press, 1985), 97–131; and Bruce I. Oppenheimer, "Legislative Influence on Policy and Budgets," in the same work, 645.

16. The typology used in this section is from Samuel C. Patterson, "The Role of the Lobbyist: The Case of Oklahoma," *Journal of Politics* 25 (Feb. 1963) :72–92.

17. Welch, "Lobbyists. . . ," 20.

18. Ibid., 19.

19. Edgar Lane, *Lobbying and the Law* (Berkeley: University of California Press, 1964), 15.

20. Compiled by the authors from data in the *1988–1989 Book of the States,* 142–44.

21. William J. Keefe and Morris S. Ogul, *The American Legislative Process* (Englewood Cliffs, NJ: Prentice Hall, 1977), 348.

22. *1990–1991 Book of the States,* 96.

23. Alan Rosenthal, *Legislative Life: People, Process and Performance* (New York: Harper & Row, 1981), 151; and Neal Tannahill and Wendell M. Bedichek, *Texas Government,* 3d ed. (Glenview, IL: Scott, Foresman, 1989), 200–203.

24. Rosenthal, *Legislative Life,* 152.

25. Details on legislative membership and organization may be found in the most recent volume of the *Book of the States* and the discussion in chapter 11.

26. Rosenthal, *Legislative Life,* chapter 8.

27. Lucinda Simon, "When Leaders Leave," *State Legislatures* 13 (Feb. 1987): 16–18.

28. Victor S. De Santis, "Council Committees," *Baseline Data Report* 19 (Washington, D.C.: International City Management Association, July/Aug. 1987).

29. See Rosenthal, *Legislative Life,* chapter 9; and Alan Rosenthal, *Legislative Performance in the States: Explorations of Committee Behavior* (New York: The Free Press, 1974).

30. The *1990–1991 Book of the States,* 167.

31. Compiled from data in the *1990–1991 Book of the States,* 160–62.

32. *Your Government,* Oct. 15, 1963.

33. See William J. Keefe, "Comparative Study of the Role of Political Parties in State Legislatures," *Western Political Quarterly* 9 (Sept. 1956): 726–42, and his citations. Also see his summary in William J. Keefe and Morris S. Ogul, *The American Legislative Process,* 6th ed. (Englewood Cliffs, NJ: Prentice Hall, 1985), 258.

34. Lester Velie, "The Secret Boss of California," *Colliers,* Aug. 13 and Aug. 20, 1949.

35. Lawrence Lowell, "The Influence of Party upon Legislature," *Annual Report of the American Historical Association for the Year 1901*, vol. 1. (New York: American Historical Association, 1901), 319–542; Warren Moscow, *Politics in the Empire State* (New York: Alfred A. Knopf, 1948). Keefe and Ogul, *American Process,* 258, describe New

York, Connecticut, Massachusetts, Rhode Island, and Pennsylvania as still having a party structure akin to the responsible two-party model.

36. Malcolm E. Jewell and David M. Olson, *Political Parties and Elections in American States,* 3d ed. (Chicago: The Dorsey Press, 1988), 225–30. We added 1988 and 1990 election results.

37. On this general point, see V. O. Key, Jr., "The Direct Primary and Party Structure: A Study of State Legislative Nominations," *American Political Science Review* 48 (March 1954) :1–26 and his many examples of this in V. O. Key, Jr., and Alexander Heard, *Southern Politics* (New York: Random House, 1949).

38. Malcolm E. Jewell, "Party Voting in American State Legislatures," *American Political Science Review* 49 (Sept. 1955): 773–91. Jewell and Olson, *Political Parties,* continue to find similar patterns in the late 1980s. See particularly chapter 7 of that work.

39. This section is taken from the discussion in Jewell and Olson, *Political Parties,* 235–44. See also Jewell and Samuel C. Patterson, *The Legislative Process in the United States,* 4th ed. (New York: Random House, 1986).

40. Jewell, "Party Voting"; and Jewell and Patterson, *Legislative Process,* are the basis for this section.

41. Wahlke et al., *The Legislative System,* 168.

42. Ibid., 169.

43. Corey M. Rosen, "Legislative Influence and Policy Orientation in American State Legislatures," *American Journal of Political Science* 18 (Nov. 1974): 681–91.

44. The study was done by Wahlke et al., *The Legislative System;* quotation and summary from Thomas R. Dye, "State Legislative Politics," in Herbert Jacob and Kenneth Vines, eds., *Politics in the American States* (Boston: Little, Brown, 1965), 175–77.

45. William T. Pound, "The State Legislatures," the *1988–1989 Book of the States,* 82.

46. The types of staff available in particular legislatures can be found in the latest edition of the *Book of the States.*

"I'M SENTENCING YOU TO 25 YEARS IN PRISON WITH NO HOPE OF PAROLE UNTIL AFTER 3 P.M. TOMORROW AFTERNOON!"

13

Law, the Judiciary, and the Criminal Justice Process

The adjudication of disputes among members of society in a manner that is relatively undisruptive of the smooth operation of that society is a common objective of social control. This generally was a task of families and extended families. But as governments became more established, part (though by no means all), of the responsibility for this function was turned over to the state and came to be administered through its judicial system. In time, certain acts by one person against another were thought of as being damaging primarily to society at large and thus to the state; these acts were called *crimes*. Other similar acts remained classified by society as being primarily wrongs against the interests, rights, or person of the second party and not of society as a whole. But even these cases came before the courts as *civil actions* to be settled through the machinery of the state. In contemporary society, the judicial branch of government, through an elaborate set of rules, administers both criminal and civil law in the name of society and largely in accord with dominant local values and interests.

Previous chapters examined legal functions of structuring and administering government. In chapter 3 we also examined the principle of rights, by looking at the role of the national and state bills of rights. This chapter will complete the examination of the role of law in the relationship between individual and government by looking at the criminal and civil law and the judicial system that administers that relationship.

The Nature of Criminal and Civil Law

In all but the simplest societies, law exists in order to perform certain functions. The first function is to define relationships among members of a society. The law explains which activities are permitted and which are prohibited. Second, law serves to control behavior and to maintain order in a society. It specifies who legitimately may exercise sanctions against other members of society, and the state has the means to enforce its rulings. Third, the law disposes of troublesome cases as they arise. Although a case may be unique in certain respects, it is expected that the law will apply existing legal norms to dispose of the case in a manner acceptable to members of the society. Last, the function of the law is to redefine relationships among individuals, organizations, and groups as technology and life-styles change.[1]

A few points should be made concerning the nature of law and the way it is administered:

1. Law is only one of the devices for social control. In both primitive and complex societies, values are important. Violation of the mores is always serious in the eyes of society and is often made a crime (e.g., "Thou shalt not kill"), whereas violation of the (less important) folkways is more likely to be controlled by gossip or ridicule, though some folkways are reinforced by law (e.g., driving on the right side of U.S. roads).

2. The law has its own logic, its own value system, its own devices for providing itself with protective coloration and for justifying its immense power to maintain social equilibrium. One of the most important of such concepts holds that justice is distributed impartially to all. In our society, the symbol of justice is a woman (gentle protectiveness), blindfolded (to ensure impartiality) and holding a balance scale (to weigh objectively the merits of the case). Justice is not actually dispensed equally and impartially to all who come before the courts, as will be discussed below, but the concept is an important part of the myth system, of the mechanism for legitimizing actions of the courts in the eyes of citizens.

3. Crime, justice, equity, for example, are all social concepts. What is a crime in one society is not in another. A crime in one American state is not always a crime in another. The harsh "justice" of class-structured England was rejected on the American frontier for a more egalitarian—but sometimes equally harsh—justice. Each represented the adjustment of a social institution to its particular environment. The notion of what is fair punishment for a crime or the conditions under which a crime may be overlooked by the prosecutor or may result in a "not guilty" verdict from a jury, even though the alleged act obviously was committed, are determined by the values of our society and not by objective standards for measuring an impartial law, as the myth portrays the system. Similarly, judicial organization and administration reflect the values of society. The institution of the jury, providing as it did judgment by one's social equals, was vital under a feudal class system but is less important under the fluid American class system. The English culture provides a system that makes it seem natural for judges to be appointed for life; the American makes it seem natural for them to be elected for a period of years.

4. Because American law and its administration are of vital importance to social control in a complex society and because law is a symbol of stability in a nation with a history of constant social change, deference is paid to the courts, and particularly to the law. It is well for the student of social institutions to recognize that this deference is a part of the method for securing compliance to the law and that an examination of the judicial process requires a look at it from outside this framework if we are to understand how it operates.[2]

Justice and the Judicial Process

Justice is a cultural concept, and the procedure by which it is pursued and accomplished is a reflection of the belief systems of a particular society. Justice may be viewed as a process by which persons wronged (by cultural definition) are able to right that wrong. In primitive societies, they may be expected to do this by securing a settlement against the person or the family and clan of the wrongdoer. In seeking justice, they may have the support of their own family and clan. The wrong may be righted in these cases through payment of a fine by the family of the wrongdoer, or a blood feud may result that continues until the wronged party believes a redress of grievances has been secured. In primitive societies, government as an institution may not be involved in the process at all.

Where government is involved, the process by which justice is secured may vary enormously, depending on the cultural concept to what is fair and who can bestow justice or determine what it is. In medieval times, for example, justice was sometimes secured through trial by combat or trial by ordeal. The former involved a physical battle between a man who believed himself wronged and the alleged wrongdoer. Medieval citizens believed that God would ensure that the proper person would win the battle. It was not even necessary for the actual litigants to be involved in the battle. The belief was that their representatives would win or lose just as readily as might the principals. Trial by ordeal involved exposure to various forms of torture. An accused wrongdoer, for example, might be forced to walk across a bed of red-hot coals or be dunked in a tub of boiling water. If he (women, except for accused witches, were not tried by ordeal) could survive the ordeal without physical damage, this was viewed as a sign from God that he was innocent.

Trial by jury is a more modern approach to justice. It had its beginnings in the twelfth century under the great English judicial reformer, King Henry II. The jury system in the United States took early form in town meetings, where the community would be asked to police itself.[3]

State legislators who today create complex systems of criminal justice still have not settled on the meaning of justice. Is the state prison designed to protect society from the dangerous (direct deterrence), to protect society by threatening stiff penalties (indirect deterrence), simply to punish because punishment is deemed right (retribution), or to change the long-term behavior of the criminally inclined (rehabilitation)? Each has been asserted at different times, and most prisons inconsistently attempt to be just by combining these contradictory notions.

Justice, then, is relative, depending in the individual case the operative ideology, attitude, diligence, interest, social class, and other considerations of the police officer, the prosecutor, the judge, the jurors, the defense attorney, the probation officer, and every other person who comes in contact with the case.

Civil and Criminal Procedure within the Subculture of Justice

In the American political process, justice is largely left to state and local governments. Few readers of this book will ever appear in federal court, but few readers of this book will be able to avoid arrest or ticketing by the local police. The judicial process involves a variety of actors interacting differently at different stages of the process. Principal actors and institutions—courts, police, judges, lawyers, juries, and corrections—will be looked at separately below. The professionals involved create a subculture—a set of special values combined uniquely within the group—in which the process of interaction takes place. This begins with a crime, conflict requiring civil adjudication, or other demand on government's judicial system. Criminal and civil procedure then take different paths.

Most crimes do not become known to the criminal justice system. For the system's process to apply, the crime must be reported, usually by first being brought to the attention of a police officer, who either must mete out justice on the scene, arrest immediately, or seek arrest after investigation. The court process begins with a complaint by the prosecutor; who has the power to discontinue the case any time before the indictment. A complaint is made to a judge under oath and alleges that a crime has been committed. At that point the judge may be asked either to issue an arrest warrant to take the accused into custody or issue a warrant to seize incriminating evidence. Then comes an examination or preliminary hearing before a judge to determine whether evidence justifies holding an individual in custody, simply ordering the accused to appear for further court processes, or whether extradition to the proper jurisdiction is necessary to carry out these procedures. At this stage, the lawyers (prosecutors and defense attorneys) become the principal actors. They must determine, not whether a crime has been committed, but what crime will be brought before the court. At this point, the accused will be charged formally through a prosecutor's *information* or a grand jury *indictment*. Bail usually is set to release the accused until trial, except when the accused is seen as dangerous or reason exists to doubt whether the accused will return for trial. Ninety percent of persons charged with crimes plead guilty. Over one-half of the remainder are found guilty after a trial. If the trial proceeds, the actions of judge and jury become the principal determinants of justice. If the defendant is found guilty then the American systems of corrections apply—fines must be paid, the guilty may go to jail or prison, or probation is arranged. In rare cases the guilty appeal to a higher court.[4] (The defendant may be found not guilty. This does not necessarily mean the same as innocent, which is not a legal finding. It simply means the person, for any one of many possible reasons, was not found to be legally guilty.)

> *Information:* **A charge made by prosecutors on their own responsibility and without grand jury action. In most states, this is the common procedure by which a charge is formally made.**

> *Presentment:* **An accusation made by a grand jury, after investigation and independently of any recommendation by a prosecutor. A charge made against a person on recommendation is an** *indictment;* **that is, the grand jury is said to have returned a** *true bill.*

Civil procedure, with the exception of some minor matters, begins when an attorney for the plaintiff files a complaint with the clerk of the court, stating the facts of the alleged wrong. A copy of the complaint is served on the defendant, who may file an answer with the court. The case is then, as in a criminal case, put on the docket for trial. The case may go before a jury, though it is increasingly the practice for civil cases to be heard by the judge alone. Witnesses are used much as they are in criminal cases, and their attendance may be required by the court. The judge or jury renders a verdict and, when applicable, determines the amount of damages that must be paid if the finding is for the plaintiff. Judges generally have more discretion in civil than in criminal cases; even when a jury is used they may direct a verdict, thereby telling the jury what it must decide, or set aside the verdict under some circumstances. Appeal in civil cases follows much the same lines as in criminal cases. (The variety and technicalities associated with civil actions are beyond the scope of this book.)

With the exception of common jurors and the litigants themselves, others in the judicial process usually have their own subculture or work in the larger subculture of the courts, with its own mysterious language, rules, and intimidating environments. Those involved know the informal rules of the game—how to make the process "work." They often know one another well and must deal with the personal biases of coworkers. Like insiders in other occupations, they protect these informal rules from infringement by outsiders. Thus on the one hand, defense attorneys are in an adversarial position representing their clients against prosecutors, but on the other hand they are lawyers with training and socialization similar to that of the prosecutor and judge. These lawyers spend more time with prosecutors, judges, police and probation officers than with outsiders.[5]

Problems with the Process of Finding Justice

The process of finding justice in practice often is criticized ("The jury was made up of corner loafers"; "It took two years to collect sixty bucks"; "The cop was prejudiced against me because I'm black"; "I needed a witness, and ten people saw the accident, but not one of them stopped"). Yet, the people who make unfavorable comments may well be the same ones who dodge jury duty (it is easy to do so, and "I didn't have time") or refuse to testify even though they suspect their testimony is essential ("Why get involved?").[6]

The process of administering justice prevents one American notion of justice—the equal application of the law—from being realized. Police officers exercise discretion; they cannot arrest every violator, nor do we want them to. Total enforcement would raise taxes beyond acceptable levels and be deemed unjust by most people. But this alone is not the problem. Police discretion is exercised for a variety of other reasons that many would see as unjust. Since the landmark case of *Miranda v. Arizona* (1966), the courts have lead the outside restriction of such discretion.[7]

Numerous delays may occur before criminal or civil cases come to trial, especially in more densely populated areas. "Justice delayed is justice denied," is a cliché, but often it is true. Witnesses die or disappear; the jury discounts an old wrong more than a recent one; evidence cannot be kept intact. The woman whose purse is stolen becomes angrier with the police if the purse is locked for a year in an evidence safe than she was with the thief. Such delays have led some to seek alternatives to court and trial. For example, in criminal cases, demand is made for informal mediation by the police officer on the street and for the plea-bargaining process detailed below. Efforts to reduce bail have had limited success.[8] Neighborhood justice centers, springing up in a number of cities, handle some minor criminal cases without formal court rules, commonly by agreement to limit the penalties to mediated fines, service, or restitution. The prospect of lower penalties appeals to the accused who is guilty. The prospect of speedy resolution and possible restitution appeals to victims. The reduction of caseloads appeals to courts and legislatures.[9] In civil cases, court-related arbitration processes or mediation centers using hired judges may be used to settle disputes, reducing the costs (particularly of time) to both parties.[10] These are employed only when the parties involved agree to an alternative to the formal system. Both criminal and civil alternatives are criticized because they may be available only to the knowledgeable and because rights may be infringed on in the absence of formal rules.

Justice is also costly, and efforts are being made to overcome this problem. The office of the public defender has developed into an institution to assist those accused of a crime; and even where such institutions are not found, lawyers are appointed to guarantee defense of the indigent. However, proof of indigence is difficult for the working poor. Although not guaranteed, varying degrees of public or privately sponsored help may be available for the poor in civil cases. But even the most able lawyers providing such services must choose whether it is worthwhile to serve many clients in routine cases or whether it is a greater service to expend large percentages of the group's resources on a few precedent-setting cases. The burden of hiring a lawyer who can best assist a client by prolonging the process is usually not worth the price or not affordable. The middle-income person finds most legal procedures a heavy financial burden, and the law, which grows ever more complicated, is totally unfathomable to the layperson. The college student unjustly charged with drinking under age at a party where many others obviously are guilty, would perhaps find it cheaper to pay the $75–$100 fine than to hire a lawyer at two or three times that price to guarantee ''justice.''[11]

The large proportion of guilty pleas is in part a result of the widespread practice of *plea bargaining*, an approach by which prosecuting attorneys tell the accused and defense attorneys what they are prepared to enter as charges. The two sides then bargain over which of a variety of charges or reduced charges to which the defendant will agree to plead guilty and perhaps as to what comments prosecutors might make to the judge concerning the case. (They might, for example, ask for leniency or tell the judge that the defendant has been cooperative in answering questions about other cases.)[12] This approach has been criticized by some civil libertarians as depriving the defendant of the right to a fair and public trial. But the accused minimizes personal risk by pleading guilty, for example, to second-degree murder rather than chancing a death sentence or life imprisonment if a first-degree charge goes to trial. Prosecutors save the time, effort, cost, and the risk of ''losing'' the case by making the agreement. Judges accept plea bargains in part because it helps keep the judicial docket backlog from growing still longer and because adult defendants have a right to plead guilty in the absence of coercion.

In the United States, justice is defined essentially by state courts and primarily by the trial courts. Appeals in criminal convictions are rarely taken and this tendency for trial court decisions to be final has been increasing in the current century. A study of 150 years of Wisconsin cases found that most of the criminal cases that came before the state appellate court did not involve the substantive concept of criminal law or the penalty imposed on those found guilty, but rather centered on questions of procedural regularity on the part of the police, the prosecutor, and the trial court:

> With rare exceptions the appellate cases only dimly reflected the great economic, social and political changes in the society. For example, the labor movement, the automobile,

the insurance industry, and the credit economy produced so few criminal appeals distinctively identified with the phenomena that one could not see their tremendous importance to the community through this window alone.[13]

Corrections affords problems, too. As mentioned earlier, serious dispute continues as to the proper use of prisons as proper places to penalize crime. Public opinion polls consistently show public demand for criminals to serve longer prison time; yet, people rarely are willing to pay the cost of building the prisons. As a result, prisons often are used more to house the dangerous criminal than to punish the guilty fairly. Federal courts have been used to uphold the rights of prisoners, which has led to prison closings, limitations on sending new prisoners to crowded prisons, and early releases for inmates.[14] Judges are seeking solutions to the traditional alternatives of fines, prison, or probation and parole—such as restitution, public service, and house arrest.

Organization of the State Courts

Because of our federal system, federal and state courts have cojurisdiction over the same territory, people, and corporations. Despite this, the ordinary citizen is likely to have contact only with state courts because the bulk of domestic law, both criminal and civil, is based on state statutes, common law, or local ordinances. Nearly all local courts are actually branches of state courts. The state courts can handle almost all of the cases that may be brought before federal courts and a large number of others besides. Many states determinedly continued using county courts or at least county justices of the peace (with limited judicial powers) until court reforms of the 1960s and 1970s. Thus in a relatively small state there might be at least as many judges as at the national level (the federal courts system has about 260 full-time, and that many additional part-time, judges). More than three thousand judges sat in New York State alone. The annual budget was greater than that of the entire federal system of courts. And the chief justice could brag that no one, including himself, could name all of the courts in the state over which his court sat in appeal. Even after reform in 1972, Florida had more judges than the national courts.[15]

Contrary to popular belief, decisions in state courts are not ordinarily subject to appeal to the federal courts. The only point at which the two systems meet is in the United States Supreme Court, and even it will review state court decisions only after all state judicial remedies are exhausted and then only in cases where a "federal question" is involved; that is, where it is argued that state law or judicial procedures contravene federal statutes or the provisions of the United States Constitution; and even then, only when the Court accepts the case.[16] (In some cases, attorneys have an option of bringing a case in either lower state or lower federal courts, or both, because laws at both levels are said to be involved. For example, a state murder charge might simultaneoulsy involve an alleged violation of federal civil rights law.)

Minor Courts

The traditional institution for locality justice is that of the justice court, which originated in England and has existed in this country since colonial times. The

Figure 13–1: Court Structure of Texas

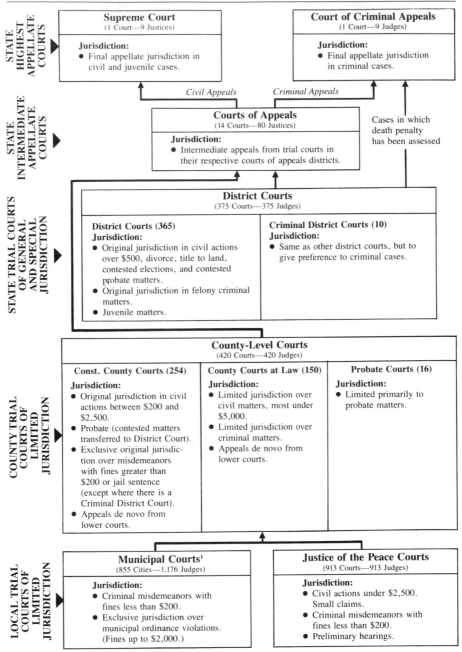

STATE HIGHEST APPELLATE COURTS

Supreme Court
(1 Court—9 Justices)

Jurisdiction:
• Final appellate jurisdiction in civil and juvenile cases.

Court of Criminal Appeals
(1 Court—9 Judges)

Jurisdiction:
• Final appellate jurisdiction in criminal cases.

STATE INTERMEDIATE APPELLATE COURTS

Civil Appeals   Criminal Appeals

Courts of Appeals
(14 Courts—80 Justices)

Jurisdiction:
• Intermediate appeals from trial courts in their respective courts of appeals districts.

Cases in which death penalty has been assessed

STATE TRIAL COURTS OF GENERAL AND SPECIAL JURISDICTION

District Courts
(375 Courts—375 Judges)

District Courts (365)
Jurisdiction:
• Original jurisdiction in civil actions over $500, divorce, title to land, contested elections, and contested probate matters.
• Original jurisdiction in felony criminal matters.
• Juvenile matters.

Criminal District Courts (10)
Jurisdiction:
• Same as other district courts, but to give preference to criminal cases.

COUNTY TRIAL COURTS OF LIMITED JURISDICTION

County-Level Courts
(420 Courts—420 Judges)

Const. County Courts (254)
Jurisdiction:
• Original jurisdiction in civil actions between $200 and $2,500.
• Probate (contested matters transferred to District Court).
• Exclusive original jurisdiction over misdemeanors with fines greater than $200 or jail sentence (except where there is a Criminal District Court).
• Appeals de novo from lower courts.

County Courts at Law (150)
Jurisdiction:
• Limited jurisdiction over civil matters, most under $5,000.
• Limited jurisdiction over criminal matters.
• Appeals de novo from lower courts.

Probate Courts (16)
Jurisdiction:
• Limited primarily to probate matters.

LOCAL TRIAL COURTS OF LIMITED JURISDICTION

Municipal Courts[1]
(855 Cities—1,176 Judges)

Jurisdiction:
• Criminal misdemeanors with fines less than $200.
• Exclusive jurisdiction over municipal ordinance violations. (Fines up to $2,000.)

Justice of the Peace Courts
(913 Courts—913 Judges)

Jurisdiction:
• Civil actions under $2,500. Small claims.
• Criminal misdemeanors with fines less than $200.
• Preliminary hearings.

[1]All justice of the peace courts and most municipal courts are not courts of record. Appeals from these courts are by trial de novo in the county-level courts, or in some instances, the district courts. Some municipal courts are courts of record. Appeals from those courts are taken on the record to the court of appeals.

Source: Office of Court Administration, Austin, Texas. Reprinted from Neal Tannahill and Wendell M. Bendichek, *Texas Government and Politics*, 3d edition (Glenview, IL: Scott, Foresman, 1989), 290.

justices of peace (JP) usually are not lawyers and probably know little law, but they are authorized to hear and settle civil actions involving small amounts of money, e.g., up to a limit of $5,000, hold preliminary hearings for felonies, try minor criminal cases, and perform some other minor legal functions, such as marrying couples. The JP was once a man of considerable prestige in his neighborhood, but this is not likely to be the case today. Instead of being a country squire whose father image allowed him to dispense a rule-of-thumb justice in neighborhood disputes in an agrarian society with a relatively simple legal system, justices are now likely to be minor local politicians of modest social standing. Normally, JPs are paid through fees assessed against the losing or processing party in each case, and they do not receive salary. The justices thus profit from each case that comes before them and may engage in advertising and in agreements with local peace officers to increase the volume of business. Justices of the peace have been criticized a great deal in recent decades. The fact that they are elected by a small constituency, often the township, gives them an opportunity to profit from nonresidents who come before the court, and they may do so with no fear of electoral recrimination. Although appeal lies from all justice and minor court decisions to the major trial court of the area, in practice the delay and cost involved in appeals usually leave the citizen at the mercy of the justice. Yet this officer is commonly untrained in the law, is responsible to no one (the professional lawyer-judge is embarrassed if criticized or overruled by a higher court, but the typical justice is not), and has a financial interest in the outcome of each case.

Under pressure from the law profession, efforts have been made to eliminate the justice courts in many states. Frequently, they have been replaced with a statewide or city system of minor courts—usually referred to as small claims courts when referring to minor civil courts—while being called magistrates court, traffic court, court of common pleas, or police court when handling minor crimes, otherwise known as misdemeanors. These courts usually are made up of salaried judges who have legal training and devote full time to the job, but the pay is likely to be poor. Beyond the administration of the law, the minor courts handling criminal matters are often concerned with raising some money in traffic or other fines or solving what some see as a local blight, such as prostitution or vagrancy.

A study of the small claims court process in California found that despite the fact that the courts originally were proposed to provide an inexpensive legal forum to solve minor disputes (in California no legal representation is permitted in court, whereas other states allow but discourage it), the courts have, to some extent, become the captive to business interests, which frequently use them to collect unpaid debts. However, the courts are not failures for the individuals who use them, usually people of the middle class. Small claims courts afford opportunities for people to have their day in court, and many are satisfied with the opportunity to tell their side of the story before a judge who appears concerned with their problems. Little concern for the legal formalities and niceties is expressed here; both litigants and judges are concerned more with an intuitive sense of justice.[17]

General Trial Courts

The principal courts for hearing civil and criminal cases "in the first instance" (for the first time) are the backbone of the American judicial system, and most cases that citizens are concerned with will come before them. The quality of justice that individuals receive and their image of the court system will depend largely on the way in which these courts are administered. In most states, they are known as county courts, districts courts, superior courts, or circuit courts, although nomenclature may not be uniform throughout a state. Larger cities in particular are likely to have their own court systems, parallel to but independent of the remainder of the state courts and often with a different nomenclature.[18] In these courts, criminal cases presented by the prosecutor or grand jury are tried (usually before a jury) for the first time, as are all but the most minor civil actions (except cases involving the probating of wills). Appeals taken from the minor courts to the general trial courts are also really heard "in the first instance," because they are started over again from the beginning (tried *de novo*, the lawyers say).

Because permanent records of the proceedings of these courts are kept, they are sometimes referred to as courts of record. Except in unusual circumstances, one judge presides over the courtroom (several judges may serve a single district if it is populous enough). In most cases, the decision of the trial court is final. Although in theory appeal can almost always be taken to a higher court, in practice this is done only in unusual circumstances: for example, in civil cases where large amounts of money are involved, or well-to-do persons or corporations wish to test the constitutionality of the law; in criminal cases with well-to-do defendants or where defense funds have been collected for them; or where a case has become a test case and is being financed by some group interested in civil liberties, such as the American Civil Liberties Union (ACLU).

Courts of Appeal

Thirty-seven states have a court of appeals above the trial courts and below the state supreme court. These courts do not hear cases over from the beginning, but, rather, receive written and oral arguments concerning points of law that were made a matter of dispute at the trial. Ordinarily, questions of fact are not reviewed by appellate courts. Because law, not fact, is being considered, no jury takes part in appeal courts and a multiple bench—from three to nine judges—is used. In some states, the decision of these intermediate courts is final unless a constitutional question is involved, in which case appeal can be made to the state supreme court. This arrangement frees the highest court for intensive consideration of the most important cases. Court reorganization has created this level of courts except in states of relatively small population, but even with additional appellate courts many supreme courts are badly overused with a chronic backlog on the docket.

Appellate courts sometimes are organized separately for criminal and civil appeals. They may be established on the basis of appellate judicial districts, or only one such court may be needed for the entire state. Titles vary, but usually they are known as the *court of appeals* or the *superior court*. Customarily, decisions are reached by a majority vote of the judges who hear the case, and one of the judges writes a formal decision explaining the facts of the case briefly, setting out the legal reasoning used (or said to have been used) by the judges in reaching their decision, and stating the ruling of the court and the disposal of the case. The latter will usually involve either sustaining the findings of the lower court or reversing them. In case of reversal, the defendant in a criminal case may be freed, but the usual order is for another trial in conformity with the findings of the decision. One must waive the protection against double jeopardy—being tried twice for the same charge—when appeal is made.

State Supreme Courts

The general function of the state supreme court (in New York and Maryland called the *court of appeals*, in Maine and Massachusetts, the *supreme judicial court*) was indicated above. Like other appeals courts, it consists of from five to nine judges and follows the same general procedure. The principal difference lies in the fact that the supreme courts are the courts of final decision from which no appeal on any ground is taken except for uncommon instances in which a case is appealed from the state supreme court to the United States Supreme Court, where cases are heard only at the Court's discretion and only when essential questions are involved.[19]

The rarity of federal questions sufficient for United States Supreme Court review allows the state supreme courts to interpret state laws in a variety of ways contrary to the precedents that might be set should the matter be handled by the United States Supreme Court. Thus, a constitutional provision found in many states may be subject to a variety of final interpretations by different state supreme courts, without being subject to higher court resolution.[20] But as a general rule, state supreme courts are more reluctant than the national court to take this activist role and therefore are less likely than the national court to produce the dissenting opinions that are common when courts become active and depart from established precedents.[21]

Unusual cases are heard by a state supreme court in original jurisdiction—that is, the case is tried initially before the court. In some states it offers advisory opinions at the request of the governor, some other state official, a legislative house, or a legislator; but in most states this function is reserved for the attorney general, and the court hears only those cases in which a real issue at law in a specific case is involved.

All courts, but especially courts of final jurisidiction, have great public policy-making powers. They must give the fine edge of meaning to legislative acts and administrative orders because they apply these general policies to specific cases. They also decide the meaning of the state constitution and apply it to cases. Although decisions are stated in the ritualistic language of the law, the court in such cases is actually serving as a political body; that is, it makes policy that has the force and effect of law. In cases where they cannot make effective policy, these courts use their power and prestige to urge other state decision makers to adopt policies they desire.[22]

Throughout our history, conflict, tension, and competition have existed between the state supreme courts and the only judicial agency that may review their decision, the United States Supreme Court. No judge likes to be reversed on appeal.

Perhaps he or she likes to be reversed least of all on questions involving basic social values; yet these are the very cases most often taken to the nation's highest court. Some involve interpretation of state statutes and constitutions by the federal high court, which is especially galling to state judges. Furthermore, the long-range trend has been for the United States Supreme Court to permit expansion of federal activities, bringing about additional jealousy from the state judges.

Special Courts

Special-purpose courts exist in many states.[23] Perhaps the most common is the probate (or surrogate) court, which has the principal responsibility for probating wills and settling estates. Juvenile courts and domestic relations courts are sometimes established as branches of probate courts, or they may be organized separately.

All state legislatures have given some recognition to the argument that juvenile offenders should be treated differently from adults. Some states have rather elaborate systems of juvenile courts, whereas others have makeshift arrangements. The first juvenile courts were established in 1899 in Chicago. Their fundamental purpose has been to emphasize rehabilitation or treatment rather than punishment, an approach based on the demonstrated fact that young criminals have better prospects for rehabilitation than do older ones. A variety of special courts are used to handle juveniles. The structure varies widely from state to state. In some states all juvenile matters are handled by the same courts, whereas in others a variety of special courts exist. Juvenile courts handle offenses and also exist to protect children. There are two different kinds of juvenile offenses: The first is delinquency, a violation of the criminal law; the second is the status offense, an offense unique to juveniles—for example, truancy or running away from home. To protect children, one category of juveniles includes those who must be protected by the courts because of abuse or lack of parent care. A final category includes juveniles who have been removed from their homes permanently where the state has terminated parental rights or the parent voluntarily placed the child for adoption. In most cases, both offenders and juvenile victims are left in their homes. The court's role is to supervise and protect the juvenile. When children are removed from the home temporarily, they may be sent to a foster home or group home where they often are mixed with other troubled juveniles under the court jurisdiction, regardless of their status. Residential treatment centers are emerging in an effort to deal with drug or alcohol abusers or children with emotional or psychological problems. For the serious offender, a juvenile correctional facility exists; these, formerly known as reform schools, during one era sought to reform youngsters with antisocial behavior. Today they may be no more than a place in which to punish the child or serve to protect the public from the offender. For the worst or habitual older offenders, courts are likely to go though an additional procedure to try the juveniles as adults, making them subject to adult penalties. When the juvenile is sent to jail, prison, or a juvenile correctional facility, chances are the inmate will learn more about crime than about the benefits of rehabilitation.

Civil libertarians sometimes argue that protection of the juvenile courts works against the interests of the juvenile. Many conventional processes to protect those in court do not automatically apply to juveniles, and when they do exist often they are not practicably applied. The informality and secretiveness of the court allow the system extraordinary power over the fate of juveniles.[24]

Court Reorganization

In many states, no one can name all of the courts. In practice, the state judicial system may really be held together only by the fact that the same laws—albeit subject to different interpretation—exist statewide. As one critic summarized:

> Terms like *state judicial systems* convey an artificial picture of order and unity. Instead, state courts usually are loose networks of semiautonomous trial and appellate courts. Individual judges and court clerks have been free to manage their courts as they see fit, without much interference or direction from state supreme courts or court administrators. Close interaction between judges and clerks and other local political officials regarding court staffing, budgets, and capital improvements has been common.[25]

In most states the move to a more integrated system began only recently, under pressure from reformers. Such a system eventually would involve consolidation of all courts in a state in a single hierarchy under the supervision of the state supreme court. The state legislature would authorize centralized funding of the courts, separate from the governor or local official's budget. Professional standards would be used to choose judges on a merit system, and policing of the court professional would have to be made more effective, with specific methods of discipline under the control of the state supreme court. Like so many state and local reform proposals, these are not inherently good; they follow assumptions about government working properly rather than tested political processes. Many vested interests oppose such reform, but the 1970s and 1980s saw some degree of reform along these lines in most states, although decentralization is still common. "Most of the evidence gathered so far shows that court reform usually fails to produce important improvements or significant changes in court behavior. Most of the assertions made by reformers also reveal a lack of understanding of how courts work and the complexity of local justice."[26] They are mainly concerned with benefits of efficiency rather than those of localism, although unintended benefits may exist (e.g., the calling up of a competent retired judge to take some of the load from a less-competent judge). The movement for court reform appears to be continuing.

The Police

The criminal justice process usually begins with the action of the police officer. The police function is one of the oldest of American towns. Police are the most frequent contact between the state and local political system and the public. Police do little to prevent crimes, but they nevertheless are called on to react when crime takes place and to provide a variety of non-law-enforcement services. As American society has become complex and as citizens feel isolated, they often call on police to solve a variety of problems.

The liberal spirit that produced the American Revolution was responsible for the fear of the police function in the early development of American towns. This fear was exacerbated by the quartering of soldiers in homes during the revolutionary war. Following the war, most places had no policing by today's standards. The first effort at policing was a night watch, which required that storekeepers (later all taxpaying families) take turns guarding the downtown area against burglars and other criminals.[27] Throughout American history policing has remained a local function, organized by city or county (sheriff) policymaking, separate from the state criminal justice process, which takes over after arrest. Police therefore have always been called on to enforce state laws, despite their being governed by local attitudes toward those laws. As the watch grew unpopular or ineffective, a small hired group usually followed. This often was in response to a perceived crime wave or as a result of a city riot. Policing became more diversified as cities became more diversified, particularly with the perceived threats posed by immigrants to the native populations. By the middle of the nineteenth century the larger cities had a dual system of night watch and daytime patrol.[28] The services remained oriented to serving the downtown business district.

With the advent of machine political systems, the police became street-corner politicians who served double duty in providing law enforcement traditionally identified with policing, coupled with the service role that machines provided. The cop on the beat was the contact with the machine, the welfare provider, and sometime "bagman" who overlooked the illegalities of the machine in return for payoffs shared by the officers and the machine hierarchy. Jobs were provided through machine patronage, usually to the young men of the neighborhoods. Police reformed as cities reformed.

Varieties of Police Behavior

Traditionally the term *professionalism* implies long periods of training in specialized knowledge of a specific nature that is recognized as beneficial to society. It involves a career and carries with it obligations for regard of public interest. By these measures, very few police could be called professional. But with twentieth-century efforts to reform police, professionalism has been a term borrowed to be applied to officers with any of a variety of desirable characteristics. To some it has meant lack of the corruption that plagued machine policing, to others the complexity of services provided and the removal of police from partisan politics. Still others have viewed professionalism as a measure of adherence to the standards of an especially trained force that emphasizes law enforcement and equal application of the law. But regardless of the values emphasized in a department, police are a reflection of the values of the local order.

The selection of police officers is governed by local administrative rules, even when they must adhere to general state practices. In the more reformed places, a merit system is attempted with a variety of formal testing procedures. But even there, selection is ultimately left to a board that must measure whether the recruit will fit into the department. In more traditional departments, selection is made by the chief, top administrators, or politicians who again seek someone to fit local values. Rarely are police officers chosen from outside the local area, unless no suitable recruits are otherwise available.

James Q. Wilson provides a frequently used typology of police behavior in which at least three different emphases are found: order maintenance, law enforcement, and service.[29] But most police departments combine these, depending on the demands of the local political system and the capacity of the locality to pay for reformed service.

The *watchman style* of behavior sterotypes both criminal and victim. Departments displaying this behavior are usually underfunded, with little specialization and few incentives for better policing. Officers have less education than those who exhibit other styles of police behavior, craftlike training, and are most susceptible to corruption. Communities that produce this behavior are most likely to be highly partisan, diversified, and have a low tax base in comparison to other cities. Police behavior will demonstrate distributive justice; that is, giving each person what the officer perceives that person deserves. When complaints are lodged, they will come either from those who believe the police are abusive in their adherence to street justice or from those who complain that the police do not offer enough protection. The law is a tool for maintaining order, rather than a statement of ends to be obeyed regardless of who is involved.

The *legalistic style* of behavior is characterized by the attempt to treat people similarly in terms of their behavior rather than in terms of who they are. Departments displaying this behavior are more hierarchical, usually better funded than watchman-style departments, with more specialized squads and greater reward for adherence to professional mores, including the use of other professionals in the legal system. This will lead to higher arrest rates, the likelihood that police will depend more on other parts of the criminal justice system, and greater reluctance on the part of officers to perform routine services. The officers are better paid and enter service with more formal education and formal training. Corruption, though rare, is taken much more seriously. Complaints usually arise from the conviction that police abuse their power by "going by the book" rather than properly recognizing the particular circumstances of each case. Reform cities are more likely to produce legalistic policing, which leads to a sense of justice based on equal application of the law.

The *service style* of police behavior is found most often in traditional suburbs, or bedroom communities. Departments displaying this behavior handle both crimes and services informally. The department is decentralized in order to maintain a sense of closeness to the service consumer. Officers are paid and trained much as are legalistic-style officers, but when they are hired a peculiar concern is sought for the desire to perform services as well as to provide law enforcement. Officers are rewarded with promotion, pay, and the informal sense of accomplishment for emphasizing service. Public appearances are of principal concern. Unlike watchman policing, little favoritism is shown to groups in the locality, but distributive justice is still the norm. The few complaints come from outsiders who are treated harshly when they are perceived as a threat to community order.

Regardless of its conventional meaning, to the police officer professionalism is usually captured in the internal sense of fitting in with other officers. But that sense will demand different behavior in different types of cities or counties.

The Police Subculture

The combination of values that police bring to their job, coupled with the values particular to the environment in which police work, form the police subculture. All professions form subcultures, but the police subculture has the greatest effect on the American criminal justice system.[30] The police enivironment is normal, but the encounter with the police is abnormal. For example, the student throwing a noisy party rarely will call on the police to come. But when the neighbors are partying too loudly, the police are called to quiet the neighborhood. Or, the student is speeding down the street, with little regard for the police, but when the speeder is pulled over to be ticketed, the driver's day is suddenly ruined. The encounter with the police is almost always going to change the perception of what is normal to the average person. On the other hand, to the police officer such encounters become normal: The party goer is disruptive and the driver is a speeder. Even when a citizen calls the police, the officer encounters abnormal expectations: When a home is burglarized, the rational homeowner should know there is little chance that stolen property will be recovered, but police are called nevertheless. They are unreasonably expected to act, to solve the crime, the crisis of the moment. (Knowledgeable victims will involve the police, however, to help provide evidence expected by their insurance company.)

The average police officer's day is not very dangerous. Despite the misleading impression conveyed by television and movies, few officers fire their weapons on the job in an average year, and few are on the receiving end of gunfire. But the occasional real threat of danger is an ongoing concern to the police officer, and officers' reaction to the *perception* of danger (whether or not accurately measured) may alter their behavior because avoidance of danger is as "normal" in the police officers' subculture as it is in the greater culture.

These factors combine to isolate police officers from the place in which they serve. Police view the public with cynicism.[31] As they settle into a career, the public may be viewed with open resentment. The maze of rules and procedures in the criminal justice system is commonly seen as an impediment to "dealing with" the criminal. Clearing the officer's cases, getting convictions easily regardless of the external measures of justice in a case, becomes the goal.

Ironically, policing may produce some degree of authoritarianism on the part of the officers.[32] To the extent that the goal of justice in America is adherence to democratic values, psychologists find police to be less likely than the average person— and much less likely than others in the criminal justice system—to believe in those values. Democratic safeguards are seen as impediments to effective police work, which could explain why the Supreme Court has been much more concerned with checking police behavior than with that of other legal actors. Particularly in the 1960s, some justices made the presumption that without supervision police would act brutally.[33]

Police Discretion

Total enforcement of the law would be impossible. Many crimes go unreported, and even the best police system would not have the resources or information necessary to catch most criminals. The likelihood is that most people would not want minor violations prosecuted when they do not pose a real threat to public order. But between the realm of full enforcement, where all crimes reported might be acted on, and the realm of actual enforcement, where crimes are acted upon, lies police discretion. Police discretion involves the decision on the part of the officer not to arrest, or the decision to arrest in abnormal circumstances when an arrest usually is not made.[34] Police departments are unlike most organizations. Rather than giving discretion to those at the top of the hierarchy who have the greatest authority, policing often requires that discretion be exercised on the scene by the officer.

Police officers in many circumstances do not make arrests. The law may be ambiguous, thus allowing officers the preferred option of using their sense of what should be done in a situation rather than arresting. With limited resources, the option not to arrest allows the department to set priorities and reduces the cost to the rest of the legal system. If the officer believes that a conviction will not follow, either because the prosecutor will not back the officer or because a violation of the rules of arrest has occurred, the officer may choose to deal with the situation by threatening, but not actually arresting. An option is rarely left to the officer if the victim does not want an arrest. This is common when the victim is a friend or family member of the accused or the victim also is guilty of criminal activity. Victims may fear giving testimony in court or may simply not want the bother or public exposure such testimony brings. In some instances arrest would result in disrespect of the officer or in political retribution. Finally, the decision not to arrest may reflect police corruption.[35]

Where arrest may reduce the strain on scarce resources, particularly when an officer has been called for the same reason repeatedly, *abnormal arrest* may occur. Such arrests may give the appearance of full enforcement or at least will increase the respect for the department. If the accused is suspected of having committed a more serious crime, abnormal arrest for a lesser crime, but more certain likelihood of conviction, may seem just. Ambiguous laws such as disorderly conduct give police the leeway to arrest simply to provide the sense of order demanded by the department or other powerful groups. Finally, abnormal arrest often is a preliminary tool in investigation. For example, the accused is arrested to trade release for information.[36]

Although curbs on police discretion have broadened since the mid-1960s, leading to increased numbers of arrests with warrant, police discretion is still a necessary part of the criminal justice system.

Judges

Judges apply the rules of society to particular cases. They are the arbitrators and authorities who may be theoreticians or the most practical of persons.

The Function of the Judge

What do judges do for society? The popular impressions is that they, like legislators or other bureaucrats, act to protect the public interest. And, unlike most other bureaucrats or legislators, judges may be impelled to consider the meaning of public interest in many of their decisions.

Some judges and judicial writers view the law as a value-neutral technical process, holding that what they would consider the "proper" decision will be made if the system is free from interference by the laity.[37] This view, once widely held, does not conform to reality. Advocates of the Platonic concept of the philosopher-king have viewed the judge as a wise, highly moral person standing above the storms of social conflict, correcting errors by legislators, and in general serving as a social engineer, making the world a better place in which to live despite the machinations of politicians and others. A realistic view, however, indicates that judges are not that qualified or that noble. They have high prestige and the best of them are very intelligent, but they do not stand above the cultural pressures that affect us all.

Judges on the bench tend to reflect, to a degree at least, their personal ideologies. These preferences, although restricted in scope by the expectations of the judicial role and by the ideology of the profession, still are to be found. The evidence is fragmentary, but it suggests that the political party affiliation of judges may have a significant bearing on their votes, at least in states where some identifiable ideological difference exists between the two major parties.[38] Furthermore, other biases appear. In one study, for instance, judges of other identifiable ethnic backgrounds tended more frequently than did Anglo-Saxon judges to find for the defense in criminal cases; to support civil rights and liberties claims; to find for the wife in divorce cases, for the debtor in conflicts with creditors, for the employee in industrial accident cases, and for the governmental administrative agent in conflicts with business concerning regulation. Ethnic and Catholic judges, in other words, were generally more liberal and working-class biased than were Anglo-Saxon judges (who had their own biases).[39] But the biases of judges are restricted by the legal system. In many cases the judge may simply be a technician who formalizes the decisions made by others outside court (e.g., the lawmakers or the precedent-setting higher courts), or the demands of the system (e.g., the realities of jail space or the capacity of the guilty to pay high fines). The judge's decision is therefore one that balances the many conflicting values and system demands.

How Judges Are Chosen

The public simultaneously wants public officials, perhaps especially judges, to be "free from political pressure to insure that their decisions are impartial," and wants them to be "accountable to the people for their official actions."[40] Because the two expectations are not entirely compatible, an ambivalent attitude results.

Because of early nineteeth-century efforts to bring government closer to the people, judgeships routinely were made elective and their terms kept to relatively short duration, e.g., two to four years. Only in the East, where the pattern of government was well established before the full impact of Jacksonian democracy was felt, was a different method adopted. In those states—and for some courts in other states— judges are appointed by the governor or elected by the legislature. Early twentieth-century reformers thought that the practice of electing judges was detrimental to the interests of society. The argument ran that not only should judges be lawyers but especially good lawyers, that they should have a good understanding of sociology, and that voters were ill equipped to select them because voters cannot evaluate the qualifications of the candidates. Appointment by the governor usually was proposed as a substitute for election.

We now know that no simple formula exists for choosing the best way to select judges. Some governors make most of their appointments from among the outstanding lawyers available; others appoint men and women of no distinction among their colleagues. Where judges are elected, various devices have been developed to help put in office persons who are qualified, at least by the standards of the local bar association. In some cities and states, the bar association makes endorsements or takes a poll on the relative qualifications of various candidates. These endorsements are given wide publicity and are influential in filling positions, particularly if no incumbent is running. Incumbent judges who seek reelection; normally are chosen over their challengers because their names are more familiar, but judges whose incompetence has become notorious risk losing their seats in the next election by that same fact of familiarity.

Some states have what is nominally an elected but virtually an appointed judiciary. Because of their tendency to stay in office until they die or until the infirmities of old age force them to retire, judges seldom fail to run for reelection. Consequently, the governor, when authorized to do so, fills most judicial vacancies by appointment. And because the incumbent normally has the advantage in elections, the new judge is then elected and reelected until death, when the governor again fills the post. This practice has created the possibility that a majority of judges in a state have been originally appointed to their posts by the chief executives; the theory thus provides for an elected judiciary, but the practice is for virtually an appointed one, with periodic review by the voters. In one study of judges formally recruited by partisan election, 40 percent initially had been appointed by the governor, as were 65 percent of those formally chosen by nonpartisan ballot. In those states whose legislatures made the selections, 72 percent similarly began their jobs by the governor's action.[41]

A variety of formal methods have developed by which to select judges. In 1990, the dominating method was by election. In thirteen states, all or most judges were chosen by election using a partisan ballot; in fifteen others, they were chosen on a nonpartisan ballot. South Carolina and Virginia judges were selected by the legislature, a method used for supreme court justices in Rhode Island. In eight states, judges were appointed by the governor. These included Connecticut, where formal selection was by the legislature but actual choice was by the governor. Missouri had its own plan of selection (one that was also used for certain positions in at least eleven other states), but even in that state some judges were chosen by election.[42] Most state judges then, are formally elected, but seldom face opposition when running for reelection and rarely are defeated. For example, throughout Wisconsin's history, only three previously elected supreme court justices have subsequently been defeated. Not until 1986 was a California supreme court justice denied retention in office when the question arose on the ballot.[43]

The Missouri Plan for Judicial Appointments

Since 1937, the American Bar Association has advocated a plan whereby the chief executive appoints each judge from a list prepared by a nominating panel composed of judges and laity. At the end of the year or at the next election and periodically thereafter, the judge's name would appear on the ballot with the question, "Shall Judge _____ be retained in office?" If the vote is unfavorable, the chief executive must appoint someone else from the nominating panel's list. The plan tends to give control over judgeships to the state and local bar associations.[44] Missouri has used it since 1940, and although several unsuccessful efforts have been made to force abandonment, it has instead spread to additional states. Today a degree of merit-panel selection is used by some courts in thirty-three states.

In Missouri, the power of the nominating panel has been increased by its own tactics. It sometimes has offered to the governor one name from the opposing party, another probably unacceptable for some reason, and a third the preference of a panel majority. The governor thus has virtually no choice in the matter. The California approach, which applies only to the supreme court and the courts of appeal, is not so highly influenced by the state bar. The governor is not restricted to a list of nominees, but appointments, by law, must be reviewed by a commission on judicial appointments consisting of the chief justice, a senior justice of a court of appeal, and the attorney general. In practice, the report of this commission usually has been quite perfunctory, however, and only in 1982 did it reject gubernatorial appointments. Ronald Reagan strongly urged the full adoption of the Missouri plan while he was governor of California, beginning in 1967. But the plan was unpopular with many rank-and-file lawyers, who thought it would "substitute the invisible politics of the State Bar for the open politics of the governor's appointments."[45] It also had little appeal to lawyers in the legislature, some of whom always hope for eventual appointment to judgeships. Other critics objected that the governor's real interest was in getting conservative Republican judges—which was what the conservative state bar leadership was likely to offer. One study found that Democratic Governor Edmund G. ("Pat") Brown had appointed Democratic judges 82 percent of the time, whereas, Republican Governor Reagan's judicial appointments were 85 percent Republican, suggesting no unwillingness of either to give party affiliation top billing.[46]

An important criticism is leveled at the Missouri plan by Supreme Court Justice Thurgood Marshall, who argued that the plan may work all too well to appoint technically qualified judges who do not meet his ideological criteria:

> But what troubles me the most about the merit system is not that it precludes the appointment of some well-qualified persons who don't meet more or less arbitrary standards. I am more concerned that the merit plan may compel or induce the appointment of judges simply because they are technically well-qualified, without regard to their basic values, philosophy, or life experience.[47]

However, in California at least, with its modified Missouri plan for the higher courts, governors have readily enough found people with the values, ideology, and life experience they have desired.

Removal of Judges

As with other public officials, means exist for the removal of judges, but some are seldom used or even attempted. The following are available:

1. *Rejection at the polls*. In states with some form of the Missouri plan, the election is not a typical election but a referendum on retention, in which the judge does not face opposition but the electorate is given the opportunity to reject the judge's retention after the present term is finished. Some form of election is perhaps the most common method, even though it may have little effect. For example, a judge with a bad reputation sometimes encounters little difficulty in securing reelection. Although one might expect that judges occasionally would have to defend specific decisions at election time, this appears to happen rarely. In fact, the public pays little attention to judicial elections. Rare exceptions occur.

2. *Impeachment*. This elaborate device generally is available, at least for judges of the principal appellate courts, but it is rarely used.

3. *Removal by the governor on request of the legislature*. This method, found in a few states, is not often used, though it is simpler than impeachment because it does not require a formal trial; however, it does involve a formal hearing.

4. *Removal by joint resolution of the legislature*. Similar to the above, but the governor does not participate.

5. *Recall*. In several states, the recall applies to judges as well as to other elective officials. It probably is used even less often for this purpose than it is against other officeholders.[48]

Tenure and Qualifications

States generally require that judges be "learned in the law," that is, that they be lawyers. This does not apply to the justices of the peace, who may be barbers, factory workers, homemakers, or almost anything else—including lawyers. Maine requires judges to have "sobriety of manners," and Maryland requires "integrity, wisdom, and sound legal knowledge," whereas some other states hold that they be "of good character"; but most make no formal requirements. Terms of office vary from election for four years (some trial courts), to appointment for life (Rhode Island). As a general rule, judges will serve longer terms than do other elected state officials.[49]

Unlike the federal court system, each state court usually is autonomous. (In metropolitan areas, the courts may be coordinated, at least as to the calendar and specialty assignments, by a chief judge; but this position may rotate annually irrespective of any administrative ability of the judge next in line. A number of metropolises reflect the complexity of life today by developing capable support organizations. Los Angeles County, with over two hundred superior court judges, has an executive office handled by a career officer who is responsible for support personnel, the budget, physical space and equipment, liaison with nonjudicial officials, and other things needed to make offices run properly. Judicial liaison is cared for by the administrative office of the chief justice of the state supreme court.) In most states, each court is autonomous and is coordinated with others only by the general laws of the state and the procedural rules laid down by the state supreme court. The latter may have specific powers of this kind, or it may have influence only through the effect of its decisions on the lower courts. One state trial judge may work hard while another loafs; one follows a set of procedures that would not be accepted by the next. Especially since about 1970, a number of states have adopted a unified court system. Reformers and bar associations have long urged that all inferior courts become branches of a single statewide court system with unified administrative supervision.[50] Under such a plan, the state supreme court would have broad rule-making power that would make it possible for the law to be administered more uniformly throughout the state. (Uniformity was, incidentally, a major goal of King Henry II in the twelfth century. Resistance to reform may show great staying power; so may reform energy.) A director of court administration under the chief justice would have power to move judges about the state from one district to another to meet varying peak loads and help clear up overcrowded dockets (e.g., from a vacancy).

Officers of the Court

In addition to the judge, who in theory represents the interests of society at large, the court of record has a clerk who prepares the technical documents used in the legal process, keeps the transcript of the court proceedings, and subpoenas witnesses and summons jurors. In some states, this officer has the imposing title of prothonotary. Clerks often are elected and may be paid on a fee, rather than salary, basis. The bailiff, commonly a deputy sheriff, serves court papers made out by the clerk, has custody of prisoners during trial, and keeps order in the courtroom. Other courtroom actors, although they are not officers of the court, include the prosecuting attorney (the title varies from state to state), who presents the case on behalf of the state; the sheriff, the traditional law enforcement officer of the county and representative of the state; and the coroner, who investigates deaths under unusual circumstances and decides, sometimes with the help of a jury, whether a deceased died a natural, suicidal, or accidental death or by the "hands of a person or persons unknown."

These officials ordinarily are all elected to office. Because of the technical job the coroner must perform—involving as it does both medical and legal knowledge—a trend exists toward abolishing the office and turning its functions over to a new one, that of medical examiner on the prosecutor's staff.

Given the diversity of additional services provided by courts today in the area of human services, a variety of other actors in the court are involved, including probation officers.

Prosecution and Defense

The Prosecutor

The prosecuting attorney, known by various titles, holds an office of great discretion. To a considerable extent, this officer decides which laws are to be enforced, how vigorously they are to be prosecuted, and in some states how heavy a penalty is to be demanded (or at least requested) of the trial judge in sentencing. Characteristically, the American prosecutor, as a key decision maker, is an elective official. In Alaska, however, district attorneys are named by the attorney general, a gubernatorial appointee; in Connecticut, the state's attorneys are appointed by superior court judges for four-year terms; in Delaware and Rhode Island, the state attorney general prosecutes all felonies; and in New Jersey, county prosecutors are appointed by the governor for five-year terms.[51] In other states, prosecutors are elected and the political system allows local values to be infused into the interpretation and prosecution of the law. (King Henry II had a problem: He wanted the law to be the same throughout the realm—that is where the term *common law* came from—but he surely expected local values to be given consideration, too. Slow means of communication allowed for this in those days, just as today we try to do it through structural forms such as elections.)

Prosecutors with political ambitions may seek to gain publicity and public approval through their actions. Local prosecutors quite often go on to various higher offices. As always in politics, a bit of luck, a well-publicized case, can offer a huge boost. Of course, many who hope to have a political career are frustrated and fail despite their ambitions. On the other hand, it appears that quite a large number of prosecutors hope to use the office only for publicity and to establish contacts potentially useful for the development of a career as a private practitioner.[52] In addition, of course, we may assume that some prosecutors, especially in small counties, are interested in public service as a temporary civic duty. In some sparsely settled areas, lawyers are so few in number that they may in turn be virtually drafted for office.

After the decision is made to proceed in a case and an indictment or information is brought, the lawyers in a prosecutor's office may be organized in a variety of ways.[53] In most heavily populated areas, assistant prosecutors (civil servants) are assigned to handle separate steps in the process. In other jurisdictions, because of the small size of the office or the importance of the case, one attorney will handle the case from beginning to final disposition. But this procedure can waste time and money when the prosecutor is ready but others involved are not.

The prosecutor's work is absorbed principally in the plea bargaining discussed above. Most prosecuting is done informally in the production of guilty pleas, which makes the trial a brief formality.

The Grand Jury

This body consists, in the common law, of a group of people (traditionally twenty-four, now often fewer) "to which is committed the duty of inquiring into crimes committed in the county from which its members are drawn, the determination of the probability of guilt, and the finding of indictments against supposed defendants."[54] The grand jury has long had two functions: to decide whether persons brought before it by the prosecutor should, according to the evidence presented, be held for trial; and to conduct investigations into the existence of a crime, or of crime generally, and to hold for trial, through a *presentment*, persons it believes may be guilty of crimes, even if the prosecutor has not acted.

The grand jury is falling into disuse as means of securing indictments. It is little used or not used at all for this purpose in about one-half of the states, although it is allowed to remain available in most of them.[55] In its native England, the grand jury has been virtually abolished. The indictment was never anything more than a finding by the jury that enough evidence of guilt existed to justify holding a person for trial. Replacing the grand jury indictment is another ancient procedure in which the prosecutor files an *information* with the appropriate court reporting that a certain person is being held for trial on some specific charge or set of charges. This method is faster and less expensive than using the grand jury. Sometimes the prosecutor still goes to the grand jury with politically sensitive cases or for headline-grabbing work, such as a search for organized crime in the county. But the body continues occasionally to perform vital service as a citizen investigating body. Whenever the prosecutor is lazy, incompetent, or corrupt, a grand jury may be the only means by which the suspected existence of crime or improper prosecution may be inquired into, although sometimes the state attorney general may act when the local prosecutor has failed to do so.

Any investigating grand jury can hold persons for trial. It has the power to require the appearance of witnesses, to punish for contempt, and to grant immunity in exchange for testimony that may be self-incriminating.

The Attorney General

The attorney general is the chief legal officer of the state, but the powers of the office vary greatly among the states. In some small states, this officer usually can enter a criminal case solely at the direction of the governor. In others (e.g., Delaware and Rhode Island), the attorney general's powers include those of local prosecutor for felonies. In some states, even some with large populations, the attorney general has responsibility for *all* criminal appeals, with local prosecutors handling only trials and retrials. One of the most important duties of the attorney general is to interpret the law. A written *opinion of the attorney general* has the force and effect of law unless overruled by the courts and can be produced much faster than can a court decision. Largely because of this, such opinions are relied on by state officers and the legislature.

Except in the smallest states, where procedures may be highly informal, requests for an opinion normally go to the deputy attorney general, who is an appointee of the attorney general (a "political" appointee). If the request is considered legitimate, it is assigned to specialists in the area concerned. Political interests are probably maximized at this point, because the deputy can decide that no opinion is necessary or that the matter should be sent to a particular division that is likely to offer the kind of interpretation the deputy would like. A well-worked draft goes to an opinion review board, which in most states consists of civil servants (typically recent law school graduates with highly orthodox concepts of the law). The board may return the draft for further work, make further modifications, or approve it as presented. The opinion then goes to the deputy and the attorney general, either of whom may reject it and send it back through the pipeline with questions and suggestions. The results are not always to the liking of the attorney general or the governor, but the opinions usually are acceptable to lawyers.

Attorneys general tend to be in positions to gain considerable attention from the mass media, settling highly publicized issues, issuing opinions that may guide or tie up some other state official or the legislature, or becoming involved in celebrated civil or criminal cases. As a result, they have been among the foremost prospects for advancement to the office of governor. Incumbents tend therefore to be, like governors, sensitive to partisan and attention-gripping issues. An unpopular opinion could slam the door of the executive mansion; one that pleases legislators could serve to recruit many campaign volunteers. The office can be one of the best and surest steps on the road to fame.

The Defense Attorney

In criminal matters, the accused has a right to a defense attorney. In our adversarial system, this person is not responsible for justice (neither is any other single person); justice is assumed to emerge, not from the individual concerns of actors, but from the outcomes of the entire interacting system. As a result, the defense attorney is responsible only for being the legal representative of his or her client.[56] The large majority of those who actually go to court for crimes are found guilty, but the defense attorney nevertheless, is concerned with defense and in most instances the best defense is gained by working out the best possible plea bargain.

Those ruled indigent by the court in cases for which a prison sentence is possible have a right to an attorney appointed by the state. In larger jurisdictions, this usually means a public defender, a county civil servant; in smaller jurisdictions, the assistance of counsel assigned by the court, usually a private lawyer who agrees to the fee paid by the court. Only a small percentage of the public is eligible for such assistance, but because a disproportionate number of arrestees are poor, these services get widespread use. Nevertheless, many who believe they are deserving are not eligible and must bear the costs themselves. For most people, securing private counsel is an expensive prospect. Because criminal cases are not very profitable, large law firms generally do not want to handle them. Persons in individual practice or in small firms may need to take numerous cases to make even a modest living, and many lawyers demand a retainer before accepting a case.[57] The few famous criminal lawyers in any given generation usually are flamboyant and able lawyers who have defended rich criminals or who take famous cases financed by such groups as the ACLU or the NAACP.

Representation in civil cases ordinarily must be paid by the participants and is therefore available mainly to those who can afford the high costs involved. Two general exceptions are legal aid, in some places provided by the national government's Corporation for Legal Assistance or by a state system, but in many areas by an organization with a history of providing aid by volunteer lawyers and donated funds; and contingency fee–based cases (that is, a lawyer will take a high portion of the award if the case is won, but will receive nothing if it is lost). People of moderate means use the lawyers of medium-size firms for routine bureaucratic services that courts administer (wills, adoptions, in some states the purchase of homes). Usually when a lawyer is hired, it is for the task at hand and the lawyer does not maintain an ongoing relationship with the client (and is not placed on retainer).

For wealthy individuals and for corporations, hiring a lawyer is a worthwhile cost in order to be able to compete in the maze of specialized rules associated with the law (for example, the entertainment business, securities law, patent law). Herbert Jacob describes this process as one of "gatekeeping" in the legal system. "To use the law one must understand its provisions, master its institutions, and pay fees and costs that accompany its invocation. These costs involve not only direct expenses such as filing fees and attorneys' retainers but also 'opportunity' costs consisting of missed opportunities that might have been pursued had one not been preoccupied with the legal action.''[58] The keys to the gate are held by those trained in the law and successful in its application:

> Individuals with potential legal problems who do not employ lawyers have [a great] disadvantage. They have no one who will open the gates of the legal system for them. They often forgo legal claims because they do not know how to pursue them, or they pursue their claims through normal negotiations without the help of an attorney and without formal litigation[59]

The Trial Jury

As a well-known judge has said, in difficult cases, "The Greeks went to the oracle at Delphi. We go to the jury. . . .''[60] In traditional legal practice, it has been the task of the judge to decide questions of law, the jury those of fact. The way juries do this in practice has been condemned by both lawyers and laypeople who say that these bodies behave with startling inconsistency, that they sometimes free persons who obviously have committed the crime with which they are charged, that the process is cumbersome and expensive, that jurors are not typical citizens but often available only because they need the extra income, that jurors cannot understand the technical testimony frequently presented in court, and that juries generally do not act very rationally.

Some of these criticisms probably are valid, but the desirability of eliminating the jury because its procedures are not very rational is questionable. The method by which the jury ''unravels truth from fiction, with all the shadings of both, is a mystery around which we reverently draw a curtain.''[61] The jury plays an important part in bringing the values of the culture to the judicial process. Undoubtedly jurors sometimes view certain kinds of criminals as heroes, and their attitudes vary according to the type of charge. They sometimes are harsh with one who murders during a family argument—a type of criminal who rarely repeats the crime and is not likely to be a threat to society—but sympathetically free a dangerous psychopath. Certainly jurors are likely to be swayed by their emotions and prejudices and may ignore all the competent technical testimony in favor of these considerations. Yet, in doing this they may help keep the law in step with changing social values.[62]

The jury is something we probably would not invent if it were not already a part of the criminal justice process. Although far older, it reflects the Jacksonian spirit of the preindustrial age, when each citizen in a town had a real opportunity to participate and could judge a neighbor by virtue of shared experiences. In the industrial age, the juror often is someone willing to serve, rather than one who shares the life experiences of those involved in the trial. Although it continues to reflect democratic practice, the jury trial is selected by defense attorneys only when they suspect that doing so will improve the defendant's chances, particularly where the accused is guilty but the attorney believes the defendant can appeal successfully to the juror's personal values. Given that most cases do not go to trial and that the majority of civil and criminal cases are not heard before a jury, jury trial deals with only a very small percentage of the total cases in the American legal system. But these are the cases that tend to be most newsworthy, controversial, conflict-ridden, dramatic, and even on occasion historic.

Selection of Jurors

Persons to be called for service on juries are selected in a variety of ways, depending on state law. A panel of names of prospective jurors may be drawn from the property tax or voters' lists, or even motor vehicle or utility lists by the judges, court clerks, jury commissioners, or sheriffs. Although in theory a "jury of one's peers" should contain a broad cross section of society, law and the practice of those making selections exclude many citizens from service, particularly persons with above-average education. Recent challenges to the fairness of juries have modified the selection process to include a greater cross section of the population by widening the list of eligible jurors and by limiting the challenges that may be made to a juror based on race, religion, ethnicity, or gender.[63]

Once the list is drawn and potential jurors are called, a process of jury selection may take longer than the trial itself. A practice known as *voir dire* allows the judge and in some states each attorney to question potential jurors and remove them by challenges for *cause* (e.g., biases against the defendant proven to the judge) or through *peremptory challenge*, which allows a certain number of challenges by each lawyer without stated reason. These challenges cannot in theory be used to discriminate on the basis of race, gender, or religion, although the purpose or intent is almost impossible to prove. The likelihood that a jury selected in this way will be biased has lead to the development of social scientific techniques—used by those clients who can afford them—that are capable of predicting which kinds of jurors are most likely to reach certain kinds of conclusions.[64]

The nonrepresentative character of the jury is one of the most telling criticisms against it. Yet, attempts to make the jury more representative have caused problems. Poor people on juries sometimes are reluctant to convict a defendant with a background similar to their own even though the accused clearly has committed the act he or she is charged with. Similarly, poor, ill-educated, naive jurors tend to favor huge civil awards (as in medical malpractice or auto accident cases) on the simplistic assumption that "nobody" really pays or is hurt by such awards. In a litigation-prone age, this has sent insurance premiums soaring and has caused increases, for example, in charges to medical patients.

Traditionally, the common-law trial jury consisted of twelve persons who were required to bring in a unanimous verdict. It is called the petit (i.e., small) jury to distinguish it from the grand (i.e., large) jury. In addition to the declining utilization of the jury, other trends include using a body fewer than twelve and dropping the requirement for a unanimous decision. The unanimity requirement is thought by some law specialists to give the defendant an undue advantage and to increase delays and expenses because it encourages hung juries. (On the other hand, independent judgment is subjected to disproportionately greater pressures for unanimity as the size of a group decreases, as every student of small-group behavior knows.)

Usually jurors are called on to spend only a few days, even a portion of one day in court. Sometimes, however, a complex case may keep them involved for several months. In important, widely publicized cases the jury may be *sequestered* in hotel rooms between court sessions, isolated from family, friends, or news media.

Folk Myth and the Jury

Judges and lawyers sometimes try to create an almost supernatural image of the court system and its procedures. The courts are, however, only another set of institutions in the governmental decision-making process. As one author pointed out:

> Decisions in court are not greatly different from those made outside the court; in that they concern, for the most part, familiar day-to-day happenings; that they involve the same kind of mental operations as are used in solving problems that arise in business or housekeeping; and that they can be and frequently are made by ordinary citizens without special training—namely, jurors.[65]

In the 1950s, the University of Chicago Law School studied the way the jury system operates in the United States.[66] One hope had been to observe juries in action, unknown to the members of the jury, and to determine how, in general, a jury reaches its verdict. This produced such criticism and was seen as such a threat to a major symbolic institution in American jurisprudence that the project had to be aborted.[67] The study of juries did produce a great deal of information, however. It examined 3,567 criminal cases and concluded that, despite popular belief, juries do not deviate as often from what those trained in the law would have done.[68] The study, however, also shows that the jury provides a unique service to justice only in rare cases. The judge (in later interviews) agreed completely with the jury's verdict 72 percent of the time. In most of the other cases, the jury was more lenient than the judge would have been. In only 9 percent of the cases did the judge consider the jury to have been legally wrong and in most of these thought the jury erred on the side of leniency. The jury differed uniquely from the judge only in its reluctance to convict in those cases where ''anyone'' could have been the guilty party—particularly in connection with violation of drunk driving, gambling, gaming, and liquor laws. But is was also somewhat more reluctant than judges in all cases to conclude that the evidence extended ''beyond reasonable doubt.'' Simulation studies more recently have reached similar conclusions about the nature of juries[69]

Corrections

A variety of penalties are available to the court once a defendant has been found guilty of a crime. A fine, probation, or incarceration have long been widely used, and restitution to the locality through service work or to the victim in some form are increasingly used. Most crimes are misdemeanors; convictions lead to fines or on occasion jail time (jails are used mainly to house those awaiting trial). Punishing the convicted criminal with a state prison sentence has always posed two dilemmas to the American justice system. We have not been able to reach a consensus about the principal reason for a system of corrections (as mentioned earlier, rehabilitation, retribution, or different types of deterrence are all reasons). Whenever such consensus has failed in the American federal system, some degree of expression has been given to each of the conflicting viewpoints. Whereas prison reform from the 1930s through the 1960s seemed to emphasize the concept of rehabilitation, social science demonstrated rather effectively that such rehabilitation rarely was achieved by the prison system. But as we entered a period with greater demand for retribution in the form of prison sentences, the second dilemma grew—public demand for prison sentences is not connected with public willingness to pay for prison space. This is not a new problem; it existed in the century after the Revolution:

> [J]ails during this period were not a source of much controversy, except when the public objected to building a new one. In early America jails often did not exist at all, and punishment normally consisted of flogging, hanging, or banishment. This was also true in the mining and shipping towns of the West. When jails were built, they often became places where criminals and debtors, men, women, and children were indiscriminately mixed. Sanitation facilities in them were minimal or nonexistent. Sometimes conditions would get so bad that reformers demanded action, but jails and their inmates were relatively invisible to the average citizen, so the proponents of economy usually prevailed.[70]

Today the reluctance to build jails and prisons continues, but the demand to send the convicted to prison produces prisons that are overflowing. Following a decline in prison sentences in the 1960s, the number of prisoners increased dramatically in the 1970s and populations doubled in the 1980s despite no accompanying increase in crime rates.[71] The patterns varied from state to state. Whereas only 60 offenders per 100,000 population in North Dakota were sentenced to prison, 288 per 100,000 in Maryland were sentenced. The ratio of the number on probation or parole to those in prison was 6 per 100 in Minnesota, but 26 per 100 in South Dakota and 24 per 100 in Missouri.[72] Increasingly the principal consideration for the judge who must decide whether to imprison someone is that of space. Sometimes this trade-off is unrealistic, given the offenses. For example, in the fall of 1988 District of Columbia jails were so full that corrections officials refused new inmates, despite the fact that "judges felt compelled to continue sentencing offenders at the rate of 100 per week."[73]

Alternatives to prison sentences are increasingly experimental for the less-dangerous criminal. Minnesota and Washington have adopted a "formula for each offense assigning a certain prescribed punishment. The reason was to assure fair, nonarbitrary sentences. But the main impact has been to allow the state to control the growth of the prison population by reserving expensive prison slots for the most violent offenders while dealing with others in county workhouses, drug treatment centers and halfway houses."[74] House arrest monitored by electronic devices is particularly popular in Florida, whereas stricter probation that requires frequent visits and drug tests are being experimented with in Georgia.[75]

Traditionally, the rights of convicted felons were held to be protected by the executive branch of government, posing separation-of-powers problems for the courts in dealing with protection of such rights. But since the passage of the 1964 Civil Rights Act, prisoners increasingly have sued in federal court to protect basic rights violated by prison practice.[76] This has made the space problem worse. In

Texas, the U.S. District Court cited a long list of deficiencies including overcrowding, failure to produce minimal security for prisoners, insufficient medical care, little psychiatric care, no provision for inmates with special needs, indiscriminate use of solitary confinement or segregated confinement, and a variety of violations of due process of law, including violation of Texas's own prison rules.[77]

A new wave in correction's reform involves the privatization of the process. Kentucky, Tennessee, Florida, and Texas have experimented with private contracts for the provision of prisons and jails.[78] Critics maintain that this process reduces the concern for inmate rights and may pose security threats, making the state potentially liable for damages on both counts. Defendants of the system once again return to the notion that prisoners do not abandon most rights by being convicted and argue that private prisons can be made as secure as others.

Although the prison problems have gotten most attention in recent years, overloading of the probation and parole process is also serious. *Probation*, a process of supervising outside of a jail or prison those found guilty of a crime, and *parole*, a process of supervising those released from prison, are also costly. A 1986 report found about three-fourths of those under state correctional supervision were on probation or parole rather than incarcerated. Probation constituted 64.6 percent of the offenders under correctional supervision, parole 10.1 percent, prison 16.9 percent and jail 8.4 percent.[79] Once again, these processes stimulate little public willingness to fund but persistent demand for improved service. Although they must be funded, probation and parole are cost savings compared to imprisonment. A Florida study found that it costs fourteen times more to incarcerate than to supervise an offender in another way,[80] again posing the question of the purposes of correctional procedures.

Concluding Notes

The American legal system grew from the principles of Madisonian federalism. Governments were decentralized and existed for a few principal purposes, one of which was the provision of a criminal justice system. Safeguards were both direct and indirect. State constitutions contained bills of rights to protect those accused of crimes. The limitations of the structural system of checks and balances were particularly geared to protecting individuals from the powers of government. Criminal law was passed at the state level, but the provision of law enforcement was a local function, physically removed from the law makers at the state capital. The courts grew around county government. The system was not designed for efficient protection against criminals. Since the 1930s, we have moved to the principles of new federalism, and the contradictions between a system of limited government and one of service provision are well illustrated in the present system of justice. This notion of federalism designed to serve rather than check will be the topic of the final chapter.

Serious efforts are being made by bar associations, legislatures, judges, social service agencies, and others to keep judicial administration abreast of the times. Many changes have taken place; others seem to be on the way. Juries are less in use; judges are more specialized; witnesses are more often sought as experts than as persons thought to have observed certain activities; nonlawyer specialists (clinical psychologists and social workers, for example) make an increasingly large portion of the major decisions that affect prosecutors, judges, and juries.

Law and the judicial process, then, are parts of the total culture in which they exist and are subjected to the same kinds of pressures that affect other institutions. In a day when most of our socially useful activities are dominated by the expert and the pattern of specialization, our courts are also coming to be dominated by the expert and to conform to the pattern of specialization.

Notes

1. E. Adamson Hoebel, *The Law of Primitive Man* (Cambridge, MA: Harvard University Press, 1968), chapter 2.

2. On this section generally, see Thurman Arnold, *Symbols of Government* (New Haven, CT: Yale University Press, 1935).

3. An excellent short review of the history of law and justice in the United States can be found in Howard Abadinsky, *Law and Justice* (Chicago: Nelson-Hall, 1988), chapter 2.

4. Herbert Jacob, *Justice in America*, 4th ed. (Boston: Little, Brown, 1984), particularly chapter 9.

5. The notion of a subculture among criminal justice professionals is developed in a variety of places, but it is best evident in regard to policing. See Jerome H. Skolnick, *Justice Without Trial*, 2d ed. (New York: John Wiley and Sons, 1975), particularly chapter 3, "A Sketch of the Policeman's Working Personality"; and Arthur Niederhoffer, *Behind the Shield* (Garden City, NY: Anchor Books, 1969).

6. See Richard A. Myren, *Law and Justice* (Pacific Grove, CA: Brooks/Cole, 1988), chapter 1. See also A. S. Cutler, "Why the Good Citizen Avoids Testifying," *Annals* 287 (May 1953): 103–109. This entire volume on 'Judicial Administration and the Common Man" deals with some of the issues discussed in this section.

7. See Skolnick, *Justice . . . Trial*; and Wayne R. La Fave, *Arrest: The Decision to Take a Suspect into Custody* (Boston: Little, Brown, 1965).

8. Malcolm Feeley, *Court Reform on Trial* (New York: Basic Books, 1983), chapter 2.

9. See the collection of articles in Roman Tomasic and Malcolm M. Feeley, eds., *Neighborhood Justice: Assessment of an Emerging Idea* (New York: Longman, 1982), particularly Daniel McGillis, "Minor Dispute Processing: A Review of Recent Developments," 60–77.

10. Paul Nejelski and Larry Ray, "Alternatives to Court and Trial," in Fannie J. Klein, ed., *The Improvement of the Administration of Justice*, 6th ed. (Chicago: American Bar Association Press, 1981), 263–82.

11. See David Caplovitz, *The Poor Pay More* (New York: The Free Press, 1967); and Jacob, *Justice in America*, particularly chapter 10.

12. On plea bargaining, see Abraham Blumberg, *Criminal Justice* (New York: Basic Books, 1964); Jacob, *Justice . . . America*, chapter 9; and Henry R. Glick, *Courts, Politics, and Justice*, 2d ed. (New York: McGraw-Hill, 1988), 177–98; and Frank W. Miller, *Prosecution* (Boston: Little, Brown, 1969).

13. Edward L. Kimball, "Criminal Cases in a State Appellate Court: Wisconsin 1839–1959," *American Journal of Legal History* 9 (Apr. 1965): 116–117.

14. James W. Marquart and Ben M. Crouch, "Judicial Reform and Prisoner Con-

trol: The Impact of *Ruiz v. Estelle* on a Texas Penitentiary," in George F. Cole, ed., *Criminal Justice Law and Politics*, 5th ed. (Pacific Grove, CA: Brooks/Cole, 1988), 416–42.

15. Robert L. Anderson and George John Miller, "Law and the Courts," in Manning J. Dauer, ed., *Florida's Politics and Government,* 2d ed. (Tallahassee: University Presses of Florida, 1984).

16. Delmar Karlen, *The Citizen in Court* (New York: Holt, Rinehart and Winston, 1964), chapter 1.

17. Kerry Kinney Fine, "Small Claims Court: Democracy in America?" (Unpublished doctoral thesis, The University of California, Riverside, 1978). See also Alfred Steinberg, "The Small Claims Court: A Consumer's Forgotten Forum," *National Civic Review* 63 (June 1974): 289ff.

18. See Henry J. Abraham, *The Judicial Process*, 4th ed. (New York: Oxford University Press, 1980), chapter IV.

19. For discussion of the jurisdiction of the United States Supreme Court in state appeals, see G. Alan Tarr and Mary Cornelia Porter, "State Constitutionalism and State Constitutional Law," *Publius* 17 (Winter 1987) :1–12, 8–9; Walter F. Murphy and C. Herman Pritchett, *Courts, Judges and Politics*, 4th ed. (New York: Random House, 1986), 88; Henry Abraham, *The Judiciary*, 2d ed. (Boston: Allyn and Bacon, 1969), 18–24.

20. See Stanley H. Friedelbaum, "Independent State Grounds: Contemporary Invitations to Judicial Activism," in Mary Cornelia Porter and G. Alan Tarr, eds., *State Supreme Courts* (Westport, CT: Greenwood Press, 1982), 23–54.

21. Patterns of dissent at the national level are discussed in Abraham, *Judicial Process*, 214–17. State dissents vary widely; for a comparative study of eight states, see Philip L. Dubois, *From Ballot to Bench* (Austin: University of Texas Press, 1980).

22. Henry R. Glick, "Policy-making and State Supreme Courts: The Judiciary as an Interest Group," *Law and Society Review* 5 (Nov. 1970): 271–88.

23. See Roger Handberg, "Specialized Courts, Turning the Clock Back or Forward," in Philip Dubois, ed., *The Politics of Judicial Reform* (Lexington, MA: Lexington Books, 1982), 99–108.

24. Glick, *Courts. . . Justice*, 363–64.

25. Henry R. Glick, "The Politics of State-Court Reform," in Dubois, *Ballot to Bench*, 17.

26. This section relies on Glick, "The Politics of State-Court Reform," in Dubois, *Ballot to Bench*; quotation at 29.

27. For the development of early policing, see Charles R. Adrian and Ernest S. Griffith, *A History of American City Government: The Formation of Traditions 1775–1870* (New York: Praeger, 1976), 85–93.

28. The best case study of police development is Roger Lane, *Policing the City: Boston 1822–1885* (New York: Atheneum Books, 1971).

29. This section relies on James Q. Wilson, *Varieties of Police Behavior* (New York: Atheneum, 1968).

30. This section relies on Skolnick, *Justice . . . Trials*, chapter 3, and Niederhoffer, *Behind the Shield*. See also the collection of articles by Abraham S. Blumberg and Elaine Niederhoffer, *The Ambivalent Force*, 3d ed. (New York: Holt, Rinehart and Winston, 1985) and the novels of Joseph Wambaugh.

31. Skolnick, *Justice . . . Trial*, chapter 3; Niederhoffer, *Behind the Shield*, chapter 4.

32. Niederhoffer, *Behind the Shield*, chapter 5.

33. Particularly in *Miranda v. Arizona*, 384 U.S. 456 (1966).

34. Joseph Goldstein, "Police Discretion Not to Invoke the Criminal Process: Low-

Visibility Decisions in the Administration of Justice," in Cole, *Criminal Justice . . . Politics*, 83–102.

35. La Fave, *Arrest: The Decision to Take a Suspect into Custody*.

36. Ibid.

37. Glendon A. Schubert, Jr., *The Public Interest* (New York: The Free Press, 1960).

38. Herbert Jacob, "Courts," in Virginia Gray, Herbert Jacob, and Kenneth N. Vines, eds., *Politics in the American States*, 4th ed. (Boston: Little, Brown, 1983), 240.

39. Stuart Nagel, "Political Party Affiliation and Judges' Decisions," *American Political Science Review* 55 (Sept. 1961): 843–51; and Stuart Nagel, "Ethnic Affiliation and Judicial Propensities," *Journal of Politics* 24 (May 1962): 92–110.

40. Carl D. McMurray and Malcom B. Parsons, "Public Attitudes Toward the Representational Role of Legislators and Judges," *Midwest Journal of Political Science* 9 (May 1965) :167–85.

41. Burton M. Atkins and Henry R. Glick, "Formal Judicial Recruitment and State Supreme Court Decisions," *American Politics Quarterly* 2 (Oct. 1974): 427–49.

42. The methods vary so widely that no summary table of methods is useful. Consult the latest edition of the *Book of the States* (Lexington, KY: Council of State Governments) for the particular method used in a given state. The figures in this paragraph are from Glick, *Courts . . . Justice*, 85.

43. Fred A. Wileman, "The Wisconsin Judiciary," in Wilder Crane, A. Clark Hagensick et al., eds., *Wisconsin Government and Politics*, 4th ed. (Milwaukee: Department of Governmental Affairs, University of Wisconsin, 1987), 181; Michael J. Ross, *California, Its Government and Politics*, 3d ed. (Monterey, CA: Brooks/Cole, 1988), 127–28.

44. Jack W. Peltason, *The Missouri Plan for Selection of Judges* (Columbia: University of Missouri Press, 1945); William J. Keefe, "Judges and Politics," *University of Pittsburgh Law Review* 20 (March 1959): 621–31.

45. Lou Cannon, *Ronnie and Jesse: A Political Odyssey* (Garden City, N.Y.: Doubleday, 1969), 303. For more recent developments, see Bernard L. Hyink, Seyom Brown, and E.W. Thacker, *Politics and Government in California*, 11th ed. (New York: Harper & Row, 1985), 194–95.

46. Cannon, *Ronnie and Jesse*, 304.

47. "Mr. Justice Marshall Comments on the Missouri Plan," in Murphy and Pritchett, *Courts . . . Politics*, 179.

48. For the particulars of a state, see the latest edition of the *Book of the States*. For specifics on the recall, see chapter 6 herein.

49. *Book of the States*, most recent edition.

50. See Ralph N. Kleps, "Reorganization and Simplification of Court Structure," in Klein, ed., *Improvement . . . Justice*, 17–34.

51. Abadinsky, *Law and Justice*, 122.

52. Jacob, *Justice in America*, chapter 5.

53. Abadinsky, *Law and Justice*, 123–25.

54. "Grand Jury," *American Jurisprudence* (Rochester, NY: Lawyers Co-operative Publishing Co., 1939), 832.

55. Abadinsky, *Law and Justice*, 154.

56. See the volume of articles, *Lawyers' Ethics*, Allan Gerson, ed. (New Brunswick, NJ: TransAction Books, 1980).

57. A good summary of defense lawyers' work in criminal cases is found in Abadinsky, *Law and Justice*, chapter 5.

58. Herbert Jacob, *Law and Politics in the United States* (Boston: Little, Brown, 1986), 123.

59. Ibid., 150–51.

60. Curtis Bok, ''The Jury System in America, '' *Annals* 287 (May 1953): 92–96.

61. Ibid., 94.

62. See Reid Hastie, Steven D. Penrod, and Nancy Pennington, *Inside the Jury* (Cambridge, MA: Harvard University Press, 1983), chapter 2.

63. Murphy and Pritchett, *Courts . . . Politics*, 355–56.

64. Abadinsky, *Law and Justice*, 156–60.

65. Karlen, *Citizen in Court*, 118.

66. D.W. Broeder, ''The University of Chicago Jury Project,'' *Nebraska Law Review* 38 (May 1959): 744–60.

67. Harry Kalven, Jr., ''Jury, the Law, and the Personal Injury Damage Award,'' *University of Chicago Law School Record* 7 (Feb. 1958) :6–21.

68. Harry Kalven, Jr., and Hans Zeisel, *The American Jury* (Boston: Little, Brown, 1966).

69. Hastie, Penrod, and Pennington, *Inside the Jury*.

70. Adrian and Griffith, *History of American City Governement*, 89.

71. Howard W. Stanley and Richard G. Niemi, *Vital Statistics on American Politics* (Washington: CQ Press, 1988), 338.

72. *Star Tribune,* Mar. 12, 1989, 14A.

73. *Star Tribune,* Mar. 13, 1989, p.1A.

74. Ibid., 4A.

75. Ibid.

76. Jack Wright, Jr., and Peter W. Lewis, *Modern Criminal Justice* (New York: McGraw-Hill, 1978), 283.

77. Wilbourn E. Benton, *Texas Politics*, 5th ed. (Chicago: Nelson-Hall, 1984), 312.

78. Timothy H. Matthews, ''Issues in Corrections,'' *1988–1989 Book of the States*, 394–97.

79. Ibid., 391–97.

80. Roger Handberg, ''The Criminal Justice System in Florida,'' in Dauer, ed. *Florida's Politics*.

"*Many of your constituents feel that a tax increase isn't appropriate to their life styles.*"

14

Fiscal Federalism

In an industrial and postindustrial society, demands on government have increased steadily. Indeed, state and local expenditures have expanded enormously since the New Deal era, as we point out in chapters 2 and 4. Some priorities remain constant. For example, public education was the largest item in the expenditure budget of governments at these levels in 1902 and will continue to be into the next century. Some priorities have changed dramatically. For instance, roads, which cost $175 million each year at the beginning of the century, have changed from rut-filled dirt lanes to hard-surfaced and often limited-access divided highways. Similar changes have taken place in almost every other area of activity as America urbanized, technology advanced, and the nation became much more populous and productive. (For data, see the most recent copies of the *Statistical Abstract of the United States* and the *Census of Governments.*)

The efforts of state and local governments have varied with political pressures that reflect contemporary concerns. Following World War I, during the fabled, care-free 1920s, the concentration beyond the myth was in fact on building high schools and hard-surfaced roads. The 1930s were devoted to the depression and most of the next decade to World War II. The 1950s, the "quiet Eisenhower years," was a time for great hope in the rehabilitation of the mentally ill; the gigantic interstate highway system was begun; and so was the desegregation of education and some other functions. The 1960s, a time of turmoil and the Vietnam War, brought calls for populistic reforms (including participatory policy making), for full racial integration of society, and application of civil rights at all levels of government. The women's movement began (or resumed from the 1920s) as women's roles gradually broke traditional restrictions.

Education and welfare remained big-spending items in the 1970s, but cutbacks occurred as society began to return to the traditional American belief that prosperity is a function of the production of greater total wealth rather than a better distribution of what exists. The 1980s, the Reagan years, were a time of nostalgic yearning for a simpler era and less-complex governments, a better-behaved citizenry, a national agenda of unified and fulfilling goals, and a return to world leadership (albeit with little evaluation of the costs of retrenchment). Reagan was a master in the manipulation of symbols. He knew better than to translate them into specific goals or to try to go beyond myth. Those left to struggle with the realities probably were shocked to find that despite great reluctance, construction and maintenance of prisons was the fastest-growing major state and local government program of the 1980s. The prison population nearly doubled during the decade as citizens demanded harsh punishment upon conviction while the courts simultaneously ordered limits to overcrowding.

In 1902, before all these changes, citizens no doubt complained of taxes as we do today. But they paid only $11.08 per capita in state *and* local taxes. By 1990, each taxpayer paid more than 140 times as much, or about 4.6 times the amount in constant dollars. Such expansion of services and their costs could not have been met without considerable effort. Part of the cost has been offset by increased productivity, an upgraded standard of living, and the consequent ability to pay; but the expanded cost has also helped to incite a search for new revenue sources. The percentage of charges for services has almost tripled since World War II, now comprising almost one-fifth of state and local revenue. The property tax remains the most important local tax, but state governments have turned to sales, excise, income, and other taxes (including gambling through legalized lotteries) as they have increasingly withdrawn from the once-dominant property tax. Local governments have sought to broaden their tax bases, looking to self-imposed sales, excise, and income taxes, as well as shared taxes and revenues from state governments. The national government also has become an important source of money for both these levels of government. But in the two generations since World War II, spending has exceeded collections and state and local debt has been rising.

This chapter will consider state and local fiscal matters in terms of federalism. Every tax in the federal system has an impact on every other revenue source. Each of the thousands of governments in the mazelike American system (described in previous chapters) must consider many others whenever a fiscal decision is made. A school district not only must consider the benefit of accepting state aid, it also must consider the degree of autonomy that might be lost in doing so. A state not only must consider the money raised by an income tax, but also the potential relocation of businesses to other states if rates are too high. Poor cities cannot simply pursue "fair" taxes, which impose on the rich more than the poor; they must consider whether sufficient numbers of upper-income people live in the area to raise the revenues necessary to provide city services. Thus, fiscal federalism cannot be explained in terms of neat economic models.

Measurement problems abound in regard to fiscal federalism. State governments measure their revenues and expenditures in different ways; combining them as the Bureau of the Census does periodically is at best only a measure of trends, not a precise measure for making comparisons. Dollar amounts can change considerably in a short period of time. Is a tax dollar collected by the state and given as a gift to a city to be considered state or local revenue? Is a state-mandated program administered by local government to be considered a state or local expenditure? In this chapter we usually will use combined state and local measures. But aggregate data can be misleading. A study of the forty-nine largest cities in the United states in 1983 found Austin twelve times more dependent on charges than Pittsburgh, and Milwaukee forty-four times more dependent on state government than Oklahoma City.[1] Nevertheless, it is almost impossible to isolate state or local responsibility for programs.[2] We will therefore emphasize the major trends and some of the political questions that must be asked when fiscal decisions are being made at the state and local levels.

A Free Lunch?

The typical citizen probably has little understanding of the relationships between government revenues and expenditures. The traditional practice of politicians is to promise more services in a better fashion at lower cost than the opposition. This probably has helped preserve the citizen's habit of making no association between service levels and costs. Everybody knows something about taxes. For example, homeowners understand their property tax—at least they can determine how much they must pay and whether it is more or less than the preceding year. The sales tax is familiar to most people because it is routinely added to the marked price of goods when they make a purchase. The income tax cannot escape the attention of the employed person in any state that levies it, especially when the filing deadline nears and state as well as national rules must be learned. Yet, the economic effects of particular taxes are unknown to most citizens. They know little more about the services that taxes buy (except that they may associate the property tax with schools); nor do they attempt to find their way through a wonderland of *grants-in-aid, shared taxes, dedicated funds, joint financing, or service charges.*

> *Shared Taxes:* **Taxes collected by one government but divided with other governments according to a prescribed formula.**

> *Grants-In-Aid:* **Payments made by voluntary appropriation from one government to another. The term is used to refer to both types described in this chapter:** *categorical grants-in-aid and block grants.*

> *Joint Financing:* **Payment by more than one government for a single project. Most local government projects are jointly financed through grants-in-aid or shared taxes.**

> *Service Charges or Fees:* **Differ from taxes in that they are based principally on benefits directly received in return for payment. Public water-supply departments commonly levy service charges, for example.**

> *Dedicated Funds:* **Produced from taxes reserved for a particular governmental function. Gasoline taxes are dedicated to street and highway building or repair.**

It is easy for people to agree with the politician or commentator who tells them that taxes are too high, for they have no criterion against which to measure. They balk from time to time when major tax increases are submitted to them on referendum, and their reluctance to pay taxes they do not associate with services has encouraged the extensive use of *dedicated funds.* By making the results of the tax more directly visible, these funds help people to understand why money is being asked and may help persuade them to accept the need for it. Thus, levying an additional penny on the gasoline tax is pledged for road building; extra millage (a mill is one-tenth of a cent, or a tax rate of 0.1 percent) on the property tax may be referred exclusively for building new schools; a state lottery may be pledged to aid school operations; fee increases for hunting and fishing licenses will go only for the stocking of more deer and trout— all are examples of dedicated funds. The use of dedicated funds has long been denounced by specialists in financial administration because of the rigidity it produces in the system. That is, it leaves less room for the executive or legislative branch to make adjustments for changing demands. But the practice undoubtedly makes the acceptance of new taxes or service charges more palatable to the typical citizen. Politicians must keep in mind the first rule of taxes; In general no one likes to pay more, and if they *must* be increased someone *else* should pay for them.

Dedication of funds is only part of the picture. State constitutions also place limitations on revenue options, localities are limited by state mandates, and national grants-in-aid come with strings attached. Thus, despite the likelihood that taxpayers will hold the last legislator to handle the tax dollar responsible, in a majority of instances legislators at the state and local levels have limited freedom in spending money. Unlike the national government, states and localities do not control their own credit and therefore cannot use indefinite deficit spending; someone must pay for every service. But the politics of revenues and expenditures within the maze of federalism often dictates that someone else be blamed for tax increases whereas credit is eagerly sought for service benefits. In the aggregate, there is no free lunch, but in particular cases, the illusion of one may tempt the taxpayer.

Expenditure Patterns

As mentioned earlier, expectations, and hence expenditure levels, have increased especially since the end of World War II. As table 14-1 shows, states and localities were spending sixty times more money (in current dollars) in 1985 than in 1942. But whereas new functions of government have been added, none have replaced the traditional ones in financial importance. Although fluctuations can be found, only higher education stands out as an area that commands a much greater percentage of state and local expenditures (from 2.7 percent to 8.0 percent) since 1945. This is explained by the priority given to higher education, led by the veterans of World War II, and the greatly increased percentage of students who have since attended college. A heavy proportion of these students have attended state universities or colleges which are subsidized by the state.

Twentieth-Century Changes

Some basic changes in the pattern have occurred since the beginning of the century, among them the following:

- New functions of government have appeared and have begun to challenge the old functions in importance, including unemployment compensation, urban re-

TABLE 14–1   Combined State and Local Expenditure Trends

	1942	1955	1965	1975	1985
Total Dollars (Millions)	10,914	40,375	86,554	269,215	656,022
Expenditure (Percentage of Total)					
Direct General Expenditure					
Education					
Higher	2.7%	3.6%	3.7%	8.1%	8.0%
Local Schools	20.3%	25.2%	17.5%	22.8%	20.1%
Other	0.7%	0.6%	0.4%	1.7%	1.3%
Total Education	23.7%	29.5%	21.6%	32.6%	29.4%
Highways	13.7%	16.0%	14.1%	8.4%	6.9%
Public Welfare	11.2%	7.8%	7.3%	10.5%	10.6%
Health	1.5%	1.2%	1.0%	1.6%	2.1%
Hospitals	4.0%	5.1%	5.2%	5.4%	5.5%
Police	3.6%	3.0%	2.9%	3.2%	3.2%
Fire Protection	2.2%	1.7%	1.5%	1.3%	1.4%
Natural Resources	2.0%	2.0%	2.0%	1.6%	1.3%
Sanitation and Sewerage	2.1%	2.8%	2.7%	2.8%	2.7%
Housing and Urban Renewal	2.2%	1.2%	1.4%	1.3%	1.6%
Local Parks and Recreation	1.2%	1.3%	1.3%	1.3%	1.4%
Financial Administration			1.5%	1.3%	1.6%
General Control	5.3%	3.6%	1.7%	1.9%	2.2%
Interest on Debt	6.5%	2.1%	2.9%	3.3%	4.9%
Total General Expenditure	84.2%	83.5%	86.1%	85.7%	84.1%
Utility and Liquor					
Water Supply System	3.4%	3.7%	2.9%	2.0%	2.2%
Electric Power Supply	2.0%	2.0%	2.3%	2.0%	3.9%
Transit System	1.8%	1.5%	1.3%	1.5%	2.1%
Gas Supply System	0.2%	0.3%	0.3%	0.2%	0.5%
Liquor Stores	2.8%	2.1%	1.4%	0.7%	0.4%
Total Utility and Liquor	10.1%	9.6%	8.2%	6.4%	9.1%
Insurance Trust Expenditure	5.7%	6.8%	5.7%	7.9%	6.7%
Total Expenditures	100.0%	100.0%	100.0%	100.0%	100.0%

Source: Percentages compiled by authors from U.S. Bureau of the Census.

development, public housing, environmental control, airports, and parking lots.

- Old functions have been greatly expanded and altered in concept. This applies to recreation, conservation, mental health, highways, higher education, health, and welfare programs. For example, until 1900, Chicago dumped its raw sewage into Lake Michigan, which was also the source of its water supply.[3] Rivers were similarly used. The nineteenth-century rule of thumb was to take the water upstream and dump the sewage downstream, but with the growth of metropolitan areas one city's downstream increasingly was another's upstream. By mid-century the movement was well under way to purify the water and to treat the problem as being areawide, first by pressure from the state and then the national government.

- State governments have assumed an increasingly important role at the state and local levels. The U.S. Census Bureau found that in 1902, state expenditures accounted for only 12 percent of total state and local expenditures. By the early 1990s, they accounted for over one-third of the total. The states have enormously expanded the number and increased the quality of their direct services to the public in this century.
- The states have gradually assumed more collection responsibilities for local governments. In the area of education particularly, state expenditure is principally payments to local governments, though states add whatever "strings" the legislature desires. Shared taxes and grants-in-aid are also important parts of other state budget items. This pattern represents, in part, the result of legislative recognition of the need for additional revenues at the local level combined with an unwillingness to delegate adequate taxing powers to local governments, so the states collect the money and then disburse it to their local governments.
- State and local expenditures have represented an increasingly large proportion of society's earnings, as measured by the gross national products (GNP). In 1913, expenditures equaled about 6 percent of the GNP; in the early 1990s, they have increased to over 12 percent.[4]
- The national government has played an increasing role in state and local governments following two periods of great expansion of grants-in-aid, during the New Deal of Franklin D. Roosevelt in the 1930s and the Great Society of Lyndon B. Johnson in the 1960s. National programs often require state or local policy changes to meet accompanying requirements and sometimes require matching of part of the national money. This is particularly true in transportation, community development, and environmental programs.

All this change has taken place within a difficult decisionmaking context, for

> the economic and institutional problems of state and local officials are, if anything, more difficult than those faced by federal officials. State and local governments do not have the ability to control the growth or stability of the economy. Moreover, state constitutions and laws include a number of limitations that federal policy-makers avoid.[5]

Decisions on taxing and spending take place within a narrowly circumscribed decision framework. We know that past expenditure patterns are the best predictors of next year's pattern, but we know little about the generation of new spending programs.[6] The budgetary process tends to be highly stylized and rich with ideological symbolism:

> Actors in the various stages of state politics are forced to act in situations which offer only a severely limited number of appropriate roles, none of which permit the exercise of full control over state finance. Lacking such control, but driven by the desire to maintain office and status, actors behave as though they are powerful by following a script

written in terms of easily understood symbols. Rationally-derived Responsibility, Economy and Service are the principal symbols.[7]

Reasonable Expenditure Levels

What are reasonable expenditure levels for state and local governments? Citizens are bombarded with propaganda, much of it conflicting, that tells them of the unfinished business of government in providing highways, mental health programs, recreation for increasing leisure time, and so forth, but also of increasing debt burdens, of the need for increased taxes if current service levels are to be maintained, and of "all-encroaching government." Citizens wonder whether a new or increased tax is fair or whether they are being taken advantage of. The questions citizens raise cannot be answered easily. Essentially, expenditure levels are culturally determined. In the 1920s, Americans would not permit elaborate welfare or unemployment compensation programs, to say nothing of public housing or limited-access highways. But since the Great Depression, Americans have come to expect government to provide a measure of security not otherwise available in an interdependent society. In the 1960s, they trusted government enough to allow it to experiment with new programs when needs were believed to exist. By the 1970s, such social experimentation, although at a slower pace, had to be masked so that it did not appear that government was "throwing money" at problems. And as discussed in chapter 2, the evolution of the social welfare state ideology entered new stages in the 1980s, particularly in regard to spending, that appear to be continuing into the 1990s.

The relative ease with which money can be raised is also important in determining expenditure levels. Congress will agree more readily than a state legislature to add a new grant-in-aid program because it is relatively easy for Congress to raise additional billions. A city or state that cannot increase services without also raising or adding new taxes will be slow to do so and will demand impressive proof of success before acting. But if a local unit of government is relatively prosperous, it is also likely to be proportionately generous in expanding its budget. Services not now performed are often in demand; the problem comes in making the marginal sacrifice necessary to pay for them. Studies of municipal costs and tax rates indicate that local expenditures vary according to the income of the local residents. In other words, as resident income increases, the marginal sacrifice involved in meeting higher budgets is less and people do not resist as much as they do in lower-income communities.[8]

Because citizens want more governmental services than they are willing to underwrite, and because they do not clearly associate tax levels with specific services, governments tend to exploit all available revenue resources and nearly always spend all funds available. This was shown in a study of the period during which West Virginia had a big increase in services. West Virginia's county governments received a fixed proportion of the local property tax. Increasing expenditures and the tax for schools in that state therefore had the effect of increasing the property tax for the counties automatically. But county functions did not expand at a rate comparable to that of the schools. Yet "with extremely rare exceptions" the counties levied the maximum permitted and spent these moneys "often on projects neither specified nor contemplated by the framers of the [state] Constitution, or by the authors of the legislative act which allocates levies.''[9]

When forming a budget, no one wants to cut pet projects in an effort to hold to a reasonable expenditure level. As attested to in earlier chapters of this work, state and local governments make public policy through a process of interest group clash. Whether reasonable or not, the expenditure levels governments finally reach are a measure of which groups succeed best in protecting their specific programs, regardless of the effect on the overall budget.

The Budget

In terms of physical size, budget documentation for a state or large city is enormous; for instance, the New York State budget comprises many volumes. Even that for smaller states (Nebraska or New Hampshire for example) is bigger in size than the summer catalog of a large mail-order house. In small villages, cities, counties, or towns, the budget document is simpler and often is printed only in the local newspapers, but where its columns of figures are unintelligible to the typical citizen.

A budget is simply a plan of action that states where money is to go and where it is to come from. Usually the budget passes like any other act in the legislative process; most jurisdictions may change the budget—within limits—once it has passed. Thus, actual expenditures and revenues often are different from those stated in the formally adopted budget. The real budget is known only after the fiscal year is completed.[10]

The Performance Budget

The trend toward centralized administration, the increasing number of government functions and the increasing complexity of those functions, have contributed to the rapid rise in the use of the executive budget in the United States since the beginning of the twentieth century. The nature of this budget and the changes it has brought about were discussed in chapter 9.

Until recent years, every budget dealt with all the minutiae needed to operate an office or function of government. Often the budget consisted of ''line items'' specifying the exact amount to be spent on a specific purpose; the funds were nontransferable from one line in the budget to another, even within the same department. The emphasis was on the things to be acquired—paper clips, snow shovels, wheelbarrows, for example—rather than on the services to be rendered. This was necessary when public funds had to be guarded at all times against ingenious attempts at fraud. It encouraged, however, the citizen's habit of disassociating taxes from services provided. Specialists in fiscal administration have long urged that the budget should propose appropriations on a lump-sum basis. Under this plan, each agency or major subdivision would receive a single sum of money, which responsible administrators would then spend as they thought best—within generally established policy guidelines of the chief executive and the legislative body. The result was flexibility that allowed for meeting emergencies and changes in service demands.

The *performance budget,* which began at the turn of the century and was used as early as 1913 in a borough of New York City, has become increasingly popular since about 1940.[11] It is a method of classifying expenditures so that each agency receives a lump sum for the operation of each of its different activities. For example, so much for snow removal, so much to purchase new park land, and so much for public welfare programs would be allocated. Although the method has its faults (it assumes competent and conscientious workers), it is designed to help make clear to both legislators and the public what funds are being used for; it makes it easier to compare past performances with future requests; and it may encourage agencies to do a better job of thinking through their needs in making requests. The budget is designed to reduce the tendency under the older budget method (appropriation by objects) to stockpile material and accelerate the purchase of services in order to exhaust appropriations. Legislators sometimes are cool toward the performance budget idea, believing that it has the effect of transferring still more fiscal power to the chief executive and the bureaucracy. The most rapid adoption of the performance budget has come in council-manager cities. It is used in other cities (some as large as Los Angeles), and some state budgets are based on it in part.

The Budget as Policy

The budgeting function is a specialized way of looking at problems in policy making. It is something of a negative view in the sense that, after the agencies and interest groups have made known their positions, the budget examiners, and ultimately the chief executive, must balance off the various interests against one another and against a plausible estimate of income, often reducing or eliminating what was requested by the agencies and interest groups. Budget making is positive in the sense that a public budget by chief executives is a basic statement of program and policy. They explain in it how they would balance off the various demands on the public funds, defend their stance on the more controversial aspects of the program, and necessarily must defend the explicit and implicit policies proposed in the budget. Many state and local governments require agencies to project capital outlay needs (land, buildings, roads, major pieces of equipment) over several (perhaps five) years, thus making this part of the budget a long-range planning instrument, because capital needs cannot be considered apart from program needs. If the mental health department, for example, must estimate its building construction needs for the next five years, it will also have to consider population and mental illness trends as well as community attitudes toward neighborhood care centers. In this way, the budget becomes a means for each agency to promote both fiscal *and* program planning.

The Parts of the Budget

A budget usually begins with a message from the chief executive and may say simply, in effect: Here is the budget for the next fiscal year. Or it may explain proposed new expenditures, tell why tax changes are requested, and otherwise explain policy positions. A brief summary of the budget for the benefit of citizens and the press usually follows. Next comes the detailed breakdown. It may start with a statement of anticipated revenues from all taxes and other sources. This will be followed by the expenditures section, broken down by funds: the general fund plus a small or large number of others, such as a highway fund, a fish-and-game fund, sometimes even a municipal bond fund. A capital outlay budget usually will be presented separately from the operations budget, as may a utilities budget (e.g., a municipal water-supply system). Provision must also be made for governmental debt service (e.g., paying interest on bonds). The budget may conclude with a statement concerning new taxes or, in local governments, the property tax levy necessary to bring the budget into balance.

Preparing the Budget

In state and local governments operating under the executive budget plan, the document is prepared by a budget officer or controller under the chief executive. In a few such governments, this job is done by an independent elected controller. In some cases, an ex-officio board prepares it. In small local government jurisdictions, legislative bodies often prepare the budgets themselves or through committees.

Budget preparation begins with the collection of estimates for the following year's needs as submitted by the various agencies. These are gone over by budget analysts, who look for padding, inaccuracies, and inconsistencies. They apply policy judgments as formulated by the chief executive. Conferences may be scheduled between the agencies and members of the budget division when differences arise, for these are likely to result from differing premises. The ideology of chief executives and their own evaluation of political strategy requirements will affect their view of how "needs" should be interpreted in each agency. The agency however, probably will use different criteria in arriving at needs, which it may base on professional concepts of standards, on the pet interests of the agency head, on demands of interest groups or on other considerations.

After detailed estimates of each department's needs for the coming year are collected, they are set out in parallel columns with statements of estimated expenditures for the same items in the current year and the actual expenditures for those items in the fiscal year just completed. The budget officer next examines the document in detail with the chief executive so that proposed changes in policy may be incorporated into the estimates.

The completely assembled budget is then ready to be sent to the legislative body. Enclosed with it also may be the political future of the governor or mayor, the career prospects of the city manager, the hopes of critics seeking new ammunition in their fight to displace the chief executive, and the welfare of all the publics that reside within the boundaries of the unit of government involved.

Enacting the Budget

The legislative body has responsibility for adopting the budget, and does so almost always with modifications. Usually it will hold budget hearings, either before the full body if it is small enough, or before the tax and appropriations committees, the heads of which normally are powerful senior legislators. For the most part, these hearings do not provide legislators any information they do not already have but serve to allow groups and individuals to vent their hope, annoyance, bitterness, or frustration. After all, they are an important part of the democratic process. A budget hearing is more likely to be attended by representatives of interest groups than by a representative cross section of the general public. Some department heads may lobby at this time to get a bigger share of the pie than was given to them by the budget office. If the chief executive is a weak administrator, this may be done quite openly; if the chief executive is strong, however, it must be done more subtly, for dissident department heads may risk their jobs if they bypass the executive. Pressure groups will take this opportunity to seek favorable hearings, and those that find the legislative climate more receptive than the executive one may succeed in getting an increase in the department budgets in which they are interested. Other groups will have to fight to retain the level of funds recommended in the executive budget as legislators strive to reestablish a balance between income and outgo. Public employees may take the opportunity to try to improve their working conditions and pay, and newspaper editors may use the occasion to view with alarm the ever-increasing cost of government.

Usually the legislative branch is free to add to, reduce, modify or leave unchanged any part of the budget. In two-house legislatures, the balance of sources and individual interests of legislators may be different in each house. Much struggling may take place before compromises are reached and budget and tax bills finally are passed. Often chief executives have the final word if they have the power of the item veto.

Administering the Budget

In local units and in states with the executive budget, the head of each department must submit a work program to the chief executive or to the controller before the beginning of each year. This program will show how much of the total appropriation for that department is desired for each month of each quarter of the coming fiscal year. This is known as the *allotment system.* After approval, the allotments are turned over to the accounting division of the controller's office, which will then refuse to allow any money to be spent by that department unless it is both authorized by the appropriations ordinance or statute and falls within the time period provided in the allotment schedule. In cases where budget administration is less organized, no allotment system may exist, and the auditor may be the only one to check for the legality of expenditure. In small units, the governing body itself may exercise the control function by passing directly on individual bills presented for payment.

The Financial Officers

The public officials most concerned with finance are the chief executive, the treasurer, the controller, the assessor, and the auditor. State fiscal administration seldom is integrated into a single department, as it frequently is in council-manager cities. It is often divided among many agencies, including perhaps an elected treasurer; an elected auditor who may exercise both control functions before agencies spend and audit functions afterward; a controller, usually appointed by the governor but sometimes elected; a state tax commission to handle property tax appeals and sometimes to administer other taxes; a secretary of state, usually elected, who handles some tax administration, especially of automobile and truck license fees; the head of the conservation department, who may have his or her own machinery for the purpose of collecting hunting and fishing license fees; and others. The division of power differs widely among the states. In Minnesota, for example, the auditor's office has far more power than does the treasurer's. Following complaints that the office had little work and should be eliminated, former Minnesota treasurer Bob Mattson was stripped of his office space in the capitol and had to sue to have resources provided to maintain an office. As discussed in chapter 7, local government practices vary widely depending on the forms of local governments and the relationships between executives and legislators.

State and Local Revenues

As might be expected in a society growing increasingly dependent on government for the performance of services, state and local revenue yields have grown enormously in the twentieth century. Sources of these revenues have become considerably diversified. Although state and local revenue totals increased almost one thousand times between 1902 and 1990, some increases have been even more spectacular. For example, state and local liquor store receipts were a mere $2 million in 1902 but would exceed $3 billion by 1990. No general state sales taxes were levied anywhere in 1902, and this source produced only $499 million in 1940. But by 1990, it was bringing in almost $150 billion in state revenues. The state personal income tax, nonexistent at the beginning of the century, produced only $206 million in 1940 but had reached almost $80 billion by 1990. Other tax sources untapped at the beginning of the century but now important bearers of revenue include the motor fuel, motor vehicle, cigarette, severance, and corporate income taxes and unemployment compensation insurance charges. The general property tax, which produced over 50 percent of state tax revenues in 1902, had declined in importance by 1967 to such an extent that it accounted for only 0.1 percent of state revenue; with small amounts still collected by Alaska and Nebraska.

Local governments received 73 percent of their tax revenues from the general property tax in 1902. This figure had declined to 46 percent by 1985. Yet, the dollar increase in property tax collections during this period amounted to more than a 300-fold rise. Personal income and especially sales tax receipts had become important for local governments, as had liquor store and utilities profits.

Compared with the beginning of the twentieth century, the most impressive change in local receipts has been in the growth of state grants and shared taxes. Local governments received less than 6 percent of their total revenue from state intergovernmental payments in 1902; this had increased to about one-third of the total by the late 1980s. By 1990, California school districts received almost 85 percent of their funds from the state.

National government direct grants have increased in importance, too, but at a far less impressive rate than the attention paid to them would indicate. In 1902, 0.4 percent of total local revenues came from national grants; in the late 1970s, when this peaked, it reached about 3 percent.

Postwar trends, which will be discussed in more detail below, can be seen in table 14-2.

Intergovernmental Payments

In the United States, financial centralization has outpaced administrative centralization faster than in other urbanized and industrialized nations. The two have a tendency to proceed in tandem in other countries, but the traditions of U.S. federalism militate against the transfer of powers to higher levels of government. We have,

TABLE 14–2   Combined State and Local Revenue Trends

	1942	1955	1965	1975	1985
Total Dollars (Millions)	13,146	37,621	87,776	264,009	720,061
			Percentage of Total Revenue		
From National Government					
Public Welfare	2.8%	3.8%	3.5%	5.4%	5.4%
Highways	1.3%	1.6%	4.6%	2.0%	1.8%
Education	1.0%	0.8%	1.9%	3.4%	2.3%
Employment Security	0.4%	0.6%	0.5%	0.6%	0.4%
Revenue Sharing				2.4%	0.6%
Other and Unallocable	1.0%	1.6%	2.1%	4.0%	4.2%
National Government Total	6.5%	8.3%	12.6%	17.8%	14.7%
From State and Local Sources					
Taxes and Charges					
Taxes					
Property	34.5%	28.5%	25.7%	19.5%	14.4%
Sales	17.9%	20.3%	19.5%	18.9%	17.6%
Income					
Individual Income	2.1%	3.3%	4.7%	8.1%	9.8%
Corporate Income	2.1%	2.0%	2.2%	2.5%	2.7%
Total Income	4.2%	5.3%	6.9%	10.6%	12.4%
Other	8.3%	8.3%	6.3%	4.6%	4.3%
Total Taxes	64.9%	62.4%	58.4%	53.6%	48.7%
Charges	7.8%	11.9%	13.4%	15.0%	19.7%
Total Taxes and Charges	72.7%	74.3%	71.7%	68.6%	68.3%
Utility and Liquor Stores					
Water Supply System	3.3%	2.9%	2.3%	1.6%	1.7%
Electric Power System	1.9%	2.3%	2.1%	1.8%	3.0%
Transit System	1.3%	1.4%	0.9%	0.5%	0.6%
Gas Supply System	0.2%	0.3%	0.3%	0.2%	0.5%
Liquor Stores	3.0%	2.9%	1.6%	0.9%	0.4%
Total Utility and Liquor	9.7%	9.8%	7.2%	5.1%	6.2%
Insurance Trust Revenue	11.1%	7.6%	8.5%	8.5%	10.7%
State and Local Total	93.5%	91.7%	87.4%	82.2%	85.3%
Revenue Total:	100.0%	100.0%	100.0%	100.0%	100.0%

Source: Percentages compiled by authors from U.S. Bureau of the Census.

therefore, sought to solve financial problems at particular levels by using shared taxes and grants-in-aid, both of which are devices for bridging the gap between the appropriate spending unit and the most efficient tax-raising unit.[12] Shared taxes and grants also are established simply in response to sufficiently powerful pressures.

The size of intergovernmental payments has been increasing over the years, particularly for the states, which then often must share the money with localities. As pointed out above, in 1902 less than 1 percent of state and local general revenues came from national grants-in-aid. By 1985, this figure had increased to 14.7 percent (down about 3 percent from a decade earlier). State and local governments also shared some revenues and received contractual payments for scientific research and certain public services (see table 14.2). State and local expenditures, however, not only are increasing faster than national domestic expenditures, but at a faster rate than all national expenditures. Indeed, in the late 1970s state and local expenditures passed total national expenditures, although the increases in defense spending and reduction of federal grants-in-aid during the Reagan years put the national spending back ahead of the states and localities by the mid-1980s.

Federal payments to states and localities came in two principal waves, as discussed in chapters 2 and 4. With the development of the ideology of social welfare state in the New Deal, grants significantly increased. A second wave followed in the Great Society programs of Lyndon B. Johnson. The changes in social values, particularly in regard to the role of the national government, explain those trends. As noted above, local governments rely far more on their state than national government. Even before the 1930s some states used shared taxes and grants-in-aid. For example, Wisconsin's shared income taxes date back to 1911. Shared gasoline taxes everywhere followed quickly with the emergence of the automobile. But the patterns vary from state to state. Even today certain types of localities must rely wholly on their own tax sources in some states. Deil S. Wright describes the 1980s and 1990s as a "contractive" period in which localities have become increasingly dependent on the state governments; the period represents decreased local autonomy.[13] Well over one-half of state payments to local governments are in the areas of education, welfare, and highways, although payments are also made for public safety, health, hospitals, non-highway transportation, housing, urban redevelopment, and natural resources, among others; some are lump-sum shared revenue for no prescribed purpose.

Criteria for Evaluating Shared Taxes and Revenues

When one level of government receives money from another, the pattern of politics changes. In order to assert itself, a government must have funds it can count on. Without a reliable source of its own money, the national government could not survive under the Articles of Confederation; the Constitution overcame this weakness. But the problem can be difficult for local governments. In recent decades, given the increased demand for property tax relief, many local school districts must find alternative sources of revenues, but no other reliable internal tax source exists; therefore, intergovernmental aid has been the response. Such aid almost always reduces the autonomy of the district, despite the traditions of localism. Grants-in-aid and shared taxes therefore must be understood in terms of a variety of values, including the following:

1. *Localism.* Intergovernmental revenues usually come with some strings attached. Conditions attached to grants vary, but the tradition of localism is usually challenged when state and local governments accept aid. For example, it is difficult to resist raising money for a sewage treatment plant when only 30 percent of the cost may be required from the local government. But without a grant-in-aid, the city probably would not build the plant. Even if no specific requirements are needed to qualify for grants-in-aid, the availability of resources from elsewhere will change public attitudes toward raising the money. Services tend to be credited to the government administering them, regardless of where the money originally came from.[14]

2. *Expertise.* At least during the period of initial development, the granting government ordinarily has greater experience and commitment to professional standards in the administration of programs. This may lead to rather elaborate programs, seemingly more expensive and more closely supervised than necessary. For example, the legislation that created the Law Enforcement Assistance Administration providing for a variety of federal law enforcement grants in the 1970s was created to "professionalize" local police departments. Apparently, congressional and interest group sponsors believed they had something of a superior concept of professionalism as compared to local decision makers.

3. *Administrative cost.* Every program costs money to administer. Only bureaucrats involved in administration see such costs positively. The reduction of these costs was a major impetus for the shift from categorical to block and revenue-sharing grants.

4. *Budget busting.* Some payments (particularly welfare programs known as *entitlements* which provide federal or state aid to individuals and usually are administered through counties) are established based on formulas and built incrementally. They are a relatively inflexible part of the budget. When such costs are at their peaks, revenues usually are at a minimum (during recessions less income or sales tax revenue is raised), increasing the likelihood of deficits.

5. *Redistributive effects.* A program may have about the same effect when paid for by a higher government as it does when paid directly. Nevertheless, as we will discuss in the following section on taxes, changing the revenue source may shift the burden of payment from one income group to another. For example, property tax relief provided by greater reliance on a shared income tax probably will shift the burden somewhat from lower- to upper-middle-class taxpayers.

6. *Program success.* Ultimately, intergovernmental programs should be judged on whether they succeed as intended or produce unintended effects. As discussed in chapter 10, many programs become part of the "system" without such auditing. For example, even after clear indications that federal revenue sharing was not meeting the expectations of some of its sponsors in the mid- to late-1970s, the program was funded again under pressure from local administrators who had grown accustomed to the yearly check from the national government and had built it into their budgets.[15] It took a considerable effort by President Reagen (some conservatives originally had been behind the program) to eliminate it in the budget cutting of the 1980s.

7. *Cheating.* Some programs have been more susceptible to fraud than others. The HUD scandals exposed in 1989 demonstrated that even programs that leave a

long paper trail may invite fraud. Virtually all forms of corruption used in the nineteenth century are still available. The risks of getting caught are higher than ever—
but so are the potential payoffs. Perhaps the most driving temptation occurs where the
public and private sectors commonly meet, e.g., in a contractual setting. The private
business seeks to win such a contract and may profit greatly from it if it is generously
written; the corrupt government official or employee also benefits in some form from
the traditional kickback or illegal, disguised return payment.

Grants-in-Aid

The amount of a grant-in-aid generally is independent of the yield from any
particular tax or other source of income. Grants come in the two types defined below.
They are distributed in one of two ways: either based on formula under which every
government that is eligible under the law and that applies, receives the grant; or as a
project for which the money is distributed with some discretion on the part of the
sending government (or its agency). Formula grants are more prone to budget busting
because the legislators establishing the formula often cannot accurately anticipate the
number made eligible by the program. Project grants are prone to "grantsmanship,"
in which the applying government may hire grant writers who can tailor the application to increase the applicant's chances of winning an award. This may mean that a
less-needy though eligible applicant may be more likely to succeed in getting a grant
than a less-skilled though more needy applicant.

Categorical Grants-in-Aid: **Grants from a higher level of government to a
lower level for a particular purpose, with specific "strings" attached.**

Block Grants: **Grants from a higher level of government to a lower level for
a general purpose with few "strings" attached. Some states refer to this
money as** *Shared Revenue.* **The control by higher governments comes principally in terms of the formula used to administer the money. When employed by the national government between 1972 and 1987, the program
was known as** *revenue sharing.*

Since about 1970, after federal and state grants had become a fixture in state
and local governments, major debates over intergovernmental revenue have not been
over whether grants should be provided but over which of the major types would be
used. *Categorical grants* are made conditionally. For example, they may require
matching funds, the use of technically trained personnel in administering them, and
the maintenance of technical standards of equipment and material. Critics argue that
these rules may reduce localism and usually are administratively top-heavy in costs.
Defenders reply that the higher government can require greater public involvement,
and they point out that although much red tape is imposed by the higher level of government in alternative grants, no guarantee exists that lower governments may not
produce their own bureaucratic costs. Furthermore, they usually argue that the
higher governments provide greater expertise and are more likely to equalize resources and benefits by paying greater attention to need. Although the trend recently

has been toward less-restrictive grants, whatever level of government raises the money (unless constitutionally restricted) can impose any restrictions it chooses. Grants are, after all , gifts that depend on the benevolence of the sending government. As a result, categorical grants, historically have been the most popular to the grantors.

Whereas *block grants* specify in broad terms the area of expenditure, those called "shared revenue" are the broadest yet, with no designation of the functional area of expenditure. These programs are distinguished from categorical grants in that the receiving government has greater discretion in spending the money. The higher government's influence comes principally through the redistributive effects of the formulas and the nonprogram stipulations that are usually attached (e.g., affirmative action rules attached to a block grant for community development).

The national government briefly experimented with revenue sharing as part of the "new" federalism proposed by Richard Nixon. The proposal was first passed in 1972 and extended in 1976 and 1980. But the Reagan administration objected in principle to raising funds at one level to be spent by another. It also sought to reduce federal involvement and spending in state and local programs. State revenue sharing was eliminated in 1982, followed by the elimination of local revenue sharing in 1987. The Reagan administration then pursued the conversion of categorical grants to block grants, but with cutbacks in appropriations made in many programs.

The pattern has been somewhat different in the states. As property taxes became more and more burdensome and the functions of government expanded in the twentieth century, taxpayers turned to the states for more money for the localities in the form of block grants to schools or shared revenue to cities and counties.

Advocates of less-restrictive grants argue that the greater expertise of higher government administrators may have existed during the period of grant development, but is no longer the case after years of experience with many of the programs. They argue that block grants and shared revenues reduce reliance on the property tax (discussed below), allow receiving governments to tailor programs to particular needs, and reduce administrative costs. Critics either prefer categorical grants (often because the strings permit control over policy) or argue that state and local governments should remain autonomous by raising their own money. Although this may prove difficult for localities, states usually have the legal power to raise taxes, even though both may object to suffering the political consequences when higher governments are willing to bear most of the costs.

Grants-in-aid appear to be a fixture in the system today. Critics nevertheless continue to level two additional objections. The first is that grants-in-aid may stimulate extravagant expenditures because the locality is spending funds that do not impose an immediate and obvious burden on local taxpayers. Thus, if local officials spend money they need not solicit from voters, they may see no need to spend it wisely or on necessities. Second, grants are held (potentially at least) to lead toward disproportionate expenditures in favor of those functions receiving grants. In other words, regardless of the merits of or need for the various functions performed, some will always have a plentiful budgetary appropriation because of the grants whereas others perhaps more needy and deserving (by local value standards), may be skimped. This criticism applies especially the more specific the grant and the more detailed are the strings attached.

Shared Taxes

A *shared tax* is one imposed by one unit of government but shared with other governments according to a formula. The amount sent to each receiving unit is sometimes intended to be representative of the portion of the tax produced within the area of that unit, but shared taxes may be distributed on any basis the collector chooses. Unlike the grant-in-aid, a shared tax delivers no fixed amount; rather, receipts depend on the yeld of the tax. Shared taxes have become increasingly popular in recent decades, and they seem to be preferred by local officials to either grants-in-aid or an enlargement of the taking powers of local governments. Part of the reason for this is that fewer strings are attached to shared taxes than to grants. Shared taxes also bring less criticism from local citizens than does the enactment of additional local taxes (usually, the higher government is blamed for the tax).

Taxes most often shared by the state with local units include those on motor fuel, motor vehicles, liquor, tobacco, sales, and income. Shared taxes are sometimes defended as being less in the nature of charity than the grant-in-aid, for although they are state-imposed and state-collected, they are levied on local wealth and hence are not a largess. Because they are viewed as a local tax with the state acting as a collecting agent, local units usually are freer to use the revenue as they see fit than they are with grants.

Many criticisms are directed at shared taxes, however. Critics argue that they cannot be adjusted to local needs. For example, some areas with little need receive more in shared taxes than they can spend, whereas others receive much less than they believe they need. (Grants-in-aid, particularly categorical grants, are better adjustable to need.) Furthermore, shared income taxes do not help stabilize local revenues; that is, they yield well in prosperous times but tend to be withdrawn by the state during less-prosperous periods, when local need for funds is most critical. Last, the manner in which shared taxes are used is less subject to control than are grants. from an ideological viewpoint this may be argued as either an advantage or a disadvantage. But from the viewpoint of imposing standards, the state cannot be so effective through shared taxes as it can be through grants.

Wisconsin provides an example of how shared taxes are used. It has relied more heavily on the income tax than other states; it was the first state to impose an income tax and within a decade, in 1911, began to share the tax. For most of its history, the tax was distributed under a formula by which 50 percent of the money went to the city or other local taxpayer jurisdiction, 40 percent went to the state, and 10 percent went to the country:

> Under this formula the municipalities in which there were many poor persons became poorer and municipalities in which there were many rich taxpayers became richer. There were, in fact, "tax islands" in which the municipality did not have to levy any property taxes because they derived so much money from the state income tax. This could be defended in that the income tax was argued to be a better tax than the property tax. Nevertheless, it seemed unfair that only richer areas could receive such extensive benefit.[16]

Under the administration of Governor Patrick Lucey (1971–1977), new formulas, subsequently modified, were developed for the shared tax. A percentage of the tax continued to be distributed based on population. Even though the yield of the tax determined the overall amount to be dispersed, the formula also considered need by basing it on the amount of property tax collected. But this allowed a government to reduce its own tax collection and rely more heavily on the shared tax. A later correction distributed part of the tax based on local tax effort. Thus, units that raised more, got more. Partisan concerns were now applied; legislators defended increases in the parts of the formula that most suited their constituents' local tax policy. Finally, in the mid-1980s, advocates of greater school aid (a block grant) were told that with limited funds neither school aids nor shared taxes could be increased. Legislators who were trying to hold down government costs tried to pit cities and towns against school districts (usually allies in this battle). This suggests that shared taxes are no less prone to value-laden considerations than are grants-in-aid. The idea often is to unload as much of the burden on people in other localities as possible; the reality may be a baffling tax system that is beyond the comprehension of nearly all taxpayers. Nevertheless, it is a system that allows local governments to finance services that would not otherwise be possible.

Taxes

All taxes ultimately derive from one of two sources: total wealth or annual income. Tax liability theoretically is based on ability to pay, although criteria used in various periods of history have not been the same. A tax appropriate to one period may prove inequitable for another time or another life-style when its justification becomes less apparent. In some instances, payments are based on a benefit theory rather than on ability to pay, but these are more in the nature of service charges than of taxes. The benefit theory is used, for example, in special assessments for street, sidewalk, streetlighting, and similar improvements. It is also applied to water and power, hunting and fishing licenses, gasoline taxes, and, to a degree, to determining motor vehicle license fees.

Another strong tradition holds that all persons have an equal obligation to pay taxes. This argument upholds the government's collection of taxes as involuntary contributions. It is also used, especially by conservatives, to argue that every adult should participate in the payment of a major tax.

Limitations on Taxing

Local governments have only those powers of taxation granted to them by the state. Rare exceptions to this rule may seem to be found in a few home-rule states, notably California, where court interpretations of the constitutional home-rule clause have given cities a general grant of powers to levy taxes (although in reality they are limited by any restrictions imposed by the legislature and no use of this ruling has been made since 1945). Through either the constitution or state statutes the taxing powers of local governments are ordinarily restricted. The law usually states a maximum tax rate relative to some limiting factor, the most common being a certain percentage of the assessed value of taxable property within the local unit of government.

The states also often impose conditions and regulations on the administration of local finances and may deprive a local unit of a portion of its tax base by exempting state property, for example, or by providing for *homestead exemptions,* which exclude part or all of the value of owner-occupied homes from the general property tax or allow for a substantial portion of the tax to be returned as an income tax credit.

There are many effects of tax restrictions. They have encouraged the creation of special districts that have low public visibility but an independent basis for taxation and hence can serve as a means of avoiding the restriction. They have encouraged borrowing under circumstances where costs could have been met from current revenues and where bonds sometimes, through interest payments, have greatly increased the cost of financing municipal services. They have required legislatures to work their way through numerous bills calling for special legislation, and they have crowded court dockets with taxpayer suits.[17]

States, too, have limited powers of taxation, as many state constitutions place specific limits on legislative taxing powers. The courts tend to hold to a narrow interpretation of authorizations to tax, and although state legislatures are less restricted than are local governing bodies, they are not free to decide taxing levels unrestrained.

Limitations on Subjects of Taxation

The subjects that may be taxed by local governments normally are controlled by the state. Nearly all of the states tell their local governments which taxes they may levy, for what period of time they may be levied, and under what conditions. A local government that finds its property tax consistently inadequate may not, for example, levy a payroll or sales tax without first being authorized by the state to place a levy on a new subject. The state government frequently is also limited as to the subjects that may be taxed. The constitution may prohibit the state from levying certain kinds of taxes or may limit the amount of the tax. Thus, some states are restricted on the use of property, income, and sales taxes.

Tax limitations result from economy pressures, and these pressures are felt especially in poor economic times. When property owners are faced with the prospect of losing their investments to the mortgage holder, it is not difficult to convince them that they should vote to limit the property tax levy. Later, when revenue is badly needed, efforts may be made to evade the limitation. Usually it is more difficult to find a way to levy a prohibited tax (e.g., a local sales tax) than it is to evade a limitation feature on an existing tax. For example, two features of the typical property tax are related: the tax rate and the assessed value of property. Each is set by the taxing government, but the state sets limits on the tax rate. As a result, localities may refuse to use 100 percent of the assessed value of the property, contrary to state law, so that increases in taxes may be imposed through an increase in assessed value when the tax levy limit is reached. Although the state usually refuses to increase levy limits, the statutory limit can be avoided by increasing another part of the formula for rasing money—the assessed value.

Criteria for Evaluating Taxes

Like grants, taxes may be evaluated using a variety of criteria. Even those with similar values may use different criteria. A legislator who must raise the tax must consider the adequacy of the tax, whereas a taxpayer naturally wants lower taxes without a subsequent decrease in service levels. The following values must be considered:

1. *Equity.* Equity is usually thought of as meaning ability to pay. In colonial America, ability to pay could best be measured in terms of property or total wealth. Today, however, most people receive a regular paycheck, so income is considered by most economists to be a better criterion. *Progressive taxes* are based on ability to pay, whereas *regressive taxes* are not. But all people do not believe that progressive taxes are good. For example, higher-income taxpayers may rationally prefer regressive taxes. Furthermore, "trickle-down" or "supply-side" politicians argue that with regressive taxes, the rich are allowed to keep more resources that they can in turn invest thereby expanding the economy or otherwise providing social benefits that extend beyond themselves. The pattern of how savings translate into social investments is not entirely clear, but this argument has been widely used and legitimized by President Reagan and President Bush.

> *Regressive Tax:* **A levy the burden of which is lessened as ability to pay increases; A *Progressive Tax* has the opposite effect. A sales tax that applies to food, medicine, fuel, or other items seen as necessities (coverage varies by states) is considered regressive, even though the rate does not vary, because persons with low incomes spend a larger percentage of it on necessities than do those with high incomes. The underlying theory is that beyond a certain point, income becomes increasingly less valuable or meaningful and hence can be taxed fairly at a higher rate.**

2. *Yield.* Politicians often expend considerable energy on taxes that produce small amounts of revenue. A tax on rutabagas for example, would discourage their use and raise little or no money (people would buy turnips instead). A tax on yachts might seem fair (it is highly progressive) but would raise little money if few people owned yachts. Since the early 1970s, the state lottery (the traditional "numbers racket") has been one of the most hotly debated low-yielding tax sources (revenue experts generally consider it to be highly regressive, or it would be if it paid much money to the state).

3. *Administrative costs.* An income tax may have very low administrative costs if little is spent auditing tax returns. After all, in most states today, taxpayers are required to submit their own returns, and the bulk of the tax is collected by employers through withholding procedures. Property taxes are generally the most expensive to administer because many levels of government are involved and achievement of equitable evaluation among properties is difficult and time consuming.

4. *Cheating.* As a general rule, taxes that are administratively complex allow the most opportunity for cheating. Often, higher-income taxpayers are accused of cheating when they take advantage of the complex nature of tax laws by finding "loopholes" that allow them to avoid part of the tax. This is not cheating, but it may appear unfair. Many people rationalize cheating, particularly in the income tax, by arguing that they "deserve" to pay less than they owe because they have already paid "their fair share." Usually this is more costly than the flagrant cheating by those who

refuse to pay taxes at all, because rationalized cheating is far more widespread. Cheating on the income tax in particular occurs at all income levels, from very-high-income persons (who may "disguise" assets to minimize—or altogether avoid—tax liability) to low-income workers (who enhance their welfare by working only for cash payments).

5. *Tax stability.* Some taxes fluctuate with the economy; others bring in relatively steady amounts of revenue. The sales tax is a very stable tax, in part because it is imposed on necessities; those items all taxpayers will buy with little regard for the health of the economy. The income tax is partly dependent on the condition of the economy. States that rely heavily on the tax tend to run surpluses when the economy is doing well and deficits in times of recession. California, with a giant economy and a relatively heavy income tax, always experiences great battles in the legislature in boom times, with conservatives wanting to return the billions of dollars in surplus to taxpayers or spend it on education and liberals wanting to use it for welfare programs for the lower classes.

6. *Visibility.* Politicians are eager to hide taxes whenever possible. That is why sales taxes, which may be the heaviest taxes on college students, often are favored by them. The tax is not collected in one lump sum but instead in small amounts. Students, as well as most taxpayers, may not realize how much is being paid. Many excise taxes are similarly hidden in the cost of the item. A $15 hat advertised in the local newspaper usually will cost at least $15.75, whereas the $15 carton of cigarettes is really $11 plus $4 in taxes. But the hat buyer will complain about the taxes on hats, whereas the cigarette buyer will complain about the high price of cigarettes, not cigarette taxes.

The General Property Tax

Although the property tax has been attacked bitterly in recent decades as unsuitable for a modern, and especially an urban, society, it remains the most important source of revenue for local government. This is true especially of local units other than cities and school districts. Cities are succeeding to some extent in diversifying their tax base and receive increasing amounts in state aid, whereas school districts are becoming increasingly dependent on state aid.

The general property tax was the principal source of income for state governments from colonial times until the Great Depression. In the 1930s, defections from the tax reached great numbers. The states needed better sources of revenue, and the whole of the property tax, to the extent that it could be collected, was needed by local governments. The result was that the states shifted to the income, especially the sales tax while at the same time diversifying as much as politically possible. E. R. A. Seligman, an authority on the property tax, once suggested that nothing is the matter with the general property tax except that it is wrong in theory and does not work in practice. There are many objections to the tax. It already has been suggested that the property tax is no longer a good measurement of ability to pay and hence is inequitable. Also, often it is administered poorly and in any case is difficult to administer. Usually the tax levy involves three steps: assessment, equalization, and rate setting. With wide variation, assessment usually is done by the county, equalization by the state, and rate setting by the taxing jurisdiction (within limits set by the state).

Assessment. Assessment is the process of determining the value of property. The pattern of local property tax assessment differs from one state to another, and although dates may not be the same, the pattern is along the following lines:

> The local government assessor must complete . . . work by December 31 of each year. By the first Monday in April, local boards of tax review must have heard any appeals made by citizens of corporations. Within the next month, county boards of equalization are expected to have "equalized," or balanced on an equitable basis, the tax burden of local units within the county. Within approximately a month thereafter, the state board of tax equalization must have decided on the equalization, or relative percentage of taxes, to be paid by each of the counties of the state. Village and city taxes are due in May or June and school and township taxes in December, by which time the local assessor has begun . . . work for the oncoming year.[18]

Assessment can be done in a variety of ways, but is usually at least partially a measure of the market value of the home, based on its most recent sales price or the sale price of a comparable piece of property. New structures may be assessed on the actual cost of building. Usually rates of appreciation (increased value over time) and depreciation (decreased value due to use) are applied at least to a degree. The urban counties of California have career assessors who apply literally the state law calling for assessment at full and fair market value. It was this practice, combined with a rapid increase in home values, that brought on the so-called taxpayers' revolt and Proposition 13 in the late 1970s. Many homeowners, especially retired persons, found that taxes had risen beyond their ability to pay. Office holders were happy with the rapid increase in tax yield, but many property owners were less than happy with accurate assessment; meanwhile, legislators could not agree on a form of tax relief. Proposition 13 then weakened further the local powers of taxation, reinforcing again the importance of fiscal federalism.

The politics of equalization. Most assessors probably are honest in their efforts, but they have little training for their jobs. Local pressures make it difficult for them to place on the tax roll everything that legally belongs there or to relate tax valuation to market value. In some cases, wide discrepancies exist in judgment by assessors, in others, influential persons and businesses are given favorable valuations. As a device designed to overcome these problems, machinery for review and equalization of property taxes exists in every taxing jurisdiction. The board of review may be a special body, or it may be the governing board.

A tendency toward competitive underassessment exists whenever assessors' figures are used as the basis for a tax by more than one unit of government. Thus, where the assessor is selected from a unit of government smaller than the county, each assessor will want to make valuations as low as possible to minimize the amount of county property tax constituents will have to pay. The same pressure exists if school or other special districts cross more than one assessing unit and if the state levies a property tax, as was once the rule. Thus equalization boards still are a necessity at the state, and often the county, levels. These bodies, whose role is to achieve equity between assessing units, differ as to powers, competence, and the effort they put into their work. Usually, equalization boards can make only a percentage increase or decrease in the total valuation of an assessing unit as a whole, but in some cases they can reassess individual properties. Therefore they may become a court of appeal for tax assessment.

Equalization boards generally have staffs that are inadequate to do the complicated work legally expected of them. Governing bodies will seldom give them the staff needed because to do so would be politically unpopular—citizens generally do not want technically competent assessment; they hope to gain favor or advantage through their own assessor and fear that effective equalization will mean higher tax bills. Equalization is further complicated by the variety of pressures involved in the process. Rural areas traditionally want few services and low assessments, but urban areas may need high assessments to overcome the debt limitations placed on them by state laws or constitutions. Debts usually may not exceed a certain percentage of assessed valuation. The higher the valuation, therefore, the better the possibilities for issuing bonds for capital outlays. In many cases, state school-aid funds are distributed partly on the basis of each district's ability to pay as determined by assessed valuation per pupil. Where this is the case, superintendents seek to make their own valuation as low as possible and to exert pressure for higher valuations in other districts in order to maximize their own state aid. In this atmosphere of numerous cross pressures, lack of public support, and inadequate staff, the equalization boards attempt to do a job which, under the best of conditions, would be extremely difficult. The degree to which districts actually are equalized varies a great deal from one state to another, but the pressures become more intense as the proportion of school-operating costs paid by the states grows larger.

Why is the property tax retained? With so many problems connected with the property tax, why is it retained as the backbone of local government finance? A number of reasons endure, including inertia and the venerable argument holding that any old tax is a good tax and any new tax is a bad tax. This argument is at least partly valid, for taxpayers have become acclimated to an old tax, but a new one may cause uncertainty.

The property tax is also one of the few taxes whose subjects will "stay put"; it is therefore the most stable local tax. Most real property (if not personal property) is not easily moved out of the taxing jurisdiction on assessment day. Local sales taxes tend to drive buyers out of the taxing jurisdiction. Taxes on income tend to cause political complications if levied on nonresidents and, if not, tend to drive homeowners, businesses, and industry outside the jurisdiction. The property tax is retained also because it produces a high yield, except in severe depressions. Local units of government are badly in need of money, and no one has suggested a satisfactory substitute to replace the tax. Cities in particular, among local units, have tried to ease the burden on the property owner by diversifying the tax base through the addition of other taxes. But these have served to supplement rather than replace the basic tax. The greatest cutbacks in the property tax occurred when mandated from above through state law, usually passed through the initiative process (most notably Proposition 13 in California and Proposition 2½ in Massachusetts in the late 1970s, which even bypassed the legislatures). During the period between 1978 and 1982, when a number of states imposed restrictions and some localities diversified on their own, local governments objected to limitations placed on the property tax, recognizing that other sources of revenues limited their autonomy.

Sales Taxes

Sales taxes and excises are levied in all states. The general sales tax applies to all (or most) items as a *retail sales, gross receipts,* or similar type of tax. It was used by forty-five states in 1987 (excepting only Alaska, Delaware, Montana, New Hampshire, and Oregon).[19] States also levy excise taxes (sales taxes on single items) on gasoline, alcoholic beverages, cigarettes, and other selected items. The objects selected for taxation usually are those that people tend to buy whether the price is relatively high or low. Thus, a specific tax on alcohol yields well because consumers see no obvious substitute for the product; a specific tax on cauliflower would yield practically nothing, because people would buy cabbage or brussels sprouts instead. Taxing alcoholic beverages, gasoline, or cigarettes is commonly justified on the grounds that these products should not be consumed or used heavily anyway and anything that discourages their use is desirable. All states levy gasoline, alcohol, and cigarette tax. The broad-based sales tax exists in several forms, the most common of which is the retail sales tax. Some states also tax charges for services, such as television repair or dental care. West Virginia has a gross income tax, which is a sales tax expanded to include rent, wages, salary, dividends, and other income. At this level, the tax becomes virtually a flat-rate personal and corporate income tax combined with a sales tax. (Other states have not followed suit, but West Virginia has relied on this tax since the 1930s.)

The sales tax has also become more popular as a secondary tax for city and even county governments since it was first used in New York in 1934. It is authorized in several states and has been especially popular in California. The broad-based state sales tax has been popular with legislators because it yields well even under relatively depressed economic conditions, with tax administrators who find it quite easy and inexpensive to collect, and with the general public, which prefers—if it must pay taxes at all—to pay a few pennies at a time rather than taxes that require budgeting and call attention to themselves at payment time, as does the income tax. The principal objections to the sales tax come first from merchants, who believe it hurts their businesses and who dislike the paperwork it imposes on them. Other objections come from persons who object to the regressive feature of the tax. But the argument on regressivity does not impress most people regardless of income, and they undoubtedly prefer the sales to the income tax.

Individual Income Taxes

Probably the most unpopular tax in America is the personal income tax, although forty-four states were using it in 1990.[20] It is unpopular because of the unending barrage of vilification directed against it over several decades by groups financed by high-income conservatives who prefer regressive taxes and fear the threat of nearly open-ended exposure to higher tax brackets; because it seems to penalize initiative; because it carries a psychological threat of confiscation; because it requires large yearly payments that are felt more than are sales taxes, which are paid each time a purchase is made; and because the national income tax, since the early 1940s has been at higher levels than the American culture will tolerate easily. The national government has been able to collect its tax despite a fairly high rate, principally because it has been justified as necessary for the defense of the nation. Despite the fact that states cannot make this argument, it has become their principal secondary tax.

State income taxes generally are only slightly graduated; that is, the tax rate increases modestly as income increases. None of the states' rates are anywhere near that of the national income tax, although to save administrative costs some states now "piggyback" on the national tax and take a flat percentage of that tax, or base their categories on that tax but allow different exemptions. For example, Vermont takes a flat 22.96 percent of the U.S. rate. On the other end of the graduation continuum six states used a flat rate in 1988. Exemptions, deductions, and progressiveness vary from one state to another, but in general the tax is most equitable as measured by progressivity. Nevertheless, the tax can create economic problems by retarding a state's economic growth. It yields well under most conditions but tends to collapse in times of recession, when state revenue needs are high. As a hedge against this problem, states that rely heavily on the tax have generated reserve or "rainyday" funds. The fund usually is a percentage of the overall revenues and can be used only in times of recession in the state. The fund is best protected against legislative temptation to spend the money when times are good by constitutional provision.

Cheating on income taxes has become epidemic in the United states and probably extends beyond measure. As described earlier, most cheating is piecemeal. The mobility of Americans makes it relatively easy to cheat a state government of the entire amount owed by crossing state lines, particularly for the self-employed. Efforts to curb cheating are costly and not very popular, but usually return more in new revenue than the administrative cost. However, this is difficult to prove to legislators who must allocate the additional money for auditing and prosecution. Over one-half the states were using amnesty programs in 1987. An amnesty program allows a taxpayer to pay delinquent taxes without penalty (although usually interest is charged). Amnesty can work only if the program has a specific time limit and taxpayers are convinced they must use the amnesty period or risk dire consequences. States have had mixed results with such programs.

The income tax has been largely preempted by state and national governments, who then may use it to fund grants-in-aid or as a basis for a shared tax. Philadelphia, however, adopted an income tax in 1939, and many other cities (including New York City during its 1970s fiscal crisis) have since done so, particularly in Pennsylvania and Ohio. Most city income taxes might more accurately be called payroll taxes, for typically they are not graduated and do not permit any deductions but are simply a certain percentage of the total amount of money earned by individuals (sometimes corporations) within a city. The Philadelphia tax, for example, applies only to earned income and not to income from stocks, bonds, and rents; as such, it is regressive in character.

The individual income tax is a supplementary tax for most states, although it is used increasingly and has roughly doubled its percentage of total tax resources since 1965 (see table 14-2). It accounted for about 30 percent of state revenues in 1990.

Corporate Income Taxes

Corporate income or profits taxes produced about 8.4 percent of state taxes in 1989, but most of the total collected is paid in only five of the forty-six states that levy one: California, Massachusetts, New York, Pennsylvania, and Wisconsin. Corporate income tax in other states is minimal and in highly industrialized Texas was not levied at all in 1989.

Politicians are regularly pressured to adopt a corporate income tax, and these reasons are especially cited. First, if individuals pay the tax, so should corporations. Second, if small businesspersons bear the burden of the sales tax with all its nuisances and possible discouragement to business, the large incorporated manufacturers should also be burdened with a tax. Finally, the tax is based only on profits and so does not hurt anyone, certainly not the small taxpayer who is burdened with the various sales taxes. The tax is, however, imposed on the most powerful and largest corporations in each state. If these firms were as powerful as populists believe, they would not allow a corporate tax. But like everyone else, the managers of these companies must live with the rest of society, and although they view it as their duty to keep costs down—and to a corporation each tax is a cost—they also accept a myth of "good corporate citizenship," getting along by going along with the paying of taxes. By openly threatening to move elsewhere in highly competitive markets, these companies fight to keep the tax low.

Economists sometimes oppose the corporate income tax on the ground that it does not measure adequately ability to pay. Their argument is that the profits of a corporation should more logically be passed along to the stockholders and the state's share should be reclaimed at that point as personal income tax. This would ensure that no truth could remain to the old claim that the corporate income tax sometimes takes bread from widows and orphans, a brass gong that is sounded each time the tax is considered. Liberals argue that corporate profits really belong to all of society and that, after stockholders are allowed a reasonable return on their investment, what is left (after the national government takes its considerable bite) properly belongs to the people of the state. For liberal politicians, the tax has another attraction: Most of their constituents are not stockholders and can be convinced that the tax will raise a lot of money without hurting anyone. Stockholders sometimes argue that the tax is unfair because it results in double taxation, once as corporate income, a second time as personal income. But double taxation is common in American government (for that matter, so is triple and quadruple taxation).

In addition to the tax on profits, all states levy taxes on corporations in the form of licenses and taxes on the privilege of doing business within its jurisdiction. These taxes are based on a variety of formulas, but profit is not a basic component. Instead, the issue is allowing a corporation the right to be recognized as an artificial person and to enjoy the various special privileges that corporations have that individual proprietorships do not have.

Other Taxes

In addition to these already mentioned, states collect a variety of other taxes. One source of income is from motor vehicle and operators' licenses. These are determined according to many criteria, and charges vary greatly. In states with mining industries or with oil and gas wells, severance levies are charged for the removal from the ground of a resource that can never be replaced. In Louisiana, Alaska, Utah, Oklahoma, and Texas, severance levies are major sources of state revenue. Large and powerful companies engaged in the extractive industries sometimes are arrayed against environmentalists who are opposed to the exploitation and exhaustion of national resources. Severance taxes were an early result of these political battles.

All states have death and gift taxes; they are of some importance as sources of revenue. Other taxes are levied on the gross receipts of public utilities (usually in lieu of property taxes) and on pari-mutuel betting. Unemployment compensation taxes are collected by all states, but they are really insurance premiums and not taxes, in the ordinary sense. Local governments may use some or all of the above taxes and others as well. They are likely to impose business taxes, sometimes to pay the cost of supervising businesses that directly affect the public health, but often these are set at a level to ensure some profit. Taxes on hotel-room occupancy are becoming popular, as are admissions taxes for theaters, motion pictures, and sports events, because theaters and stadiums (if not the teams that use them) are relatively immovable.

Nontax Revenues

State and local governments receive some money annually from fines and fees. The fines are from ordinance and law violations. The fees are from charges for certain services, such as issuing licenses or transferring real estate. They also make some profits from operating what are essentially business enterprises. These include the sale of water, fertilizer (from sewage-disposal plants), and liquor, and the operation of ferryboats, toll bridges, and roads. Some states have a monopoly over the wholesale distribution or retail sale of liquor. This is defined as aiding in the policing of the liquor business at all levels of operation; it is also enormously profitable. State and local governments operate retail liquor stores—usually package sales only, but sometimes also liquor by the drink.

In an effort to make the raising of revenues more palatable, state-operated lotteries have become common. New Hampshire was the first to establish a state lottery; by 1990 over half the states had done so and many others were interested, some in conjunction with other states, sharing costs and profits. The typical lottery ticket sells for a dollar to make it affordable for low-income persons. Only 45 percent of the "take" goes for prize money (as compared with nearly 90 percent at a racetrack). Public lotteries have been criticized for encouraging the compulsive gambler and the poor to spend money they can ill afford against very poor odds. Public lotteries are also eyed as a subtle device for increasing the tax burden on the poor. Most important, perhaps, state lotteries have been poor revenue sources, raising far less than proponents originally asserted because expenses have been high and rate of sales slower than expected. But their attraction continues to expand, particularly after a few regular multimillion-dollar payoffs, which replaced a larger number of more modest awards.

Service Charges

Rather than pay for many services from general taxes, local governments often levy *service charges*. As noted above, these fees have risen most dramatically as a percentage of state and locally raised revenues since World War II. Used traditionally for water supply and sometimes electricity, they have also been levied in the form of charges on sewage disposal, garbage collection, streetlighting and streetcleaning, snow removal, weed cutting, and other services. Charges often are levied as a means of avoiding an increase in the general tax rate. It is a way of causing the tax level to appear to be lower than it actually is. Service charges also can be used to promote equity in local taxation by making it possible to charge tax-exempt property, of which much is found in some cities, and by forcing industries that contribute disproportionate amounts of waste to the sewage system to pay appropriate costs. Service charges also are useful when local governments have come close to their legal tax limits, because they usually are not counted as taxes under limitation provisions. The "tax revolt" of the late 1970s in California and elsewhere resulted in a big increase in service charges when taxes were frozen and residents still demanded services.

In addition to service charges, another important means of paying for services under the benefit theory is the *special assessment*. This is often used when covering neighborhoods from rural to urban by putting in sidewalks and changing from septic tank to sewer lines, although often the "benefits" are not wanted by the residents who are charged.

> *Special Assessment:* **An extra levy on specific pieces of property designed to defray the costs of services or conveniences of particular value to that property. Practices in their application vary widely, as do the rules by which the property owner pays for them.**

Debt Policies and Issues

A conflict that arises in every state or local unit of government from time to time centers on the alternatives of paying for capital improvements by issuing bonds or by increasing taxes and paying cash. The principles of borrowing on these levels are different from those on the national level. As Governor Thomas P. Salmon commented in a 1975 message, "Unlike the Federal government, the State of Vermont cannot print money and cannot consciously program a deficit." The national government itself is the principal institution for the establishment of credit-creating institutions, chiefly the banks. If the national government borrows from banks, it is borrowing credit made possible largely by its own rules. Furthermore, the internally held national debt is not passed on to other generations. However, in the late 1970s, for the first time in the twentieth century, the national government began to borrow funds abroad. This practice, if it became common enough, would cause a noticeable portion of the debt to be passed on to future generations. An internal debt only moves the money around among Americans, but a foreign debt requires a lowering of the domestic standard of living if bondholders abroad are to be repaid.

The borrowing power of the national government is limited only by the faith the

American people have in their government, and that faith is enormous. Except in national defense emergencies, the national government can manage to borrow mostly in times of economic recession, when interest rates are low, and the money pumped into the system thereby serves to prime the economic pump. State and local governments enjoy none of the borrowing advantages of the national government: they cannot create credit. State and local governments usually have to borrow money in boom times to provide services a prosperous people want. But they must pay high interest rates to get the money. In contrast, when people need jobs, interest rates are usually low and borrowing conditions therefore favorable, state and local governments tend to decrease spending and avoid borrowing. The public faith in any given state or community is also immensely less than the faith in the United States. In turn, state and local government borrowing power is also limited. Except as they contain nontaxable income features, bonds of these units of government are treated with no more respect on the open market than are the bonds of private corporations.

When to Borrow

Almost all economists agree that a state or local unit of government should not borrow money to meet current operating expenses. In the past this has happened, either because a depression had dried up the revenue sources and the situation was desperate, or because public officials desired to keep taxes low as a vote-attracting technique. The most notorious case occurred in New York City. It continued over many years until the city found itself in a genuine financial crisis in the mid-1970s. Borrowing to pay for permanent improvements is another matter, especially if the bonds are to be paid off before the improvement becomes obsolete or dilapidated. Issuing bonds to cover a period greater than the life of the improvement is not economically sound, although it may be politically attractive.

Sometimes the question of whether to borrow never actually confronts the governing body, for the conditions governing indebtedness are often prescribed by state constitution or city charter. These vary in detail; some of them may be waived by popular referendum.

Types of Bonds

Limitations on the borrowing power of state and local governments apply particularly (although not exclusively) to the pledging of the full faith and credit of the government to *general-obligation bonds*, whereby the local government jurisdiction agrees to levy whatever tax is necessary to pay the interest and eventually to retire the debt. If the issuing of these bonds is limited (sometimes it is completely prohibited) by statute or constitution, the governing body can turn to *mortgage bonds* or *revenue bonds*.

> *Mortgage Bonds:* **Bonds normally used in connection with the purchase or construction of utilities or other income-producing properties, and a mortgage on the utility serves as security. This type of bond usually requires a higher interest rate than bonds of general obligation (because no popular**

vote is required and the purchasers are less certain of getting their money back). Sometimes mortgage bonds also involve a pledge of full faith and credit, however, in which case the interest rate is lowered.

Revenue Bonds: Bonds that are retired from the income of the utility or any other property for which they were issued.

Revenue bonds have become increasingly popular since the 1930s. Generally, fewer constitutional and other legal rules restrict their issue, and no popular referendum is required, as is almost always the case with general-obligation bonds. Their interest rate usually is higher, however, than if full faith and credit is pledged. These bonds are secured by a pledge of the revenue from a self-liquidating project. Toll roads or bridges, tunnels, electrical-generation or -distribution plants, water-supply systems, stadiums, field houses, auditoriums, and college dormitories may be financed in this way. Governments must agree to set rates high enough to pay the debt charges. Sometimes the bondholders are also given a mortgage on the utilities.

Slightly over 70 percent of the outstanding state debt in 1987 was nonguaranteed; that is, was based on revenue or mortgage bonds rather than general-obligation bonds. In 1948, only 14 percent of debt had been of this type.

Repayment of Bonds

Traditionally, state and local government bonds have been retired by the establishment of a *sinking fund*, which would, supposedly, provide sufficient funds to retire the bonds when they came due. Most bonds of this type would be issued so that all of them would fall due at the same time. The sinking-fund method has proved to be defective in several respects, however, particularly, because (1) the governing body often failed to make adequate appropriations to the fund, which must be built up systematically, or the fund was otherwise tampered with, e.g., by being borrowed from but without prompt repayment; and (2) the sinking fund could come to disaster if its investments failed.

More recently, a trend has been toward the use of *serial bonds*. A certain percentage of these mature each year. The governing body, instead of appropriating money into a sinking fund, appropriates the necessary amount for the direct retirement of part of the debt. This is the same plan that is so popular in bank loans to private individuals (e.g., auto loans) because part of the principal is paid back each month, thus simplifying planning for the retirement of the debt.

Bond Prices and National Government Policies

Two national government policies have had important effects on the bond market for state and local government issues. The monetary policies of the national government are a major factor in determining the interest rates that must be paid on bonds. When the national government follows an easy-credit policy, state and local governments are encouraged to borrow; possibly they are encouraged beyond what they later may consider to have been prudent. When the national government follows a hard-credit policy, state and local governments find it more expensive to borrow money to make improvements they believe to be needed. In a time of expanding school-age populations, for example, it may be necessary to build schools regardless of the current cost of borrowing money. Federal policies are tied to political ideologies or to the business cycle; they do not consider current state and local needs and may work hardships on these units of government.

A second national government money policy of importance to state and local governments was that of exempting the income from their bonds from taxation by the national government. A series of nineteenth-century U.S. Supreme Court decisions established the principle of intergovernmental tax immunity, according to which one government cannot tax the instrumentalities of another. This principle in effect was set aside by the Supreme Court around 1940, but Congress only began narrowing the tax exemptions in the 1980s, doing so despite opposition from lower units of governments, from bond houses, and from potential buyers of the bonds. Tax exempt bonds carry a lower interest rate than taxable bonds. This encourages state and local governments to go into debt. The only people who find buying them to be advantageous are high-income persons and banks. The exemption feature in effect subsidizes those who least need it. The benefitting units of government nevertheless prefer to keep the present system even though it raises some questions of equity, because it saves huge sums of money for local governments that issue bonds. Public employee unions have become major purchasers of tax-exempt bonds by investing their pension funds, thus increasing demand and lowering interest rates still further. In return for helping the governments in this way, the unions hope to have leverage over the borrowing practices of their employers.

Public Attitudes toward Debt

Since the end of World War II, state and local borrowing has increased greatly. Highway construction has been the main reason for borrowing by state governments; education, by local governments. The need for local utilities (water, electrical, and gas supply) and transit systems has also been responsible for much indebtedness. Between 1985 and 1986—in just one year—state indebtedness increased by 17 percent to over $129 billion. If the outstanding debt were paid in one year, it would amount to almost one-third of the total state expenditure.[21]

The fiscal crisis in the City of New York between 1975 and 1978 brought borrowing at the local level to national attention, which had not happened since the Great Depression.[22] This crisis, followed by those in Cleveland and Philadelphia and in school districts in San Jose and Chicago, demonstrated that local governments may overborrow, overspend, and have to turn to extraordinary cutbacks, and state (or in the case of New York, national) bailouts. But major governments do not go bankrupt from borrowing; they may however, default on some loans, leaving themselves open to higher interest rates and short-term policy cutbacks.

A few items should be noted about borrowing patterns:

- Cultural values and the priorities they establish are important factors in determining what the public will go into debt for. Thus, it is easier to gain approval for bonds for school construction than for sewage-disposal plants; for highway construction than for mental hospitals.

- The public sometimes will refuse to permit a general-obligation bond issue at a referendum but will not seriously oppose a revenue bond issue intended for the same purpose. The latter usually does not require a referendum, generally provokes little interest, and the complaints that follow its approval by the governing body often are mild, whereas they might be vigorous if a referendum campaign were conducted, provoking public curiosity and concern.
- Economic conditions and interest rates affect public attitudes toward bond issues. In 1953, when interest rates were low, 90 percent of the referendums on general-obligation bond issues in Michigan passed; in 1956, when interest rates were the highest in decades, only 42 percent passed. In the 1970s, high interest rates and a recession were probably factors in negative voting on referendums. Rates subsided in the economic good times of the late 1980s, despite some national concern and bewilderment about the national government's deficit.
- Per capita debt tends to increase with the population of local governmental units and is likely to be higher in growing that in stable communities. Growing communities must build new schools and other services, many of them expensive.
- A direct relationship exists between the degree of urbanism of a state and its per capita debt. In addition, debt patterns tend to be grouped geographically. The East and Oregon, Alaska, and Hawaii have relatively high debts. All of the eastern states north of Virginia have higher per capita debts than the national average, except for Pennsylvania. These figures indicate that debt patterns are related to cultural values, although other factors explain them in part.[23]

Concluding Note

Public finance is not a science. Although economists can give technical advice concerning the approximate yield of a particular tax under certain conditions, and although they have fairly well-developed ideas about the way in which the burden of a tax is distributed—that is, whether it is regressive or progressive, is borne by the persons or things taxed, or is passed on to others—information will be only one of the factors considered by legislators in passing tax laws. Two things are more important: the value patterns of the society, which will have to pay any tax adopted, and the balance of forces among the interest groups pressuring the legislative body. Out of these two considerations, balanced against the service demands of that same society and the same pressure groups, will come a tax system—or more likely a group of poorly coordinated taxes. These will be combined with various other sources of government revenue in such a manner as to make possible the rough balancing of a budget. Such is the tentative character of governmental action.

Notes

1. See Deil S. Wright, *Understanding Intergovernmental Relations,* 3d ed. (Pacific Grove, CA: Brooks/Cole, 1988), 168–69. This is the best source of intergovernmental fiscal trends.

2. Ibid., 167–72.

3. Charles R. Adrian, *A History of American City Government, The Emergence of the Metropolis, 1920–1945* (Lanham, MD: University Press of America, 1987), 275–77.

4. Wright, *Understanding . . . Relations,* 190.

5. Ira Sharkansky, *The Politics of Taxing and Spending* (Indianapolis: Bobbs-Merrill, 1969), 83.

6. Ibid., chapter 7.

7. Thomas J. Anton, "Roles and Symbols in the Determination of State Expenditures," *Midwest Journal of Political Science* 11 (Feb. 1967) :43.

8. See U.S. Bureau of the Census, *Historical Statistics on State and Local Government Finances.*

9. *Report of the Trend in Costs of Maintaining Functions of County Government in West Virginia* (Charleston: West Virginia Chamber of Commerce, 1957).

10. Most of the many good texts on budgeting emphasize the complex administrative process. Among the best on the political process involved are the works of Aaron Wildavsky, which focus, however, on the national government. In particular see Aaron Wildavsky, *The New Politics of the Budgetary Process* (Glenview, IL: Scott, Foresman, 1988); and Aaron Wildavsky, *Budgeting* (Boston: Little, Brown, 1975).

11. On performance budgeting, see Fremont J. Lyden and Marc Lindenberg, *Public Budgeting in Theory and Practice* (New York: Longman, 1983).

12. See chapters 2, 4, and 7 herein; see also Wright, *Understanding . . . Relations,* and for national grants of the types cited, Michael D. Reagan and John G. Sanzone, *The New Federalism,* 2d ed. (New York: Oxford University Press, 1981).

13. Wright, *Understanding . . . Relations,* 193.

14. Ibid., 99.

15. Reagan and Sanzone, *New Federalism,* chapter 4.

16. See Michael Fine and Mort Sipress, "Budget and Finance," in Wilder Crane, A. Clarke Hagensick et al., eds., *Wisconsin Government and Politics,* 4th ed. (Milwaukee Department of Governmental Affairs, University of Wisconsin, 1987), 246–47.

17. U.S. Advisory Commission on Intergovernmental Relations, *State Constitutional and Statutory Taxing Powers,* 1962.

18. Charles Press, *A Michigan Local Property Tax Primer* (East Lansing: Institute for Community Development, Michigan State University, 1962).

19. Consult the latest edition of *The Book of the States* (Lexington, KY: Council of State Governments). The figures in this section were taken from pp. 333–34 of the 1990–91 edition.

20. *1990–1991 Book of the States,* 331–32.

21. Calculated by the authors from the *1988–1989 Book of the States,* 246–47.

22. See the collection of articles on the New York predicament, Charles Brecher and Raymond D. Horton, eds., *Setting Municipal Priorities* (New York: New York University Press, 1984).

23. *Statistical Abstract of the United States,* 1989 edition, 278.

Index